Lecture Notes in Bioinformatics 8590

Subseries of Lecture Notes in Computer Science

T0212917

De-Shuang Huang   Kyungsook Han
Michael Gromiha (Eds.)

Intelligent Computing in Bioinformatics

10th International Conference, ICIC 2014
Taiyuan, China, August 3-6, 2014
Proceedings

 Springer

Volume Editors

De-Shuang Huang
Tongji University
Machine Learning and Systems Biology Laboratory
School of Electronics and Information Engineering
4800 Caoan Road, Shanghai 201804, China
E-mail: dshuang@tongji.edu.cn

Kyungsook Han
Inha University
Department of Computer Science and Engineering
Incheon, South Korea
E-mail: khan@inha.ac.kr

Michael Gromiha
Indian Institute of Technology (IIT) Madras
Department of Biotechnology
Chennai 600 036, Tamilnadu, India
E-mail: gromiha@iitm.ac.in

ISSN 0302-9743   e-ISSN 1611-3349
ISBN 978-3-319-09329-1   e-ISBN 978-3-319-09330-7
DOI 10.1007/978-3-319-09330-7
Springer Cham Heidelberg New York Dordrecht London

Library of Congress Control Number: 2014943596

LNCS Sublibrary: SL 8 – Bioinformatics

Typesetting: Camera-ready by author, data conversion by Scientific Publishing Services, Chennai, India

Printed on acid-free paper

Springer is part of Springer Science+Business Media (www.springer.com)

Preface

The International Conference on Intelligent Computing (ICIC) was started to provide an annual forum dedicated to the emerging and challenging topics in artificial intelligence, machine learning, pattern recognition, bioinformatics, and computational biology. It aims to bring together researchers and practitioners from both academia and industry to share ideas, problems, and solutions related to the multifaceted aspects of intelligent computing.

ICIC 2014, held in Taiyuan, China, during August 3–6, 2014, constituted the 10th International Conference on Intelligent Computing. It built upon the success of ICIC 2013, ICIC 2012, ICIC 2011, ICIC 2010, ICIC 2009, ICIC 2008, ICIC 2007, ICIC 2006, and ICIC 2005 that were held in Nanning, Huangshan, Zhengzhou, Changsha, China, Ulsan, Korea, Shanghai, Qingdao, Kunming, and Hefei, China, respectively.

This year, the conference concentrated mainly on the theories and methodologies as well as the emerging applications of intelligent computing. Its aim was to unify the picture of contemporary intelligent computing techniques as an integral concept that highlights the trends in advanced computational intelligence and bridges theoretical research with applications. Therefore, the theme for this conference was "**Advanced Intelligent Computing Technology and Applications**". Papers focused on this theme were solicited, addressing theories, methodologies, and applications in science and technology.

ICIC 2014 received 667 submissions from 21 countries and regions. All papers went through a rigorous peer-review procedure and each paper received at least three review reports. Based on the review reports, the Program Committee finally selected 235 high-quality papers for presentation at ICIC 2013, included in three volumes of proceedings published by Springer: one volume of *Lecture Notes in Computer Science* (LNCS), one volume of *Lecture Notes in Artificial Intelligence* (LNAI), and one volume of *Lecture Notes in Bioinformatics* (LNBI).

This volume of *Lecture Notes in Bioinformatics* (LNBI) includes 58 papers.

The organizers of ICIC 2014, including Tongji University and North University of China, Taiyuan Normal University, Taiyuan University of Science and Technology, made an enormous effort to ensure the success of the conference. We hereby would like to thank the members of the Program Committee and the referees for their collective effort in reviewing and soliciting the papers. We would like to thank Alfred Hofmann, executive editor from Springer, for his frank and helpful advice and guidance throughout and for his continuous support in publishing the proceedings. In particular, we would like to thank all the authors for contributing their papers. Without the high-quality submissions from the authors, the success of the conference would not have been possible. Finally, we are especially grateful to the IEEE Computational Intelligence Society, the International Neural Network Society, and the National Science Foundation of China for their sponsorship.

May 2014   De-Shuang Huang
                                                            Kyungsook Han
                                                            Michael Gromiha

ICIC 2014 Organization

General Co-chairs

De-Shuang Huang, China
Vincenzo Piuri, Italy
Yan Han, China

Jiye Liang, China
Jianchao Zeng, China

Program Committee Co-chairs

Kang Li, UK
Juan Carlos Figueroa, Colombia

Organizing Committee Co-chairs

Kang-Hyun Jo, Korea
Valeriya Gribova, Russia

Bing Wang, China
Xing-Ming Zhao, China

Award Committee Chair

Vitoantonio Bevilacqua, Italy

Publication Chair

Phalguni Gupta, India

Workshop/Special Session Co-chairs

Jiang Qian, USA
Zhongming Zhao, USA

Special Issue Chair

M. Michael Gromiha, India

Tutorial Chair

Laurent Heutte, France

International Liaison

Prashan Premaratne, Australia

Publicity Co-chairs

Kyungsook Han, Korea   Abir Hussain, UK
Ling Wang, China   Zhi-Gang Zeng, China

Exhibition Chair

Chun-Hou Zheng, China

Program Committee Members

Khalid Aamir, Pakistan   Minrui Fei, China
Andrea F. Abate, USA   Juan Carlos Figueroa-García,
Sabri Arik, Korea   Colombia
Vasily Aristarkhov, Australia   shan Gao, China
Costin Badica, Japan   Liang Gao, China
Waqas Bangyal, Pakistan   Dun-wei Gong, India
Vitoantonio Bevilacqua, Italy   Valeriya Gribova, China
Shuhui Bi, China   Michael Gromiha, China
Jair Cervantes, Mexico   Xingsheng Gu, China
Yuehui Chen, China   Kayhan Gulez, USA
Qingfeng Chen, China   Ping Guo, China
Wen-Sheng Chen, China   Phalguni Gupta, India
Xiyuan Chen, China   Kyungsook Han, Korea
Guanling Chen, USA   Fei Han, China
Yoonsuck Choe, USA   Laurent Heutte, France
Ho-Jin Choi, Korea, Republic of   Wei-Chiang Hong, Taiwan
Michal Choras, Colombia   Yuexian Hou, China
Angelo Ciaramella, China   Jinglu Hu, China
Youping Deng, Japan   Tingwen Huang, Qatar
Primiano Di Nauta, Italy   Peter Hung, Taiwan
Salvatore Distefano, USA   Abir Hussain, UK
Ji-Xiang Du, China   Saiful Islam, India
Jianbo Fan, China   Li Jia, China

Zhenran Jiang, China

Kang-Hyun Jo, Korea

Dah-Jing Jwo, Korea

Seeja K.R, India

Vandana Dixit Kaushik, India

Gul Muhammad Khan, Pakistan

Sungshin Kim, Korea

Donald Kraft, USA

Yoshinori Kuno, Japan

Takashi Kuremoto, Japan

Jaerock Kwon, USA

Vincent Lee, Australia

Shihua Zhang, China

Guo-Zheng Li, China

Xiaodi Li, China

Bo Li, China

Kang Li, UK

Peihua Li, China

Jingjing Li, USA

Yuhua Li, UK

Honghuang Lin, USA

Meiqin Liu, USA

Ju Liu, China

Xiwei Liu, China

Shuo Liu, China

Yunxia Liu, China

Chu Kiong Loo, Mexico

Zhao Lu, USA

Ke Lu, China

Yingqin Luo, USA

Jinwen Ma, USA

Xiandong Meng, China

Filippo Menolascina, Italy

Ivan Vladimir Meza-Ruiz, Australia

Tarik Veli Mumcu Mumcu, Turkey

Roman Neruda, Turkey

Ben Niu, China

Seiichi Ozawa, Korea

Paul Pang, China

Francesco Pappalardo, USA

Surya Prakash, India

Prashan Premaratne, Australia

Daowen Qiu, China

Angel Sappa, USA

Li Shang, China

Dinggang Shen, USA

Fanhuai Shi, China

Shitong Wang, China

Wilbert Sibanda, USA

Jiatao Song, China

Stefano Squartini, Italy

Badrinath Srinivas, USA

Zhan-Li Sun, China

Evi Syukur, USA

Joaquín Torres-Sospedra, Spain

Rua-Huan Tsaih, USA

Antonio Uva, USA

Jun Wan, USA

Yong Wang, China

Ling Wang, China

Jim Jing-Yan Wang, USA

Xuesong Wang, China

Bing Wang, China

Ze Wang, USA

Junwen Wang, HK

Hong Wei, UK

Wei Wei, Norway

Yan Wu, China

QingXiang Wu, China

Junfeng Xia, China

Shunren Xia, China

Bingji Xu, China

Gongsheng xu, China

Yu Xue, China

Xin Yin, USA

Xiao-Hua Yu, USA

Zhigang Zeng, China

Shihua Zhang, China

Jun Zhang, China

Xing-Ming Zhao, China

Hongyong Zhao, China

Xiaoguang Zhao, China

Zhongming Zhao, USA

Bojin Zheng, China

Chunhou Zheng, China

Fengfeng Zhou, China

Yongquan Zhou, China

Hanning Zhou, China

Li Zhuo, China

Xiufen Zou, China

Reviewers

Jakub Šmíd	Giuseppe Carbone
Pankaj Acharya	Raffaele Carli
Erum Afzal	Jair Cervantes
Parul Agarwal	Aravindan Chandrabose
Tanvir Ahmad	Yuchou Chang
Musheer Ahmad	Deisy Chelliah
Syed Ahmed	Gang Chen
Sabooh Ajaz	Songcan Chen
Haya Alaskar	Jianhung Chen
Felix Albu	David Chen
Dhiya Al-Jumeily	Hongkai Chen
Israel Alvarez Villalobos	Xin Chen
Muhammad Amjad	Fanshu Chen
Ning An	Fuqiang Chen
Mary Thangakani Anthony	Bo Chen
Masood Ahmad Arbab	Xin Chen
Soniya be	Liang Chen
Sunghan Bae	Wei Chen
Lukas Bajer	Jinan Chen
Waqas Bangyal	Yu Chen
Gang Bao	Junxia Cheng
Donato Barone	Zhang Cheng
Silvio Barra	Feixiong Cheng
Alex Becheru	Cong Cheng
Ye Bei	Han Cheng
Mauri Benedito Bordonau	Chi-Tai Cheng
Simon Bernard	Chengwang Xie
Vitoantonio Bevilacqua	Seongpyo Cheon
Ying Bi	Ferdinando Chiacchio
Ayse Humeyra Bilge	Cheng-Hsiung Chiang
Honghua Bin	Wei Hong Chin
Jun Bo	Simran Choudhary
Nora Boumella	Angelo Ciaramella
Fabio Bruno	Azis Ciayadi
Antonio Bucchiarone	Rudy Ciayadi
Danilo Caceres	Danilo Comminiello
Yiqiao Cai	Carlos Cubaque
Qiao Cai	Yan Cui
Guorong Cai	Bob Cui
Francesco Camastra	Cuco Curistiana
Mario Cannataro	Yakang Dai
Kecai Cao	Dario d'Ambruoso
Yi Cao	Yang Dan

Farhan Dawood
Francesca De Crescenzio
Kaushik Deb
Saverio Debernardis
Dario Jose Delgado-Quintero
Sara Dellantonio
Jing Deng
Weilin Deng
M.C. Deng
Suping Deng
Zhaohong Deng
Somnath Dey
Yunqiang Di
Hector Diez Rodriguez
Rong Ding
Liya Ding
Sheng Ding
Sheng Ding
Shihong Ding
Dayong Ding
Xiang Ding
Salvatore Distefano
Chelsea Dobbins
Xueshi Dong
Vladislavs Dovgalecs
Vlad Dovgalecs
Gaixin Du
Dajun Du
Kaifang Du
Haibin Duan
Durak-Ata Lutfiye
Malay Dutta
Tolga Ensari
Nicola Epicoco
Marco Falagario
Shaojing Fan
Ming Fan
Fenghua Fan
Shaojing Fan
Yaping Fang
Chen Fei
Liangbing Feng
Shiguang Feng
Guojin Feng
Alessio Ferone

Francesco Ferrise
Juan Carlos Figueroa
Michele Fiorentino
Carlos Franco
Gibran Fuentes Pineda
Hironobu Fujiyoshi
Kazuhiro Fukui
Wai-Keung Fung
Chun Che Fung
Chiara Galdi
Jian Gao
Yushu Gao
Liang Gao
Yang Gao
Garcia-Lamont Farid
Garcia-Marti Irene
Michele Gattullo
Jing Ge
Na Geng
Shaho Ghanei
Rozaida Ghazali
Rosalba Giugno
Fengshou Gu
Tower Gu
Jing Gu
Smile Gu
Guangyue Du
Weili Guo
Yumeng Guo
Fei Guo
Tiantai Guo
Yinan Guo
Yanhui Guo
Chenglin Guo
Lilin Guo
Sandesh Gupta
Puneet Gupta
Puneet Gupta
Shi-Yuan Han
Fei Han
Meng Han
Yu-Yan Han
Zhimin Han
Xin Hao
Manabu Hashimoto

Tao He
Selena He
Xing He
Feng He
Van-Dung Hoang
Tian Hongjun
Lei Hou
Jingyu Hou
Ke Hu
Changjun Hu
Zhaoyang Hu
Jin Huang
Qiang Huang
Lei Huang
Shin-Ying Huang
Ke Huang
Huali Huang
Jida Huang
Xixia Huang
Fuxin Huang
Darma Putra i Ketut Gede
Haci Ilhan
Sorin Ilie
Saiful Islam
Saeed Jafarzadeh
Alex James
Chuleerat Jaruskulchai
James Jayaputera
Umarani Jayaraman
Mun-Ho Jeong
Zhiwei Ji
Shouling Ji
Yafei Jia
Hongjun Jia
Xiao Jian
Min Jiang
Changan Jiang
Tongyang Jiang
Yizhang Jiang
He Jiang
Yunsheng Jiang
Shujuan Jiang
Ying Jiang
Yizhang Jiang
Changan Jiang

Xu Jie
Jiening Xia
Taeseok Jin
Jingsong Shi
Mingyuan Jiu
Kanghyun Jo
Jayasudha John Suseela
Ren Jun
Fang Jun
Li Jun
Zhang Junming
Yugandhar K.
Tomáš Křen
Yang Kai
Hee-Jun Kang
Qi Kang
Dong-Joong Kang
Shugang Kang
Bilal Karaaslan
Rohit Katiyar
Ondrej Kazik
Mohd Ayyub Khan
Muhammed Khan
Sang-Wook Kim
Hong-Hyun Kim
One-Cue Kim
Duangmalai Klongdee
Kunikazu Kobayashi
Yoshinori Kobayashi
Takashi Komuro
Toshiaki Kondo
Deguang Kong
Kitti Koonsanit
Rafal Kozik
Kuang Li
Junbiao Kuang
Baeguen Kwon
Hebert Lacey
Chunlu Lai
Chien-Yuan Lai
David Lamb
Wei Lan
Chaowang Lan
Qixun Lan
Yee Wei Law

Tien Dung Le
My-Ha Le
Yongduck Lee
Jooyoung Lee
Seokju Lee
Shao-Lun Lee
Xinyu Lei
Gang Li
Yan Li
Liangliang Li
Xiaoguang Li
Zheng Li
Huan Li
Deng Li
Ping Li
Qingfeng Li
Fuhai Li
Hui Li
Kai Li
Longzhen Li
Xingfeng Li
Jingfei Li
Jianxing Li
Keling Li
Juan Li
Jianqing Li
Yunqi Li
Bing Nan Li
Lvzhou Li
Qin Li
Xiaoguang Li
Xinwu Liang
Jing Liang
Li-Hua Zhang
Jongil Lim
Changlong Lin
Yong Lin
Jian Lin
Genie Lin
Ying Liu
Chenbin Liu
James Liu
Liangxu Liu
Yuhang Liu
Liang Liu

Rong Liu
Liang Liu
Yufeng Liu
Qing Liu
Zhe Liu
Zexian Liu
Li Liu
Shiyong Liu
Sen Liu
Qi Liu
Jin-Xing Liu
Xiaoming Liu
Ying Liu
Xiaoming Liu
Bo Liu
Yunxia Liu
Alfredo Liverani
Anthony Lo
Lopez-Chau Asdrúbal
Siow Yong Low
Zhen Lu
Xingjia Lu
Junfeng Luo
Juan Luo
Ricai Luo
Youxi Luo
Yanqing Ma
Wencai Ma
Lan Ma
Chuang Ma
Xiaoxiao Ma
Sakashi Maeda
Guoqin Mai
Mario Manzo
Antonio Maratea
Erik Marchi
Carlos Román Mariaca Gaspar
Naoki Masuyama
Gu Meilin
Geethan Mendiz
Qingfang Meng
Filippo Menolascina
Muharrem Mercimek
Giovanni Merlino
Hyeon-Gyu Min

Martin Renqiang Min
Minglei Tong
Saleh Mirheidari
Akio Miyazaki
Yuanbin Mo
Quanyi Mo
Andrei Mocanu
Raffaele Montella
Montoliu Raul
Tsuyoshi Morimoto
Mohamed Mousa Alzawi
Lijun Mu
Inamullah Muhammad
Izharuddin Muhammed
Tarik Veli Mumcu
Francesca Nardone
Fabio Narducci
Rodrigo Nava
Patricio Nebot
Ken Nguyen
Changhai Nie
Li Nie
Aditya Nigam
Evgeni Nurminski
Kok-Leong Ong
Kazunori Onoguchi
Zeynep Orman
Selin Ozcira
Cuiping Pan
Binbin Pan
Quan-Ke Pan
Dazhao Pan
Francesco Pappalardo
Jekang Park
Anoosha Paruchuri
Vibha Patel
Samir Patel
Lizhi Peng
Yiming Peng
Jialin Peng
Klara Peskova
Caroline Petitjean
Martin Pilat
Surya Prakash
Philip Pretorius

Ali Qamar
Xiangbo Qi
Shijun Qian
Pengjiang Qian
Bin Qian
Ying Qiu
Jian-Ding Qiu
Junfeng Qu
Junjun Qu
Muhammad Rahman
Sakthivel Ramasamy
Tao Ran
Martin Randles
Caleb Rascon
Muhammad Rashid
Haider Raza
David Reid
Fengli Ren
Stefano Ricciardi
Angelo Riccio
Alejo Roberto
Abdus Samad
Ruya Samli
Hongyan Sang
Michele Scarpiniti
Dongwook Seo
Shi Sha
Elena Shalfeeva
Li Shang
Linlin Shen
Yehu Shen
Haojie Shen
Jin Biao Shen
Ajitha Shenoy
Jiuh-Biing Sheu
Xiutao Shi
Jibin Shi
Fanhuai Shi
Yonghong Shi
Yinghuan Shi
Atsushi Shimada
Nobutaka Shimada
Ji Sun Shin
Ye Shuang
Raghuraj Singh

Dushyant Kumar Singh

Haozhen Situ

Martin Slapak

Sergey Smagin

Yongli Song

Yinglei Song

Meiyue Song

Bin Song

Rui Song

Guanghua Song

Gang Song

Sotanto Sotanto

Sreenivas Sremath Tirumala

Antonino Staiano

Jinya Su

Hung-Chi Su

Marco Suma

Xiaoyan Sun

Jiankun Sun

Sheng Sun

Yu Sun

Celi Sun

Yonghui Sun

Zengguo Sun

Jie Sun

Aboozar Taherkhani

Shinya Takahashi

Jinying Tan

Shijun Tang

Xiwei Tang

Buzhou Tang

Ming Tang

Jianliang Tang

Hissam Tawfik

Zhu Teng

Sin Teo

Girma Tewolde

Xiange Tian

Yun Tian

Tian Tian

Hao Tian

Gao Tianshun

Kamlesh Tiwari

Amod Tiwari

Kamlesh Tiwari

Andrysiak Tomasz

Torres-Sospedra Joaquín

Sergi Trilles

Yao-Hong Tsai

Naoyuki Tsuruta

Fahad Ullah

Pier Paolo Valentini

Andrey Vavilin

Giuseppe Vettigli

Petra Vidnerová

Villatoro-Tello Esaú

Ji Wan

Li Wan

Lin Wan

Quan Wang

Zixiang Wang

Yichen Wang

Xiangjun Wang

Yunji Wang

Hong Wang

Jinhe Wang

Xuan Wang

Xiaojuan Wang

Suyu Wang

Zhiyong Wang

Xiangyu Wang

Mingyi Wang

Yan Wang

Zongyue Wang

Huisen Wang

Yongcui Wang

Xiaoming Wang

Zi Wang

Jun Wang

Aihui Wang

Yi Wang

Ling Wang

Zhaoxi Wang

Shulin Wang

Yunfei Wang

Yongbo Wang

Zhengxiang Wang

Sheng-Yao Wang

Jingchuan Wang

Qixin Wang

Yong Wang

Fang-Fang Wang

Tian Wang

Zhenzhong Wang

Panwen Wang

Lei Wang

Qilong Wang

Dong Wang

Ping Wang

Huiwei Wang

Yiqi Wang

Zhixuan Wei

Zhihua Wei

Li Wei

Shengjun Wen

Shiping Wen

Di Wu

Yonghui Wu

Chao Wu

Xiaomei Wu

Weili Wu

Hongrun Wu

Weimin Wu

Guolong Wu

Siyu Xia

Qing Xia

Sen Xia

Jin Xiao

Min Xiao

Qin Xiao

Yongfei Xiao

Zhao Xiaoguang

Zhuge Xiaozhong

Minzhu Xie

Zhenping Xie

Jian Xie

Ting Xie

Chao Xing

Wei Xiong

Hao Xiong

Yi Xiong

Xiaoyin Xu

Dawen Xu

Jing Xu

Yuan Xu

Jin Xu

Xin Xu

Meng Xu

Li Xu

Feng Xu

Zhenyu Xuan

Hari Yalamanchili

Atsushi Yamashita

Mingyuan Yan

Yan Yan

Zhigang Yan

Bin Yan

Zhile Yang

Dan Yang

Yang Yang

Wankou Yang

Wenqiang Yang

Yuting Yang

Chia-Luen Yang

Chyuan-Huei Yang

Deng Yanni

Jin Yao

Xiangjuan Yao

Tao Ye

Xu Ye

Fengqi Yi

Wenchao Yi

Kai Yin

James j.q. Yu

Helen Yu

Jun Yu

Fang Yu

Xu Yuan

Lin Yuan

Jinghua Yuan

Lin Yuling

Faheem Zafari

Xue-Qiang Zeng

Haimao Zhan

Yong-Wei Zhang

Jing Zhang

Shuyi Zhang

Kevin Zhang

Ming Zhang

Zhenmin Zhang

Xuebing Zhang
Minlu Zhang
Jianping Zhang
Xiaoping Zhang
Yong Zhang
Qiang Zhang
Guohui Zhang
Chunhui Zhang
Yifeng Zhang
Wenxi Zhang
Xiujun Zhang
Long Zhang
Jian Zhang
Boyu Zhang
Hailei Zhang
Hongyun Zhang
Jianhua Zhang
Chunjiang Zhang
Peng Zhang
Jianhai Zhang
Hongbo Zhang
Lin Zhang
Xiaoqiang Zhang
Haiying Zhang
Jing Zhang
Wei Zhang
Qian Zhang
Hongli Zhang
Guohui Zhang
Liping Zhang
Hongbo Zhang
Sen Zhao
Yaou Zhao
Jane Zhao
Liang Zhao

Yunlong Zhao
Miaomiao Zhao
Xinhua Zhao
Xu Zhao
Guodong Zhao
Liang Zhao
Feng Zhao
Juan Zhao
Junfei Zhao
Changbo Zhao
Yue Zhao
Min Zheg
Dong Zhen
Guang Zheng
Xiaolong Zheng
Huanyu Zheng
Shenggen Zheng
Shan Zhong
Qi Zhou
Mian Zhou
Yinzhi Zhou
Jiayin Zhou
Songsheng Zhou
Bo Zhou
Qiang Zhou
Lei Zhu
Lin Zhu
Yongxu Zhu
Nanli Zhu
Xiaolei Zhu
Majid Ziaratban
Xiangfu Zou
Brock Zou
Tanish
Qiqi Duan

Table of Contents

Machine Learning

Neural Networks

Image Processing

Computational Systems Biology and Medical Informatics

Biomedical Informatics Theory and Methods

Special Session on Advances in Bio-inspired Computing: Theories and Applications

Special Session on Protein and Gene Bioinformatics: Analysis, Algorithms and Applications

Predicting the Outer/Inner BetaStrands in Protein Beta Sheets Based on the Random Forest Algorithm

Li Tang[1,2,*], Zheng Zhao[1], Lei Zhang[3,*], Tao Zhang[3,**], and Shan Gao[3,**]

[1] School of Computer Science and Technology, Tianjin University, Tianjin, P.R. China
tangli0831@yeah.net
[2] Information Science and Technology Department,
Tianjin University of Finance and Economics, Tianjin, P.R. China
[3] Key Lab. of Bioactive Materials, Ministry of Education and The College of Life Sciences,
Nankai University, Tianjin, P.R. China
{zhni,zhangtao,gao_shan}@nankai.edu.cn

Abstract. The beta sheet, as one of the three common second form of regular secondary structure in proteins plays an important role in protein function. The best strands in a beta sheet can be classified into the outer or inner strands. Considering the protein primary sequences have determinant information to arrange the strands in the beta sheet topology, we introduce an approach by using the random forest algorithm to predict outer or inner arrangement of a beta strand. We use nine features to describe a strand based on the hydrophobicity, the hydrophilicity, the side-chain mass and other properties of the beta strands. The random forest classifiers reach the best prediction accuracy 89.45% with 10-fold cross-validation among five machine learning methods. This result demonstrates that there are significant differences between the outer beta strands and the inner ones in beta sheets. The finding in this study can be used to arrange beta strands in a beta sheet without any prior structure information. It can also help better understanding the mechanisms of protein beta sheet formation.

Keywords: beta sheet, beta strand, protein secondary structure, random forest algorithm.

1   Introduction

Protein secondary structure is an important bridge to understand the protein's three-dimensional structure from its amino acid sequence[1-3]. Investigation of the protein secondary structure helps the determination of the protein structure, as well as the design of new proteins[4]. The beta sheet (also β-pleated sheet) is one of the three common second form of regular secondary structure in proteins. The statistical data of the PDB database[5] showed more than 75% of proteins with known structures

---

* These authors contributed equally to this paper.
** Corresponding author.

D.-S. Huang et al. (Eds.): ICIC 2014, LNBI 8590, pp. 1–9, 2014.
© Springer International Publishing Switzerland 2014

contain beta sheets. To predict these beta sheet containing proteins, assigning beta strands to a beta sheet can reduce the search space in the ab initio methods[13, 45]. Moreover, beta sheets play some important roles in protein functions, particularly in the formation of the protein aggregation observed in many human diseases, notably the Alzheimer's disease.

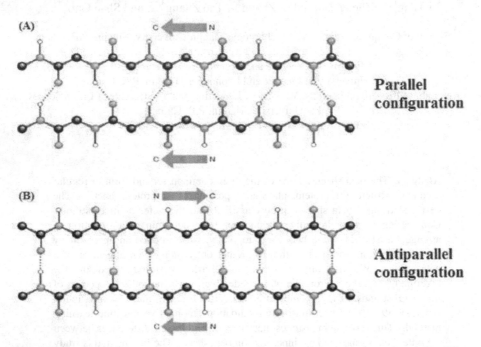

Fig. 1. Illustration of beta strands pairs and configurations. Arrows show the amide (N) to carbonyl (C) direction of beta strands. Hydrogen bonds are represented by dotted lines.

In a beta sheet, beta strands are paired by the interactive hydrogen bonds in parallel or antiparallel arrangement (Fig.1). A beta sheet forms a topology (Fig.2b), which can be described by three components: the group of beta strands in the beta sheet, the orders of these beta strands on the sequence level (Fig.3), and the configuration of beta strand pairs (parallel or antiparallel). The order of beta strands arranged in a beta sheet topology differs with the order of beta strands on sequence level (Fig.2). As described in the Protein Data Bank Contents Guide[6], beta strands are listed and numbered according to their orders on the sequence level. In this study, the first and the last strand in a beta sheet are defined as outer strands, whereas the other strands are defined as inner strands (Fig.3).

Many studies have been proposed to reach the different levels of understanding the beta sheet topology. The mechanisms and rules of beta sheet formation are investigated and simulated by theoretical and experimental method[7-10]. Some efforts focus on the prediction of residue contact maps, which can be used to construct the beta sheet topology[11, 12]. Other researcher predicted the parallel/antiparallel beta strand pairs[13-15], based on the non-random distribution and pairing preferences of amino acids in parallel and antiparallel beta strand pairs[16-19]. Utilizing machine learning algorithms, several methods are proposed to predict the topology of some certain kinds of beta sheets[2, 20, 21]. Although much achievements have been acquired in some aspects of beta sheet studies, the mechanisms of beta strands to form beta sheets have not yet to be fully understood[7].

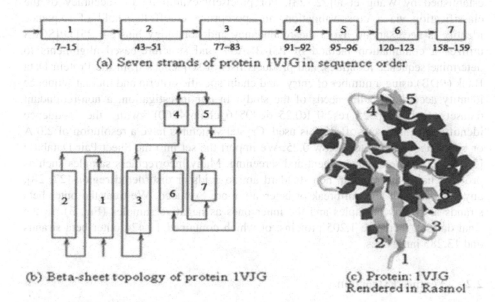

Fig. 2. (a) Seven strands of protein 1VJG in sequence order. (b) Beta-sheet topology of protein 1VJG. (c) Protein 1VJG rendered in Rasmol.

Considering the two outer beta strands take the starting and terminal location in one beta sheet, we suggest beta strands probably have different conservative properties in the outer and inner strands on the sequenced level. In this study, we predict the outer/inner beta strands in beta sheets using the Random Forest (see Materials and Methods), extracting the features from the protein primary sequences.

```
HELIX     9   9 GLN A 184  ASN A 197 1                                    14
HELIX    10  10 TRP A 198  ASN A 203 1                                     6
SHEET    ①  A 5 TYR A  43  GLY A  51 0
SHEET    2   A 5 THR A   7  GLY A  15 1  N PHE A 13  O LEU A 50
SHEET    3   A 5 ASN A  77  SER A  83 1  O VAL A 81  N VAL A 14
SHEET    4   A 5 VAL A 120  ILE A 123 1  O ILE A 123 N PHE A 82
SHEET    ⑤  A 5 TYR A 158  LEU A 159 1  O LEU A 159 N MSE A 122
SHEET    1   B 2 LEU A  91  GLU A  92 0
SHEET    2   B 2 LYS A  95  PRO A  96 -1 O LYS A 95  N GLU A 92
```

Fig. 3. Illustration of beta strands number in the beta sheets of protein 1VJG in the PDB file. The number 1 and 5 marked with circles denote the outer beta strands; whereas the number marked with the box denote inner ones. The number 1 strand, ranging from the sequence number of residue 43 to 51, corresponds to the second strand in sequence order.

2   Materials and Methods

2.1   Datasets

The protein structure dataset we used is from a database server named PISCES, established by Wang et al[22, 23]. For precisely examining the accuracy of the classification via a cross-validation, an appropriate cutoff threshold of sequence identity is necessary to avoid the redundancy and homology bias[24, 25]. PISCES utilizes a combination method of PSI-BLAST and structure-based alignments to determine sequence identities, and products lists of sequences from the Protein Data Bank (PDB) using a number of entry- and chain-specific criteria and mutual sequence identity according to the needs of the study. In our investigation, a non-redundant dataset   (cullpdb_pc25_res2.0_R0.25_d090516_chains4260)   with   the   sequence identity percentage cut-off 25% is used. Crystal structures have a resolution of 2.0 Å or better and an R-factor below 0.25. We import the set into the Sheet Pair Database [26] for easier data management and screening. Many incorrectness samples such as protein chains that contain non-standard amino acids or disordered regions[27, 28], any patterns with a chain break or heteroatom are excluded. We treat the outer beta strands as positive samples and the inner ones as negative samples (Fig. 3). In the final dataset, there are 1,205 proteins, of which contained 11,424 outer beta strands and 13,285 inner ones.

2.2   Feature Extraction

Protein folding is a collaborative process but mainly driven by the hydrophobic interaction[29]. The balance of the interaction between hydrophobicity and hydrophilicity is a notable feature of the stability of protein structure[29,30]. The previous studies also showed that the amino acid hydrophobicity and molecular size are two important factors that cause differences of amino acid conservative[31]. In this study, we used nine features to describe a beta strand. Seven of nice features are based on three physical and chemical properties of the amino acids, which are the hydrophobicity value (H_1) from Tanford[32], the hydrophilicity value (H_2) from Hopp and Woods[33], and the mass of side chain of amino acid(M).   The other two features are from the Pseudo-Amino Acid Composition (PseAAC), which was originally introduced by Chou for the prediction of protein subcellular localization and membrane protein type[34]. The PseAAC includes not only the main feature of amino acid composition but also sequence order information beyond amino acid composition. It can represent a protein sequence comprehensively with additional sequence order effects reflected by a series of sequence correlation factors with different tiers of correlation.

A beta strand chain can be represented by a 9-dimension numeric vector $X = \{x_1 x_2 x_3 \ldots x_7 x_8 x_9\}$. Each value in the vector can be calculated by such formulas:

$$x_1 = \frac{1}{L}\Sigma_{i=1}^{L}H_1(R_i), x_2 = \frac{1}{L}\Pi_{i=1}^{L}H_1(R_i), x_3 = \Sigma_{i=1}^{L}H_1(R_i), x_4 = \frac{1}{L}\Sigma_{i=1}^{L}H_2(R_i) \qquad (1\text{-}4)$$

$$x_5 = \frac{1}{L}\Pi_{i=1}^{L}H_2(R_i), x_6 = \Sigma_{i=1}^{L}H_2(R_i), x_7 = \frac{1}{L}\Sigma_{i=1}^{L}M(R_i) \qquad (5\text{-}7)$$

$$x_8 = \frac{1}{L-1}\Sigma_{i=1}^{L-1}\Theta(R_i, R_{i+1}), x_9 = \frac{\dfrac{w}{L-1}\Sigma_{i=1}^{L-1}\Theta(R_i, R_{i+1})}{\Sigma_{i=1}^{20}f_i + \dfrac{w}{L-1}\Sigma_{i=1}^{L-1}\Theta(R_i, R_{i+1})} \qquad (8\text{-}9)$$

Where, $H_1(R_i), H_2(R_i)$ and $M(R_i)$ are the hydrophobicity value, hydrophilicity value, and side-chain mass of the amino acid R_i after the **standard conversion**, respectively.

The element x_8 is the first-tier correlation factor defined in PseAAC[34].Since the length of a beta strand sequence is usually not long, only the first-tier correlation factor is calculated which can reflect the sequence order correlation between all the most contiguous residues along a beta strand sequence[34]. Correspondingly, the element x_9 is the 21st component of PseAAC. In Eq.(9), f_i is the normalized occurrence frequency of the 20 amino acids in the beta strand and w is the weight factor for the sequence order effect and is set to default value 0.05 in the current study [34]. In Eq.(8) and Eq.(9), $\Theta(R_i, R_{i+1})$ is calculated by the following equation as described in PseAAC:

$$\Theta(R_i, R_{i+1}) = \frac{1}{3}\{[H_1(R_{i+1}) - H_1(R_i)]^2 + [H_2(R_{i+1}) - H_2(R_i)]^2 + [M(R_{i+1}) - M(R_i)]^2\} \qquad (10)$$

The **standard conversion** from $H_1^0(R_i)$ to $H_1(R_i)$ is described by the forrmula (11) as below. $H_1^0(R_i), H_2^0(R_i)$ and $M^0(R_i)$ are the raw values of the amino acid hydrophobicity, hydrophilicity and side-chain mass.

$$H_1(R_i) = (H_1^0(R_i) - \Sigma_i^{20}\frac{H_1^0(R_i)}{20}) / \sqrt{\frac{\Sigma_{i=1}^{20}(H_1^0(R_i) - \Sigma_i^{20}\frac{H_1^0(R_i)}{20})^2}{20}} \qquad (11)$$

2.3   The Random Forest Algorithm

Random Forest (RF), as a machine learning algorithm, was originally introduced by Breiman[35]. RF generates decision trees by randomly sampling subspaces of the input features, and then makes the final decisions by a majority voting from these trees. RF has a good predictive performance even though the dataset has much noise [36]. With the increased number of decision trees, RF avoids the overfitting problem or the dependence on the training data sets[35]. In view of the good characteristics of Random Forest, it has been applied successfully to deal with many classification or prediction problems in varied biological fields[37-41]. In this study, we used theWeka software package[42] to implement the RF classification of the outer/inner beta strands. There are three parameters to run RF in Weka developer version 3.6.2, which are I: the number of trees constructed in the forest; K: the number of features calculated to define each of the nodes in a tree; and S:random number seed. In this study, we used the default setting without model selection.

2.4   Performance Measures

To assess the performance of classifiers we used the following measures: the number of true positives (TP), the number of false positives (FP), the number of true negatives (TN), the number of false negatives (FN) , sensitivity of positive examples(Sn^+), specificity of positive examples(Sp^+), sensitivity of negative examples(Sn^-), specificity of negative examples(Sp^-), accuracy(Ac) and Matthews correlation coefficient(MCC), as described in[43].

3   Results

In order to compare the prediction performance of different algorithms with that of Random Forest (RF), BayesNet, support vector machine (SVM), multilayer perceptron (MLP) and K-nearest-neighbor (IBk) were used to classify the outer/inner beta strands with the default parameter setting. The SVM algorithm was implemented by the LibSVM 2.86 [44], while the other three algorithms were implemented in Weka. Ten-fold cross-validation test was used to evaluate the accuracy of each prediction algorithm. The prediction accuracy of outer/inner beta strands in beta sheets reaches 89.45% Ac and 0.79 MCC by using RF (see 2.3). From Table 1, we can see that RF reaches the best performance among five algorithms. The prediction accuracy of RF is about 2% higher than the K-nearest-neighbor classifier, significantly ahead of the Naive Bayes, SVM and MLP classifiers.

Table 1. The prediction result of theouter/inner beta strands

Algorithm	Sn^+	Sp^+	Sn^-	Sp^-	Ac	MCC
BayesNet	0.61	0.71	0.78	0.70	70.14%	0.40
SVM	0.75	0.66	0.74	0.81	74.38%	0.48
MLP	0.73	0.77	0.81	0.78	77.35%	0.54
IBk	0.86	0.87	0.89	0.88	87.53%	0.75
RF	**0.87**	**0.90**	**0.92**	**0.89**	**89.45%**	**0.79**

4 Conclusion and Discussion

In this study, we proposed an approach based on the Random Forest (RF) classification to predict the outer/inner beta strands in beta sheets using nine features. Seven of the nine features were extracted based on the hydrophobicity, the hydrophilicity, and the side-chain mass of the beta strands. The other two features are from the Pseudo-Amino Acid Composition (PseAAC). Using RF, the accuracy of prediction of outer/inner beta strands reaches 89.45% with 10-fold cross-validation. The RF performance defeated other four machine learning methods on datasets used in this study. This RF prediction result can provide useful information about the arrangement of beta strands in a beta sheet, especially for the beta sheets which include no more than four beta strands.

The high prediction accuracy demonstrates that there are significant differences between the outer beta strands and the inner ones on the sequence level. The primary sequences of proteins contain determinant information to arrange a strand in an outer or inner location. However, the best accuracy reaches 89.45%. There must be some other factors which take effects on the arrangement of strands in a beta sheet.

Acknowledgements. This work was supported by grants from the National Natural Science Foundation of China (31171053) and Tianjin research program of application foundation and advanced technology (12JCZDJC22300).

References

1. Hua, S., Sun, Z.: A Novel Method of Protein Secondary Structure Prediction with High Segment Overlap Measure: Support Vector Machine Approach. J. Mol. Biol. 308(2), 397–407 (2001)
2. Cheng, J.L., Baldi, P.: Three-Stage Prediction of Protein Beta-Sheets by Neural Networks, Alignments and Graph Algorithms. Bioinformatics 21(suppl.1), I75–I84 (2005)
3. Chen, C., et al.: Prediction of Protein Secondary Structure Content by Using the Concept of Chou's Pseudo Amino Acid Composition and Support Vector Machine. Protein Pept. Lett. 16(1), 27–31 (2009)
4. Kuhlman, B., et al.: Design of a Novel Globular Protein Fold with Atomic-Level Accuracy. Science 302(5649), 1364–1368 (2003)
5. Zhang, C., Kim, S.H.: The Anatomy of Protein Beta-Sheet Topology. J. Mol. Biol. 299(4), 1075–1089 (2000)
6. Balbach, J.J., et al.: Supramolecular Structure in Full-Length Alzheimer's Beta-Amyloid Fibrils: Evidence for a Parallel Beta-Sheet Organization from Solid-State Nuclear Magnetic Resonance. Biophysical Journal 83(2), 1205–1216 (2002)
7. Wathen, B., Jia, Z.C.: Protein Beta-Sheet Nucleation is Driven by Local Modular Formation. Journal of Biological Chemistry 285(24), 18376–18384 (2010)
8. Piana, S., et al.: Computational Design and Experimental Testing of the Fastest-Folding Beta-Sheet Protein. J. Mol. Biol. 405(1), 43–48 (2011)
9. Zhang, L., et al.: Studies on the Rules of Beta-Strand Alignment in a Protein Beta-Sheet Structure. Journal of Theoretical Biology 285(1), 69–76 (2011)

10. Goh, B.C., et al.: The Mechanism of Antiparallel Beta-Sheet Formation Based on Conditioned Self-Avoiding Walk. Eur. Phys. J. E Soft. Matter. 35(4), 9704 (2012)
11. Zhang, G.Z., Huang, D.S., Quan, Z.H.: Combining a Binary Input Encoding Scheme with RBFNN for Globulin Protein Inter-Residue Contact Map Prediction. Pattern Recognition Letters 26(10), 1543–1553 (2005)
12. Cheng, J.L., Baldi, P.: Improved Residue Contact Prediction Using Support Vector Machines and A Large Feature Set. BMC Bioinformatics 8, 113–121 (2007)
13. Steward, R.E., Thornton, J.M.: Prediction of Strand Pairing in Antiparallel and Parallel Beta-Sheets Using Information Theory. Proteins-Structure Function and Bioinformatics 48(2), 178–191 (2002)
14. Zhang, N., et al.: The Interstrand Amino Acid Pairs Play a Significant Role in Determining The Parallel or Antiparallel Orientation of Beta-Strands. Biochemical and Biophysical Research Communications 386(3), 537–543 (2009)
15. Zhang, N., et al.: Prediction of the Parallel/Antiparallel Orientation of Beta-Strands Using Amino Acid Pairing Preferences and Support Vector Machines. Journal of Theoretical Biology 263(3), 360–368 (2010)
16. Lifson, S., Sander, C.: Specific Recognition in the Tertiary Structure of Beta-Sheets of Proteins. Journal of Molecular Biology 139(4), 627–639 (1980)
17. Hubbard, T.J.: Use of Beta-Strand Interaction Pseudo-Potentials in Protein Structure Prediction and Modelling. In: Proceedings of The Biotechnology Computing Track, Protein Structure Prediction Minitrack of The 27th HICSS. IEEE Computer Society Press (1994)
18. Wouters, M.A., Curmi, P.M.: An Analysis of Side Chain Interactions and Pair Correlations Within Antiparallel Beta-Sheets: The Differences Between Backbone Hydrogen-Bonded and Non-Hydrogen-Bonded Residue Pairs. Proteins-Structure Function and Bioinformatics 22(2), 119–131 (1995)
19. Fooks, H.M., et al.: Amino Acid Pairing Preferences in Parallel Beta-Sheets in Proteins. Journal of Molecular Biology 356(1), 32–44 (2006)
20. Kato, Y., Akutsu, T., Seki, H.: Dynamic Programming Algorithms and Grammatical Modeling for Protein Beta-Sheet Prediction. Journal of Computational Biology 16(7), 945–957 (2009)
21. Aydin, Z., Altunbasak, Y., Erdogan, H.: Bayesian Models and Algorithms for Protein Beta-Sheet Prediction. IEEE/ACM Trans. Comput. Biol. Bioinform. 8(2), 395–409 (2011)
22. Wang, G.L., Dunbrack, R.L.: PISCES: A Protein Sequence Culling Server. Bioinformatics 19(12), 1589–1591 (2003)
23. Wang, G.L., Dunbrack, R.L.: PISCES: Recent Improvements to A PDB Sequence Culling Server. Nucleic Acids Research 33, W94–W98 (2005)
24. Chou, K.C., Shen, H.B.: Recent Progress in Protein Subcellular Location Prediction. Analytical Biochemistry 370(1), 1–16 (2007)
25. Chou, K.C.: Some Remarks on Protein Attribute Prediction and Pseudo Amino Acid Composition. Journal of Theoretical Biology 273(1), 236–247 (2011)
26. Zhang, N., et al.: SHEETSPAIR: A Database of Amino Acid Pairs in Protein Sheet Structures. Data Science Journal 6, S589–S595 (2007)
27. Linding, R., et al.: Protein Disorder Prediction: Implications for Structural Proteomics. Structure 11(11), 1453–1459 (2003)
28. Ferron, F., et al.: A Practical Overview of Protein Disorder Prediction Methods. Proteins-Structure Function and Bioinformatics 65(1), 1–14 (2006)
29. Parisien, M., Major, F.: Ranking The Factors That Contribute to Protein B-Sheet Folding. Proteins: Structure, Function, and Bioinformatics 68(4), 824–829 (2007)

30. Wang, L.H., et al.: Predicting Protein Secondary Structure by a Support Vector Machine Based on a New Coding Scheme. Genome Inform. 15(2), 181–190 (2004)
31. French, S., Robson, B.: What Is a Conservative Substitution? J. Mol. Evol. 19, 171–175 (1983)
32. Tanford, C.: Contribution of Hydrophobic Interactions to the Stability of the Globular Conformation of Proteins. Journal of The American Chemical Society 84(22), 4240–4247 (1962)
33. Eisenberg, D., Wilcox, W., Mclachlan, A.D.: Hydrophobicity and Amphiphilicity in Protein Structure. J. Cell Biochem. 31(1), 11–17 (1986)
34. Chou, K.C.: Prediction of Protein Cellular Attributes Using Pseudo-Amino Acid Composition. Proteins-Structure Function and Bioinformatics 43(3), 246–255 (2001)
35. Breiman, L.: Random Forests. Machine Learning 45(1), 5–32 (2001)
36. Hua, J.P., et al.: Optimal Number of Features as a Function of Sample Size for Various Classification Rules. Bioinformatics 21(8), 1509–1515 (2005)
37. Qi, Y., Klein-Seetharaman, J., Bar-Joseph, Z.: Random Forest Similarity for Protein-Protein Interaction Prediction From Multiple Sources. In: Pac. Symp. Biocomput., pp. 531–542 (2005)
38. Diaz-Uriarte, R., Alvarez De Andres, S.: Gene Selection and Classification of Microarray Data Using Random Forest. Bmc Bioinformatics 7, 3 (2006)
39. Jain, P., Hirst, J.D.: Automatic Structure Classification of Small Proteins Using Random Forest. Bmc Bioinformatics 11, 364 (2010)
40. Jia, S.C., Hu, X.Z.: Using Random Forest Algorithm to Predict Beta-Hairpin Motifs. Protein and Peptide Letters (2011)
41. Kandaswamy, K.K., et al.: AFP-Pred: a Random Forest Approach for Predicting Antifreeze Proteins From Sequence-Derived Properties. Journal of Theoretical Biology 270(1), 56–62 (2011)
42. Witten, I.H., Frank, E., Hall, M.A.: Data Mining: Practical Machine Learning Tools and Techniques, 3rd edn. Morgan Kaufmann (2011)
43. Gao, S., et al.: Prediction of Function Changes Associated with Single-Point Protein Mutations Using Support Vector Machines (Svms). Human Mutation. 30(8), 1161–1166 (2009)
44. Chang, C.C., Lin, C.J.: LIBSVM: a Library for Support Vector Machines (2001)
45. Kolinski, A., et al.: Generalized Comparative Modeling (GENECOMP): A Combination of Sequence Comparison, Threading, and Lattice Modeling for Protein Structure Prediction and Refinement. Proteins-Structure Function and Genetics 44(2), 133–149 (2001)

Extract Features Using Stacked Denoised Autoencoder

Yushu Gao[1], Lin Zhu[1], Hao-Dong Zhu[2], Yong Gan[2], and Li Shang[3]

[1] College of Electronics and Information Engineering, Tongji University Shanghai, China
[2] School of Computer and Communication Engineering,
ZhengZhou University of Light Industry
Henan Zhengzhou, 450002, China
[3] Department of Communication Technology, College of Electronic Information Engineering,
Suzhou Vocational University, Suzhou 215104, Jiangsu, China

Abstract. In this paper, a novel neural network, DenoisedAutoEncoder (DAE) is introduced first. This neural network is applied for extracting the features. In this paper, we proved that stacked DAE can extract good features for classification task. We apply the stacked DAE to extract features of leave pictures, and then we classify leaves using those features with SVM, the result suggests that this method surpass pure SVM.

Keywords: Stacked DAE, classification, feature extracting.

1 Introduction

When proposed an efficient way to train deep architecture through pre-training [1], deep neural network re-boomed. Deep architectures have an advantage in feature extracting, because they can get much more complex and abstract features than shallow architectures[2][3]. In this paper, we extract features through stacked DAE and then do classification using these features. The results prove that the performance surpass pure SVM.

2 Prerequisites

2.1 Basic AutoEncoder

AE neural is an unsupervised learning algorithm that applies back propagation,Setting the output equal to the input. It directly encodes the input layer and then decodes the hidden layer. The aim of an AE is to learn a compressed or sparse representation (encoding) for a set of data. The architecture of AE is shown in figure 1:

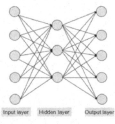

Input layer   Hidden layer   Output layer

Fig. 1. The architecture of AE. The input and output are equal, and there is only one hidden layer.

D.-S. Huang et al. (Eds.): ICIC 2014, LNBI 8590, pp. 10–14, 2014.

In the AE, we should first define a feature extracting function called encoder in a special parameterizedclosed form. With the encoder, we can straightforward compute the feature vector efficiently. The formula is:

$$h = f_\theta(x) \tag{1}$$

where h is the feature vector or sometimes called representation, f is the encoder function, x is the input vector and theta is the parameter vector. To get the output, we should define another function called decoder: $r = g_\theta(h)$

where r is the output, g is the decoder function, h is the feature vector from (1) and theta is the parameter vector. So the AE is defined by its encoder and decoder, and there are many different kind of training principle. Theta is earned simultaneously on the task of reconstructing as well as possible the original input. One of most popular training principle is attempting to lowest the reconstruct error defined as: $\min_\theta L(r,x)$

Basic AE training consists in finding a value of parameter vector theta minimizing reconstruction error

$$\vartheta(\theta) = \sum_t L\left(x^{(t)}, g_\theta\left(f_\theta\left(x^{(t)}\right)\right)\right) \tag{2}$$

where x is the training example. This minimization is usually carried out by stochastic gradient descent as in the training mulit-layer-perceptrons(MLP). The most commonly used encoder and decoder are:

$$f_\theta(x) = s_f(b + Wx)$$

$$g_\theta(h) = s_g(d + W'h)$$

where s_f and s_g are non-linear.

2.2   DAE

Vincent proposed the DAE in [4][5], In the DAE, we should first corrupt the input data. There are two common way to corrupt the raw data, to add Gaussian noise or binary masking noise. Here we donate the original data and the corrupt data, if you add Gaussian noise, we can get $\tilde{x} = x + N(0, \sigma^2 I)$.

Then, the DAE is optimized using the artificially corrupted input. In the DAE, learn the identity in not enough because the learner must capture the input distribution in order to undo the effect of the corrupt process [6].

Formally, the objective optimized by such a DAE is:

$$\vartheta_{DAE} = \sum_t E_{q\left(\tilde{x}|x^{(t)}\right)}\left[L\left(x^{(t)}, g_\theta\left(f_\theta\left(\tilde{x}\right)\right)\right)\right]$$

where $E_{q\left(\tilde{x}|x^{(t)}\right)}[\cdot]$ denotes the expectation over corrupted examples ~x drawn from

corruption process $q\left(\tilde{x}|x^{(t)}\right)$. In practice this is optimized by stochastic gradient

descent, where the stochastic gradient is estimated by drawing one or a few corrupted versions of x(t) each time x(t) is considered.

3   The Architecture Used in this Paper

In this paper, the author combined the stacked DAE and SVM.for clarity, the architecture is shown in figure 2:

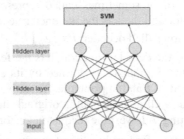

Fig. 2. The architecture used in this paper

The algorithm is in table 1:

Table 1. Training algorithm

---

1. Activation[0]=input data.
2. For i=1, 2, 3...n
    Train the AE[i],use activation[i-1] as the input, and get the weight w[i]
3. Unfold these AE in a deep neural network.
4. Fine tune the deep neural network gained in step 2
5. Add a SVM to the highest level for classification task, to train the SVM,taking the deep neural network's highest level hidden layer's activation as input and corresponding labels as the output.

---

4   Experiment

In the experiment, we chose sigmoid activation function for the DAE, the sigmoid function is: $sigmoid\left(x\right)=\dfrac{1}{1+e^{-x}}$, We chose binary masking noise, denote the noised data as $\tilde{x}$, we can get:

$$\tilde{h}=sigmoid\left(W\,\tilde{x}+b\right) \tag{3}$$

Where W is the weight and b is the bias.

Subsequently, we can get the reconstructed version of input x by

$$r=sigmoid\left(W^{T}\,\tilde{h}+d\right)$$

Where W^{T} is the reverse of W^{T} in (5) and d is the bias.

Finally, we get the optimize object: $\underset{W,b,d}{minimize} L_{DAE} = \dfrac{1}{2N} \sum_N \left(x^{(i)} - r^i\right)^2$

For all the samples, the fraction of training samples and testing samples is 2:1. We first transform those pictures into 32*32 gray pixels.

In our experiment, the architecture is 1024-2048-512-2048-1024 and we choose the 3rd lay to perform classify. We choose the binary masking noise to corrupt the original data.

Table 2. The parameters used in our experiment

	Learning rate	Activation function	poach	Batch size	Masked fraction
DAE{1}	0.01	sigmoid	10	10	0.15
DAE{2}	0.01	Sigmoid	10	10	0.3
Unfold Net	0.05		5	10	

The result of this experiment is shown in table 3, and in the two method, the parameters of SVM are same:

Table 3. The result of this experiment

Method	accuracy
SVM	88%
Stacked DAE+SVM	90%

5   Conclusion

AE can extract good features through restricting the input and the output, DAE is a generative of AE aiming at robust through corrupt the input and try to make the output to be same to clean input data. Our experiment show that stacked DAE can get better feature, so the result beat pure SVM.

Acknowledgments. This work is supported by the Science and Technology Innovation Outstanding Talent Plan Project of Henan Province of China under Professor De-Shuang Huang (No.134200510025), the National Natural Science Foundation of China (Nos. 61373105, 61373098 & 61133010).

References

[1] Bengio, Y.: Learning deep architectures for AI. Foundations and Trends® in Machine Learning 2(1), 1–127 (2009)
[2] Bengio, Y., Courville, A., Vincent, P.: Representation learning: A review and new perspectives, p. 1 (2013)
[3] Bourlard, H., Kamp, Y.: Auto-association by multilayer perceptrons and singular value decomposition. Biological Cybernetics 59(4-5), 291–294 (1988)

[4] Rumelhart, D.E., Hinton, G.E., Williams, R.J.: Learning representations by back-propagating errors. Nature 323(6088), 533–536 (1986)

[5] Hinton, G.E.: Training products of experts by minimizing contrastive divergence. Neural Computation 14(8), 1771–1800 (2002)

[6] Vincent, P., Larochelle, H., Bengio, Y., Manzagol, P.-A.: Extracting and composing robust features withdenoising AEs. In: ICML 2008 (2008)

[7] Vincent, P., Larochelle, H., Lajoie, I., Bengio, Y., Manzagol, P.-A.: Stackeddenoising AEs: Learning useful representations in a deep network with a local denoising criterion. J. Machine Learning Res. 11 (2010)

[8] Wang, X.F., Huang, D.S., Xu, H.: An efficient local Chan-Vese model for image segmentation. Pattern Recognition 43(3), 603–618 (2010)

[9] Li, B., Huang, D.S.: Locally linear discriminant embedding: An efficient method for face recognition. Pattern Recognition 41(12), 3813–3821 (2008)

[10] Huang, D.S., Du, J.-X.: A constructive hybrid structure optimization methodology for radial basis probabilistic neural networks. IEEE Trans. Neural Networks 19(12), 2099–2115 (2008)

[11] Huang, D.S.: Radial basis probabilistic neural networks: Model and application. Int. Journal of Pattern Recognit., and Artificial Intell. 13(7), 1083–1101 (1999)

[12] Huang, D.S., Horace, H.S.Ip, Chi, Z.-R.: A neural root finder of polynomials based on root moments. Neural Computation 16(8), 1721–1762 (2004)

Cancer Classification Using Ensemble
of Error Correcting Output Codes

Zhihao Zeng, Kun-Hong Liu, and Zheyuan Wang

Xiamen University, School of Software
{zengzhihao5star,wang1987}@gmail.com, lkhqz@xmu.edu.cn

Abstract. We address the microarray dataset based cancer classification problem using a newly proposed ensemble of Error Correcting Output Codes (*E-ECOC*) method. To the best of our knowledge, it is the first time that ECOC based ensemble has been applied to the microarray dataset classification. Different feature subsets are generated from datasets as inputs for some problem-dependent ECOC coding methods, so as to produce diverse ECOC coding matrixes. Then, the mutual difference degree among the coding matrixes is calculated as an indicator to select coding matrixes with maximum difference. Local difference maximum selection(*L-DMS*) and global difference maximum selection(*G-DMS*) are the strategies for picking coding matrixes based on same or different ECOC algorithms. In the experiments, it can be found that E-ECOC algorithm outperforms the individual ECOC and effectively solves the microarray classification problem.

Keywords: ECOC, ensemble learning, Cancer classification, feature selection.

1 Introduction

In the field of machine learning and pattern recognition, the goal of a classification problem is looking for a map function: f: S – K, in which S is a set of attributes that describes series of properties of the samples, and K is the corresponding labels that belong to each sample. Function f maps each sample belonging to S into a unique class label k. Consider a binary problem, there has been widespread application of mature machine learning algorithm for estimating the function f. However, for multi-class problems, with the increasing categories, a single learner is usually hardly competent to produce accurate outputs. |And there are many classifier that can only deal with binary class problem. An alteration for solving the multi-class problem is the divide and conquer method, which means, the original classification problem is decomposed into multiple binary classification problems. By solving each binary classification independently, we can solve a multi-class classification task with some integration strategies, such as voting. Under the guidance of this idea, there are three basic solutions: flat strategy, hierarchical strategy, Error-Correcting Output Codes (ECOC). In flat strategy, a fixed decomposition method is used, such as One vs. One or One vs. All, and the final label is decided directly by voting. On the other hand,

D.-S. Huang et al. (Eds.): ICIC 2014, LNBI 8590, pp. 15–24, 2014.

hierarchical strategy build a binary tree based on the relationship among categories for the multi-class problem, and each branch node represents a binary classifier and the leaf node represents a final class. ECOC algorithm framework[1] consists of two key steps: in encoding phase, the original multi-classification problem is decomposed into multiple binary classification problem, which is represented by an M*N encoding matrix δ. In a coding matrix, each row represents a unique class, and each column illustrates specifically the decomposition method from a multi-class problem into a set of binary problem. In decoding phase, by comparing the distance between outputs of the multiple binary classifier and each code word in the coding matrix, the label with the minimum distance is selected as the final label for a unknown sample[2]. In a sense, ECOC algorithm framework can be considered as a more general solution than flat and hierarchical strategies. In the coding phase, the methods of decomposing multi-class contain all of the possible ways of division from the former two strategies. In addition, Dieterich and Kong[3] proved that ECOC algorithm framework can reduce bias and variance errors produced by the binary classification algorithms. It's worth noting that the number of the binary classifiers has been reduced to [$10\log_2 N$, $15 \log_2 N$][4]. The coding matrix is not difficult to construct even when N is large enough. However, it is very difficult to filter the optimum coding matrix.

In the past few years, the ECOC algorithm framework were studied by researchers from different perspectives. Algorithms to construct suitable and effective coding matrix, and the decoding strategies have been extensively studied. Moreover, Masulli and Valentini[5] analyzed the different factors that affect the effectiveness of ECOC algorithm, and the correlation between the coding matrix and the binary classifier. Effectiveness of ECOC depends on code word correlation, structure and accuracy of dichotomizers, and the complexity of the multiclass learning problem. It is noticeable that the predefined coding matrix, like one vs. one, one vs. all, and the random-based coding matrix, are not suitable for the problems. The reason is that all those algorithms neglect the distribution characteristics of the data itself. Therefore, researchers take the distribution features of the data into consideration when constructing the encoding matrix and proposed many data dependent encoding algorithms to decompose the original multi-class problem into dichotomizer. DECOC[6] method builds N-1 binary classifier. Moreover, Crammer and Singer[7] proved that searching for the optimal coding matrix which are associated to the problem domain is a NP-complete problems. Recent research works use Genetic Algorithms in the coding phase to obtain higher accuracy of coding matrix along with reducing the number of dichotomizer. Bautista et al.[8] focused on optimizing ECOC coding matrix based on the standard genetic algorithm (GA), which is known as Minimal ECOC. The final result was that the number of binary classifiers is reduced to [$\log_2 N$] and at the same time, the degree of differentiation among classes are guaranteed. Garcia-Pedrajas and Fyfe[9] used the CHC based genetic algorithm to optimize the Sparse Random ECOC Matrix. In their work, the length of coding matrix is limited within [30, 50], and is independent of both the distribution of data sets and the number of classes. It is obvious that the techniques involved are simple and direct. Lorena and Carvalho [10]combined GA with the Sparse Random coding matrix too, and limited the length of code in [$\log_2 N$, N]. Furthermore, Miguer and Sergio

[11]proposed a new genetic operator to avoid invalid individuals and reduce the search space of the genetic algorithm.

Although there are already many papers discussing ECOC, the application of ECOC on microarray data is just at the beginning. Different from regular datasets, due to the small sample size of microarray data, a validation set is not affordable in the classification process, so it is much more complicated. In this paper, we propose a novel ensemble of ECOC(E-ECOC) system work by integrating different ECOC coding matrix with local difference maximum selection(LDMS) or global difference maximum selection(GDMS) strategies. And the experiments on some microarray datasets proves that our method is effective.

The rest of the paper is organized as follows: Section 2 overviews the background of ECOC framework. In Section 3, we present the E-ECOC framework. Section 4 is devoted to presenting the experimental results. Finally, Section 5 concludes the paper.

2   Error Correcting Output Codes

Let K denotes a set of unique labels, $K = \{k_1, k_2, \dots, k_N\}$, where N means the number of classes (N > 2). Let S denotes a set of samples, $S = \{(X_1, y_1), (X_2, y_2), \dots, (X_L, y_L)\}$. X_i is the features vector represent the sample S_i, and y_i is the class label to which S_i belongs. Besides, $y_i \in K$. L means the number of samples. And Let D denotes a set of dichotomizers according to the ECOC coding matrix $D = \{d_1, d_2, \dots, d_M\}$.

The basis of ECOC framework is building a unique "code word" for each class. The elements within the coding matrix of size M * N belong to the set {-1, +1} or {-1, 0, +1}. Each row represents a class, and there are M classes totally. Meanwhile, each column is interpreted as a binary classifier, and the original class label is re-calibrated into binary classes, which is named as meta-class. For instance, suppose a sample (X, y) belonging to class i. It will be re-labeled as positive in j-th dichotomizer when $ECOC(i, j) = 1$; otherwise (X, y) will be re-labeled as negative when $ECOC(i, j) = -1$. Moreover, (X, y) will be neglected when $ECOC(i, j) = 0$.

(a)   Encoding Algorithms

Encoding matrix plays an important role in ECOC framework, because it describes how to decompose a multi-class classification into a set of binary problem. In [12], the researchers summarized the methods to build coding matrix into two categories: static method and dynamic method. The static method commonly constructs coding matrix independent of base classifiers and datasets. There are four kinds of static coding design schemes, including One Vs. One, One Vs. All, dense random, and sparse random. Dynamic methods construct problem-dependent encoding matrixes, so they are more flexible comparing with static schemes.

The researchers take two factors into consideration: row separation/column separation and matrix validity. Row separation refers to the distance between any pair of code words, and column separation indicates the difference degree within each binary classifier pair. Both should be as large as possible, so as to reduce the correlation between base classifiers.

The coding matrix may not be correctly constructed, and there are some essential rules to check the legality of the matrix, as shown in equation 1-4[13]. Equation 1 indicates that each column of the encoding matrix comprises at least one +1 and -1. AHD represents attenuated Hamming distance. Equation 2 shows that the minimum Hamming distance between two rows should be at least one, which means all 0s, all +1s and all -1s are not correct. Equation 3 means if there is converse relationship between any two rows, the encoding matrix is invalid. Equation 4 indicates that the number of binary classifiers should be at least $\log_2 M$. Validity checking can provide pseudo integrity protection while constructing coding matrix.

$$\min\left(\delta AHD\left(r^i, r^l\right)\right) \geq 1, \forall i, k : i \neq k \neq, i, k \in [1, \ldots, N]. \tag{1}$$

$$\min\left(\delta HD\left(d^j, d^l\right)\right) \geq 1, \forall j, l : j \neq l, j, l \in [1, \ldots, M]. \tag{2}$$

$$\min\left(\delta HD\left(d^j, -d^l\right)\right) \geq 1, \forall j, l : j \neq l, j, l \in [1, \ldots, M]. \tag{3}$$

$$N \geq \log_2 M \tag{4}$$

(b)   Decoding Strategies

When testing an unlabeled sample X*, each binary classifier gives an output, and the group of outputs makes up a vector V* with length L. Then, the distance between the output vector and code words within the coding matrix is calculated, and the code word with the minimum distance will be the class label to which X* belongs. The procedure is called decoding. There are different decoding strategies. Among them, hamming decoding is the most commonly used, as is shown in equation 5-6. It has obvious drawbacks, because it requires each binary classifier produces hard outputs, +1 or -1. With Euclidean decoding strategy, this problem can be solved, and the output of each classifier could be the confidence to positive class or negative class as shown in equation 7.

$$HD\left(V^*, y_i\right) = \sum_{j=1}^{n} \frac{\left(1 - sign\left(V^{*j} \times y_i^j\right)\right)}{2}. \tag{5}$$

$$y = \min_{i=\{1,\ldots,n\}} HD\left(V^*, y_i\right). \tag{6}$$

$$ED\left(V^{*}, y_{i}\right) = \sqrt{\sum_{j=1}^{n}\left(V^{*j} - y_{i}^{j}\right)^{2}} \,. \tag{7}$$

Besides distance based decoding strategies, researchers also proposed some other schemes based on loss function[4]. The loss function is calculated firstly according to the output vector V* as shown in equation 8. Loss function $L\left(\theta\right)$ depends on the characteristics of the base classifier, and the most commonly used functions are $L\left(\theta\right) = -\theta$ (LLD) and $L\left(\theta\right) = e^{-\theta}$ (ELD). Then, the code word with the minimum loss function value is picked as the class label for a sample. . Moreover, decoding strategies based on probability have been proposed, which take probability estimation and confidence into consideration.

$$LB\left(V^{*}, y_{i}\right) = \sum_{j=1}^{n}L\left(V^{*j} \times y_{i}^{j}\right). \tag{8}$$

3   Ensemble of ECOC

The most important purpose while designing ECOC coding matrix is to improve the error correction capability of the matrix. According to the theory of error-correcting, the matrix could fix d bits' error if the code matrix's minimum hamming distance equals 2d + 1. Therefore, many random-based algorithms and data-dependent algorithms try to maximize the minimum hamming distance. However, the ability to detect and correct errors depends on whether the errors occur independently. In the ECOC framework, the efforts to improve the binary classifiers' mutual independence is reasonable and essential. In [12], researchers uses different feature subsets for each dichotomizer, leading to more independent classifiers.

We design a new method to ensemble ECOC coding matrixes called *E-ECOC*. The strategy consists of designing multiple ECOC coding matrixes, and then ensemble the matrices with high diversity. That is, a multi-class problem is solved by a set of different ECOC coding matrixes consequently, so as to increase the overall system accuracy. And the coding matrices are produced based on different problem dependent algorithms, and different feature subsets are used to construct the matrix within one same algorithm. The notation used to measure the difference is show in equation 9. We design two strategies to ensemble ECOC coding matrixes, the first one called as Local Difference Maximum Selection (L-DMS). Different feature subsets to construct the problem dependent coding matrix, and the top coding matrixes are chosen to solve the original multi-class problem. The second is called as Global Difference Maximum Selection (G-DMS). Different algorithms are applied to construct coding matrices, and for each algorithm, different feature subsets are used. Then, we calculate the global difference degree and choose top coding matrixes with maximum difference degree. The process of choosing coding matrices is shown in Figure 1.

$$Diff\left(E\left(M,N^{*}\right),E\left(M,N\right)\right)=\sum_{i=1}^{N^{*}}\min_{j=1}^{N}\left(L\left(d_{i},d_{j}\right)\right) \tag{9}$$

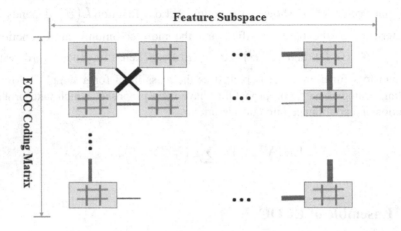

Fig. 1. ECOC coding matrixes' mutual difference degree, basis for ECOC ensemble. Red lines mean the local diversity among one same ECOC algorithm with different feature subsets (L-DMS). Purple lines and dark lines including the red lines indicate the global diversity among different ECOC coding matrixes with different feature subsets (G-DMS). The thickness of the line illustrates the difference degree.

4   Experiments and Analysis

ECOC library [14]is used to implement the ECOC algorithm framework, and three ECOC methods are used: DECOC[6], forest-ECOC[15], and ECOC-One[16]. The decoding method uses the default Hamming distance function. Two kinds of base classifiers are applied: KNN (k=3), and SVM (Lib-SVM library[17]). Other parameters use the default settings. The feature selection methods include Su[18], Laplacian Score[19] and t-test[20]. Moreover, the feature size within a same ECOC coding matrix increases from 20 to 200, and the step size is 20. We apply E-ECOC method to two well-known cancer datasets: Cancers [21], and Breast cancer dataset [22]. Table 1 shows the performance for each single ECOC coding matrix, and Table 1, 2 summarizes the ensemble results. Methods (a), (b), and (c) mean one single ECOC coding matrix with feature selection. Methods (d), (e), and (f) select from one same encoding algorithm with different feature subsets, which is called as L-DMS. Method (g) selects ECOC coding matrixes from different encoding algorithms and each constructed with different features, which is named as G-DMS.

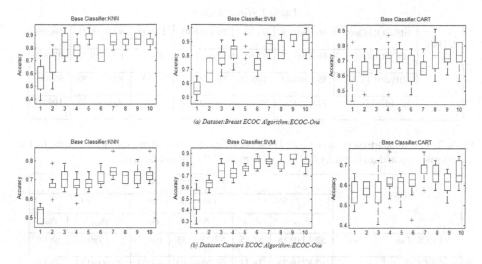

(a) Dataset:Breast ECOC Algorithm:ECOC-One

(b) Dataset:Cancers ECOC Algorithm:ECOC-One

Fig. 2. Typical results of classification accuracy obtained by individual ECOC-One with different number of genes selected by Laplacian Score: (a) Dataset: Breast (b) Dataset: Cancers

Table 1. The comparison of average and best classification accuracies among individual ECOC coding matrixes and different ECOC ensemble method for dataset Breast

Breast		Base Classifier: KNN					
		Su		Laplacian Score		t-test	
		A_{avg}	A_{best}	A_{avg}	A_{best}	A_{avg}	A_{best}
(a)ECOC-One		56.52±1.09	73.91	69.13±1.07	82.61	69.13±0.35	78.26
(b)DECOC		65.65±0.61	78.26	72.61±0.17	78.26	62.17±0.51	73.91
(c)Forest-ECOC		63.04±0.47	73.91	76.52±0.39	82.61	64.35±1.42	82.61
L-DMS	(d)ECOC-One	73.04±0.79	**86.96**	82.61±0.67	**100.00**	**92.61±0.21**	**100.00**
	(e)DECOC	75.22±0.21	82.61	84.78±0.26	91.30	89.13±0.22	95.65
	(f)Forest-ECOC	73.91±0.42	82.61	**89.13±0.30**	95.65	89.57±0.30	95.65
(g)G-DMS		**78.26±0.42**	**86.96**	83.91±0.21	91.30	87.39±0.27	95.65
Breast		Base Classifier: SVM					
		Su		Laplacian Score		t-test	
		A_{avg}	A_{best}	A_{avg}	A_{best}	A_{avg}	A_{best}
(a)ECOC-One		55.65±0.29	65.22	68.26±0.59	78.26	63.04±1.10	82.61
(b)DECOC		63.91±0.25	69.57	66.96±0.39	73.91	59.13±0.93	73.91
(c)Forest-ECOC		68.26±0.30	73.91	78.26±0.34	86.96	64.35±1.08	82.61

Table 1. (*Continued.*)

L-DMS	(d)ECOC-One	86.96±0.08	91.30	**99.13±0.03**	**100.00**	**92.61±0.21**	**100.00**
	(e)DECOC	88.26±0.21	91.30	87.39±0.27	95.65	89.13±0.22	95.65
	(f)Forest-ECOC	**89.13±0.43**	**100.00**	86.52±0.27	91.30	89.57±0.30	95.65
(g)G-DMS		77.83±0.52	91.30	86.09±0.12	91.30	93.04±0.26	**100.00**

Table 2. The comparison of average and best classification accuracies among individual ECOC coding matrixes and different ECOC ensemble method for dataset Cancers

Cancers		Base Classifier: KNN					
		Su		Laplacian Score		t-test	
		A_{avg}	A_{best}	A_{avg}	A_{best}	A_{avg}	A_{best}
(a)ECOC-One		52.13±0.18	57.45	57.23±0.38	63.83	59.15±0.47	68.09
(b)DECOC		**67.87±0.23**	**78.72**	61.06±0.19	68.09	70.00±0.15	76.60
(c)Forest-ECOC		56.17±0.40	65.96	43.83±0.18	51.06	54.04±0.49	63.83
L-DMS	(d)ECOC-One	57.23±0.30	65.96	73.40±0.16	78.72	79.15±0.06	80.85
	(e)DECOC	63.62±0.31	72.34	74.47±0.10	78.72	**80.43±0.16**	**87.23**
	(f)Forest-ECOC	60.43±0.29	74.47	**76.17±0.43**	**89.36**	79.36±0.25	**87.23**
(g)G-DMS		65.96±0.35	74.47	74.04±0.15	80.85	78.09±0.18	82.98
Cancers		Base Classifier: SVM					
		Su		Laplacian Score		t-test	
		A_{avg}	A_{best}	A_{avg}	A_{best}	A_{avg}	A_{best}
(a)ECOC-One		48.30±1.49	65.96	46.81±0.33	55.32	50.21±0.63	65.96
(b)DECOC		63.19±0.22	70.21	52.34±0.11	59.57	61.70±0.46	76.60
(c)Forest-ECOC		57.87±0.14	61.70	59.15±0.24	48.94	58.51±0.44	65.96
L-DMS	(d)ECOC-One	81.49±0.11	87.23	86.17±0.25	93.62	87.23±0.27	**95.74**
	(e)DECOC	79.79±0.31	**89.36**	82.55±0.11	87.23	84.47±0.11	89.36
	(f)Forest-ECOC	78.51±0.26	85.11	**87.45±0.18**	**95.74**	**91.49±0.06**	**95.74**
(g)G-DMS		**83.40±0.11**	**89.36**	85.96±0.43	93.62	87.23±0.11	93.62

From Fig. 2, it can be found that the performance of the ECOC-One methods varies greatly with different feature subsets, which indicates the performance of data-dependent ECOC coding matrixes vary greatly. Comparing with individual ECOC coding matrixes, E-ECOC ensembles achieve better results. From Table. 1 and table. 2, E-ECOC with SVM generally has better average results. For dataset Breast, the best results reach 99.13±0.03. Its parameters include ECOC-One, SVM as base classifier and t-test for feature selection. For dataset Cancers, the best results reach 91.49 ± 0.06. Its parameters include forest-ECOC, SVM as base classifier and t-test for feature selection. Furthermore, L-DMS has similar performance comparing with G-DMS.

5   Conclusions

In this paper, we applied ECOC framework to tackle the microarray data classification problem. In this ensemble scheme, individual ECOC coding matrixes are selected according to the mutual diversity measures. Therefore, ECOC ensemble are used to solve the original multi-class classification problem. Two strategies including different feature subsets and different data-dependent ECOC coding matrixes are applied to promote diversity. The experimental results show that ECOC ensemble algorithm is an effective method for microarray classification, which usually leads to better accuracy. Furthermore, ECOC ensemble is more robust method comparing with individual ECOC.

References

1. Dietterich, T.G., Bakiri, G.: Solving multiclass learning problems via error-correcting output codes. arXiv preprint cs/9501101 (1995)
2. Escalera, S., Pujol, O., Radeva, P.: On the decoding process in ternary error-correcting output codes. IEEE Transactions on Pattern Analysis and Machine Intelligence 32(1), 120–134 (2010)
3. Kong, E.B., Dietterich, T.G.: Error-Correcting Output Coding Corrects Bias and Variance. In: ICML 1995 (1995)
4. Allwein, E.L., Schapire, R.E., Singer, Y.: Reducing multiclass to binary: A unifying approach for margin classifiers. The Journal of Machine Learning Research 1, 113–141 (2001)
5. Masulli, F., Valentini, G.: Effectiveness of error correcting output codes in multiclass learning problems. In: Kittler, J., Roli, F. (eds.) MCS 2000. LNCS, vol. 1857, pp. 107–116. Springer, Heidelberg (2000)
6. Pujol, O., Radeva, P., Vitria, J.: Discriminant ecoc: A heuristic method for application dependent design of error correcting output codes. IEEE Transactions on Pattern Analysis and Machine Intelligence 28(6), 1007–1012 (2006)
7. Crammer, K., Singer, Y.: On the learnability and design of output codes for multiclass problems. Machine Learning 47(2-3), 201–233 (2002)
8. Bautista, M.Á., et al.: Minimal design of error-correcting output codes. Pattern Recognition Letters 33(6), 693–702 (2012)
9. García-Pedrajas, N., Fyfe, C.: Evolving output codes for multiclass problems. IEEE Transactions on Evolutionary Computation 12(1), 93–106 (2008)
10. Lorena, A.C., Carvalho, A.C.: Evolutionary design of multiclass support vector machines. Journal of Intelligent and Fuzzy Systems 18(5), 445–454 (2007)
11. Escalera, S., et al.: Subclass problem-dependent design for error-correcting output codes. IEEE Transactions on Pattern Analysis and Machine Intelligence 30(6), 1041–1054 (2008)
12. Bagheri, M.A., Montazer, G.A., Kabir, E.: A subspace approach to error correcting output codes. Pattern Recognition Letters 34(2), 176–184 (2013)

13. Bautista, M.Á., et al.: On the design of an ECOC-Compliant Genetic Algorithm. Pattern Recognition 47(2), 865–884 (2014)
14. Escalera, S., Pujol, O., Radeva, P.: Error-Correcting Ouput Codes Library. J. Mach. Learn. Res. 11, 661–664 (2010)
15. Escalera, S., Pujol, O., Radeva, P.: Boosted Landmarks of Contextual Descriptors and Forest-ECOC: A novel framework to detect and classify objects in cluttered scenes. Pattern Recognition Letters 28(13), 1759–1768 (2007)
16. Escalera, S., Pujol, O., Radeva, P.: ECOC-ONE: A novel coding and decoding strategy. In: 18th International Conference on Pattern Recognition, ICPR 2006. IEEE (2006)
17. Chang, C.-C., Lin, C.-J.: LIBSVM: a library for support vector machines. ACM Transactions on Intelligent Systems and Technology (TIST) 2(3), 27 (2011)
18. Yu, L., Liu, H.: Efficient feature selection via analysis of relevance and redundancy. The Journal of Machine Learning Research 5, 1205–1224 (2004)
19. He, X., Cai, D., Niyogi, P.: Laplacian score for feature selection. In: NIPS (2005)
20. Ding, C., Peng, H.: Minimum redundancy feature selection from microarray gene expression data. Journal of Bioinformatics and Computational Biology 3(2), 185–205 (2005)
21. Su, A.I., et al.: Molecular classification of human carcinomas by use of gene expression signatures. Cancer Research 61(20), 7388–7393 (2001)
22. Perou, C.M., et al.: Molecular portraits of human breast tumours. Nature 406(6797), 747–752 (2000)

Early Detection Method of Alzheimer's Disease Using EEG Signals

Dhiya Al-Jumeily[1], Shamaila Iram[1], Abir Jaffar Hussain[1], Vialatte Francois-Benois[2], and Paul Fergus [1]

[1] Applied Computing Research Group, Liverpool John Moores University,
Byroom Street, Liverpool, L3 3AF, UK
[2] Laboratoire SIGMA, ESPCI ParisTech, Paris, France
{D.Aljumeily,P.Fergus,A.Hussain}@ljmu.ac.uk,
francois.vialatte@espci.fr

Abstract. Different studies have stated that electroencephalogram signals in Alzheimer's disease patients usually have less synchronization as compare to healthy subjects. Changes in electroencephalogram signals start at early stage but clinically, these changes are not easily detected. To detect this perturbation, three neural synchrony measurement techniques have been examined with three different sets of data. This research work have successfully reported the experiment of comparing right and left temporal of brain with the rest of the brain area (frontal, central and occipital), as temporal regions are relatively the first ones to be affected by Alzheimer's disease. A new approach using principal component analysis before applying neural synchrony measurement techniques has been presented and compared with to other existing techniques. The simulation results indicated that applying principal component analysis before synchrony measurement techniques show significantly improvement over the lateral one. The results of the experiments were analyzed using Mann-Whitney U test.

Keywords: Electroencephalogram signals, EEG Signals, Alzheimer's Disease.

1 Introduction

Mild Cognitive Impairment (MCI) is characterized by impaired memory state of brain probably leads towards mild Alzheimer's disease (MiAD) or Alzheimer's disease (AD). This prodromal stage of AD is under a great influence of research for long time [1-3]. Different research work reported that 6-25% of MCI are transformed to AD annually and 0.2-4% transformed from healthy person to AD [2, 4], revealing the fact that MCI is a transition state of MiAD and AD.

Loss of functional connectivity between cortical and hippocampus has long been an important focus of many investigation to examine the cause of cognitive dysfunction in AD [5, 6]. Functional connectivity is a term which has been used to study the functional interaction among times series recorded from different brain areas [7]. Due to destructive characteristics of AD, it has also been characterized as a

D.-S. Huang et al. (Eds.): ICIC 2014, LNBI 8590, pp. 25–33, 2014.

neocortical "disconnection syndrome" [8]. Brain's visualization as a complex network of subsystems has led us to find out the factors that can best identify functional disorders in the brain [9]. There is now ample evidence that formation of dynamic links in term of synchronization constitutes the functional integration of brain [10-12].

Electroencephalogram (EEG) signals are considered functional example to evaluate cognitive disturbances and a diagnostic tool, especially when a diagnostic doubt exists even after the initial clinical procedures [13, 14]. A great deal of research has already been conducted to detect the fluctuations in EEG signals [2, 5, 15]. Alteration in the regional cerebral blood flow (rCBF) has been considered one of the causes of abnormality in EEG signals of AD [16, 17]. Studies on MCI have shown a decrease of alpha power [18, 19] and an increase of theta (4-8 Hz) power [20] in cortio-cortical and subcortical parts of the brain. Babiloni et al [2] claimed that the reduction of the synchronization likelihood occurs both at inter-hemispherical (delta-beta2) and fronto-parietal (delta-gamma) electrodes. Topographically analyzing the EEG signals, Micheal et al [22] reported a less synchronization of upper alpha band between central and temporal cortex. In line, a correlation between higher low-frequency amplitude and alpha-beta activity at frontal region may reflect an early sign of cortical atrophy during the course of AD. The concept of local and global methods is used to analyze synchronization between pairs of signals and entire EEG channels at the same time, respectively [15]. This paper proposes a novel approach using principal component analysis before applying neural synchrony measurement techniques; the proposed technique was benchmarked with other existing techniques. The simulation results indicated that applying principal component analysis before synchrony measurement techniques show significantly improvement over the lateral one. The reminder of this paper is organised as follows. Section 2 will discuss synchrony measurement techniques while section 3 will shows the data description and filtering. Section 4 is concerned with the methodology and section 5 shows the conclusion and future direction.

2   Synchrony Measurement Techniques

In this section, we briefly review the synchrony measurement techniques that we have implemented on our datasets which include phase synchrony, cross correlation and coherence.

2.1   Phase Synchrony (Hilbert Transform)

Synchronization of two periodic non-identical oscillators refers to the adjustment of their rhythmicity, i.e. the phase locking between the two signals. It refers to the interdependence between the instantaneous phases $\varphi_1(t)$ and $\varphi_2(t)$ of the two signals $s_1(t)$ and $s_2(t)$, respectively. It is usually written as:

$$\varphi_{n,m} = n\varphi_1(t) - m\varphi_2(t) = constant \tag{1}$$

Where n and m are integers indicating the ratio of possible frequency locking, and $\varphi_{n,m}$ is their relative phase or phase difference. To compute the phase synchronization, the instantaneous phase of the two signals should be known. This can be detected using analytical signals based on Hilbert Transform [9].

$$z(t) \quad x(\tau) \mid i\tilde{x}(t) \tag{2}$$

Here z(t) is complex value with x(t) is a real time series and $\tilde{x}(t)$ is its Hilbert transform.

2.2   Cross Correlation

Cross correlation is a mathematical operation used to measure the extent of similarity between two signals. If a signal is correlated to itself, it is called auto-correlated. If we suppose that *x(n)* and *y(n)* are two time series then the correlation between them is calculated as:

$$\hat{R}_{xy}(m)$$
$$\begin{cases} \sum_{n=0}^{N-m-1} x_{n+m} y_n & m \geq 0 \\ R_{yx}(m) & m < 0 \end{cases} \tag{3}$$

Cross correlation returns a sequence of length 2*M−1 vector, where x and y are of length N vectors (N>1). If x and y are not of the same length then the shorter vector is zero-padded. Cross correlation returns value between −1 and +1. If both signals are identical to each other the value will be 1, otherwise it would be zero [15].

2.3   Magnitude Squared Coherence

The coherence functions estimates the linear correlation of signals in frequency domain [15]. The magnitude squared coherence is defined as the square of the modulus of the mean cross power spectral density (PSD) normalized to the product of the mean auto PSDs. The coherence $C_{xy}(f)$ between two channel time series is computed as:

$$C_{xy}(f)$$
$$\frac{|P_{xy}(f)|}{P_{xx}(f) P_{yy}(f)} \tag{4}$$

$P_{xy}(t)$ is the cross PSD estimate of x and y. $P_{xx}(f)$ and $P_{yy}(t)$ are the PSD estimates of x and y respectively. For computation, each signal is divided into a section of 650ms and default value of 50% is used. Coherence returns the values between 0 and 1, showing how well the input x corresponds to the output y at each frequency.

3   Data Description and Data Filtering

3.1   Data Description

The datasets we are analyzing, have been recorded from three different countries of European Union. Specialist at memory clinic referred all patients to the EEG department of the hospital. All patients passed through a number of recommended tests; Mini Mental State Examination (MMSE). The Rey Auditory Verbal Learning Test, Benton Visual Retention test and memory recall tests. The results are scored and interpreted by psychologists and a multidisciplinary team in the clinic. After that, each patient is referred to hospital for EEG assessment to diagnose the symptoms of AD. Patients were advised to be in a resting state with their eyes closed. The sampling frequency and number of electrodes for three datasets are all different. Detailed information is described in the following sections.

3.1.1   Database A
The EEG dataset A contains 17 MiAD patients (10 males; aged 69.4 ± 11.5 years) while 24 healthy subjects (9 males; aged 77.6 ± 10 years). They all are of British nationality. These data were obtained using a strict protocol from Derriford Hospital, Plymouth, U.K. and had been collected using normal hospital practices. EEG signals were obtained using the modified Maudsley system which is similar to the traditional 10-20 international system. EEGs were recorded for 20 sec at a sampling frequency of 256 Hz (later on sampled down to 128 Hz) using 21 electrodes.

3.1.2   Database B
This EEG dataset composed of 5 MiAD patients (2 males; aged 78.8 ± 5.6 years) as well as 5 healthy subjects (3 males; aged 76.6 ± 10.0 years). They all are of Italian nationality. Several tests, for instance; MMSE, the clinical dementia rating scale (CDRS) and the geriatric depression scale (GDS) were conducted to evaluate the cognitive state of the patients. The MMSE result for healthy subjects is (29.3 ± 0.7) while for MiAD patients is (22.3 ± 3.1). EEGs were recorded for 20 sec at a sampling frequency of 128 Hz using 19 electrodes at the University of Malta, Msida MSD06, Malta.

3.1.3   Database C
This dataset consists of 8 MiAD patients (6 males; aged 75 ± 3.4 years) and 3 healthy subjects (3 males; aged 73.5 ± 2.2 years). They all are of Romanian Nationality. The AD patients have been referred by a neurologist for EEG recordings. All subjects are diagnosed with AD by means of psychometric tests (MMSE, CDR, OTS), neuroimaging (CT) and clinical examination (gender, age, disease, duration, education and medication). The MMSE result for healthy subjects is (28-30) while for MiAD patients is (20-25). EEG data is recorded using a large equidistant 22-channel arrangement conforming to the international federation of clinical neurophysiology (IFCN) standards for digital recording of clinical EEG from the Ecological University

of Bucharest. The time series are recorded for 10 to 20 min at a sampling frequency of 512 Hz using 22 electrodes. The signals are notch filtered at 50 Hz.

For current research work, we have obtained a version of data that is already preprocessed of artifacts by using Independent Component Analysis (ICA), a blind source separation technique (BSS). Details of these procedures can be found in [43]. For ICA processed data, least corrupted 20s recordings have been selected for further analysis.

3.2 Data Filtering into Five Frequency Bands

EEG time series are classified into five frequency bands. Each frequency band has its own physiological significance [6].

1. Delta (δ: $1 \leq f \leq 4$ Hz): these are characterized for deep sleep and are correlated with different pathologies.
2. Theta (θ: $4 \leq f \leq 8$ Hz): they play important role during childhood. High theta activities in adults are considered abnormal and associated with brain disorders.
3. Alpha (α: $8 \leq f \leq 12$ Hz): they usually appear during mental inactive conditions and under relaxation. They are best seen during eye closed and mostly pronounced in occipital location.
4. Beta (β: $12 \leq f \leq 25$ Hz): they are visible in central and frontal locations. Their amplitude is less than alpha waves and they mostly enhance during tension.
5. Gamma (γ: $25 \leq f \leq 30$ Hz): they are best characterized for cognitive and motor functions.
6. Bandpass filter is applied to each EEG channel to extract the EEG data in specific frequency band [F:(F+W)] Hz. Butterworth filters were used (of 2nd order) as they offer good transition band characteristics at low coefficient orders; thus, they can be implemented efficiently.

4   Methodology

In this research work, a novel methodology using PCA and neural synchrony measurement of the brain is proposed. We have compared our proposed method with other method which takes the average of synchrony measures for all channels in one region of the brain. As mentioned previously, we are comparing right and left temporal with frontal, central and occipital so there are total 7 comparisons of the brain ((left temporal-right temporal (LT-RT)), (left temporal-frontal (LT-F)), (left temporal-central (LT-C)), (left temporal-occipital (LT-O)), (right temporal-frontal (RT-F)), (right temporal-central (RT-C)), and (right temporal-occipital (RT-O))) for all frequency bands (δ, θ, α, β, γ). A brief description of these methods is given below.

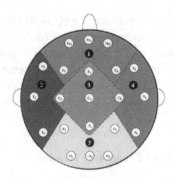

Fig. 1. The 21 Channels used for EEG recording

4.1   First Method (Taking Average of Synchrony Measures)

First we apply neural synchrony measurement technique on each channel pair (time series of two channels) of two different regions for all frequency bands and then we take the average of those results. For instance, we apply phase synchrony measure on each channel pair of right and left temporal ((F7-F8), (F7-T4), (F7-T6), (T3-F8), (T3-T4), (T3-T6), (T5-F8), (T5-T4), (T5-T6) and then we take the average result of right temporal-left temporal. We compare the left temporal with frontal (FP1, FP2, FPz, F3, F4), central (Fz, C3, Cz, C4, Pz) and occipital (P3, P4, O1, O2, Oz). Similarly, we compare the right temporal (F8, T4, T6) to rest of the brain area.   The same technique has been used for rest of the synchrony measures i.e. cross correlation and coherence.

After getting the results, we compare the neural synchronization of AD patients and healthy subjects, for all three measurement techniques (phase synchronization, cross correlation and coherence), by Mann-Whitney U test. Figure 2 shows all the steps of our Average method.

4.2   Second Method (PCA Based Neural Synchrony Measure)

In this method, instead of applying synchrony measurement technique directly on the filtered data, first we apply Principal Component Analysis (PCA) technique on all channels of one region. This eliminates any redundant information that a region could provide. For instance, we apply PCA on all three channels of left temporal (F7, T3, T5) and consequently it provides a single signal without any redundant information. Then we apply PCA on all channels of right temporal (F8, T4, T6). After that, we apply synchrony measure on these two regions. Similarly, we apply PCA on all other channels of a region; frontal (FP1, FP2, FPz, F3, F4), central (Fz, C3, Cz, C4, Pz) and occipital (P3, P4, O1, O2, Oz) and compute the synchrony measure with left and right temporal. Rest of the procedure is similar to the first proposed method.

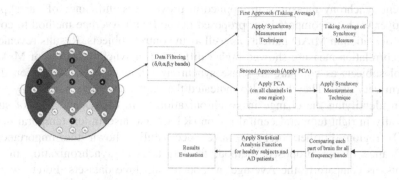

Fig. 2. Average and PCA Methods

4.2.1 Principal Component Analysis (PCA)

The basic purpose of PCA is to reduce the dimensionality of a dataset to convert it to uncorrelated variables providing maximum information about a data while eliminating interrelated variables. In other words it transforms highly dimensional dataset (of m dimensions) into low dimensional orthogonal features (of n dimension) where n<m.

In our case we apply PCA on all channels in one particular region, for instance, the application of PCA for the left temporal as is shown in Fig.3 (a) using channel (F7, T3, T5) are converted into a single signal as shown in Fig. 3(b). The generated temporal signal contains almost all information from the left temporal while eliminating any redundant information.

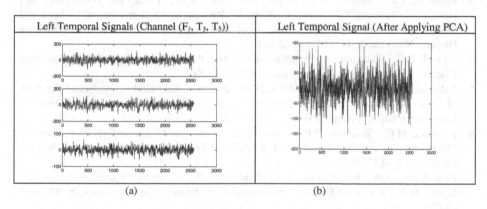

Fig. 3. Application of PCA on left temporal channels signals

5   Conclusion

The aim of the current study was to show the significance of applying PCA method to eliminate redundant information from the datasets to get more reliable results. In this study, three different datasets are selected with different specifications and three different synchrony measures are applied to prove the significance of our approach. Moreover we have compared our proposed method with Average method to compute synchronization in MiAD patients as well as in control subjects. Results revealed that cross correlation measure showed higher difference in synchronization of MiAD and control subjects as compare to phase synchrony while coherence function did not perform very well. They have also indicated that alpha and theta bands play a major role in identifying the change in synchronization from MiAD and control subjects especially in right temporal-central region (RT-C) and also in left temporal-occipital (LT-O) region. Furthermore, we have successfully shown the importance and significance of our proposed method, to detect lower synchronization in MiAD patients, as compare to the Average method for all three datasets. Future work will involve the study of much significant results of lower synchronization in case of datasets B and datasets C as compare to dataset A.

References

1. Rogers, J., Webster, S., Lue, L.F., Brachova, L., Civin, W.H., Emmerling, M., Shivers, B., Walker, D., Mcgeer, P.: Inflammation and Alzheimer's Disease Pathogenesis. Neurobiology of Aging 17, 681–686 (1996)
2. Babiloni, C., Ferri, R., Binetti, G., Cassarino, A., Forno, G.D., Ercolani, M., Ferreri, F., Frisoni, G.B., Lanuzza, B., Miniussi, C., Nobili, F., Rodriguez, G., Rundo, F., Stam, C.J., Musha, T., Vecchio, F., Rossini, P.M.: Fronto-Parietal Coupling of Brain Rhythms in Mild Cognitive Impairment: A Multicentric EEG Study. Brain Research Bulletin 69, 63–73 (2006)
3. Babiloni, C.G., Frisoni, B., Pievani, M., Vecchio, F., Lizio, R., Buttiglione, M., Geroldi, C., Fracassi, C., Eusebi, F., Ferri, R., Rossini, P.M.: Hippocampal Volume and Cortical Sources of EEG Alpha Rhythms in Mild Cognitive Impairment and Alzheimer Disease. Neuroimage 44, 123–135 (2009)
4. Frisoni, G.B., Padovani, A., Wahlund, L.O.: The Predementia Diagnosis of Alzheimer Disease. Alzheimer. Dis. Assoc. Disord. 18, 51–53 (2004)
5. Jelles, B., Scheltens, P., Van Der Flier, W.M., Jonkman, E.J.: Global Dynamical Analysis of The EEG in Alzheimer's Disease: Frequency-Specific Changes of Functional Interactions. Clinical Neurophysiology 119 (2008)
6. Faustino, M.C., Serquiña, R.P., Rapp, P.E., Albano, A.M.: Phase Synchronization of Electroencephalographic Signals in The Different Frequency Bands. Philippine Science Letters 5, 131–137 (2012)
7. Fingelkurts, A.A., Fingelkurts, A.A., Kähkönen, S.: Functional Connectivity in The Brain—Is It An Elusive Concept? Neuroscience & Biobehavioral Reviews 28, 827–836 (2005)
8. Delbeuck, X., Van Der Linden, M., Collette, F.: Alzheimer' Disease As A Disconnection Syndrome? Neuropsychology Review 13, 79–92 (2003)
9. Stam, C.J., Nolte, G., Daffertshofer, A.: Phase Lag Index: Assessment of Functional Connectivity From Multi Channel EEG and MEG With Diminished Bias From Common Sources. Human Brain Mapping 28, 1178–1193 (2007)
10. Singer, W.: Neuronal Synchrony: A Versatile Code for The Definition of Relations? Neuron 24 (1999)

11. Fries, P.: A Mechanism for Cognitive Dynamics: Neuronal Communication Through Neuronal Coherence. Trends in Cognitive Sciences 9, 474–480 (2005)
12. Varela, F., Lachaux, J.P., Rodriguez, E., Martinerie, J.: The Brainweb: Phase Synchronization and Large-Scale Integration. Neuroscience 2 (2001)
13. Claus, J.J., Strijers, R.L.M., Jonkman, E.J., Ongerboer De Visser, B.W., Jonker, C., Walstra, G.J.M., Scheltens, P., Van Gool, W.A.: The Diagnostic Value of Electroencephalography in Mild Senile Alzheimer's Disease. Clinical Neurophysiology 110, 825–832 (1999)
14. Gallego-Jutgla, E., Elgendi, M., Vialatte, F., Sole-Casals, J., Cichocki, A., Latchoumane, C., Jaesung, J., Dauwels, J.: Diagnosis of Alzheimer's Disease From EEG By Means of Synchrony Measures in Optimized Frequency Bands. In: International Conference (EMBC), pp. 4266–4270 (2012)
15. Dauwels, J., Vialatte, F.B., Cichocki, A.: A Comparative Study of Synchrony Measures for The Early Detection of Alzheimer's Disease Based on EEG. In: Ishikawa, M., Doya, K., Miyamoto, H., Yamakawa, T. (eds.) ICONIP 2007, Part I. LNCS, vol. 4984, pp. 112–125. Springer, Heidelberg (2008)
16. JÓHannesson, G., Brun, A., Gustafson, I., Ingvar, D.H.: EEG in Presenile Dementia Related to Cerebral Blood Flow and Autopsy Findings. Acta Neurologica Scandinavica 56, 89–103 (1977)
17. Szelies, B., Grond, M., Herholz, K., Kessler, J., Wullen, T., Heiss, W.D.: Quantitative EEG Mapping and PET in Alzheimer's Disease. Journal of the Neurological Sciences 110, 46–56 (1992)
18. Huang, C., Wahlund, L.O., Dierks, T., Julin, P., Winblad, B., Jelic, V.: Discrimination of Alzheimer's Disease and Mild Cognitive Impairment By Equivalent EEG Sources: A Cross-Sectional and Longitudinal Study. Clinical Neurophysiology 111, 1961–1967 (2000)
19. Grunwald, M., Busse, F., Hensel, A., Kruggel, F., Riedel-Heller, S., Wolf, H., Arendt, T., Gertz, H.J.: Correlation Between Cortical Theta Activity and Hippocampal Volumes in Health, Mild Cognitive Impairment, and Mild Dementia. J. Clin. Neurophysiol. 18 (2001)
20. Fonseca, L.C., Tedrus, G.M., Prandi, L.R., Andrade, A.C.: Quantitative Electroencephalography Power and Coherence Measurements in The Diagnosis of Mild and Moderate Alzheimer's Disease. Arq Neuropsiquatr 69 (2011)
21. Stam, C.J., Jones, B.F., Manshanden, I.A., Van Cappellen Van Walsum, M., Montez, T., Verbunt, J.P.A., De Munck, J.C.B., Van Dijk, W., Berendse, H.W., Scheltens, P.: Magnetoencephalographic Evaluation of Resting-State Functional Connectivity in Alzheimer's Disease. Neuroimage 32, 1335–1344 (2006)
22. Hogan, M.J., Swanwick, G.R., Kaiser, J.J., Rowan, M., Lawlor, B.: Memory-Related EEG Power and Coherence Reductions in Mild Alzheimer's Disease. International Journal of Psychophysiology 49, 147–163 (2003)

Tumor Clustering Using Independent Component Analysis and Adaptive Affinity Propagation

Fen Ye[1], Jun-Feng Xia[2], Yan-Wen Chong[3], Yan Zhang[1], and Chun-Hou Zheng[1,*]

[1] College of Electrical Engineering and Automation, Anhui University, Hefei, China
zhengch99@126.com
[2] Institute of Health Sciences, Anhui University, Hefei, China
[3] State Key Laboratory for Information Engineering in Surveying,
Mapping and Remote Sensing, Wuhan University, Wuhan, China

Abstract. Tumor clustering is a powerful method in tumor subtype discovery for more accurately and reliably clinical diagnosis and prognosis. In order to further improve the performance of tumor clustering, we introduce a new tumor clustering approach based on independent component analysis (ICA) and affinity propagation (AP). Particularly, ICA is initially employed to select a subset of genes so that the effect of irrelevant or noisy genes can be reduced. The AP and its extensions, adaptive affinity propagation (adAP), are then used for tumor clustering on the selected genes.

Keywords: Clustering, independent component analysis (ICA), gene expression data, affinity propagation (AP), adaptive affinity propagation (adAP).

1   Introduction

Cluster of patients can be used to assess the distinct clinical outcomes and interpret the biological processes contribute to understand the mechanisms of human disease. With the rapid advance of DNA microarray technologies, it is possible for us to know about the underlying human disease, and then nip the underlying disease in the bud. The microarray data contain tens of thousands of genes for each chip typically, and the number of the collected tumor samples is much smaller than genes. So it is a typical "large p, small n" problem [1], i.e., the number of predictor variables p is much greater than that of available samples n. The particular condition $p\gg n$ makes most of the standard statistical methods difficult to use from both analytical and interpretative points of view [2].

There are many approaches to gene selection (feature selection), such as nonnegative matrix factorization (NMF) [2]. There are also many approaches for dimensionality reduction, such as Linear Discriminate Analysis (LDA) [3]. Independent component (IC) analysis (ICA) can be employed to select a subset of genes that might be relevant to different tumors [2].

---

* Corresponding author.

D.-S. Huang et al. (Eds.): ICIC 2014, LNBI 8590, pp. 34–40, 2014.

Up to now, many unsupervised clustering approaches have been applied in clustering analysis successfully. Wang et al. [4] have employed adaptive affinity propagation (adAP) to twelve kinds of data sets, and achieved good cluster results.

The successful use of gene selection and adAP in processing simulated data and clinical data inspires us to improve the clustering performance.

2   Methods

(a)   Gene Selection by ICA

In this part, we first describe the ICA algorithm simply and then we describe the AP algorithm and the adAP algorithm briefly. ICA is a linear transformation technique for data feature extraction. Now we briefly introduce the ICA proposed by Hyvarinen A et al. [5] and [2]. Consider a gene expression data set that consists of p genes in n samples. We denote it by a matrix X of size $p \times n$.

gene
expression data

independent
coefficients

eigengenes

Fig. 1. The ICA model of gene expression data used in this paper

Then the standard mathematical ICA model can be written as:

$$X = AS = \sum_{k=1}^{n} a_k s_k \qquad (1)$$

Where A is a matrix of size $p \times n$ and S is a mixing matrix of size $n \times n$.

$X = (X_1, X_2, ... X_n)^T$, which is n-dimensional random mixing signals, the observed signals. A is a constant mixing matrix of size $n \times n$, $S = (S_1, S_2, ... S_n)^T$, which is component independent source signals. Formula (1) implies that the columns of X are linear mixtures of the ICs, in order to seek out the right linear combinations of the observed variables, we use another form to express the mixing matrix as follow.

$$A = XS^{-1} = XW \qquad (2)$$

Vectors a_q, which are the columns of A, are called the ICs of A and are assumed to be statistically independent. The mission of the ICA is to find out the $n \times n$ mixed matrix $W = (W_1, W_2, ... W_n)^T$ to make recovery signal each component independent as far as possible when we only know the observation signal X.

The ICA gene selection method is based on a ranking of the p genes, the ranking process is showed as follow [2],

Step 1. z-ICs $A_1, A_2, ... A_z$ with zero mean and unit variance are extracted from the gene profiles data by ICA.

Step 2. For gene $l(l = 1,2,...p)$, the absolute score are computed on each component $|a_{ij}|$. By retaining the maximum one, these z scores (the actual number of ICs) are synthesized and denoted by $g_l = \max_j |a_{ij}|$.

Step 3. According to the maximum absolute scores $\{g_1, ..., g_p\}$, the p genes are sorted in increasing order, and the rank $r(l)$ is computed for each gene.

When we perform the experiments again and again, we found the selected genes by ICA is difficult to be reproducible [6] because of local optima of the ICA [7]. In this paper, we selected the IC number z experimentally, and we found that the appropriate value of z to make the experiment results have weak randomness. Lastly, the number of selected gene is decided according to the cluster methods experimentally.

(b)   Cluster with adAP

Affinity Propagation (AP) [8] is a new clustering algorithm proposed in Science. AP algorithm adopts the similarity between n data points to cluster samples, the similarity which can be symmetrical or asymmetric. Wang et. al. [4] proposed that AP has two limitations: the oscillations can not be eliminated automatically if occurs and it is hard for us to know what value of "preference" can get an optimal clustering result. Hence, they proposed adAP instead of AP to solve the above limitations, including eliminating oscillations by adaptive adjustment of the damping factor, decreasing value of p when adaptive damping methods don't work, and finding out the optimal and suitable clustering solution through adaptive searching the space of p. The adaptive escaping technique is designed below,

Step 1. when lam (lam is damping factor; $lam \in [0,1]$) is large (e.g., lam is increased to 0.85) and oscillations occur, decrease p step by step until oscillations disappear in the iterative process, this could be added in the step 2.

Step 2. increase lam by a step when oscillations occur; if $lam \geq 0.85$, go to step 1 or decrease p by step ps.

The adaptive preference scanning technique is designed as follows,

step 1. start the algorithm by a designated large preference (p).

step 2. runs an iteration to generate K exemplars.

step 3. check whether K exemplars are converged.

step 4. if K exemplars are converged, go to step 5; otherwise go to step 2.

step 5. if K exemplars converge too in additional dy iterations decrease the value of p by step ps, otherwise go to step 2.

step 6. go to step 2. For details, please refer to [4]. The approaches of evaluate the solutions is numerous, in this paper, we choose Silhouette index [9].

$$S_{il}(t) = \frac{b(t) - a(t)}{\max\{a(t), b(t)\}} \tag{3}$$

Where $a(t)$ is the average distance of sample t in cluster C_j to all other samples in cluster C_j, $d(t, C_j)$ is average distance of sample t in cluster C_j to all samples in another cluster C_i, then $b(t) = \min\{d(t, C_i)\}, i = 1, 2, ..., k, i \neq j$.

The value of $S_{il}(t)$ beyond 0.5 indicates that the each cluster can be separated perfectly, less than 0.5 indicates that certain clusters exist overlap, and less than 0.2 illustrates the lack of substantial cluster structure. The optimal cluster results correspond to the largest value among all value of Silhouette[9, 10].

3   Data

The follicular lymphoma gene expression data were derived from 106 samples (patients with follicular lymphoma), which was produced by the SMRT array platform [11] and contain 26266 genes (probes) per samples [12, 13]. The expected cluster for these 106 samples predicted by HMM-Mix method is 6 groups and WKM method is 4 groups [14].

4   Experimental Results

Up to present, numerous gene selection approaches have been raised [15-18]. The most important reason that we choose ICA as the gene selection method is that ICA-based gene selection does not need to know the labels of samples, so ICA is very suitable for AP and adAP cluster. Besides, ICA has been demonstrated to be a valid gene selection technique in tumor classification [18] and there is a reasonable biological explanation of ICA model for gene expression data. In order to show the efficiency of our methods, we also use the genevarfilter method, which filters genes with small profile variance.

In our study, we find that selected genes have the best stability when we select $z = 1$ for ICA. The number of selected genes is 10 in table 1 and the number of selected genes is 20 in table 2 when we perform the ICA. When Pearson coefficients are used as similarity measure we find it is hard to obtain a good result, so our results are based on Euclidean distances. Please note that we excluded the category when there is only one sample in this category. Because the dataset have no true class labels so that we cannot calculate the error rate and FM value, and we determined the number of groups using the maximum Silhouette coefficient.

Table 1. The experimental result on the FL data (z=1, m=10)

Experimental Method	Class Number	Value of silhouette
ICA + adAP	2	0.513713
ICA + AP	25	0.454998
Genevarfilter + ICA + adAP	4	0.572212
Genevarfilter + ICA + AP	27	0.371547

Table 2. The experimental result on the FL data (z=1, m=20)

Experimental Method	Class Number	Value of silhouette
ICA + adAP	2	0.554458
ICA + AP	27	0.301090
Genevarfilter + ICA + adAP	4	0.483395
Genevarfilter + ICA + AP	27	0.399124

From the tables 1 and 2, obviously, we can find the cluster results by adAP are better than the results by AP. We also selected 10927 genes by genevarfilter before we used ICA. The clustering effect is better when we initialized the model by genevarfilter. The value of silhouette by ICA and adAP both beyond 0.5 which indicate the each cluster can be separated perfectly when the samples are full into two groups. In table 1, Apply Genevarfilter before ICA works better than without use Genevarfilter, we could get 4 clusters, and the value of silhouette is more than 0.5, which indicates that the each cluster can be separated perfectly. However in table 2, we could find that adAP combined with ICA is better than adAP combined with ICA and Genevarfilter. Hence, in order to obtain a best result, the larger the probability, we should do a large of experiments. In addition, the value of parameters z, m are determined experimentally. We find when we make z=1, and m=10 the fluctuation in results is on the small side.

5   Conclusion

In this work, we first applied ICA to model the gene expression data for gene selection, and then we employed adAP to cancer clustering using the selected genes. ICA is a multipurpose statistical approach in which the observed random data can be served as the estimation of a latent variable model. The results of adAP algorithm is better than AP algorithm indeed. The main purpose of this paper is to study the combination gene selection and clustering. There are numerous gene selection methods and numerous cluster methods, we could take advantage of the kind of combination, thus all kinds of novel combination techniques could be used for dealing with gene expression data, that is, we should choose the best combination so that we obtain most effective approaches to cluster cancers. We are also find approaches to model selection to prevent choosing the number of grounds at run time. The method could be applied in different areas such as biomedical signal processing, image processing, and telecommunication.

Acknowledgments. This work was supported by the National Science Foundation of China under Grant nos. 61272339 and 31301101, the Key Project of Anhui Educational Committee, under Grant no. KJ2012A005, the Anhui Provincial Natural Science Foundation under Grant no. 1408085QF106, and the Fundamental Research Funds for the Central Universities under Grant no.2042014kf0242.

References

1. West, M.: Bayesian Factor Regression Models in the "large p, small n" Paradigm. Bayesian Statistics 7, 723–732 (2003)
2. Zheng, C.H.: Tumor Clustering Using Nonnegative Matrix Factorization with Gene Selection. Information Technology in Biomedicine 13, 599–607 (2009)
3. Haeb Umbach, R., Ney, H.: Linear Discriminant Analysis for Improved Large Vocabulary Continuous Speech Recognition. In: IEEE International Conference on Acoustics, Speech, and Signal Processing, ICASSP 1992, vol. 1(5), pp. 13–16 (1992)
4. Wang, K.: Adaptive Affinity Propagation Clustering. arXiv preprint arXiv (2008)
5. Hyvärinen, A., Oja, E.: Independent Component Analysis: Algorithms and Applications. Neural Networks 13(4), 411–430 (2000)
6. Liebermeister, W.: Linear Modes of Gene Expression Determined by Independent Component Analysis. Bioinformatics 18(1), 51–60 (2002)
7. Chiappetta, P., Roubaud, M.C., Torrésani, B.: Blind Source Separation and the Analysis of Microarray Data. Journal of Computational Biology 11(6), 1090–1109 (2004)
8. Frey, B.J., Dueck, D.: Clustering by Passing Messages between Data Points. Science, 972–976 (2007)
9. Dudoit, S., Fridlyand, J.: A Prediction-based Resampling Method for Estimating the Number of Clusters in A Dataset. Genome Biology 3(7), 1–21 (2002)
10. Velamuru, P.K.: Robust Clustering of Positron Emission Tomography Data. In: Joint Interfce CSNA (2005)
11. Ishkanian, A.S.: A Tiling Resolution DNA Microarray with Complete Coverage of the Human Genome. Nature Genetics 36(3), 299–303 (2004)
12. Cheung, K.J.J.: Genome-wide Profiling of Follicular Lymphoma by Array Comparative Genomic Hybridization Reveals Prognostically Significant DNA Copy Number Imbalances. Blood 113(1), 137–148 (2009)
13. Höglund, M.: Identification of Cytogenetic Subgroups and Karyotypic Pathways of Clonal Evolution in Follicular Lymphomas. Genes, Chromosomes and Cancer 39(3), 195–204 (2004)

14. Shah, S.P.: Model-based Clustering of Array CGH Data. Bioinformatics 25(12), 30–38 (2009)
15. Huang, D.S., Zheng, C.H.: Independent Component Analysis-based Penalized Discriminant Method for Tumor Classification using Gene Expression Data. Bioinformatics 2(15), 1855–1862 (2006)
16. Furlanello, C.: Entropy-based Gene Ranking without Selection Bias for the Predictive Classification of Microarray Data. BMC Bioinformatics 4(1), 54 (2003)
17. Dudoit, S., Fridlyand, J., Speed, T.P.: Comparison of Discrimination Methods for the Classification of Tumors using Gene Expression Data. Journal of the American Statistical Association 97(457), 77–87 (2002)
18. Calò, D.G.: Variable Selection in Cell Classification Problems: A Strategy based on Independent Component Analysis, pp. 21–29. Springer (2005)

Research of Training Feedforward Neural Networks Based on Hybrid Chaos Particle Swarm Optimization-Back-Propagation

Fengli Zhou and Xiaoli Lin

Faculty of Information Engineering,
City College Wuhan University of Science and Technology, Wuhan 430083, China
{thinkview,aneya}@163.com

Abstract. This paper proposed a new method to train feedforward neural networks(FNNs) parameters based on the iterative chaotic map with infinite collapses particle swarm optimization(ICMICPSO) algorithm. This algorithm made full use of the information of BP's error back propagation and gradient. It used ICMICPS as the global optimizer to adjust the neural networks' weights and thresholds, when network parameters converge around global optimum. And it used gradient information as a local optimizer to accelerate the modification at a local scale. Compared with other algorithms, results show that the performance of the ICMICPSO-BPNN method is superior to the contrast methods in training and generalization ability.

Keywords: Feedforward Neural Networks, Back-propagation Neural Networks, Particle Swarm Optimization, Chaos Map.

1   Introduction

In recent years, neural network is widely used in pattern recognition, data mining, intelligent control and other fields. The three-layer feedforward neural network is a kind of mentor learning algorithm, which used gradient descent method based on error back propagation(BP) for training[1]. However, this method is sensitive to the initial weights choice and is easy to fall into local minima. These are made worse neural network training effect, so the performance of BP neural network is affected.

Particle Swarm Optimization(PSO) algorithm is a Swarm intelligence optimization algorithm proposed by Kennedy and Eberhart in 1995[2]. PSO has many advantages of fast convergence speed, simple modeling and implementation, and existing PSO has fast convergence speed in the pre-search and easily fall into local optimal value in the latter. Chaos is a common phenomenon that exists in nonlinear system, and can obtain the motion state of randomness by deterministic equations. Chaotic motion has many characteristics of random, universality and regularity. It can traverse all states within a certain range in accordance with its non-repetition of own laws.

This paper presents an ICMIC particle swarm method(ICMICPSO), then combines ICMICPSO with gradient descent and become a mixed ICMICPSO-BP algorithm to

D.-S. Huang et al. (Eds.): ICIC 2014, LNBI 8590, pp. 41–47, 2014.

train feedforward neural networks (FNNs). The algorithm uses PSO for global search in the initial stages, then uses chaotic search to led the particles escape from local optimal solution when premature convergence, at the same time, accelerate local search near the globally optimal solution by using gradient descent. The proposed ICMICPSO-BP algorithm is used to train FNNs' weights and thresholds. Finally we use four Benchmark standard function questions to test the algorithm and compared the results with literature result, show the effectiveness of this algorithm.

2   BPNN, PSO and Chaotic Mapping

2.1   Neural Network Based on Error Back-propagation (BPNN)

BP neural network's learning process is divided into forward propagation and backward propagation under the instructors' guidance. It has been demonstrated that a three-layer BP neural network can approximate nonlinear function by any accuracy. The mean square error function calculation formula is as follows:

$$E = \sum_{j=1}^{q} E_j / (q*k) \quad where \quad E_j = \sum_k \varepsilon_k^2 = \sum_k (d_k - c_k)^2 \tag{1}$$

Where q is input samples' number, ε_k is the k-node's output error, d_k is the k-node's desired output value, c_k is the k-node's actual output value.

2.2   Particle Swarm Optimization Algorithm (PSO)

The standard particle swarm algorithm is an optimization algorithm based on populations, individual in the particle swarm is called particle. Assume that a certain group size is N in the D-dimensional search space, the position of its *i-th* particle's t-generation in this search space is $X_i^t = (x_{i1}^t, x_{i2}^t, \cdots, x_{iD}^t)$, $i = 1, 2, \cdots N$, velocity is $V_i^t = (v_{i1}^t, v_{i2}^t, \cdots, v_{iD}^t)$, individual history optimal position is $P_i^t = (p_{i1}^t, p_{i2}^t, \cdots, p_{iD}^t)$, global optimal position of t-generation is $P_g^t = (p_{g1}^t, p_{g2}^t, \cdots, p_{gD}^t)$, the *i-th* particle changes its velocity and position according to the following equations[2][3]:

$$V_i^{t+1} = \omega \times V_i^t + c_1 \times r_1 \times (P_i^t - X_i^t) + c_2 \times r_2 \times (P_g^t - X_i^t) \tag{2}$$

$$X_i^{t+1} = X_i^t + V_i^{t+1} \tag{3}$$

Where c_1 and c_2 are constants and are known as acceleration coefficients; r_1, r_2 are random values in the range of (0, 1)[3].

2.3   Chaotic Mapping

Chaos is a common phenomenon that exists in nonlinear system, it can traverse all states within a certain range in accordance with its non-repetition of own laws. We can combine this traversal state and PSO algorithms, which is helpful for particles to escape from local optima region and enhance the global search ability[4]. Reversible one-dimensional mapping is the simplest chaotic motion system, He et al. has proposed iterative chaotic map with infinite collapses (ICMIC) and discussed its chaos rigorously from the perspective of mathematics[5]. In this paper, we use ICMIC mapping to generate chaotic variables, and the variable sequence will be distributed between -1 and 1:

$$x_{k+1} = \sin(a / x_k) \qquad 1 \leq x_k \leq 1, x_k \neq 0 \qquad (4)$$

Where x_k is the k-th component, a is control parameter and its general value is 5.65. Chaos is sensitive to initial value, so we can get N-chaotic variables of different locus by taking N-initial particles.

3   ICMICPSO-BP Algorithm and FNNs Training

3.1   Mixed ICMICPSO-BP Algorithm

ICMICPSO-BP has combined ICMIC chaotic mapping and gradient descent method based on the error back propagation. PSO has strong search capability of global optimal solution, but the search speed will become slow and be prone to premature when searching is close to optimal solution. In order to solve the algorithm's drawbacks, this paper introduces ICMIC and gradient descent algorithm based on error back propagation to improve the performance of PSO. When PSO algorithm falls into local optimal solution by premature judgment mechanism, introduce chaotic mapping, lead the local population to escape local extreme point, continue to search in the global scope and avoid premature phenomenon.

3.2   Training Feedforward Neural Networks by ICMICPSO-BP Algorithm

Take the FNNs' weights and thresholds as the particles' position vectors, and then train network parameters by using proposed algorithm.

This algorithm can obtain the diversity of population by using chaotic mapping, and accelerate PSO's local search capability by using gradient descent information, so particles can search the entire space globally under the premise of fast local search, specific steps are as follows:

(1) Initialize each parameter of algorithm

(a) Set M as particle population's size, T as algorithm's total iterations, TN as algorithm's current iteration, λ as minimum training stop error, P_m as chaotic transition probability, c_1 and c_2 as learning factors, ω as inertia weight, C as fitness variance threshold, T_{BP} as BP algorithm's iteration, η as learning rate, α as momentum factor.

(b) Initialize particle's velocity $V_i = (v_{i1}\ v_{i2} \cdots v_{iD})^T$ and position $X_i = (x_{i1}\ x_{i2} \cdots x_{iD})^T$ randomly to characterize weights and thresholds of the neural network, where D is the sum of neural network weights and thresholds dimension.

(c) Calculate particle's fitness value $f(x_i)$, select particle with best fitness value in the initial population, the value is also treated as global extreme position p_g of initial search algorithm and p_{best} of whole algorithm, make TN=1.

(2) If $TN \geq T$, save $\min\{f(p_g), f(p_i)\}$ as optimal results, the algorithm finishes. Otherwise, perform the following steps:

(a) According to formula (2) and (3), update particles' speed v_i and position x_i.

(b) Update p_i and p_g by each particle's information, and record global optimal particle subscript.

(3) If $\sigma^2 \leq C$, proceed with the following steps, otherwise, return to Step (2).

(4) Take global optimal particle's position $X_{g_{best}}$ as the initial point, call BP algorithm, update $X_{g_{best}}$, p_i and TN.

(5) If $TN \geq T$, save $\min\{f(p_g), f(p_i)\}$ as optimal results, algorithm finishes. Otherwise, continue.

(6) Generate a random number r in the range of (0, 2) for each particle, if $r \leq P_m$ and $i \neq g_{best}$, carry on ICMIC chaotic mapping in the chaotic search space, calculate new position's target value f_i^{k+1}, update TN and p_g.

(7) Return to step (2).

3.3   Performance Analysis of ICMICPSO-BP Algorithm

ICMICPSO-BP algorithm has combined particle swarm, chaotic mapping and BP algorithm. ICMICPSO-BP's complexity is equal with PSO-BP and GA-BP et al, particles will have a stronger global search capability based on chaotic mapping mechanism, and particles' local search capability will be accelerated by BP, PSO's performance will get a good play.

4   Simulation

4.1   Function List and Experimental Parameters

In this paper, four typical Benchmark functions that shown in Table1 are used to test algorithm's effectiveness, then compare the results to literature[5].

Table 1. Test Benchmark Function Set

Test Functions	Range
$f_1 = 100 \times (x_1^2 - x_2)^2 + (1 - x_1)^2$	$x_i \in [-10,10], i = 1,2$
$f_2 = x_1^2 + x_2^3 - x_1 x_2 x_3 + x_3 - \sin x_2^2 - \cos(x_1 x_3^2)$	$x_i \in [-2\pi, 2\pi], i = 1,2,3$
$f_3 = x_1^{x_1^3} + x_3^{x_3^5}$	$x_i \in [0,2], i = 1,2,...,5$
$f_4 = \sum_{i=1}^{8} x_i^i$	$x_i \in [-1,1], i = 1,2,...,8$

In order to maintain the consistency of training parameter settings in comparative literature, parameters are set as follows: $M = 40$, $T = 1000$, $\lambda = 10^{-6}$, $c_1 = c_2 = 1.4$, network weights and thresholds are initialized to [-1,1], ω is in the range of [0.4, 0.9],

r_1 and r_2 are random values in the range of (0, 1). Assume particles' max speed is 10, min speed is -10. By using ICMIC mapping as chaotic mapping, set $p_m = 0.2$, $c = 0.01$, $v_{max} = (x_{max} - x_{min})/2$, $v_{min} = v_{max}$, particle's position and velocity dimension $D = i \times h + h \times 1 + h + 1$, where i represents neurons number of input layer and h represents neurons number of hidden layer. Assume that BP's learning rate $\eta = 0.7$, momentum factor $\alpha = 0.3$, max iterations of BP subroutine is 30. In the range of independent variable values, initialize 150 training samples randomly and generalize 50 samples. Then compare the proposed algorithm with literature's results, E_1 is training MSE, E_2 is generalization MSE, E_3 is training average absolute error, E_4 is generalization average absolute error, E_5 is all sample average absolute error.

When function $f_1 \sim f_4$ have different nodes number h of hidden layer, errors $E_1 \sim E_5$ are shown in Table2~5, error comparison of ICMICPSO-BPNN and contrast algorithms for four functions is shown in Table6.

Table 2. Training Error Comparison of Different Network Structures By Function f_1

Nodes Number h	Algorithm	E_1	E_2	E_3	E_4	E_5
6	ICMICPSO-BPNN	3.63E – 06	0.000547	0.001782	0.023257	0.007149
	PSO-BPNN	6.06E – 06	0.009995	0.001906	0.074016	0.019933
7	ICMICPSO-BPNN	1.04E – 06	4.284E – 05	0.000867	0.010234	0.003201
	PSO-BPNN	4.87E – 06	2.98E – 04	0.001886	0.014980	0.005160
8	ICMICPSO-BPNN	8.37E – 06	0.000797	0.001032	0.018561	0.005414
	PSO-BPNN	4.75141E – 05	0.001074	0.005482	0.030187	0.011658
9	ICMICPSO-BPNN	1.26E – 05	0.000864	0.001932	0.024634	0.007607
	PSO-BPNN	3.33E – 05	0.003742	0.004869	0.039807	0.013603

Table 3. Training Error Comparison of Different Network Structures By Function f_2

Nodes Number h	Algorithm	E_1	E_2	E_3	E_4	E_5
7	ICMICPSO-BPNN	4.39E – 05	8.23E – 05	0.003326	0.011254	0.007808
	PSO-BPNN	2.86E – 04	5.15E – 04	0.012571	0.018063	0.013944
8	ICMICPSO-BPNN	3.54E – 05	0.000863	0.003746	0.022758	0.008493
	PSO-BPNN	4.75141E – 05	0.001524	0.004963	0.030166	0.011264
9	ICMICPSO-BPNN	1.26E – 05	0.007651	0.002973	0.021415	0.007581
	PSO-BPNN	3.33E – 05	0.019533	0.005353	0.112832	0.032223
10	ICMICPSO-BPNN	1.05E – 05	0.004132	0.002865	0.027159	0.008936
	PSO-BPNN	1.70E - 05	0.006777	0.005272	0.064394	0.020052

Table 4. Training Error Comparison of Different Network Structures By Function f_3

Nodes Number h	Algorithm	E_1	E_2	E_3	E_4	E_5
7	ICMICPSO-BPNN	0.007165	0.007268	0.031723	0.046526	0.035424
	PSO-BPNN	0.007343	0.007399	0.057853	0.062319	0.058970
8	ICMICPSO-BPNN	0.006472	0.008562	0.021652	0.047184	0.028033
	PSO-BPNN	0.011044	0.009478	0.074014	0.070769	0.073203
9	ICMICPSO-BPNN	0.004125	0.006318	0.024963	0.042541	0.029355
	PSO-BPNN	0.009145	0.013129	0.065892	0.079063	0.069184
10	ICMICPSO-BPNN	0.003156	0.003264	0.020015	0.032815	0.023215
	PSO-BPNN	0.005850	0.003419	0.044258	0.043698	0.044118

Table 5. Training Error Comparison of Different Network Structures By Function f_4

Nodes Number h	Algorithm	E_1	E_2	E_3	E_4	E_5
7	ICMICPSO-BPNN	0.008192	0.006742	0.041791	0.062839	0.047052
	PSO-BPNN	0.012823	0.008337	0.068605	0.068605	0.069402
8	ICMICPSO-BPNN	0.008292	0.009281	0.042655	0.068547	0.049012
	PSO-BPNN	0.009363	0.013577	0.079761	0.100246	0.084882
9	ICMICPSO-BPNN	0.008192	0.009347	0.052163	0.074152	0.057660
	PSO-BPNN	0.012823	0.015750	0.092703	0.103527	0.095409
10	ICMICPSO-BPNN	0.008292	0.009728	0.063276	0.075251	0.067265
	PSO-BPNN	0.009363	0.010234	0.077145	0.076798	0.077059

Table 6. Error Comparison of ICMICPSO-BPNN and Contrast Algorithms for Four Functions

Algorithm	Error	f_1(2-7-1)	f_2(3-6-1)	f_3(5-10-1)	f_4(8-7-1)
ICMICPSO-BPNN	E_1	1.04E − 06	4.67E − 06	0.003156	0.005228
	E_2	4.28E − 05	8.29E − 05	0.007764	0.006742
	E_3	0.000867	0.002835	0.020015	0.041791
	E_4	0.010234	0.016457	0.032815	0.062839
	E_5	0.003201	0.006488	0.023215	0.047052
Improved PSO-BPNN	E_1	4.87E − 06	3.56E − 05	0.005850	0.007367
	E_2	2.98E − 04	9.26E − 04	0.003419	0.008337
	E_3	0.001886	0.004992	0.044258	0.068605
	E_4	0.014980	0.025081	0.043698	0.071793
	E_5	0.005160	0.010014	0.044118	0.069402
Traditional PSO-BPNN	E_1	4.16E − 05	2.54E − 04	0.008941	0.015331
	E_2	0.110844	0.066119	0.002599	0.019901
	E_3	0.005701	0.013349	0.061929	0.098510
	E_4	0.250629	0.224780	0.041604	0.111654
	E_5	0.066933	0.066207	0.056848	0.101796
GA-BPNN	E_1	5.37E − 04	3.30E − 04	0.009272	0.011973
	E_2	0.041519	0.064065	0.003002	0.016747
	E_3	0.017857	0.015369	0.058552	0.086193
	E_4	0.197877	0.221804	0.045065	0.105106
	E_5	0.062862	0.066978	0.055180	0.090921
Basic BPNN	E_1	9.9995E − 05	3.6850E − 04	0.0114	0.0120
	E_2	0.4178	0.1350	0.1949	0.0132
	E_3	0.0082	0.0151	0.0730	0.0857
	E_4	0.5980	0.3629	0.3813	0.0944
	E_5	0.2075	0.1361	0.2001	0.1172

4.2   Simulation Results and Analysis

From table 2 it can be seen that ICMICPSO-BPNN's training error E_1 and generalization error E_2 is less than comparison algorithm significantly, also are reflected on E_3, E_4 and E_5, algorithm has good learning ability and adaptive for new samples.

From table 3 it can be seen that ICMICPSO-BPNN's errors $E_1 \sim E_5$ is less than comparison algorithm significantly. These results fully illustrate the importance of chaotic mapping in PSO, which has led particles escape from local optima.

From table 4 it can be seen when $h=6$, the rest training error and generalization error results are better than comparison algorithms. These are also fully explained that ICMICPSO-BPNN has higher training precision and better learning ability.

From table 5 it can be seen that $E_3 \sim E_5$ is less than comparison algorithms' results, ICMICPSO-BPNN's network output value is closer to the true value.

Table 6 compares ICMICPSO-BPNN with improved PSO-BPNN, traditional PSO-BPNN, GA-BPNN and BPNN which are proposed in Literature[5], where the network structure of four functions are 2-7-1, 3-6-1, 5-10-1 and 8-7-1. From the results it can be seen that ICMICPSO-BPNN's five test indicators are superior to other algorithms. The proposed algorithm has higher training accuracy.

5   Conclusion

This paper proposed a new method to train feedforward neural networks(FNNs) parameters based on the iterative chaotic map with infinite collapses particle swarm optimization(ICMICPSO) algorithm. This algorithm made full use of the information of BP's error back propagation and gradient. And it used gradient information as a local optimizer to accelerate the modification at a local scale. Compared with other algorithms, results show that the performance of the ICMICPSO-BPNN method is superior to the contrast methods in training and generalization ability.

Acknowledgement. The work in this paper is in part supported by the education department foundation of hubei province of China under Grant No. B2013258

References

1. Hornik, K., Stinchcombe, M., White, H.: Multilayer Feedforward Networks are Universal Approximators. Neural Networks 2(5), 359–366 (1989)
2. Kennedy, J., Eberhart, R.C.: Particle Swarm Optimization. In: Proceedings IEEE International Conference on Neural Networks, Perth, pp. 1942–1948 (1995)
3. Shi, Y.H., Eberhart, R.C.: Empirical Study of Particle Swarm Optimiaztion. In: Proc of IEEE Congress on Evolutionary Computation, pp. 1945–1950. IEEE Press, Washington, DC (1999)
4. Gao, S., Yang, J.Y.: Swarm Intelligence Algorithm and Applications, pp. 112–117. China Water Power Press, Beijing (2006)
5. Li, Z.Y., Wang, J.Y., Guo, C.: A New Method of BP Network Optimized Based on Particle Swarm Optimization and Simulation Test. ACTA Electronic Sinica 36(11), 2224–2228 (2008)

Training Deep Fourier Neural Networks
to Fit Time-Series Data

Michael S. Gashler and Stephen C. Ashmore

University of Arkansas, Fayetteville AR, 72701, USA
{mgashler,scashmor}@uark.edu

Abstract. We present a method for training a deep neural network containing sinusoidal activation functions to fit to time-series data. Weights are initialized using a fast Fourier transform, then trained with regularization to improve generalization. A simple dynamic parameter tuning method is employed to adjust both the learning rate and regularization term, such that stability and efficient training are both achieved. We show how deeper layers can be utilized to model the observed sequence using a sparser set of sinusoid units, and how nonuniform regularization can improve generalization by promoting the shifting of weight toward simpler units. The method is demonstrated with time-series problems to show that it leads to effective extrapolation of nonlinear trends.

Keywords: neural networks, time-series, curve fitting, Fourier decomposition.

1   Introduction

Finding an effective method for predicting nonlinear trends in time-series data is a long-standing challenge with numerous potential applications, including weather prediction, market analysis, and control of dynamical systems. Fourier decompositions provide a mechanism to make neural networks with sinusoidal activation functions fit to a training sequence [1,2,3], but it is one thing to fit a curve to a training sequence, and quite another to make it extrapolate effectively to predict future nonlinear trends. We present a new method that uses deep neural network training techniques to transform a Fourier neural network into one that can facilitate practical and effective extrapolation of future nonlinear trends.

Nonlinear curve-fitting approaches tend to be very effective at interpolation, predicting values among those for which it was trained, but they often struggle with extrapolation, predicting values outside those for which it was trained. Because extrapolation requires predicting in a region that is separated from all available samples, any superfluous complexity in the model tends to render predictions very poor. Thus far, only very simple models, such as linear regression, have been generally effective at extrapolating trends in time-series data. Finding an effective general method for nonlinear extrapolation remains an open challenge.

We use a deep artificial neural network to fit time-series data. Artificial neural networks are not typically considered to be simple models. Indeed, a neural network

D.-S. Huang et al. (Eds.): ICIC 2014, LNBI 8590, pp. 48–55, 2014.
© Springer International Publishing Switzerland 2014

with only one hidden layer has been shown to be a universal function approximator [4]. Further, deep neural networks, which have multiple hidden layers, are used for their ability to fit to very complex functions. For example, they have been very effective in the domain of visual recognition [5,6,7]. It would be intuitive to assume, therefore, that deep neural networks would be a poor choice of model for extrapolation. However, we show that a careful approach to regularization can enable complex models to extrapolate effectively, even with complex periodic and chaotic nonlinear trends.

2   Related Works

Many papers have surveyed the various techniques for using neural networks to forecast time-series data [8,9,10,11,12,13]. Therefore, in this section, we review only the works necessary to give a high-level overview of how our method fits among the existing techniques. The various approaches for training neural networks to model time-series data may be broadly categorized into three major groups, which we refer to as pattern-based, recurrent, and extrapolation.

Pattern-based methods are the most common, and perhaps simplest, methods for time-series prediction. They involve feeding sample values from the past into the model to predict sample values in the future [12,14]. These methods require no recurrent connections, and can be implemented without the need for any training techniques specifically designed for temporal data. Consequently, these can be easily implemented using many available machine learning toolkits, not just those specifically designed for forecasting time-series data. These convenient properties make these methods appealing for a broad range of applications. Unfortunately, they also have some significant limitations: The window size for inputs and predictions must be determined prior to training. Also, they essentially use recent observations to represent state, and they are particularly vulnerable to noise in the observed values.

A more sophisticated group of methods involves neural networks with recurrent connections [15]. These produce their own internal representation of state. This enables them to learn how much to adjust their representations of state based on observed values, and hence operate in a manner more robust against noisy observations. Training recurrent neural networks is notoriously difficult because long training times are often required [16,17], and recurrent neural networks are particularly vulnerable to chaotic responses in their error surfaces due to the feedback connections [18]. However, recurrent neural network models have found significant success with time-series problems [19], and recent advances in deep neural network learning have also helped to improve the training of recurrent neural networks [20,21,22,23].

The third, and most relevant, group of methods for forecasting time-series data is extrapolation. Extrapolation with linear regression has long been a standard method for forecasting trends. Extrapolating nonlinear trends, however, has generally been ineffective. For this reason, this branch of time-series forecasting has been much less studied, and remains a relatively immature field. Our work attempts to promote research in this branch by presenting a practical method for extrapolating nonlinear trends in time-series data.

The idea of using a neural network that can combine basis functions to reconstruct a signal, and initializing its weights with a Fourier transform, has been previously proposed [1,24], and more recently methods for training them have begun to emerge [2,3]. These studies, however, do not address the important practical issues of stability during training and regularizing the model to promote better generalization. Our work treats the matter of representing a neural network that can combine basis functions as a solved problem, and focuses on the more challenging problem of refining these networks to achieve reliable nonlinear extrapolation.

3   Algorithm Description

Our algorithm uses a deep artificial neural network with a mixture of activation functions. We train with stochastic gradient descent [25]. Each unit in the artificial neural network uses one of three activation functions, sinusoid: $f(x) = \sin(x)$, softplus: $f(x) = \log_e(1 + e^x)$, or identity: $f(x) = x$. Using the "identity" activation function creates a linear unit, which is only capable of modeling linear components in the data. Nonlinear components in the data require a nonlinear activation function. The softplus units enable the network to fit to non-repeating nonlinearities in the training sequence. The sinusoid units enable the network to fit to repeating nonlinearities in the data.

Initializing Weights: Before training begins, we measure the standard deviation, σ, of the training sequence to serve as a baseline for accuracy. The output layer of our neural network is a single linear unit. We call this layer 4. The layer that feeds into the output layer, layer 3, contains k sinusoid units, 12 softplus units, and 12 linear units, where k is the number of samples in the training sequence. We use the Fast Fourier Transform to initialize the sinusoid units. This technique has been well-established [1,2,3], and our implementation is included in the *Waffles* machine learning toolkit [26]. We initialize the other units to approximate the identity function. For the softplus units, we do this by setting the weights to the identity matrix, then we increase the bias by 10, and decrease each weight w_j that feeds out from the softplus unit into the next layer by $10w_j$. Layers 1 and 2 each contain 12 softplus and 12 linear units. Only one input value (representing time) feeds into layer 1. Layers 1 and 2 are also initialized to approximate the identity function. These layers serve the important purpose of enabling the model to "warp time" as needed to fit the training data with fewer sinusoid units. In other words, these layers enable the model to find simple repeating patterns, even in real-world data where some of the oscillations may not occur at precisely regular intervals. Because these layers are further from the output end of the model, backpropagation will refine them more slowly than the other layers. This is desirable because warping time in the temporal region of the training sequence is a "last resort" method for "explaining away" superfluous complexity in the training sequence. Finally, we complete our initialization of the weights by slightly perturbing all the weights in the network.

The initialized weights result in a model that predicts the training sequence will repeat in the future, as depicted in Figure 1. Such models fit the training data well, but generalize poorly. Our purpose in training, therefore, is not to improve how well it fits to the training data, but to simplify the model.

Regularization: For the first half of our training epochs, we use weight decay, also known as L^2 regularization. This is implemented by multiplying all the network weights by $1 - \eta\lambda$ just before the presentation of each training pattern. (η is the learning rate for training, and λ is a small term that controls how strongly the network is regularized.) L^2 is effective at making all weights small, which tends to distribute the weight somewhat evenly among the various units. During the second half of training, we use L^1 regularization. This is implemented by subtracting the term $1 - \eta\lambda$ from all positive weights, and adding that term to all negative weights. L^1 regularization tends to promote sparsity in the neural network. It causes the network to utilize few non-zero weights, while still fitting the training data. Thus, L^2 regularization helps to draw weight away from the sinusoid units, and the final L^1 regularization helps the weight to settle into a small number of units, preventing the overfit that typically occurs with large networks.

In order to further promote shifting weight onto the simpler units, we use a non-uniform regularization term. For sinusoid units, we regularize with the standard term $1 - \eta\lambda$. For softplus units, we use $1 - 0.1\eta\lambda$. For linear units, we use $1 - 0.01\eta\lambda$. Thus, the strongest regularization is applied to the sinusoid units, while only very weak regularization is applied to the linear units. These constant factors (1, 0.1, and 0.01) were selected intuitively. We attempted to optimize them, but in our experiments small variations tended to have little influence on the final results.

Dynamic Parameter Tuning: Stochastic gradient descent relies on being able to update the network weights without visiting every pattern in the training data. This works well with logistic activation functions because its derivative is close to zero except where the net pre-activation is close to zero. This gives it a very local region of influence, such that each pattern presentation will only significantly change a few relevant weights in the whole network. The three activation functions we use in our algorithm, however, all have non-local regions of influence. In other words, each pattern presentation will usually affect many of the weights in the network. This has the effect of giving the network a strong tendency to diverge unless an extremely small learning rate is used. In our experiments we found that even learning rates as small as 10^{-6}, would eventually result in divergence at some point during training. The only static learning rates that always lead to convergence were so small that training became impractical. Therefore, the crux of our training algorithm relies on dynamically adjusting the learning rate η, and regularization term λ.

After initializing the weights, the network already fits to the training data with a very small root-mean squared error (RMSE), much smaller than 0.1σ. As training proceeds, we use stochastic gradient descent to keep the RMSE near 0.1σ, and we use regularization to improve generalization. As training completes, the model no longer predicts that the training data will repeat, but predicts a continuation of the nonlinear trends exhibited in the training data.

It is important that η and λ be dynamically adjusted using different mechanisms, so the ratio between them is free to change. After each epoch of training, if the RMSE is less than 0.1σ, then $\lambda = \lambda * 1.001$ else $\lambda = \lambda / 1.001$. In contrast with this approach, we always make η bigger after every epoch, such that $\eta = 1.01\eta$. Eventually, this will lead to divergence, which we detect when the RMSE is greater than 0.2σ. When that occurs, we restore the network weights to the last point where the RMSE score was below 0.1σ, and we set $\eta = 0.1\eta$. Naturally, all of these constants could be optimized, but we anticipate only a nominal amount of performance gain by doing so. Due to space limitations, we must omit an explanation of the intuition motivating this dynamic tuning approach, but suffice it to say that this approach is much more effective at independently tuning λ and η than many other approaches we tried.

4   Validation

This section presents visual results showing that our method is able to anticipate nonlinear trends into the future. Deliberately absent in this section are quantitative comparisons with recurrent neural networks and other methods. Because non-linear extrapolation is a less-mature method for time-series forecasting, we seek only to demonstrate effectiveness with this approach. We do not attempt to establish it as the new state-of-the-art in forecasting. If the research community were to only focus on improving the method with the highest precision, then it would risk becoming stuck in a local optimum. By advancing this alternative approach, we intend to help open the way for research interest in an area that could potentially lead to different use-cases or a long-term shift in how time-series forecasting is done.

Our first experiment shows results with a toy problem involving a sine wave with the addition of a linear trend, $f(t) = \sin(t) + 0.1t$. For training, we used this equation to generate a sequence of 128 values. After initializing the weights, the model predicts that the training sequence repeats into the future, as shown in Figure 1. This model assigns significant weight to many of its sinusoid units. As training proceeds, however, the model is greatly simplified while still fitting with the training sequence. The final model assigns nearly all of its weight to just two units: a sinusoid unit and a linear unit, which matches the equation that was used to generate the training sequence. The results are shown in Figure 2. The blue dots spanning the left half of the plot represent the training sequence. The red dots spanning the right half of the plot are test values generated by continuing to sample from the same equation. These were withheld from our algorithm during training. The green curve shows the continuous predictions of the trained model.

We tested our method with the Mackey-Glass series. This test is interesting because it involves a chaotic series, rather than a periodic series. Results with this data are given in Figure 3. We note that the model begins to prematurely descend very early in the test sequence (at approximately time 1.02), which causes its predictions to be slightly out of phase for the remainder of the test sequence. Nevertheless, the model clearly exhibits similar patterns to those in the test set. Significantly, these patterns do not repeat those in the training sequence, nor does the model repeat its earlier predictions. This shows that our method can be effective for predicting even non-repeating trends in the near term.

Fig. 1. Weights initialized with the FFT predict that the training data repeats

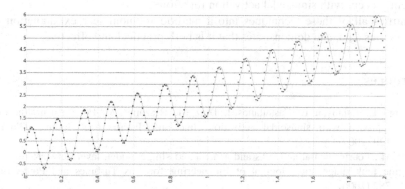

Fig. 2. After training, the model is much simpler, and generalizes well

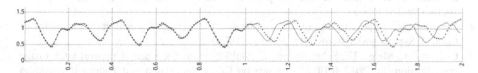

Fig. 3. Results with predicting the Mackey-Glass chaotic series. Although the extrapolated part of the model is slightly of phase, it anticipates nonlinear trends effectively. This is significant because this problem does not repeat the training data.

Other experiments were performed, and positive results were obtained, but these could not be reported here due to space limitations. These can be found in the longer preprint version of this paper at http://arxiv.org/abs/1405.2262.

5   Summary of Contributions

We presented a method for fitting a neural network to time-series data for the purpose of extrapolating nonlinear trends in the data. This paper makes several contributions to the current knowledge, which we itemize here:

1. It proposes new theoretical intuition for why deep neural networks can actually facilitate finding simpler predictive models than can be found with shallow networks. Specifically, the deeper layers provide a mechanism to "warp time" in the temporal region of the training sequence, allowing subsequent layers to "explain" the training data with fewer sinusoid units.
2. It shows that shifting weight toward simpler units can be promoted during training by regularizing the complex units more heavily.
3. It describes a dynamic method for simultaneously tuning both the learning rate and regularization terms, while allowing them to find independent values. It also shows that dynamic tuning can be an effective solution to the instability problems that inherently occur with sinusoidal activation functions.
4. It unifies all of these techniques into a method for nonlinear extrapolation with time-series data, and demonstrates that it is both practical and effective.

References

1. Mingo, L., Aslanyan, L., Castellanos, J., Diaz, M., Riazanov, V.: Fourier neural networks: An approach with sinusoidal activation functions. International Journal ITA 11(1), 126–129 (2004)
2. Tan, H.: Fourier neural networks and generalized single hidden layer networks in aircraft engine fault diagnostics. Journal of Engineering for Gas Turbines and Power 128(4), 773–782 (2006)
3. Zuo, W., Zhu, Y., Cai, L.: Fourier-neural-network-based learning control for a class of nonlinear systems with flexible components. IEEE Transactions on Neural Networks 20(1), 139–151 (2009)
4. Cybenko, G.: Approximation by superpositions of a sigmoidal function. Mathematics of Control, Signals and Systems 2(4), 303–314 (1989)
5. Ciresan, D., Meier, U., Schmidhuber, J.: Multi-column deep neural networks for image classification. In: 2012 IEEE Conference on Computer Vision and Pattern Recognition (CVPR) (2012)
6. Krizhevsky, A., Sutskever, I., Hinton, G.: Imagenet classification with deep convolutional neural networks. Advances in Neural Information Processing Systems 25 (2012)
7. Taigman, Y., Yang, M., Ranzato, M., Wolf, L.: DeepFace: Closing the Gap to Human-Level Performance in Face Verification. In: Conference on Computer Vision and Pattern Recognition (CVPR) (2014)
8. Dorffner, G.: Neural networks for time series processing. In: Neural Network World (1996)
9. Kaastra, I., Boyd, M.: Designing a neural network for forecasting financial and economic time series. Neurocomputing 10(3), 215–236 (1996)
10. Zhang, G.P.: Time series forecasting using a hybrid ARIMA and neural network model. Neurocomputing 50, 159–175 (2003)
11. Zhang, G., Eddy Patuwo, B., Hu, M.Y.: Forecasting with artificial neural networks: The state of the art. International Journal of Forecasting 14(1), 35–62 (1998)
12. Frank, R.J., Davey, N., Hunt, S.P.: Time series prediction and neural networks. Journal of Intelligent and Robotic Systems 31(1-3), 91–103 (2001)
13. De Gooijer, J.G., Hyndman, R.J.: 25 years of time series forecasting. International Journal of Forecasting 22(3), 443–473 (2006)

14. Abarbanel, H.D., Brown, R., Sidorowich, J.J., Tsimring, L.S.: The analysis of observed chaotic data in physical systems. Reviews of Modern Physics 65(4), 1331 (1993)
15. Nerrand, O., Roussel-Ragot, P., Urbani, D., Personnaz, L., Dreyfus, G.: Training Recurrent Neural Networks: Why and How? An Illustration in Dynamical Process Modeling (1994)
16. Sjöberg, J., Zhang, Q., Ljung, L., Benveniste, A., Deylon, B., Glorennec, P.Y., Hjalmarsson, H., Juditsky, A.: Nonlinear Black-Box Modeling in System Identification: a Unified Overview. Automatica (31), 1691–1724 (1995)
17. Sontag, E.: Neural Networks For Control. Essays on Control: Perspectives in the Theory and its Applications 14, 339–380 (1993)
18. Cuéllar, M.P., Delgado, M., Pegalajar, M.C.: An Application of Non-linear Programming to Train Recurrent Neural Networks in Time Series Prediction Problems. In: Enterprise Information Systems VII, pp. 95–102 (2006)
19. Hochreiter, S., Schmidhuber, J.: Long short-term memory. Neural Computation 9(8), 1735–1780 (1997)
20. Oh, K.-S., Jung, K.: GPU implementation of neural networks. Pattern Recognition 37(6), 1311–1314 (2004)
21. Cottrell, G.W.: New Life for Neural Networks. Science 313(5786), 454–455 (2006)
22. Gashler, M.S., Martinez, T.R.: Temporal Nonlinear Dimensionality Reduction. In: The International Joint Conference on Neural Networks (2011)
23. Graves, A., Mohamed, A.-R., Hinton, G.: Speech recognition with deep recurrent neural networks. In: 2013 IEEE International Conference on Acoustics, Speech and Signal Processing (ICASSP) (2013)
24. Silvescu, A.: Fourier neural networks. In: International Joint Conference on Neural Networks, IJCNN 1999 (1999)
25. Wilson, D.R., Martinez, T.R.: The general inefficiency of batch training for gradient descent learning. Neural Networks 16(10), 1429–1451 (2003)
26. Gashler, M.S.: Waffles: A Machine Learning Toolkit. Journal of Machine Learning Research. MLOSS (12), 2383–2387 (2011)

Regularized Dynamic Self Organized Neural Network Inspired by the Immune Algorithm for Financial Time Series Prediction

Haya Al-Askar[1], Abir Jaafar Hussain[1], Dhiya Al-Jumeily[1], and Naeem Radi[2]

[1] Liverpool John Moores University, Byroom Street, Liverpool, L3 3AF, UK
{h.alaskar,a.hussain,d.aljumeily}@2011.ljmu.ac.uk
[2] Al-Khawarizmi International College, P.O. Box 25669, Abu Dhabi, United Arab Emirates
n.radi@khawarizmi.com

Abstract. A novel type of recurrent neural network, the regularized Dynamic Self Organised Neural Network Inspired by the Immune Algorithm, is presented. The Regularization technique is used with the Dynamic self-organized multilayer perceptrons network that is inspired by the immune algorithm. The regularization has been addressed to improve the generalization and to solve the over-fitting problem. The results of an average 30 simulations generated from ten stationary signals are demonstrates. The results of the proposed network were compared with the regularized multilayer neural networks and the regularized self organized neural network inspired by the immune algorithm. The simulation results indicated that the proposed network showed better values in terms of the annualized return in comparison to the benchmarked networks.

Keywords: Dynamic neural network, exchange rate time series, and financial time series prediction.

1   Introduction

Financial time series analysis is a fundamental subject that has been addressed widely in economic fields. The analysis of financial time series is primary importance in the economic world. A time series is a collection of observations of a particular problem measured during a period of time. The analysis of financial time series has an economic importance. It is a promising and crucial task for any future investment used for making decisions in different areas, such as businesses and financial institutions [1]. Financial time series involve different time scales such as intraday (high frequency), hourly, daily, weekly, monthly, or tick-by-tick stock prices of exchange rates. The distance between variables in financial time series is influenced by real economic activity [2]. The effect of this activity has been represented by a mixture of hills and bumps in financial time series charts [3]. Thus, the prediction aims to forecast these activities. Financial data analysis usually provides the fundamental basis for decision models [4] to achieve good returns, which is the first and the most important factor for any investor. This can help to improve companies' strategies and decrease the risk of potentially high losses [5]. Furthermore, it can help

D.-S. Huang et al. (Eds.): ICIC 2014, LNBI 8590, pp. 56–62, 2014.
© Springer International Publishing Switzerland 2014

investors to cover the potential market risk to establish some techniques to progress the quality of financial decisions. Financial data are naturally dynamic, nonlinear, nonparametric, complex, and chaotic [6]. This type of time series is non-stationary, has a high level of uncertainty, is highly noisy, and has an unstructured nature which includes regular structural breaks. In addition, the financial time series holds several types of information, which are incomplete, unclear and unlimited [7]. Furthermore, financial time series such as the stock market are facing dramatic changes, as well as rapid information exchange all the time. Hence, the prediction of its economic activity in the future is extremely challenging.

Several models and techniques have already been developed to enhance the forecasting ability of neural networks, such as the regularization methods. This method is based on using weight decay in order to improve the training of the neural network. Mahdi et al has used regularization technique in Self-organized Multilayer network inspired by the Immune Algorithm (SONIA) network in order to forecasting physical time series data as well as financial time series data [8], [9]. Their result demonstrated that the weight decay has improved the predication performance of SONIA network.

In this paper the Regularization technique is applied with Dynamic Self-organized Multilayer neural network which is inspired by Immune Algorithm (R-DSMIA). The aim is to improve the generalization capability of the R-DSMIA network for time series forecasting. The main goal of this simulation is to evaluate the forecasting performance of the proposed neural network. The proposed R-DSMIA is used to predict ten financial time series.

2   Dynamic of Self-organized Multilayer Network Inspired by Immune Algorithm (DSMIA)

The proposed Dynamic Self-organised Multilayer network Inspired by the Immune Algorithm (DSMIA) is used to predict financial time series. The structure of the DSMIA network is shown in Fig. 1. The DSMIA network has three or more layers: the input, the self-organised hidden layer, and the output layers with feedback connections from the output layer to the input layer. The input layer holds copies of the current inputs as well as the previous output produced by the network. This provides the network with memory. As such, the previous behaviour of the network is used as an input affecting current behaviour. Similar to the Jordan recurrent network[10] the output of the network is fed back to the input through the context units.

Suppose that N is the number of external inputs $x(t)$ to the network, and $y(t-1)$ is the output of the network from the previous time step while O refers to the number of outputs. In the proposed DSMIA, the total input to the network will be the component of $x(t)$ and the previous output where

$$U(n) = \begin{cases} x_i(n) & i = 1,....N \\ y_i(n-1) & i = 1,....,O \end{cases}$$

(1)

The output of the hidden layer is computed as

$$v_{hj}(n) = \alpha \sqrt{\sum_{i=1}^{N}(w_{hj} - x_{hj}(n))^2}$$

(2)

$$z_{hj}(n) = \beta \sqrt{\sum_{k=1}^{O}(wz_{hjk} - y_k(n-1))^2} \tag{3}$$

$$D_{hj}(n) = v_{hj}(n) + z_{hj}(n) \tag{4}$$

$$x_{hj}(n) = f_{ht}(D_{hj}(n)) \tag{5}$$

The output of the network is computed as:

$$\hat{y}_k = f_{ot}\left(\sum_{j=1}^{N_H} w_{ojk}\, x_{Hj} + B_{ok}\right) \tag{6}$$

Where f_{ht}, f_{ot} are nonlinear activation functions, N is the number of external inputs, O is the number of output units. w_{ojk} is the weight corresponds to the external input while wz_{hjk} is the weight corresponding to the previous output, and n is the current time step, while α, β are selected parameters with $0 < \alpha$ and $0 < \beta$.

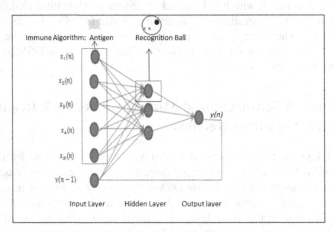

Fig. 1. The structure of the proposed DSMIA network

The first layer of the DSMIA is a self-organised hidden layer trained similar to the recursive self-organized map RecSOM [11]. In this case, the training rule for updating the weights is based on the same technique for updating the weights of the self-organized network inspired by the immune algorithm (SONIA) network [12]. The change in the proposed network is that the weights of the context nodes are also updated in the same way as the weights of the external inputs. This is done by first finding D, which is the distance between the input units and the centroid of the j_{th} hidden units:

$$D_{hj}(n) = \alpha \sqrt{\sum_{i=1}^{N}(w_{hji} - x_{hj}(n))^2} + \beta \sqrt{\sum_{k=1}^{O}(wz_{hjk} - y_k(n-1))^2} \tag{7}$$

The position of the closest match will be determined as:

$$c(n) = \arg\min(D_{hj}(n)) \tag{8}$$

If the shortest distance is less than the stimulation level value, s1 (0, 1), then the weight from the external input vector and the context vector are updated as follows:

$$W_{hji}(n+1) = W_{hji}(n) + \gamma D_c(n) \tag{9}$$

$$Wz_{hji}(n+1) = Wz_{hjk}(n) + \gamma D_c(n) \tag{10}$$

Where wz_{hjk} is the weight of the previous output and w_{hji} is the weight for the external inputs, and γ is the learning rate which is updated during the epochs.

3   Regularized DSMIA Network (R-DSMIA)

The regularization technique has been used on DSMIA to improve the performance of the proposed network. The main aim of the regularization is to decrease the generalization error. Regularization is the technique of adding a penalty term Ω to the error function, which can help obtain a smoother network mapping. It is given by

$$E_{reg} = E_{std} + \lambda\Omega \tag{11}$$

Where E_{std} represents one of the standard cost functions such as the Sum-of-squares error and the parameter λ controls the range of the penalty term Ω in which it can influence the form of the solution. The network training should be implemented by minimizing the total error function E_{reg} [13] .

Weight decay is based on the sum of the squares of the adaptive parameter in the network.

$$\Omega = \frac{1}{2}\sum_i w_i^2 \tag{12}$$

The idea is that every weight once updated, is simply decayed or shrunk as follows:

$$w^{new} = w^{old}(1 - \lambda) \tag{13}$$

Where $0 < \lambda < 1$, The weight decay is performed by adding a bias term to the original objective function E_{std}, thus the weight decay cost function is determined as follows [24]:

$$E_{reg} = E_{std} + (\lambda/2)\,B \tag{14}$$

Where λ is the weight decay rate, B represents the penalty term.
The simplest form of calculating the penalty term B is:

$$B = \sum W_{ij}^2 \tag{15}$$

Where w_{ij} is the weight connections between the ith units and j^{th} nodes in the next layer. In the R-DSMIA network, the weight decay was used to adjust the weights between the hidden and the output units. The change of weights using weight decay method could be calculated as follows:

$$\Delta w_{ojk}/wd = \Delta w_{ojk} - \eta\lambda w_{ojk} \tag{16}$$

Where Δw_{oik} is the updated weight that connects the hidden and the output units. The significant role of weight decay is to manage the complexity of the cost function. This will improve the neural network performance.

4　Financial Time Series Data

Three different types of financial time series are applied in this research work: the exchange rate prices, stock opening and closing prices, and the oil price. The exchange rate time series and the stock process are daily time series for the period from 1st July 2002 to 11th November 2008, giving 1,605 trading days. The oil price data is monthly data and covers the period between 1st January 1985 and 1st November 2008, with a total of 389 trading months. The source of the data can be found at http://www.economagic.com/ecb.htm.

Since most of the published papers about financial time series prediction have focused on exchange rate prediction, this research has used six series exchange rate signals. The foreign exchange market is considered to be the largest market, with more than $1 trillion traded everyday. The US dollar is the most significant currency in the market and it has been used as a reference currency. Another time series used in this research is the West Texas Intermediate (WTI) crude oil spot prices. Crude oil is well known as a central source of energy. The future oil price has a great impact on governments and industries and companies' activities.

5　Modelling DSMIA for Financial Time Series Prediction

The original raw non-stationary signals are transformed into stationary signals before sending them to the neural network, by a transformation technique known as Relative Difference in Percentage of price (RDP) [14]. The input variables are computed from four lagged RDP values based on five-day periods (RDP-5, RDP-10, RDP-15, and RDP-20) and one transformed signal (EMA15) which is computed by subtracting a 15-day exponential moving average from the raw signals [15].

There are different evaluation functions that have been applied to estimate the network performance; some of them are related to financial measurement and some of them are statistical methods. The performance of the proposed network is measured with four financial metrics [16] and five statistical metrics [17] which measure the accuracy of the prediction signal.

6　The Simulation Results

In this section, the simulation results of the regularization Dynamic Self-organized Multilayer network inspired by Immune Algorithm are presented. In this research work, the networks were tested on five steps ahead predictions of financial time series. In term of evaluating the performance of the network based on Annualized return measures (AR). The R-DSMIA has obtained the highest percentage compared to DSMIA network except for the NASDAQC time series. The comparison between the performance of DSMIA and R-DSMIA networks showed that using regularization techniques on R-DSMIA network has significantly improved the performance of DSMIA. In term of the maximum drawdown (MDD) measure, the R-DSMIA has achieved the highest value of maximum drawdown when predicting the USDUK, JPYUSD NASDAQC, NASDAQO, DJIAO, DJUAO, DJUAC OIL time series. However, DSMIA network achieved good result on maximum drawdown when predicting the USDEUR signal.

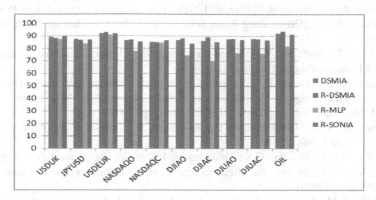

Fig. 2. The Annualised Return result of the benchmarks networks and the R-DSMIA in Stationary signals

The comparison between R-DSMIA and other networks is illustrated in Figure 2. The proposed network was compared with the Regularized MLP (R-MLP) and the Regularized SONIA (R-SONIA) neural networks. The R-DSMIA has obtained the highest percentage compared to the benchmarks network except USDUKP, JPYUSD, NASDAQC and DJUAC time series. The R-SONIA has achieved the best values of AR on USDUKP and NASDAQC time series. The R-MLP networks achieved the lowest profits on average for all ten time series. The R-DSMIA successfully obtained the best profits in comparison to other Regularized neural networks.

7   Conclusion

In this paper a novel neural network architecture based on the regularization is proposed which is called the regularized dynamic self-organized neural network inspired by the immune algorithm. The proposed network was utilized for the prediction of financial time series. The financial data was transformed into stationary signal and the results for 5 step ahead prediction were shown. The simulation results indicated that using recurrent links with regularization techniques can significantly improve the results due to the temporal aspect of the financial time series.

Future work will involve the use of one step and multi-step ahead prediction for stationary and nonstationary financial time series prediction. For nonstationary prediction, the financial data will be presented to the neural network directly to test the performance of the proposed network to extract the information and model the financial signals data. Another direction of research will involve the use of the proposed neural network for the prediction of physical time series such as the earthquake and the sunspot time series which exhibit extreme nonlinearity and nonstationary behaviours.

References

1. Kamruzzaman, J.: ANN-Based Forecasting of Foreign Currency Exchange Rates. Neural Information Processing - Letters and Reviews 3(2), 49–58 (2004)
2. Espinoza, R., Lombardi, M.J., Fornari, F.: The role of financial variableS in PredicTing economic activity. ECB Working Paper Series, vol. (1108). Frankfurt am Main, Germany (2009)
3. Leondes, C.T.: Intelligent Knowledge-Based Systems: Business and Technology in the New Millennium illustrate. Springer (2010)
4. Kamruzzaman, J., Sarker, R.: Forecasting of currency exchange rates using ANN: a case study. In: Proceedings of the 2003 International Conference on Neural Networks and Signal Processing, vol. 1, pp. 793–797. IEEE, Nanjing (2003)
5. Krollner, B.: Risk Management in the Australian Stockmarket using Artificial Neural networks, PhD Thesis (2011)
6. Tan, T.Z., Quek, C., Ng, G.S.: Brain-inspired Genetic Complementary Learning for Stock Market Prediction. In: IEEE Congress on Evolutionary Computation, vol. 3, pp. 2653–2660 (2005)
7. Ahmadifard, M., Sadenejad, F., Mohammadi, I., Aramesh, K.: Forecasting stock market return using ANFIS: the case of Tehran Stock Exchange. International Journal of Advanced Studies in Humanities and Social Science 1(5), 452–459 (2013)
8. Mahdi, A.: The Application of Neural Network inFinancial Time Series Analysis and Prediction Using Immune System. Liverpool John Moores University (2010)
9. Mahdi, A., Hussain, A., Al-Jumeily, D.: The Prediction of Non-Stationary Physical Time Series Using the Application of Regularization Technique in Self-organised Multilayer Perceptrons Inspired by the Immune Algorithm. E-systems Eng., 213–218 (September 2010)
10. Jordan, M.I.: Attractor dynamics and parallelism in a connectionist sequential machine. In: Artificial Neural Networks, NJ, USA, pp. 112–127. IEEE Press, Piscataway (1990)
11. Voegtlin, T.: Recursive self-organizing maps. Neural Netw. 15(8-9), 79–91 (2002)
12. Widyanto, M.R., Nobuhara, H., Kawamoto, K., Hirota, K., Kusumoputro, B.: Improving recognition and generalization capability of back-propagation NN using self-organized network inspired by immune algorithm. Appl. Soft Comput. 6, 72–84 (2005)
13. Bishop, C.M.: Neural Networks for Pattern Recognition, Cambridge, UK (1995)
14. Thomason, M.: The practitioner method and tools. J. Comput. Intell. Financ. 7(3), 36–45 (1999)
15. Cao, L.J., Tay, F.E.H.: Financial Time Series Forecasting. IEEE Trans. Neural Networks 14(6), 1506–1518 (2003)
16. Dunis, C.L., Williams, M.: Applications of Advanced Regression Analysis for Trading and Investment. John Wiley & Sons, Ltd. (2003)
17. Cao, L.J., Tay, F.E.H.: Support Vector Machine with Adaptive Parameters in Financial time Series Forecasting. IEEE Trans. Neural Networks 14(6), 1506–1518 (2003)

Multi-scale Level Set Method for Medical Image Segmentation without Re-initialization

Xiao-Feng Wang[1,2], Hai Min[2,3], Le Zou[1], and Yi-Gang Zhang[1]

[1] Key Lab of Network and Intelligent Information Processing,
Department of Computer Science and Technology, Hefei University,
Hefei, Anhui 230601, China
[2] Intelligent Computing Lab, Hefei Institute of Intelligent Machines,
Chinese Academy of Sciences, P.O. Box 1130, Hefei, Anhui 230031, China
[3] Department of Automation, University of Science and Technology of China,
Hefei, Anhui 230027, China
xfwang@iim.ac.cn, minhai361@gmail.com, zoule1983@163.com,
yxygz@sina.com

Abstract. This paper presents a novel level set method to segment medical image with intensity inhomogeneity (IIH). The multi-scale segmentation idea is incorporated and a new penalty energy term is proposed to eliminate the time-consuming re-initialization procedure. Firstly, the circular window is used to define the local region so as to approximate the image as well as IIH. Then, multi-scale statistical analysis is performed on intensities of local circular regions center in each pixel. The multi-scale energy term can be constructed by fitting multi-scale approximation of inhomogeneity-free image in a piecewise constant way. In addition, a new penalty energy term is constructed to enforce level set function to maintain a signed distance function near the zero level set. Finally, the multi-scale segmentation is performed by minimizing the total energy functional. The experiments on medical images with IIH have demonstrated the efficiency and robustness of the proposed method.

Keywords: intensity inhomogeneity, level set method, multi-scale segmentation, penalty energy term, re-initialization.

1   Introduction

Medical Image segmentation is usually formulated as a minimization problem where the predefined energy functional specifies the segmentation criterion and the unknown variables describe the object contours. The most representative method within this context is the level set method (LSM) whose popularity and success is due to its ability to deal with topological changes (contour splitting or merging) without additional functions. Besides, extensive numerical solutions based on Hamilton-Jacobi equations can provide the stable contour evolution for LSM.

Generally, the existing level set methods can be classified into edge-based methods and region-based methods. Edge-based methods [1-4] are efficient for segmenting object with edge defined by gradient. However, they are quite sensitive to the initial

D.-S. Huang et al. (Eds.): ICIC 2014, LNBI 8590, pp. 63–71, 2014.

conditions and often suffer from serious boundary leakage problems at weak edge. Region-based methods [5-7] have a better performance for image with weak object boundaries and are less sensitive to initial conditions. However, they usually fail to segment images with intensity inhomogeneity (IIH). Recently, local region-based methods have been proposed [8-10] which assume that the intensities are homogeneous in local regions. By fitting the image in terms of local regions rather than global region, they have advantage to segment image with IIH. Huang et al. [11-16] proposed designing neural network for image recognition and segmentation. However, the scale of local region is generally fixed in the existing local region-based methods, which may produce failed segmentation for medical image with severe IIH. To solve this problem, multi-scale segmentation idea can be introduced.

In practical implementation, level set function (LSF) is initially represented by a signed distance function (SDF) to keep numerical stability and accuracy of LSM. During the level set evolution, LSF often becomes very flat or steep near zero level set, which in turn affect the numerical stability. Therefore, a remedy procedure called re-initialization is applied periodically to enforce the degraded LSF being an SDF. However, it is hard to build a trade-off between speed (re-initialization is particularly time-consuming) and accuracy (LSM will develop irregularities if without re-initialization). Recently, Li et al [2, 17] proposed constraining the LSF to preserve an SDF during contour evolution and hence re-initialization can be efficiently avoided.

In this paper, we propose a new level set method which incorporates the multi-scale segmentation idea. Besides, a new penalty energy term is constructed to make our method be completely free of re-initialization. Here, we utilize circular window to define a local region so as to approximate the image as well as IIH. Then, multi-scale statistical analysis is performed on intensities of local circular regions center in each pixel. The multi-scale energy term is constructed by fitting multi-scale approximation of inhomogeneity-free image in a piecewise constant way. To avoid re-initialization, we propose a new double-well potential and construct the penalty energy term which can maintain the signed distance property of LSF near zero level set. Finally, the multi-scale segmentation is performed by minimizing the overall energy functional.

The rest of this paper is organized as follows: The detail of the proposed method is presented in Section 2. In Section 3, we provide the experimental results on several medical images with IIH. Finally, the conclusive remark is included in Section 4.

2   Proposed Method

(a)   Intensity Inhomogeneity

The intensity inhomogeneity (IIH) is frequently encountered in medical images. It is a systematic intensity change on both object and background which are originally homogeneous. The presence of IIH can greatly degrade the medical image segmentation performance since the intensities vary significantly for the pixels within the same class of tissue and overlap between the pixels belonging to the different classes of tissues. Generally, IIH can be regarded as a multiplicative component of image and is independent of noise. So, the image with IIH can be modeled as follows:

$$I(x) = b(x)J(x) + n(x), \qquad (1)$$

where I is the given image and J is the inhomogeneity-free image which is hypothetically piecewise constant. b denotes the IIH which often manifests itself as a smooth spatially varying function. n is noise which can be approximated by a zero-mean Gaussian distribution. To simplify the computation, the noise can be ignored:

$$I(x) = b(x)J(x). \qquad (2)$$

The emergence of IIH in medical image is attributed to a number of reasons. Many of IIH arise from the non-uniform artificial illumination which usually presents circular scattered shape. Here, we illustrated three examples of IIH in Fig.1. It can be easily observed that they are slowly changing in circular scattered shape. Inspired by this observation, we use circular shape to define the local region rather than square shape in traditional methods. By approximating the image with local circular regions, more precise intensity information can be used to guide the contour evolution.

Fig. 1. Illustrations of three examples of IIH

(b)   Multi-scale Energy Term

Generally, IIH influences the intensity distribution of non-boundary pixels (low-frequency part), whereas for that of boundary pixels (high-frequency part), the influence is relatively small. By reducing the value of low-frequency components, we can make the variation of b less significant. So, we need to perform the local statistical analysis based on filtering technology, which implies a separation of the low-frequency IIH from the higher frequencies of image structures. In this paper, the Homomorphic Unsharp Masking (HUM) method [18] is adopted:

$$J'(x) = I(x)/b(x) = I(x)C_N / LPF(x), \qquad (3)$$

where J' is an approximation of inhomogeneity-free image J. LPF means low-pass filtering and C_N is a normalized constant to preserve the mean intensity of J'.

Among the low-pass filtering methods, mean filtering is used in our method due to its particularly simple analytical form. As mentioned above, fixing radius for all local circular regions is unreasonable. Thus, we consider introducing the multi-scale segmentation idea and constructing the multi-scale mean filtering as follows:

$$LPF_r(x) = \frac{1}{k}\sum_{y \in R_r} I(y), \quad R_r : \{y : \sqrt{(y_1 - x_1)^2 + (y_2 - x_2)^2} \le r\}, \quad r = 1...m, \quad (4)$$

where $LPF_r(x)$ is the mean filtering at scale of r. R_r denotes the local circular region with radius also being r. k denotes the number of pixels belonging to R_r and m is the number of scales. Accordingly, HUM in (3) can be reformulated as follows:

$$J'_r(x) = I(x)C_{N,r} / LPF_r(x), \quad r = 1...m, \quad (5)$$

where J'_r denotes the approximation of inhomogeneity-free image J at scale of r. The normalized constant $C_{N,r}$ is the average intensity of $LPF_r(x)$. Then, the mean of $J'_r(x)$ is computed as the multi-scale approximation of inhomogeneity-free image J :

$$\overline{J}(x) = \frac{1}{m}\sum_{r=1}^{m} J'_r(x). \quad (6)$$

By reducing the low-frequency components in a multi-scale way, the intensity contrast between object boundary and background in $\overline{J}$ can be significantly increased. The separation of object boundary and background may be performed even in the image with severe IIH. However, $\overline{J}$ is still hard to segment since the substantial IIH still remains. Hence, the level set segmentation should be performed and the multi-scale energy term can be constructed in a piecewise constant way:

$$E_m^D(c_1, c_2, C) = \int_{inside(C)} \left|\overline{J}(x) - c_1\right|^2 dx + \int_{outside(C)} \left|\overline{J}(x) - c_2\right|^2 dx, \quad (7)$$

where c_1 and c_2 are intensity averages of $\overline{J}$ inside and outside evolving contour C.

(c)   Regularization Energy Term

To avoid the re-initialization problem, Li et al [17] proposed constructing the penalty energy term based on a double-well potential function with two minimum points as $s = 0$ and $s = 1$. It can efficiently maintain the signed distance property of LSF near the zero level set and keep LSF as a constant at locations far away from the zero level set. This paper takes the idea of [17] a few steps further by constructing the following double-well potential function based on polynomial instead of trigonometric function.

$$P_2(s) = \begin{cases} \dfrac{1}{2}s^2(s-1)^2 + \dfrac{1}{2}s^3(s-1)^3, & \text{if } s \le 1 \\ \dfrac{1}{2}(s-1)^2, & \text{if } s > 1 \end{cases}, \tag{8}$$

$P_2(s)$ has the same property with the double-well potential function proposed in [17] but has a less computation complexity due to the usage of polynomial. Thus, our penalty energy term can be constructed as follows:

$$R(\phi) = \int_\Omega P_2(|\nabla\phi(x)|)dx, \tag{9}$$

The gradient flow of (9) can be described as follows:

$$\frac{\partial\phi}{\partial t} = div(d(|\nabla\phi|)\nabla\phi), \tag{10}$$

where div denotes the divergence operator and $d(s)$ is defined by $P_2'(s)/s$. Here, we gave the illustrations of $P_2(s)$ and $d(s)$ in Fig. 2.

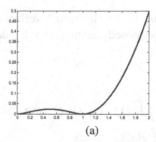 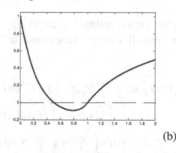

(a)   (b)

Fig. 2. Illustration of $P_2(s)$ and $d(s)$. (a) Illustration of $P_2(s)$. (b) Illustration of $d(s)$.

It can be seen from Fig.2 that $d(s)$ satisfies the following relationship:

$$|d(s)| < 1, \quad s \in [0,\infty] \quad \text{and} \quad \lim_{s\to0}d(s) = \lim_{s\to\infty}d(s) = 1, \tag{11}$$

Regarding (10) as a diffusion equation with the diffusion rate being $d(|\nabla\phi|)$, we can analyze the effect of our penalty energy term as follows:

1. If $|\nabla\phi| > 1$, $d(|\nabla\phi|)$ is positive and diffusion is forward so as to decrease $|\nabla\phi|$ to 1;
2. If $0.5 < |\nabla\phi| < 1$, $d(|\nabla\phi|)$ is negative and diffusion is backward so as to increase $|\nabla\phi|$ to 1;

3. If $|\nabla\phi| < 0.5$, $d(|\nabla\phi|)$ is positive and diffusion is forward so as to decrease $|\nabla\phi|$ to 0.

Our penalty energy term will make LSF preserve an SDF near the zero level set and be a constant at locations far away from the zero level set. Hence, the re-initialization can be efficiently avoided. In addition, the frequently used length energy term $L(\phi)$ should also be included to control the smoothness of evolving contour. Thus, the regularization energy term E^R of the proposed method consists of two parts:

$$E^R(\phi) = \mu \cdot L(\phi) + R(\phi) = \mu \cdot \int_\Omega \delta(\phi(x))|\nabla\phi(x)|dx + \int_\Omega P_2(|\nabla\phi(x)|)dx. \qquad (12)$$

where μ controls the length penalization effect and δ is the Dirac delta function.

(d)   Level Set Formulation

By introducing the penalty energy term in (9), the binary step function can be utilized as the initial LSF:

$$\phi_0(x) = \begin{cases} 1, & x \text{ is inside initial contour } C_0 \\ -1, & \text{otherwise} \end{cases}. \qquad (13)$$

Implicitly representing the evolving contour C by the zero level set of the LSF ϕ, the overall energy functional of the proposed method can be described as follows:

$$
\begin{aligned}
E_m(c_1, c_2, \phi) &= E_m^D(c_1, c_2, \phi) + E^R(\phi) \\
&= \int_\Omega |\overline{J}(x) - c_1|^2 H_\varepsilon(\phi(x))dx + \int_\Omega |\overline{J}(x) - c_2|^2 (1 - H_\varepsilon(\phi(x)))dx \qquad (14) \\
&\quad + \mu \cdot \int_\Omega \delta_\varepsilon(\phi(x))|\nabla\phi(x)|dx + \int_\Omega P_2(|\nabla\phi(x)|)dx,
\end{aligned}
$$

where $H_\varepsilon(z)$ is the smoothed approximation of Heaviside function and $\delta_\varepsilon(z)$ is the regularized approximation of Dirac delta function.

$$H_\varepsilon(z) = \frac{1}{2}\left|1 + \frac{2}{\pi}\arctan\left|\frac{z}{\varepsilon}\right|\right|, \quad \delta_\varepsilon(z) = \frac{1}{\pi} \cdot \frac{\varepsilon}{\varepsilon^2 + z^2}. \qquad (15)$$

Fixing ϕ, we minimize (14) with respect to $c_1(\phi)$ and $c_2(\phi)$. Then, c_1 and c_2 can be computed by calculus of variations as follows:

$$c_1(\phi) = \frac{\int_\Omega \overline{J}(x) H_\varepsilon(\phi(x))dx}{\int_\Omega H_\varepsilon(\phi(x))dx}, c_2(\phi) = \frac{\int_\Omega \overline{J}(x)(1 - H_\varepsilon(\phi(x)))dx}{\int_\Omega (1 - H_\varepsilon(\phi(x)))dx}. \qquad (16)$$

Keeping c_1 and c_2 fixed and minimizing $E(c_1,c_2,\phi)$ with respect to ϕ, we can deduce the associated gradient flow equation for ϕ:

$$\frac{\partial \phi}{\partial t} = \delta_\varepsilon(\phi)\{(\overline{J}(x) - c_2)^2 - (\overline{J}(x) - c_1)^2) + \mu div(\frac{\nabla\phi}{|\nabla\phi|})\} + div(d(|\nabla\phi|)\nabla\phi) \ . \quad (17)$$

To solve the above equation, the finite difference scheme is used in this paper.

3   Experimental Results

In this section, we demonstrated the experiments of the proposed method on several medical images with IIH. The proposed method was implemented by Matlab R2010a on a computer with Intel Core 2 Duo 2.2GHz CPU, 8G RAM. We used the same parameters, i.e. $\Delta t = 0.1$, $\varepsilon = 1$, $m = 32$, $\mu = 0.01 \times 255^2$ for all experiments.

Firstly, we used the images with slight IIH to test our method (as shown in Fig.3). The first row shows three vessel images which have been regarded as the benchmark images to test the performance of local region methods. To show the good ability of our method, we placed the initial contours (green circles) near the vessels rather than on the vessels (as shown in the first row). The final segmentation results of our method are shown as the red curves in the second row. The experimental records show that the evolving contours successfully arrived at each vessel boundaries at the 25th iteration, 34th iteration and 28th iteration.

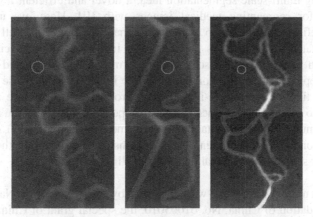

Fig. 3. Segmentation for medical images with slight IIH by using our method. The first row: Initial contours. The second row: Final segmentation results.

Next, we shall validate the performance of our method on segmenting images with severe IIH. In Fig.4, we provided three medical images where severe IIH appears due to the low imaging quality and inhomogeneity of reception coil sensitivity. The initial contours were still placed near the target objects as shown in the first row of Fig.4.

The second row shows that our method has achieved successful segmentation on all three images despite the presence of severe IIH. The iteration numbers for three segmentations were 36, 66 and 89, respectively.

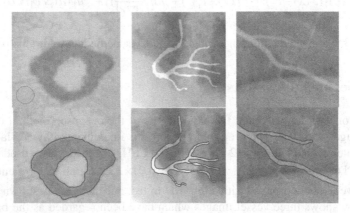

Fig. 4. Segmentation for medical images with severe IIH by using our method. The first row: Initial contours. The second row: Final segmentation results.

4   Conclusions

By introducing multi-scale segmentation idea, a novel and efficient level set method is proposed for segmenting medical images with IIH. Here, we utilize circular window to define local region so as to approximate the image as well as IIH. Then, multi-scale statistical analysis is performed on intensities of local circular regions center in each pixel. The multi-scale energy term can be constructed by fitting the multi-scale approximation of inhomogeneity-free image in a piecewise constant way. To avoid the time-consuming re-initialization procedure, we propose a new penalty energy term to maintain the signed distance property of LSF near the zero level set. Finally, the multi-scale segmentation is performed by minimization of the overall energy functional. The experiments have demonstrated that our method is efficient and robust for segmenting medical images with slight or severe IIH.

Acknowledgements. This work was supported by the grant of the National Natural Science Foundation of China, No. 61005010, the special grant of China Postdoctoral Science Foundation, No. 2012T50582, the grant of Anhui Provincial Natural Science Foundation, No. 1308085MF84, the grant of China Postdoctoral Science Foundation, No. 20100480708, the grant of the Key Scientific Research Foundation of Education Department of Anhui Province, No. KJ2010A289, the grant of Scientific Research Foundation for Talents of Hefei University, No. 11RC05, the grant of Training Object for Academic Leader of Hefei University, No. 2014dtr08, the grant of DAAD.

References

1. Caselles, V., Kimmel, R., Sapiro, G.: Geodesic Active Contours. Int. J. Comput. Vision 22(1), 61–79 (1997)
2. Li, C., Xu, C., Gui, C., Fox, M.D.: Level Set Formulation without Re-initialization: A New Variational Formulation. In: Proc. CVPR, vol. 1, pp. 430–436 (2005)
3. Wang, X., Huang, D.: A Novel Density-Based Clustering Framework by Using Level Set Method. IEEE Trans. Knowl. Data Eng. 21(11), 1515–1531 (2009)
4. Gao, X., Wang, B., Tao, D., Li, X.: A Relay Level Set Method for Automatic Image Segmentation. IEEE Trans. Syst., Man, Cybern. B, Cybernetics 41(2), 518–525 (2011)
5. Chan, T.F., Vese, L.A.: Active Contours without Edges. IEEE Trans. Image Process. 10(2), 266–277 (2001)
6. Paragios, N., Deriche, R.: Geodesic Active Regions and Level Set Methods for Supervised Texture Segmentation. Int. J. Comput. Vision 46(4), 223–247 (2002)
7. Gao, S., Bui, T.D.: Image Segmentation and Selective Smoothing by Using Mumford-Shah Model. IEEE Trans. Image Process. 14(10), 1537–1549 (2005)
8. Li, C., Kao, C., Gore, J.C., Ding, Z.: Minimization of Region-Scalable Fitting Energy for Image Segmentation. IEEE Trans. Image Process. 17, 1940–1949 (2008)
9. Wang, X., Huang, D., Xu, H.: An Efficient Local Chan-Vese Model for Image Segmentation. Pattern Recognition 43(3), 603–618 (2010)
10. Sun, K., Chen, Z., Jiang, S.: Local Morphology Fitting Active Contour for Automatic Vascular Segmentation. IEEE Trans. Biomed. Eng. 59(2), 464–473 (2012)
11. Huang, D., Du, J.: A Constructive Hybrid Structure Optimization Methodology for Radial Basis Probabilistic Neural Networks. IEEE Trans. Neural Networks 19(12), 2099–2115 (2008)
12. Huang, D.: Radial Basis Probabilistic Neural Networks: Model and Application. Int. J. Pattern Recognit. Artificial Intell. 13(7), 1083–1101 (1999)
13. Huang, D., Chi, Z., Siu, W.C.: A Case Study for Constrained Learning Neural Root Finders. Applied Mathematics and Computation 165(3), 699–718 (2005)
14. Huang, D., Horace, H.S., Ip, C.Z.: A Neural Root Finder of Polynomials Based on Root Moments. Neural Computation 16(8), 1721–1762 (2004)
15. Huang, D.: A Constructive Approach for Finding Arbitrary Roots of Polynomials by Neural Networks. IEEE Trans. on Neural Networks 15(2), 477–491 (2004)
16. Zhao, Z., Huang, D., Sun, B.: Human Face Recognition Based on Multiple Features Using Neural Networks Committee. Pattern Recognition Letters 25(12), 1351–1358 (2004)
17. Li, C., Xu, C., Gui, C., Fox, M.D.: Distance Regularized Level Set Evolution and its Application to Image Segmentation. IEEE Trans. Image Process. 19(12), 3243–3254 (2010)
18. Brinkmann, B.H., Manduca, A., Robb, R.A.: Optimized Homomorphic Unsharp Masking for MR Grayscale Inhomogeneity Correction. IEEE Trans. Med. 17(2), 161–171 (1998)

A Novel Local Regional Model
Based on Three-Layer Structure

Hai Min[1,2] and Xiao-Feng Wang[2,3,*]

[1] Department of Automation, University of Science and Technology of China,
Hefei Anhui 230027, China
[2] Intelligent Computing Lab, Hefei Institute of Intelligent Machines,
Chinese Academy of Sciences, P.O. Box 1130, Hefei Anhui 230031, China
[3] Key Lab of Network and Intelligent Information Processing, Department of Computer
Science and Technology, Hefei University, Hefei Anhui 230601, China
minhai361@gmail.com, xfwang@iim.ac.cn

Abstract. In this paper, considering the local variance of intensity inhomogeneity, we propose a novel local regional level set model based on a so-called Three-Layer structure to segment images with intensity inhomogeneity. The local region intensity mean idea is used to construct region descriptor. Especially, three descriptors separately based on 'large', 'median' and 'small' scales of local regions are utilized to derive the Three-Layer structure. Compared to the traditional methods based on fixed scale for all local regions, the Three-Layer structure is more reliable for capturing local intensity information. Then, the Three-Layer structure is incorporated into the level set energy functional construction. As a result, more effective local intensity information is incorporated into the level set evolution. Finally, the experimental results demonstrate that the proposed method yields results comparative to and even better than the existing popular models for segmenting images with intensity inhomogeneity.

Keywords: local information, level set, intensity inhomogeneity, three-Layer structure.

1   Introduction

The level set methods for capturing dynamic interface and shape [1] are the state-of-the-art techniques for image segmentation [2]. The fundamental idea of the level set function is to represent a contour as the zero level set of a higher dimensional function and formulate the motion of the contour as the evolution of the level set function.

Recently, many region-based models are proposed to segment images with intensity inhomogeneity by utilizing local intensity information, such as the local region based model (LRB) model [3], the local binary fitting (LBF) model [4], the local intensity clustering (LIC) model [5], the local Chan-Vese model [6], the local

---

[*] Corresponding author.

D.-S. Huang et al. (Eds.): ICIC 2014, LNBI 8590, pp. 72–79, 2014.

image fitting (LIF) model [7], etc. However, some drawbacks are existed in these local region-based models. The Dirac functional used there is restricted to a neighborhood around the zero level set, which makes level set evolution act locally. Therefore, the local minima often occur in LRB model. For LBF model, the local region descriptor function is utilized to describe each local region in the whole image. However, the intensity inhomogeneity of local regions is different to some extent. The local region descriptor with fixed scale cannot accurately describe all local regions of image. Besides, the LIC model can also be seemed as the locally weighted K-means clustering. Unfortunately, the cluster variance is not considered in LIC model. Therefore, it is unavailable for images with sever intensity inhomogeneity.

However, it is difficult to determine the desired local region scale for each model. Meanwhile, it is also a difficult problem to utilize local region descriptor with single certain scale to describe all local regions. Thus, some desirable hybrid structures [8-10] and neural networks [11-14] are proposed and proved to be more effective than traditional methods. Motivated by these methods, a novel local regional level set model based on Three-Layer structure is proposed to segment images with intensity inhomogeneity. By analyzing the role of local region information, we propose using local region descriptor based on Three-Layer structure to describe the local regions. The local region descriptor based on Three-Layer structure is composed by three descriptors separately based on 'large', 'median' and 'small' scales. It works with three local regions each of which is created based on a specific kind of local region, and fuses the descriptors in the level set energy functional. Firstly, the three kernel functions with different variance scales are given. Then, the local region mean idea is used to represent the each local region descriptor. Finally, the local operation based on Three-Layer structure is incorporated into level set method and the overall energy functional is constructed.

The rest of the paper is organized as follows. The proposed method and variational formulation are described in Section 2. In Section 3, we verify the effectiveness of our method by some experiments. The conclusion is presented in Section 4.

2   Model Description

(a)   Three-Layer Structure

As described above, the local information is used to describe images with intensity inhomogeneity. However, the local region with predefined single scale generally cannot capture enough desirable intensity distribution information. Fig.1 shows three local regions with different scales s_1, s_2, s_3 and the same center point (red point) are exhibited in the input image I. While the local region scale is s_1, the local region does not include the intensity inhomogeneity or boundary information. Then, the descriptor derived from the local region cannot capture the intensity inhomogeneity feature. If the value s_3 is selected as the local region scale, many of intensity information is included in the local region with scale of s_3. However, the descriptor based on intensity mean cannot accurately describe the local region feature with included information. It can be seen that s_2 may be a desired scale of local region. It includes some intensity inhomogeneity information and the local region descriptor based on intensity mean can represent the intensity feature of local region. Thus, for the center point, the desired local region scale s can be determined in the interval $[s_1, s_3]$. Similarly, for all the other points of image, the desired local region scales can also be determined as s_q (q denote the different points of image) which separately locate in some other intervals. Due to the local variance of intensity inhomogeneity, all these intervals may be not identical.

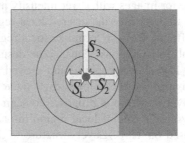

Fig. 1. The illustration of local region scales of image with intensity inhomogeneity

Therefore, considering the uncertainty of optimal scale, we propose a so-called Three-Layer structure to solve the intensity inhomogeneity problem. Since the desirable local region scale located in different intervals, the 'large' (L), 'median' (M) and 'small' (S) local region scales are used to construct the local region descriptors. The aim is to make the intersections between three scales and each desirable scale interval be non-zero.

Firstly, we need to determine the three local regions with L, M, S scales for each point of image. Here, as formula (1) shows, the Gaussian kernel function is used to determine the local regions by setting different variances.

$$k_{\sigma_j}(x-y) = \frac{1}{2\pi^{1/2}\sigma_j^2} e^{-|x-y|^2/2\sigma_j^2} \ (j = L, M, S), (\sigma_j = 4 \cdot j + 1). \tag{1}$$

The three predefined scales (L, M, S) represent the values located in different intervals. Thus, our method based on Three-Layer structure can include enough local region information. Meanwhile, it is noticed that the three descriptors are derived. The local information is extracted by three descriptors based on intensity mean. Then, we fuse the three descriptors by summing the description differences. The illustration of Three-Layer structure is shown in Fig.2. The Gaussian kernel functions k_{σ_L}, k_{σ_M} and k_{σ_S} are used to process the image I. Based on the Three-layer structure idea, the data term of our level set energy functional can be written as the following:

$$E_D = \int_{\Omega\,inside(C)} \int \varepsilon_1 dy dx + \int_{\Omega\,outside(C)} \int \varepsilon_2 dy dx \tag{2}$$

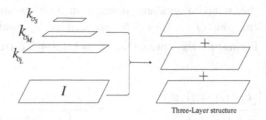

Fig. 2. The illustration of Three-Layer structure

where ε_1 and ε_2 are computed as follows:

$$\varepsilon_1 = k_{\sigma_L}(x-y)(I(y)-m_1(x))^2 + k_{\sigma_M}(x-y)(I(y)-m_2(x))^2$$
$$+k_{\sigma_S}(x-y)(I(y)-m_3(x))^2,$$

(3)

$$\varepsilon_2 = k_{\sigma_L}(x-y)(I(y)-m_4(x))^2 + k_{\sigma_M}(x-y)(I(y)-m_5(x))^2$$
$$+k_{\sigma_S}(x-y)(I(y)-m_6(x))^2,$$

(4)

where C denotes the evolving contour, k_{σ_L}, k_{σ_M} and k_{σ_S} denote the three Gaussian kernel functions with L, M and S scales as formula (1) shows. m_i ($i = 1,2,3,4,5,6$) denote the local region intensity mean of inside or outside of C.

(b)   Numerical Computation

In this paper, we utilize level set method to solve the energy functional in (2). In level set method, the contour C is represented by zero level set of a Lipschitz function ϕ, which is called a level set function. We use $H(x)$ to denote the Heaviside function. Then, the data term in (2) can be formulated as follows:

$$E_D = \iint \varepsilon_1 \cdot H(\phi)dydx + \iint \varepsilon_2 \cdot (1-H(\phi))dydx$$

(5)

Here, $H(x)$ and its derivative, i.e. Dirac delta $\delta(x)$, are approximated by the following formula:

$$H(x) = \frac{1}{2}[1+\frac{2}{\pi}.\arctan(\frac{x}{\varepsilon})], \quad \delta(x) = H'(x) = \frac{1}{\pi}\frac{\varepsilon}{\varepsilon^2+x^2}.$$

(6)

Besides, the regularization terms proposed in [4] are also introduced to regulate the level set function. Finally, the overall energy functional is written as:

$$E = \iint \varepsilon_1 \cdot H(\phi)dydx + \iint \varepsilon_2 \cdot (1-H(\phi))dydx$$
$$+\mu \int_\Omega (\nabla H(\phi(x)))dx + v \int_\Omega (\nabla \phi(x)-1)^2 dx$$

(7)

Then, we use the standard gradient descent method to solve the numerical computation problem. m_i ($i = 1,2,3,4,5,6$) are derived by minimizing the energy functional in (7). Fixing ϕ, the optimal m_i ($i = 1,2,3,4,5,6$) can be obtained as follows:

$$m_1(x) = \frac{\int_\Omega k_L * (I(x) \cdot H(\phi)) dx}{\int_\Omega k_L * H(\phi) dx}, m_2(x) = \frac{\int_\Omega k_M * (I(x) \cdot H(\phi)) dx}{\int_\Omega k_M * H(\phi) dx}, \tag{8}$$

$$m_3(x) = \frac{\int_\Omega k_S * (I(x) \cdot H(\phi)) dx}{\int_\Omega k_S * H(\phi) dx}, m_4(x) = \frac{\int_\Omega k_L * (I(x) \cdot (1 - H(\phi))) dx}{\int_\Omega k_L * (1 - H(\phi)) dx}, \tag{9}$$

$$m_5(x) = \frac{\int_\Omega k_M * (I(x) \cdot (1 - H(\phi))) dx}{\int_\Omega k_M * (1 - H(\phi)) dx}, m_6(x) = \frac{\int_\Omega k_S * (I(x) \cdot (1 - H(\phi))) dx}{\int_\Omega k_S * (1 - H(\phi)) dx}. \tag{10}$$

The function m_i ($i = 1,2,3,4,5,6$) given in (8-10) are weighted averages of intensities in a neighborhood. It is noticed that the scales of local neighborhoods are proportional to the scale parameters L, M and S. In practical implementation, L, M and S are predefined by us according to experience.

Keeping m_i ($i = 1,2,3,4,5,6$) fixed, we minimize the energy functional. It can be achieved by using standard gradient descent method:

$$\frac{\partial \phi}{\partial t} = \underbrace{\delta(\phi)(\varepsilon_1 - \varepsilon_2)}_{data\ term} + \underbrace{\mu \delta(\phi).div(\frac{\nabla \phi}{|\nabla \phi|}) + v(\nabla^2 \phi - div(\frac{\nabla \phi}{|\nabla \phi|}))}_{regularization\ term}. \tag{11}$$

where ∇ is gradient operator and $div(.)$ is the divergence operator.

(c)   Algorithm Summary

1. Place the initial contour and initialize the level set function ϕ: if x is located inside initial contour, $\phi(x) = 1$ or else $\phi(x) = -1$.
2. Set parameters v, μ, L, M, S, $\sigma_j = 4j + 1$ ($j = L, M, S$).
3. Evolve ϕ according to the gradient flow equation described in (11).
4. Extract the zero level set from the final level set function.

3   Experimental Results

In this section, the experiment results of our model shall be shown on some synthetic and real medical images. Besides, we also compared our method with the popular LBF and LIF model, respectively. The LBF model extracts the intensity information of local region at a controllable scale. It demonstrates that the problem of intensity inhomogeneity can be solved. The LIF model introduces a local image fitting energy to extract the local image information where the Gaussian kernel with predefined scale is utilized to process original image. Here, we make experiments by Matlab 7.0 on a PC with Intel double core, 2.2GHZ CPU. We shall use the same parameters, i.e. $v=1$, $\mu=0.001\times255^2$, $L=19$, $M=11$, $S=3$, for all experiments in this section.

In Fig.3, we made the comparison between the LBF model and our method on segmenting two medical images. The initial contours are shown in the first column. The segmentation result of LBF model and our method are shown in the second and third columns, respectively. Obviously, our method achieved better segmentation performance than LBF model. This is because the LBF model based on certain scale parameter could not describe the local variance of intensity inhomogeneity. On the contrary, the local regions with scale parameters L, M and S in our method can efficiently extract more desired local intensity information.

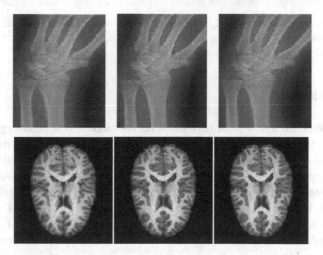

Fig. 3. The comparison between LBF model and our method on segmenting two medical images. Column1: Initial contours. Column2: The segmentation results of LBF model. Column3: Final segmentation results of our method.

The comparison between the LIF model and our method on segmenting two medical images is shown in Fig.4. The initial contours and original images are shown in the first column. The segmentation results of the LIF model and our method are separately shown in the second and third columns. It can be seen that our method is more robust to intensity inhomogeneity than LIF model. Although the local image information is considered in LIF model, the fixed local region is not reliable for describing image. In our method, more desirable local image information can be extracted based on proposed Three-Layer structure. Hence, the better segmentation results were obtained by our method.

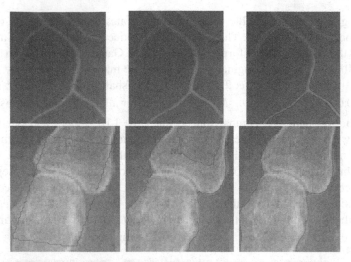

Fig. 4. The comparison between LIF model and our method on segmenting two medical images. Column1: Initial contours. Column2: The segmentation results of LIF model. Column3: Final segmentation results of our method.

4   Conclusion

This paper proposed a new local regional level set model for segmenting images with intensity inhomogeneity. Based on the local variance of intensity inhomogeneity, the local intensity mean idea is utilized to extract more local intensity information. By fusing the proposed Three-Layer structure into the level set method, we successfully derived a novel local regional level set energy functional. Experimental results have demonstrated the superior performance of our method in terms of accuracy for segmenting images with intensity inhomogeneity. In future, the Three-Layer structure shall be further studied and extended to solve the existing complex image segmentation problem.

Acknowledgements. This work was supported by the grant of the National Natural Science Foundation of China, No. 61005010, the special grant of China Postdoctoral Science Foundation, No. 2012T50582, the grant of Anhui Provincial Natural Science Foundation, No. 1308085MF84, the grant of China Postdoctoral Science Foundation, No. 20100480708, the grant of the Key Scientific Research Foundation of Education Department of Anhui Province, No. KJ2010A289, the grant of Scientific Research Foundation for Talents of Hefei University, No. 11RC05, the grant of Training Object for Academic Leader of Hefei University, No. 2014dtr08, the grant of DAAD.

References

1. Osher, S., Sethian, J.: Fronts Propagating With Curvature-Dependent Speed: Algorithms Based on Hamilton-Jacobi Formulations. J. Comput. Phys. 79, 12–49 (1988)
2. He, L., Peng, Z., Everding, B., Wang, X., Han, C.Y., Weiss, K.L., Wee, W.G.: A Comparative Study of Deformable Contour Methods on Medical Image Segmentation. Image Vis. Comput. 26(2), 141–163 (2008)
3. Lankton, S., Tannenbaum, A.: Localizing Region-Based Active Contours. IEEE Trans. Image Process. 17(11), 2029–2039 (2008)
4. Li, C., Kao, C., Gore, J.C., Ding, Z.: Minimization of Region-Scalable Fitting Energy for Image Segmentation. IEEE Trans. Image Process. 17(10), 1940–1949 (2008)
5. Li, C., Huang, R., Ding, Z., Gatenby, C., Metaxas, D., Gore, J.C.: A Level Set Method for Image Segmentation in the Presence of Intensity Inhomogeneities with Application to MRI. IEEE Trans. Image Process. 20(7), 2007–2016 (2011)
6. Wang, X., Huang, D., Xu, H.: An Efficient Local Chan-Vese Model for Image Segmentation. Pattern Recognition 43(3), 603–618 (2010)
7. Zhang, K., Song, H., Zhang, L.: Active Contours Driven by Local Image Fitting Energy. Pattern Recognition 43(4), 1199–1206 (2010)
8. Wang, X., Huang, D.: A Novel Density-Based Clustering Framework by Using Level Set Method. IEEE Trans. Knowl. Data Eng. 21(11), 1515–1531 (2009)
9. Li, B., Huang, D.: Locally Linear Discriminant Embedding: An Efficient Method for Face Recognition. Pattern Recognition 41(12), 3813–3821 (2008)
10. Huang, D., Du, J.: A Constructive Hybrid Structure Optimization Methodology for Radial Basis Probabilistic Neural Networks. IEEE Trans. Neural Networks 19(12), 2099–2115 (2008)
11. Huang, D.: Radial Basis Probabilistic Neural Networks: Model and Application. Int. J. Pattern Recognit. Artificial Intell. 13(7), 1083–1101 (1999)
12. Huang, D., Chi, Z., Siu, W.C.: A Case Study for Constrained Learning Neural Root Finders. Applied Mathematics and Computation 165(3), 699–718 (2005)
13. Huang, D., Horace, H.S., Ip, C.Z.: A Neural Root Finder of Polynomials Based on Root Moments. Neural Computation 16(8), 1721–1762 (2004)
14. Huang, D.: A Constructive Approach for Finding Arbitrary Roots of Polynomials by Neural Networks. IEEE Trans. on Neural Networks 15(2), 477–491 (2004)

Multi-modality Medical Case Retrieval
Using Heterogeneous Information

Menglin Wu[1,2] and Quansen Sun[1]

[1] School of Computer Science and Engineering, Nanjing University of Science and Technology,
210094 Nanjing, China
wumenglin@njtech.edu.cn
[2] College of Electronics and Information Engineering, Nanjing Tech University,
211816 Nanjing, China
sunquansen@njust.edu.cn

Abstract. Real-life clinical cases are important sources for computer diagnosis and pathologic analysis. In this paper, we propose a novel medical case retrieval framework based on multi-graph semi-supervised learning. The presented framework aims to retrieve multi-modality medical cases consisting of images together with diagnostic information. In particular, we first introduce a multi-graph semi-supervised learning method, which unifies both visual and textual information during learning by minimizing the cost function on a fusion graph. Then, a manifold ranking scheme is generated based on this multi-graph structure for retrieval. Experiments on the LIDC dataset and the mammographic patches dataset validate the effectiveness of the proposed method.

Keywords: medical case retrieval, image ranking, multi-graph semi-supervised learning, multi-graph fusion.

1   Introduction

One main task in computer-aided diagnosis is automatically searching relevant medical cases from a variety of medical image datasets and archival systems to generate a reliable diagnosis. It assists a radiologist to compare a new case to previously solved cases and makes a medical decision based on his or her experience. The underlying idea is the assumption that analogous problems have similar solutions. Therefore, efficient retrieval of medical case combining images and structured-textual information becomes an active area of research.

Content-based image retrieval (CBIR), which queries relevant medical images based on their visual content similarity, is one of the promising solutions to medical case retrieval [1]. The core of the medical CBIR is the extraction of the visual features that can effectively represent the medical image. These features typically include color, texture [2], and shape [3] for representing the specific categories of medical images such as mammography, brain MR, lung CT and so on. Especially, for the large scale image retrieval, bag of words (BOW) and fusion features are applied to describe the medical images with diverse models [4]. To improve the performance of

D.-S. Huang et al. (Eds.): ICIC 2014, LNBI 8590, pp. 80–91, 2014.
© Springer International Publishing Switzerland 2014

the retrieval system, some prototypes treat the relevant medical image searching as a machine learning problem. Yang et al. proposed a boosting based metric learning algorithm seeking to preserve both visual and semantic similarities in medical retrieval procedures [5]. In addition, support vector machine (SVM) based frameworks are also popular in medical image retrieval system during image filtering and dynamic features fusion [6]. However, the low-level features may not be able to characterize the medical sense of the images, known as semantic gap.

Medical case retrieval becomes even more challenging because the data of the medical case originates from heterogeneous information including visual and textual information. Recently, some literatures have proposed several models for medical case retrieval [7-12]. The main purpose of these methods is to combine the content of digit image and textual information by using fusion strategies or representing the various modalities in a unified model. However, these methods have a major obstacle that the labeled medical cases are limited for retrieval in practical applications. The semi-supervised learning aims to develop the machine learning model combining labeled data and a huge of unlabeled data. Based on this idea, we propose a novel medical case retrieval framework based on multi-graph semi-supervised learning, which views medical case searching as a multi-modality information retrieval problem. The main contributions of this paper are: (1) integrating both medical image features and clinical diagnostic descriptors for medical case retrieval; (2) introducing a new multi-graph semi-supervised learning model for multi-modality information retrieval; (3) conducting extensive experiments to demonstrate the effectiveness of the proposed framework.

2   Related Works

In recent years, multi-modality medical case retrieval has arisen as an active research topic. To search relevance medical cases based on both visual and semantic similarity, some algorithms for heterogeneous information retrieval were proposed on this subject. Shao et al. introduced a brain CT retrieval system linearly combining textual information and visual content in a common similarity measure [7]. In [8-9], a decision tree model and a Bayesian network were proposed for medical case retrieval based on various sources of medical information, respectively. To retrieval similar patient cases by time-series medical data, a dynamic time warping fusion scheme was presented in [10]. Ko et al. proposed a medical image annotation algorithm and keyword-based image retrieval framework with relevance feedback [11]. Besides, in [12], a graph-based retrieval approach concerning spatial proximity of tumors and organs was proposed for multi-modality medical image retrieval. Most of these methods aimed to integrate clinical annotations and images into a regular feature vector using fusion scheme, or represent them by a unified model.

Other studies suggest medical case retrieval is a cross-modal multimedia retrieval problem. Burdescu et al. adopted a cross relevance model for medical image retrieval using both medical annotation and visual features [13]. In [14], Lacost et al. proposed an automatic indexing of images and associate texts for retrieval using unified medical language system. Although these approaches have demonstrated effectiveness in retrieval, they depend on the precision of the image segmentation.

More recently, graph-based semi-supervised learning methods have attracted widely attention due to their effectiveness and computational efficiency. Most methods in this filed define a graph where nodes are labeled and unlabeled sample in the dataset, and weighted edges denote the pairwise similarity between the samples. Then the scores of the labeled samples are spread to unlabeled samples by diffusing the similarity values through the graph [15]. These methods are widely applied in data classification [16], multimedia annotation [17], and image retrieval [18]. Especially, several approaches focus on multi-modal image classification and annotation, which construct a multi-graph model for learning task [19]. Motivated by graph regularization model in [15], we proposed a multi-graph semi-supervised learning based retrieval framework and applied it to medical case retrieval in this paper.

3   The Medical Case Retrieval Framework

In this section, we propose a multi-graph semi-supervised learning based medical case retrieval framework. Firstly, graph models are built for both visual and textural information. Secondly, we propose a multi-graph fusion based learning method according to the basic function of graph regularization model. Thirdly, a manifold ranking scheme is implemented based on this multi-graph fusion structure.

3.1   Graph-Based Semi-supervised Learning

First we describe the basic notation for graph-based semi-supervised learning. Given the dataset as $\chi = \{\chi_L, \chi_U\} = \{x_1, ..., x_l, ..., x_n\}$. The first l samples are labeled by $y_L = \{y_1, ..., y_l\}$, where $y_i \in L = \{1, ..., c\}$. The goal of learning is to infer the missing labels $y_U = \{y_{l+1}, ..., y_n\}$ corresponding to the unlabeled set χ_U.

Assume that an undirected weighted graph $G = (V, W)$ is converted from the input dataset χ. Its vertex set is $V = \chi$ and weight matrix is $W = \{w_{ij}\}_{n \times n}$, where the edge w_{ij} represents the similarity between x_i and x_j. Here w_{ij} is given by Gaussian kernel of width σ:

$$w_{ij} = \exp(- \| x_i - x_j \|^2 / 2\sigma^2) \tag{1}$$

According the manifold assumption that nearby samples or samples on the same manifold structure are likely to have the same label, graph-based semi-supervised learning methods attempt to predict the soft labels $F = \{f_1^T, ..., f_l^T, ..., f_n^T\} \in R^{n \times c}$ through minimizing a cost function defined over the graph. One of these methods is Guassian fields and harmonic function (GFHF). In this approach, the quadratic cost function integrates the combined contributions of smoothness term and the local fitting term. This graph regularization based cost function is defined as [15]:

$$F^* = \arg\min_F \sum_{i,j} \frac{w_{ij}}{d_{ii}} (f_i - f_j)^2 + \infty \sum_{i \in L} (f_i - y_i)^2 \tag{2}$$

where $W = \{w_{ij}\}_{n \times n}$ is the weight matrix and $D = \{d_{ii}\}_{n \times n}$ is the diagonal matrix with $d_{ii} = \sum_j w_{ij}$. The first term of the right side is smoothness term, which indicates the nearby sample should not charge too much according to the structure of the graph, while the second term is local fitting term, which requires that the initial labels of the annotation samples should not change in the label propagation.

Let $S = D^{-1}W$ be the transfer matrix of the graph G. Splitting the matrix S after the l-th row and the l-th column, we have

$$S = \begin{bmatrix} S_{LL} & S_{LU} \\ S_{UL} & S_{UU} \end{bmatrix} \tag{3}$$

According to [15], we can obtain the solution of (2) as $F_U^* = (I - S_{UU})^{-1} S_{UL} y_L$. Then each of the unlabeled samples can be assigned a soft label.

3.2   Multi-graph Learning Model

Digital image and diagnostic information are heterogeneous information in medical cases. Therefore, their manifold structures should be represented by two different graph models, which are denoted by $W^g = \{w_{ij}^g\}_{n \times n}$ and $W^c = \{w_{ij}^c\}_{n \times n}$. Based on the basic notion of GFHF, we define a multi-graph learning function as:

$$F^* = \arg\min_F \left\{ \eta \sum_{i,j} \frac{w_{ij}^g}{d_{ii}^g} (f_i - f_j)^2 + (1 - \eta) \sum_{i,j} \frac{w_{ij}^c}{d_{ii}^c} (f_i - f_j)^2 \right\} \tag{4}$$

$$s.t. \quad f_i \equiv y_i \, (1 \le i \le l)$$

where $d_{ii}^g = \sum_j w_{ij}^g$ and $d_{ii}^c = \sum_j w_{ij}^c$. The parameter η denotes a tradeoff between two graph models. This function can be viewed as an extension of formula (2) for multi-graph fusion structure. The first term of right side indicates that the labels of nearby samples should not change too much according to the graph structure for visual content, while the second term denotes that the labels of nearby samples should not change too much according to the graph structure for textual information. The constraint requires that the initial labels should not change in the label propagation.

The multi-graph learning structure is shown in Fig.1. In this structure, the top graph represents the manifold structure of visual content, the bottom graph represents the manifold structure of textual information, and the middle graph is the fusion graph. The label propagation procedure executes on top and bottom graph, both of which supervise each other through the fusion graph.

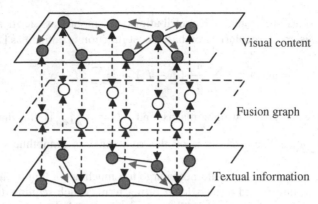

Fig. 1. The multi-graph learning structure and label propagation procedure. The labeled samples are denoted by red circles. The score of labeled samples are spread to unlabeled samples by diffusing the similarity values through the graph.

To solve the optimization problem in (4), we rewrite it as a matrix form:

$$F^* = \arg\min_F \{\eta F^T L^g F + (1-\eta) F^T L^c F\}$$
$$s.t. \quad F_L = Y_L \tag{5}$$

where $L^g = I - (D^g)^{-1} W^g$ and $L^c = I - (D^c)^{-1} W^c$ are the graph Laplacians of two graphs, respectively. D^g and D^c are diagonal matrices with diagonal elements d_{ii}^g and d_{ii}^c. We assume the multi-graph transfer matrix as:

$$S^M = \eta S^g + (1-\eta) S^c = \eta (D^g)^{-1} W^g + (1-\eta)(D^c)^{-1} W^c \tag{6}$$

Then the formula (5) can be rewritten as:

$$F^* = \arg\min_F \{F^T (I - S^M) F\}$$
$$s.t. \quad F_L^* = Y_L \tag{7}$$

We differentiate with respect to F and set it to zero. By splitting S and F like (3):

$$\begin{cases} F_U^* = S_{UL}^M F_L^* + S_{UU}^M F_U^* \\ F_L^* = Y_L \end{cases} \tag{8}$$

The solution of (8) is $F_U^* = (I - S_{UU}^M)^{-1} S_{UL}^M Y_L$, which indicates the soft labels of the unlabeled samples. This solution then can be represented as an iterative form:

$$F_U^{(t+1)} = S_{UU}^M F_U^t + S_{UL}^M Y_L \tag{9}$$

3.3   The Medical Case Retrieval Algorithm

Based on the multi-graph learning model, we generate a manifold ranking scheme on the fusion graph to implement medical case retrieval. Manifold ranking is a typical application of graph-based semi-supervised learning, which obtains the scores by label propagation on the graph and returns the query results according to their ranking score. It can be viewed as a binary-class classification problem of graph based semi-supervised learning. The label y_i is set to 1 if x_i is a relevant medical case; otherwise, y_i is set to 0. Therefore, we can apply the multi-graph learning model to medical case retrieval by converting the initial label matrix to a binary vector.

For clarity, we summarize the medical case retrieval approach in algorithm 1:

Algorithm1. Multi-graph semi-supervised learning based medical case retrieval
Input: Medical cases $\chi = \{x_1, ..., x_l, ..., x_n\}$. The first l samples are medical cases of queries and the rest are medical cases in dataset.
1. Create Graph $G^g = (V^g, W^g)$ and $G^c = (V^c, W^c)$ for visual content and textual information using (1), respectively.
2. Construct initial vector $Y = [y_1, .., y_l, ..., y_n]^T$. If x_i is relevant sample or query sample, $y_i = 1$; otherwise $y_i = 0$.
3. Calculate the multi-graph transfer matrix S^M using (6).
4. Iterate $F_U^{(t+1)} = S_{UU}^M F_U^t + S_{UL}^M Y_L$ until convergence. The element of vector F_U denotes the ranking score of corresponding medical case.
5. Return the top K medical cases by listing the ranking scores in descend order.

4   Experiments and Analysis

4.1   Experiment Setup

To evaluate the performance of the proposed framework, we carried out experiments on the LIDC dataset [20] and the mammographic patches dataset [21]. The summary of the details of each dataset is follows:

1. LIDC dataset is a popular benchmark dataset for the development, training and evaluation for lung cancer detection and classification. In this paper, we selected 876 samples from the dataset as the training set. Each sample includes a CT scan, a contouring of nodule marking by the expert thoracic radiologists and 9 pathological properties of each nodule. According to the assessment of each tumor, we classified these samples as 5 categories: Highly unlikely, moderate unlikely, indeterminate, moderately suspicious, and highly suspicious.
2. Mammographic patches dataset consists of texture patches from screen mammography. It includes 2796 patches annotated by IRMA code [21]. Each patch contains a region of interest (ROI), which is resized to 512×512. According

to the tumor stating, we group these mammographic patches into 5 categories: normal, benign, probably benign, suspiciously abnormal, and malignant.

In LIDC dataset, visual contents are represented by the features of lung nodules including: co-occurrence, Gabor, Markov features, shape and intensity, while the textual information is described by 8 characteristics of the lesion [20]. In mammographic patches dataset, each patch is represented by patch-based visual words and medical annotation is described by IRMA code [21].

4.2   Compare with CBIR Methods

To evaluate the performance of the medical case retrieval framework, we compare the proposed approach in this paper with CBIR methods. For LIDC dataset, the comparative methods are: (1) manifold ranking-based image retrieval (MRBIR) [18]; (2) Euclidean distance measurement based on texture and shape features [20]. For mammographic patches dataset, the comparative methods are: (1) MRBIR; (2) bag of words (BOW) [4] and Jensen-Shannon divergence-based measurement; (3) mammogram retrieval based on Gabor feature [2]. All algorithms in our experiments are implemented in MATLAB and run on a computer with 2.8 GHZ CPU and 16GB RAM.

For the proposed approach, we set $K = 60$ to computer the KNN similarity matrix by (1) according to the sample distribution, where $\sigma^g = 0.5$ and $\sigma^c = 0.1$ for visual and textual information, respectively. In addition, we set the fusion parameter η in (5) to 0.4 and 0.2 for LIDC dataset and mammographic patches dataset by cross validation, respectively. In the experiment, according to the dataset scale, we randomly select 200 and 500 samples from former and later dataset as query medical cases, and leave the rest for retrieval. A query example on LIDC datasets is shown in Fig.2.

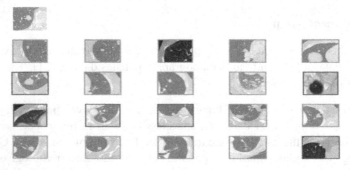

Fig. 2. A query example on LIDC dataset (Only the ROIs are shown). The left upper image is the query medical case and others are top 20 returned results. Green framed images denote the relevant medical cases and red framed images denote the irrelevant medical cases.

For comparison, a popular and straightforward measure is the PR-curve, which depicts the relationship between precision and recall of a specific retrieval system. In this paper, we draw the PR-curves for different retrieval algorithms on both datasets. These results are shown in Fig. 3 and Fig.4.

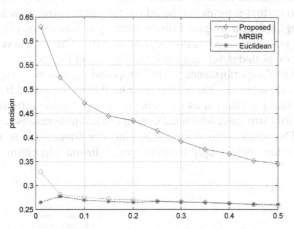

Fig. 3. The PR-curves of three algorithms on LIDC

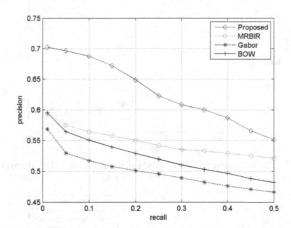

Fig. 4. The PR-curves of four algorithms on mammographic patches dataset

As these figures show, it is evident that the proposed approach explicitly outperforms the other CBIR algorithms on both datasets. Although the performance of all the compared methods degenerates with the recall increasing, the proposed approach still achieves highest accuracy because it integrates the visual and textual information for retrieval. The CBIR algorithms only concern the visual similarity of the medial images, but they ignore the semantic information of the medical annotation. Therefore, their average precisions are lower than the proposed approach. In addition, the BOW descriptor is more effectiveness than the Gabor feature for mammogram retrieval. The MRBIR performs better than BOW-based algorithm due to the fact that MRBIR concerns more about the manifold structure rather than pairwise similarity between images.

4.3   Compare with Fusion Based Methods

In order to verify the effectiveness of exploiting the visual and textual information in medical case retrieval, we evaluate the proposed framework with three fusion-based multi-modality information retrieval schemes. Scheme 1 uses early fusion combining visual content and textual information based on canonical correlation analysis (CCA) [22], scheme 2 applies linear weighted fusion strategy as late fusion [7], and scheme 3 is a multi-graph learning based fusion algorithm [19]. The PR-curves for different retrieval methods on both datasets are shown in Fig. 5 and Fig. 6.

We observe that the performance of the proposed approach is superior to other fusion-based retrieval schemes. The results indicate that the proposed framework treats the visual and textual information as two kinds of compensation information and fuse them on the manifold structure, which achieves more accurate results than early fusion and late fusion. The results also demonstrate that our framework is more effective for retrieval than the multi-graph learning based fusion algorithm of scheme 3.

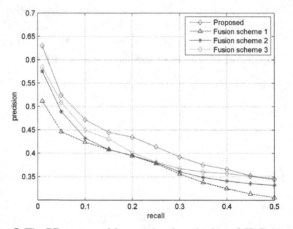

Fig. 5. The PR-curves of four retrieval methods on LIDC dataset

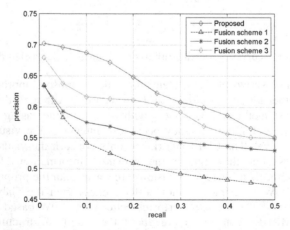

Fig. 6. The PR-curves of four retrieval methods on mammographic patches dataset

In addition, we notice that the late fusion scheme achieves a better performance than early fusion, although its computation complexity is higher, because there are two manifold ranking procedures generated for visual and textual information, respectively. The comparisons of average time costs in one query for four methods are shown in table 1, which obviously illustrate that the proposed framework is more efficient than other three methods in both datasets.

Table 1. Comparisions of time cost

Dataset	Method	Executing Time (s)	Dataset	Method	Executing Time (s)
LIDC	Scheme1	0.556	Mammographic patches	Scheme1	2.088
	Scheme2	0.929		Scheme2	6.569
	Scheme3	0.236		Scheme3	1.413
	proposed	**0.090**		proposed	**0.480**

For the purpose of computer-aid diagnosis, radiologists always pay more attention on the top results of the retrieval list. Therefore, we apply the NDCG (Normalized Discounted Cumulative Gain) to evaluate the retrieval performance, where the contribution of each result is proportional to its relevancy to the query and the position in the ranking list. The NDCG is defined as follows:

$$\text{NDCG}(n) = Z_n \sum_{i=1}^{n} (2^{r(i)} - 1) / \log_2(1+i) \qquad (10)$$

where $r(i)$ denotes the relevance degree of the *i-th* sample. Z_n is the normalized parameter which is set to the NDCG value of the best retrieval result. Table 2 demonstrates the NDCG evaluations of the three methods on both datasets. The results explicitly show that the proposed approach achieves a higher NDCG value than other fusion-based retrieval methods.

Table 2. The NDCG evaluation of three retrieval methods on both dataset

Dataset	Method	NDCG value of top K medical cases				
		10	20	30	40	50
LIDC	Scheme1	0.6227	0.6065	0.5978	0.5896	0.5812
	Scheme 2	0.6421	0.6110	0.5938	0.5834	0.5731
	Scheme 3	0.6374	0.6233	0.6015	0.5946	0.5831
	Proposed	**0.6734**	**0.6416**	**0.6268**	**0.6115**	**0.5980**
Mammographic patches	Scheme1	0.6371	0.6082	0.5896	0.5770	0.5661
	Scheme 2	0.6715	0.6612	0.6545	0.6482	0.6427
	Scheme 3	0.7177	0.7049	0.6982	0.6956	0.6909
	Proposed	**0.7594**	**0.7547**	**0.7454**	**0.7330**	**0.7176**

5   Conclusion and Discussion

In this paper, we proposed a novel medical case retrieval framework using heterogeneous information. The proposed framework bases on multi-graph semi-supervised learning and aims to unify the visual and texture information by minimizing the cost function of the fusion graph. We first introduced the basic function of graph regularization model and extended it to multi-graph learning for retrieval. Then we generate a manifold ranking scheme on this multi-graph manifold structure for medical case retrieval based on visual content and textual information. The results demonstrate the effectiveness of the proposed framework to integrate the two kinds of information for retrieval. In the further we will combine the proposed framework with relevance feedback strategy, which can improve the performance of the retrieval system by user feedback.

Acknowledgement. This work is supported by the National Natural Science Foundation of China under Grant No. 61273251 and the Fundamental Research Funds for the Central Universities under Grant No. 30920140111004.

References

1. Müller, H., Michoux, N., Bandon, D., Geissbuhler, A.: A Review ofContent-Based Image Retrieval Systems in Medical Applications-Clinical Benefits and Future Directions. Int. J. Med. Inform. 73, 1–23 (2004)
2. Wei, C.H., Li, Y., Li, C.T.: Effective Extraction ofGabor Features for Adaptive Mammogram Retrieval. In: IEEE International Conference on Multimedia and Expo 2007, pp. 1503–1506. IEEE Press (2007)
3. Xu, X., Lee, D.J., Antani, S., Long, L.R.: A Spine X-Ray Image Retrieval System Using Partial Shape Matching. IEEE. T. Inf. Technol. B. 12, 100–108 (2008)
4. Avni, U., Greenspan, H., Konen, E., Sharon, M.: X-Ray Categorization and Retrieval on The Organ and Pathology Level, Using Patch-Based Visual Words. IEEE. T. Med. Imaging 30, 733–746 (2011)
5. Yang, L., Jin, R., Mummert, L., Sukthankar, R.: A Boosting Framework for Visuality-Preserving Distance Metric Learning and Its Application to Medical Image Retrieval. IEEE. T. Pattern. Anal. 32, 30–44 (2010)
6. Rahman, M.M., Antani, S.K., Thoma, G.R.: A Learning-Based Similarity Fusion and Filtering Approach for Biomedical Image Retrieval Using SVM Classification and Relevance Feedback. IEEE. T. Inf. Technol. B. 15, 640–646 (2011)
7. Shao, H., Cui, W.C., Zhao, H.: Medical Image Retrieval Based on Visual Contents and Text Information. In: IEEE International Conference on Systems, Man and Cybernetics, pp. 1098–1103. IEEE Press (2004)
8. Quellec, G., Lamard, M., Bekri, L.: Medical Case Retrieval From A Committee ofDecision Trees. IEEE. T. Inf. Technol. B. 14, 1227–1235 (2010)
9. Quellec, G., Lamard, M., Cazuguel, G.: Case Retrieval in Medical Databases by Fusing Heterogeneous Information. IEEE. T. Med. Imaging 30, 108–118 (2011)

10. Tsevas, S., Iakovidis, D.K.: Dynamic Time Warping Fusion for The Retrieval ofSimilar Patient Cases Represented by Multimodal Time-Series Medical Data. In: IEEE International Conference on Information Technology and Applications in Biomedicine, pp. 1–4. IEEE Press (2010)
11. Ko, B.C., Lee, J., Nam, J.: Automatic Medical Image Annotation and Keyword-Based Image Retrieval Using Relevance Feedback. J. Digit. Imaging 25, 454–465 (2012)
12. Kumar, A., Kim, J., Wen, L.: A Graph-Based Approach for The Retrieval ofMulti-Modality Medical Images. Med. Image. Anal. 18, 330–342 (2013)
13. Burdescu, D., Mihai, G.C., Stanescu, L.: Automatic Image Annotation and Semantic Based Image Retrieval for Medical Domain. Neurocomputing 109, 33–48 (2013)
14. Lacoste, C., Lim, J., Chevallet, J., Le, D.T.H.: Medical-Image Retrieval Based on Knowledge-Assisted Text and Image Indexing. IEEE. T. Circ. Syst. Vid. 17, 889–900 (2007)
15. Zhu, X.: Semi-Supervised Learning with Graphs, Ph.D. Dissertation, Carnegie Mellon Univ., Pittsburgh, PA (2005)
16. Subramanya, A., Bilmes, J.: Semi-Supervised Learning with Measure Propagation. J. Mach. Learn. Res. 12, 3311–3370 (2011)
17. Tang, J.H., Li, H.J., Qi, G.: Image Annotation by Graph-Based Inference with Integrated Multiple/Single Instance Representations. IEEE. T. Multimedia 12, 131–141 (2010)
18. He, J.R., Li, M.J., Zhang, H.J.: Generalized Manifold-Ranking-Based Image Retrieval. IEEE. T. Image. Process. 15, 3170–3177 (2006)
19. Lee, W.Y., Hsieh, L., Wu, G., Hsu, W.: Graph-Based Semi-Supervised Learning with Multi-Modality Propagation for Large-Scale Image Datasets. J. Vis. Commun. Image. R. 24, 295–302 (2013)
20. Muhammad, M.N., Raicu, D.S., Furst, G.D., Varutbangkul, E.: Texture Versus Shape Analysis for Lung Nodule Similarity in Computed Tomography Studies. In: Proceedings of the SPIE, vol. 6919 (2008)
21. Oliveira, J., Machado, A., Chavez, G., Lopes, A., Deserno, T.M., AraÚJo, A.: Mammosys: A Content-Based Image Retrieval System Using Breast Density Patterns. Comput. Meth. Prog. Bio. 99, 289–297 (2010)
22. Sun, Q.S., Zheng, S.G., Liu, Y.: A New Method ofFeature Fusion and Its Application in Image Recognition. Pattern Recogn. 38, 2437–2448 (2005)

An Incremental Updating Based Fast Phenotype Structure Learning Algorithm

Hao Cheng[1], Yu-Hai Zhao[2,*], Ying Yin[2], and Li-Jun Zhang[2]

[1] College of Sciences, Northeastern University, China
[2] College of Information Science and Engineering, Northeastern University, China
zhaoyuhai@ise.neu.edu.cn

Abstract. Unsupervised phenotype structure learning is important in microarray data analysis. The goal is to (1) find groups of samples corresponding to different phenotypes (e.g. disease or normal), and (2) find a subset of genes that can distinguish different groups. Due to the large number of genes and a mass of noise in microarray data, the existing methods are often of some limitations in terms of efficicency and effectiveness. In this paper, we develop an incremental updating based phenotype structure learning algorithm, namely FPLA. With a randomly selected initial state, the algorithm iteratively tries three possible adjustments, i.e. gene addition, gene deletion and sample move, to improve the quality of the current result. Accordingly, four incremental updating based optimization strategies are devised to eliminate the redundancy computations in each iteration. Further, by utilizing a harmonic quality function, it improves the result accuracy by penalizing the "outlier" effect. The experiments conducted on several real microarray datasets show that FPLA outperforms the two representative competing algorithms on both effectiveness and efficiency.

Keywords: data mining, microarray data, phenotype structure, bioinformatics.

1   Introduction

The high-throughput microarray technology enables to simultaneously monitor the expression levels of tens of thousands of genes. However, it is often that only a small number of genes will interest the biologists [1]. So, finding such genes is a significant task in microarray data analysis.

Generally, the task can be considered from two different scenarios. In supervised case, it is described as an informative gene selecting problem, where the genes showing differential expression levels among different phenotypes are selected. In unsupervised case, the task is described as a phenotype structure learning problem, the goal of which is to find (1) an exclusive and exhaustive partition of the samples that samples of each group within the partition represent a unique phenotype; and (2) a set of informative genes manifesting this partition that each informative gene

---

* Corresponding author.

D.-S. Huang et al. (Eds.): ICIC 2014, LNBI 8590, pp. 92–103, 2014.
© Springer International Publishing Switzerland 2014

displays approximately invariant signals on samples of the same phenotype and highly differential signals for samples between different phenotypes. Obviously, the unsupervised task is much more difficult than the former, since the information of sample labels, which can be utilized as a reference to guide gene selection, is not available. In this case, many statistical methods cannot be applied.

In this paper, we focus on the unsupervised task, which is more challenging and tougher. An intuitive solution to this problem is an iterative method. That is, we first design a criterion, say Q, for the clustering quality evaluation. Then, starting from a randomly initialized clustering, perform an iterative updating, where any addition or deletion operation of a sample or a gene is tried for every cluster in the current clustering to make clustering proceed towards Q increasing. There are two major drawbacks in this intuitive method. First, Q has to be computed from scratch in each iteration if no any optimization; Second, some outliers may heavily influence the clustering result so that some resulting clusters are too extreme, that is, some clusters only contain very few samples and genes. In this paper, we tackle this problem by developing an incremental updating based fast phenotype structure learning algorithm, namely FPLA. We claim the contributions as follows.

1.   We adopt the incremental updating strategies to optimize the iterative process. Particularly, four incremental updating based optimization strategies are devised. By integrating them into the iterative learning, the quality evaluation in each iteration need not to be calculated from stratch. Thus, the running time is greatly reduced.
2.   We consider the impact of the number of samples to the result quality. By utilizing a harmonic quality function, which harmonizes the pattern quality with the pattern weight, the "outlier" effect is penalized and the result accuracy is improved.
3.   We conduct the experiments on several real microarray datasets. The result show that FPLA outperforms the two related competing algorithms on both effectiveness and efficiency.

The remainder of this paper is organized as follows. Section 2 gives some preliminaries and the problem statement. Section 3 describes the quality measurements. The algorithm is detailed in Section 4. Experimental results are given in Section 5. Section 6 introduces some related work. Finally, Section 7 concludes this paper.

2   Preliminary

A gene expression matrix M consists of a set of rows $R = \{r_1, r_2, ..., r_m\}$, which represent a set of genes, and a set of columns $C=\{c_1, c_2, ..., c_m\}$, which represent all considered samples. Then, the data matrix can be represent as $M = \{a_{i,j} | 1 \leq i \leq m, 1 \leq j \leq n\}$, where $a_{i,j}$ corresponds to the value of gene r_i on sample c_j. For example, Table 1 gives an illustrative gene expression matrix.

Definition 1. The empirical phenotypes refer to the samples controlled by the biologist in a gene expression experiment (e.g. diseased or normal samples). The sample partition corresponding to the empirical phenotypes is called an empirical sample pattern, and each subset of samples of the partition is called a sample group.

Definition 2. An informative gene is a gene that can manifest the empirical sample pattern. So, an informative gene should express the similar values in every sample groups but the differential values in different groups. The set of informative genes is called the informative gene space.

Table 1. An illustrated gene expression matrix

	c_1	c_2	c_3	C_4	c_5	C_6
r_1	10	10	70	70	30	30
r_2	10	10	30	30	70	70
r_3	6	13	65	75	26	32
r_4	7	12	27	36	66	77
r_5	40	40	40	40	40	40
r_6	10	68	48	35	15	53
r_7	20	100	20	20	100	20

Problem Statement: Given a gene expression matrix M and the number of sample phenotypes K, the goal is to find a sample partition of K groups matching the empirical phenotype and a subset of genes that can manifest this special pattern.

3   Quality Measurable Function of Sample Patterns and Informative Genes

We first give a general view of quality measure function of sample patterns and informative genes. Accordingly, Intra-pattern-Variance and Inter-pattern-Mean are introduced respectively. Moreover, the Sample-number-Influence is taken into account. In what follows, let $C^* \subseteq C$ be a sample group, $R^* \subseteq R$ be a subset of genes, and $M_{R*,C*} = \{a_{i,j} | i \in R^*, j \in C^*\}$ be the corresponding submatrix of C^* projected on R^*.

3.1   Intra-pattern-Variance

The similarity of values in one group is measured by Intra-pattern-Variance that is defined as the average row variance of the projected submatrix. The formula is expressed as follows:

$$Intra(R^*, C^*) = \frac{1}{|R^*|} \sum_{i \in R^*} \frac{\sum_{j \in C^*} (a_{i,j} - \bar{a}_{i,C^*})^2}{|C^*| - 1}$$

$$= \frac{1}{|R^*| \times (|C^*| - 1)} \sum_{i \in R^*} \sum_{j \in C^*} (a_{i,j} - \bar{a}_{i,C^*})^2 \qquad (1)$$

where $\overline{a}_{i,c^*} = (\sum_{j \in C^*} a_{i,j})/|C^*|$ is the mean expression value of samples in C^*. The variance of each row indicates the distribution of the values of the samples in a group on the given genes. The smaller the variance, the more similar the expression values of these samples on the genes. Thus, it is reasonable to infer that the small value of Intra-pattern-Variance indicates a good sample group. This is intuitively because the expression values with little change mean the stability and the similarity within the corresponding submatrix. *Note*: Tang et al. [2] have showed that two common local similarity metrics, residue and mean squared residue, are not suitable Intra-pattern-variance.

3.2   Inter-pattern-Mean

Inter-pattern-Mean is introduced to qualify how different the two exclusive groups $(C_1 \subset C, C_2 \subset C$ and $C_1 \cap C_2 = \varnothing)$ projected on the same subset of genes (denote as R^*). We use the difference of the mean values to measure the divergence between two groups. The formula is

$$Inter(R^*, C_1, C_2) = \frac{\sum_{i \in R^*} |\overline{a}_{i,C_1} - \overline{a}_{i,C_2}|}{|R^*|} \qquad (2)$$

where $\overline{a}_{i,C_1}$ is the mean value of the samples in C_1 expressed on genes R^*, and $\overline{a}_{i,C_2}$ is the mean value of the samples in C_2 expressed on genes R^*. We could clearly conclude that if the value of Inter-pattern-Mean is large, the discrepancy of the expression values of the samples in different groups on the same set of genes is large.

3.3   Pattern Quality

Given a set of samples C, which are divided into K mutually exclusive groups $(C_i \cap C_j = \varnothing, 1 \leq i, j \leq k$ and $i \neq j)$. The pattern quality, Q, should be able to qualify how well the pattern partitions the samples given a subset of genes (R^*). Thus, it is measured by the reciprocal of the square root of the sum of Intra-pattern-Variance divided by the Inter-pattern-Mean between different groups. The formula is as follows:

$$Q = \frac{1}{\sum_{C_i, C_j} \sqrt{\dfrac{Intra(R^*, C_i) + Intra(R^*, C_j)}{Inter(R^*, C_i, C_j)}}} \qquad (3)$$

3.4   Pattern Weight

Microarray data is often of high noise. So, only using the pattern quality, Q, is not enough. Consider such a case that a gene, which similarly expresses on almost all the samples, has the similar over-expression value on the other few samples due to noise. Eq.(3) may identify such a case as a pattern of good quality due to the small intra-group difference and the large inter-group difference. Such fake patterns conceal the real empirical pattern that we want to find.

To address this issue, we introduce another measurement, namely pattern weight (*Pw* for short), which is defined as the product of the sample numbers of each group divided by the total number of samples. The formula of pattern weight is

$$Pw = \prod_{i=1}^{K} \frac{|C_i|}{|C|} \qquad (4)$$

The pattern weight helps to reduce the influence of outliers. It is obvious that *Pw* is large when the number of samples in each group is identical. By this way, we can adjust the weight of a pattern.

4   FPLA Algorithms

The empirical sample pattern detecting problem is NP-hard [2]. In this section, we give a heuristic searching algorithm, which is an enhanced version of the method proposed by Tang et al [2].

4.1   An Heuristic Searching Algorithm

The algorithm proposed by Tang et al. [2] is iterative, which consists of two major steps: initialization and iterative adjustment. In the initialization phase, an initial state, i.e. k groups and a subset of genes, is randomly selected and the corresponding pattern quality, Q, is calculated. In the iterative adjustment phase, the current phenotype structure is adjusted by trying adding genes, deleting genes or moving samples, receptively. Then, the corresponding quality increment, $\triangle Q$, is calculated, and the operation corresponding to the highest $\triangle Q$ is adopted to raise the quality of the adjusted status. However, such a way is not efficient since it calculates the intra pattern variance of the submatrix from scratch in each iteration and only one gene or sample is changed in every adjustment. Instead, we design an incremental method, which directly derives the updated intra pattern variance based on the just previously adjusted status. Since many repeated computations are avoided, the running time is greatly reduced.

4.2   The FPLA Algorithm

In this section, we detail the proposed algorithm, namely FPLA. Besides adopting an incremental manner to adjust the current status towards increasing Q, FPLA takes into account the influence of noise (or say outliers). As explained in Section 3.4, the outlier samples may interfere the value of pattern quality. FPLA penalizes the extreme sample partition by the pattern weight, and thus reduces the negative impact of outliers. The FPLA algorithm is shown in Figure 1.

FPLA Algorithm(K)

Initialization phase:
1. Create K groups each with several randomly selected samples and a set of genes R^*
2. Use Eq. (3) and (4) to calculate the quality of the initial state.
Iterative adjustment phase:
3. Arrange the sequence of genes and samples randomly.
4. For each element in the sequence do
5.   if the element is a gene
6.   if the gene is in the informative gene set
7.   compute Q using the optimization strategy 2
8.   else   compute Q using the optimization strategy 1
9.   else if the element is a sample
10.   incrementally compute Q for the best movement using optimization strategies 3 and 4
12.   Compute Q using Eq. (3) and (4) and then compute $\triangle Q$
13.   if $\triangle Q{\geq}0$, then conduct the best movement

14.   else if $\triangle Q{<}0$, then conduct the adjustment with the probability $p = \exp(\dfrac{\Delta Q}{Q \times T(i)})$

15. Output the final sample partition.

Fig. 1. The FPLA algorithm

In each iterative adjustment phase, the possible operations, i.e. gene adding, gene deleting and sample moving, are tested one by one. If the informative genes contain the current tested gene, remove it from the set of informative genes. If not, add it into the set of informative genes. For every sample, it can be put into the other $k-1$ groups. Then, the corresponding quality increments $\triangle Q$ are calculated, respectively. The adjustment of the maximum quality increment $\triangle Q$ is conducted if it is positive. Otherwise, if $\triangle Q{<}0$, conduct the adjustment with the possibility $p = \exp(\dfrac{\Delta Q}{Q \times T(i)})$.

Note: $\triangle Q/Q$ is the slope of the declining pattern quality [3]. The smaller $\triangle Q$, the smaller the possibility of the adjustment. $T(i) = \dfrac{1}{1+i}$ is an annealing function, where $T(0) = 1$ and i is the number of iterations. With the iteration proceeding, $T(i)$ gradually decreases.

To further improve the efficiency, some useful optimization strategies are introduced. One of the major optimization strategies is the incremental calculation of the pattern quality. First, we give some lemmas, which are used to derive the strategies.

Lemma 4.1. *Suppose that the mean value of n samples is $\overline{X}_n$ and the value of the $(n+1)$-th sample is X_{n+1}, we conclude that the mean value of the $n+1$ samples is that*

$$\overline{X}_{n+1} = \frac{n \times \overline{X}_n + X_{n+1}}{n+1} \tag{5}$$

Lemma 4.2. *Suppose that the sample variance of n samples on a given gene is $\widetilde{S}_n^2$. Then, after inserting a sample X_{n+1} into the group, the sample variance of the $n+1$ samples should be $S_{n+1}^2 = \frac{n-1}{n} S_n^2 + \frac{1}{n+1} \times (X_{n+1} - \overline{X}_n)^2$, where X_n is the mean value of the n samples.*

Similar to lemma 4.2, we can derive that if a sample is removed from a group, the updated sample variance should be $\widetilde{S}^2_{n-1} = \frac{n-1}{n-2} \times \widetilde{S}^2_n + \frac{n-1}{(n-2)\times n} \times (X_n - \overline{X}_{n-1})^2$, where X_n is the removed sample and $\overline{X}_{n-1}$ is the mean value of the remaining $n-1$ samples.

As such, we can devise different optimal strategies for three basic adjusting operations, i.e. gene adding, gene deleting, sample moving. In what follows, we give these optimization strategies, where R^* denotes the informative gene set and C^* denotes the set of samples within a group before the adjustment.

Optimization Strategy 1: When a gene is added into the set of informative genes, the updated intra pattern variance should be where $\overline{a}_{|R^*|+1, C^*}$ is the mean expression value of the new added gene on the sample set C^*.

$$Intra_{new}(R^* + 1, C^*) = \frac{1}{|R^*|+1} \times (Intra_{old} \times |R^*| + \frac{\sum_{j \in C^*} (a_{|R^*|+1, j} - \overline{a}_{|R^*|+1, C^*})^2}{|C^*|-1}) \qquad (6)$$

Proof: The sum of the intra pattern variance of the former $|R^*|$ genes on the sample set $|C^*|$ is $Intra\_old \times |R^*|$, and the intra pattern variance of the added $(|R^*|+1)$-th gene on the sample set $|C^*|$ is $\frac{\sum_{j \in C^*} (a_{|R^*|+1, j} - \overline{a}_{|R^*|+1, C^*})^2}{|C^*|-1}$. Eq.(6) can be derived from Eq.(1).

Optimization Strategy 2: When a gene is deleted from the set of informative genes, the updated intra pattern variance should be

$$Intra_{new}(R^* - 1, C^*) = \frac{1}{|R^*|-1} \times (Intra_{old} \times |R^*| - \frac{\sum_{j \in C^*} (a_{i,j} - \overline{a}_{i,C^*})^2}{|C^*|-1}) \qquad (7)$$

where i is the number ID of the gene removed and $\overline{a}_{i,C^*}$ is the mean expression value of the deleted gene on the sample set C^*.

Proof: The proof is similar to that for Eq.(6).

Optimization Strategy 3: When a sample is inserted into a group of samples, the updated intra pattern variance should be

$$Intra_{new}(R^*, C^* + 1) = \frac{|C^*|-1}{|C^*|} \times Intra_{old} + \frac{\sum_{i \in R^*} (a_{i,C^*+1} - \overline{a}_{i,C^*})^2}{(|C^*|+1) \times |R^*|} \qquad (8)$$

where $\overline{a}_{i,C^*}$ is the mean expression value of gene i on the sample set C^* and a_{i,C^*+1} is the expression value of gene i on the inserted sample C^*+1.

Proof: For a group of n samples and one gene, Lemma 4.2 gives the formula to incrementally updating the intra pattern variance. Since the informative gene set R^* contains $|R^*|$ genes, we can derive Eq.(8) by summing up such $|R^*|$ formulas of the similar form in Lemma 4.2.

Optimization Strategy 4: When a sample is removed from a group of samples, the updated intra pattern variance should be

$$Intra_{new}(R^*, C^* - 1) = \frac{|C^*| - 1}{|C^*| - 2} \times Intra_{old} + \frac{(|C^*| - 1) \times \sum_{i \in R^*} (a_{i,j} - \overline{a}_{i,C^*-1})^2}{(|C^*| - 2) \times |C^*| \times |R^*|} \tag{9}$$

where j is the sample removed from the group and $\overline{a}_{i,C^*-1}$ is the mean expression value of gene i on the remaining $C^* - 1$ samples.

Proof: The proof is similar to that for Eq.(8).

Note: Optimizations 1 and 2 correspond to gene addition and gene deletion, respectively. Both optimization 3 and 4 correspond to sample move, since moving a sample from group A to B indicates deleting the sample in group A and adding it to group B. Utilizing the four optimization strategies, the updating of the intra pattern variance can be directly performed in an incremental manner. That is, instead of computing from scratch, we only need to accumulate the increment to the just previous result. Thus, the cost of computing the pattern quality is greatly reduced.

As mentioned, only the pattern quality Q, is not enough for the empirical phenotypes discovery since microarray data is often highly noisy. So, we propose a method to reduce the negative impact of the outliers by taking into account the proportion of the samples within each group. As discussed, the pattern weight function can be used to harmonize the pattern quality Q in Eq.(3). For example, Eq.(10) and Eq.(11) are two alternative harmonic quality functions, the performance of which are given in the performance evaluation section.

$$Q_{final} = 1 / (1 / Q + 1 / Pw) \tag{10}$$

$$Q_{final} = {}^{\kappa}\sqrt{Q} \times Pw \tag{11}$$

5   Perpformance Evaluation

In this section, we study the performance of FPLA by evaluating its effectiveness and efficiency. The algorithm is coded in C++. ALL experiments are conducted on a 2.33GHz Intel Core 2 HP PC with 2GB memory running Windows XP.

5.1   Experimental Datasets

Real Datasets: we use the clinical data on Leukemia [4], DLBCL Tumor [5] and Hereditary Breast Cancer (HBC) [6]. In Table 2, we give the description for each real dataset in the Data size column.

Synthetic Datasets: The synthetic data generator takes the following parameters: (1) m, the number of genes, (2) n, the number of samples, (3) k, the number of classes.

5.2   Effectiveness Evaluation

The Rand Index [7], denoted as *RI*, measures the extent to which the ground-truth phenotypes (T) agree with the conducted partition (R). Thus, it is adopted to evaluate the effectiveness of FPLA.

Table 2. Rand Index value of different methods

Data set	ALL_AML	ALL_AML	ALL	DLBCL	DLBCL	HBC	HBC
Data size	5000×38	5000×38	5000×27	7129×77	7129×77	3226×22	3226×22
K	2	3	2	2	3	2	3
J-Express	0.510	0.425	0.497	0.494	0.407	0.486	0.411
SOTA	0.602	0.424	0.492	0.495	0.420	0.493	0.411
CLUTO	0.578	0.512	0.487	0.493	0.498	0.680	0.636
SOM	0.510	0.486	0.492	0.497	0.472	0.602	0.584
Kmeans	0.659	0.553	0.492	0.487	0.453	0.613	0.584
δ-cluster	0.501	0.440	0.454	0.480	0.437	0.498	0.471
HS	0.868	0.758	0.755	0.885	0.703	0.779	0.750
FPLA	0.957	0.816	0.982	0.989	0.805	0.863	0.840

To show the effectiveness of the proposed FPLA algorithm, we test *RI* of FPLA on several real datasets. For comparison, we also report the results of some other respresentative methods, such as HS [2], J-Express [8], SOTA [9], CLUTO [10], SOM [11], *K*-means [12], δ-cluster [13]. The detailed experimental results are given in Table 2. It is not difficult to see that the proposed FPLA algorithm always behaves the best *RI* on all the tested datasets. This is because that J-press, CLUTO, SOTA, SOM and *K*-means partition the samples using the full set of genes. However, it is well known that only a small number of genes are relevant to the sample partition [13]. Thus, the accuracy of the sample partition using the full set of genes will be depressed due to the large number of irrelevant genes included in the full set of genes. δ-cluster [13] is an effective subspace clustering algorithm. It reduces the dimensionality of genes by adopting PCA. However, the principal components in PCA do not necessarily capture the group structure of the data. Therefore, it is not surprising that the subspace clustering method δ-cluster is not effective to find the phenotypes and informative genes precisely. Further, because it is more susceptible to the large noise of microarray data, the Rand Index of HS algorithm is lower than the proposed FPLA algorithm.

5.3   Efficiency Evaluation

In this section, we first evaluate the efficiency of FPLA by studying how response time varies w.r.t. #sample and #gene. Moreover, two representative unsupervised phenotype structure learning algorithms, HS [2] and SDC [15], are used as the alternatives for comparison. In this set of experiments, K are respectively set to two or three. In Figure 2, the number of samples is set to 30, and the number of genes varies from 1000 to 7000 with step 1000. In Figure 3, the number of genes is set to 3000, and the number of samples varies from 10 to 40 with step 5. It is easy to see that the response time of FPLA becomes longer as #gene or #sample increases and it is much less than that of HS or SDC. Moreover, FPLA behaves much better than the two alternatives as #gene or #sample increases. This is because HS calculates the pattern quality from scratch in each iteration, and SDC has to enumerate all possible combinations of genes. However, due to the incremental computation, FPLA greatly reduces the cost of computing the pattern quality.

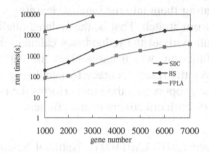

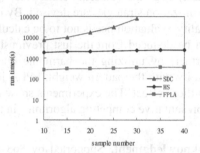

Fig. 2. time vs. #gene when K=2   **Fig. 3.** time vs. #gene when K=2

6   Related Work

The exiting methods fall into two major classes: supervised analysis and unsupervised analysis.

The supervised approach assumes that phenotype information is attached to the samples. There are some popular supervised methods, such as the neighborhood analysis [4], the support vector machine [16], the tree harvesting method [17], the decision tree method [18] and so on. In these methods, a subset of samples is used as training set to find a subset of informative genes, where some criteria are used to rank the genes and guide the gene selection. All the given samples are classified based on these genes.

Some unsupervised methods without knowing the phenotype information are also proposed to find the phenotypes of samples, such as K-means [12], self-organizing maps [11], hierarchical clustering [9], graph based clustering [19] or pattern-based clustering [20]. However, these traditional methods are all based on the full set of genes. They are not suitable for microarray data due to the large number of redundancy genes. Accordingly, some subspace based methods are presented to address the problem. Specially, HS [2] and SDC [15] are two such representative unsupervised methods. The former is a simple iteration-based heuristic searching algorithm, where the updated pattern quality has to be recomputed from stratch in each iteration. The latter is a breadth-first based exhaustive enumeration algorithm, where the Apriori property is used to prune the unnecessary computations. However, it is well known that learning phenotype structure in an unsupervised manner is an NP-hard problem.

7   Conclusion

In this paper, we propose an unsupervised phenotypes and informative genes detection algorithm with outlier consideration, namely FPLA. Starting with a randomly selected initial state, the algorithm iteratively tries three possible adjustments, i.e. gene addition, gene deletion and sample move, to improve the quality of the current state. Accordingly, four incremental updating based optimization strategies are devised. By integrating them into the iterative learning, the quality evaluation needs not to be calculated from stratch. That is, the updated quality can be deduced from the just previously result without the redundancy calculations. Further, by utilizing the harmonic quality function, which harmonizes the pattern quality with the pattern weight, FPLA improves the result accuracy by penalizing the "outlier" effect. The experiments show that the proposed method outperforms the two representative competing algorithms in terms of both effectiveness and efficiency.

Acknowledgment. Supported by 863 program (2012AA011004), National Science Fund for Distinguished Young Scholars (61025007), State Key Program of National Natural Science of China (60933001, 61332014), National Natural Science Foundation of China (61272182, 61100028, 61073063, 61173030), New Century Excellent Talents (NCET-11-0085), China Postdoctoral Science Foundation (2012T50263, 2011M500568) and Fundamental Research Funds for the Central Universities ((N130504001).

References

1. Zhao, Y.H., Wang, G.R., Li, Y., Wang, Z.H.: Finding Novel Diagnostic Gene Patterns Based on Interesting Non-Redundant Contrast Sequence Rules. In: ICDM, pp. 972–981 (2011)
2. Kirkpatrick, S., Gelatt Jr., C.D., Vecchi, M.P.: Optimization by Simulated Annealing. Science 220, 671–680 (1983)
3. Tang, C., Zhang, A.D., Pei, J.: Mining Phenotypes and Informative Genes From Gene Expression Data. In: SIGKDD 2003, Washington, DC, USA, pp. 655–660 (2000)
4. Golub, T.R., Slonim, D.K., et al.: Molecular Classification of Cancer: Class Discovery and Class Prediction by Gene Expression Monitoring. Science 286, 531–537 (1999)
5. Shipp, M.A., Ross, K.N., Tamayo, P., et al.: Diffuse Large B-Cell Lymphoma Outcome Prediction by Gene-Expression Profiling and Supervised Machine Learning. Nat. Med. 8(1), 68–74 (2002)
6. Hedenfalk, I., Duggam, D., et al.: Gene-Expression Profiles in Hereditary Breast Cancer. N. Eng. J. Med. 344(8), 539–548 (2001)

7. Rand, W.M.: Objective Criteria for Evaluation of Clustering Methods. L. Am. Stat. Assoc., 846–850 (1971)
8. Rhodes, D.R., Miller, J.C., Haab, B.B., Furge, K.A.: CIT: Identification Of Differentially Expressed Clusters of Genes From Microarray Data. Bioinformatics 18, 205–206 (2001)
9. Herrero, J., Valencia, A., Dopazo, J.: A Hierarchical Unsupervised Growing Neural Network for Clustering Gene Expression Patterns. Bioinformatics 17(1), 126–136 (2001)
10. Schloegel, K., Karypis, G.: CRPC Parallel Computing Handbook, Chapter Graph Partitioning for High Performance Scientific Simulations. Morgan Kaufmann (2002)
11. Toronen, P., Kolehmainen, M., Wong, G., et al.: Analysis of Gene Expression Data Using Self-Organizing Maps. FEBS Lett. 45(1), 142–146 (1999)
12. Ding, C., He, X.: Principal Components and K-Means Clustering. In: Proc. of the 4th SIAM International Conference on Data Mining, pp. 23–32 (2004)
13. Yang, J., Wang, W., et al.: Δ-Cluster: Capturing Subspace Correalation in Alarge Data Set. In: Proceedings of 18th International Conference on Data Engineering (ICDE 2002), pp. 517–528 (2002)
14. Thomas, J.G., Olson, J.M., Tapscott, S.J., Zhao, L.P.: An Efficient and Robust Statistical Modeling Approach to Discover Differentially Expressed Genes Using Genomic Expression Profiles. Genome Research 11(7), 1227–1236 (2001)
15. Fang, G., Kuang, R., Pandey, G., et al.: Subspace Differential Coexpression Analysis: Problem Definition and A General Approach. In: Pacific Symposium on Biocomputing, pp. 145–156 (2010)
16. Zintzaras, E., Kowald, A.: Forest Classification Trees and Forest Support Vector Machines Algorithms: Demonstration Using Microarray Data. Comp. in Bio. and Med. (CBM) 40(5), 519–524 (2010)
17. Hastie, T., Tibshirani, R., Boststein, D., Brown, P.: Supervised Harvesting of Expression Trees. Genome Biol. 2(1), 0003.1–0003.12 (2001)
18. Horng, J.T., Wu, L.C., et al.: An Expert System to Classify Microarray Gene Expression Data Using Gene Selection by Decision Tree. Expert Syst. Appl. (ESWA) 36(5), 072-9081 (2009)
19. Yu, W., Wong, H.S., Wang, H.Q.: Graph-Based Consensus Clustering for Class Discovery From Gene Expression Data. Bioinformatics 23(21), 2888–2896 (2007)
20. Zhao, Y.H., et al.: Maximal Subspace Coregulated Gene Clustering. IEEE Trans. on Knowledge and Data Engineering 20(1), 83–98 (2008)

A Multi-Instance Multi-Label Learning Approach for Protein Domain Annotation

Yang Meng[1,2], Lei Deng[1,*], Zhigang Chen[1], Cheng Zhou[1], Diwei Liu[1],
Chao Fan[1], and Ting Yan[1]

[1] School of Software, Central South University, Changsha, China
[2] School of Software, Shanghai Jiaotong University, Shanghai, China
leideng@csu.edu.cn

Abstract. Domains act as structural and functional units of proteins, playing an essential role in functional genomics. To investigate the annotation of finite protein domains is of much importance because the functions of a protein can be directly inferred if the functions of its component domains are determined. In this paper, we propose PDAMIML based on a novel multi-instance multi-label learning framework combined with auto-cross covariance transformation and SVM. It can effectively annotate functions for protein domains. We evaluate the performance of PDAMIML using a benchmark of 100 protein domains and 10 high-cycle functional labels. The experiment results reveal that PDAMIML yields significant performance gains when compared to the state-of-the-art approaches. Furthermore, we combine PDAMIML with the other two existing methods by using majority voting, and obtain encouraging results.

Keywords: domain annotation, multi-instance multi-label, SVM, auto-cross covariance transformation.

1 Introduction

One of the most challenging and intriguing problems in the post-genomic era is the characterization of the biochemical functions of proteins. Accurate computational assignment of protein function is becoming a useful resource for both the community at large and the curators that eventually assign function to proteins. It is known that domains appear either singly or in combination with other domains as building blocks in a protein [1,2], and play important roles in the process of protein-protein interactions [3]. It will be much easier to infer the function of proteins if the functions of their component domains are determined.

Traditional work of annotation of functions is based on the physicochemical properties of special structure and primarily conducted manually, which is a time-consuming, inefficient and experience-dependent process. Some researchers have paid attention to the field of domain annotation using computational methods. Schug et al. [4] described a heuristic algorithm for annotating Gene Ontology (GO) [5].

---

* Corresponding author.

D.-S. Huang et al. (Eds.): ICIC 2014, LNBI 8590, pp. 104–111, 2014.
© Springer International Publishing Switzerland 2014

Lu et al. [6] utilized protein-domain mapping (P2D) features to investigate the associa-tion rules between target domains and GO terms.

Based on the previous work, Zhao and Wang [7] designed two methods, the threshold-based classification method and the SVM method, for protein domain func-tion prediction by integrating heterogeneous information sources, improving predic-tion accuracy and annotation reliability. The threshold-based classification method outperforms the SVM method according to their experiments.

However, in those formalizations, each domain is represented by an instance and associated with single GO term. Actually, each domain usually exists in multiple proteins, which can be described by a feature vector, and it may belong to multiple categories since it is associated with several different functions.

In this paper, we propose a novel Multi-Instance Multi-Label Learning (MIML) [8] based framework, PDAMIML, to predict functions of protein domains. PDAMIML combines MIML model, SVM [9] and auto-cross covariance (ACC) [10] to overcome the multi-label classification problem and effectively utilizes the features of Position-Specific Scoring Matrix (PSSM) [11]. Furthermore, we design an ensemble method, PDAMIML-Ensemble, which integrates PDAMIML and other two eminent threshold-based approaches (CDD and P2D)[7] with majority voting strategy. Our experimental results show that PDAMIML-Ensemble significantly outperforms the state-of-the-art domain annotation approaches.

2　　Materials and Methods

2.1　　Datasets

Relationships between proteins and domains are obtained from InterPro Database [12] and the function annotations of domains are generated from GOA Database [13]. Through analyzing the databases, we find that around 76% domains are annotated with more than one GO term, and every domain has 2.5 GO terms on average. We choose the top 100 domain with the most GO terms as target domains, and select the most frequent 10 GO terms as target labels.

In each experiment, the whole data set is randomly partitioned into two parts, a training set, accounting for 70% of the data set, and a test set, 30%. The training set is used to build classifiers, and the test set is used to evaluate the performance of the corresponding classifier. The whole experiment is repeated for 10 times to get an average and common performance, and every time, all the model parameters are tuned with 10-fold cross validation on the training set to optimize the model performance.

2.2　　MIML Model for Domain Annotation

In this section, we first describe in detail how to formulate protein domain annotation as an MIML problem.

In biology, many proteins consist of several structural domains; meanwhile one domain may appear in a variety of different proteins. Besides, in a multi-domain protein, each domain may fulfill its own functions independently, or in a concerted man-ner with its neighbors [14]. Since proteins interact with each other through domain interactions, the functions of domains determine the functions of their host proteins. Domains act as the structural and functional units, and each domain is associated with multiple proteins and multiple GO terms, as illustrated in Fig.1.

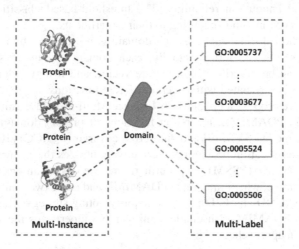

Fig. 1. Diagram for MIML learning in protein domain annotation

Let $\aleph$ denote the instance space and $\Re$ the set of class labels. In our research, every protein containing some particular domain is an instance and every GO term is a label. Then the task is to learn a function *func*: $\aleph \rightarrow \Re$ from a given data set $\{(X_i, Y_i) \mid 1 \le i \le M\}$, where $X_i \subseteq \aleph$ is a set of instances $\{x_1^{(i)}, x_2^{(i)}, ..., x_{ni}^{(i)}\}$, $x_j^{(i)} \in \aleph$, and $Y_i \subseteq \Re$ is a set of labels $\{y_1^{(i)}, y_2^{(i)}, ..., y_{li}^{(i)}\}$, $y_k^{(i)} \in \Re$ associated with X_i .

Concisely, we use $X_i = \{x_t\}$ to stand for the collection of all the local feature vectors of i-th domain, and Y_i are the annotation flags assigned to this domain. The annotation task is to predict the proper labels Y of a test bag X when given a train set $\{(X_i, Y_i) \mid 1 \le i \le M\}$.

We train an exclusive SVM classifier for a label every time. In this study, the Libsvm package is used to as an implementation of SVM.

For each label $y \in \Re$, let $\phi(X_i, y) = +1$ if $y \in Y_i$ and -1 otherwise. Then the formulation of the corresponding SVM is as follows:

$$\min_{w,b,\xi} \frac{1}{2} \|w\|^2 + C^+ \sum_{\phi(X_i,y)=+1} \xi_i + C^- \sum_{\phi(X_i,y)=-1} \xi_i$$

s.t. $\phi(X_i, y)(w\phi(X_i) + b) \ge 1 - \xi_i, \xi_i \ge 0 (i = 1,2,..., n)$

where $\phi(X_i)$ is the mapping function that maps bag of instances X_i into a kernel space; $\phi(X_i, y)$ indicates whether y is a proper label of X_i; ξ_i is the hinge loss; n is the number of domains in the training set; and w and b are parameters for representing a linear discrimination function in the kernel space. C^+ and C^- are the penalty parameters for errors resulting from positive bags and negative bags, respectively.

Then the discriminant function of the final classifier can be demonstrated as:

$$h_y(X) = \sum_{i=1}^{\#sv} \alpha_i \phi(X_i, y) K_{MI}(X_i, X) + b$$

where $\#sv$ is the number of support vectors; α_i is the parameter learned from the dual form of the SVM formulation described above.

Since convolution kernel is one of famous kernels used to deal with those multi-attribute vectors, we adopt the Gaussian RBF kernel [15] combined with convolution kernel to describe the kernel function, and then the kernel K_{MI} is defined as:

$$K_{MI}(X, X) = \sum_{x_i \in X} \sum_{x_j \in X} e^{-\gamma \|x_i - x_j\|^2}$$

2.3   PDAMIML Framework

Two predictors (PDAMIML and PDAMIML-Ensemble) are implemented as shown in Fig.2.

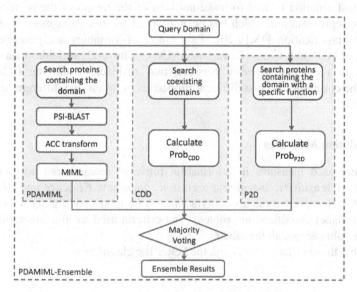

Fig. 2. Overview of PDAMIML and PDAMIML-Ensemble

PDAMIML is based on MIML learning framework and ACC transformation, while PDAMIML-Ensemble is an ensemble classifier built to combine the outputs of PDAMIML and other two existing methods. It can be formulated as:

$$R = R_{PDAMIML} \oplus R_{CDD} \oplus R_{P2D}$$

where R_{PDAMIM}, R_{CDL} and R_{P2D} stand for the predicted results of PDAMIML, CDD and P2D respectively, sign $\oplus$ means the operation of voting, R is the final result. For detailed implementation of CDD, P2D and CDD+P2D, please refer to the paper of Zhao[7].

2.4   Position-Specific Scoring Matrix(PSSM)

Each protein sequence can be represented as a time sequence of physical-chemical properties. In this study, we select PSSMs as the features to transform protein sequences to simple quantitative matrices. PSSMs are taken from multiple sequence alignment obtained by PSI-BLAST searching against NCBI non-redundant database(ftp://ftp.ncbi.nih.gov/blast/db/), with parameters j = 3 and e = 0.001 [11,16,17].

2.5   Auto-Cross Covariance Transformation

PSSM contains wealthy information about the evolutionary relationship of proteins and often has different lengths, while many machine learning methods, for instance, SVM, usually require fixed length data.

ACC transformation is used to make uniform of the length of the proteins. It is a new feature representation, which has been adopted by more and more investigators for protein classification [18,19,20]. Two kinds of variables are generated: Auto Covariance (AC) and Cross Covariance (CC). The AC variable measures the correlation of the same property between two residues, while the CC variable measures the correlation of two different properties between two different residues in some distance.

2.6   Evalution Measures

Some widely used measures in information retrieval research are adopted in this study, such as *sensitivity*, *specificity*, *precision*, *accuracy*, *F1-score* and *AUC* (Area Under ROC). However, these six criteria have to be modified slightly to be suitable for the multi-label classification problem. The criteria used for the annotation task is the average value across all the labels.

The higher those criteria scores are, the better the classifier is.

3 Results and Discussions

3.1 The Impact of Parameter during ACC Transformation

In the study, each protein sequence is represented as a vector of either AC variable or ACC variable that is a combination of AC and CC. The maximum value of distance between the residues, LG, can influence the performance of transformation to some extent. The maximum value of variable LG is 30 for the sequences we use. Fig.3 shows the average accuracy of prediction performance on different values of LG.

According to Fig.3, it is obvious that ACC variable has a better performance than AC variable, and it is sound to choose 15 as the optimal value for LG, so we choose ACC variable to present protein and LG takes 15 in all relative processes.

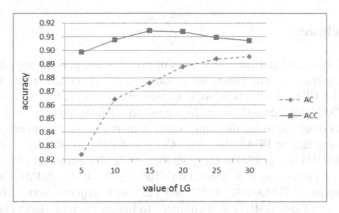

Fig. 3. Average accuracy versus LG value

3.2 Performance Comparison with the State-of-the-Art Approaches

To evaluate the proposed methods, we performed computational experiments and compared them with CDD, P2D and CDD+P2D. The performance of each model is measured by six metrics: *accuracy*, *sensitivity*, *specificity*, *precision*, *AUC* and *F1-score*. Higher score means better performance.

Table 1. Performance comparison with existing methods on multiple labels

	accuracy	sensivity	specificity	precision	AUC	F1-score
CDD	0.923±0.021	0.661±0.168	0.962±0.043	0.802±0.135	0.647±0.160	0.698±0.142
P2D	0.897±0.016	**0.900±0.105**	0.877±0.018	0.601±0.092	0.805±0.113	0.699±0.095
CDD+P2D	0.907±0.013	0.891±0.114	0.886±0.013	0.636±0.116	0.855±0.114	0.718±0.112
PDAMIML	0.914±0.017	0.744±0.090	0.936±0.013	0.822±0.075	0.908±0.051	0.757±0.058
PDAMIML-Ensemble	**0.953±0.010**	0.823±0.061	**0.974±0.010**	**0.894±0.065**	**0.934±0.017**	**0.843±0.062**

Table 1 shows the detailed results of comparing our method with the existing methods. Our approaches (PDAMIML and PDAMIML-Ensemble) show dominant advantages over the existing methods in the metrics of AUC, F1-score and precision. PDAMIML-Ensemble has the best performance among all of the methods, with the AUC of 0.934, F1-score of 0.843, specificity of 0.974, precision of 0.894, and accuracy of 0.953, while PDAMIML achieves the second best performance in the measures of AUC, F1-score and precision. Only in sensitivity, P2D and CDD+P2D per-form better than our methods. The results in Table 1 verify the effectiveness of the proposed MIML-based algorithm and the ensemble method with majority voting. It is worth emphasizing that PDAMIML doesn't need to know the whole protein sequences and annotations of other coexisting domains, which is much more direct and convenient than other methods.

4   Conclusion

Domains are structural and functional units of proteins and play an important role in functional genomics. In this paper, we construct a novel multi-instance multi-label SVM classifier (PDAMIML) with ACC transformation to predict the annotation of domains. PDAMIML doesn't need to know the whole protein sequences and annotations of other coexisting domains, which is more direct and convenient.

Further, we combine PDAMIML with CDD and P2D, to establish a new voting system (PDAMIML-Ensemble) to integrate their particular advantages to improve the comprehensive performance of annotation. The result of PDAMIML-Ensemble is based on outputs of PDAMIML, CDD and P2D with majority voting. Final result demonstrates that PDAMIML is well-equipped to handle the multi-label classification problem, and the ensemble method PDAMIML-Ensemble obtains the best performance when compared with the state-of-the-art methods.

As for the future work, more effective features and transform methods will be investigated. Other machine learning algorithms such as neural network, decision tree and Bayesian network will also be considered in the ensemble classifier.

Acknowledgement. This work was supported by the National Natural Science Foundation of China under grants nos. 61309010 and 61379057 and Specialized Research Fund for the Doctoral Program of Higher Education of China under grant no. 20130162120073.

References

1. Apic, G., Gough, J., Teichmann, S.A.: Domain Combinations in Archaeal, Eubacterial and Eukaryotic Proteomes. Journal of Molecular Biology 310, 311–325 (2001)
2. Wang, M.L., Caetano, A.G.: Global Phylogeny Determined by The Combination of Protein Daomains in Proteomes. Mol. Boi. Evol. 23(12), 2444–2454 (2006)
3. Bork, P.: Shuffled Domains in Extracellular Proteins. FEBS Letters 286(1-2), 47–54 (1991)

4. Schug, J., Diskin, S., Mazzarelli, J., et al.: Predicting Gene Ontology Functions From Prodom and CDD Protein Domains. Genome Res. 12(4), 648–655 (2002)
5. Ashburner, M., Ball, C.A., Blake, J.A., et al.: Gene Ontology: Tool For The Unification of Biology. The Gene Ontology Consortium. Nat Genet. 25, 25–29 (2000)
6. Lu, X., Zhai, C., Gopalakrishnan, V., Buchanan, B.G.: Automatic Annotation of Protein Motif Function With Gene Ontology Terms. BMC Bioinformatics 5, 122 (2004)
7. Zhao, X.M., Wang, Y., Chen, L., Aihara, K.: Protein Domain Annotation With Integration of Heterogeneous Information Sources. Proteins 72, 461–473 (2008)
8. Zhou, Z.H., Zhang, M.L., Huang, S.J., Li, Y.F.: Multi-Instance Multi-Label Learning. Artificial Intelligence 176(1), 2291–2320 (2012)
9. Vapnik, V.: Statistical Learning Theory. John Wiley and Sons, New York (1998)
10. Wold, S., Jonsson, J., Sjöström, M., et al.: Dna and Peptide Sequences and Chemical Processes Mutlivariately Modelled by Principal Component Analysis and Partial Least-Squares Projections To Latent Structures. Anal. Chim. Acta. 277(2), 239–253 (1993)
11. Altschul, S.F., Madden, T.L., et al.: Gapped BLAST and PSI-BLAST: A New Generation of Protein Database Search Programs. Nucleic Acids Research 25(17), 3389–3402 (1997)
12. Hunter, S., Jones, P., Mitchell, A.: Interpro in 2011: New Developments in The Family and Domain Prediction Database. Nucleic Acids Research 40, 306–312 (2011)
13. Camon, E., Magrane, M., Barrell, D., Lee, V., et al.: The Gene Ontology Annotation (GOA) Database:Sharing Knowledge in Uniprot With Gene Ontology. Nucleic Acids Research 32, 262–266 (2004)
14. Heringa, J., Domains, P.: Encyclopedia of Genetics, Genomics, Proteomics and Bioinformatics. Wiley Interscience (2005)
15. Steinwart, I., Hush, D., Scovel, C.: An Explicit Description of The Reproducing Kernel Hilbert Spaces of Gaussian RBF Kernels. IEEE Transactions on Information Theory 52, 4635–4643 (2006)
16. Deng, L., Guan, J., Dong, Q., et al.: Semihs: An Iterative Semi-Supervised Approach For Predicting Protein-Protein Interaction Hot Spots. Protein Pept. Lett. 18(9), 896–905 (2011)
17. Deng, L., Guan, J., Wei, X., et al.: Boosting Prediction Performance of Protein-Protein Interaction Hot Spots by Using Structural Neighborhood Properties. Journal of Computational Biology 20(11), 878–891 (2013)
18. Wen, Z.N., Li, M.L., Li, Y.Z., Guo, Y.Z., Wang, K.L.: Delaunay Triangulation With Partial Least Squares Projection To Latent Structures: A Model For G-Protein Coupled Receptors Classification and Fast Structure Recognition. Amino Acids 32, 277–283 (2007)
19. Guo, Y., Yu, L., Wen, Z., Li, M.: Using Support Vector Machine Combined With Auto Co-Variance To Predict Protein-Protein Interactions From Protein Sequences. Nucleic Acids Research 36(9), 3025–3030 (2008)
20. Deng, L., Guan, J., Dong, Q., et al.: Prediction of Protein-Protein Interaction Sites Using An Ensemble Method. BMC Bioinformatics 10, 426 (2009)

An Advanced Machine Learning Approach to Generalised Epileptic Seizure Detection

Paul Fergus, David Hignett, Abir Jaffar Hussain, and Dhiya Al-Jumeily

Liverpool John Moores University, Applied Computing Research Group,
Byrom Street, Liverpool, L3 3AF, UK
{P.Fergus,D.Hignett,A.Hussain,D.Aljumeily}@ljmu.ac.uk

Abstract. Epilepsy is a chronic neurological condition that affects approximately 70 million people worldwide. Characterised by sudden bursts of excess electricity in the brain manifesting as seizures, epilepsy is still not well understood when compared with other neurological disorders. Seizures often happen unexpectedly and attempting to predict them has been a research topic for the last 20 years. Electroencephalograms have been integral to these studies, as they can capture the brain's electrical signals. The challenge is to generalise the detection of seizures in different regions of the brain and across multiple subjects. This paper explores this idea further and presents a supervised machine learning approach that classifies *seizure* and *non-seizure* records using an open dataset containing 543 electroencephalogram segments. Our approach posits a new method for generalising seizure detection across different subjects without prior knowledge about the focal point of seizures. Our results show an improvement on existing studies with 88% for *sensitivity*, 88% for *specificity* and 93% for the area under the curve, with a 12% global error, using the *k-NN* classifier.

Keywords: Seizure, non-seizure, machine learning, classification, Electroencephalogram, oversampling.

1 Introduction

Epilepsy is a chronic condition of the brain, and causes repeated seizures, commonly referred to as fits. Epilepsy is said to affect one in every 103 people in the UK (500,000 approximately), according to epilepsy research UK[1], and 70 million people worldwide (Fazel, Wolf, Langstrom, Newton, & Lichtenstein, 2013). The risk of developing epilepsy is greatest at the extremes of life with incidences more common in the elderly than the young (Engel, 2013).

Seizures can be focal (partial) and exist in one part of the brain only, or they can be general and affect both halves of the brain. In a focal seizure, the excess electrical activity is confined to the occipital lobes, parietal lobes, frontal lobes, or temporal lobes. During a focal seizure, the person may be conscious and unaware that a seizure

---

[1] http://www.epilepsyresearch.org.uk

D.-S. Huang et al. (Eds.): ICIC 2014, LNBI 8590, pp. 112–118, 2014.
© Springer International Publishing Switzerland 2014

is taking place, or they may have uncontrollable movements or unusual feelings and sensations. During a general seizure, consciousness is normally lost and muscles may stiffen and jerk[2]. A diagnosis of epilepsy is made if a patient has had two or more unprovoked seizures[3], and diagnosis is made with the help of an electroencephalogram (*EEG*), which measures the electrical activity in the brain.

The majority of previous works on seizure detection have focused on patient-specific predictors, were a classifier is trained on one person and tested on the same person (Carney, Myers, & Deyer, 2011; Maiwald et al., 2004; Mormann, Andrzejak, Elgar, & Lehnertz, 2007; Shoeb, 2009). However, in this paper, the emphasis is on using *EEG* classification to generalise detection across all regions of the brain using multiple subject records, without prior knowledge of which region of the brain the seizure occurred. Several classifiers are evaluated using 171 *seizure* and 171 *non-seizure* blocks extracted from the 543 *EEG* segments of 24 patients suffering with epilepsy.

The structure, of the remainder, of this paper is as follows. Section 2 describes the underlying principles of Electroencephalography and the type of features extracted from Electroencephalography signals. Section 3 discusses the approach taken in this paper, while Section 4 describes the evaluation. The results are discussed in Section 5 before the paper is concluded in Section 6.

2   Electroencephalography and Feature Extraction

Electroencephalography (EEG) is the term given for the recording of electrical activity resulting from ionic current flows generated by neurons in the brain (Libenson, 2009) and is mainly used to evaluate seizures and epilepsy. In order to retrieve *EEG* signals, electrodes are placed on the scalp where odd numbered electrodes are placed on the left side of the scalp and even numbered electrodes on the right. The letters that precede the numbers represent brain regions (*Fp*) frontopolar, (*F*) frontal, (*T*) temperal, (*P*) parietal, (*C*) central, and (*O*) occipital (Libenson, 2009).

The collection of raw *EEG* signals is always temporal. However, for analysis and feature extraction purposes, translation, into other domains, is possible and often required. In order to obtain frequency parameters, several of the studies reviewed, have used Power Spectral Density (*PSD*). *Peak Frequency* is one of the features also considered in many studies. It describes the frequency of the highest peak in the *PSD*. During a seizure, *EEG* signals tend to contain a major cyclic component, which shows itself as a dominant peak in the *frequency domain* (Sanei & Chambers, 2007).

Meanwhile, Ning *et al.* (Ning & Lyu, 2012) found that *Median Frequency* displayed significant differences between *seizure* and *non-seizure* patients. By segmenting the *EEG* signal into five separate frequency bands for *delta* (δ: $0.5 \leq f \leq 4$ Hz), *theta* (θ: $4 \leq f \leq 8$ Hz), *alpha* (α: $8 \leq f \leq 12$ Hz): *beta* (β: $12 \leq f \leq 25$ Hz), and *gamma*

---

[2] http://www.epilepsy.org.uk
[3] http://www.who.int

(γ: 25 ≤ f), it was possible to predict 79 of 83 *seizures*, with a *sensitivity* value of 95.2%.

Root Mean Square (*RMS*) has also been considered a useful feature for distinguishing between *seizure* and *non-seizure* events. *RMS* measures the magnitude of the varying quantity and is a good signal strength estimator in *EEG* frequency bands (Abdul-latif, Cosic, Kimar, & Polus, 2004; Patel, Chern-Pin, Fau, & Bleakley, 2009).

Entropy has been used as a measure of the complexity, or uncertainty, of an *EEG* signal, were the more chaotic the signal is, the higher the *entropy* (Greene et al., 2008; Sanei & Chambers, 2007). Many authors agree that during a *seizure*, the brain activity is more predictable than during a normal, *non-seizure*, phase and this is reflected by a sudden drop in the *entropy* value (Aarabi, Fazel-Rezai., & Aghakhani, 2009; Diambra, de Figueiredo, & Malta, 1999; Greene et al., 2008; Iasemidis, 2003; Kelly et al., 2010). All of the above features are extracted from the raw dataset in this paper.

3   Generalisation of Epileptic Seizure Detection

The study in this paper focuses on discriminating between *seizure* and *non-seizure* *EEGs* across a group of 24 subjects. The classifiers are trained on all patient records and therefore, classification is generalised across all subjects using features from channels that capture the *EEG* in all parts of the brain.

3.1   Methodology

The *CHB-MIT* dataset used in this paper is a publicly available database from physionet.org that contains 686 scalp *EEG* recordings from 24 patients treated at the Children's Hospital in Boston. The subjects had anti-seizure medication withdrawn, and *EEG* recordings were taken for up to several days after.

3.1.1 Data Pre-processing

In the *CHB-MIT* database, each record was sampled at 256Hz, with 16-bit resolution. Signals were recorded simultaneously through twenty-three different channels, via 19 electrodes and a ground attached to the surface of the scalp.

A bandpass filter was applied to each of the 543 *EEG* segments to extract the *EEG* data in each of the frequency bands. This results in four columns of additional data; *delta* (δ: $0.5 \leq f \leq 4$ Hz), *theta* (θ: $4 \leq f \leq 8$ Hz), *alpha* (α: $8 \leq f \leq 12$ Hz): and *beta* (β: $12 \leq f \leq 25$ Hz). Finally, all frequency bands in each of the 543 *EEG* segments were normalised to a common scale between zero and one.

3.1.2 Classification

Following an analysis of the literature, the study in this paper adopts simple, yet powerful algorithms. These include the *linear discriminant classifier* (*LDC*), *quadratic discriminant classifier* (*QDC*), *uncorrelated normal density based classifier* (*UDC*), *polynomial classifier* (*POLYC*), *logistic classifier* (*LOGLC*), *k-nearest neighbour*

(*KNNC*), *decision tree* (*TREEC*), *parzen classifier* (*PARZENC*) and the *support vector machine* (*SVC*) (van der Heijde, Duin, de Ridder, & Tax, 2005).

4   Evaluation

4.1   Results Using Top Twenty Uncorrelated Features Ranked Using LDA Backward Search Feature Selection

In this evaluation, the top twenty uncorrelated features, extracted from each of the frequency bands within each of the *EEG* channels, and nine classifiers are used. The performance for each classifier is evaluated using the *sensitivity*, *specificity*, and *AUC* values with 100 simulations and randomly selected training and test sets for each simulation.

4.1.1   Classifier Performance
The first evaluation uses all the *seizure* and *non-seizure* blocks from all subjects in the *CHB-MIT* dataset (171 *seizures* and 171 *non-seizures*). Table 1, shows the mean averages obtained over 100 simulations for the *sensitivity*, *specificity*, and *AUC*.

Table 1: Classifier Performance Results for Top 20 Uncorrelated Features

Classifier	Sensitivity	Specificity	AUC
LDC	70%	83%	54%
QDC	65%	92%	62%
UDC	39%	95%	65%
POLYC	70%	83%	83%
LOGLC	79%	86%	89%
KNNC	84%	85%	91%
TREEC	78%	80%	86%
PARZENC	61%	86%	54%
SVC	79%	86%	88%

As shown in Table 2, the *sensitivities* (*seizure*), in this initial test, are lower for all classifiers. This is interesting given that the number of *seizure* and *non-seizure* blocks is equal. One possible reason for this is that the *ictal* length across the 171 records was 60 seconds. However, in the *CHB-MIT* records *ictal* periods ranged between 6 and 752 seconds. It is possible that some *ictal* blocks resemble *non-seizure* records resulting in misclassification (particularly blocks that contain 6 seconds of *ictal* data).

4.2   Results Using Top Five Uncorrelated Features Ranked Using LDA Backward Search Feature Selection from Five Head Regions

In the second evaluation, the top five uncorrelated features, extracted from five main regions across the head, are used to determine whether the detection of *seizures* can be improved. Again, the performance for each classifier is evaluated using the *sensitivity*, *specificity*, and *AUC* values with 100 simulations and randomly selected training and test sets for each simulation.

4.2.1   Classifier Performance

As shown in Table 2, the *sensitivities* (*seizure*), for most of the algorithms have improved, including the *specificity* values. The *AUC* results also showed improvements for several of the classifiers, with 93% achieved by the *KNNC* classifier. This is encouraging given that *sensitivities* are more important in this research than *specificities*. From the previous results, we find a 4% increase in *sensitivities*, a 3% increase in *specificities* and a 2 % increase in the performance of the *KNNC* classifier, with other classifiers improving with similar increases.

Table 1. Classifier Performance Results from Top five Uncorrelated Features from Five Head Regions

Classifier	Sensitivity	Specificity	AUC
LDC	78%	88%	55%
QDC	84%	86%	60%
UDC	51%	91%	70%
POLYC	78%	88%	89%
LOGLC	82%	84%	90%
KNNC	88%	88%	93%
TREEC	82%	81%	89%
PARZENC	81%	93%	61%
SVC	85%	86%	90%

5   Discussion

The study in this paper focused on discriminating between *seizure* and *non-seizure* EEG records across a group of 24 subjects, rather than a single individual. The classifiers are trained using all 24 patients, and therefore, classification is generalised across the whole population contained in the *CHB-MIT* database. To achieve this, features from all the channels that capture the *EEG* in all parts of the brain were used. In the initial classification results, the top 20 uncorrelated features from the whole of the head (not region-by-region) were extracted from 805 possible features. This has been accomplished using the *linear discriminant analysis backward search* technique to rank features. This approach achieved reasonably good results, using the *KNNC* classifier, with 84% for *sensitivity*, 85% for *specificity*, 91% for the *AUC*, with a global error of 15%.

Interestingly, the features used in this initial evaluation, involved channels from the four lobes of the brain, *occipital*, *parietal*, *frontal*, and *temporal*, but not the channels spread across the centre of the head. This implied that rather than having generalised seizures across the whole of the brain, a majority of focal seizures occurred in each of the lobes.

Using the top five uncorrelated features from *EEG* channels specific to the five main regions of the head improved the *sensitivities* and *specificities*, while producing high *AUC* values. The best classification algorithm was again the *KNNC* classifier, which achieved 88% for *sensitivity*, 88% for *specificity,* and an *AUC* value of 93% with a 12% global error. This was followed closely by the *SVC* classifier, which achieved 85% for *sensitivity*, 86% for *specificity,* and an *AUC* value of 90% with a 14% global error.

Generally, this paper produced good results and in many cases better than several papers reported in the literature. Where papers reported better results than ours, a patient-specific seizure detector was used, in contrast to the generalised detector approach taken in this paper. Consequently, it is challenging to make a like-for-like comparison and it is difficult to determine if the higher results produced in our study are, in fact, better than the results produced in patient-specific studies.

6   Conclusions and Future Work

Epilepsy is one of the most common neurological conditions, and one of the least understood. The seizures that characterise epilepsy are frequently unannounced and affect a sufferer's quality of life, as well as increasing the risk of injury or possibly death. A strong body of evidence has suggested that these epileptic seizures can be predicted by analysis of *EEG* recordings.

Within a supervised-learning paradigm, this paper utilises *EEG* signals to classify *seizure* and *non-seizure* records. Most of the previous work in this area has focused on detecting seizures of individual patients, but this paper generalises seizure detection across a group of 24 subjects from the open CHB-MIT database.

A rigorous, methodical, approach to pre-processing of the data was undertaken, and features were extracted from the raw *EEG* signal using several feature-ranking techniques. From our evaluations, the highest result, achieved with the *KNNC* classifier, was 93% for the *AUC*, 88% for *sensitivity*, and 88% for *specificity*.

Despite these encouraging results, more in-depth research is still required. For example, regression analysis, using a larger number of observations would be interesting. This would help to predict the early signs of a seizure, not just when the seizure happens. In addition, more advanced classification algorithms, and techniques, will be considered, including advanced artificial neural network architectures. The investigation and comparison of features, such as *fractal dimension* and *cepstrum analysis*, *autocorrelation zero crossing* and *correlation dimension*, has also not been performed. Future work will investigate these techniques in a head-to-head comparison, with linear methods.

References

1. Aarabi, A., Fazel-Rezai, R., Aghakhani, Y.: A Fuzzy Rule-Based System for Epileptic Seizure Detection in Intracranial EEG. Clinical Neurophysiology 2 120(9), 1648–1657 (2009)
2. Abdul-Latif, A.A., Cosic, I., Kimar, D.K., Polus, B.: Power Changes of EEG Signals Associated With Muscle Fatigue: The Root Mean Square Analysis of EEG Bands. In: IEEE Proceedings of Intelligent Sensors, Sensor Networks and Information Processing Conference, pp. 531–534 (2004)
3. Carney, P.R., Myers, S., Deyer, J.D.: Seizure Prediction: Methods. Epilepsy Behaviour 22, S94–S101 (2011)
4. Diambra, L., De Figueiredo, J.C.B., Malta, C.P.: Epileptic Activity Recognition in EEG Recording. Physica A: Statical Mechanics and its Applications 273(3-4), 495–505 (1999)
5. Engel, J.: Seizures and Epilepsy, p. 736 (2013)
6. Fazel, S., Wolf, A., Langstrom, N., Newton, C.R., Lichtenstein, P.: Premature Mortality in Epilepsy and the Role of Psychiatric Comorbidity: A Total Population Study. The Lancet 382(9905), 1646–1654 (2013)
7. Greene, B.R., Faul, S., Marnane, W.P., Lightbody, G., Korotchikova, I., Boylan, G.B.: A Comparison of Quantitative EEG Features Fro Neonatal Seizure Detection. Clinical Neurophysiology 119(6), 1248–1261 (2008)
8. Iasemidis, L.D.: Epileptic Seizure Prediction and Control. IEEE Transactions on Biomedical Engineering 50(5), 549–558 (2003)
9. Kelly, K.M., Shiau, D.S., Kern, R.T., Chien, J.H., Yang, M.C.K., Yandora, K.A., Sackellares, J.C.: Assessment of a Scalp EEG-Based Automated Seizure Detection System. Clinical Neurophysiology 121(11), 1832–1843 (2010)
10. Libenson, M.: Practical Approach to Electroencephalography, p. 464 (2009)
11. Maiwald, T., Winterhalder, M., Aschenbrenner-Scheibe, R., Voss, H.U., Shulze-Bonhage, A., Timmer, J.: Comparison of Three Nonlinear Seizure Prediction Methods by Means of the Seizure Prediction Characteristic. Physica D: Nonlinear Phenomena 194, 357–368 (2004)
12. Mormann, F., Andrzejak, R.G., Elgar, C.E., Lehnertz, K.: Seizure Prediction the Long and Winding Road. Brain 130, 314–333 (2007)
13. Ning, W., Lyu, M.R.: Exploration of Instantaneous Amplitude and Frequency Features for Epileptic Seizure Prediction. In: 12th IEEE International Conference on Bioinformatics and Bioengineering, pp. 292–297 (2012)
14. Patel, K., Chern-Pin, C., Fau, S., Bleakley, C.J.: Low Power Real-Time Seizure Detection for Ambulatory EEG. In: 3rd International Conference on Pervasive Computing Technologies for Healthcare, pp. 1–7 (2009)
15. Sanei, S., Chambers, J.A.: EEG Signal Processing, p. 312 (2007)
16. Shoeb, A.H.: Application of Machine Learning to Epileptic Seizure Onset and Treatment (2009)
17. Van Der Heijde, F., Duin, R.P.W., De Ridder, D., Tax, D.M.J.: Classification, Parameter Estimation and State Estimation, p. 440 (2005)

Structure-Based Prediction of Protein Phosphorylation Sites Using an Ensemble Approach

Yong Gao[1,*], Weilin Hao[1,2,*], Zhigang Chen[1], and Lei Deng[1,**]

[1] School of Software, Central South University, Changsha, China
[2] School of Electronics Engineering and Computer Science, Peking University, Beijing, China
leideng@csu.edu.cn

Abstract. As one of the most prevailing post-translational modifications, phosphorylation is vital in regulating almost every cellular behavior. In this paper, we propose a new computational method that can effectively identify phosphorylation sites by using optimally chosen properties. The highlight of our method is that the optimal combination of features was selected from a set of 165 novel structural neighborhood properties by a random forest feature selection method. And then an ensemble learning method based on support vector machine was used to build the prediction model. Experimental results obtained from cross validation and independent test suggested that our method achieved a significant improvement on the prediction quality. Promising results were obtained after being compared with the state-of-the-art approaches using independent dataset.

1   Introduction

Reversible phosphorylation is one of the most prevailing post-translational modifications[1, 2]. It is estimated that about 30~50% of the proteins can be phosphorylated in a eukaryotic cell[3], but most of the phosphorylation substrates still remain to be unrecognized. Despite the fact that there are already around 40 phosphorylation site prediction tools being established, they vary from one tool to another with respect to several particular attributes. For example, DISPHOS[4] and NetPhos[5] are both non-kinase-specific phosphorylation site prediction tools, and NetPhosK, GPS[6], PPSP[7] as well as KinasePhos2.0[8] are all kinase-specific phosphorylation site prediction tools. While DISPHOS takes position-specific amino acid frequencies and disorder information as its crucial features, NetPhos and NetPhosK are based on neural-network. GPS came up with their own algorithm named Group-based Phosphorylation Scoring algorithm, and PPSP implements an algorithm of Bayesian decision theory (BDT). In our experiment, a full set of 165 features including both sequence and structural information as well as their novel structural neighborhood properties were obtained. Then, a random forest feature selection method was used to select a subset of optimal features. Finally, SVM-

---

[*] These authors contributed equally to this work.
[**] Corresponding author.

D.-S. Huang et al. (Eds.): ICIC 2014, LNBI 8590, pp. 119–125, 2014.

based ensemble models were built to identify phosphorylation sites with less bias and better performance.

2   Methods

2.1   Dataset

2143 phosphoprotein chains which have at least one phosphorylated site were exacted from Phospho3D database[9, 10] in the first step. A tool named CD-HIT[11] was then used here to remove the redundant (or highly similar) chains with 90% sequence identity. Several well-known families—PKA, PKC, CK2, MAPK and SRC were chosen in our experiment to be discussed after we grouped the remained 817 phosphoprotein chains according to their respective kinase family. Then, from the non-redundant dataset, we extracted sequences centering on S, T and Y with a window size of 5.

To construct positive dataset, we extracted sequences with the center residue annotated as phosphorylation site in Phospho3D. The remained sequences were considered as negative control. As shown in table 1, there are 40, 42, 22, 24 and 35 phosphoprotein chains, 58, 68, 37, 30, 47 phosphorylation sites and 955, 1280, 579, 612, 1371 none-phosphorylation sites in PKA, PKC, CK2, MAPK and SRC, respectively.

Table 1. Number of Protein Chains, Phosphorylation Sites and Non-phosphorylation Sites of Each of the Five Families

	PKA	PKC	CK2	SRC	MAPK
number of protein chains	40	42	22	24	35
number of phosphorylation sites	58	68	37	30	47
number of non-phosphorylation sites	955	1280	579	612	1371

In hope to have a more impartial estimation, we decided to use all chains discovered after the year of 2008 to construct the benchmark dataset. It should be pointed out that because of the lack of data after 2008 of family CK2 and PKA in Phospho3D, discussion about independent testing on CK2 and PKA was not included in this paper. The remaining chains composed the training set.

2.2   Features

Site Features and Structural Neighborhood Properties
In our experiment, a large variety of 55 sequence, structural, and energy attributes are selected for classification, including disorder score, PSSM score, evolutionary conservation score, ASA features, pair potential, atom contacts and residue contacts, et al. For each residue, its feature vector not only including the above 55 attributes of the residue itself, but also including these 55 attributes of its two types structural

neighborhood residues defined by Euclidean distance and Voronoi diagram[12, 13] , that is , there are $55 \times 3 = 165$ features for each residue.

Feature Selection
In this experiment, we assessed the feature vector elements using the mean decrease Gini index (MDGI) calculated by the RF package in R[12] . MDGI represents the importance of individual feature vector elements for correctly assigning a residue into phosphorylation site and non–phosphorylation site. Here, for family of CK2, MAPK, PKA, PKC and SRC, we selected the top 19,112,33,25,20 features with MDGI Z-Score larger than 2.5 respectively.

2.3   Ensemble Learning Process

- A test set was constructed with both 10% of the positive set and negative set by a random selection.
- We generated training set by combining the remaining 90% positive examples and the same or similar size of negative examples which was randomly sampled with replacement from the remaining 90% negative set.
- Step II was repeated for $m = 20$ times, therefor we got 20 subsets for classifiers. Each sub-set was adopted to train a corresponding SVM classifier. Each training model of the classifier was tested by the test set obtained from step I and the final prediction result was determined by averaging raw outputs from all m classifiers for further processing with 10-fold cross validation.

Support Vector Machines
In this experiment, we employed the Support Vector Machines (SVMs)[13] as the underlying supervised learning algorithm in the ensemble approach. A public SVM library, namely LIBSVM, is applied for training the predictive models. The SVM kernel function of radial basis function (RBF) is selected. The SVM cost values and SVM gamma values are optimized for maximizing the sum of predictive Auc, Acc, Sn and Sp.

2.4   Performance Evaluation

The performance of the proposed prediction method is evaluated by 10-fold cross-validation. The following measures of predictive performance of the trained models are defined:

Specificity(Sp)=TN/(FP+TN), Precision(Pre)=TP/(TP+FP),
Sensitivity (Sn)=TP/(TP+FN), F1=(2*Pre*Sn)/(Pre+Sn),
Acracy(Acc)=(TP+TN)/(TP+FP+TN+FN),
and CC=(TP*TN-FP*FN)/$\sqrt{(TP+FN)(TP+FP)(TN+FN)(TN+FP)}$

Above, the TP, FP, TN, and FN are abbreviations of true positives, false positives, true negatives, and false negatives, respectively. The AUC score is the normalized area under the ROC curve. The ROC curve is plotted with TP as a function of FP for various classification thresholds.

3   Results and Discussions

3.1   Performance Comparison: SVM-F vs. SVM-Sub

We implemented 10-fold cross-validation using two distinctive feature sets, namely full set of features (SVM-F) and subselected feature set (SVM-Sub).

Table 2. Performance comparison on SVM-F and SVM-Sub

		AUC	Accuracy	Sensitivity	Specificity	CC	F1
CK2	SVM-Sub	0.877	0.963	0.433	0.992	0.433	0.429
	SVM-F	0.842	0.954	0.350	0.986	0.370	0.366
MAPK	SVM-Sub	0.839	0.952	0.483	0.973	0.480	0.480
	SVM-F	0.833	0.959	0.400	0.985	0.424	0.423
PKA	SVM-Sub	0.858	0.948	0.375	0.980	0.426	0.432
	SVM-F	0.846	0.926	0.335	0.959	0.279	0.310
PKC	SVM-Sub	0.857	0.952	0.303	0.985	0.396	0.363
	SVM-F	0.821	0.948	0.226	0.984	0.282	0.274
SRC	SVM-Sub	0.900	0.951	0.558	0.973	0.510	0.499
	SVM-F	0.890	0.946	0.241	0.985	0.317	0.294

Table 2 shows the detailed results of comparing SVM-F with SVM-Sub. On test set, SVM-Sub shows dominant advantages over SVM-F in four metrics: auc, sensitivity, CC, and F1-score for all five families. As to accuracy and specificity, SVM-F narrowly outperformed SVM-Sub in MAPK and SRC, but still not good enough than SVM-Sub in other three families. Concretely, as for MAPK, considering the size of its optimal feature set, maybe it indicates that there doesn't exist a few of features that can discriminate MAPK significantly. Table 2 indicate that our feature selection method based on RFC can effectively improve the prediction performance with less computational cost and reduce the risk of over-fitting.

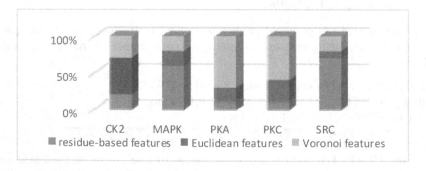

Fig. 1. The proportions of residue-based features, Euclidean features and Voronoi features on the top 10 list ranked by MDGI Z-Score for 5 families

We investigated three types of features-site, Euclidean, and Voronoi features. The proportions of the three types of features on the top 10 list by MDGI Z-Score for 5 families are presented in Figure 1. From Figure 1, we can find that for all families except SRC and MAPK, structural neighborhood properties (Euclidean or Voronoi) dominated the top 10 list. To be more specific, CK2 are mainly influenced by Euclidean features while Voronoi features are the most prominent features to PKA and PKC, suggesting that structural neighborhood properties are more predictive for those four families. Opposed to the former 3 families, Figure 1 indicated that the residue-based features dominated top 10 list for SRC and MAPK.

3.2   Performance Evaluation by Independent Test Comparison with Other Kinase-Specific Prediction Tools and SVM

We carried out the comparison of kinase-specific predictions using our method, SVM and four widely used kinase-specific prediction tools (PPSP, NetPhosK 1.0, KinasePhosK 1.0 and GPS 2.1) based on the independent test dataset. Results of the independent test are presented in Table 3. It is need to be noted that unfair comparison may generate if our test data are included in the training set of other tools, and thus leading a fake high performance of other existing ones and underestimation of ours.

Table 3. Performance Comparison of MAPK, PKC and SRC on the Independent Test Dataset

Tools	Kinase	Acc	Sn	Sp	CC	F1
PPSP_DEFAULT	MAPK	0.938895	0.157025	0.998735	0.362594	0.267606
	PKC	0.747826	0.6	0.761905	0.22981	0.292682
	SRC	0.856868	0.591703	0.882527	0.367532	0.421789
KinasePhos_100%	MAPK	0.936545	0.107438	1	0.317125	0.19403
	PKC	0.878261	0	0.961905	-0.05858	0
	SRC	0.924099	0.150655	0.998944	0.357936	0.259398
KinasePhos_95%	MAPK	0.919506	0.132231	0.97976	0.173842	0.189349
	PKC	0.886957	0.1	0.961905	0.085534	0.133333
	SRC	0.919091	0.170306	0.991549	0.308001	0.270834
KinasePhos_90%	MAPK	0.90658	0.272727	0.955092	0.244424	0.293333
	PKC	0.773913	0.5	0.8	0.202085	0.277778
	SRC	0.917742	0.224891	0.984788	0.329501	0.325435
NetPhosK_DEFAULT	MAPK	0.937133	0.115702	1	0.329193	0.207407
	PKC	0.791304	0.4	0.828571	0.163743	0.25
	SRC	0.921595	0.19214	0.992183	0.341029	0.301887
GPS	MAPK	0.940658	0.181818	0.998735	0.393516	0.303448
	PKC	0.852174	0.1	0.92381	0.024979	0.105263
	SRC	0.946253	0.475983	0.99176	0.611564	0.609791
SVM-Sub	MAPK	0.938895	0.140496	1	0.363076	0.246377
	PKC	0.960452	0.133333	0.99705	0.286519	0.222222
	SRC	0.911963	0.262009	0.974857	0.320564	0.344333
Ensemble-SVM-Sub	MAPK	0.8866	0.644628	0.786844	0.258225	0.291045
	PKC	0.9237	0.6	0.938	0.3892	0.4
	SRC	0.8996	0.5044	0.9379	0.416	0.47

For the family of MAPK, recall value reached nearly three times as high as the average value of others. Cc and F1-score are also the highest among these methods. Although the accuracy and specificity of the ensemble learning method decreased, ensemble learning method did make a better balance between the positive dataset and negative dataset, and thus, acquired an outperformance in comprehensive strength (the sum of accuracy, recall, specificity, cc and F-score) compared with SVM and other prediction tools. For the family of PKC, the high recall leads to a high cc and F1-score, and wins an absolutely victory in comprehensive strength. For the family of SRC, although ensemble learning method has a good performance, GPS performed better. Note that for SRC, GPS only considers about Y, while S, T and Y are all taken into account in our method, which may lead to a less-explicate prediction result compared with GPS. In any case, the prediction performance of our method is at least comparable with other kinase-specific prediction tools.

4   Conclusion

In this work, we presented a novel phosphorylation site prediction approach combining structural neighborhood properties. Experimental results revealed that the proposed method outperformed most existing kinase specific prediction methods. Two key factors are responsible for our success. First, 165 features providing much more thorough clues for phosphorylation identification. Second, significant lower computational cost and lower risk of overfitting was achieved by random feature selection. Although our method wins an absolutely victory in comprehensive strength compared with other tools,   the ensemble learning method leads to an decrease on Sp at the same time, which is the demerit of this method. The conclusions derived from this paper might help to accelerate accumulation of our knowledge on phosphorylation mechanism and guide corresponding experimental validation.

Acknowledgements. This work was supported by the National Natural Science Foundation of China under grants nos. 61309010 and 61379057 and Specialized Research Fund for the Doctoral Program of Higher Education of China under grant no. 20130162120073.

References

1. Steen, H., Jebanathirajah, J.A., Rush, J., Morrice, N., Kirschner, M.W.: Phosphorylation Analysis by Mass Spectrometry Myths, Facts, and the Consequences for Qualitative and Quantitative Measurements. Molecular & Cellular Proteomics 5(1), 172–181 (2006)
2. Delom, F., Chevet, E.: Phosphoprotein Analysis: From Proteins to Proteomes. Proteome Science 4(1), 15 (2006)
3. Pinna, L.A., Ruzzene, M.: How Do Protein Kinases Recognize Their Substrates?: Biochimica et Biophysica Acta (BBA)-Molecular Cell Research 1314(3), 191–225 (1996)
4. Iakoucheva, L.M., Radivojac, P., Brown, C.J., O'Connor, T.R., Sikes, J.G., Obradovic, Z., Dunker, A.K.: The Importance of Intrinsic Disorder for Protein Phosphorylation. Nucleic Acids Research 32(3), 1037–1049 (2004)

5. Blom, N., Gammeltoft, S., Brunak, S.: Sequence and Structure-Based Prediction of Eukaryotic Protein Phosphorylation Sites. Journal of Molecular Biology 294(5), 1351–1362 (1999)

6. Xue, Y., Ren, J., Gao, X., Jin, C., Wen, L., Yao, X.: Gps 2.0, a Tool to Predict Kinase-Specific Phosphorylation Sites in Hierarchy. Molecular & Cellular Proteomics 7(9), 1598–1608 (2008)

7. Xue, Y., Li, A., Wang, L., Feng, H., Yao, X.: Ppsp: Prediction of Pk-Specific Phosphorylation Site with Bayesian Decision Theory. BMC Bioinformatics 7(1), 163 (2006)

8. Wong, Y.-H., Lee, T.-Y., Liang, H.-K., Huang, C.-M., Wang, T.-Y., Yang, Y.-H., Chu, C.-H., Huang, H.-D., Ko, M.-T., Hwang, J.-K.: Kinasephos 2.0: A Web Server for Identifying Protein Kinase-Specific Phosphorylation Sites Based on Sequences and Coupling Patterns. Nucleic Acids Research 35(suppl. 2), W588–W594 (2007)

9. Zanzoni, A., Ausiello, G., Via, A., Gherardini, P.F., Helmer-Citterich, M.: Phospho3d: A Database of Three-Dimensional Structures of Protein Phosphorylation Sites. Nucleic Acids Research 35(suppl. 1), D229–D231 (2007)

10. Zanzoni, A., Carbajo, D., Diella, F., Gherardini, P.F., Tramontano, A., Helmer-Citterich, M., Via, A.: Phospho3d 2.0: An Enhanced Database of Three-Dimensional Structures of Phosphorylation Sites. Nucleic Acids Research 39(suppl. 1), D268–D271 (2011)

11. Huang, Y., Niu, B., Gao, Y., Fu, L., Li, W.: Cd-Hit Suite: A Web Server for Clustering and Comparing Biological Sequences. Bioinformatics 26(5), 680–682 (2010)

12. Deng, L., Guan, J., Wei, X., Yi, Y., Zhang, Q.C., Zhou, S.: Boosting Prediction Performance of Protein–Protein Interaction Hot Spots by Using Structural Neighborhood Properties. Journal of Computational Biology 20(11), 878–891 (2013)

13. Liaw, A., Wiener, M.: Classification and Regression by Randomforest. R News 2(3), 18–22 (2002)

Concept Mining of Binary Gene Expression Data

Ping He[*], Xiaohua Xu[*], Yongsheng Ju, Lin Lu, and Yanqiu Xi

Department of Computer Science, Yangzhou University, Yangzhou 225009, China
{angeletx,arterx}@gmail.com

Abstract. In this paper, we address the concept mining of binary gene expression data. To deal with this problem, we first compute the left and right singular vector matrices from the input binary gene expression matrix, and then information entropy is employed to determine whether column-clustering or row-clustering is performed first. Finally, the column-clustering and the row-clustering are repeated iteratively until the stopping criterion is satisfied. Experimental results show that our algorithm can identify the non-overlapping biclusters effectively.

Keywords: Concept Mining, Biclustering, Gene Expression Data.

1 Introduction

In biological experiments, gene expression levels can be simplified into two cases: active or inactive. It corresponds to binary matrix which contains only two values, 0 and 1. Clustering technology is often used during the exploratory of data analysis procedure, so we can use a clustering algorithm to analyze 0/1 gene expression data.

Singular value decomposition employs the product of several smaller and simpler matrices to represent a complex matrix. These sub-matrices are found to encode important properties of the 0/1 matrix. By far, there have been several work dedicated to biclustering of binary gene expression data. The first is a fast divide-and-conquer algorithm (Bimax) [1], which is time consuming and produces a list of insignificant biclusters. Second is Cmnk [2] introduced to find statistically significant biclusters, yet it returns biclusters that contain a large number of predicted elements, where most of these predicted biclusters are not part of the true bicluster. This is later improved by [3] to detect bicluters in sparse genomic data sets even in noisy background with a much lower false positive rate. Taking into consideration the instance-level constraints, Pensa et al. [4] come up with a CDK-Means for co-clustering 0/1 data. Recently, [5] puts forward a tabu-research heuristic and address block modelling of the binary network matrices; and [6] introduces a BiBit method aiming to discover bit-patterns from binary data. Seokho Lee, Jianhua Z. Huang [7] recently proposed a biclustering algorithm for binary matrices based on penalized Bernoulli likelihood.

---

[*] Corresponding authors.

D.-S. Huang et al. (Eds.): ICIC 2014, LNBI 8590, pp. 126–133, 2014.

Inspired by the recent research of [8], this article utilizes Singular Value Decomposition to select focus areas of energy (element 1), while removing a certain amount of noise at the same time. The 0/1 biclusters are obtained by iteratively perform row clustering or column clustering, whose order is determined by the information entropy computation. The iteration is supposed to terminate when the number of element 1 in a sub-matrix meets threshold's requirements. This paper can also distinguish overlapping and non-overlapping sub-matrices, and dig out those who are not overlapped. For those who are in the overlapping area, the degree of similar differences can be used to classify row sets and column sets. Thus, we can get rid of the background elements and achieve all-1 matrix or biclusters fulfilling the similar difference limitations.

2   Preliminaries

Suppose a gene collection G and a condition collection C, where $G = \{ g_1, g_2, ..., g_m\}$ represents a collection of genes and $C = \{ t_1, t_2, ..., t_n\}$ represents a collection of conditions. The data to be mined under a boolean context is $R \subseteq G \times C = \{0,1\}^{m \times n}$, where the elements of R, i.e., $(g_i, t_j) \in R$ indicates that the jth condition supports the ith gene, or in another word, ith gene reacts under the jth condition.

Definition 1: Frequency of 1
A collection of bi-set binary (G, C), $G=\{ g_1, g_2, ..., g_m\}$, $C=\{ t_1, t_2, ..., t_n\}$,$(g_i, t_j)=1$ indicates that ith gene reacts under the jth condition. Frequency of 1 is

$$f(G, C) = size((g_i, t_j)=1)/size((G,C)) \tag{1}$$

where $size((g_i,t_j)=1)$ denotes the number of 1 in set (G, C),and $size((G,C))=|G| \times |C|$.

Definition 2: 1-matrix and 0-matrix
A bi-set (G, C) is a 1-matrix if and only if $\forall g \in G$, $\forall t \in C$ and $(g, t) \in R$; a collection of bi-set binary (G,C) is 0-matrix if and only if $\forall g \in G$, $\forall t \in C$ and $(g, t) \notin R$.

Definition 3: Concept [10]
Suppose a 0/1 gene matrix $R_{m \times n}$, $(G,C) \in 2^{\{1,...,m\}} \times 2^{\{1,...,n\}}$ called a Concept if and only if

    (1) $\forall g \in G$, $\forall t \in C$: $(g,t) \in R$
    (2) $\nexists (G',C') \in 2^{\{1,...,m\}} \times 2^{\{1,...,n\}}$, where $\forall g' \in G$, $\forall t' \in C$: $(g',t') \in R$ and $G \subseteq G' \wedge C \subseteq C' \wedge (G',C') \neq (G,C)$.

Therefore, a Concept is also known as a maximum 1-matrix, which means it cannot be extended in either dimension.

Definition 4: Frequent Concept [11]
Given a concept (G, C), if its Frequency of 1 meets that $f(G, C) \geq \sigma$ ($0 < \sigma \leq 1$), where σ is the user-specified threshold value, then we call it a Frequent Concept.

3   Biculstering Algorithm

The Singular Value Decomposition [12] technique refers to the following equation.

$$R = USV^T, \quad S = \begin{bmatrix} \Sigma & 0 \\ 0 & 0 \end{bmatrix} \tag{2}$$

$$\Sigma = diag\ (\sigma_1, \sigma_2, ..., \sigma_p), \sigma_1 \geq \sigma_2 \geq ... \geq \sigma_p > 0$$

By using SVD, a matrix can be decomposed into a left singular vector matrix U, a diagonal matrix S, and a right singular vector matrix V.

Since the larger value of a singuar value σ_i indicates the greater important of the corresponding left singular vector u_i and right singular vector v_i, we sort the singular vectors according to their singular values in descent order. We start from analyzing the row vector u_1 and the column vector v_1, and use them for biclustering.

Row vector $u_1=(r_1, r_2, ..., r_m)$ reflects the energy distribution of rows in the 0/1 matrix, the greater the number of element 1 in a row i, the bigger   value r_i of u_1. Assume that the values in u_1 are rearranged from large to small $u_1=(r_1, r_2, ..., r_m)$ ($r_1 \geq r_2 \geq ... \geq r_m$), the row clustering of 0/1 matrix R equals to the clustering of row vector u_1; vector $v_1=(c_1, c_2, ..., c_m)$ reflects the energy distribution of the columns in 0/1 matrix, similarly, the column clustering is the clustering of the column vector v_1.

Given a row vector $u_1=(r_1, r_2, ..., r_m)$ and column vector $v_1=(c_1, c_2, ..., c_m)$ after SVD decomposition of R, we try to determine the order of column and row clustering. In view of this, we introduce the information entropy [13], which is a concept in information theory aiming to measure the amount of information. Assuming a variable X, it may have n different possible values, namely $x_1, x_2, ..., x_n$, the probabilities for X to take each value are $P_1, P_2, ..., P_n$ respectively, then the entropy of X is defined as:

$$H(X) = H(P_1, P_2, ..., P_n) = -\sum_{i=1}^{n} P_i \times \log_2 P_i \tag{3}$$

For a 0/1 gene matrix $R_{m \times n}$, $g \in G \equiv \{ 1, ..., m \}$, G expresses the collection of genes in matrix $R_{m \times n}$, then the matrix $R_{m \times n}$ can also be represented by the row vector g, $R_G = (g_1, g_2, ..., g_m)^T$, and the ith row vector $g_i=(R_{i1}, R_{i2}, ..., R_{in})$; $t \in C \equiv \{1, ..., n\}$, C expresses the collection of conditions in matrix $R_{m \times n}$, then the matrix $R_{m \times n}$ can also be represented by the row vector t, i.e., $R_C = (t_1, t_2, ..., t_n)$, the ith column vector $t_i=(R_{1i}, R_{2i}, ..., R_{mi})$。

Now we know, 0/1 gene matrix $R_{m \times n}$ has two expression forms R_G and R_C, and they carry different amount of information, i.e., different information entropy. For row matrix R_G, its information entropy is:

$$H(R_G) = -\sum_{i=1}^{m} P_i \times log_2 P_i, \ P_i = \frac{r_i}{\sum_k (u_k)} \tag{4}$$

u_k denotes the kth row characteristic vector. For column matrix R_C, its information entropy is:

$$H(R_C) = -\sum_{i=1}^{m} P_i \times log_2 P_i, \ P_i = \frac{c_i}{\sum_k (v_k)} \tag{5}$$

v_k denotes the kth characteristics column vector. If $H(R_G) \geq H(R_C)$ then row clustering is the prior choice; otherwise, column clustering is. Assume the row clustering first, Algorithm 1 is described as follows.

Algorithm 1. SVD Biclustering for Frequency Concept Mining

Input: 0/1 matrix R; noise threshold δ_o $(\delta_o{\geq}0)$•row similarity threshold Ψr, column similarity threshold•1-Frequency threshold $w(w{>}0)$.

Output: Frequency concept array A

[1] Decompose matrix R with SVD:

$R = USV^T$, $U=(u_1, u_2, \ldots, u_r)$, $V=(v_1, v_2, \ldots, v_r)$;

if $(\sigma_1+\ldots+\sigma_k)/(\sigma_1+\ldots+\sigma_r)\geq 98\%$, then output k;

[2] Compute the entropy of R_G and R_C

$H(R_G) = -\sum_{i=1}^{m} P_i \times log_2 P_i, \ P_i = \frac{r_i}{\sum_k(u_k)}$

$H(R_C) = -\sum_{i=1}^{m} P_i \times log_2 P_i, \ P_i = \frac{c_i}{\sum_k(v_k)}$

if $H(R_G) \geq H(R_C)$

```
  l= u₁=(r₁, r₂, ..., rₘ), Ψ=Ψᵣ
else
  l= v₁=(c₁, c₂, ..., cₘ), Ψ=Ψ_c
endif
sort(l)•l=(l₁, l₂, ..., lₘ) (l₁≥l₂≥... ≥lₘ≥0)
if lₙ ≥ δ₀ and l_{N+1} < δ₀
  l'=(l₁, l₂, ..., lₙ)
endif
```

[3] for $i = 2$ to N

```
    s(i-1)= lᵢ- l_{i-1}
endfor
if (s(i)<  || size(lᵢ)<3),
  merge the iᵗʰ and (i-1)ᵗʰ rows
  if size(lᵢ)<3
    if s(i)<s(i-1),
      merge the iᵗʰ and (i+1)ᵗʰ rows
    else
      merge the iᵗʰ and (i-1)ᵗʰ rows
    endif
  endif
endif
M={M₁, ..., M_g}(M= G or C)
```

[4] for $i=1$ to g

```
    Compute the 1-frequency of M_l, denoted as f(Mᵢ)
  if f(Mᵢ)>w
    return Mᵢ
  else
    goto 2
  endif
Endfor
```

5. Jump back to 2 unless the exit conditions are met

Fig. 1. SVD Biclustering Algorithm for Concept Discovery

In step 1 of Algorithm 1, SVD decomposes 0/1 matrix R into U, S and V. We find out the first k energy concentrated singular values. Limitation proportion is used in this article to interception when $(\sigma_1+...+\sigma_k)/(\sigma_1+...+\sigma_r) \geq \theta$, where θ is a threshold which we set 98%. Then the row vector u_1 and column vector v_1, which correspond to the maximum singular, are extracted respectively. In step 2, we determine the priority of column and row clustering. According to our assumption that row clustering is conducted first, we sort the u_1 to ordered vector $u_1=(r_1, r_2, ..., r_m)$ $(r_1 \geq r_2 \geq ... \geq r_m \geq 0)$. To remove the background signal and other noises, we set a threshold δ_0 $(\delta_0 \geq 0)$, and obtain $u_1 = (r_1, r_2,..., r_{NG})$ $(r_1 \geq r_2 \geq ... \geq R_{NG} > 0)$ which is free of background signal and noises with $r_{NG} \geq \delta_0$ and $r_{NG+1} < \delta_0$. Next, in the third step, since u_1 is well ordered, we calculate the similarity of the adjacent rows in a vector $s(r)=(s(r)_1, s(r)_2, ..., s(r)_{NG-1})$ with $s(r)_i=|r_{i+1}- r_i|$. To merge adjacent rows into clusters, there are two conditions: first $s(r)_i < \Psi_r$, where Ψ_r is the similarity threshold for row clustering; second $size(l_i) < 3$, where $size(l_i)$ is the least number of genes in cluster l_i. This step is to merge rows with the adjacent rows whose values are most similar to r_i. After row clustering, we obtain a sub-matrix set $G=\{G_1, ..., G_g\}$. The step 4 is to judge if the 1-Frequency of G_i is above threshold w. If yes, then G_i is a Frequent Concept, otherwise we need to continue in Frequent Concept Mining. Therefore, in step 5, our algorithm jumps back to the second step until the exit condition is met.

4   Experiments

In this experiment, we test our algorithm on both artificial and real-world data sets. Both data sets contain noise. Our algorithm is implemented in Matlab.

4.1   Artificial 0/1 Data Set with Noise

We create a matrix of 100 rows and 100 columns, and generate three 1-matrices as shown in Fig. 2. To simulate noise, we replace some elements in the original 1-matrices with a small amount of element 0. Our aim is to identify the Frequent Concept.

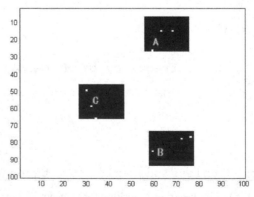

Fig. 2. Artificial data with noise

We now use Algorithms 1 to cluster the scattered noisy 0/1 data. From Fig. 3, where the x axis is gene and the y axis is condition, we find that A and B can be merged into a single high-quality Frequent Concept, while A as well as B is orthogonal with C, so the row vector u_1 and the column vector v_1 are unable to dig out C, but the row vector u_2 and the column vector v_2 are capable.

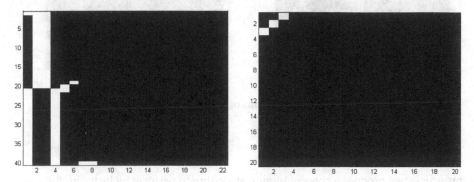

Fig. 3. Result by u_1 and v_1 and result by u_2 and v_2

4.2   Real-World Data Set (yeast)

We adopt two real-world data sets and transform them into binary data. This process includes standardization of the original matrix and then discretization with a threshold t. Element 1 means any real data above the threshold t, 0 otherwise.

Fig. 4 (left) illustrates a real-world data set containing 858 genes and 17 conditions. The threshold is t =0.0315, and the w threshold for 1-Frequency is w=75%. Fig. 4 (right) is another real-world data set, which includes 1979 genes and 17 conditions, with threshold t =0.0210, w=75%.

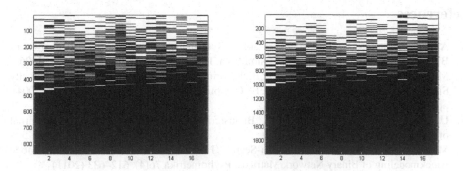

Fig. 4. Binary data sets transformed from real data sets

Fig. 5 (left) is the biclustering result of Fig. 4 (left). It covers all the conditions and 634 different genes. Fig. 5 (right) denotes the biclustering result of Fig. 4 (right), which covers all the conditions and 1515 genes. The 1-Frequencies of both biclusters are above 90%.

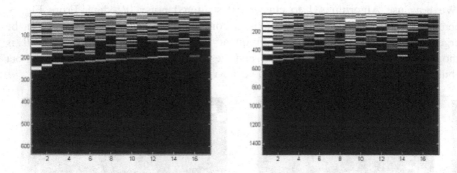

Fig. 5. Biclustering results of real-world data sets

5   Conclusions

In this article, we propose a concept mining algorithm to perform biclustering for gene expression data with SVD. It can help us understand the binary gene expression matrix easier and find the frequent concept of element 1. The experiments show the effectiveness of our method.

Acknowledgments. This work was supported in part by the Chinese National Natural Science Foundation under Grant nos. 61003180, 61379066 and 61103018, Natural Science Foundation of Education Department of Jiangsu Province under contracts 13KJB520026 and 09KJB20013, Natural Science Foundation of Jiangsu Province under contracts BK2010318 and BK2011442, and the New Century Talent Project of Yangzhou University.

References

1. Amela, P., Stefan, B., Phillip, Z., et al.: A Systematic Comparison and Evaluation of Biclustering Methods for Gene Expression Data. Bioinformatics 22(9), 1122–1129 (2006)
2. Mehmet, K., Wojciech, S., Ananth, G.: Biclustering Gene-Feature Matrices for Statistically Significant Dense Patterns. In: IEEE Comput. Sys. Bio. Coference (CSB 2004), pp. 480–484 (2004)
3. Uitert, M., Meuleman, W., Wessels, L.: Biclustering sparse Binary Genomic Data. Journal of Comput. Bio. 15, 1329–1345 (2008)
4. Michael, B., Douglas, S.: A Tabu-Search Heuristic for Deterministic Two-Mode Blockmodeling of Binary Network Matrices. Psyhometrika 76(4), 612–633 (2011)
5. Ruggero, G.P., Celine, R., Jean-Francois, B.: Constraint-driven co-clustering of 0/1 data. CRC Press LLC (2008)
6. Domingo, S.R., Antonio, J.P., Jesus, S.A.: A Biclustering Algorithm for Extracting Bit-Pattern from Binary Datasets. Bioinformatics 27(19), 2733–2745 (2011)
7. Lee, S., Huang, J.Z.: A biclustering algorithm for binary matrices based on penalized Bernoulli likelihood. Statistics and Computing (2013)

8. Chen, H.C., Zou, W., Tien, Y.J., Chen, J.J.: Identification of Bicluster Regions in a Binary Matrix and Its Applications. PLoS ONE 8(8), e71680
9. Jeremyn, B., Celine, R., Jean-Francois, B., Sophie, R.: Constraint-based concept mining and its application to microarray data analysis. Intelligent Data Analysis 9(1), 59–82 (2005)
10. Wille, R.: Restructuring lattice theory: an approach based on hierarchies of concepts. In: Rival, I. (ed.) Ordered Sets, pp. 445–470 (1982)
11. Ng, R., Lakshmanan, L., Han, J., Pang, A.: Exploratory mining and pruning optimizations of constrained associations rules. In: Proceedings ACM SIGMOD 1998, pp. 13–24. ACM Press (1998)
12. Alter, O., Brown, P.O., Botstein, D.: Singular value decomposition for genome-wide expression data processing and modeling. PNAS 97(18), 10101–10106 (2000)
13. Bagyamani, J., Hangavel, K., Rathipriya, T.R.: Biological Significance of Gene Expression Data using Similarity based Biclustering Algorithm. International Journal of Biometrics and Bioinformatics 4(6), 201–216 (2011)

Inference of Dynamic Gene Regulatory Relations with Multiple Regulators

Jeonghoon Lee, Yu Chen, and Kyungsook Han[*]

Department of Computer Science & Engineering, Inha University, Incheon, Korea
sosal@hanmail.net, chenyu@live.com, khan@inha.ac.kr

Abstract. Gene expression in complex regulatory interactions is often governed by more than one gene, so a gene involved in such interactions may have multiple regulators. We developed a method for identifying dynamic gene regulations of several types from the time-series gene expression data. The method can find gene regulations with multiple regulators that work in combination or individually as well as those with single regulators. The method has been implemented and tested on several gene expression datasets. The algorithms and program developed in our study will be useful for identifying multiple regulators, especially those that jointly regulate the expression level of a target gene.

Keywords: gene regulatory interactions, multiple regulators, regulatory network.

1 Introduction

A regulatory interaction between genes is a fundamental mechanism of a cell to develop and adapt to the environment. Biological processes in living cells are controlled by complex regulatory interactions between genes rather than by a single gene [1].

Recent studies report that some genes tend to cooperate with others in playing a role of regulator of another gene although each of them does not have a regulatory relation with the target gene independently [2, 3]. So far, most studies for finding gene regulations from gene expression data have focused on identifying regulatory relations between individual genes or co-regulated genes which have the same regulator, so they cannot find gene regulatory relations with multiple activators or inhibitors that jointly regulate the expression level of a target gene.

We developed a new method that identifies regulatory interactions between a group of genes and a single gene. It constructs a dynamic network of gene regulatory interactions of several types, which have not been considered by existing methods. We tested the method on the data of the yeast cell cycle [5]. The rest of this paper presents the method and its experimental results.

---

[*]To whom correspondence should be addressed.

D.-S. Huang et al. (Eds.): ICIC 2014, LNBI 8590, pp. 134–140, 2014.
© Springer International Publishing Switzerland 2014

2   Methods

(a)   Scoring Scheme for Gene Regulatory Relationships

The gene expression data of m genes with n samples is represented as an $m \times n$ matrix, where rows represent genes and columns represent various samples such as experimental conditions or time points in a biological process. Each element of the matrix represents the expression level of a particular gene.

We analyze the gene expression matrix for similarity between gene expressions. The similarity of gene expressions is often measured using several metrics such as Pearson correlation coefficient [7], Euclidean distance [8] and Spearman correlation [9]. To evaluate the regulatory relation between two genes, we modified the Pearson correlation coefficient. $R1(X, Y, i, p)$ in Equation 1 represents the score of a regulation between gene X at time point i and gene Y at time point $i + p$. p is the time delay of the gene regulation.

$$R1(X,Y,i,p) = \frac{\sum_{k=1}^{N}(X_k - \overline{X})(Y_{k+p} - \overline{Y})}{\sqrt{(\sum_{k=1}^{N}(X_k - \overline{X})^2)(\sum_{k=1}^{N}(Y_k - \overline{Y})^2)}} \tag{1}$$

In Equation 1, N is the total number of time points contained in the time span, X_k and Y_k are the expression levels of genes X and Y at time k, and $\overline{X}$ and $\overline{Y}$ are the average gene expression levels at all time points of the time section. The $R1$ score is in range of [-1, 1]. Among the total $i \times p$ candidate regulations, the regulation with the maximum absolute value of $R1(X, Y, i, p)$ above a threshold value is selected as the regulatory relation between X and Y. By default the threshold value is set to include 80% of the $R1$ scores of all identified gene pairs, but can be changed to a different value by the user.

Using the $R1$ score, we can determine whether gene X is a candidate activator or inhibitor of gene Y. If the expression level of gene X increases before that of Y increases, X is a candidate activator of gene Y; if the expression level of gene X increases before that of Y decreases, X is a candidate inhibitor of Y.

Algorithm 1 provides the top-level description of the algorithm for constructing an initial regulation list using $R1$ scores.

(b)   Inferring Gene Regulatory Relationships with Multiple Regulators

We consider two types of multiple regulators in gene regulations. What we call multiple-separate regulators have a same target gene, and each of the regulators has an individual regulatory relation with the target gene. The regulators X and Y which satisfy all the conditions below are grouped as multiple-separate regulators, and the regulation with multiple-separate regulators is denoted by $\{X, Y\} \rightarrow Z$ in the regulation list.

1). The regulators X and Y should have a same target gene Z.
2). The regulations $X \rightarrow Z$ and $Y \rightarrow Z$ must appear at the same time point.
3). The regulations must be of the same type (either activation or inhibition).

Algorithm 1. Construct an initial regulation list

1: For each pair of genes X and Y, compute $R1(X, Y, t, p)$ at every time point t and time delay $0 < p \leq 8$.
2: Select the regulation with the maximum absolute value of $R1(X, Y, t, p)$ as a candidate regulatory relation.
3: Classify the regulation into one of the four types, $+X(t) \rightarrow +Y(t + p)$, $-X(t) \rightarrow +Y(t+p)$, $+X(t) \rightarrow -Y(t+p)$, $-X(t) \rightarrow -Y(t+p)$, and add it to the regulation list.
4: If the new gene regulation is already in the regulation list, merge it with the previous regulation.
5: Go to step 2 to find the next gene regulation until no more regulation found.
6: Sort the candidate regulations in the regulation list with respect to their $R1$ scores, and remove those with $R1$ score $< d$.

In the other type of multiple regulators, the target gene is not regulated by any single gene of the multiple regulators, but rather by a combination of the multiple genes. We call these genes multiple-combined regulators, and the regulation with multiple-combined regulators is denoted by $\{X, Y\} \rightarrow Z$. Unlike multiple-separate regulators, regulation by multiple-combined regulators X and Y cannot be found by examining individual gene regulations since individual gene regulations $X \rightarrow Z$ and $Y \rightarrow Z$ do not exist. Regulation by multiple-combined regulators is identified using the information on transcription factors of potential regulators and their binding to target genes.

Genes X and Y that satisfy the following conditions are identified as multiple-combined regulators of their target gene Z.

1). Individual regulatory relations $X \rightarrow Z$ and $Y \rightarrow Z$ do not hold (i.e., the relations are not included in the gene regulation list).
2). The transcription factors of X and Y should satisfy one of these:
   1.   Genes X and Y have a same transcription factor that binds to a target gene (Figure 1A).
   2.   Genes X and Y have different transcription factors that constitute a cis-regulatory element and bind to a target gene in a promoter region (Figure 1B).

Given a time-series data of gene expression, it first identifies regulations between individual genes using the $R1$ score. From the gene regulation list, it then finds the gene regulations with multiple-separate regulators by grouping regulations with a same target gene. For multiple-combined regulators, it first extracts data of transcription factors for all genes left after filtering out housekeeping genes and unexpressed genes. For every pair of genes with transcription factors known, it examines whether there is no regulatory relation between them (i.e., their relation is not included in the gene regulation list) and their transcription factors have a same target gene. If so, the pair of genes is a potential multiple-combined regulator of their target gene.

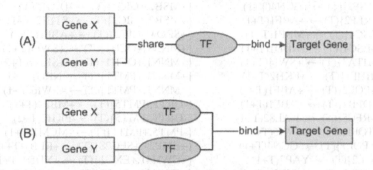

Fig. 1. Two cases of multiple-combined regulators of a target gene. (A) Genes *X* and *Y* have a same transcription factor that binds to a target gene. (B) Genes *X* and *Y* have different transcription factors that constitute a cis-regulatory element and bind to a target gene.

3   Results and Discussion

The algorithms have been implemented as the second version of GeneNetFinder (hereafter called GeneNetFinder2) using Microsoft Visual C#. GeneNetFinder2 is executable on any Windows systems. Given a time-series data of gene expressions in log-ratios, it identifies gene regulatory interactions of several types and visualizes them. This section shows the experimental results of GeneNetFinder2 with the gene expression data of yeast cell cycle.

We tested GeneNetFinder2 on the dataset of the yeast cell cycle obtained from the Yeast Genome Project [5], which contains a total of 6,178 yeast genes. After removing redundant genes, 1,290 yeast genes were selected for identification of regulations. Using the $R1$ score, 1,378 gene regulations were identified between the 1,290 yeast genes. 1,083 (78.6%) out of the 1,378 gene regulations have supporting evidences in literatures or databases [1-8, 10] and previous studies [11, 12]. The remaining 295 gene regulations are considered uncertain.

From the gene regulations with supporting evidences, we found 60 multiple-separate regulations by grouping those with the same target gene at the same time point (Table 1). For example, genes RHC18 and RAD27 activate gene MBP1 after a short delay, so their regulatory relation is represented by {+RHC18, +RAD27}(T) → +MBP1(T+1). For every pair of genes with known transcription factors, we also found multiple-combined regulations in which a target gene is not regulated by any single gene of the multiple regulators but by a combination of them (Table 2).

Table 1. Gene regulations with multiple-separate regulators in the yeast cell cycle. Two genes X and Y have individual regulatory relation with their target gene Z.

{X, Y} → Z	
{+ABF1,+CAC2}(T) → +SWI6(T+1)	{+BNI4,-GIN4}(T) → -NRG1(T+1)
{+MIF2,-ASF2}(T) → +GCN4(T+1)	{+MSB2,+GIC2}(T) → -DIG1(T+1)
{+ASF2,+RLF2}(T) → +ABF1(T+1)	{+MSB2,+GIC2}(T) → -STE12(T+1)
{-ASF1,-ESC4}(T) → +MBP1(T+1)	{+SRO4,+GIC2}(T) → +ABF1(T+1)
{+CBF2,+ESC4}(T) → -NDD1(T+1)	{+MNN1,+OCH1}(T) → +SWI4(T+1)
{-HTA1,+HTA3}(T) → +SWI4(T+1)	{+MNN1,+OCH1}(T) → +SKN7(T+2)
{-HTA1,-HHF1}(T) → +FKH2(T+1)	{+MNN1,+PMT1}(T) → -NRG1(T+1)
{+RFA2,+POL2}(T) → +ABF1(T+2)	{+MNN1,+PMT1}(T) → +SWI6(T+1)
{+CTF4,+DPB2}(T) → +ABF1(T+1)	{-QRT1,-PMT5}(T) → +MBP1(T+1)
{-POL30,-RFC5}(T) → -DAL82(T+1)	{-QRT1,-PMT5}(T) → -FKH2(T+2)
{-CDC2,-TOF1}(T) → +SWI6(T+1)	{-PMT5,+PMT1}(T) → -MCM1(T+1)
{+CDC9,+POL1}(T) → -GCN4(T+1)	{+EMP24,+SEC28}(T) → +REB1(T+1)
{-PRI2,-POL2}(T) → -YAP7(T+1)	{+CWH41,+EXG1}(T) → +NDD1(T+1)
{-POL12,-POL1}(T) → +MBP1(T+1)	{+CWH41,+EXG1}(T) → +FKH2(T+2)
{-CDC2,-DPB2}(T) → +MBP1(T+2)	{-GAS1,+EXG1}(T) → +MBP1(T+1)
{+GAS1,+EXG1}(T) → +SWI6(T+1)	{+PHO3,+PHO5}(T) → -FKH2(T+1)
{+CWP1,+CWP2}(T) → +SWI4(T+1)	{+PHO3,+PHO5}(T) → +MSN2(T+2)
{+EPT1,-LPP1}(T) → -INO4(T+1)	{-MET1,-MET28}(T) → -NRG1(T+1)
{+LPP1,+PSD1}(T) → -INO2(T+2)	{+MET16,+MET17}(T) → +UME6(T+1)
{+CNM67,-SPC42}(T) → +SWI4(T+1)	{+MET30,-CLB5}(T) → -RFC3(T+1)
{+RHC18,+RAD27}(T) → +MBP1(T+1)	{-RNR1,-RNR3}(T) → -GCN4(T+1)
{+RAD54,+RAD27}(T) → +SUT1(T+1)	{+BNI4,-BUD9}(T) → -SWI5(T+1)
{+RAD54,+RHC18}(T) → +REB1(T+1)	{+BNI4,+MSB2}(T) → +SKN7(T+1)
{-DUN1,+OGG1}(T) → +FKH2(T+1)	{+BNI4,-GIN4}(T) → +MBP1(T+1)
{-DUN1,-UNG1 }(T) → +SWI6(T+1)	{+BNI4,-GIN4}(T) → +SWI6(T+2)
{+RDH54,-UNG1}(T) → +SWI4(T+1)	{-BUD9,+MSB2}(T) → +SWI6(T+1)
{+RAD5,+RAD51}(T) → +MET31(T+1)	{-BUD9,+MSB2}(T) → +SWI4(T+2)
{-BNI4,+GIN4}(T) → +SWI4(T+1)	{+MET6,+MET10}(T) → +MET4(T+1)
{-MET13,+MET6}(T) → -GCN4(T+1)	{+MET6,+MET14}(T) → +CBF1(T+1)
{+MET6,+MET14}(T) → -MET32(T+1)	{+MET10,-MET28}(T) → +CBF1(T+1)

Table 2. Gene regulations with multiple-combined regulators in the yeast cell cycle. The target gene Z is not regulated by any of X and Y individually, but only by a combination of X and Y.

{X + Y} → Z	
{PHO2+SWI5} → BAS1	{MNN1+PMT5} → NRG1
{ORC1+SPG4} → NDE1	{SWH1+PDR3} →APN2
{MNN1+ORC1} →SKN7	{PAH1+CTL1} → SGS1
{URA7+GRX7} → UBP14	{CUP2+CUP9} → NDD1
{SCJ1+SKY1} → HRB1	{ORC3+BOP2} → SUR4
{HTT2+APP1} → RIO2	{MRP51+VPS30} → PRM4
{RAD50+CAF40} → DDI3	{SGO1+RPO31} → RET1
{HTZ1+GSH2} → HPF1	{ESA1+SLY41} → ECM23
{MNN1+ORC1} → SWI4	

4   Conclusions

This article presented the development of a method for reasoning dynamic gene regulatory relations from the time-series gene expression data. Unlike most methods that focus on finding regulations between individual genes, our method can identify regulations by single regulators and those by multiple regulators that work individually or in combination. From the time-series data of gene expression, it infers gene regulatory interactions and the temporal aspects of the regulatory interactions. The identified gene regulatory interactions and their temporal aspects are stored in the regulation list and visualized as a gene regulatory network.

The methods for identifying gene regulations have been implemented as GeneNetFinder2. We tested GeneNetFinder2 on the yeast cell cycle data. In the yeast cell cycle data, GeneNetFinder2 identified 1,378 gene regulations, and 78.6% of them (1,083 regulations) were verified. Seventeen regulations involve multiple-combined regulators, and 60 regulations have multiple-separate regulators. The approach of GeneNetFinder2 would be useful for identifying gene regulatory interactions of several types, especially those with multiple regulators that work in combination or individually, and for analyzing and refining known regulatory relations.

Acknowledgement. This research was supported by the Basic Science Research Program through the National Research Foundation of Korea (NRF) funded by the Ministry of Science, ICT & Future Planning (NRF-2012R1A1A3011982) and in part by the Ministry of Education (2010-0020163).

References

1. Slivescu, A., Honavar, V.: Temporal Boolean network models of genetic networks and their inference from gene expression time series. Complex Systems 13, 61–78 (2001)
2. Hobert, O.: Gene Regulation by Transcription Factors and MicroRNAs. Science 319, 1785–1786 (2008)
3. Snel, B., Noort, V.V., Huynen, M.A.: Gene co-regulation is highly conserved in the evolution of eukaryotes and prokaryotes. Nucleic Acids Research 32, 4725–4731 (2004)
4. Chen, Y., Park, B., Han, K.: Qualitative reasoning of dynamic gene regulatory interactions from gene expression data. BMC Genomics 11, S14 (2010)
5. Spellman, P.T., Sherlock, G., Zhang, M.Q., Iyer, V.R., Anders, K., Eisen, M.B., Brown, P.O., Bostein, D., Futcher, B.: Comprehensive Identification of Cell Cycle-regulated Genes of the Yeast Saccharomyces cerevisiae by Microarray Hybridization. Molecular Biology of the Cell 9, 3273–3297 (1998)
6. Whitfield, M.L., Sherlock, G., Saldanha, A.J., et al.: Identification of Genes Periodically Expressed in the Human Cell Cycle and their Expression in Tumors. Mol. Biol. Cell 13, 1977–2000 (2002)
7. Lee Rodgers, J., Nicewander, W.A.: Thirteen Ways to Look at the Correlation Coefficient. The American Statistician 42, 59–66 (1988)

8. Danielsson, P.: Euclidean Distance Mapping. Computer Graphics and Image Processing 14, 227–248 (1980)
9. Spearman, C.: The proof and measurement of association between two things. American Journal of Psychology 15, 72–101 (1904)
10. Yitzhak, P., Priya, S., George, M.C.: Identifying regulatory networks by combinational analysis of promoter elements. Nature Genetics 29, 153–159 (2001)
11. Knapp, D., Bhoite, L., Stillman, D.J., et al.: The Transcription Factor Swi5 Regulates Expression of the Cyclin Kinase Inhibitor p40SIC1. Mol. Cell. Biol. 16, 5701–5707 (1996)
12. Lovrics, A., Csikász-Nagy, A., Zsély, I.G., et al.: Time Scale and Dimension Analysis of a Budding Yeast Cell Cycle Model. BMC Bioinformatics 7, 494 (2006)

Evolving Additive Tree Model for Inferring Gene Regulatory Networks

Guangpeng Li, Yuehui Chen, Bin Yang, Yaou Zhao, and Dong Wang

Computational Intelligence Lab, School of Information Science and Engineering,
University of Jinan, Shandong, Jinan 250022, P.R. China
yhchen@ujn.edu.cn

Abstract. Gene regulatory networks have been studied in the past few years and it is still a hot topic. This paper presents a different evolutionary method for inferring gene regulatory networks (GRNs) using a system of ordinary differential equations (ODEs) as a network model based on time-series microarray data. An evolutionary algorithm based on the additive tree-structure model is applied to identify the structure of the model and genetic algorithm (GA) is used to optimize the parameters of the ODEs. The experimental results show that the proposed method is feasible and effective for inferring gene regulatory networks.

Keywords: Gene Regulatory Networks, Evolutionary Algorithms, Additive tree model, Ordinary differential equations, Genetic programming.

1 Introduction

With the development of biological technology and computer techniques, more and more methods and models for identifying GRNs are proposed. Erina Sakamoto used the ordinary genetic programming (GP) to identify the structures and the least mean square (LMS) to evolve the parameters of the ODEs [1]. Lijun Qian applied the GP to identify the structure of model and Kalman filter to estimate the parameters [2]. Vilela identified neutral biochemical network models from time-series data, combining Monte Carlo method to evolve the parameters [3]. Yang used flexible neural tree model to reconstruct the GRNs [4].

In this paper, we propose a new hybrid evolutionary method to identify the GRNs using the system of the ODEs. We apply the evolutionary algorithm based on the additive tree model to identify the structures and the improved genetic algorithm to estimate the parameters in the ODEs. The partitioning method [5] is applied in the process of identifying the structure of the system. Each equation in the ODEs is separately inferred.

The paper is organized as followed. We describe concrete methods in section 2 and perform two different experiments to validate our method in section 3. In section 4, discussions and conclusions are finally made.

D.-S. Huang et al. (Eds.): ICIC 2014, LNBI 8590, pp. 141–147, 2014.

2   Method

2.1   Structure Optimization of Models

2.1.1   The Introduction of the Additive Tree Model

GP is a popular method to identify the structure of the system of the ODEs. But its encoding representation is complex and its running efficiency is low. So we evolve its encoding method and propose the tree-structure based evolution algorithm to identify the structure of the additive tree models [6]. To fit our needs, we encode the right-hand part of the ODEs into an additive tree individual, as shown in Figure.1.

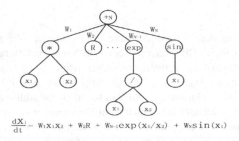

$$\frac{dX_i}{dt} = W_1 x_1 x_2 + W_2 R + W_{N-1} \exp(x_1/x_2) + W_N \sin(x_1)$$

Fig. 1. An additive tree model which represents an ODE

In the generation of the additive tree, instruction and operator sets I0 and I1 are adopted as: I0 = {+2, +3, ..., +N}, I1 = FUT = {*, /, sin, cos, exp, rlog, x, R}

Here F = {*, /, sin, cos, exp, rlog } are the function sets and T = {x, R} are the terminal sets, where +N,*, /, sin, cos, exp, rlog, x, and R denote addition, multiplication, division, sine, cosine, exponent, logarithm, system inputs, random constant number taking N, 2, 2, 1, 1, 1, 1, 0 and -1 arguments respectively. N is an integer number which is the maximum number of the ODE terms, I0 is the instruction set of the root node and I1 is the instruction set of other nodes.

As the evolving process is so complex and time-consuming, we take the partitioning method in inferring the system of the ODEs. Through the use of the partitioning method, a candidate equation for a signal variable is integrated by substituting references to other variables with data from the observed time series [5]. Therefore each equation is evolved independently in parallel.

2.1.2   The Process of Evolving the Structure of the ODEs

Our structural evolutionary process is the standard evolutionary process. The genetic operators are adopted as followed.

(1) Selection. We adopt EP-style tournament selection method to select the parents for the next generation.

(2) Crossover. Through the comparison of the predefined crossover probability Pc and the randomly generated probability, we select two individuals to perform the crossover operation. And we randomly select one nonterminal node for each additive tree. Then we swap the selected subtree of these two individuals.

(3) Mutation. We have three different mutation operators to generate the next offspring from the parents.

    1) Randomly select a terminal node and replace it with another terminal node which is randomly selected from the T terminal sets, or replace it with a subtree which is randomly generated using the predefined generation method.

    2) Randomly select a functional node and replace it with a terminal node which is randomly selected from the T terminal sets.

2.2   Fitness Definition

In our study, fitness evaluation function is used in both structure and parameters optimization. As we infer the GRNs from gene expression time-series data, the sum of squared error (SSE) may be the optional fitness function, which is defined as:

$$fitness(i) = \sum_{k=0}^{T-1} \left(x_i^{'}(t_0 + k\Delta t) - x_i(t_0 + k\Delta t) \right)^2 \tag{1}$$

where t_0 is the starting time, Δt is the time interval, T is the number of all data points, $x_i(t_0 + k\Delta t)$ is the actual time-series data of the i-th sample, and $x_i^{'}(t_0 + k\Delta t)$ is the actual evaluation value of the ODEs we finally infer. $x_i^{'}(t_0 + k\Delta t)$ is calculated using approximate fourth-order Runge-Kutta method.

2.3   Parameter Optimization of Models

2.3.1   Encoding.

Each equation as an individual can be represented as a vector with varying dimensions. As each equation has many different parameters and they will be changed with the evolution of the equation, we adopt floating point numbers to represent the parameters of the ODEs.

2.3.2 Fitness Evaluation

As we have already defined the fitness evaluation function above, we could adopt the same fitness function in the GA..

2.3.3.   The Process of Evolving the Parameters of the ODEs Using Improved GA

    (1) Selection. In this paper, we adopt Roulette Wheel Selection method to select the individuals which have higher degree of fitness values for next generation.

    (2) Crossover and Mutation. In our study, we adopt the standard FGA operator method to generate our crossover and mutation operators.

2.4   Summary of the Proposed Algorithm

As the construction and parameters of the ODEs are evolved separately, the construction optimization or the parameter optimization is performed while the other one stays the same. The procedure of the evolution of the ODEs can be described as followed:

(1) Randomly initialize a population.

(2) Structure optimization is performed using the additive tree models until we get the predefined generation.

(3) Parameter optimization is performed using GA while the structure of the equation is fixed.

(4) If the optimal solution is found, then stop; otherwise go to step (2).

3   Experimental Results

In our study, we select one biochemical system and one real GRN to confirm the effectiveness of our proposed method. We run our program in a PC with 2.00GHz Pentium Dual processor and 2 GB of RAM. Experimental parameters are summarized in Table 1. As GA algorithm is very time-consuming, we could adopt parallel genetic algorithm while referring the large network.

Table 1. Parameters for experiments

	Exp.1	Exp.2
Population size	50	200
Generation	100	100
Crossover rate	0.7	0.7
Mutation rate	0.1	0.1
Step size	0.01	0.01
Data point	30	10

3.1   E-Cell Simulation

In our first experiment, we use the data of E-cell system which is a metabolic network and consists of three substances. E-cell simulation is a software package for cellular and biochemical modeling and simulation [7]. This metabolic network can be represented approximately as follows:

$$\frac{dx_1}{dt} = -k_1 x_1 x_3$$

$$\frac{dx_2}{dt} = k_1 x_1 x_3 - k_2 x_2 \qquad (2)$$

$$\frac{dx_3}{dt} = -k_1 x_1 x_3 + k_2 x_2$$

Note that the parameters k1, k2 and k3 are unknown for the simulation experiment. We use three time-series datasets generated by E-cell system with different initial values for the experiment. Experimental parameters are shown in Table 1. By applying our method, we obtain the following equations:

$$\frac{dx_1}{dt} = -10.263 \, x_1 x_3$$

$$\frac{dx_2}{dt} = 9.576 \, x_1 x_3 - 17.462 \, x_2 \tag{3}$$

$$\frac{dx_3}{dt} = -9.583 \, x_1 x_3 + 17.406 \, x_2$$

The time-series data generated by Eq. (3) is shown in Fig. 2. The system of Eq. (3) gets the MSE (mean square error) is $1.628 * 10^{-9}$. Through comparing two curves in Fig. 2, we can see that the models are almost identical to the target ODEs.

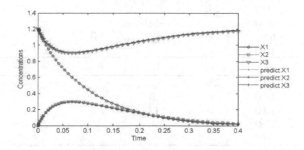

Fig. 2. Time series of the acquired model for E-cell simulation

We also have made further comparison to examine the effectiveness of our proposed approach with GP+RLS and GP+KF. Obviously, the parameters of our model are closer to the targeted model than GP+RLS and GP+KF. And the GP+KF need 1000 individuals while our initial population size is just only 50.

Table 2. Obtained Parameters by GP+RLS[8],GP+KF[2] and Our Method

	True value	GP+RLS	GP+KF	Our Method
w_{11}	-10.32	-9.64	-10.34	-10.263
w_{21}	9.72	13.42	8.87	9.576
w_{22}	-17.5	21.8	-17.42	-17.462
w_{31}	-9.7	-5.63	-9.74	-9.583
w_{32}	-17.5	12.64	17.15	17.406

3.2   Regulator and Effector Gene Interaction Network

In the next two experiments, we use our method for the S-system to infer the GRNs. The S-system [9] is a type of power-law formalism described as follows:

$$\frac{dX_i}{dt} = \alpha_i \prod_{j=1}^{n} X_j^{g_{ij}} - \beta_i \prod_{j=1}^{n} X_j^{h_{ij}}$$

(4)

Where X is the vector of dependent variable, α and β are vectors of non-negative rate constants and g and h are the matrix of kinetic orders, n is the number of state variables or reactants Xi.

To confirm the effectiveness of our proposed algorithm, we adopt the modeling of the dynamics of the small-scale gene network as a case study [10]. The parameters of the genetic network are given in Table 3. Experimental parameters are shown in Table 1. The used instruction set I0 = {+2, +3, +4}, F = {*, ax}, and we get the inferred parameters for this model in Table 4. We can see that the parameters we obtained are very close to those in the original system.

Table 3. Parameters of the genetic network system

i	α_i	g_{i1}	g_{i2}	g_{i3}	g_{i4}	g_{i5}
1	5.0			1.0		-1.0
2	10.0	2.0				
3	10.0		-1.0			
4	8.0			2.0		-1.0
5	10.0				2.0	
	β_i	h_{i1}	h_{i2}	h_{i3}	h_{i4}	h_{i5}
1	10.0	2.0				
2	10.0		2.0			
3	10.0		-1.0	2.0		
4	10.0				2.0	
5	10.0					2.0

Table 4. Parameters estimated by our method

i	α_i	g_{i1}	g_{i2}	g_{i3}	g_{i4}	g_{i5}
1	4.839			0.865		-0.927
2	9.896	1.826				
3	9.923		-0.839			
4	7.872			1.928		-1.162
5	4.839				1.817	
	β_i	h_{i1}	h_{i2}	h_{i3}	h_{i4}	h_{i5}
1	9.726	1.792				
2	9.879		1.858			
3	9.916		-0.853	1.921		
4	9.861				1.932	
5	10.293					1.824

4   Conclusion

In this paper, we proposed a hybrid evolutionary method for referring GRNs. The experimental results show the effectiveness and accuracy of our proposed method. Our method has two advantages: (1) the evolved additive tree model is robust and easy to analyze by using traditional techniques. Because the evolved additive tree model is simple in form, we can acquire the best structures of the ODEs only by a small population in referring the GRNs; (2) with partitioning, each ODE of the ODEs can be inferred separately and the research space reduces rapidly, so we can acquire the best system very fast.

Acknowledgement. This research was partially supported by the Natural Science Foundation of China (Grant No. 61201428, 61070130, 61302028) and the Natural Science Foundation of Shandong Province (ZR2011FZ003).

References

1. Iba, H., et al.: Inferring a system of differential equations for a gene regulatory network by using genetic programming. In: Proc. Congress on Evolutionary Computation, pp. 720–726 (2001)
2. Qian, L., et al.: Inference of Noisy Nonlinear Differential Equation Models for Gene Regulatory Networks Using Genetic Programming and Kalman Filtering. IEEE Transactions on Signal Processing 56(7), 3327–3339 (2008)
3. Vilela, M., et al.: Identification of neutral biochemical network models from time series data. BMC Systems Biology 3, 47 (2009)
4. Yang, B., et al.: Reverse engineering of gene regulatory networks using flexible neural tree models. Neurocomputing (2012)
5. Bongard, J., Lipson, H.: Automated reverse engineering of nonlinear dynamical systems. Proceedings of the National Academy of Science 104(24), 9943–9948 (2007)
6. Chen, Y., Yang, J., et al.: Evolving Additive tree models for System Identification. International Journal of Computational Cognition 3(2), 19–26 (2005)
7. Tomita, M., et al.: E-cell: software environment for whole-cell simulation. Bioinformatics 15, 72–84 (1999)
8. Ando, S., Sakamoto, E., Iba, H.: Evolutionary modeling and inference of gene network. Inf. Sci. 145, 237–259 (2002)
9. Savageau, M.A.: Biochemical Systems Analysis: A Study of Function and Design in Molecular Biology. Addison-Wesley, Reading (1976)
10. Hlavacek, W.S., Savageau, M.A.: Rules for coupled expression of regulator and effector genes in inducible circuits. J. Mol. Biol. 255, 121–139 (1999)

Analyzing Support Vector Machine Overfitting on Microarray Data

Henry Han

Department of Computer and Information Science, Fordham University,
New York NY 10458 USA
Quantitative Proteomics Center, Columbia University, New York 10027 USA
xhan9@fordham.edu

Abstract. Support vector machines (SVM) are a widely used state-of-the-art classifier in molecular diagnostics. However, there is little work done on its overfitting analysis to avoid deceptive diagnostic results. In this work, we investigate the important problem and prove that a SVM classifier would inevitably encounter overfitting for gene expression array data under a standard Gaussian kernel due to the built-in large data variations from DNA amplification mechanism in the transcriptional profiling. We have found that SVM demonstrates its own special overfitting characteristics on array data, in addition to showing that feature selection algorithms may not contribute to overcoming overfitting, and discussing overfitting in biomarker discovery algorithm.

Keywords: Support vector machines, Overfitting, DNA amplification, Biomarker.

1   Introduction

As a state-of-the art machine learning algorithm, the standard support vector machine (SVM) and its variants are widely employed in microarray and other omics data classification and biomarker discovery [1-3]. However, it often suffers from overfitting problem, which is a less addressed problem in machine learning community but plays an essential role in robust diagnostics in translational bioinformatics. The overfitting simply means that a learning machine loses its learning generalization capabilities. Although it may achieve some good results on some training data, it has no way to generalize to new testing data. Given its importance in omics data analysis and machine learning, SVM overfitting deserves a serious investigation [2]. In this work, we mainly focus on analyzing SVM overfitting by using benchmark microarray datasets, i.e., gene expression array data.

As a special high-dimensional data, gene expression arrays can be represented as a $n \times m, n \ll m$ matrix $X = [x_1, x_2 \cdots x_n]^T$ after preprocessing, where each row represents a single sample (observation) that is a diseased or healthy subject, and each column represents a gene (variable). The number of genes is usually much greater than the

D.-S. Huang et al. (Eds.): ICIC 2014, LNBI 8590, pp. 148–156, 2014.

number of samples. Although there are a large number of genes, only a small number of them have meaningful contributions to data variations.

The standard support vector machine (SVM) algorithm for microarray data classification can be described as follows, if we assume they are linearly non-separable. Given a gene expression training dataset consisting of n samples across total m genes and corresponding label information $\{x_i, c_i\}_{i=1}^d$, where $X = [x_1, x_2 \cdots x_n]^T$, $x_i \in \mathbb{R}^m$ and $c = [c_1, c_2 \cdots c_n]^T$, $c_i \in \{-1, 1\}$, the SVM algorithm calculates an optimal separating hyperplane $O_h : w^T x + b = 0$ in $\mathbb{R}^m$ to attain the maximum margin between the '-1' (negative) and '+1' (positive) sample types. This is equivalent to solving the following quadratic programming problem:

$$\min_{w, \xi, b} \frac{1}{2} \| w \|^2 + C \sum_{i=1}^n \xi_i$$
$$s.t. \ c_i (w^T u_i + b) \geq 1 - \xi_i, \ i = 1, 2 \cdots n, \tag{1}$$
$$\xi_i \geq 0$$

It employs a decision function $f(x') = sign(\sum_{i=1}^n \alpha_i c_i k(x_i, x') + b)$ to determine the type of an unknown sample $x' \in \mathbb{R}^m$, where the vector $\alpha = [\alpha_1, \alpha_2 \cdots \alpha_n] \geq 0$ is the solution of the dual problem of the QP in Eq. (1) and $k(x_i, x')$ is a kernel function mapping samples x_i, x' into a same or higher dimensional feature space. Although different kernel choices are available, we focus on two most representative kernels: linear and standard Gaussian kernels (where bandwidth sigma is set as 1) due to their popularity in this work. The former and latter map two samples into a same dimensional or an infinite dimensional feature space respectively in SVM classification.

In our studies, we have investigated SVM overfitting on microarray classification using six benchmark datasets, and had following interesting findings. First, contrary to a general assumption that a nonlinear decision boundary is more effective in SVM classification [1], we found that a SVM classifier will suffer from overfitting under Gaussian kernels and demonstrate their own characteristics. Second, we rigorously proved that SVM would *inevitably* encounter overfitting under a standard Gaussian kernel, besides demonstrating feature-selection algorithms maynot overcome it. Third, we provided that the biological reason for SVM overfitting, in addition to discussing the role of overfitting in biomarker discovery.

This paper is organized as follows. Section 2 presents the details of SVM overfitting and conducts a rigorous kernel structure analysis. Section 3 demonstrates that the transform-based and filtering-based feature-selection algorithms are unable to overcome overfitting and improve SVM performance, besides investigating related biological reasons for overfitting. Finally, we discuss the role of overfitting in biomarker discovery and our ongoing and future work before concluding our paper.

2   Analysis of Support Vector Machine Overfitting

We employ six benchmark data in our experiment, whose detailed information on these data can be found in Table 1 [3-8]. To demonstrate our results' generality, we implement SVM for each dataset under a 50% holdout cross-validation (HOCV) model selection, where 100 trials of training and test data are randomly generated for each dataset. Compared to other model selections such as k-fold and leave-one-out cross validation (LOOCV), it has a large number of trials in training and test to obtain robust analysis results. Table 2 illustrates SVM performance under linear and Gaussian kernels on six datasets in terms of three classification measures and their standard deviations. It is interesting that overfitting can be easily detected from the complementary average sensitivities and specificities under the Gaussian kernel. For example, the average sensitivities for *Stroma* and *Colon* data are 100% and their corresponding average specificities are 0.0%. On the other hand, there is no overfitting associated with the '*linear*' kernel, though the classification performance is far from the expectations from a molecular diagnostic viewpoint. The question is '*why does a SVM classifier encounter overfitting under the Gaussian kernel?*' We answer this question by conduct SVM kernel matrix analysis as follows.

Table 1. Six benchmark gene expression array data sets

Dataset	#Genes	#Samples
Stroma	18995	13 inflammatory breast cancer + 34 non-inflammatory breast cancer
Colon	2000	22 controls + 40 cancers
Medulloblastoma	5893	25 classic + 9 desmoplastic
Prostate	12625	59 controls + 77 cancers
BRCA1	3226	7 BRCA1 mutations +15 non-BRCA1 mutations
BREAST	24188	46 breast cancer patients with distant metastasis within 5 year + 51 breast cancer patients remain disease-free within 5 years

Table 2. SVM classification results and standard deviations under the 50% HOCV

Dataset	Average Classification Rates (%)	Average Sensitivity(%)	Average Specificity (%)
kernel:'Gaussian'			
Stroma	72.70±06.48	100.0±00.00	00.00±00.00
Colon	62.81±06.41	100.0±00.00	00.00±00.00
Medulloblastoma	73.47±07.55	00.00±00.00	100.0±00.00
Prostate	55.81±06.06	95.00±21.90	05.00±21.90
BRCA1	65.82±12.20	98.00±14.07	02.00±14.07
BREAST	47.25±05.08	69.00±46.48	31.00±46.48
kernel:'linear'			
Stroma	73.83±07.02	92.87±06.58	25.45±15.82
Colon	80.74±07.20	87.46±07.38	70.91±16.67
Medulloblastoma	78.18±09.72	48.23±31.49	95.68±19.34
Prostate	91.37±03.20	90.37±04.36	92.78±05.80
BRCA1	74.18±11.32	92.04±10.50	45.78±33.40
BREAST	63.04±05.48	65.81±11.20	61.59±13.17

As an interface between input data and a learning machine, a kernel matrix contains all priori knowledge for an SVM classifier and derives its generalization bound. It is natural to turn to kernel matrices to analyze overfitting. Interestingly, we have found that SVM kernel matrices of all datasets are the identity or near identity matrices under the standard Gaussian kernel. A near identity matrix is a matrix whose diagonal entries are all '1's but its non-diagonal elements are zero or approximately zero. Specially, we treat population data are viewed as the training dataset to calculate the kernel matrix, which includes all possible training samples in an SVM implemented by any cross validations. Obviously, such a kernel matrix not only makes an SVM lose its generalization, but also demonstrates special characteristics in classification.

Figure 1 illustrates that all six Gaussian kernel matrices are identity or near the identity matrices. The sub-figure 1 in Figure 1 shows that the minimum values of all possible square distances between the samples $\|x_i - x_j\|^2$ are in the interval $(2^{7.501}, 2^{11.687})$. It is easy to find that any non-diagonal kernel entry is $< \exp(-2^{3.136})$ for the prostate data, and they all are $< \exp(-2^{7.501})$ for the other five datasets. Such findings are further highlighted by the sums of non-diagonal entries in each kernel matrix (the sub-figure 2), where the sums are zero for all five data except the prostate data. Although the non-diagonal kernel entry sum on *prostate* data is $\sum_{i \neq j} k_{ij} = 3.156 \times 10^{-4}$, the sub-figure 3 shows there are only 18 lower-triangle elements $> 10^{-10}$ in its kernel matrix i.e., the matrix is a near identity matrix with all eigenvalues equal to 1.

Since an identity or near identity kernel matrices can only represent the concept of identity and have no way to generalize to other new data, it is the reason why an SVM classifier with the Gaussian kernel encounters overfitting. However, all linear kernel matrices are regular Gram matrices with a unique eigenvalue corresponding to each sample. The sub-figure 4 shows the eigenvalues of the linear and Gaussian kernel matrix of *Prostate* data, which indicates that their SVM kernel matrices are a normal matrix and near-identity matrix from an eigenvalue standing point.

In fact, an SVM classifier will demonstrate special characteristics in gene expression array classification due to overfitting: *it can only recognize the majority type of a training data no matter the type of a test sample*. The following theorem states the special characteristic in classification and its proof is skipped for the limit of space.

Theorem 1. Let $X = [x_1, x_2, \cdots x_n]^T$, $x_i \in \mathbb{R}^m$ be a binary training dataset with label information: $c = [c_1, c_2 \cdots c_n]^T$, $c_i \in \{-1, 1\}$, drawn from a population microarray profile $D \in \mathbb{R}^{N \times m}$ ($N > n$), inputted to a SVM specified by Eq. (1) with a kernel $k(x \cdot y)$. If the kernel term is zero or approximately zero, i.e., $k(x_i \propto x_j) \sim 0$ for $\forall x_i, x_j \in D, i \neq j$, then, (1) the bias term in Eq. (1) $b = \frac{n_1 - n_2}{2n}$, where $n_1 = |\{c_i | c_i = 1\}|$ and $n_2 = |\{c_i | c_i = -1\}|$.

(2) $\forall x' \in D - X$, its class type can be determined by $f(x') = sign(n_1 - n_2)$, i.e.,

where $f(x')=0$ means SVM cannot determine the class type of x' and the corresponding classification rate will be zero

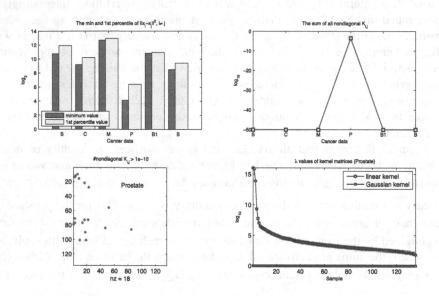

Fig. 1. The sub-fig 1 (NW) shows that the minimum values of all possible square distances between the samples; sub-fig 2 (NE) shows the sums of all kernel matrix non-diagonal entries; sub-fig 3 (SW) visualizes the non-diagonal entries $>10^{-10}$ in the lower triangle Gaussian kernel matrix for the prostate data; sub-fig 4 (SE) displays the eigenvalues of the linear and Gaussian kernel matrix of prostate data

Note that choosing different sigma values instead of setting σ^1 in the Gaussian kernel still cannot avoid overfitting or increase classification performance. For instance, we selected the σ^2 value as the mean of non-diagonal elements in the kernel matrix for *Colon* and *Medulloblastoma* data and implemented SVM with the Gaussian kernel under 1000 trials of 50% HOCV. We had the following results: the average classification, sensitivity, and specificity and their STD are 0.689742 ± 0.098169, 0.932122 ± 0.072402, 0.292699 ± 0.257365 for the colon data; and 0.729882 ± 0.078509, 0.012167 ± 0.099167, 0.996115 ± 0.047601 for the medulloblastoma data. They still encountered overfittting in spite the change of values of the sigma, and their kernel matrices are still identity or near the identity matrix. Similar cases also happened for the other data sets.

3   SVM Overfitting under Feature Selection

We have found that general feature selection algorithms can not overcome SVM overfitting. The feature selection algorithms range from statistical tests based filtering algorithms (e.g., t-tests) to transform-based feature selection techniques such as principal component analysis (PCA), independent component analysis (ICA), nonnegative matrix factorization (NMF), and their different variants [9-11,4]. We first employed Bayesian two-sample t-test as a representative to investigate the impact of filtering-based feature selection algorithms on overfitting [12]. As such, we selected top 100, 50 and 10 differentially expressed genes ranked by it from each dataset, which will work as input data for an SVM classifier. We have found that the low-dimensional data generally are unable to avoid overfitting under the standard Gaussian kernel for all three model selections: 100 trials of 50% HOCV, LOOCV, and k-fold CV (k=10). This result suggests that SVM overfitting seems to have less relationship with input data dimensionality. Moreover, we run each gene under an SVM classifier with the standard Gaussian kernel, and found that some single genes even suffered from overfitting under LOOCV also, that is, the SVM classifier can only recognize the majority sample type for this single gene.

Note that selected top genes ranked by the Bayesian t-test show some level improvements in classification on some data under the linear kernel. However, the improvements are not consistent for all data. For example, SVM classification of the 100 top-ranked genes, the average classification rate for *Colon* data is 83.97%, which is greater than the original 80.12% performance on full data. But the average classification rate of *Prostate* data is 85.75%, which is much less than the original 91.37% level performance on its full data.

Moreover, we have found that overfitting cannot be avoided or overcome through integrating SVM with transform-based feature selection algorithms. We implemented PCA-SVM, ICA-SVM and NMF-SVM algorithms in our experiments. Specially, we employed a 100% explained variance percentage (EVP) to conduct PCA feature selection, which is a ratio between the accumulative variance from the selected data and the total data variance. For example, the explained variance percentage ρ_r from

the first r PCs is defined as, $\rho_r = \sum_{i=1}^{r} \lambda_i / \sum_{j=1}^{n} \lambda_j$, where λ_i is the data variance on the ith

PC. We employed a projected-gradient nonnegative matrix factorization (PG-NMF) and FastICA algorithm to implement NMF and ICA respectively for their fast and robust convergence [12,10]. The number of independent components (ICs) was selected as the dimension of the input data in ICA-SVM. The matrix decomposition rank is selected as $r = 2 \sim 10$ in NMF-SVM. Specially, the best average classification rate among the 9 rounds of 100 trials of classifications is counted as the final average classification rate for the NMF-SVM algorithm.

We have the following findings based on our simulations. First, it seems that PCA-SVM, ICA-SVM, and NMF-SVM classifiers have no statistically significant advantages over SVM in performance under the liner kernel (data not shown). Second, it seems that none of them can be free from overfitting under the Gaussian kernel, though NMF-SVM may avoid overfitting on some datasets due to NMF's parts-based learning mechanism occasionally. Table 3 includes the average classification rates, sensitivities, and specificities and their standard deviations of the three algorithms under the Gaussian kernel on three datasets.

It is clear that PCA-SVM and ICA-SVM overfittings are still rooted in the built-in large data variations between samples: $\parallel x_i - x_j \parallel^2$, which are further amplified in the transform-based projections in following SVM classifiers. Finally, the exponential transform in Gaussian kernels causes distances between two different samples to be zero or approximately zero in the feature space such that the classifiers lose discriminant capabilities and encounter overfitting. Although NMF-SVM demonstrates potential in overcoming overfitting by avoiding this term involved in computing kernel entries, the NMF's stochastic nature and high-complexity limit its consistency, stability, and its application to large datasets with more samples.

Table 3. PCA-SVM, ICA-SVM, and NMF-SVM classification performance

Dataset	Average Classification Rates (%)	Average Sensitivity (%)	Average Specificity (%)
pca-svm-gaussian			
Stroma	72.70±06.48	100.0±00.00	00.00±00.00
Medulloblastoma	73.47±07.55	00.00±00.00	100.0±00.00
BREAST	47.25±05.08	69.00±46.48	31.00±46.48
ica-svm-gaussian			
Stroma	71.70±06.48	100.0±00.00	00.00±00.00
Medulloblastoma	73.47±07.55	00.00±00.00	100.0±00.00
BREAST	47.25±05.08	69.00±46.48	31.00±46.48
nmf-svm-gaussian			
Stroma	72.70±06.48	100.0±00.00	00.00±00.00
Medulloblastoma	82.18±08.99	58.98±27.03	91.98±08.11
BREAST	58.13±06.99	65.05±12.62	52.53±16.50

Biological Root for Overfitting. Up to now, all our experimental results suggest that the large built-in variations between biological samples are responsible for SVM overfitting. The question is 'which biological factors are responsible for the large built-in variations between biological samples?' The answer is rooted in DNA molecule amplification process in transcriptional profiling technologies used in array technologies. DNA amplification techniques are essential for array expression data to detect cancers in a molecular level through monitoring gene expression changes. Microarray techniques generally amplify DNA molecules as targets for hybridization by quantitative polymerase chain reaction (PCR) amplification in the case of cDNA arrays, or direct synthesis in the case of oligonucleotide arrays [14]. The raw PCR fluorescence data is fitted into an exponential curve and the exponential nature of the quantitative PCR amplification determines the exponential increase of the biological sample expression variations in profiling [14]. Moreover, since all DNA and RNA molecules follow similar hybridization kinetics, a heterogeneous probe can simultaneously hybridize thousands of DNA sequences arrayed on a solid substrate in the microarray technology. The heterogeneous hybridizations mechanism contributes to the increase of the already exponentially amplified transcription signal variations between samples. Thus, a microarray profile is characterized by large built-in variation between samples.

4   Discussion and Conclusion

In this work, we analyzed SVM overfitting on gene expression array data and theoretically proved that an SVM classifier will inevitably encounter overfitting by demonstrating special classification characteristics by only recognizing the majority type for any test samples. In addition, we demonstrated that general transform-based and filtering-based feature selection algorithms actually cannot contribute to overcoming overfitting effectively by integrating with an SVM classifier. In addition to pointing out the biological root of overfitting, we showed that SVM classifiers integrated with PCA, ICA, and NMF have same level performance in microarray data classification as the a standard SVM classifier. It is noted that single-gene overfitting can be employed to identify effective biomarkers for gene expression array data, if we view such overfitting as a gene-switch mechanism, i.e., a gene encounters overfitting means its gene switch 'closed' for providing meaningful diagnostic information. We designed a filter-wrapper biomarker identification algorithm by taking advantage of signee-gene overfitting to search biomarkers among the top-ranked genes without overfitting (algorithm details not shown). We applied it to *medulloblastoma* data and identified two biomarkers: NDP and CDC25A identified among 178 top-ranked non-overfitting genes by using Bayesian t-test. The total SVM accuracy achieved under the two biomarkers achieves 97.06% with 100.0% specificity and 88.89% sensitivity, which is much higher than all previous at most 82% level classification. Moreover, both biomarkers were reported as meaningful gene markers related to brain tumor diseases in previous studies [15].

It is worthy to point out that simply changing Gaussian kernel parameters will not contribute to overcoming SVM overfitting. However, we would like to further investigate potential overfitting overcome algorithms by integrating improved NMF algorithms in support vector machine classifications. In the future work, we plan to employ sparse coding techniques or nonnegative parameter argument approaches to improve the generality and robustness of data representation in NMF and decrease the complexities of NMF by exploring embedding wavelet based multi-resolution techniques in NMF [16].

References

1. Vapnik, V.N.: Statistical Learning Theory. John Wiley & Sons, New York (1998)
2. Han, X.: Nonnegative Principal component Analysis for Cancer Molecular Pattern Discovery. IEEE/ACM Transaction of Computational Biology and Bioinformatics 7(3), 537–549 (2010)
3. Han, H., Li, X.-L.: Multi-resolution Independent Component Analysis for High-Performance Tumor Classification and Biomarker Discovery. BMC Bioinformatics 12(S1), S7 (2011)

4. Boersma, B.J., et al.: A stromal gene signature associated with inflammatory breast cancer. Int. J. Cancer 122(6), 1324–1332 (2008)
5. Brunet, J., Tamayo, P., Golub, T., Mesirov, J.: Molecular pattern discovery using matrix factorization. Proc. Natl Acad. Sci. USA 101(12), 4164–4169 (2004)
6. Singh, D., et al.: Gene expression correlates of clinical prostate cancer behavior. Cancer Cell 1(2), 203–209 (2002)
7. Hedenfalk, I., et al.: Gene-Expression Profiles in Hereditary Breast Cancer. The New England Journal of Medicine 344, 539–548 (2001)
8. van 't Veer, L.J., et al.: Gene Expression Profiling Predicts Clinical Outcome of Breast Cancer. Nature 415(6871), 530–536 (2001)
9. Jolliffe, I.T.: Principal Component Analysis, 2nd edn. Springer Series in Statistics. Springer, NY (2002)
10. Hyvärinen, A., Karhunen, J., Oja, E.: Independent Component Analysis. Wiley, New York (2001)
11. Lin, C.: Projected gradient methods for non-negative matrix factorization. Neural Computation 19(10), 2756–2779 (2007)
12. Fox, R., Dimmic, M.: A two-sample Bayesian t-test for microarray data. BMC Bioinformatics 7(126) (2006)
13. Twyman, R., Primrose, S.: Principles of gene manipulation and genomics, 7th edn. Blackwell Publishing (2006)
14. Stein, A., et al.: A Serial Analysis of Gene Expression (SAGE) Database Analysis of Chemosensitivity: Comparing Solid Tumors with Cell Lines and Comparing Solid Tumors from Different Tissue Origins. Cancer Research 64, 2805–2816 (2004)
15. Pomeroy, S.L., et al.: Prediction of central nervous system embryonal tumour outcome based on gene expression. Nature 415(6870), 436–442 (2002)
16. Han, H.: A novel profile-biomarker diagnosis for mass spectral proteomics. In: Pacific Symposium on Biocomputing (PSB), vol. 19, pp. 340–351 (2014)

Evolutionary Design of Synthetic Gene Networks by Means of a Semantic Expert System

Paolo Pannarale and Vitoantonio Bevilacqua

Department of Electrical and Information Engineering, Politecnico di Bari, Bari, 70125 Italy
vitoantonio.bevilacqua@poliba.it

Abstract. In the last decade many researchers proposed tools and methods for the automatic generation of synthetic biological devices with desired functions. However, advances in synthetic biology have been limited by a lack of frameworks meeting the essential requirements of standardization, modularity, complexity and re-use. The present work tries to cope with the standardization issue by the adoption of model exchange standards like CellML, BioBrick standard biological parts and standard signal carriers for modeling purpose. The generated models are made of SVP modular components. Model complexity includes more interaction dynamics than previous works. The inherent software complexity has been handled by a rational use of ontologies and rule engine. The database of parts and interactions is automatically created from publicly available whole system models. Built on this automatic modeling component, a genetic algorithm has been implemented, that searches the space of possible genetic circuits for an optimal circuit meeting user defined input-output dynamics. The system has been successfully tested on two test cases. This work proposes a new approach able of pushing forward the complexity managed by genetic circuits automatic design tools.

Keywords: Biological system modeling, Design automation, DNA, Expert systems, Genetic algorithms.

1   Introduction

Historically, biology has made less use of a mathematical approach, compared to other scientific disciplines (such as physics and chemistry). However, biology is now closely linked to information science that tries to make up for this shortcoming by providing the typical results of biochemistry and molecular biology with a set of analytical and numerical tools, models, algorithms, and databases.

The definition of standardized interfaces for genetic components (e.g. PoPs and RIPs) has led to the development of drag-and-drop tools, in which the components are taken from a palette and placed on the design for being connected with hypothetical wiring as can be seen in many software for the design of electronic circuits [1]. One of the first tools of this kind is Biojade [2], followed by very flexible software, like TinkerCell [3]. An interesting approach to modularity has been achieved with Asmparts [4], which describes each biological component with a SBML file.

D.-S. Huang et al. (Eds.): ICIC 2014, LNBI 8590, pp. 157–163, 2014.

Also web applications like GenoCAD [5] appeared recently, which implements an algorithm of syntax check of the circuits designed [6].

In addition to aided design, tools for the automatic design and optimization of genetic circuits have appeared [7], also specifically for BioBrick systems [8][9]. They can assist the designer through the generation, storage, research and simulation of synthetic biological networks but with some limitations. The existing tools may not adopt standard signal carriers as PoPs and RiPs, may not accurately model the transcription and translation steps, may not take into account non genetic interactions, may use hypothetical components, may produce not exchangeable output, may be difficult to be configured or to be extended with additional biological parts, may not label the entities with standard identifiers, may not represents the parts as modules, may require the user to define the network topology. A sequence of biological components can be automatically transformed into a set of reactions, for the simulation of the resulting system. In most cases it is however necessary human intervention, for example to set the value of certain kinetic parameters. To our best knowledge no tool exists which does not show a couple of these limitations.

This is the context of the present work, a tool named ARChITeCt (Automatic geneRation of genetic CIrcuiT models from biobriCk parts), which aims at building a system capable of generating gene networks that have desired input-output characteristics overcoming some of the limitations of the previous approaches.

Moreover, our tool is the only capable of using a library of parts, dynamically generated from other system models available from public databases [10]. The tool automatically infers the chemical and genetic interactions occurring between entities of the repository models and applies them in the target model if opportune. The repository models have to be modeled by a specific CellML standard, the Standard Virtual Parts (SVP) [11] formalism and the components have to be annotated with OWL for unique identifiers [12], or more in the future. We believe that this detail could foster the characterization of biological components [13][14].

The output of the automatic process is a sequence of readily composable biological components, deposited in the registry of parts, and a complete CellML kinetic model of the system. A stimulation protocol can be specified by CellML. The kinetic parameters are automatically extracted from the models in public repositories. Accordingly, a model can be generated and simulated from a sequence of BioBrick, without any human intervention.

The major part of the existing tools applies only to very simple systems with a limited number of interaction dynamics. This is due to the exponential increase of complexity that arises from a more realistic scenario. Actual tools present a moderated degree of accuracy in the prediction of the behavior, principally due to the lack of consideration of many cellular factors [15]. Despite the advances in molecular construction, modeling and fine-tuning the behavior of synthetic circuits remains extremely challenging [16]. We tried to cope with this issue of scalability by means of ontologies coupled with a rule engine [17]. Model complexity includes more interaction dynamics than previous works, including gene regulation, interaction between small molecules and proteins but also protein-protein and post-transcriptional regulation. Ontologies are now pervasive in biomedicine [18] and represent a powerful tool for the researchers working in this field. In fact, to achieve our goal we used OWL ontologies for the description of the domain and Jess rules for adding complex logic. Ontologies have been yet used in conjunction with CellML [19][20] and to address the problem of collaboration among system biologists [21][22].

A genetic algorithm can then search in the space of gene networks that better exhibit the desired input-output behavior. The system has been tested using the existing SVP models archive on the web for the generation of two sample systems.

2   Material and Methods

The search algorithm used is a genetic algorithm defined in such a way that the chromosomes represent real biological plasmids. The candidate solutions are transformed into a CellML model by an expert system, called MCE (Model Construction Engine). The engine adopts a hybrid strategy based on OWL and Jess rules. This choice allows the use of the many ontologies created for the world of molecular biology, to exploit the effectiveness of ontologies in the representation of the entities of a domain, but also exploits the flexibility and simplicity of implementation of Jess rules. The whole path from genotype to fitness can be summarized in the following steps:

- The Genetic algorithm chromosome is translated into a syntactically checked sequence of biological genes on one or more plasmids;
- The CellML models in the repository are translated in OWL ontologies and are joint to an intensive domain ontology;
- The OWL ontologies are translated in Jess facts organized as triples;
- Also the candidate biological system is represented as Jess triples;
- The Jess engine uses OWL inference rules and domain rules to infer the occurring biological interactions;
- The resulting system is represented as a modular CellML model;
- An ode simulation of the model is compared to the target behavior to compute the fitness.

Different versions of the genetic algorithm were implemented. The population is randomly initialized and then enters the evolutionary cycle. The first step is the determination of the value of fitness for each individual. In the elitist version the best individual is selected to be added back in the next generation. The genetic operators are single point crossover and mutation operators. Two different natural selection strategies have been tested: Weighted Roulette and Best Chromosomes. A given percentage of individuals is selected for the next generation, which is repopulated randomly to replace the non-selected individuals. The GA parameters have been settled based on heuristics and a trial and error process. The algorithm has been developed using the JGAP (Java Genetic Algorithms Package) framework.

2.1   Model Construction Engine

The model construction step (Fig. 1) involves the reconstruction of the molecular dynamics, the process of transcription, translation, regulation of transcription and the interactions between chemical species, between enzymatic species and between chemical species and enzymatic species. This has to be contextualized to the host cell and quantified. The necessary information could be scattered in multiple models of the repository. Once logically reconstructed, the model has to be translated into a CellML model, in terms of components, variables, connections, sums of flows, flow equations, initial values and multiple encapsulations. This process normally engages an experienced researcher for many hours, combining different tools and data sources [23, 24], both in the reconstruction phase and the implementation phase, not without generating errors and often severe headaches. In the transition from CellML to Jess an additional stage has been introduced: the introduction of a semantic layer based on OWL-DL.

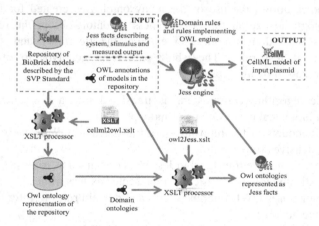

Fig. 1. The Model Construction Engine uses a combination of OWL ontologies and Jess rules to achieve its task. The transition between CellML to OWL and from OWL to Jess is performed by XSLT transformations.

3   Results

The architectural choices give important effects in terms of implementation complexity. The total code volume is high for the Java and C++ components, while it is limited for the remaining components, which actually enclose most of the complexity of the system. The Jess components are characterized by a high number of compact and fragmented rules.

In the first testing scenario the BugBuster and ElectrEcoBlu iGEM project models were taken from the CellML repository and dropped in the ARChITeCt models repository folder. The target model is a hybrid system, which produces pyocianin, as ElectrEcoBlu [25], in order to be able to detect the output signal electrically, but which responds to the presence of pathogenic organisms, as in BugBuster [26], rather than to pollutants. The system found several admissible solutions for the given design objective. The repressilator is an oscillatory synthetic gene network designed by Elowitz *et al.* [27]. The network has been implemented in the bacterium Escherichia coli and is obtained through three genes connected in mutual repression, in such a way that each gene represses the next gene in the circuit. The output of the model obtained by the Construction Engine Model includes 30 components, 23 import, 6 equations, 24 variables, 56 connections and 2 units and takes some hours to be developed by hand but a few minutes with the aid of ARChITeCt. The Model Construction Engine processing time is strongly dependent on the dimensionality of the repository, and is in the order of a few tens of seconds. Also the phenotype length affects the elaboration.

4   Discussion

The MCE component proved to handle properly the automatic generation of the kinetic models of systems characterized by different mechanisms of gene regulation, interaction between small molecules and proteins but also protein-protein and post-transcriptional regulation, and by means of PoPs and RIPs signal carriers. The logic required is enclosed in a few thousand lines of code. The search algorithm has been able to identify optimal solutions in the formulated test cases. In the first test case there are biological components and interactions coming from two different models of the repository. The genetic algorithm showed sensitivity to parameter variations and premature convergence issues. A proper setting of the parameters, however, guarantees to obtain the optimal solution. The same configuration of the first test case, named ElectrEco-Buster, was valid in the Repressilator test case.

ARChITeCt is the only system capable of generating a system directly from the sequence of its component parts which considers non genetic interactions. Only TinkerCell and ARChITeCt have a database of parts automatically populated. In fact, TinkerCell can connect to RegulonDB in order to get a qualitative list the parts and of their interactions, but also with the Standard Biological Parts knowledgebase (SBPkb) [28], which build on the previous work of the Provisional BioBrick Language (PoBoL) [29], but does not contain kinetic information. These databases are the result of a manual data insert. Only ARChITeCt automatically builds its knowledge base from whole system models. Finally, ARChITeCt is the only system that can harness the power of semantic knowledge representation and rule business logic modeling.

5   Conclusion

This work, which represents a proof of concept rather than a ready-to-use tool, based on what has been done by Cooling *et al.*, offers an innovative way to the characterization of biological components. The intelligent system and the combinatorial optimization algorithm developed, allow the automatic design and automatic modeling of genetic circuits, based on the reuse of models built according to synthetic biology standards, and encourage the characterization of new biological components. This work also proposes a technological approach to handle the high complexity and evolving nature of its biological domain, in accordance with technological standards already established in this field, such as ontologies. The creation of a web-based platform, built on ARChITeCt, that stores and makes available models of characterized biological components, for flexible sharing among researchers, represents the following development step. To make ARChITeCt usable in practice two factors should also be considered: robustness and biological feasibility. The delivered systems robustness with respect to parameter uncertainties, systemic uncertainties, noise, etc. should be included in fitness calculation, also through the use of multi-objective genetic algorithms; It is also important to enrich the rules, with constraints that ensure as much as possible the identified systems being biologically feasible. Finally, future reworks should adopt the more widely spread and interoperable SBML language, taking benefits of the recent introductions in the standard and of several experiments [30], combining the knowledge coming from genomics, proteomics, transcriptomics and dynamical systems theory. Moreover with SBML it is possible to convert the SBML into multiple modeling approaches, e.g. ode, stochastic, flux balance, Boolean, whereas in CellML this is not possible. The tool source code is available at http://tinyurl.com/ky8mwrk .

References

1. Kelly, J.R.: Biological Engineering Division, Tools and Reference Standards Supporting the Engineering and Evolution of Synthetic Biological Systems. Massachusetts Institute of Technology, Biological Engineering Division (2008)
2. Knight Jr., T., Goler, J., et al.: Biojade: A Design and Simulation Tool for Synthetic Biological Systems, Ph.D. dissertation, Massachusetts Institute of Technology (2004)
3. Chandran, D., Bergmann, F.T., Sauro, H.M.: TinkerCell: Modular CAD Tool for Synthetic Biology. Journal of Biological Engineering 3, 19 (2009)
4. Rodrigo, G., Carrera, J., Jaramillo, A.: Asmparts: Assembly of Biological Model Parts. Systems and Synthetic Biology 1(4), 167–170 (2007)
5. Cai, Y., Wilson, M.L., Peccoud, J.: GenoCAD for iGEM: a Grammatical Approach to the Design of Standard-Compliant Constructs. Nucleic Acids Research 38(8), 2637–2644 (2010)
6. Cai, Y., Hartnett, B., Gustafsson, C., Peccoud, J.: A Syntactic Model to Design and Verify Synthetic Genetic Constructs Derived from Standard Biological Parts. Bioinformatics 23(20), 2760–2767 (2007)
7. Marchisio, M.A., Stelling, J.: Computational Design Tools for Synthetic Biology. Current Opinion in Biotechnology 20(4), 479–485 (2009)
8. Weeding, E., Houle, J., Swiniarski, B., Smadbeck, P., Lindblad, K., Volzing, K., Srivastava, P., Sotiropoulos, V., Biliouris, K., Kaznessis, Y.: Bbf Rfc 40: How to Build Kinetic Models of Biobricks. The BioBricks Foundation, Tech. Rep. (2009)
9. Wang, Z., Liao, C., Jiang, H., Yao, X., Jiang, K.: Bbf Rfc 55: Standard Biological Part Automatic Modeling Database Language (Model). The BioBricks Foundation, Tech. Rep. (2010)
10. Beard, D.A., Britten, R., Cooling, M.T., et al.: CellML Metadata Standards, Associated Tools and Repositories. Philosophical Transactions. Series A, Mathematical, Physical, and Engineering Sciences 367(1895), 1845–1867 (2009)

11. Cooling, M.T., Rouilly, V., Misirli, G., et al.: Standard Virtual Biological Parts: a Repository of Modular Modeling Components for Synthetic Biology. Bioinformatics (Oxford, England) 26(7), 925–931 (2010)
12. Novère, N.L., Finney, A., Hucka, M., et al.: engMinimum Information Requested in the Annotation of Biochemical Models (Miriam). engNat Biotechnol. 23(12), 1509–1515 (2005)
13. Kelly, J.R., Rubin, A.J., Davis, J.H., et al.: Measuring the Activity of Biobrick Promoters Using an in Vivo Reference Standard. Journal of Biological Engineering 3, 4 (2009)
14. Conboy, C., Braff, J., Endy, D.: Definitions and Measures of Performance for Standard Biological Parts (2006)
15. Rodrigo, G., Carrera, J., Landrain, T., Jaramillo, A.: Perspectives on the Automatic Design of Regulatory Systems for Synthetic Biology. FEBS Letters 586(15), 2037–2042 (2012)
16. Lu, T.K., Khalil, A.S., Collins, J.J.: Next-Generation Synthetic Gene Networks. Nature Biotechnology 27(12), 1139–1150 (2009)
17. Pannarale, P., Catalano, D., De Caro, G., et al.: Gidl: a Rule Based Expert System for Genbank Intelligent Data Loading Into The Molecular Biodiversity Database. BMC Bioinformatics 13(suppl. 4), S4 (2012)
18. Hoehndorf, R., Dumontier, M., Gkoutos, G.V.: engEvaluation of Research in Biomedical Ontologies. engBrief Bioinform (2012)
19. Wimalaratne, S.M., Halstead, M.D.B., Lloyd, C.M., et al.: A Method For Visualizing Cellml Models. Bioinformatics (Oxford, England) 25(22), 3012–3019 (2009)
20. Shimayoshi, T., Komurasaki, K., Amano, A., Iwashita, T., Matsuda, T., Kanazawa, M.: A Method to Support Cell Physiological Modelling Using Description Language and Ontology. IPSJ Digital Courier 2(1), 726–735 (2006)
21. Sun, Z.: Using Ontology and Semantic Web Services to Support Modeling in Systems Biology: Ph.D. dissertation, University College London (2009)
22. Matos, E.E., Campos, F., Braga, R., Palazzi, D.: CelOWS: An Ontology Based Framework for The Provision of Semantic Web Services Related to Biological Models. Journal of Biomedical Informatics 43(1), 125–136 (2010) (Online)
23. Wierling, C., Herwig, R., Lehrach, H.: Resources, Standards and Tools for Systems Biology. Brief Funct Genomic Proteomic 6, 240–251 (2007)
24. Ng, A., Bursteinas, B., Gao, Q., Mollison, E., Zvelebil, M.: engResources for Integrative Systems Biology: from Data Through Databases to Networks and Dynamic System Models. engBrief Bioinform. 7(4), 318–330 (2006)
25. Gilbert, D., Rosser, S.: Electrecoblu. In: iGEM (2007)
26. Aylward, M., Chalder, R., Nielsen-Dzumhur, N., Taschuk, M., Thompson, J., Wappett, M.: Bugbuster: Computational Design of a Bacterial Biosensor. In: iGEM (2008)
27. Elowitz, M., Leibler, S.: A Synthetic Oscillatory Network of Transcriptional Regulators. Nature 403(6767), 335–338 (2000)
28. Galdzicki, M., Rodriguez, C., Chandran, D., Sauro, H.M., Gennari, J.H.: Standard Biological Parts Knowledgebase. PLoS ONE 6(2), e17005 (2011)
29. Galdzicki, M., Chandran, D., Nielsen, A., Morrison, J., Cowell, M., Grünberg, R., Sleight, S., Sauro, H.: BBF RFC #31: Provisional Biobrick Language (pobol). Tech. Rep. (2009)
30. Bevilacqua, V., Pannarale, P., Abbrescia, M., Cava, C.A., Tommasi, S.: Comparison of Data-merging Methods with SVM attribute Selection and Classification in Breast Cancer Gene Expression. BMC Bioinformatics 13(suppl. 7), S9 (2012) (Online)

Stability and Oscillation of the Solutions for a Coupled FHN Model with Time Delays

Yuanhua Lin

School of Mathematics and Statistics, Hechi University, Yizhou, Guangxi 546300, China
lyh4473@163.com

Abstract. A FitzHugh–Nagumo (FHN) model with delayed coupling is considered to investigate the stability and oscillatory behavior of the solutions due to the coupling strength and delay. Two theorems of sufficient conditions are given to guarantee the stability and oscillation of the solutions by constructing of Liapunov functional and applying the Chafee's limit cycle criterion. Computer simulations are provided to illustrate the correctness of our theoretical analysis. Some results in the literature about coupled FHN systems are extended.

Keywords: coupled FHN model, equilibrium, instability, oscillation.

1   Introduction

It is well known that the FitzHugh–Nagumo (FHN) model with delayed coupling will exhibit rich dynamical behavior than a simplified version of FHN equation. In the past two decades, many researches have studied the various dynamical behaviors such as stability, oscillation, bifurcation and periodic solutions for different models [1-8]. In [1], the authors have investigated the effects of time delay on bifurcation and synchronization in two synaptically coupled FHN neurons as follows:

$$\frac{dv_1}{dt} = -v_1^3 + av_1 - w_1 + c_1 \tanh\left(v_2\left(t-\tau\right)\right),$$

$$\frac{dw_1}{dt} = v_1 - b_1 w_1,$$

$$\frac{dv_2}{dt} = -v_2^3 + av_2 - w_2 + c_2 \tanh\left(v_1\left(t-\tau\right)\right), \tag{1}$$

$$\frac{dw_2}{dt} = v_2 - b_2 w_2.$$

where $v_1\left(t\right)$ and $v_2\left(t\right)$ represent the transmembrane voltages, $w_1\left(t\right), w_2\left(t\right)$ model the time dependence of several physical quantities related to electrical variables. Some bifurcation diagrams are obtained numerically or analytically from

D.-S. Huang et al. (Eds.): ICIC 2014, LNBI 8590, pp. 164–174, 2014.
© Springer International Publishing Switzerland 2014

the mathematical model and the parameter regions of different behavior are clarified. Fan and Hong extended model (1) to two delays system:

$$x_1'(t) = -x_1^3(t) + ax_1(t) - x_2(t) + c_1 \tanh(x_3(t - \tau_1)),$$
$$x_2'(t) = x_1(t) - b_1 x_2(t),$$
$$x_3'(t) = -x_3^3(t) + ax_3(t) - x_4(t) + c_2 \tanh(x_1(t - \tau_2)),$$
$$x_4'(t) = x_3(t) - b_2 x_4(t).$$

(2)

The authors regarded the delay $\tau = \tau_1 + \tau_2$ as a parameter to investigate the stability and bifurcation to the model (2). They have shown that under certain assumptions the steady state of the model is asymptotically stable. Under another set of conditions, there is a critical value of the parameter, the steady state is stable when the parameter is less than the critical value and unstable when the parameter is greater than the critical value [2]. Zhen and Xu have consider a three coupled FHN neural system with one delay as follows [3]:

$$u_1'(t) = -\frac{1}{3}u_1^3(t) + cu_1^2(t) + du_1(t) - u_2(t) + \alpha u_1^2(t)$$
$$+ \beta\left[f(u_3(t - \tau)) + f(u_5(t - \tau)) \right],$$
$$u_2'(t) = \varepsilon(u_1(t) - bu_2(t)),$$
$$u_3'(t) = -\frac{1}{3}u_3^3(t) + cu_3^2(t) + du_3(t) - u_4(t) + \alpha u_3^2(t)$$
$$+ \beta\left[f(u_1(t - \tau)) + f(u_5(t - \tau)) \right],$$
$$u_4'(t) = \varepsilon(u_3(t) - bu_4(t)),$$
$$u_5'(t) = -\frac{1}{3}u_5^3(t) + cu_5^2(t) + du_5(t) - u_6(t) + \alpha u_5^2(t)$$
$$+ \beta\left[f(u_1(t - \tau)) + f(u_3(t - \tau)) \right],$$
$$u_6'(t) = \varepsilon(u_5(t) - bu_6(t)).$$

(3)

where $f(u_i(t - \tau))$ $(i = 1,3,5)$ are sufficiently smooth sigmoid amplification functions such as $\tanh(x)$ and $\arctan(x)$. The method of Lyapunov functional is used to obtain the synchronization conditions of the neural system. While Murza [4] has discussed the oscillation patterns in a symmetric network of modified FHN neurons. The author described the building block structure of a three-dimensional lattice shaped as a torus, and identify the symmetry group acting on the coupled differential systems located at the nodes of the lattice. By means of the explicit expressions for eigenvalues and eigenvectors, the existence of limit cycles arose from the Hopf bifurcation which depends on the interneuronal couplings is shown. Motivated by the above models, in this paper, we will discuss the following n coupled FHN model:

$$u_1'(t) = -u_1^3(t) + c_1 u_1^2(t) + d_1 u_1(t) - u_2(t)$$
$$+ \beta_1 \Big[\tanh(u_3(t-\tau)) + \tanh(u_5(t-\tau)) + \cdots + \tanh(u_{2n-1}(t-\tau)) \Big],$$
$$u_2'(t) = \varepsilon_1 u_1(t) - b_2 u_2(t),$$
$$u_3'(t) = -u_3^3(t) + c_3 u_3^2(t) + d_3 u_3(t) - u_4(t)$$
$$+ \beta_3 \Big[\tanh(u_1(t-\tau)) + \tanh(u_5(t-\tau)) + \cdots + \tanh(u_{2n-1}(t-\tau)) \Big], \qquad (4)$$
$$u_4'(t) = \varepsilon_3 u_3(t) - b_4 u_4(t),$$

$$\cdots\cdots\cdots\cdots\cdots\cdots\cdots\cdots\cdots\cdots\cdots\cdots\cdots\cdots\cdots\cdots$$

$$u_{2n-1}'(t) = -u_{2n-1}^3(t) + c_{2n-1} u_{2n-1}^2(t) + d_{2n-1} u_{2n-1}(t) - u_{2n}(t)$$
$$+ \beta_{2n-1} \Big[\tanh(u_1(t-\tau)) + \tanh(u_3(t-\tau)) + \cdots + \tanh(u_{2n-3}(t-\tau)) \Big],$$
$$u_{2n}'(t) = \varepsilon_{2n-1} u_{2n-1}(t) - b_{2n} u_{2n}(t).$$

Where $c_i, d_i, \beta_i, \varepsilon_i \ (i = 1,3,5,\cdots,2n-1)$, and $b_{2i} \ (i=1,2,\cdots,n)$ are constants, $0 < \varepsilon_i \ll 1$.

By means of Chafee's criterion: If a class time delay system has a unique unstable equilibrium point, all solutions of this system are bounded, this system will generate a limit cycle. Namely, the system has a non-constant periodic solution. We will investigate the existence of periodic solutions for model (4).

Preliminaries

The linearization of system (4) about the zero point leads to the following

$$u_1'(t) = d_1 u_1(t) - u_2(t) + \beta_1 u_3(t-\tau) + \beta_1 u_5(t-\tau) + \cdots + \beta_1 u_{2n-1}(t-\tau),$$
$$u_2'(t) = \varepsilon_1 u_1(t) - b_2 u_2(t),$$
$$u_3'(t) = d_3 u_3(t) - u_4(t) + \beta_3 u_1(t-\tau) + \beta_3 u_5(t-\tau) + \cdots + \beta_3 u_{2n-1}(t-\tau),$$
$$u_4'(t) = \varepsilon_3 u_3(t) - b_4 u_4(t), \qquad (5)$$

$$\cdots\cdots\cdots\cdots\cdots\cdots\cdots\cdots\cdots\cdots\cdots\cdots\cdots\cdots\cdots\cdots$$

$$u_{2n-1}'(t) = d_{2n-1} u_{2n-1}(t) - u_{2n}(t) + \beta_{2n-1} u_1(t-\tau)$$
$$+ \beta_{2n-1} u_3(t-\tau) + \cdots + \beta_{2n-1} u_{2n-3}(t-\tau),$$
$$u_{2n}'(t) = \varepsilon_{2n-1} u_{2n-1}(t) - b_{2n} u_{2n}(t).$$

The matrix form of system (6) is as follows:

$$U'(t) = PU(t) + QU(t-\tau) \tag{6}$$

where $U(t) = \left[u_1(t), u_2(t), u_3(t), \cdots, u_{2n}(t)\right]^T$,

$U(t-\tau) = \left[u_1(t-\tau), u_2(t-\tau), u_3(t-\tau), \cdots, u_{2n}(t-\tau)\right]^T$, and matrices P and Q are the following:

$$P = \begin{bmatrix}
d_1 & -1 & 0 & 0 & 0 & \cdots & 0 & 0 & 0 \\
\varepsilon_1 & -b_2 & 0 & 0 & 0 & \cdots & 0 & 0 & 0 \\
0 & 0 & d_3 & -1 & 0 & \cdots & 0 & 0 & 0 \\
0 & 0 & \varepsilon_3 & -b_4 & 0 & \cdots & 0 & 0 & 0 \\
\cdots & \cdots & \cdots & \cdots & \cdots & \cdots & \cdots & \cdots & \cdots \\
0 & 0 & 0 & 0 & 0 & \cdots & 0 & d_{2n-1} & -1 \\
0 & 0 & 0 & 0 & 0 & \cdots & 0 & \varepsilon_{2n-1} & -b_{2n}
\end{bmatrix},$$

$$Q = \begin{bmatrix}
0 & 0 & \beta_1 & 0 & \beta_1 & \cdots & 0 & \beta_1 & 0 \\
0 & 0 & 0 & 0 & 0 & \cdots & 0 & 0 & 0 \\
\beta_3 & 0 & \beta_3 & 0 & \beta_3 & \cdots & 0 & \beta_3 & 0 \\
0 & 0 & 0 & 0 & 0 & \cdots & 0 & 0 & 0 \\
\cdots & \cdots & \cdots & \cdots & \cdots & \cdots & \cdots & \cdots & \cdots \\
\beta_{2n-1} & 0 & \beta_{2n-1} & 0 & \beta_{2n-1} & \cdots & 0 & \beta_{2n-1} & 0 \\
0 & 0 & 0 & 0 & 0 & 0 & 0 & 0 & 0
\end{bmatrix}.$$

Let $A = P + Q$, hence

$$A = \begin{bmatrix}
d_1 & -1 & \beta_1 & 0 & \beta_1 & \cdots & 0 & \beta_1 & 0 \\
\varepsilon_1 & -b_2 & 0 & 0 & 0 & \cdots & 0 & 0 & 0 \\
\beta_3 & 0 & \beta_3+d_3 & -1 & \beta_3 & \cdots & 0 & \beta_3 & 0 \\
0 & 0 & \varepsilon_3 & -b_4 & 0 & \cdots & 0 & 0 & 0 \\
\cdots & \cdots & \cdots & \cdots & \cdots & \cdots & \cdots & \cdots & \cdots \\
\beta_{2n-1} & 0 & \beta_{2n-1} & 0 & \beta_{2n-1} & \cdots & 0 & \beta_{2n-1}+d_{2n-1} & -1 \\
0 & 0 & 0 & 0 & 0 & \cdots & 0 & \varepsilon_{2n-1} & -b_{2n}
\end{bmatrix}.$$

Lemma 1. Suppose that matrix $A(=P+Q)$ is a nonsingular matrix. Then, system (6) has a unique equilibrium point.

Proof. An equilibrium point $U^* = \left[u_1^*, u_2^*, u_3^*, \cdots, u_{2n}^*\right]^T$ is the solution of the following algebraic equation:

$$PU^* + BU^* = AU^* = 0 \tag{7}$$

Assume that U^* and V^* are two equilibrium points of system (7), then we have

$$P(U^* - V^*) + Q(U^* - V^*) = A(U^* - V^*) = 0 \tag{8}$$

Since A is a nonsingular matrix, implying that $U^* - V^* = 0$ and $U^* = V^*$. This means that system (6) has a unique equilibrium point. Obviously, this equilibrium point is exactly the zero point. Noting that the activation function $\tanh u(t)$ is a monotone increasing function, and only $\tanh(0) = 0$. This implies that system (4) has only a unique equilibrium point.

Lemma 2. Suppose that the constants $b_{2i} > 0 (i = 1, 2, \cdots, n), d_i < 0, 0 < \varepsilon_i \ll 1$, and $c_i^2 + 4d_i < 0 (i = 1, 3, 5, \cdots, 2n - 1)$. Then all solutions of system (4) are bounded.

Proof. Note that the activation function $\tanh u(t)$ is continuous nonlinear function, and $|\tanh u(t)| \leq 1$. Since $d_i < 0$ and $c_i^2 + 4d_i < 0 (i = 1, 3, 5, \cdots, 2n - 1)$, this implies that there exist constants $k_i > 0$ such that for any values u_i we have

$$-(u_i^2 - c_i u_i - d_i) \leq -k_i < 0 (i = 1, 3, 5, \cdots 2n - 1) \tag{9}$$

From (4) we get

$$\frac{d|u_1(t)|}{dt} \leq -k_1|u_1(t)| + |u_2(t)| + 2(n-1)|\beta_1|,$$

$$\frac{d|u_2(t)|}{dt} \leq -b_2|u_2(t)| + \varepsilon_1|u_1(t)|,$$

$$\frac{d|u_3(t)|}{dt} \leq -k_3|u_3(t)| + |u_4(t)| + 2(n-1)|\beta_3|,$$

$$\frac{d|u_4(t)|}{dt} \leq -b_4|u_4(t)| + \varepsilon_3|u_3(t)|, \tag{10}$$

$$\cdots\cdots\cdots\cdots\cdots\cdots\cdots\cdots$$

$$\frac{d|u_{2n-1}(t)|}{dt} \leq -k_{2n-1}|u_{2n-1}(t)| + |u_{2n}(t)| + 2(n-1)|\beta_{2n-1}|,$$

$$\frac{d|u_{2n}(t)|}{dt} \leq -b_{2n}|u_{2n}(t)| + \varepsilon_{2n-1}|u_{2n-1}(t)|.$$

Noting that (10) is a first order linear differential system. Since $b_{2i} > 0, k_{2i-1} > 0$ $(i = 1, 2, \cdots, n)$, it is easy to know that the eigenvalues of system (10) are negative

as $\dfrac{1}{2}\left[(b_{2i} + k_{2i-1})^2 - 4(k_{2i-1}b_{2i} - \varepsilon_{2i-1}) \right] > 0 \, (i = 1, 2, \cdots, n)$; or are complex

numbers with negative real parts as $\dfrac{1}{2}\left[(b_{2i} + k_{2i-1})^2 - 4(k_{2i-1}b_{2i} - \varepsilon_{2i-1}) \right] < 0$

$(i = 1, 2, \cdots, n)$. Thus, all solutions of system (10), as well as the system (4) are bounded based on the theory of the first order linear system of differential equations with constant coefficients.

2   Stability and Oscillations of the Solutions

In this paper, we adopt the following norms of vectors and matrices [11]:
$$\|u(t)\| = \sum_{i=1}^{2n} |u_i(t)| \quad, \quad \|P\| = \max_j \sum_{i=1}^{2n} |p_{ij}| \quad, \quad \|Q\| = \max_j \sum_{i=1}^{2n} |q_{ij}| \quad,$$
$$\mu(P) = \lim_{h \to \infty} \frac{\|E + hP\| - 1}{h} \quad, \quad \text{where } E \text{ is the identity matrix, which for the}$$

chosen norms reduce to $\mu(P) = \max_{1 \le j \le 2n} \left(p_{jj} + \sum_{i=1, i \ne j}^{2n} |p_{ij}| \right)$.

Theorem 1. Suppose that $A(= P + Q)$ is a nonsingular matrix, and the eigenvalues of matrix A are less than zero. Constants $b_{2i} > 0 \, (i = 1, 2, \cdots, n)$, $d_i < 0$, $0 < \varepsilon_i \ll 1$, $0 < \beta_i$ and $c_i^2 - 4d_i < 0 \, (i = 1, 3, 5, \cdots, 2n - 1)$. And

$$k_{2i-1} > 1 + \beta_{2i-1}, \ b_{2i} > \varepsilon_{2i-1} \, (i = 1, 2, 3, \cdots, n). \tag{11}$$

Then the trivial solution of system (4) is stable.

Proof. Under the assumptions, the zero point is a unique equilibrium point of model (4). We shall prove that all solutions converge to the trivial solution as t tends toward to infinity. Noting that $0 < \beta_i \, (i = 1, 3, 5, \cdots, 2n - 1)$. Consider the Liapunov functionals as follows:

$$V_{2i-1}(t) = |u_{2i-1}(t)| + \sum_{j=1, j \ne i}^{n} \beta_{2j-1} \int_{t-\tau}^{t} |u_{2j-1}(s)| ds,$$
$$V_{2i}(t) = \sum_{i=1}^{n} |u_{2i-1}(t)| \, (1 = 1, 2, \cdots, n) \tag{12}$$

Note that $\left|\tanh\left(u_i\left(t-\tau\right)\right)\right| \le \left|u_i\left(t-\tau\right)\right|$, thus,

$$\sum_{j=1,j\ne i}^{n} \beta_{2j-1}\left|\tanh\left(u_{2j-1}\left(t-\tau\right)\right)\right| + \sum_{j=1,j\ne i}^{n} \beta_{2j-1}\left(\left|u_{2j-1}\left(t\right)\right| - \left|u_{2j-1}\left(t-\tau\right)\right|\right)$$

$$\le \sum_{j=1,j\ne i}^{n} \beta_{2j-1}\left(\left|u_{2j-1}\left(t\right)\right|\right)$$

Calculating the upper right derivative $D^+V_{2i-1}\left(t\right)$ of $V_{2i-1}\left(t\right)$ along the solutions of (4), using (9), we get

$$D^+V_{2i-1}\left(t\right) = Sgnu_{2i-1}\frac{du_{2i-1}\left(t\right)}{dt} + \sum_{j=1,j\ne i}^{n} \beta_{2j-1}\left(\left|u_{2j-1}\left(t\right)\right| - \left|u_{2j-1}\left(t-\tau\right)\right|\right)$$

$$\le -\left[u_{2i-1}^2\left(t\right) - c_{2i-1}u_{2i-1}\left(t\right) - d_{2i-1}\right]\left|u_{2i-1}\left(t\right)\right| - \left|u_{2i}\left(t\right)\right|$$

$$+ \sum_{j=1,j\ne i}^{n} \beta_{2j-1}\left(\left|u_{2j-1}\left(t\right)\right|\right), \quad \left(i = 1,2,\cdots,n\right)$$

and

$$D^+V_{2i}\left(t\right) = Sgnu_{2i}\frac{du_{2i}\left(t\right)}{dt} \le -b_{2n}\left|u_{2i}\left(t\right)\right| + \varepsilon_{2i-1}\left|u_{2i-1}\left(t\right)\right|\left(i=1,2,\cdots,n\right) \quad (13)$$

Let $V = \left[V_1,V_2,\cdots,V_{2n}\right]^T$, then we have

$$D^+V \le A\left|U\left(t\right)\right|. \tag{14}$$

Since all eigenvalues of matrix A are less than zero, this means that $D^+V < 0$, implying that all solutions converge to the trivial solution.

Theorem 2. Suppose that $A\left(= P + Q\right)$ is a nonsingular matrix, constants $b_{2i} > 0$, $\left(i = 1,2,\cdots,n\right)$, $d_i < 0$, $0 < \varepsilon_i \ll 1$, and $c_i^2 + 4d_i < 0$ $\left(i = 1,3,5,\cdots,2n-1\right)$. In addition that

$$\left(\|Q\|\tau e\right)\exp\left(-\tau\left|\mu\left(p\right)\right|\right) > 1. \tag{15}$$

Then all solutions of system (4) are oscillatory.

Proof. Under the restrictive condition, system (4) has a unique equilibrium point, and all solutions of system (4) are bounded. We shall prove that the unique equilibrium point is unstable. From (4), we have

$$\frac{d|u_1(t)|}{dt} \le -\left[u_1^2(t) - c_1 u_1(t) - d_1\right]|u_1(t)| - |u_2(t)| + \sum_{j=2}^{n}|\beta_{2j-1}|\left(|u_{2j-1}(t)|\right),$$

$$\frac{d|u_2(t)|}{dt} \le -b_2|u_2(t)| + \varepsilon_1|u_1(t)|,$$

$$\frac{d|u_3(t)|}{dt} \le -\left[u_3^2(t) - c_3 u_3(t) - d_3\right]|u_3(t)| - |u_4(t)| + \sum_{j=1, j\ne 2}^{n}|\beta_{2j-1}|\left(|u_{2j-1}(t)|\right),$$

$$\frac{d|u_4(t)|}{dt} \le -b_4|u_4(t)| + \varepsilon_3|u_3(t)|,$$

$$\cdots\cdots\cdots\cdots\cdots\cdots$$

$$\frac{d|u_{2n-1}(t)|}{dt} \le -\left[u_{2n-1}^2(t) - c_{2n-1}u_{2n-1}(t) - d_{2n-1}\right]|u_{2n-1}(t)| - |u_{2n}(t)|$$

$$+ \sum_{j=1}^{n-1}|\beta_{2j-1}|\left(|u_{2j-1}(t)|\right),$$

$$\frac{d|u_{2n}(t)|}{dt} \le -b_{2n}|u_{2n}(t)| + \varepsilon_{2n-1}|u_{2n-1}(t)|.$$

$$(16)$$

Let $v(t) = \sum_{i=1}^{2n}|u_i(t)|$, then $v(t) \ge 0$ for any $t > 0$ and system (16) can be rewritten as a matrix form

$$\frac{dv(t)}{dt} \le \mu(P)v(t) + \|Q\|\|u(t-\tau)\| \tag{17}$$

Consider the scalar delay differential equation

$$\frac{dz(t)}{dt} = \mu(P)z(t) + \|Q\|\|z(t-\tau)\| \tag{18}$$

According to the comparison theorem of differential equation, there exists a $t^* > 0$, such that $v(t) = z(t), t \in \left[t^*, t^* + \tau\right]$, and $v(t) \le z(t), t \ge t^* + \tau$. We claim that the trivial solution is unstable under the assumptions. If this is not true, then the characteristic equation associated with (18) given by

$$\lambda = \mu(P) + \|Q\|e^{-\lambda\tau} \tag{19}$$

Will have a real non-positive root say $\lambda^* < 0$. Thus, $e^{-\lambda^* \tau} = e^{|\lambda^* \tau|}$, from (19) one can obtain

$$|\lambda^*| \geq \|Q\| e^{|\lambda^* \tau|} - |\mu(P)| \tag{20}$$

Therefore

$$1 \geq \frac{\|Q\| e^{|\lambda^* \tau|}}{|\lambda^*| + |\mu(P)|} = \frac{\left(\tau \|Q\| e^{-|\mu(P)|\tau}\right) e^{|\lambda^* \tau| + |\mu(p)|\tau}}{|\lambda^*|\tau + |\mu(P)|\tau} \tag{21}$$

Using formula $e^{|\lambda^* \tau|} \geq e\left(|\lambda^* \tau|\right)$, from (21) we have

$$1 \geq \frac{\left(\tau \|Q\| e^{-|\mu(P)|\tau}\right) e^{|\lambda^* \tau| + |\mu(p)|\tau}}{|\lambda^*|\tau + |\mu(P)|\tau} \geq \left(\|Q\| e\tau\right) e^{-|\mu(P)|\tau} \tag{22}$$

Inequality (22) contradicts (15). Hence, the trivial solution is unstable. Based on the Chafee's criterion, system (4) generates a limit cycle. Namely, there exists an oscillatory periodic solution.

3   Computer Simulations

Example 1. In system (4), Let $n = 6$, Consider a six coupled FHN system.
We first select the parameters as follows: $c_1 = 1.48$, $c_3 = 1.55$, $c_5 = 1.75$, $c_7 = 1.65$, $c_9 = 1.35$, $c_{11} = 1.65$; $d_1 = -8.95$, $d_3 = -7.58$, $d_5 = -6.65$, $d_7 = -6.68$, $d_9 = -4.8$, $d_{11} = -5.5$; $\beta_1 = 1.25$, $\beta_3 = 1.45$, $\beta_5 = 0.45$, $\beta_7 = 0.55$, $\beta_9 = 0.35$, $\beta_{11} = 0.85$; $\varepsilon_1 = 0.085$, $\varepsilon_3 = 0.095$, $\varepsilon_5 = 0.105$, $\varepsilon_7 = 0.102$, $\varepsilon_9 = 0.098$, $\varepsilon_{11} = 0.085$; $b_2 = 0.45$, $b_4 = 0.26$, $b_6 = 0.45$, $b_8 = 0.28$, $b_{10} = 0.38$, $b_{12} = 0.45$, time delay selected as $\tau = 1.5$. Thus, the conditions of Theorem 1 are satisfied. The trivial solutions of this system are convergent (see Figure 1). When the parameter values are selected as $c_1 = 0.27$, $c_3 = 0.58$, $c_5 = 0.89$, $c_7 = 0.68$, $c_9 = 0.62$, $c_{11} = 0.65$; $d_1 = -0.95$, $d_3 = -0.58$, $d_5 = -0.65$, $d_7 = -0.68$, $d_9 = -0.8$, $d_{11} = -0.5$; $\beta_1 = 0.55$, $\beta_3 = -0.85$, $\beta_5 = 0.95$, $\beta_7 = -0.45$, $\beta_9 = 0.85$, $\beta_{11} = -1.35$; $\varepsilon_1 = 0.085$, $\varepsilon_3 = 0.095$, $\varepsilon_5 = 0.075$, $\varepsilon_7 = 0.098$, $\varepsilon_9 = 0.09$,

$\varepsilon_{11} = 0.092$; $b_2 = 0.25$, $b_4 = 0.16$, $b_6 = 0.24$, $b_8 = 0.18$, $b_{10} = 0.28$,

$b_{12} = 0.24$, time delay selected as $\tau = 0.8$. It is easy to check that the conditions of Theorem 2 are satisfied. The trivial solutions of this system are oscillatory (see Figure 2). To our knowledge, no results about such oscillation analysis of six coupled FHN model were appeared in the literature. Thus, our criterion is new method.

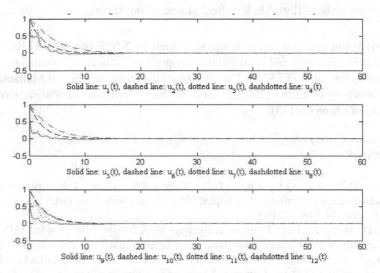

Fig. 1. Covergence of the solutions for a six coupled FHN system, delay: 1.5

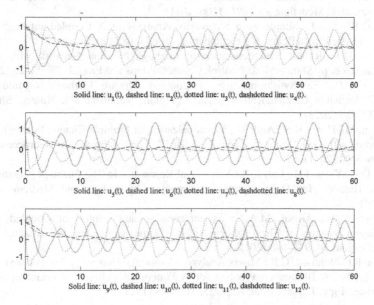

Fig. 2. Oscillation of the solutions for a six coupled FHN system, delay:0.8

4   Conclusion

This paper discusses an any n coupled FHN neurons model in which the synaptic strength of self-connection for each neuron is different. Two theorems are provided to determine the stability and periodic oscillatory behavior of the solutions based on constructing of the Liapunov functional and the Chafee's criterion of limit cycle. Computer simulations illustrate the effectiveness of our criteria.

Acknowledgements. This research was supported by NNSF of China(11361010), the high school specialty and curriculum integration project of Guangxi Zhuang Autonomous Region (GXTSZY2220), the Key Discipline of Applied Mathematics of Hechi University of China (200725), and the Key Discipline of Statistics of Hechi University of China (20133).

References

1. Wang, Q.Y., Lu, Q.S., Chen, G.R., Feng, Z.S., Duan, L.X.: Bifurcation and Synchronization of Synaptically Coupled FHN Models with Time Delay. Chaos, Solitons and Fractals 39, 918–925 (2009)
2. Fan, D., Hong, L.: Hopf Bifurcation Analysis in A Synaptically Coupled FHN Neuron Model with Delays. Commun. Nonlinear Sci. Numer. Simulat. 15, 1873–1886 (2010)
3. Zhen, B., Xu, J.: Bautin Bifurcation Analysis for Synchronous Solution of a Coupled FHN Neural System with Delay. Commun. Nonlinear Sci. Numer. Simulat. 5, 442–458 (2010)
4. Murza, A.C.: Oscillation Patterns in Tori of Modified FHN Neurons. Applied Mathematical Modelling 35, 1096–1106 (2011)
5. Zhen, B., Xu, J.: Simple Zero Singularity Analysis in A Coupled Fitzhugh–Nagumo Neural System with Delay. Neurocomputing 73, 874–882 (2010)
6. Zhang, Q.J.: Robust Synchronization of Fitzhugh–Nagumo Network with Parameter Disturbances by Sliding Mode Control. Chaos, Solitons and Fractals 58, 22–26 (2014)
7. Yang, D.D.: Self-Synchronization of Coupled Chaotic Fitzhugh–Nagumo Systems with Unreliable Communication Links. Commun. Nonlinear Sci. Numer. Simulat. 18, 2783–2789 (2013)
8. Rehan, M., Hong, K.S., Aqil, M.: Synchronization of Multiple Chaotic Fitzhugh–Nagumo Neurons with Gap Junctions Under External Electrical Stimulation. Neurocomputing 74, 3296–3304 (2011)
9. Hu, D.L., Yang, J.H., Liu, X.B.: Vibrational Resonance in The Fitzhugh Nagumo System with Time-Varying Delay Feedback. Computers in Biology and Medicine 45, 80–86 (2014)
10. Ambrosio, B., Alaoui, M.A.A.: Synchronization and Control of Coupled Reaction–Diffusion Systems of The Fitzhugh–Nagumo Type. Computers and Mathematics with Applications 64, 934–943 (2012)
11. Horn, R.C., Johnson, C.R.: Matrix Analysis. Cambridge University Press (1985)
12. Chafee, N.: A Bifurcation Problem for A Functional Differential Equation of Finitely Retarded Type. J. Math. Anal. Appl. 35, 312–348 (1971)

A Restrained Optimal Perturbation Method
for Solving a Kind of Inverse Problem
with Variable Coefficient

Bo Wang[1,2], Yujing Yuan[3], and Guang-an Zou[4,5]

[1] Henan University, Institute of Applied Mathematics, Kaifeng, P.R. China
[2] Henan University, College of Mathematics and Information Science, Kaifeng, P.R. China
Wangbo_sdu@163.com
[3] Shandong University, Mathematic College, Jinan, P.R. China
yuanyujing88@163.com
[4] Key Laboratory of Ocean Circulation and Wave, Institute of Oceanology,
Chinese Academy of Sciences, Qingdao, P.R. China
[5] University of Chinese Academy of Sciences, Beijing, P.R. China

Abstract. A restrained optimal perturbation method is proposed to study one-dimensional variable coefficient backward inverse heat conduction problem. We determine the initial temperature distribution from final measurement data. Owning to the ill-posedness of this problem, a regularization term is introduced in the objective function, which based on the thought of regularization technique. And we give a brief description about the application in Genetic regulatory networks. Numerical experiments show that the method is feasibility in the determination of initial condition.

Keywords: Genetic regulatory networks, backward heat conduction problem, restrained optimal perturbation method, finite difference method.

1   Introduction

As we all known, evolution partial differential equation can be used in heat diffusion procedure, ocean acoustic propagation, physical or mathematical systems with a time variable and processes that behave essentially like heat diffusing through a solid. In this paper, we aim to solve a kind of inverse problems of evolution equation.

Inverse heat conduction problems appear in many important engineering science and technological fields, and they have been applied to obtain accurate thermal quantities such as surface temperatures, heat flux distributions, heat sources, thermal conductivity and heat transfer coefficients [1] and so on. These problems have been studied by many authors and many different methods have been applied to solve the inverse heat conduction problems [2-10]. However, in many dynamic heat conduction situations, it is also necessary to calculate the initial temperature with some temperature measurements given at time $t=T>0$, this is usually referred as the backward heat conduction problem (BHCP). Generally, it is severely ill-posed and it belongs to inverse heat conduction problems. There have been many approaches

D.-S. Huang et al. (Eds.): ICIC 2014, LNBI 8590, pp. 175–185, 2014.

developed for solving the BHCP, such as regularization techniques [14,15], fictitious time integration method [17], iterative boundary element method [1,16], finite difference method [18], finite element method [12], quasi-reversibility method [19], and other methods[11,13,20].

In this paper, we consider the backward inverse problem in the reverse process of heat transfer equation. Inspired by the conditional nonlinear optimal perturbation (CNOP) method, which is proposed by Mu.M et al. [21,22], we propose a restrained optimal perturbation method to estimate the initial temperature.

This paper is organized as follows. In the next section, we will present the mathematical formulation of the BHCP. We will use the finite difference approximation to discrete the space derivative in section 3, with transforming the heat conduction problem into the system of ordinary differential equations (ODEs). In section 4, we will give a brief description of the restrained optimal perturbation method and apply it to solve the BHCP, and the spectral projected gradient algorithm is used to obtain the optimal perturbation. In the fifth section, we give the sensitivity analysis of the initial problem. In section 6, an outline how the retrained optimal perturbation method was used to solve the genetic regulatory networks is listed. In the last section, numerical experiments will be given to investigate the applications of this method, and we give numerically test for the stability of this method. The conclusion and discussion are presented in section 7.

2   Mathematic Formulation of the Inverse Problem

In this section, we will consider the variable coefficient backward heat transfer problem governed by the equation

$$\rho c \frac{\partial u(x,t)}{\partial t} = \alpha(t) \frac{\partial^2 u(x,t)}{\partial x^2}, \quad 0 \le x \le 1, \quad 0 < t \le T, \tag{1}$$

with the initial condition

$$u(x,0) = f(x), 0 \le x \le 1, \tag{2}$$

and the boundary conditions

$$u(0,t) = u(1,t) = 0, 0 < t \le T, \tag{3}$$

where the constants $\rho > 0$, $c > 0$ are density and specific heat of the material respectively, $\alpha(t)$ is the known thermal conductivity. The direct heat problem aims to determine the temperature distribution $u(x,t)$ for a given boundary heat status and an initial temperature distribution. The inverse problem is to approximate the initial temperature $f(x)$ with the overspecified data at time $t=T$ as follows:

$$u(x,T) = g(x), \quad 0 \le x \le 1, \tag{4}$$

in which $g(x)$ is considered as a known function.

3   Finite Difference Approximation

We divide the interval $[0,1]$ into M mesh points with spatial step size $h = 1/M$ in the x direction, and mesh points x_i are given by $x_i = ih$, $i = 0,1,2\cdots M$, where M is an integer number.

Consider the central difference with respect to the space derivative in equation (1), we have the following semi-discrete equation:

$$\rho c \frac{\partial u_i(t)}{\partial t} = \alpha(t) \frac{u_{i+1}(t) - 2u_i(t) + u_{i-1}(t)}{h^2} , \tag{5}$$

where $u_i(t)$ is the approximation of $u(ih,t)$.

If we note $U = (u_1(t), u_2(t), \cdots, u_{M-1}(t))^T$, and apply equation (5) to all the $M-1$ interior mesh points of the interval $[0,1]$, the problem (1)-(3) can be replaced by the system of ordinary differential equations (ODEs) as following:

$$\frac{\partial U}{\partial t} = F(U) , \tag{6}$$

$$U\big|_{t=0} = U_0 , \tag{7}$$

in which $F(\vec{X}) = \alpha(t)A\vec{X}$, $U_0 = (f_1, f_2, \cdots, f_{M-1})^T$, and $t \in (0,T]$, where F is a linear operator, the matrix A is of order $M-1$, and will be given by

$$A = \frac{1}{\rho c h^2} \begin{pmatrix} -2 & 1 & 0 & 0 & \cdots & 0 & 0 & 0 \\ 1 & -2 & 1 & 0 & \cdots & 0 & 0 & 0 \\ \vdots & \vdots & \vdots & \vdots & \ddots & \vdots & \vdots & \vdots \\ 0 & 0 & 0 & 0 & \cdots & 1 & -2 & 1 \\ 0 & 0 & 0 & 0 & \cdots & 0 & 1 & -2 \end{pmatrix}.$$

4   A Restrained Optimal Perturbation Method

4.1   A Brief Introduction

In this section, we will give a brief introduction to the restrained optimal perturbation method. Assuming that the mathematical model is as following:

$$\frac{\partial U}{\partial t} = F(U) , \tag{8}$$

$$U\big|_{t=0} = U_0 , \tag{9}$$

in which $U = (u_1(t), u_2(t), \cdots u_{M-1}(t))^T$, F is a nonlinear (or linear) operator, and $(x,t) \in \Omega \times [0,T]$, Ω is a domain in R^n and $T < +\infty$, U_0 is the initial estimate value which can be obtained from the long experience value. Supposing R is the propagator from 0 to time T, hence, for the fixed point $T > 0$, the solution $U(x,t) = R(U_0)(T)$ is well defined. Let $U(x,t)$ and $U(x,t) + u(x,t)$ be the solution to problem (8)-(9) with initial estimate value $U_0 + u_0$, where u_0 is the initial perturbation. We have

$$U(T) = R(U_0)(T),$$ (10)

$$U(T) + u(T) = R(U_0 + u_0)(T).$$ (11)

So $u(T)$ describes the evolution of the initial perturbation u_0. The perturbation $u_{0\delta}$ is called the optimal perturbation, if and only if

$$J(u_{0\delta}) = \min_{u_0} J(u_0).$$ (12)

It must satisfy the following condition:

$$E = \left\| R(U_0 + u_{0\delta})(T) - G(T) \right\| \le \delta,$$ (13)

here, the error E is sufficiently small, where $G(T)$ are discrete values of the observational data.

Generally, the inverse problem belongs to ill-posed problem, in order to overcoming the difficulty of ill-posedness, a regularization term is introduced in the objective function, so $J(u_0)$ can be defined as

$$J(u_0) = \left\| R(U_0 + u_0)(T) - R(U_0)(T) \right\| + \lambda \left\| U_0 \right\|,$$ (14)

where $\lambda > 0$ is a regularizing parameter.

The above constrained optimization minimum value problems can be transformed into the following Lagrangian problem:

$$J(u_{0\delta}) = \min_{u_0} J(u_0) + \mu \left\| R(U_0 + u_0)(T) - G(T) \right\|,$$ (15)

where $\mu > 0$ is a Lagrange multiplier.

In this paper, spectral projected gradient (SPG) algorithm is adopted to solve the above Lagrangian problem, and the detailed description of this algorithms can be found in Birgin et al. [23,24].

4.2   Application of This Method

Now, we will use restrained optimal perturbation method to determine the initial distribution.

Firstly, the Euler scheme is adopted to solve the ordinary differential equations (ODEs) (6), the time interval $(0,T]$ is divided into N small cells equally and let the time step size $k = T/N$. The notation U^j are used for the approximations of the $U(jk)$, so we have the following scheme

$$U^{j+1} = U^j + kF(U^j),\qquad(16)$$

where $U^j = (u_1(jk), u_2(jk), \cdots, u_{M-1}(jk))^T$, and for $j = 1, 2, \cdots, N$.

Secondly, we give the initial estimates for the initial values U_0, as the description of restrained optimal perturbation method in section 4.1, and our aim is searching for $u_{0\delta}$. In this paper, the discrete values of the additional condition are $G(T) = (g_1, g_2, \cdots g_{M-1})^T$.

When we find out the $u_{0\delta}$, the initial estimates U_0 plus $u_{0\delta}$ can be treated as the initial values, then inverse heat conduction problem is changed into the direct problem.

5   Stability Analysis

In this section, we give the sensitivity analysis of the initial problem.

Firstly, we introduce the inner product in Hilbert Space $H = L_2(\Omega)$, which defined as

$$(u, v) = \int_\Omega uvdx,\qquad(17)$$

and the corresponding norm is

$$\|u\| = (u, u)^{\frac{1}{2}} = \left(\int_\Omega u^2 dx\right)^{\frac{1}{2}}.\qquad(18)$$

Next, we define the operator

$$Lu = -\frac{\partial^2 u}{\partial x^2}, 0 \le x \le 1,\qquad(19)$$

then equation (1) can be written as

$$\frac{\partial u}{\partial t} + m(t)Lu = 0,\qquad(20)$$

$$u(0) = u_0,\qquad(21)$$

in which, $m(t) = \dfrac{\alpha(t)}{\rho c} > 0$.

To check the sensitivity, we also need to introduce the following lemma firstly.

Lemma 1. The solution of problem (20)-(21) satisfies the following a priori error estimate:

$$\|u(t)\| \le \|u_0\|, \quad \forall\, t \in [0,T].$$ (22)

Proof. Multiplying equation (20) by $u(t)$, we get

$$(\frac{\partial u}{\partial t}, u) + (m(t)Lu, u) = 0.$$ (23)

Considering the boundary condition, we have

$$(m(t)Lu, u) = m(t)(Lu, u) = m(t)\int_0^1 (\frac{\partial u}{\partial x})^2 dx > 0.$$ (24)

By using the Cauchy-Schwarz inequality, we obtain

$$(\frac{\partial u}{\partial t}, u) = \frac{1}{2}\frac{\partial}{\partial t}\|u\|^2 = \|u\|\frac{\partial}{\partial t}\|u\| \le 0,$$ (25)

thus

$$\frac{\partial}{\partial t}\|u\| \le 0,$$ (26)

Integrating equation (26) from 0 to t, it is not difficulty to get the estimate

$$\|u(t)\| \le \|u(0)\| = \|u_0\|.$$ (27)

Finally, we briefly discuss about the dependence of the solution on the continuous initial values. Giving the initial condition a small perturbation u_0^*, the corresponding solution denotes as u^*. Therefore, the equation (20)-(21) can be rewritten as:

$$\frac{\partial u^*}{\partial t} + m(t)Lu^* = 0, 0 < t \le T,$$ (28)

$$u^*(0) = u_0^*.$$ (29)

then, we have the following corollary:

Corollary 2. Suppose we have $\|u_0 - u_0^*\| \le \varepsilon$, here $\varepsilon > 0$, then the following results holds

$$\|u^*(t) - u(t)\| \le \varepsilon.$$ (30)

Proof. We denote $\delta u_0 = u_0 - u_0^*$, $\delta u = u(t) - u^*(t)$, from (20), (21), (28), (29), we can obtain the problem

$$\frac{\partial \delta u}{\partial t} + m(t)L\delta u = 0, \tag{31}$$

with the initial condition

$$\delta u(0) = \delta u_0. \tag{32}$$

From lemma 1, we get

$$\|\delta u\| \le \|\delta u_0\| \le \varepsilon. \tag{33}$$

6   An Outline of the Application in Genetic Regulatory Networks

Genetic regulatory networks is the system that contain DNA, RNA, protein and other small molecule and the interaction and influence with each other. The aim of genetic regulatory networks analysis is build a mathematic model and research the interrelationships between the molecules.

Now, there are many tools using in genetic regulatory networks, such as directed graphs [25], Boolean networks [25,26], Bayesian networks [25,27], differential equations [25,29], stochastic equations [29] and so on. Directed graphs and Boolean networks are simple models, so the simulations are qualitative and rough. Bayesian networks is a probability model, it can quantitatively and randomly describe the regulatory networks. Differential equations can quantitatively and exactly predict the whole system. Though stochastic equations can give an exact simulation, it seldom uses in practical application because of the computation difficulty. Here we give two differential equation models and illustrate the reasons why restrained optimal perturbation method can be used in genetic regulatory networks.

The first model is an ordinary differential equation:

$$\frac{dc_i}{dt} = f_i(c), 0 \le i \le 1. \tag{34}$$

This equation is always called kinetic equation or rate equation. Here, $c = [c_1, c_2, \cdots c_n]^T \ge 0$ are the concentration of different components, $f_i : R^n \to R$ are nonlinear functions. In most cases, nonlinear equations can better describe the real situation of the organism, so we often consider $f_i(x)$ are continuous, differential and monotonical increasing functions. The simplest example is sigmoid function or hyperbolic function. The simplest ordinary differential equation model is:

$$\frac{dc_i}{dt} = \sum_{j=1}^{p} \omega_{ij} c_j + b_i, \tag{35}$$

where ω_{ij} indicates how much the level of gene j influence gene i, b_i is a constant bias term and it model the activation level of the gene in the absence of any other regulatory input.

In equation (35), knowing the parameters ω_{ij} and the initial condition, we can give an exact description to the regulatory networks. But ω_{ij} are usually unknown, then we can use the experimental dates to estimate the parameter, this is the so-called reverse engineering. On the other hand, we find that equation (35) are the same with the model, which the restrained can be used to solve, so we can infer that ROP can be used to solve the genetic regulatory networks.

The second model is a partial differential equation as following:

$$\frac{\partial c_i}{\partial t} = f_i(x) + d_i \frac{\partial^2 c_i}{\partial x^2}, \ 1 \le i \le n, \ 1 < x < l, \tag{36}$$

on the boundary $x = 0$ and $x = l$, suppose no diffusion occurs, then the boundary can be

$$\frac{\partial^2}{\partial x^2} c_i(0,t) = \frac{\partial^2}{\partial x^2} c_i(l,t) = 0. \tag{37}$$

Equation (36)-(37) is a reaction diffusion equation [25] and is similar to heat conduction equation, so the restrained optimal perturbation method can also be used to solve the problem.

7   Numerical Examples

In this section, we do some numerical implementations on the restrained optimal perturbation method by giving two examples, numerical results are presented for small values of the final time, we take $T = 0.1, 0.2$.

7.1   Example 1

We consider the backward heat conduction problem with the following given data

$$\alpha(t) = \sin(t), u(x,t) = \sin(\pi x)\exp(\cos(t)). \tag{38}$$

Giving $\rho = c = \pi$, $h = 0.1$, $k = 0.001$, with a uniform mesh containing $N = 100$, we give the initial estimate $U_0 = lu(x,0)[1 + \delta_0 ran(x)]$, where the $ran(x) \in (-1,1)$ for $x \in [0,1]$ is standard random numbers, $l \in (0,1)$ is a constant, δ_0 is the percentage of noise. The initial estimate value, optimal perturbation, numerical solution and the exact solution are given in Figuers 1-2.

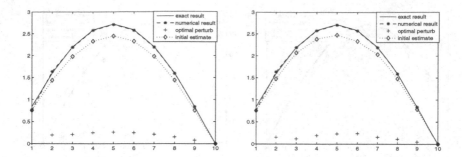

Fig. 1. The left figure shows the exact results and numerical results for the solution $f(x)$ when $\lambda = 0.78$, $\mu = 50$, $l = 0.90$, $\delta_0 = 0$. The right figure shows the exact results and numerical results for the solution $f(x)$ when $\lambda = 0.80$, $\mu = 50$, $l = 0.90$, $\delta_0 = 0.08$.

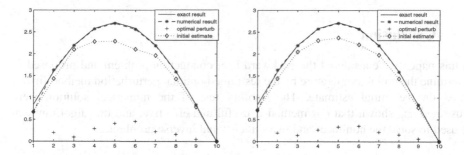

Fig. 2. The left figure shows the exact results and numerical results for the solution $f(x)$ when $\lambda = 0.80$, $\mu = 40$, $l = 0.80$, $\delta_0 = 0.20$. The right figure shows the exact results and numerical results for the solution $f(x)$ when $\lambda = 0.80$, $\mu = 40$, $l = 0.85$, $\delta_0 = 0.15$.

7.2   Example 2

Since there are no theoretical results available about the stability of this method proposed, we give numerical stability analysis of the solution with respect to the random noisy data

$$u^*(x,T) = [1 + \delta_1 ran(x)]u(x,T), \tag{39}$$

where $ran(x) \in (-1,1)$ for $x \in [0,1]$ is the standard random number, $u(x,T)$ is the exact final value obtained by solving the direct problem and δ_1 is the percentage of noise. Now we consider the noisy input data for this example, other given data are as in example 1, and we give $N = 200$, the results are given in Figure 3.

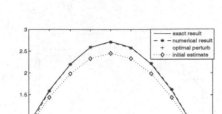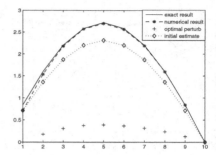

Fig. 3. The left figure shows the exact results and numerical results for the solution $f(x)$ when $\lambda = 0.60$, $\mu = 50$, $l = 0.90$, $\delta_0 = 0$, $\delta_1 = 0.05$. The right figure shows the exact results and numerical results for the solution $f(x)$ when $\lambda = 0.85$, $\mu = 40$, $l = 0.85$, $\delta_0 = 0$, $\delta_1 = 0.15$.

8   Conclusion

In this paper, we considered the backward heat conduction problem and proposed to determine the initial temperature by the restrained optimal perturbation method firstly, based on the initial estimate. The stability test of the numerical solution were illustrated and shown that our method is useful and effective, and this algorithm can be used to solve the nonlinear and two-dimensional inverse problem.

Acknowledgments. The project is supported by National Natural Science Foundation of China (No.40805020), and by the Natural Science Foundation of Henan Province (No.112300410054).

References

1. Mera, N.S., Elliott, L., Ingham, D.B., Lesnic, D.: An iterative boundary element method for solving the one-dimensional backward heat conduction problem. Int. J. Heat Mass Transfer 44, 1937–1946 (2001)
2. Cannon, J.R., Duchateau, P.: Structural identification of an unknown source term in a heat equation. Inverse Problems 14, 535–551 (2001)
3. Molhem, H., Pourgholi, R.: A numerical algorithm for solving a one-dimensional inverse heat conduction problem. J. Math. Statis. 4, 60–63 (2008)
4. Jia, X.Z., Wang, Y.B.: A boundary integral method for solving inverse heat conduction problem. J. Inv. Ill-posed Problem 14, 375–384 (2006)
5. Dehghan, M.: Numerical computation of a control function in a partial differential equation. Appl. Math. Comput. 147, 397–408 (2004)
6. Lesnic, D., Elliott, L., Ingham, D.B.: Application of the boundary element method to inverse heat conduction problems. J. Heat and Mass Transfer 39, 1503–1517 (1996)
7. Wang, B., Zou, G.A., Zhao, P.: Finite volume method for solving a one-dimensional parabolic inverse problem. Appl. Math. Comput. 217, 5227–5235 (2011)

8. Geng, F.Z., Lin, Y.Z.: Application of the variational iteration method to inverse heat source problem. Comput. Math. Appl. 58, 2098–2102 (2009)
9. Shidfar, A., Karamali, G.R., Damichi, J.: An inverse heat conduction problem with a nonlinear source term. Nonlinear Anal. 65, 615–621 (2006)
10. Chen, Q., Liu, J.J.: Solving an inverse parabolic problem by optimization from final measurement data. J. Comput. Appl. Math. 193, 183–203 (2006)
11. Han, H., Ingham, D.B., Yuan, Y.: The boundary element method for the solution of the backward heat conduction equation. J. Comput. Phys. 116, 292–299 (1995)
12. Liu, J.J.: Numerical solution of forward and backward problem for 2-D heat conduction equation. J. Comput. Appl. Math. 145, 459–482 (2002)
13. Liu, C.S.: Group preserving scheme for backward heat conduction problems. Int. J. Heat Mass Transfer 47, 2567–2576 (2004)
14. Chang, J.R., Liu, C.S., Chang, C.W.: A new shooting method for quasi-boundary regularization of backward heat conduction problems. Int. J. Heat Mass Transfer 50, 2325–2332 (2007)
15. Cheng, J., Liu, J.J.: A quasi Tikhonov regularization for a two-dimensional backward heat problem by a fundamental solution. Inverse Problems 24, 065012, doi:10.1088/0266-5611/24/6/065012
16. Lesnic, D., Elliott, L., Ingham, D.B.: An iterative boundary element method for solving the backward heat conduction problem using an elliptic approximation. Inverse Problems in Engineering 6, 255–279 (1998)
17. Chang, C.W., Liu, C.S.: A new algorithm for direct and backward problems of heat conduction equation. Int. J. Heat Mass Transfer 53, 5552–5569 (2010)
18. Shidfar, A., Zakeri, A.: A numerical technique for backward inverse heat conduction problems in one-dimensional space. Appl. Math. Comput. 171, 1016–1024 (2005)
19. Xiong, X.T., Fu, C.L., Qian, Z.: Two numerical methods for solving a backward heat conduction problem. Appl. Math. Comput. 179, 370–377 (2006)
20. Kabanikhin, S.I., Penenko, A.V.: Convergence analysis of gradient descend methods generated by two different functionals in a backward heat conduction problem. J. Inv. Ill-posed Problems 17, 713–732 (2009)
21. Mu, M., Duan, W.S., Wang, B.: Conditional nonlinear optimal perturbation and its applications Nonlin. Processes Geophys. 10, 493–501 (2003)
22. Mu, M., Duan, W.S.: A new approach to studying ENSO predictability: conditional nonlinear optimal perturbation. Chinese Sci. Bull. 48, 1045–1047 (2003)
23. Birgin, E.G., Martinez, J.M., Raydan, M.: Nonmonotone spectral projected gradient methods on convex sets. SIAM Journal on Optimization 10, 1196–1211 (2000)
24. Birgin, E.G., Martinez, J.M., Raydan, M.: Inexact spectral projected gradient methods on convex sets. SIAM Journal of Numerical Analysis 23, 539–559 (2003)
25. Jong, H.D.: Modeling and simulation of genetic regulatory systems: a literature review. J. Comput. Boil. 9, 67–103 (2002)
26. Somogyi, R., Sniegoski, C.A.: Modeling the complexity of genetic networks: understanding multigenic and pleiotropic regulation. Complexity 1, 45–63 (1996)
27. Friedman, N., Linial, M., Nachman, I., Pe'er, D.: Using Bayesian networks to analyze expression data. In: Proceedings of the Fourth Annual International Conference on Computational Molecular Biology. ACM Press, New York (2000)
28. D'Haeseleer, P., Wen, X., Fuhrman, S., Somogyi, R.: Linear modeling of mRNA expression levels during CNS development and injury. In: Pacific Symposium on Biocomputing, vol. 4, pp. 41–52 (1999)
29. McAdams, H.M., Arkin, A.: Stochastic mechanism in gene expression. Proceedings of the National Academy of Science of the USA 94, 814–819 (1997)

A Knowledge-Guided Approach for Inferring Gene Regulatory Networks

Yu-Ting Hsiao and Wei-Po Lee

Department of Information Management, National Sun Yat-sen University,
Kaohsiung, Taiwan

Abstract. In the reconstruction of gene regulatory networks (GRNs) from time expression data, a reverse engineering approach is often adopted to reproduce possible fitting models of GRNs. However, two major tasks must be undertaken: one is to optimize the accuracy of inferred network behaviors; and the other is to designate valid biological topologies for target networks. To achieve the above two goals, this work presents an integrative modeling framework that combines knowledge-based and data-driven input sources to infer gene regulatory networks. Experiments have been conducted to validate the proposed approach. The results show that our framework can successfully infer solutions.

Keywords: reverse engineering, systems biology, knowledge-driven, structural correctness, optimization.

1 Introduction

The purpose of developing a computational framework to infer GRNs is to elucidate the causality of gene expression processes to generate new possible pathways. To achieve these objectives, biologists employ modern high-throughput experimentation, e.g., DNA microarrays, to capture a large number of regulatory interactions among genes in a time-series format. The temporal measurements are thus made available to be the input of a mathematical function. Ideally, the above data-driven inference should be able to apply the gene expression data to model GRNs and would at the same time characterize both the magnitude of the genetic interactions and the scaffolding of the network [1]. In practice, however, the parameter values of a computational model cannot provide detailed guidance regarding a biological system, because the information on genetic processes that is recorded by the time series is mainly implicit [2]. Therefore, scientists now advocate inferring the computational models by integrating knowledge-based data (i.e., prior knowledge datasets, PKDs) into the original modeling methods [3].

To construct the correct pathways, biological scientists have collected prior knowledge datasets as precisely as possible, regarding the gene functions, the causal links, and the partial topology of the biological systems (e.g., [4, 5]). Although PKDs still contain different degrees of data inconsistency on account of the various experimental settings and purposes, these databases serve as useful resources for providing the

D.-S. Huang et al. (Eds.): ICIC 2014, LNBI 8590, pp. 186–192, 2014.
© Springer International Publishing Switzerland 2014

structural relationships as a practical guideline for inferring genetic networks. Therefore, applying qualitative behavior that is obtained from PKDs to network modeling has been considered to be a complementary strategy to construct the genetic dynamics in a way that has biological meaning.

In this study, we propose an integrative framework that exploits the advantages of knowledge-based and data-driven inference strategies to derive a computational model of gene regulatory networks. The goal of this procedure is not only to fulfill the deficiencies of prior research on knowledge-based GRN modeling but also to have a better understanding of how to exploit the existing literature and bio-software, to help us to build a comprehensive framework. To validate the proposed approach, we used different datasets taken from the literature to examine and demonstrate how our approach operates in practice.

2   The Proposed Method

2.1   PKD Source Selection and Data Pre-processing

The first step of a knowledge-based approach is to select the prior knowledge resources. Without losing generality, in the following we take the network of yeast DNA repair genes as an example to explain how the proposed framework works.

Once the target network and the dataset are determined, the source of PKDs from the existing literature is then selected. For this dataset, we can exploit the software YeastNet version 2 [6] as the main source of genetic structures of yeast DNA repair genes. The software has calculated confidences in pair-wise genetic interactions from the collected databases, and it suggests 102,803 linkages among 5,483 yeast genes.

To form the regulatory network of DNA repair genes and construct useable prior knowledge, we can reference two benchmark papers, including [7] and [8], then incorporate genes labeled 'repair' into a regulatory network according to the biological function. Furthermore, based on this network, we can use YeastNet to build the connection relationships (i.e. an adjacency matrix) among the chosen genes. Once the matrix for the genes is built, the procedure of constructing desired prior knowledge, which includes 71 paired connections in the network, is then completed.

2.2   Mapping Knowledge onto the Computational Model

In the GRN modeling, equations are often used to represent the network structure and to describe some extent of simplicity of chemical dynamics. To date, one of the most prominent and well-researched ordinary differential equations (ODEs) models, S-system, has been considered suitable to characterize the gene regulations [9]. It consists of a set of tightly coupled ODEs, in which the synthesis and degradation process are approximated by the power law functions. The corresponding S-system model can be described as follows:

$$\frac{dX_i}{dt} = \underbrace{\alpha_i \prod_{j=1}^{N} X_j^{g_{i,j}}}_{synthesis} - \underbrace{\beta_i \prod_{j=1}^{N} X_j^{h_{i,j}}}_{degradation}, \forall\, i \tag{1}$$

In the above equation, X_i is the expression level of gene i and N is the total number of genes in a genetic network. The parameters α_i and $\beta_i \in [0,10]$ are rate constants; $g_{i,j}$ and $h_{i,j} \in [-3,3]$ are kinetic orders that reflect the interactions from gene j to i in the synthesis and degradation processes, respectively.

To simplify the task of network inference, Maki *et al.* [10] proposed an efficient strategy to decouple the above tightly coupled model into N independent differential equations, each of which refers to one gene. In general, the most advantageous feature of S-system for parameter estimations is that the range of kinetics can be set either by a default or an indicative search range representing the intensity and the regulatory relationship. In the first case, if the structural information remains unknown, we can then set $g_{i,j}$ and $h_{i,j}$ within the default range: usually [-3, +3]. In contrast, if knowledge can indicate some structural interactions, the kinetics can be identified within a specific range or an exact value. For instance, if the regulation from gene j to gene i has been known as a positive relationship, then the range of its kinetics is set into (0, +3]. The kinetics value is set to zero if the regulation does not exist.

Before going through the process of knowledge mapping, we firstly exhibit how the components of S-system can be used to represent a network topology. Figure 1a shows the visualized topology transformed from the adjacency matrix constructed. In the graph, we take gene UNG1 (with a link toward OGG1), as an example to illustrate the network topology. The corresponding pathway diagram is expressed in Figure 1b. As shown, the input magnitude (flux-in) of UNG1 may be affected by OGG1 (i.e. gung1, ogg1), and this is the synthesis process of UNG1 (equation 2). Meanwhile, the output magnitude (flux-out) of UNG1 depends on the concentration level of UNG1 (i.e. hung1, ung1) and may be affected by OGG1 (i.e. hung1, ogg1) as well. They are depicted in equation 3. The concentration of UNG1 at the next time step is determined by a calculation of the magnitude of synthesis minus that of degradation (equation 4). Similarly, a larger example from the perspective of OGG1 in Figure 1c with the same computation process can be completed through equations 5 to 7.

$$synthesis\ process\ S = \alpha_{ung1}\ OGG_1^{\,g_{ung1,\,ogg1}} \tag{2}$$

$$degradation\ process\ D = \beta_{ung1}\ UNG_1^{\,h_{ung1,\,ung1}} OGG_1^{\,h_{ung1,\,ogg1}} \tag{3}$$

$$\dot{UNG}_1 = S - D \tag{4}$$

$$synthesis\ process\ S = \alpha_{ogg1}\ UNG_1^{\,g_{ogg1,\,ung1}} MSH_2^{\,g_{ogg1,\,msh2}} MSH_6^{\,g_{ogg1,\,msh6}} \tag{5}$$

$$degradation\ process\ D = \beta_{ogg1}\ OGG_1^{\,h_{ogg1,\,ogg1}} UNG_1^{\,h_{ogg1,\,ung1}} MSH_2^{\,h_{ogg1,\,msh2}} MSH_6^{\,h_{ogg1,\,msh6}} \tag{6}$$

$$\dot{OGG}_1 = S - D \tag{7}$$

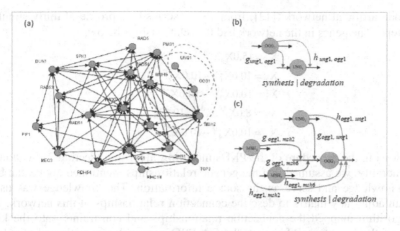

Fig. 1. Network topology for the S-system representation

2.3   PKD Modeling Algorithm Using the Reverse-Engineering Approach

To infer numerical values for the kinetic orders in S-system, an efficient reverse-engineering approach is needed. Here, we adopt the hybrid GA-PSO approach, (described in our previous work [11]) which combines two optimization procedures, genetic algorithm and particle swarm optimization, to exploit their respective advantages. In this study, we implement the PKD modeling algorithm with the GA-PSO approach to train the decoupled S-system by a proposed objective function as below.

$$f_{obj}(i) = \text{MSE}(i) + \text{Structure}(i), \quad \text{for } i = 1, 2, 3, \dots, N \tag{8}$$

In the above equation, the first part of the function is the mean squared error (MSE) of gene i over the time period t. The second part of the objective function is to prioritize a preferred network topology for an inferred GRN model in which the estimated skeletal structure can dovetail with the structure given by prior knowledge. With the structural priority defined in the proposed objective function as the guidance for the skeletal structure, the computational algorithm is able to find a preferred network structure that is in accordance with the suggested structure (prior knowledge). In this way, a target network structure can be derived during the process of evaluating candidate structures.

3   Experimental Results and Discussion

To validate the proposed framework, we performed different sets of experiments to exploit the PKDs modeling algorithm. Due to the space limitation, here we take a small popular artificial network as an example to illustrate how the proposed framework works. In this set of experiments, our method was employed to model the five-node artificial network ([12]) from a time series data profile of thirty simulation time steps. The genes in the network had the relationships below:

$$\dot{X}_1 = 15.0X_3X_5^{-0.1} - 10.0X_1^{2.0}$$
$$\dot{X}_2 = 10.0X_1^{2.0} - 10.0X_2^{2.0}$$
$$\dot{X}_3 = 10.0X_2^{-0.1} - 10.0X_2^{-0.1}X_3^{2.0}$$
$$\dot{X}_4 = 8.0X_1^{2.0}X_5^{-0.1} - 10.0X_4^{2.0}$$
$$\dot{X}_5 = 10.0X_4^{2.0} - 10.0X_5^{2.0}$$

Following the procedure of the PKDs modeling algorithm (section 2), without losing generality, we assumed that the genetic relationships mentioned above can be the prior knowledge and serve as the source information. The knowledge was used to build an adjacency matrix to describe connection relationships of this network. Then, the algorithm mapped the connection relationships and constraints onto the kinetic orders of the S-system. After that, the GA-PSO approach was activated to infer the gene expression profiles and the numerical values of kinetic orders according to the proposed objective function (i.e. equation 8). Thirty independent runs were conducted; each of which continued for 1,500 iterations with a population size 800.

After the runs of inferring GRN models were performed, the algorithm summed up the numerical values in the parameter sets for the S-system, in which 50 parameters (i.e., $g_{i,j}$ and $h_{i,j}$) of each run were analyzed. The numbers of runs in which the parameters $g_{i,j}$ and $h_{i,j}$ violated the structure priority were then calculated (due to the space limitation, the details of these violations are not shown here).

To determine a final inferred model with the desired kinetic orders, there are two model selection strategies used. First, if there were some runs in which all parameters fitted the suggestion about the connection relationships, and then the model with the lowest MSE value was chosen. Second, if there was no single run that can produce a model to fit the structural suggestion for all genes (this usually happens in a real dataset), drawing on the nature of a decoupled S-system, the algorithm chose to take the best structural fitting model with a desired MSE (i.e. smaller than the threshold) of genes in different runs. In this set of experiments, the first strategy was adopted.

Figure 2 compares the inferred (produced by the selected model) and target gene expression profiles (i.e. network behaviors), in which the behavior of the inferred model (left) is almost identical to that of the target network (right). In addition, a comparison between the values of the chosen and expected kinetic orders was made and the results are shown in Table 1. As can be seen, very similar values can be obtained by the proposed approach.

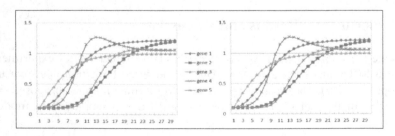

Fig. 2. Overview of the network behaviors of the five-gene artificial network

Table 1. Comparison of kinetic orders between the inferred and the expected numerical values

Gene-id i		$g_{i,1}$	$g_{i,2}$	$g_{i,3}$	$g_{i,4}$	$g_{i,5}$	$h_{i,1}$	$h_{i,2}$	$h_{i,3}$	$h_{i,4}$	$h_{i,5}$	α_i	β_i
1	(expected)	0	0	1	0	-0.1	2	0	0	0	0	15	10
	(inferred)	0	0	0.9926	0	-0.1221	2.0013	0	0	0	0	14.0093	9.2967
2	(expected)	2	0	0	0	0	0	2	0	0	0	10	10
	(inferred)	2.0000	0	0	0	0	0	2.0000	0	0	0	10.0000	10.0001
3	(expected)	0	-0.1	0	0	0	0	-0.1	2	0	0	10	10
	(inferred)	0	-0.0934	0	0	0	0	-0.0951	2.0064	0	0	10.1508	10.1553
4	(expected)	2	0	0	0	-1	0	0	0	2	0	8	10
	(inferred)	1.9963	0	0	0	-0.9903	0	0	0	1.9632	0	8.1886	10.2462
5	(expected)	0	0	0	2	0	0	0	0	0	2	10	10
	(inferred)	0	0	0	2.0000	0	0	0	0	0	2.0000	10.0000	10.0000

The above results show that, the most important contribution of our framework is to discover the plausible pathway diagram(s) (see Figure 3), which can be drawn through the inferred kinetic orders (Table 1). Taking this five-gene network as an example, we can find that although the final inferred GRN model coordinated with the expected structures perfectly, and therefore the plausible pathways of the model were consistent with those of the expected model, there were still some gene regulations (i.e., $g_{i,j}$ or $h_{i,j}$) out of the preferred connection relationships. Further examination shows that $g_{3,1}$ and $g_{3,4}$ were against the suggestion in 2 and 9 runs out of 30 runs, respectively. Under such situation, in considering the plausible pathways of a network, one needs to keep in mind that there are two possible scenarios behind the diagram(s) as described below.

First, in spite of fitting all genetic relationships of the inferred model, some kinetic orders still deviated from the preferred topology given by the prior knowledge. The reason is that it is easier to the inferred models to meet the targeted network dynamics by behaving this way. In this case, one can examine the unfitted kinetic orders by looking into the biological meanings of the corresponding genes. These unfitted topologies are perhaps essential for the further in vivo experiments. Second, if the final inferred model did not match all the genetic relationships, the existence of some links can thus not be sure. These links were in contravention of the expected structures. One possible solution to such a situation is to give a threshold for looking into these most unfitted genes and for considering whether to design new experiments in terms of biological context.

Obviously, this set of experiments lies in the first scenario. Since the artificial dataset was used, we considered the suggested topology is equal to the 'true' topology. Hence, $g_{3,1}$ and $g_{3,4}$ were regarded as the parameters which tried to capture the target network behaviors. We thus discarded additional analyses of these two genes. These results demonstrated that if we derive connection relationships from the existing biological knowledge and directly encode the information in the form of topology constraints to prioritize the search solutions, then the meaningful solutions corresponding to similar network behaviors can be obtained. In this way, the inferred kinetic orders will suggest some attempts at new experimental design. These results indicated the effectiveness of the presented framework that has successfully integrated the PKDs into the GA-PSO network modeling approach with an objective function weighting both the curve-fitting and the structural priorities.

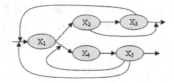

Fig. 3. Overview of the pathway diagram of the five-gene artificial dataset

4   Conclusion

The need of integrating the knowledge-based and data-driven inference strategies has been emphasized and addressed in order to construct network models with both correct network structures and behaviors. This study proposes a systematic framework that combines the strength of both knowledge and data to construct the ODEs network model. Experiments have been reported to validate the proposed approach. The results show that the knowledge-driven modeling approach is able to derive the parameter set implied by the available biological meanings and to reconstruct the corresponding gene expression profiles. The results confirm that the proposed approach can take advantages of using PKDs to interpret the network regulatory relationships.

References

1. Voit, E.O.: Biochemical systems theory: a review. ISRN Biomathematics 2013, 1–53 (2013)
2. Engl, H.W., Flamm, C., Kügler, P., Lu, J., Müller, S., et al.: Inverse problems in systems biology. Inverse Problems 25, 123014 (2009)
3. Alterovitz, G., Ramoni, M.F.: Knowledge-Based Bioinformatics: from Analysis to Interpretation. Wiley, Chichester (2010)
4. Ogata, H., Goto, S., Sato, K., Fujibuchi, W., Bono, H., et al.: KEGG: Kyoto encyclopedia of genes and genomes. Nucleic Acids Research 27, 29–34 (1999)
5. Pico, A., Kelder, T., van Iersel, M., Hanspers, K., Conklin, B.R., et al.: WikiPathways: pathway editing for the people. PLoS Biology 6, e184 (2008)
6. Cho, R.J., Campbell, M.J., Winzeler, E.A., Steinmetz, L., Conway, A., et al.: A genome-wide transcriptional analysis of the mitotic cell cycle. Molecular Cell 2, 65–73 (1998)
7. Lee, I., Li, Z., Marcotte, E.M.: An improved, bias-reduced probabilistic functional gene network of baker's yeast, Saccharomyces cerevisiae. PloS One 2, e988 (2007)
8. Spellman, P.T., Sherlock, G., Zhang, M.Q., Iyer, V.R., Anders, K., et al.: Comprehensive identification of cell cycle-regulated genes of the yeast Saccharomyces cerevisiae by microarray hybridization. Molecular Biology of the Cell 9, 3273–3297 (1998)
9. Kikuchi, S., Tominaga, D., Arita, M., Takahashi, K., Tomita, M.: Dynamic modeling of genetic networks using genetic algorithm and S-system. Bioinformatics 19, 643–650 (2003)
10. Maki, Y., Ueda, T., Okamoto, M., Uematsu, N., Inamura, K., et al.: Inference of genetic network using the expression profile time course data of mouse P19 cells. Genome Informatics, 382–383 (2002)
11. Lee, W.P., Hsiao, Y.T.: An adaptive GA-PSO approach with gene clustering to infer S-system models of gene regulatory network. The Computer Journal 54, 1449–1464 (2011)
12. Cao, H., Kang, L., Chen, Y., Yu, J.: Evolutionary modeling of systems of ordinary differential equations with genetic programming. Genetic Programming and Evolvable Machines 1, 309–337 (2000)

A Framework for Automatic
Hair Counting and Measurement

Qian Zhang

Department of Information Science and Technology, Taishan University
Taian City, Shandong Province, China
aazhqg@hotmail.com

Abstract. Alopecia is a research focus in clinical dermatology. Compare with other skin diseases diagnosis, it is a tough task to measure the effects of hair treatment. In the paper, we propose a framework for hair analysis and measurement based on digital image, which includes hair numbers in the region of interested, hair diameter and hair length. Several techniques are considered in our research: an improved classical iterative thresholding method for hair image segmentation motivated by divide and conquer design paradigm, skeleton extraction method for hair counting, and curvature analysis method for cross hair partition. Experiments are performed to demonstrate the effectiveness and robustness of our system.

Keywords: Hair counting, Hair measurement, Iterative thresholding method, Skeleton extraction, Image segmentation, Gauss Curvature.

1 Introduction

Hair loss is very common that most of the time it is considered a normal variation and not a disease. Most people lose about 50 to 100 head hairs a day. These hairs are replaced — they grow back in the same follicle on your head. If you're losing more than that, though, something may be wrong. The medical term for hair loss — losing enough hair that a person has visibly thin or balding patches — is alopecia [1]. Hair counting and measurement is an important part to discriminate alopecia from hair normal physiology variation.

Researchers began hair loss measurement from 1983. All of them majored in choosing valid region and analysis method in medical. At first, they selected sample hair region and observed the hair organization cell through microscope [2]. In 1996, Courtois M et al [3] reported the data using phototrichogram method in 10 male subjects, balding and non-balding, by observations at monthly intervals over a period of 8-14 years. In 2002, Amornsiripanitch invented a new method to measure all parameters of hair cycles which called DIHAM (Digital Image for Hair Analysis and Measurement). The method would help identifying the defects of hair cycle in all men and women. These defects could be monitored in general follow up, in specific treatment and in research to find a better hair cycle control factors. In addition, experiment shows that more than 320 hairs per image cannot be measured with 100% reproducibility by hand [4].

D.-S. Huang et al. (Eds.): ICIC 2014, LNBI 8590, pp. 193–202, 2014.
© Springer International Publishing Switzerland 2014

Hairs' magnification in the image is different with camera parameters setting. For example, there are about 400 hairs in a 1600*1200 image, and also hair number can change to 30 with the same resolution. Influenced by hair magnification, a robust image segmentation algorithm is necessary. There are many image segmentation algorithms in the current, such as threshold method, level set method, k-means, watershed, and so on. Among them, threshold method is chosen with less parameter, more efficient and less manual intervention. In our paper, we proposed an improved iterative thresholding method for hair image segmentation, and also give a proof for our improvement. For hair counting, a simple way is hair thinning through skeleton selection, which records the two ends of single hair and also the cross-points of crossed hairs. For hair measurement, crossed hairs are separated based on Gauss Curvature considering image noises.

Aside from the introductory section, the remainder of this paper is organized in five sections. Section 2 is devoted to an improvement iterative thresholding method for hair region segmentation. Hair counting and measurement is explained in section 3 and 4. We guarantee the performance of our system by experiments in section 5. Fnally, section 6 draws the conclusion and our future works.

2   An Improved Iterative Thresholding Method

2.1   Iterative Thresholding Method and Convergence Analysis

The iterative selection method proposed by Ridler and Calvard [5] is based on a two-classes segmentation problem. At iteration n, a new threshold T_n is established using the average of the interested object and the background class means [6]. The iterations termination is decided by the changes $|T_{n+1} - T_n|$. When the change is sufficiently small, the current T_{n+1} is the two-class segmentation threshold. Leung and Fam [7] and Trussel [8] realized two similar methods. Yanni and Horne [9] improved initialization of threshold by the two assumed peaks as $T_1 = (g_{max} + g_{min})/2$ where g_{max} is the highest nonzero gray level and g_{min} is the lowest one. Level set method is based on the curve evolution with a speed from initial defined curve to totally disappearing. Suppose the initial arbitrary curve as two class separation boundary, it can be recorded by an initial threshold T_1, and in the method threshold changes from $T_1 \sim 0$. Compared with level set method, the solution space of iterative thresholding method is from $T_1 \sim T_{n+1}$, and actually it is a very narrow space. The discussion and convergence analysis of thresholding method is in the following.

Consider the two-classes image segmentation. The initial threshold is $T_1 = (g_{max} + g_{min})/2$, and it is $|T_n| = (\overline{G}_{+(n)} + \overline{G}_{-(n)})/2$ after nth iteration, where $\overline{G}_{+(n)}$ and $\overline{G}_{-(n)}$ are the mean gray value of ROI intra-region and its extra-region respectively. Iteration terminates when the changes $|T_{n+1} - T_n| = |\Delta \overline{G}_{+(n)} + \Delta \overline{G}_{-(n)}|/2$ is near to zero. $\Delta \overline{G}_{+(n)}$ and $\Delta \overline{G}_{-(n)}$ are calculated as follows.

$$\Delta \overline{G}_{+(n)} = \overline{G}_{+(n+1)} - \overline{G}_{+(n)}$$
$$= \frac{\iint_{\Omega_+ - \Delta\Omega} I dxdy}{\iint_{\Omega_+ - \Delta\Omega} dxdy} - \frac{\iint_{\Omega_+} I dxdy}{\iint_{\Omega_+} dxdy} \tag{1}$$

where, I is pixel gray value with its coordinate (x, y), and $\Delta \overline{G}_{\Delta\Omega}$ is the mean gray value in evolutional region in nth iteration. Similarly, we can get

$$\Delta \overline{G}_{-(n)} = \frac{\iint_{\Omega} dxdy}{\iint_{\Omega_- + \Delta\Omega} dxdy} (\overline{G}_{\Delta\Omega} - \overline{G}_{-(n)}) \tag{2}$$

As iteration, the interested object region is reduced gradually until object is separated from its background by the current threshold. Suppose object gray value smaller than background in range [0~255], we know $\overline{G}_{+(n)} - \overline{G}_{\Delta\Omega} \leq 0$, and also $\overline{G}_{\Delta\Omega} - \overline{G}_{-(n)} \leq 0$. So $\Delta \overline{G}_{+(n)} \leq 0$ and $\Delta \overline{G}_{-(n)} \leq 0$. We summary formula (1) and (2) to get

$$\Delta \overline{G}_{+(n)} + \Delta \overline{G}_{-(n)} = \iint_{\Delta\Omega} dxdy \cdot \left[\frac{1}{\iint_{\Omega_+ - \Delta\Omega} dxdy} (\overline{G}_{+(n)} - \overline{G}_{\Delta\Omega}) + \frac{1}{\iint_{\Omega_- + \Delta\Omega} dxdy} (\overline{G}_{\Delta\Omega} - \overline{G}_{-(n)}) \right] \tag{3}$$

Suppose $\Omega_+ \leq \Omega_-$, which means object region in image is smaller than its background region. We get

$$2 \cdot \frac{\iint_{\Delta\Omega} dxdy}{\iint_{\Omega_- + \Delta\Omega} dxdy} (\overline{G}_{-(n)} - \overline{G}_{+(n)}) \leq |T_{n+1} - T_n| \leq 2 \cdot \frac{\iint_{\Delta\Omega} dxdy}{\iint_{\Omega_+ - \Delta\Omega} dxdy} (\overline{G}_{-(n)} - \overline{G}_{+(n)}) \tag{4}$$

When $\Delta\Omega \to 0$, the threshold descends near to zero, and when $\Delta\Omega \to \Omega_+$, $(\Omega_- + \Delta\Omega) \to \Omega_{image}$. If we want to expand the segmentation threshold range, one way is that we can change the ratio between Ω_+ and Ω_- which means to increase proportion of object region in the image.

2.2   An Improved Iterative Thresholding Method

In our research, we proposed an improved iterative thresholding method. We divides the original image into n blocks, choose one block of them to keep the original color and others are masked with pixel RGB value (0, 0, 0). A new image is created. The new image is executed via the iterative thresholding method. In our pipeline, number of n new images are created and processed via segmentation algorithm orderly. The segmentation threshold will reduce rapidly as we expect. Our algorithm is illustrated in Figure 1.

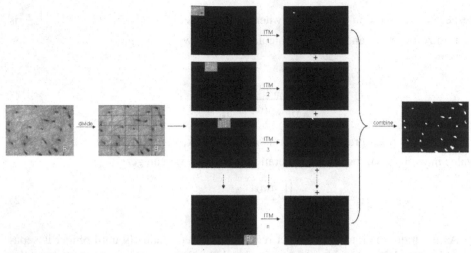

Fig. 1. Illustration for our proposed algorithm. Input image is divided into *n* parts. There are *n* images are segmented via iterative thresholding method (ITM) orderly. Lastly, we combine them as one image.

In the improved algorithm, the segmentation parameter is the block number n. In order to divide an image into n parts, integer n is factorized as the product of two numbers with a constraint given by:

$$minimize \ \ n_1 + n_2$$
$$subject \ to \ \ n = n_1 \times n_2 \tag{5}$$
$$n_1, n_2 > 0 \ \ and \ \ integer$$

In hair images, we found that many hairs crossed together, and also pseudo-cross phenomena were caused by image segmentation. Figure 2 in the following shows an example of hair segmentation results. We can see the contours evolution with n setting. Other results will be illustrated in experiments.

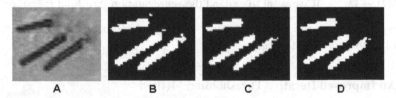

Fig. 2. Isocontours plot of image segmentation with *n* blocks. A is the original hair image, and B, C, D show the segmentation results with *n*=0, *n*=2, and *n*=4 respectively.

3   Hair Counting

How many hairs are in the region of interested (ROI)? The similar computer aided problems are involved in blood cell image recognition, crop seed detection in observation area, human face recognition, etc. For the problem of hair counting, there are several situations as usual: single hair, double hairs crossed, and three or more hairs crossed. One method is to partition them one by one, and then to count number of objects. It is a complex problem to segment hairs into partitions with single hair one by one exactly. Instead of it, a simple way is to find intersection points in each labeled hair region. If returned number of intersection points was zero, it means that a single hair lies in the region. Similarly, we can know how many hairs are in each partition.

Skeleton preserves 2D or 3D shapes topological and size characteristics of the original. Binary image skeleton solves the problem of intersection points via junction points in hairs' skeleton. In this technique thinning algorithms reduce binary images to their skeletons by an iterative shrinking process in which each contour pixel is analyzed. If certain removal criteria are satisfied, that pixel is deleted. In our framework, we mainly refer to Alexandru Telea's approach [10], which is an improvement of fast matching method (FMM) through an arbitrary boundary parameterization. It is robust and efficient with respect to noisy boundaries for endpoints and junctions of the skeleton. So the total hair number in ROI is the sum of total junctions number plus the total single hair number. One example of hair skeleton and counting is show in Figure 3. In labeled region a, hair number is 4, and in regions b, c, d, e, hair number is 3, 4, 3, 2 respectively.

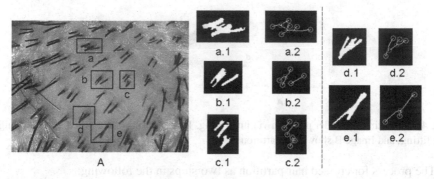

Fig. 3. Hair counting via junction points in skeleton. Image A is the original image with hair regions labeled with a, b, c, d and e, and right part is the process of labeled regions in steps image segmentation and junction points' detection in skeleton.

4   Hair Segmentation and Measurement

Hair measurement helps doctors to analyze the biological parameters of hair growth, which includes hair diameter and hair length basically. It is observed that only half hairs are single, nearly half hairs are double crossed together, and seldom hairs are three or more crossed together. For single hair, we can get its diameter and length through minimum ellipse labeling. Hair diameter equals to the shortest ellipse axis and hair length equals to the longest ellipse axis. For crossed hair, we take double crossed case as an example to illustrate our algorithm.

To begin with, we quote the definition of curvature K in the plane curve [11] as follows:

$$K(u,\sigma) = \frac{\dot{X}(u,\sigma)\ddot{Y}(u,\sigma) - \ddot{X}(u,\sigma)\dot{Y}(u,\sigma)}{[\dot{X}(u,\sigma)^2 + \dot{Y}(u,\sigma)^2]^{3/2}} \qquad (6)$$

Where $\dot{X}(u,\sigma) = x(u) \otimes \dot{g}(u,\sigma)$, $\ddot{X}(u,\sigma) = x(u) \otimes \ddot{g}(u,\sigma)$, $\dot{Y}(u,\sigma) = y(u) \otimes \dot{g}(u,\sigma)$, and $\ddot{Y}(u,\sigma) = y(u) \otimes \ddot{g}(u,\sigma)$. $\otimes$ is the convolution operator, while $g(u,\sigma)$ denotes a Gaussian of width σ , and $\dot{g}(u,\sigma)$, $\ddot{g}(u,\sigma)$ are the first and second derivatives of $g(u,\sigma)$ respectively. The partition point on the contours is the point with minimum curvature, which is a negative quantity.

A line crossing through two contour points is the partition border. The first point with minimum curvature lines on the contour, and it is necessary to find another point. We have calculated the junction via skeleton algorithm and we can fit a straight line between two points (partition point *a* and junction point *b*). This line has intersection points with contour. We select the right point *d* as another partition point. Because point *d* and point *a* should be located on both sides of point *b*. Figure 4 shows the process of line fitting.

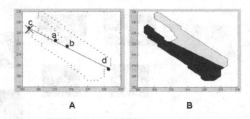

Fig. 4. Illustration of border partition via line fitting. Image A shows the processing of straight line fitting, and Image B shows the partition result.

The process for crossed hair partition as two steps in the following:

Step 1: Curvature calculated
In the step, we extract the edge contours from the edge-map, and fill the gaps in the contours. Then compute curvature at a low scale for the contour.
Step 2: Line fitting
It is to find the minimum curvature and its contour points. Line fitting is done between two points: contour points and junction point. We calculate all intersection points and their position relation. Make sure the right point as another contour points, and partition crossed hairs with three points.

5   Results and Evaluation

To demonstrate the performance of our research, experiments were done on an Intel Dual Core Processor 1.66GHz computer with 2G memory. Hair image database was provided by Ellead Company in Korea. First, we show the image segmentation results using our proposed algorithm. Second, hair counting and measurement results were shown via the comparison with manually counting. Third, for hair measurement performance are tested also via the comparison with manually partition.

5.1   Hair Segmentation Experiments

As we mentioned in section 2, pseudo-cross phenomena are caused by image segmentation. An example is shown in Figure 5. Actually, hairs inside the black rectangle are two single hairs, but they are crossed after image segmentation. Skin color is influenced by light and hair shadow. The properties of refraction and reflection make skin darker around hairs. In special cases, parts of hair roots are hidden under the skin. Our proposed algorithm can avoid the problem as much as possible. In hair images, it is the common situation that hairs are close together without crossing. In the example, the segmentation threshold reduces from 105 to 80 in gray value [0~255].

Fig. 5. Image segmentation. Left image is the original image, middle image is pseudo-cross phenomena, and left image shows the correct result with our proposed algorithm.

5.2   Hair Counting Evaluation and Measurement

The hair counting results through our proposed method (P.M.), and the manual evaluation (M.E.) as well as the absolute and relative differences are shown in Table 1. The absolute error is controlled below 6, and relative error is about below 10%. Hair width and hair length are the average of all single hair with pixels measurement. The crossed hair measurement is only a reference when a doctor focuses on one hair region as his case study. The test data and its' results were listed in Figure 6.

In automatic counting system, the robustness of image segmentation algorithm is critical. In Figure 7, we showed the measurement results with our segmentation algorithm and iterative thresholding method respectively. We can see the influence caused by the image segmentation (special in regions with black box). The evaluation results were shown in Table 2. We can see the errors in A.1 which were caused by image segmentation. In hair counting and average of hair length, the error is in an acceptable range. But the average of hair width has a large error. Because the connect region was detected as a single hair, which enlarged the hair in width direction. And also, as error occurred, system was running with a longer time.

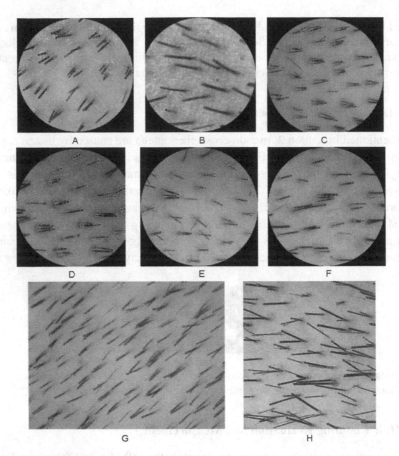

Fig. 6. Hair image and its' counting results from A to H. The read points are the junctions in the crossed hair region.

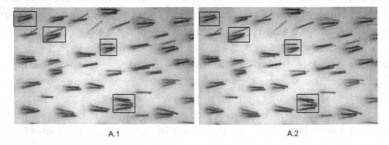

Fig. 7. Comparison with iterative thresholding method (A.1) and our improved algorithm with $n=4$ (A.2)

To demonstrate the processing of hair measurement, Figure 8 shows the partition result visually, and the evaluation is shown in Figure 9. We select the single hairs in original images using Photoshop software manually. For hair diameter manual result is 6.6879 pixels, and our method result is 6.5612 pixels. Absolute error is 0.1267 pixels, and relative error is 1.89%. For hair length manual result is 37.1663 pixels, and our method result is 35.3406 pixels. Absolute error is 1.8257 pixels, and relative error is 4.91%.

Fig. 8. Two examples for crossed hair partition. There is an example in each row. From left to right they are original images, segmented images, line fitting with points on the contours, and partition result.

            manually   manually   automatic

Fig. 9. Evaluation of crossed hair partition. From left to right they are the crossed hair with manual partition, the manual visual result, and the automatic visual result.

Table 1. Hair counting results comparison between proposed method and manually counting

Image No.	Image size	P.M.	M.E.	abs. Diff.	rel. Diff.	Hair width	Hair Length	CPU time (s)
A	287*210	32	33	1	3.03%	6.6501	40.4291	3.4063
B	253*270	13	13	0	0.00%	7.8937	90.2869	3.3125
C	278*320	45	49	4	8.16%	7.4405	44.7577	5.2500
D	297*297	33	33	0	0.00%	6.5702	44.5838	5.2813
E	348*353	32	35	3	8.58%	5.4099	48.9374	4.3594
F	324*337	24	23	1	4.35%	6.6825	57.6405	4.4531
G	397*525	147	153	6	3.92%	5.0203	38.0637	19.1719
H	437*391	105	108	3	2.78%	4.0944	41.4821	16.7969

Table 2. Comparison with iterative thresholding method and our improved algorithm with $n=4$

Image No.	Image size	P.M.	M.E.	abs. Diff.	rel. Diff.	Hair width	Hair Length	CPU time (s)
A.1	365*554	83	80	3	3.75%	8.3348	40.6492	14.5469
A.2	365*554	78	80	2	2.50%	4.8555	37.9398	6.3594

6   Conclusion and Future Works

In the paper, we proposed a framework for digital hair analysis and measurement. To avoid the pseudo-cross phenomena caused by image segmentation, we improved the classical iterative thresholding method with divide and conquer design paradigm using number of (n-1) masks. It can enlarge the candidate threshold space. The curvature of plane curve is useful for crossed hairs partition. Experiments demonstrate our method is efficient with high performance. There still have some problems caused by image segmentation, skeleton, and partition. For example, the tiny hairs in our images couldn't be detected, and in the current system, we detect them manually. We will continue to improve our system in the follow-up research.

Acknowledgments. This research was supported by the Shandong Provincial Natural Science Foundation, China (ZR2013FQ029); by the Higher Educational Science and-Technology Program of Shandong Province, China (J11LG58).

References

1. Dudda-Subramanya, R., Alexis, A.F., Siu, K., Sinha, A.A.: Alopecia Areata: Genetic Complexity Underlies Clinical Heterogeneity. European Journal of Dermatology EJD 17(5), 367–374 (2007)
2. Rushton, D.H., James, K.C., Mortimer, C.H.: The Unit Area Trichogram in The Assessment of Androgen-Dependent Alopecia. British Journal Dermatol (109), 429–437 (1983)
3. Karam, J.M., Courtois, B., Holjo, M., Leclercq, J.L., Viktorovitch, P.: Collective Fabrication of Gallium Arsenide Based Microsystems. In: Proc. SPIE's 1996 Symposium on Micromachining and Microfabrication, pp. 99–129 (1996)
4. Ulrike, B.P., Antonella, T., David, A.W., Ralph, M.T.: Hair Growth and Disorders, pp. 138–142. Springer (2008)
5. Ridler, T.W., Calvard, S.: Picture Thresholding Using an Iterative Selection Method. IEEE Trans. Syst. Man Cybern, SMC-8, 630–632 (1978)
6. Sezgin, M., Sankur, B.: Survey over Image Thresholding Techniques and Quantitative Performance Evaluation. Journal of Electronic Imaging 13(1), 146–165 (2004)
7. Leung, C.K., Lam, F.K.: Performance Analysis of a Class of Iterative Image Thresholding Algorithms. Pattern Recognition 29(9), 1523–1530 (1996)
8. Trussel, H.J.: Comments on Picture Thresholding using Iterative Selection Method. IEEE Trans. Syst. Man Cybern, SMC-9, 311 (1979)
9. Yanni, M.-K., Horne, E.: A New Approach to Dynamic Thresholding. In: 9th European Conf. Sig. Process., vol. 1, pp. 34–44 (1994)
10. Telea, A., Wijk, J.: An Augmented Fast Marching Method for Computing Skeletons and Centerlines. In: Proc. IEEE vissym 2002, pp. 251–260 (2002)
11. He, X.C., Yung, N.H.C.: Corner Detector Based on Global and Local Curvature Properties. Optical Engineering 47(5), 057008 (2008)

A Deep Learning Method for Classification
of EEG Data Based on Motor Imagery

Xiu An, Deping Kuang, Xiaojiao Guo, Yilu Zhao, and Lianghua He

The Key Laboratory of Embedded System and Service Computing, Ministry of Education,
Tongji University, Shanghai 201804, China
Department of Computer Science and Technology, Tongji University, Shanghai 201804, China
anxiuaijia88@sina.cn

Abstract. Effectively extracting EEG data features is the key point in Brain Computer Interface technology. In this paper, aiming at classifying EEG data based on Motor Imagery task, Deep Learning (DL) algorithm was applied. For the classification of left and right hand motor imagery, firstly, based on certain single channel, a weak classifier was trained by deep belief net (DBN); then borrow the idea of Ada-boost algorithm to combine the trained weak classifiers as a more powerful one. During the process of constructing DBN structure, many RBMs (Restrict Boltzmann Machine) are stacked on top of each other by setting the hidden layer of the bottom layer RBM as the visible layer of the next RBM, and Contrastive Divergence (CD) algorithm was also exploited to train multilayered DBN effectively. The performance of the proposed DBN was tested with different combinations of hidden units and hidden layers on multiple subjects, the experimental results showed that the proposed method performs better with 8 hidden layers. The recognition accuracy results were compared with Support vector machine (SVM) and DBN classifier demonstrated better performance in all tested cases. There was an improvement of 4 – 6% for certain cases.

Keywords: Deep Learning, Motor Imagery, EEG, Brain-computer interface, Ada-boost.

1 Introduction

Brain-computer interface is a communication control system without depending on the normal output pathways that composed by brain, peripheral nerve and muscles, that can transfer brain information and realize control by using computer or electrical device to analyze the brain activities under specific task [1].

A lot of studies have done by Shang-Lin Wu and his follows indicates that using the common spatial pattern (CSP) for feature extraction from EEG and the linear discriminate analysis (LDA) for motor imagery classification obtained an average classification accuracy of 80% for two subjects [4]. Additionally, Yohimbe Tom ita et al. proposed bimodal approach that using near infrared spectroscopy (NIRS) simultaneously with EEG to measure the hemodynamic fluctuations in the brain during stimulation with steady-state visual evoked potentials (SSVEP) made the wrong classification for 9 classes for 13 subjects [7,18]. The studies conducted by Like's

D.-S. Huang et al. (Eds.): ICIC 2014, LNBI 8590, pp. 203–210, 2014.

group demonstrated that combining multi-scale filters and Principal Component Analysis (PCA) to enhance the classification performance in identifying EEG signals works and achieve a classification accuracy of 91.13% [2].

Deep Learning is a new field in itself in the machine learning whose motivation is to simulate the human brain's mechanism to explain the data by the composition of multiple non-linear transformations of the data, with the goal of obtain more abstract and ultimately more useful representation [3-5].

Despite the success of DBN, its application in Electroencephalogram (EEG)-based Brain Computer Interaction (BCI) is still rare. The main difficulty is the enormously high feature dimensionality spanning EEG channel, frequency, and time [10]. Deep Learning algorithm has shown superior learning and classification performance in fields such as computer vision, natural language processing and other areas for its excellent feature extraction capabilities except the field of EEG data analysis [15]. In this paper, a classify method was proposed based on deep learning with Ada-boost algorithm. Using this method, the misclassification rate of EEG signals decreased even using fewer channels. The final powerful classifier is combined by several weak classifiers which are trained using single channel data.

The sections below are our learning method and experiments. Section 2 mainly describes the RBM and DBN method and Section 3 presents our experimental results on MI EEG dataset.

2   Method

2.1   Theory of Deep Learning

Deep learning algorithm focus on learning multiple levels of representation of raw data automatically, using a deep architecture which composed of many hidden layers. This algorithm automatically extracts the high-level features necessary for classification which involving more meaningful information that hierarchically depends on other features. Here we use DBN model which formed by a plurality of RBM, each RBM is trained greedily and unsupervised [5].

An RBM has a single layer of hidden layer that are disconnected with the units in the same layer and have undirected, symmetrical connections to the units in the visible layer which makes it easy to compute the conditional probabilities. The key issue of training the RBM is to get generative weights. As shown in Fig. 1, W represents the weights between visible and hidden layers, b, c correspond to the bias of visual and hidden layer respectively [3].

The type of RBM we employed in this work is Gaussian RBMs which use real-valued visible units for training the first layer of the DBNs. Fig. 1 shows the structure of the RBM:

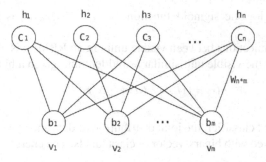

Fig. 1. Structure of RBM

2.2   Classification of MI Based on Deep Belief Net

Now, let v represents the feature vector containing only one channel features. An RBM defines a joint distribution on it, regard as the visible units in DBN and h, the hidden units as follow format [13]:

$$p(v) = \frac{\sum_{h} e^{-E(v,h)}}{\sum_{u}\sum_{g} e^{-E(u,g)}} \tag{1}$$

Where E is the energy function defined as

$$E(v,h) = \sum_{j \in visible} a_j v_j - \sum_{j \in hidden} b_j h_j - \sum_{i,j} v_j h_j \omega_{ij} \tag{2}$$

Where V_j, h_j are the binary states if visible unit i and hidden unit j, a_i, b_j are their biases and w_{ij} is the weight between them. The network assigns a probability to every possible pair of a visible and a hidden vector via this energy function:

$$p(v,h) = \frac{1}{Z} e^{-E(v,h)} \tag{3}$$

The probability that the network assigns to a training data can be optimized by adjusting the weights and biases to lower the energy of it. The derivative of the log probability of a training vector with respect to a weight calculated as follow:

$$\frac{\partial \log p(v)}{\partial \omega_{ij}} = \frac{\sum_{v \in D} \partial \log p(v)}{\partial \omega_{ij}} = E_{data}\left[\frac{\partial E(v,h)}{\partial \omega_{ij}}\right] - E_{model}\left[\frac{\partial E(u,g)}{\partial \omega_{ij}}\right] \tag{4}$$

Where the first item is the expectation of $\partial E(v,h)/\partial w_{ij}$ responds to the training set D and the hidden variables are sampled according to the conditional distribution of the dataset on $p(h/v)$, given a randomly selected training sample, v, the binary state, h_j, of each hidden unit, j, is set to 1 with probability

$$p(h_j = 1 | v) = \sigma(b_j + \sum v_j w_{ij}) \tag{5}$$

Where $\sigma(x)$ is the logistic sigmoid function $1/(1+exp(-x))$. $v_i h_j$ is then an unbiased sample.

For no direct connections between visible units in an RBM, it is also the way to get unbiased sample of the visible unit similar as hidden unit, given a hidden vector

$$p(v_i = 1 \mid h) = \sigma(\alpha_i + \sum_j h_j \omega_{ij})$$ (6)

For training an RBM classifier, the joint distribution of data and class labels, the visible vector is concatenated with binary vector of class labels. The energy function becomes:

$$E(v,l,h) = -\sum_i \alpha_i v_i - \sum_j b_j h_j - \sum_{i,j} \omega_{ij} - \sum_y c_y l_y - \sum_{y,j} \omega_{yj} h_j l_y$$ (7)

Where l is the binary class label and w_{ij} is the weights between hidden and label units.

2.3   Boost of the Single Channel Deep Belief Net

Based on the former test performance of the single channel, we adopt the idea of Ada-boost algorithm [8] that combine the weak classifier to one more powerful classifier [19][20]. Here the channel C3, C4, Fc4 were chose as the meta data and the combination tactics to boost each weak classifiers refer to follow [15][16]:

$$M_k(X) = \sum_{k=1}^{k} c_k f_k(X)$$ (8)

Where c_k is the estimated coefficient for each DBN model and each DBN model is produces a discrete classification for input data [17].

The whole structure of our model based on DBN shows as follow:

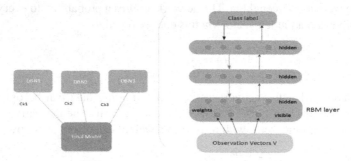

Fig. 2. Structure of the final model

3   Experiment

3.1   Experimental Data

The experimental data was collected from 4 subjects, all of them are students, male and without brain disease history. 30 trials left-hand imagination EEG data and 30 right ones were selected as sample for analysis for each subject. Fig. 3 shows the way to get the final data which contained 7s data, of which the search adopted the data from 3s to 7s, sample rate is 250HZ/s and each of them contained 4s data, which means that each of them have 1000 sample points.

For the EEG data, de-noising processing and filtering were applied such as Elec-tro-Oculogram (EOG) as well as separated the data according to the channel. The EOG is removed by the Neuroscan software. And for the filtering work, this paper mainly analyzes the frequency band of 8-30Hz. So an elliptic filter was designed, with band-pass from 8 to 30Hz. And then converted the time domain data to frequency domain data via FFT (Fast Fourier Transformation) algorithm.

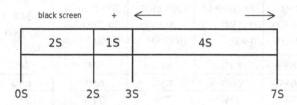

Fig. 3. Experiment time distribution for one trial

3.2   Test on Combine of the Single Channel

For each subject, 20 trials were selected as the train set from the total data with the remaining data to be the test samples from each channel. The weights were randomly initialized and the turning parameters were set as: learning rate for weight and biases = 0.07, momentum=0.5 and weight decay = 0.002. Four to sixteen layers were trained and tested for each channel of every subject. The results for eight layers worked better than others and the performance of nine and ten or more layers were very similar. In the paper we have not shown results for all of the layers due to space limitations. Table 1 shows the result of the classification performance with 7,8, 9, 10 layers respectively, using a fixed layer size of 2048 under the same condition and the result shows that the average recognition rate of DBN with 8 hidden layers is 0.81 which is higher than others.

The result for every subject with different hidden layers lists as Table 1 and the number represent the recognition accuracy rate:

Table 1. Performance of DBN with different layers

Subjects	DBN			
	7 hidden layers	8hidden layers	9 hidden layers	10 hidden layers
SHY	73%	85%	83%	80%
XB	56%	65%	59%	58%
ZJH	44%	77%	78%	74%
WDM	82%	95%	94%	96%

According to the results above which shows that the DBN classifier outperform others with 8 hidden layers, then we did the test for the different combination of hidden units under this condition, the result shows that there's no obvious effect on the performance. Table 2 shows the final performance of the recognition rate of all cases.

Table 2. Performance of DBN with different hidden nodes

Subjects	DBN_8 layers					
	2000-800 -700-600 -500-300 -200-900	3000-1800-1 700-1600-15 00-1300-120 0-900	4000-1100- 1200-1300- 1400-1500- 1600-900	5000-2100-2 200-2300-24 00-2500-260 0-900	6000-310 0-3200-33 00-3400-3 500-3600- 1900	8000-2100- 2200-2300- 2400-2500- 2600-1900
SHY	83%	84%	84%	85%	84%	85%
XB	65%	66%	65%	65%	65%	64%
ZJH	73%	75%	77%	77%	75%	74%
WDM	96%	94%	93%	95%	95%	95%

The performances of SVM based on the same input features was further investigated.Fig.4 shows the contradistinction of recognition accuracy for DBN and SVM, the performance of SVM is inferior to that of DBN and the discrepancy is particularly evident for subject ZJH and WDM.

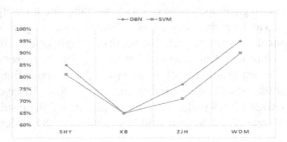

Fig. 4. The recognition accuracy of DBN vs. SVM

3.3   Experiment on Time Series

The experimental data was by time segments, and each section contains 1s as data to be classified. Fig.4 presents the performance of classification with different subjects. From the figure we can see that the average recognition rate of first 2 seconds can reach 83%, while the last 2 seconds is lower, we can explain that at the beginning of the experiment the subjects can preferably focus on the motor imagery experiment, but with the passage of time, the subjects may get absent-minded which would affect the validity of the experimental data, and finally leads to the low recognition accuracy.

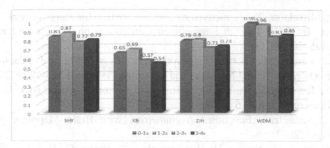

Fig. 5. Classification accuracy of time series

4   Conclusion

In this paper, a DBN classifier model for the classification of MI pattern is proposed. In the research, results showed consistent improvements for all tested cases over SVM through multiple cross-validation experiments. The test on different combination of hidden units was conducted, and it is found that the number of nodes had no obvious effect on the performance of classification. The experimental results showed that Deep Learning algorithm performs effectively on the task of classification with MI data. And the experimental results of time series show that the performance of classification depends on concentration of the subjects, for the accuracy rate is affected greatly by the status of the subject. Deep learning plays an important role in the process of classification because it can learn the advanced abstract representation from numerous unlabeled data. Our study suggests that DBN has great potential to be a powerful tool for the BCI research.

For the next stage, we'll try to employ this algorithm into classification of Multi-class based on EEG data, and merge more channels in order to take full use of the EEG data information to achieve better recognition results.

References

1. Reza, K., Chai, Q.: A Brain-Computer Interface for classifying EEG correlates of chronic mental stress. In: Proceedings of International Joint Conference on Neural Networks, pp. 757–762 (2011)
2. Li, K., Rui, Q.: Classification of EEG Signals by Multi-Scale Filtering and PCA. In: IEEE International Conference on Intelligent Computing and Intelligent Systems, ICIS 2009, pp. 362–366 (2009)
3. Gorge, H.S.O.: A fast learning algorithm for deep belief nets. Neural Computation, 1527–1554 (2006)
4. Wu, S., Wu, W.: Common Spatial Pattern and Linear Discriminant Analysis for Motor Imagery Classification. In: 2013 IEEE Symposium on Computational Intelligence, Cognitive Algorithms, Mind, and Brain (CCMB), pp. 146–151 (2013)
5. Yoshua, B., Pascal, L.: Greedy layer-wise training of deep networks. NIPS (2006)
6. Jarrett, K., Kavukcuoglu, K.: What is the best – stage architecture for object recognition. In: ICCV (2009)

7. Yohei, Y., Mitsukura, Y.: Hemodynamic characteristics for improvement of EEG-BCI performance. In: 2013 The 6th International Conference on Human System Interaction (HSI), pp. 495–500 (2013)
8. Yohei, T., Yasue, M.: Boosted Network Classifiers for Local Feature Selection. IEEE Transactions on Neural Networks and Learning Systems, 1767–1778 (2012)
9. Plamen, D., Jesse, S.: Classification of Imagined Motor Tasks for BCI. In: 2008 IEEE Region 5 Conference, pp. 1–6 (2008)
10. Karl, J.: Characterizing Functional Asymmetries with Brain Mapping, pp. 161–186. The MIT Press (2003)
11. Guger, C., Schlogl, C., Neuper, D., Walterspacher, T., Strein, G.: Rapid prototyping of an EEG-based brain computer interface (BCI). IEEE Trans. on Neural Systems and Rehabilitation Engineering, 49–58 (2001)
12. Wolpaw, J., Birbaumer, N.: Brian-computer interfaces for communication and control. Clinical Neurophysiology, 767–791 (2002)
13. Bengio, Y., Lecun, Y.: Scaling learning algorithms towards AI. Large-Scale Kernel Machines, 1–34 (2007)
14. Jonathan, R., Wolpaw, N., Birbaumer, D.: Brain-computer interfaces for communication and control. Clin. Neurophysiol., 767–791 (2002)
15. Kirkup, L., Searle, A.: EEG-based system for rapid on-off switching without prior learning. Medical and Biological Engineering and Computing, 504–509 (2007)
16. Hochberg, L., Serruya, M.: Neuronal ensemble control of prosthetic devices by a human with tetraplegia. Nature, 164–170 (2006)
17. Cheng, M., Gao, X.: Design and implementation of a brain-computer interface with high transfer rates. IEEE Transactions on Biomedical Engineering, 1181–1186 (2002)
18. Shoker, L., Sanei, S.: Distinguishing between left and right finger movement from EEG using SVM. In: Engineering in Medicine and Biology 27th Annual Conference, pp. 5420–5423 (2005)
19. Ohkawa, Y., Suryanto, C.: Image set-based hand shape recognition using camera selection driven by multi-class Ada Boosting. Advances in Visual Computing, 555–566 (2011)
20. Shen, C., Li, H.: Boosting through optimization of margin distributions. IEEE Trans. Neural Netw. Learn. Syst., 659–666 (2010)

Investigation of New Statistical Features for BCI Based Sleep Stages Recognition through EEG Bio-signals

Ibrahim Sefik[1], Furkan Elibol[2], Ibrahim Furkan Ince[3], and Ilker Yengin[4]

[1] TÜBİTAK MAM, Energy Institute,
Baris Mah. Dr. Zeki Acar Cad. No:1 P.K. 21, 41470, Gebze, Kocaeli, Turkey
ibrahim.sefik@tubitak.gov.tr
[2] TÜBİTAK BİLGEM, National Research Institute of Electronics and Cryptology,
Baris Mah. Dr. Zeki Acar Cad. No:1 P.K. 21, 41470, Gebze, Kocaeli, Turkey
furkan.elibol@tubitak.gov.tr
[3] Hanwul Multimedia Communication Co. Ltd. 1012-1015, Ace High Tech21,
1470, U-dong, Haeundae-gu, Busan, Republic of Korea
furkan@hanwul.com
[4] A*STAR, Institute of High Performance Computing,
1 Fusionopolis Way ,#16-16 Connexis North, 138632, Singapore
yengini@ihpc.a-star.edu.sg

Abstract. Electroencephalogram (EEG) is one of the oldest techniques available to read brain data. It is a methodology to measure and record the electrical activity of brain using sensitive sensors attached to the scalp. Brain's electrical activity is visualized on computers in form of signals through BCI tools. It is also possible to convert these signals into digital commands to provide human-computer interaction (HCI) through adaptive user interfaces. In this study, a set of statistical features: mean entropy, skew-ness, kurtosis and mean power of wavelets are proposed to enhance human sleep stages recognition through EEG signal. Additionally, an adaptive user interface for vigilance level recognition is introduced. One-way ANOVA test is employed for feature selection. EEG signals are decomposed into frequency sub-bands using discrete wavelet transform and selected statistical features are employed in SVM for recognition of human sleep stages: stage 1, stage 3, stage REM and stage AWAKE. According to experimental results, proposed statistical features have a significant discrimination rate for true classification of sleep stages with linear SVM. The accuracy of linear SVM reaches to 93% in stage 1, 82% in stage 3, 73% in stage REM and 96% in stage AWAKE with proposed statistical features.

1   Introduction

Human-Computer Interaction (HCI) research is not only based on mouse and keyboard actions anymore; nowadays, HCI research includes interface interaction in environments where sensor-equipped systems collect data to know more about users' activities, preferences, needs and interactions [1]. The new techniques and sensors provide a real-time data acquisition to understand users' daily activities. These

D.-S. Huang et al. (Eds.): ICIC 2014, LNBI 8590, pp. 211–224, 2014.
© Springer International Publishing Switzerland 2014

advancements may be helpful to increase the occurrence of expected outcomes such as improving performance of the users in their daily activities [2]. Using such extensive knowledge about the users' states, it is possible to design of new adaptive systems and interfaces which will bring new perspectives into the HCI research field [3].

There are various methods to obtain user data [4]. However, most of them don't address the need of having direct and real time extensive data to understand users' neurophysiological states to design adaptive systems accordingly [5, 6]. For these purposes, Brain Computer Interface (BCI) technologies provide new sensing techniques to collect data [7]. BCI technologies enables HCI researchers to understand the state of users relying on changes in electrical, chemical and blood flow due to reaction of brain toward specific stimuli [8]. Techniques in BCI aim to provide a communication system that understand users' states by interpreting brain signals and react accordingly through an output device like computers [9] – [13].

HCI researchers suggest that using electroencephalogram (EEG) is very feasible and relatively cheaper to obtain neurophysiological states of users [14, 15]. Using EEG data, it is possible to design adaptive user interfaces that understand users' real states [16, 17]. There are quite a number of such systems suggested by HCI researchers [18, 19]. For instance, researchers proposed the possible interfaces may be designed to adjust information flow, manage interruptions and cognitive load and sense users' cognitive and emotional levels (e.g. confusion – frustration and satisfaction – realization etc.) based on neurophysiological and cognitive states of users [20].

It is also possible to design real-time adaptive interfaces that sense users' neurophysiological and cognitive states such as alertness and vigilance. Detecting alertness and vigilance is an important and challenging HCI topic that requires advanced system design for processes controls [21, 22]. Detecting alertness and vigilance is very critical because lack of alertness and vigilance may cause serious consequences in tasks where users and operators should interact with machines and systems such as power plant control, air traffic control and military equipment [23].

More than in industry related tasks, being at the state of lack of alertness and vigilance is also a serious problem in daily life activities such as driving [24, 25].

To address the issues that may cause due to lack of alertness and vigilance, HCI researchers proposed systems that use real-time analysis of EEG data to detect the alertness and vigilance levels of the users and operators of critical systems [26] – [28].

Using a real time system that continuously monitor user states based on EEG analysis, the general objective of such systems is to provide mechanisms to avoid potential accidents due to the decreased vigilance. Researchers believe that EEG-based technologies are "gold standard" in detection of vigilance and alertness with their technological advantages to provide a task independent, non-disruptive method for detection [29]. They also believe that using EEG detection; it is possible to design systems that improve users' vigilance and alertness to provide safety in critical tasks (e.g. driving and operating mission critical machines etc.) [30] – [32].

Although theoretically EEG-based technologies are "gold standard" in detection of vigilance and alertness, EEG technology has its own technical issues [33]. For instance, EEG signals are non-stationary and non-linear patterns causing difficulty to identify the cognitive tasks since EEG bio-signals are highly subjective and chaotic due to brain's multi-functional activities such as body movements, eye gaze, hearing, smelling which create various wave patterns behave as noise for particular pattern recognition tasks through EEG signals [34].

In this study, addressing the similar problem stated above, a systematic of EEG signal processing for detecting the alertness states of users in their night sleep is introduced. Several statistical features are proposed for linear model construction. A linear SVM classifier [35] is employed for vigilance level classification. Moreover, a prototype adaptive interface that sense users' alertness and vigilance is presented. This study would be helpful for HCI and BCI researchers who seek for a method to accurately interpret EEG signals to detect users' alertness and vigilance states. This paper also would be a guideline for designers who wish to create interfaces that detect users' states for critical tasks such as driving.

2   Materials and Methodology

Sleep stages are good way of identification of the level of alertness of the users [36]. In this study, it is aimed to achieve a true classification using linear SVM to distinguish sleep stages. Following the traditional terminology [37], sleep states are labeled as Stage W (Wakefulness), Stage N1 (NREM 1 sleep), Stage N2 (NREM 2 sleep), Stage N3 (NREM 3 sleep), Stage R (REM sleep) [38].

Using EEG, it is possible to classify sleep vigilance in terms of sleep stages [39]. In this kind of formalization, vigilance could be addressed as wakefulness - sleep and between the levels of vigilance state [40]. To formalize the spectrum ranges, the EEG signals are subdivided into categories of δ (1–4 Hz), θ (4–8 Hz), α(8–13 Hz), β (13–30 Hz) and γ (>30 Hz) [41].

Active wakefulness is a state where the eyes are open [42]. In wakefulness state α EEG signal frequency power is low [43]. On the other hand, the EEG α power is high if the users are in a state of resting [44]. A transition from resting state to sleeping is also possible to detect with EEG [45]. In transition, α power decreases and q power increases moderately [46]. In extended wakefulness, there is a negative correlation with α power and positive correlation with θ power [47]. In this sense, the brain activity could be categorized by interpreting the signal power, in theory [48].

As discussed in introduction section, it is well known that EEG signals are hard to distinguish from each other due to their dynamic, stochastic, non-linear and non-stationary nature [49]. Thus, in order to detect the alertness and vigilance states' of the users by comparing the concurrent state toward a set of classes, alternative methods are required to compensate the shortcomings of traditional ones [50].

2.1   BCI (Brain-Computer Interface) Set up

As suggested by researchers, a typical BCI system should have a set-up with 4 main steps which are EEG signal reading, pre-processing, pattern recognition and output [51]. These main steps are illustrated in Figure 1 as follows:

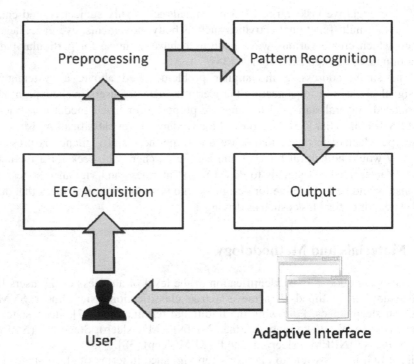

Fig. 1. Main steps in BCI's framework

In EEG acquisition step, EEG signals are recorded using electrodes placed on the users' scalps. After this process, signals are transferred to the pre-processing procedure. The pre-processing procedure is employed to remove any occurrence of noise in EEG signals. The pattern recognition process classifies the features into commands for an output. The output step takes the command and regulates the rest of the system. In output step, it is possible to generate a feedback for users or regulate the information flow of the system to provide an adaptive interface. The design of proposed prototype adaptive interface is discussed in the following sections of this paper.

2.2   Data Acquisition and Pre-processing

In EEG acquisition step, silver-plated electrodes are employed for the recordings. Following 10–20 international electrode placement procedure [52], C3–A2 standard settlement is applied [53]. EEG signal recordings are acquired using a Grass Model-78 Polysomnography [54].

After EEG acquisition, a filter is applied for the EEG recordings between 0.3 and 50 Hz and digitized them (12-bit resolution with sampling rate of 128 Hz per channel) to enable using all eight channels of the instrument simultaneously [55, 56]. With almost 1000 Hz sampling rate, each channel could be read distinctly which also help to have a real-time data processing [57].

2.3   Pattern Recognition from EEG Signals Using DWT

Discrete wavelet transform (DWT) is generally used for discriminating the non-stationary signals with various frequency patterns while Fourier Transform is applied to stationary signals [58]. Since EEG like signals contain plenty of non-stationary patterns, the discrete wavelet transform is chosen instead of Fourier Transform for signal analysis [59]. Basically, the discrete wavelet transform is a decomposition of signals into a set of wavelets which are continuous functions obtained by dilation, contraction and shifting of a single particular function called wavelet prototype [60] as follows:

$$\Psi_{a,b}(t) = \frac{1}{\sqrt{|a|}} \Psi(\frac{t-b}{a}) \tag{1}$$

The function $\Psi_{a,b}(t)$ represents the continuous wavelet family where (a, b) are continuous and real valued shift and scale parameters given by

$$a = a_0^j \quad b = kb_0 a_0^j \tag{2}$$

and where j and k are discretized integer parameters of $\Psi_{a,b}(t)$ as

$$\Psi_{j,k}(t) = a_0^{-j/2} \Psi(a_0^{-j}t - kb_0) \tag{3}$$

where $\Psi_{j,k}(t)$ is the base of discrete wavelet transform (DWT) and the time variable of the transform is still continuous. The coefficients of DWT may be extracted from the continuous time function as

$$d_{j,k} = \langle f_w(t), \Psi_{j,k}(t) \rangle = \frac{1}{a_0^{j/2}} \int f_w(t) \Psi(a_0^{-j}t - kb_0) dt \tag{4}$$

After the DWT basis $\Psi_{j,k}(t)$ is set, a function can be represented in wavelet form as

$$f_w(t) = \sum_j \sum_k \langle f_w(t), \Psi_{j,k}(t) \rangle \Psi_{j,k}(t) \tag{5}$$

Discrete wavelet coefficients play an important role in feature extraction from real-time data. The major priority to analyze the data with DWT is continuity of signals. Another issue typically takes place in the number of decomposition levels of DWT setup which is important for adjusting signal multi-resolution. The number of decomposition levels is generally selected from the dominant frequency component of the signal and levels are selected from the parts of signal which have high correlation with frequencies needed for true classification. Since EEG signals don't contain highly useful frequency components above 30 Hz, the number of levels of decomposition is selected as 4 from D1 to D4 and a final approximation A4 is also employed as shown in Table 1.

Table 1. Decomposition levels with corresponding frequency ranges

Decomposed signal	Frequency range (Hz)
D1	32-64
D2	16-32
D3	8-16
D4	4-8
A4	0-4

The usage of optimum wavelet types is also important since different wavelet types yield different efficiency in different data types. If the data is more like discontinuous, sharp wavelet types such as Haar wavelets are generally used; otherwise smooth wavelets are employed.

On the other hand, another important issue for pattern recognition takes place in true features that can discriminate the classes. In this study, several features are employed for feature selection by means of one-way ANOVA test which is generally used for measuring the discriminating significance of independent variables in statistical analysis [61].

For this purpose, such features: mean entropy, skew-ness, kurtosis and mean power of wavelet segments are extracted from DWT signals (number of epochs = 14400) and those features are evaluated whether they are significantly discriminating features for pattern recognition.

Entropy is often used as a measure of disorder or complexity in pattern recognition. The wavelet energy entropy of each segment of EEG signal can also be a good feature for pattern discrimination. Wavelet mean entropy is calculated from the wavelet spectra of any input signal $x(t)$ in N scaled time-frequency window area where $E = E_1, E_2, E_3, E_4...E_N$ represents the total signal power of each area E_j on different scale domains in which p_j becomes $\dfrac{E_j}{E}$ to normalize distribution of each component that satisfies $\sum\limits_{j=1}^{N} E_j = 1$ for wavelet mean entropy $S_{WT}(p)$ estimation.

Mean entropy of wavelets show the average complexity of entire signal in time-frequency domain such that it does not vary depending on the time or frequency changes.

Similarly, skew-ness is employed to find asymmetry of probability distribution around its mean while kurtosis is used for finding the peakedness degree of corresponding distribution. Skew-ness and kurtosis degree of each wavelet can be a good indicator of particular patterns in EEG signal.

Mean power is also used to find similarity in segments of signal in terms of potential of EEG signal. Table 2 shows the equations of proposed features with their corresponding signals from a 15 minutes Stage REM sleep as follows:

Table 2. Signals of proposed features from a 15 minutes Stage REM sleep

Signals Obtained From Coefficients of Proposed Features	Equations
entropy	$$S_{WT} \equiv S_{WT}(p) = -\sum_{j<0} p_j \cdot \ln(p_j)$$
skewness	$$S_{K_{MC}} = \frac{\sum_{i=1}^{N} \frac{(x_i - \bar{x})^3}{N}}{\left[\sum_{i=1}^{N} \frac{(x_i - \bar{x})^2}{N}\right]^{\frac{3}{2}}}$$
kurtosis	$$K_{MC} = \frac{\sum_{i=1}^{N} \frac{(x_i - \bar{x})^4}{N}}{\left[\sum_{i=1}^{N} \frac{(x_i - \bar{x})^2}{N}\right]^{2}} - 3$$
power of beta band power of alpha band	$$\bar{x} = \frac{1}{N}\sum_{i=1}^{N} x_i$$

A collection of 72000 rows of data is prepared with corresponding classes and one-way ANOVA test is applied for feature selection. Table 3 shows the ANOVA results as follows:

Table 3. One-way ANOVA test results

		Sum of Squares	df	Mean Square	F	Sig.
Mean Entropy	Between Groups	87,702	4	21,925	3875,398	,000
	Within Groups	407,318	71995	,006		
	Total	495,020	71999			
Kurtosis	Between Groups	3272,715	4	818,179	246,937	,000
	Within Groups	238541,332	71995	3,313		
	Total	241814,047	71999			
Skew-ness	Between Groups	454,057	4	113,514	236,762	,000
	Within Groups	34517,588	71995	,479		
	Total	34971,645	71999			
Mean power (Alpha Band)	Between Groups	13962307617471,470	4	3490576904367,868	876,474	,000
	Within Groups	286721572295297,500	71995	3982520623,590		
	Total	300683879912769,000	71999			
Mean power (Beta Band)	Between Groups	3375047581652,782	4	843761895413,196	371,331	,000
	Within Groups	163591404194001,600	71995	2272260631,905		
	Total	166966451775654,300	71999			

According to ANOVA test; proposed features have a significant relation with corresponding classes with p-value < 0.001. Finally, 4 numbers of selected features: mean entropy, skew-ness, kurtosis and mean power of wavelets are employed in linear SVM [62] for true classification of sleep stages.

3   Experimental Results

Proposed BCI system is tested with participants (n=20; 9 females and 11 males) at "Dr.Suat Seren Breast Illnesses Education and Research Hospital". The subject group with an age rate of 18 to 65 years (average=33.5) and a Body Mass Index (BMI) of $7.3 kg/m^2$ is asked to participate in the experimental study. All the subjects are reported as healthy and normal (passed the neurological screening, not sleep-deprived, no medication and alcohol during the course of the study and no deviations from usual circadian cycle). EEG recordings are obtained and inspected by two well-trained neurologists with years of EEG experiences. Also, neurologists are employed to verify the EEG readings' accuracy for the state of indicated alert, drowsy or sleepy states of subjects. Stage 2 is not evaluated in the experiment due to lack of data obtained at the hospital. Table 4 shows the performances of linear SVM in sleep stages recognition with proposed features as follows:

Table 4. classification performance of SVM with proposed features in sleep stages

Classes	Classifier	Type	True	False	Accuracy
Stage 1	SVM	Linear	6696	504	0.93
Stage 3	SVM	Linear	5904	1296	0.82
Stage REM	SVM	Linear	5256	1944	0.73
Stage AWAKE	SVM	Linear	6912	288	0.96

SVM classification results in very successful accuracies with proposed features: mean entropy, skew-ness, kurtosis and mean power of wavelets in time-frequency domain. Here, totally 7200 feature vectors are gone through a classification process. These total 7200 vectors are obtained from 15 minute EEG signals that their classes are predetermined manually by 2 Head Doctors at Dr.Suat Seren Breast Illnesses Education and Research Hospital. According to experimental results, the accuracy of linear SVM reaches to 93% in stage 1, 82% in stage 3, 73% in stage REM and 96% in stage AWAKE with proposed statistical features.

4   Design Adaptive Interface for Attention Levels

The set of proposed BCI system is described in previous parts and illustrated in Figure 1. Accordingly, the last step is to give feedback to users on their alertness levels. Although it is not implemented in the actual system, a simple adaptive interface is developed which works as a display that assists users of the system on their level of alertness as well as changing the nature of the work flow when it is necessary. In monitoring states, the alertness levels of the users is displayed as a visual feedback as in Figure 2.

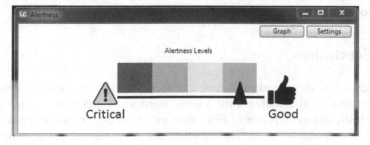

Fig. 2. Visual feedback interface for alertness levels

Accordingly, the four level bars show the alertness levels of the users (from critical to good). For example, proposed framework uses the pitch of the sound to indicate the degree of the sleep level, as well as displaying images in forms of icons to show the alertness levels. Users may click on the differently painted attention level bar to hear a sound that resembles their attention level. It is also possible to view a linear graphic to follow the level of the alertness by clicking the "graph" button.

The monitoring interface changes if there is a change in attention levels which may be mission critical. For instance, if the system detects the users' level of alertness and vigilance is dropping down to critical states that may create some implications on operational tasks of the users, an audio-visual warning is provided to alert the user as illustrated in Figure 3.

Fig. 3. Warning interface for operational tasks

The system is designed to combine visual and audio signals in a way to create a meaningful interaction where the forms of the alert carry information. Once the users are warned about their attention status, they are also provided a question to stop their operation and take a rest. Hence, the information flow and the operation of the system modify the way of interaction. Additionally, it is also possible to share the real time data of the users' alertness in a network for alternative uses. For instance, in systems where the operations are carried by multiple users depending on each other's actions (e.g. driving in a highway, military operations etc.), when there is a user with low level of alertness, the system may alert the other users in the system so the other users may follow their tasks precociously.

5   Conclusions

This study introduces an adaptive user interface for vigilance level recognition that applies a linear SVM classifier using a set of statistical features: mean entropy, skewness, kurtosis, and mean power of EEG wavelets in time-frequency domain. One-way ANOVA test is employed for feature selection. EEG signals are decomposed into frequency sub-bands with discrete wavelet transform (DWT) and selected statistical features are employed in SVM for recognition of human sleep stages (stage 1, stage 3, stage REM and stage AWAKE). Empirical results significantly supports that the proposed statistical features achieved an accuracy of linear SVM reaches to 93% in stage 1, 82% in stage 3, 73% in stage REM and 96% in stage AWAKE. Thus, the proposed method would be helpful to accurately interpret EEG signals to detect users' alertness and vigilance states. Based on the method, it is possible to design an adaptive interface which detects users' states for critical tasks. Such an adaptive interface design is also introduced as a part of this study. This study would guide HCI and BCI researchers who would like to design similar systems for critical tasks such as drowsiness detection for drivers.

References

1. Nijholt, D., Anton, S.T.: Brain-computer interfaces (2010)
2. Wolpaw, J., Wolpaw, E.W.: Brain-computer interfaces: principles and practice. Oxford University Press (2012)
3. Rogers, Y., Sharp, H., Preece, J.: Interaction design: beyond human-computer interaction. John Wiley & Sons (2011)
4. Lazar, J., Feng, J.H., Hochheiser, H.: Research methods in human-computer interaction. John Wiley & Sons (2010)
5. Knapp, R.B., Kim, J., André, E.: Physiological signals and their use in augmenting emotion recognition for human–machine interaction. In: Emotion-Oriented Systems, pp. 133–159. Springer (2011)
6. Konstantinidis, E.I., Frantzidis, C.A., Pappas, C., Bamidis, P.D.: Real time emotion aware applications: a case study employing emotion evocative pictures and neuro-physiological sensing enhanced by Graphic Processor Units. Computer Methods and Programs in Biomedicine 107(1), 16–27 (2012)
7. He, B., Gao, S., Yuan, H., Wolpaw, J.R.: Brain-Computer Interfaces. In: Neural Engineering, pp. 87–151. Springer (2013)
8. Valente, S., Ringwood, J., Mangourova, V., Lowry, J.: Investigation of events in the EEG signal correlated with changes in both oxygen and glucose in the brain. In: Signals and Systems Conference (ISSC 2012), pp. 1–6. IET Irish (2012)
9. Wolpaw, J.R., Birbaumer, N., McFarland, D.J., Pfurtscheller, G., Vaughan, T.M.: Brain–computer interfaces for communication and control. Clinical Neurophysiology 113(6), 767–791 (2002)
10. Lotte, F., Congedo, M., Lécuyer, A., Lamarche, F., Arnaldi, B., et al.: A review of classification algorithms for EEG-based brain–computer interfaces. Journal of Neural Engineering 4 (2007)
11. Teplan, M.: Fundamentals of EEG measurement. Measurement Science Review 2(2), 1–11 (2002)
12. Niedermeyer, E., Da Silva, F.H.L.: Electroencephalography: basic principles, clinical applications, and related fields. Lippincott Williams & Wilkins (2005)
13. Wang, Y., Gao, X., Hong, B., Gao, S.: Practical designs of brain–computer interfaces based on the modulation of EEG rhythms. In: Brain-Computer Interfaces, pp. 137–154. Springer (2010)

14. Lee, J.C., Tan, D.S.: Using a low-cost electroencephalograph for task classification in HCI research. In: Proceedings of the 19th Annual ACM Symposium on User Interface Software and Technology, pp. 81–90 (2006)
15. Sridhar, S.S., Shivaraman, R.: Feasibility Study for Implementing Brain Computer Interface Using Electroencephalograph. In: Proceedings of International Conference on Internet Computing and Information Communications, pp. 207–218 (2014)
16. Jacob, R.J.K., Girouard, A., Hirshfield, L.M., Horn, M.S., Shaer, O., Solovey, E.T., Zigelbaum, J.: Reality-based interaction: unifying the new generation of interaction styles. In: CHI 2007 Extended Abstracts on Human Factors in Computing Systems, pp. 2465–2470 (2007)
17. Hirshfield, L.M., Solovey, E.T., Girouard, A., Kebinger, J., Jacob, R.J.K., Sassaroli, A., Fantini, S.: Brain measurement for usability testing and adaptive interfaces: an example of uncovering syntactic workload with functional near infrared spectroscopy. In: Proceedings of the SIGCHI Conference on Human Factors in Computing Systems, pp. 2185–2194 (2009)
18. Curran, E.A., Stokes, M.J.: Learning to control brain activity: a review of the production and control of EEG components for driving brain-computer interface (BCI) systems. Brain and Cognition 51(3), 326–336 (2003)
19. Kübler, A., Kotchoubey, B., Kaiser, J., Wolpaw, J.R., Birbaumer, N.: Brain-computer communication: unlocking the locked in. Psychological Bulletin 127(3), 358–375 (2001)
20. Nijholt, A., Tan, D.: Playing with your brain: brain-computer interfaces and games. In: Proceedings of the International Conference on Advances in Computer Entertainment Technology, pp. 305–306 (2007)
21. Stubler, W.F., O'Hara, J.M.: Human factors challenges for advanced process control. In: Proceedings of the Human Factors and Ergonomics Society Annual Meeting, vol. 40(19), pp. 992–996 (1996)
22. Meister, D.: The history of human factors and ergonomics. CRC Press (1999)
23. Dinges, D.F.: An overview of sleepiness and accidents. Journal of Sleep Research 4(s2), 4–14 (1995)
24. Lim, J., Dinges, D.F.: Sleep deprivation and vigilant attention. Annals of the New York Academy of Sciences 1129(1), 305–322 (2008)
25. Ting, P.H., Hwang, J.R., Doong, J.L., Jeng, M.C.: Driver fatigue and highway driving: A simulator study. Physiology & Behavior 94(3), 448–453 (2008)
26. Berka, C., Levendowski, D.J., Cvetinovic, M.M., Petrovic, M.M., Davis, G., Lumicao, M.N., Zivkovic, V.T., Popovic, M.V., Olmstead, R.: Real-time analysis of EEG indexes of alertness, cognition, and memory acquired with a wireless EEG headset. International Journal of Human-Computer Interaction 17(2), 151–170 (2004)
27. Duru, D.G., Duru, A.D., Barkana, D.E., Sanli, O., Ozkan, M.: Assessment of surgeon's stress level and alertness using EEG during laparoscopic simple nephrectomy. In: Proceedings of the 6th International IEEE/EMBS Conference on Neural Engineering, pp. 452–455 (2013)
28. Hansen, L.K., Hansen, S.T., Stahlhut, C.: Mobile real-time EEG imaging Bayesian inference with sparse, temporally smooth source priors. In: Proceedings of the International Winter Workshop on Brain-Computer Interface (BCI), pp. 6–7 (2013)
29. Johnson, R.R., Popovic, D.P., Olmstead, R.E., Stikic, M., Levendowski, D.J., Berka, C.: Drowsiness/alertness algorithm development and validation using synchronized EEG and cognitive performance to individualize a generalized model. Biological Psychology 87(2), 241–250 (2011)

30. Liu, N.H., Chiang, C.Y., Hsu, H.M.: Improving driver alertness through music selection using a mobile EEG to detect brainwaves. Sensors 13(7), 8199–8221 (2013)
31. Mardi, Z., Ashtiani, S.N.M., Mikaili, M.: EEG-based Drowsiness Detection for Safe Driving Using Chaotic Features and Statistical Tests. Journal of Medical Signals and Sensors 1(2), 130 (2011)
32. Woźniak, D., Rumian, S., Szpytko, J.: Transport device operator stress features analysis. Journal of KONES 18, 577–586 (2011)
33. Allen, J.J.B., Coan, J.A., Nazarian, M.: Issues and assumptions on the road from raw signals to metrics of frontal EEG asymmetry in emotion. Biological Psychology 67(1), 183–218 (2004)
34. Guo, L., Wu, Y., Zhao, L., Cao, T., Yan, W., Shen, X.: Classification of mental task from EEG signals using immune feature weighted support vector machines. IEEE Transactions on Magnetics 47(5), 866–869 (2011)
35. Park, Y., Luo, L., Parhi, K.K., Netoff, T.: Seizure prediction with spectral power of EEG using cost-sensitive support vector machines. Epilepsia 52(10), 1761–1770 (2011)
36. Subasi, A., Gursoy, M.I.: EEG signal classification using PCA, ICA, LDA and support vector machines. Expert Systems with Applications 37(12), 8659–8666 (2010)
37. Oken, B.S., Salinsky, M.C., Elsas, S.M.: Vigilance, alertness, or sustained attention: physiological basis and measurement. Clinical Neurophysiology 117(9), 1885–1901 (2006)
38. Silber, M.H., Ancoli-Israel, S., Bonnet, M.H., Chokroverty, S., Grigg-Damberger, M.M., Hirshkowitz, M., Kapen, S., Keenan, S.A., Kryger, M.H., Penzel, T., et al.: The visual scoring of sleep in adults. Journal of Clinical Sleep Medicine 3(2), 121–131 (2007)
39. Zheng, X., Yang, B., Li, X., Zan, P., Dong, Z.: Classifying EEG using incremental support vector machine in BCIs. In: Li, K., Jia, L., Sun, X., Fei, M., Irwin, G.W. (eds.) LSMS 2010 and ICSEE 2010. LNCS, vol. 6330, pp. 604–610. Springer, Heidelberg (2010)
40. Rechtschaffen, A., Kales, A.: A manual of standardized terminology, technics and scoring system for sleep stages of human subjects (1968)
41. Piryatinska, A., Terdik, G., Woyczynski, W.A., Loparo, K.A., Scher, M.S., Zlotnik, A.: Automated detection of neonate EEG sleep stages. Computer Methods and Programs in Biomedicine 95(1), 31–46 (2009)
42. Vural, C., Yildiz, M.: Determination of Sleep Stage Separation Ability of Features Extracted from EEG Signals Using Principle Component Analysis. Journal of Medical Systems 34(1), 83–89 (2010)
43. Hsu, Y.L., Yang, Y.T., Wang, J.S., Hsu, C.Y.: Automatic sleep stage recurrent neural classifier using energy features of EEG signals. Neurocomputing 104, 105–114 (2013)
44. Koley, B., Dey, D.: An ensemble system for automatic sleep stage classification using single channel EEG signal. Computers in Biology and Medicine 42(12), 1186–1195 (2012)
45. Bajaj, V., Pachori, R.B.: Automatic classification of sleep stages based on the time-frequency image of EEG signals. Computer Methods and Programs in Biomedicine 112(3), 320–328 (2013)
46. Rajendra, A.U., Faust, O., Kannathal, N., Chua, T., Laxminarayan, S.: Non-linear analysis of EEG signals at various sleep stages. Computer Methods and Programs in Biomedicine 80(1), 37–45 (2005)
47. Fraiwan, L., Lweesy, K., Khasawneh, N., Wenz, H., Dickhaus, H.: Automated sleep stage identification system based on time-frequency analysis of a single EEG channel and random forest classifier. Computer Methods and Programs in Biomedicine 108(1), 10–19 (2012)

48. Krajča, V., Petránek, S., Mohylová, J., Paul, K., Gerla, V., Lhotská, L.: Neonatal EEG sleep stages modelling by temporal profiles. In: Moreno Díaz, R., Pichler, F., Quesada Arencibia, A. (eds.) EUROCAST 2007. LNCS, vol. 4739, pp. 195–201. Springer, Heidelberg (2007)
49. Güneş, S., Polat, K., Yosunkaya, Ş.: Efficient sleep stage recognition system based on EEG signal using k-means clustering based feature weighting. Expert Systems with Applications 37(12), 7922–7928 (2010)
50. Kerkeni, N., Alexandre, F., Bedoui, M.H., Bougrain, L., Dogui, M.: Automatic classification of sleep stages on a EEG signal by artificial neural networks. In: Proceedings of the 5th WSEAS International Conference on Signal, Speech and Image Processing (SSIP 2005), pp. 128–131. World Scientific and Engineering Academy and Society (WSEAS), Stevens Point (2005)
51. Van Hese, P., Philips, W., De Koninck, J., Van de Walle, R., Lemahieu, I.: Automatic detection of sleep stages using the EEG. In: Proceedings of the 23rd Annual International Conference of the IEEE Medicine and Biology Society, vol. 2, pp. 1944–1947 (2001)
52. Huang, R.J., Chang, S.Y., Hsiao, Y.Y., Shih, T.S., Lee, S.D., Ting, H., Lai, C.H.: Strong Correlation of Sleep Onset between EOG and EEG Sleep Stage 1 and 2. In: Proceedings of the 2012 International Symposium on Computer, Consumer and Control (IS3C 2012), pp. 614–617. IEEE Computer Society, Washington, DC (2012)
53. Krakovská, A., Mezeiová, K.: Automatic sleep scoring: A search for an optimal combination of measures. Artificial Intelligence in Medicine 53(1), 25–33 (2011)
54. Chouvarda, I., Rosso, V., Mendez, M.O., Bianchi, A.M., Parrino, L., Grassi, A., Terzano, M., Cerutti, S.: Assessment of the EEG complexity during activations from sleep. Computer Methods and Programs in Biomedicine 104(3), e16–e28 (2011)
55. Ić, M., Šoda, J., Bonković, M.: Automatic classification of infant sleep based on instantaneous frequencies in a single-channel EEG signal. Computers in Biology and Medicine 43(12), 2110–2117 (2013)
56. Brignol, A., Al-Ani, T., Drouot, X.: Phase space and power spectral approaches for EEG-based automatic sleep-wake classification in humans: A comparative study using short and standard epoch lengths. Computer Methods and Programs in Biomedicine 109(3), 227–238 (2013)
57. Subasi, A.: Automatic recognition of alertness level from EEG by using neural network and wavelet coefficients. Expert Systems with Applications 28(4), 701–711 (2005)
58. Daubechies, I., Bruce, J.B.: Ten lectures on wavelets. Acoustical Society of America Journal 93, 1671 (1993)
59. Daubechies, I.: Where do wavelets come from? A personal point of view. Proceedings of the IEEE 84(4), 510–513 (1996)
60. Rioul, O., Martin, V.: Wavelets and signal processing. IEEE Signal Processing Magazine 8 (LCAV-ARTICLE-1991-005), 14–38 (1991)
61. Tabachnick, B.G., Linda, S.F.: Using multivariate statistics (2001)
62. Hearst, M.A., et al.: Support vector machines. IEEE Intelligent Systems and their Applications 13(4), 18–28 (1998)

Discrimination of ADHD Based on fMRI Data
with Deep Belief Network

Deping Kuang, Xiaojiao Guo, Xiu An, Yilu Zhao, and Lianghua He

The Key Laboratory of Embedded System and Service Computing,
Ministry of Education, Tongji University, Shanghai 201804, China
Department of Computer Science and Technology, Tongji University, Shanghai 201804, China
kuangdp1990@gmail.com

Abstract. Effective discrimination of attention deficit hyperactivity disorder
(ADHD) using imaging and functional biomarkers would have fundamental
influence on public health. In this paper, we created a classification model using
ADHD-200 dataset focusing on resting state functional magnetic resonance
imaging. We predicted ADHD status and subtype by deep belief network (DBN).
In the data preprocessing stage, in order to reduce the high dimension of fMRI
brain data, brodmann mask, Fast Fourier Transform algorithm (FFT) and
max-pooling of frequencies are applied respectively. Experimental results
indicate that our method has a good discrimination effect, and outperform the
results of the ADHD-200 competition. Meanwhile, our results conform to the
biological research that there exists discrepancy in prefrontal cortex and
cingulate cortex. As far as we know, it is the first time that the deep learning
method has been used for the discrimination of ADHD with fMRI data.

Keywords: ADHD, fMRI, Deep Learning, Deep Belief Network.

1   Introduction

Attention deficit hyperactivity disorder (ADHD) is one of the most common childhood
disorder and can continue through adolescence and adulthood with the problems of
attention, hyperactivity, or acting impulsively [1]. The American Psychiatric
Association's Diagnostic and Statistical Manual, Fifth edition (DSM-5) [2], is usually
used by mental health professionals to help diagnose ADHD. However, diagnose based
on sole clinical and rating measure may be unreliable for it may have relationship with
the clinicians, cultures and countries. Therefore, objective methods for diagnose of
ADHD have great importance.

Functional magnetic resonance imaging (fMRI) is a functional neuroimaging
technology, depending on blood oxygenation level dependent (BOLD), which defines
activity in the healthy and diseased human brain [3]. In recent years, a growing number
of functional neuroimaging have been applied in the research of ADHD. It is reported
that abnormality of areas in the dorsal anterior cingulate cortex (dACC), ventro medial
prefrontal cortex (vmPFC), and cerebellum when analysis task-related fMRI data [4-5].
Wolf et al. [4] applied to 12 healthy and 12 ADHD adults using independent

D.-S. Huang et al. (Eds.): ICIC 2014, LNBI 8590, pp. 225–232, 2014.
© Springer International Publishing Switzerland 2014

component analysis in a working memory task. Zhu et al. [6] for the first time proposed a resting-state fMRI based PC-FDA classifier using features of regional homogeneity (ReHo) to discriminate children with ADHD. The leave-one-out cross-validation accuracy can be as high as 85%. But the subjects for the experiments were only 20. Due to the scarcity of data, few studies were for the automated diagnose of ADHD. Fortunately, the 1000 Functional Connectomes Project (FCP) provided a model which includes large-scale datasets [7]. Upon this model, ADHD-200 Consortium established aggregate resting-state fMRI dataset and phenotypic data. On the global ADHD-200 competition, Eloyan A et al. [8] from Johns Hopkins University achieved the best score. They mainly use rs-fc-fMRI based on decomposition of CUR along with gradient boosting. Furthermore, a motor network segmentation and random forest algorithm are used for prediction. In this paper, three datasets from ADHD-200 competition are applied to discriminate ADHD with typical controls.

Deep belief network (DBN) is a generative probabilistic model which has raised a lot of interest since the successful implication of greedy layer-wise training using restricted Boltzmann machine (RBM) [9-11]. DBN has been used to the application of image processing [9], audio classification [12], object recognition [13-14], natural language processing [15] and so on. However, DBN has never been applied to the discrimination of ADHD.

A deep belief network with three hidden layers is utilized to discriminate the ADHD of three types with control. From the experimental results, it achieves higher accuracy than ever. The sections below are our learning method and experiments. Section 2 mainly describes the RBM and DBN method and Section 3 presents our experimental results on ADHD dataset.

2   Method

The building blocks of a Deep Belief Network (DBN) are the Restricted Boltzmann Machines (RBMs), which are used to represent each layer of a DBN architecture.

(a)   Restricted Boltzmann Machine

A DBN is a hierarchical structure consisting of multiple stacked RBM. RBMs are undirected graphical models including two layers: visible units and hidden units (see Fig. 1). The visible units that represent observations connect to the hidden units that represent features. But no connections are established within visible units or hidden units. The simplest RBM use Bernoulli distributed units in which the visible and hidden units are both binary. To adapt to the real-valued data, the Gaussian-Bernoulli RBMs with real-valued input for visible units and binary output for hidden units are used. It makes RBMs suitable to build blocks to learn DBNs for its valid greedy learning method.

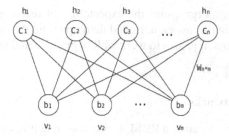

Fig. 1. Structure of RBM

In RBMs, the joint probability distribution between v and h can be written as:

$$p(v,h) = \frac{1}{z}\exp(-E(v,h)) \tag{1}$$

Where v is visible unit, h is hidden unit, E is an energy function defined by:

$$E(v,h) = -\sum_{i=1}^{V}\sum_{j=1}^{H} v_i h_j w_{ij} - \sum_{i=1}^{V} b_i v_i - \sum_{j=1}^{H} a_j h_j \tag{2}$$

Where $v_i, h_j \in \{0, 1\}$, w_{ij} is the weight between v_i and h_j, b_i is the bias of visible unit and a_j is the bias of hidden unit. Z is obtained by the sum of $e^{-E(v,h)}$. The probability of a visible unit which is assigned by the model is:

$$p(v) = \sum_{h} e^{-E(v,h)} / \sum_{v}\sum_{h} e^{-E(v,h)} \tag{3}$$

The conditional distributions $p(v/h)$ and $p(h/v)$ are given by:

$$p(h_j = 1|v;\theta) = \sigma\left(\sum_{i=1}^{V} w_{i,j} v_i + a_j\right) \quad p(v_i = 1|h;\theta) = \sigma\left(\sum_{j=1}^{H} w_{i,j} h_j + b_i\right) \tag{4}$$

Where $\theta = (w,b,a)$ and $\sigma(x) = (1+e^{-x})^{-1}$.

An RBM is pre-trained to maximize the log-likelihood $\log p(v)$. The derivative of the log probability with respect to the weights is given by:

$$\partial \log p(v) / \partial w_{ij} = <v_i h_j>_v - <v_i h_j>_{model} \tag{5}$$

The update rule for the weights follows the gradient of the log likelihood as:

$$\Delta w_{ij} = \varepsilon\left(<v_i h_j>_{data} - <v_i h_j>_{model}\right) \tag{6}$$

Where ε is the learning rate and the angle brackets manifested the expectations relative to the distribution specified in the subscript. It takes exponential time to compute the exact value of term $<v_i h_j>_{model}$. The Contrastive Divergence (CD) [16] approximation to the gradient can be used. Then the new update rule is :

$$\Delta w_{ij} = \varepsilon\left(<v_i h_j>_{data} - <v_i h_j>_{recon}\right) \tag{7}$$

Where the term $<v_ih_j>_{recon}$ represents the expectation of reconstructions produced by initializing the data from the hidden units and then updating the hidden units according to the data as visible units, it proves to work well in practice and to detect good features adequately.

2.1   Deep Belief Networks

After understanding how to build a RBM, It becomes much easier to construct a DBN by stacking RBMs. While the first RBM consisting of visible layer and first hidden layer is trained, the parameters, θ_1, of this RBM is also obtained. It defines a prior distribution over first hidden units which are obtained by marginalizing over the space of visible units. The idea behind the DBN, which is training by a stack of RBMs, is to keep the $p(v/h,\theta_1)$ defined by the first RBM, but to improve $p(v)$ by replacing $p(h/\theta_1)$ by a better prior over the hidden units. The better prior must have a smaller KL divergence than $p(h/\theta_1)$ from the aggregated posterior to improve $p(v)$.

Considering training second RBM, which is the network formed by using samples from the aggregated posterior of first RBM as training data. It is simple to initialize the second RBM which has the visible and hidden units swapped in first RBM. Then the second RBM has visible units h and hidden units h_2. We makes $p(h/\theta_2)$ be a better model of the aggregated posterior of $p(h/\theta_1)$ as the same of first RBM.

In the same way we could train a stack of RBMs. Then a feed-forward network of multiple layers can be initialized by the bottom-up recognition weights of the resulting DBN. The network can be fine-tuned by the back-propagating err derivatives, which is given by a final "softmax" layer that computes a probability over class labels. Softmax regression is also called multinomial logistic regression, which can deal with classification problem of the multi-class. In other words, it can be seen as the expansion of logistic regression. The weights in all lower layers are fine-tuned and the weights of final layer are back-propagated by the derivative of the log probability of the correct class. The process of bottom-up training and up-bottom fine-tuning is displayed in Fig. 2. Red arrows stand for the generative process and green arrows for the fine-tuning process.

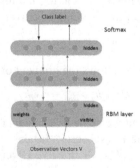

Fig. 2. Architecture of DBN

3   Experiments

3.1   Process of Data

MRI data and scan parameters of ADHD were released on the ADHD-200 Global Competition website (http://fcon_1000.projects.nitrc.org/indi/adhd200/). The fMRI data is time-series of 3D images which size is 49*58*47. Due to the inevitable interference during the experimental procedure, in order to analysis data effectively, a series of preprocessing are conducted in spm8 [17] such as realign, slice time, co-register, normalize, smooth. More information about the preprocessing steps can be found in [18].

To reduce the dimension, three strategies are involved. First, divide the 3D images to 48 areas according to brodmann template which is a region of human cerebral cortex defined on its cytoaerchitectonics, or structure and organization of cells. Then, assume that the highest frequency of voxels in some areas may be different during the scanning procedure. So the fast Fourier transform algorithm (FFT) is used to transform data from time domain to frequency domain. At last, execute max-pooling of frequencies in each voxel to select the frequency which has the maximum value of amplitude. After FFT and max-pooling every voxels have only one property and the number of properties in each area depends on the number of voxels. We can use the properties for analysis after preprocessing.

3.2   Application of DBN to ADHD Data

In this paper, we apply DBN to the preprocessed ADHD data for learning features of each area. The properties in each area are viewed as the observations of the first layer in the DBN, which is composed of three hidden layers training with greedy RBMs. The data collected by different institutions came from various experimental environment and scan parameters, so we discriminate the ADHD vs. Typically Developing Controls (TDC) separately by training different DBNs for different sites. The diagnose of each subject is given according to the DSM-5 with regard to the score of inattentive, hyper/impulsive, IQ measure and so on. Actually, for the data of every site we train 48 DBNs, and discriminate the class of subject by every DBN, for the numbers of observations are different from one area to another. Also, in order to exclude the occasionality of the data collected from individual area, we combined properties from some areas to one vector of features.

4   Results

The ADHD-200 Global Competition divided the datasets into training and test sets. We test the DBN on the ADHD hold-out set for KKI, Peking-1 and NYU, with softmax as the classifier. For KKI dataset, the training subjects are 83, and test subjects are 11; for Peking-1 dataset, the training subjects are 85, and test subjects are 50; and for NYU the training subjects and test subjects are 222 and 41 respectively.

As NYU dataset in the ADHD-200 competition achieved the lowest discrimination results. So in this paper, the proposed method was particularly tested on the NYU dataset of 48 areas to discriminate control with ADHD (regardless of subtypes). The results of 48 regions (excluding 7 empty regions) are shown in Fig. 3. It can be inferred that the average discrimination performs effectively in the area of 9, 10 and 11, 18, 30. On the other hand, according to brodmann definition [19], area 9, 10, 11 stands for prefrontal cortex, area 18 plays a role in the visual cortex and area 30 is part of cingulated cortex and the average accuracies of the visual cortex and cingulated cortex are more than 50%. Thus we combine the data of prefrontal cortex (area 9, 10 and 11) to one vector of features, and carried the same operation for the data of visual cortex (area 17, 18 and 19) and the data of   cortex (area 23, 24, 26, 29, 30, 31 and 32). Then use them as the input observations of the DBN.

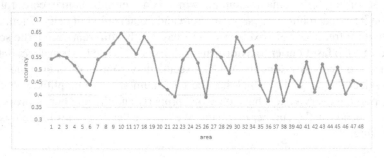

Fig. 3. Discrimination accuracy of NYU in 48 areas

The average accuracy of the four classes, including control and three ADHD subtypes, is shown in Table 2. It can be seen that the accuracy of the method we proposed above is better than the discrimination accuracy achieved by the team in the ADHD-200 competition which are 35.19%, 51.05% and 61.90% for NYU, Peking-1 and KKI respectively. By performing DBN on prefrontal cortex, our average accuracies are 37.41%, 54.00% and 71.82%. Compared with the competition results, our accuracy respectively improved 2.22 percent, 2.95 percent and 9.92 percent, which is shown in Table 3. Meanwhile, the accuracies on cingulated cortex are 37.07%, 54.00% and 72.73%, which is also higher than the accuracies of ADHD-200 competition. However, the accuracies are lower on visual cortex since the subjects were scanning on the resting state. The results are receivable as it has been confirmed that there indeed exists disparity in prefrontal cortex and cingulated cortex between control and ADHD [20]. The details are shown in Table 1. All the results above demonstrate that our method can obtain a better performance.

Table 1. Discrimination accuracy

Site	ADHD-200	Prefrontal cortex	Visual cortex	Cingulate cortex
NYU	35.19	37.41	34.39	37.07
Peking-1	51.05	54.00	51.20	54.00
KKI	61.90	71.82	68.82	72.73

In addition, the prediction of ADHD is conducted using the neural network with one hidden layer. The data used for prediction in the model is from the prefrontal cortex. The neural network performs little better than the DBN in one dataset. In general, the proposed method by this paper performs better. The comparison of DBN and NN with two different numbers of layers is shown in Fig. 4.

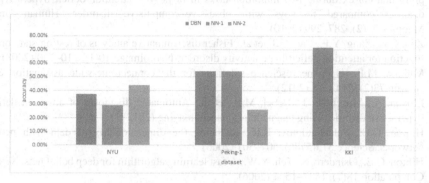

Fig. 4. The comparison of DBN and NN

5   Conclusion

In this paper, deep belief network, one of the deep learning models, is applied for feature extraction. Experiments were carried out on NYU, Peking-1 and KKI. The proposed method was proved to be effective in discriminating between ADHD and control. And the accuracy of prediction has improved in some degree compared with the results published in ADHD-200 competition. It may be feasible to apply this method to other studies on psychiatric disorders.

The results use part of brain regions but achieves better performance, and verifies that there is difference between ADHD and control in prefrontal cortex and cingulated cortex. In the future, we will expand our research brain regions, which may leads to a better discrimination performance. In addition, the DBN with different layers will be realized to achieve better performance. By considering the above factors, there is a reason to believe that the discrimination performance based on the proposed method can be more effective.

References

1. Kooij, S.J.J., Bejerot, S., Blackwell, A., et al.: European consensus statement on diagnosis and treatment of adult ADHD: The European Network Adult ADHD. BMC Psychiatry 10(1), 67 (2010)
2. American Psychiatric Association: Diagnostic and Statistical Manual of Mental Disorders, 5th edn. American Psychiatric Association, Arlington (2013)
3. Huettel, S.A., Song, A.W., McCarthy, G.: Functional magnetic resonance imaging. Sinauer Associates, Sunderland (2004)

4. Wolf, R.C., Plichta, M.M., Sambataro, F., et al.: Regional brain activation changes and abnormal functional connectivity of the ventrolateral prefrontal cortex during working memory processing in adults with attention-deficit/hyperactivity disorder. Human Brain Mapping 30(7), 2252–2266 (2009)
5. Rubia, K., Cubillo, A., Smith, A.B., et al.: Disorder-specific dysfunction in right inferior prefrontal cortex during two inhibition tasks in boys with attention-deficit hyperactivity disorder compared to boys with obsessive–compulsive disorder. Human Brain Mapping 31(2), 287–299 (2010)
6. Zhu, C.Z., Zang, Y.F., Cao, Q.J., et al.: Fisher discriminative analysis of resting-state brain function for attention-deficit/hyperactivity disorder. Neuroimage 40(1), 110–120 (2008)
7. Milham, M.P.: Open neuroscience solutions for the connectome-wide association era. Neuron 73(2), 214–218 (2012)
8. Eloyan, A., Muschelli, J., Nebel, M.B., et al.: Automated diagnoses of attention deficit hyperactive disorder using magnetic resonance imaging (2012)
9. Hinton, G.E., Salakhutdinov, R.R.: Reducing the dimensionality of data with neural networks. Science 313(5786), 504–507 (2006)
10. Hinton, G.E., Osindero, S., Teh, Y.W.: A fast learning algorithm for deep belief nets. Neural Computation 18(7), 1527–1554 (2006)
11. Bengio, Y., Lamblin, P., Popovici, D., et al.: Greedy layer-wise training of deep networks. Advances in Neural Information Processing Systems, 19–153 (2007)
12. Lee, H., Pham, P.T., Largman, Y., et al.: Unsupervised feature learning for audio classification using convolutional deep belief networks. In: NIPS, vol. 9, pp. 1096–1104 (2009)
13. Lee, H., Grosse, R., Ranganath, R., et al.: Unsupervised learning of hierarchical representations with convolutional deep belief networks. Communications of the ACM 54(10), 95–103 (2011)
14. Ranzato, M., Huang, F.J., Boureau, Y.L., et al.: Unsupervised learning of invariant feature hierarchies with applications to object recognition. In: IEEE Conference on Computer Vision and Pattern Recognition, CVPR 2007, pp. 1–8. IEEE (2007)
15. Sarikaya, R., Hinton, G.E., Deoras, A.: Application of Deep Belief Networks for Natural Language Understanding
16. Hinton, G.E.: Training products of experts by minimizing contrastive divergence. Neural Computation 14(8), 1771–1800 (2002)
17. Statistical parametric mapping, version 8 (2009), http://www.fil.ion.ucl.ac.uk/spm/
18. Huettel, S.A., Song, A.W., McCarthy, G.: Functional magnetic resonance imaging. Sinauer Associates, Sunderland (2004)
19. Wanchai. Cortical Functions. Trans. Cranial Technologies ldt. (2012)
20. Bush, G., Valera, E.M., Seidman, L.J.: Functional neuroimaging of attention-deficit/hyperactivity disorder: a review and suggested future directions.

ADHD-200 Classification Based on Social Network Method

Xiaojiao Guo, Xiu An, Deping Kuang, Yilu Zhao, and Lianghua He

The Key Laboratory of Embedded System and Service Computing, Ministry of Education,
Tongji University, Shanghai 201804, China
Department of Computer Science and Technology, Tongji University, Shanghai 201804, China
xiaojiaoguo12@gmail.com

Abstract. Attention Deficit Hyperactivity Disorder (ADHD) is one of the most common diseases in school aged children. In this study, we proposed a method based on social network to extract the features of the ADHD-200 resting state fMRI data between ADHD conditioned and control subjects. And the classification is done by using the support vector machine. The innovation of this paper lies in that: firstly, in the social network, the edge is defined by correlation between two voxels, where the threshold is proposed based on the optimal properties of small world; secondly, in the procedure of feature extraction, besides the traditional network features, we also exploit the new features such as assortative mixing and synchronization. We obtain an average accuracy of 63.75%, which is better than the average best imaging-based diagnostic performance 61.54% achieved in the ADHD-200 global competition. Compared with the proposed method, the result of the method based on traditional features is 61.04% , which verified that the proposed method based on new features is better than traditional one.

Keywords: ADHD, fMRI, social network features, svm.

1 Introduction

Attention Deficit Hyperactivity Disorder(ADHD), one of the most commonly found behavioral disorders, is characterized by inappropriate inattention and hyperactivity. And these behaviors may last for a particular length of time and result in impairment throughout their life[1]. At present, the information that leads to this disorder is limited and the existing diagnoses rely largely on the physiopathologic symptoms. In fact, it is very difficult to classify the ADHD symptoms and normal by medicine clinical diagnoses accurately. Thus, there have great significance on the further studies on objective diagnosis of ADHD.

Functional magnetic resonance imaging (fMRI) is a widespread tool to measure brain activity in a non-invasive way, because fMRI images obtained using blood oxygen level dependent (BOLD) contrast show signal fluctuations at rest. These fluctuations have been shown to be coherent across widely separated brain regions such as sensorimotor cortices [2-3]. Studies have demonstrated ADHD related abnormalities

D.-S. Huang et al. (Eds.): ICIC 2014, LNBI 8590, pp. 233–240, 2014.
© Springer International Publishing Switzerland 2014

in the interactions among brain regions supporting the implementation and maintenance of attention control [4]. And we use the resting state brain fMRI data as comparison to reflect the abnormalities in ADHD brains.

Recent advances in graph theoretical approaches have allowed us to characterize properties of brain networks. As one of the typical features of social network, the small world properties of brain networks are affected by normal aging and brain diseases [5] such as Alzhermer's [6] disease, epilepsy [7] and schizophrenia [8]. fMRI data can provide us the time-series of intensity values for each voxel, then the brain network can be constructed based on the correlation of the time-series. We choose social network features such as small world properties and degree of connectivity to discriminate the difference of ADHD and control brains fMRI data.

In this study, we use a large dataset from the ADHD-200 Global Competition challenged teams. It provides us an important opportunity to test fMRI data diagnosis for the reason that the ADHD-200 dataset collects data from 776 participants from multiple institutions contrast to the previous studies on fMRI-based diagnoses only included 39 participants on average [9]. The details of the dataset and methods used in our study are explained in Section 2. The experimental results including the description of the experiment are presented in Section 3 and the conclusion from the experiment shows in Section 4.

2   Materials and Methods

2.1   Dataset and Processing

The data used in the present work is from the New York University Child Study Center (NYU) and Kennedy Krieger Institute (KKI) , which are part of the eight datasets of ADHD-200 Global Competition. Because the classification results on NYU dataset are the worst among ADHD-200 datasets at present, we choose it to compare with the average best results. NYU dataset contains a total number of 216 subjects including 118 ADHD whose age range from 7.17 to 17.61 (mean age 11.13) and 98 healthy controls whose age range from 7.17 to 17.96 (mean age 12.15). For processing, the resting state fMRI data are first subjected to a series of preprocessing steps, including 1) removement of a central spike caused by magnetic resonance signal offset, 2) slice timing, 3)realign, 4) image registration to make image fuse between various imaging ways, 5) normalization, 6) spatial smoothing [10].

Then the Brodmann's Interactive Atlas is applied to measure the functional connectivity among brain regions, which facilitates fMRI analysis understanding by providing access to all of the functions that have been associated with each of the Brodmann areas or corresponding gyri [11]. The details of Brodmann areas for brain are provided in Fig. 1. As known, social network analysis have been applied in various field such as mathematics, physics,information science, economics and scientific cooperation[12]. As for brain network, few properties such as small world properties are used and we will apply other more features of better effects in this paper.

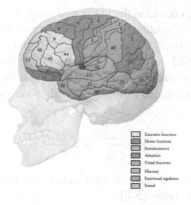

Fig. 1. Brodmann Cortical Areas

2.2   Network Construction

fMRI data can be viewed as 4-D video so that the 3-D volumn of brain is divided into small voxels. The correlation of intensity time-series can be an indication of how synchronous the activities of two voxels are. Symmetric correlation matrixes are produced by Pearson's correlation coefficients between the time series of each possible pair of voxels of brain regions for each subject[13]. Each correlation matrix is thresholded into a binary graph to investigate the properties of brain functional networks.

There is no definitive way currently to select a precise threshold in brain networks studies. In the present study, we use a new method to choose the proper threshold to obtain the most economical network. To diagnose small world properties, the characteristic path length and clustering coefficient were compared with the same metrics estimated in random networks configured with the same number of nodes, mean degree K_{ran}, and degree distribution as the network of interest, under the constraint that $K_{ran} > log(n)$. Typically, in a small world network, we expect the ratio $\gamma > 1$ and the ratio $\lambda \approx 1$ [14-15]. Based on these, we select a threshold that makes γ and λ optimal under the constraints at the same time, thus the most economical network can be constructed.

2.3   Small World Properties

Small world parameters of a network were originally proposed by Watts and Strogatz. The clustering coefficient $C_i(0 < C_i < 1)$ is a ratio that defines the proportion of possible connections[16]. The average of the clustering coefficients over all nodes C_{net} quantifies the local inter-connectivity of a network and can be written

$$C_{net} = \frac{3 \times \text{number of triangles on the network}}{\text{number of connected triples of nodes}} \tag{1}$$

And high values of C_i imply the most of nearest neighbors of that nodes are also nearest neighbors of each other. The L_{net} of a L_i network is the mean of the n-1 minimum path lengths (L_i) between the index node and all other nodes in the network. L_{net} is an indicator of overall routing efficiency of a network[17]. To evaluate the small world properties, we generated 100 degree-matched random networks and scaled the C_{net} and the L_{net} of the real networks with the mean γ and λ (2) of all the random networks[18]. Typically, a small world network should fulfill the following conditions: $\gamma>1$ and $\lambda\approx1$[15]. A scalar summary of small-worldness is therefore the ratio σ, which is typically >1 [19].

$$\gamma = \frac{C_{net}}{C_{ran}} \quad \lambda = \frac{L_{net}}{L_{ran}}$$ (2)

These conventional measures have been recently applied to many structural and functional brain networks studies[5-6].

2.4   Assortative Mixing

Assortative mixing is one of social network features and a network is said to show assortative mixing if the nodes in the network that have many connections tend to be connected to other nodes with many connections. Many networks show assortative mixing on their degrees, a preference for high degree nodes to attach to other high degree nodes while others show dis-assortative mixing that high degree nodes attach to low degree ones[20]. Assortative mixing can have a substantial effect on the behavior of networked systems.

The networks that we might want to break up such as the social networks appear to be assortative and therefore are resilience, at least against simple targeted attacks. And yet at the same time the networks, including technological networks such as the Internet, appear to be dis-assortative and are hence particularly vulnerable[21]. In this paper, we use the assortative mixing as one of the brain network features to distinguish the ADHD brains form controls. For the practical purpose of evaluating r (assortative mixing) on an observed network, we can define as

$$r = \frac{M^{-1}\sum_i j_i k_i - \left[M^{-1}\sum_i \frac{1}{2}(j_i + k_i)\right]^2}{M^{-1}\sum_i \frac{1}{2}(j_i^2 + k_i^2) - \left[M^{-1}\sum_i \frac{1}{2}(j_i + k_i)\right]^2}$$ (3)

Where j_i, k_i are the degrees of the nodes at the ends of ith edge, with $i=1,...,M$.

2.5   Other Properties and the Classification Method

Other properties of the social network are applied in the study, which may have better performance in the analysis. We quantify the dynamical implications of the small-world phenomenon by considering the generic synchronization of oscillator networks of arbitrary topology. The small world route produces synchronizability more efficiently than standard deterministic graphs, purely random graphs and ideal constructive schemes. However, the small world property does not guarantee synchronizability, the synchronization threshold lies within the boundaries, but linked to the end of the small world region[22]. The synchronization is quantified by the ratio $S(5)$ with λ_2 and λ_N indicating the second smallest eigenvalue and the largest eigenvalue of the coupling matrix of the network, respectively.

$$S = \frac{\lambda_2}{\lambda_N} \tag{4}$$

The hierarchical organization implies that small groups of nodes organize in a hierarchical manner into increasingly large groups while maintaining a scale-free topology. The degree of clustering characterizing the different groups follows a strict scaling law, which can be used to identity the presence of a hierarchical organization in real networks[23]. And we define the hierarchical exponent β as

$$C(k) \sim k^{-\beta} \tag{5}$$

Support Vector Machine (SVM) can be characterized as a machine learning algorithm which maximizes the predictive accuracy without over-fitting the data to be trained and is capable of resolving linear and nonlinear classification problems. SVM works by mapping data to a high dimensional feature space and categorized, even when the data are not linearly separable. A separator between the categories is found and the data are then drawn into a hyperplane. Then, the characteristics of new data can be used to predict the group where a new record should belong. The boundary among the two categories can be defined by a hyperplane after the transformation. The kernel function of mathematical function is used in transformation. It supports the linear, Radial basis function (RBF) Polynomial and Sigmoid kernel types.

3   Experimental Results

The data preprocessing is applied to all resting state fMRI data from the ADHD-200 Global Competition, and the detailed steps have been described in Section 2. The preprocessed fMRI data that written into MNI space at 3 mm * 3 mm * 4 mm voxel resolution are divided into 48 regions according to the Brodmann areas. It is noneffective on some regions of 12, 13, 14, 15, 16, 31 and 33, for the data in these regions are empty. Then the network of each region is constructed by the correlation coefficient in the datasets of NYU and KKI. We calculate the properties of the social network such as small world properties and synchronization in each region network, and then train our SVM classifier with these properties. During the training and testing of SVM classifier, we used each subject in the dataset once as the validation data, and selected the optimal arguments by repeating this process the same times as the number of subjects with grid search algorithm. By a certain SVM training, we can obtain the average classification accuracy of 63.75% and 78.21% corresponding to NYU and KKI dataset respectively, which is better than the average best imaging-based diagnostic performance of 61.54%, achieved in the ADHD-200 global competition[24]. Particularly emphasized, among the ADHD-200 global competition, NYU dataset achieves the lowest classification accuracy.

Table 1. The average accuracy of different features used

		NYU	KKI
All features		0.6375	0.7821
Small	world	0.6104	0.7786
properties			
Others		0.6316	0.7750

In order to make comparison, the classification has been performed in three ways to test the accuracy between the ADHD brain and controls, also to test the effect of social network features. The three ways are respectively features of small world properties only, all features of social network analysis, and the other properties. The results of the average accuracy are shown in Table 1. And the results of detailed region in three ways show in Fig. 2. The best accuracies of the NYU and KKI dataset are 72.22% and 85.71% , separately appear in the region of 40 and 9.

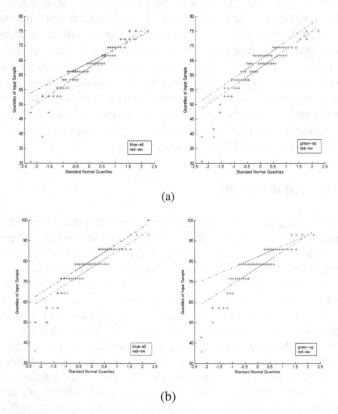

Fig. 2. NYU and KKI experimental results. (a) shows the accuracy of detailed regions in three ways of NYU dataset. (b) shows the accuracy of detailed regions in three ways of KKI dataset. The blue indicates the accuracy of all features in classification while the red indicates the accuracy of small world properties used. On the right one, the green means the accuracy of the other features used in the classification.

Seen from Fig. 2, we can find that the average accuracy among regions by using all features of social network is higher than that by only using small world properties. And also it can be seen that, there exists the same trend between the new features only and small world properties for both datasets, which in some degree verifies that the proposed method has a better effect than the one based on small world properties.

4   Conclusion

In this paper, a feature selection method based on social network analysis is applied, which can obviously reduce the computational complexity before SVM training. Nine kinds of features were extracted from the brain images and then used for training classifiers. It can be concluded from the experimental results that, the proposed method obtain a good performance of classification between ADHD diagnosed and control subjects. Also, we found that the features of assortative mixing and synchronization can be more effective in the classification than the traditional small world properties. The region of intermediate frontal, granular frontal and supramarginal gyrus corresponding to the area 8, 9 and 40, apparently have better performance in the classification, thus we have reason to consider that there exists obvious difference in these regions between ADHD and healthy subjects.

In the future work, we will verify the feasibility of the method for classification of other brain diseases, since we obtain a good result by applying the proposed method to classify between the ADHD diagnosis and controls in this paper. On the other hand, the classification accuracy may improve effectively if personal characteristic factor such as age, IQ etc. are also taken into account. And Future research will be needed to focus on this question.

References

1. Biederman, J., Mick, E., Faraone, S.V.: Age-dependent decline of symptoms of attention deficit hyperactivity disorder: impact of remission definition and symptom type. American Journal of Psychiatry 157(5), 816–818 (2000)
2. Biswal, B., Zerrin Yetkin, F., Haughton, V.M., Hyde, J.S.: Functional connectivity in the motor cortex of resting human brain using echo-planar mri. Magnetic Resonance in Medicine 34(4), 537–541 (1995)
3. Cordes, D., Haughton, V.M., Arfanakis, K., Wendt, G.J., Turski, P.A., Moritz, C.H., Meyerand, M.E.: Mapping functionally related regions of brain with functional connectivity MR imaging. American Journal of Neuroradiology 21(9), 1636–1644 (2000)
4. Castellanos, F.X., Margulies, D.S., Kelly, C., Uddin, L.Q., Ghaffari, M., Kirsch, A., Milham, M.P.: Cingulate-precuneus interactions: a new locus of dysfunction in adult attention-deficit/hyperactivity disorder. Biological Psychiatry 63(3), 332–337 (2008)
5. Achard, S., Bullmore, E.: Efficiency and cost of economical brain functional networks. PLoS Computational Biology 3(2), e17 (2007)
6. Stam, C.J., Reijneveld, J.C.: Graph theoretical analysis of complex networks in the brain. Nonlinear Biomedical Physics 1(1), 3 (2007)

7. Ponten, S.C., Bartolomei, F., Stam, C.J.: Small-world networks and epilepsy: Graph theoretical analysis of intracerebrally recorded mesial temporal lobe seizures. Clinical Neurophysiology 118(4), 918–927 (2007)
8. Micheloyannis, S., Pachou, E., Stam, C.J., Breakspear, M., Bitsios, P., Vourkas, M., Zervakis, M.: Small-world networks and disturbed functional connectivity in schizophrenia. Schizophrenia Research 87(1), 60–66 (2006)
9. Shinkareva, S.V., Ombao, H.C., Sutton, B.P., Mohanty, A., Miller, G.A.: Classification of functional brain images with a spatio-temporal dissimilarity map. NeuroImage 33(1), 63–71 (2006)
10. Matthews, P.M., Jezzard, P.: Functional magnetic resonance imaging. Journal of Neurology, Neurosurgery & Psychiatry 75(1), 6–12 (2004)
11. Brauer, J., Anwander, A., Friederici, A.D.: Neuroanatomical prerequisites for language functions in the maturing brain. Cerebral Cortex 21(2), 459–466 (2011)
12. Sabater, J., Sierra, C.: Reputation and social network analysis in multi-agent systems. In: Proceedings of the First International Joint Conference on Autonomous Agents and Multiagent Systems: part 1, pp. 475–482. ACM (2002)
13. Benjamini, Y., Hochberg, Y.: Controlling the false discovery rate: a practical and powerful approach to multiple testing. Journal of the Royal Statistical Society. Series B (Methodological), 289–300 (1995)
14. Watts, D.J., Strogatz, S.H.: Collective dynamics of small-world§ networks. Nature 393(6684), 440–442 (1998)
15. Montoya, J.M., Sole, R.V.: Small world patterns in food webs. Journal of Theoretical Biology 214(3), 405–412 (2002)
16. Latora, V., Marchiori, M.: Efficient behavior of small-world networks. Physical Review Letters 87(19), 198–701 (2001)
17. Newman, M.E.: The structure and function of complex networks. SIAM Review 45(2), 167–256 (2003)
18. Maslov, S., Sneppen, K.: Specificity and stability in topology of protein networks. Science 296(5569), 910–913 (2002)
19. Humphries, M.D., Gurney, K., Prescott, T.J.: The brainstem reticular formation is a small-world, not scale-free, network. Proceedings of the Royal Society B: Biological Sciences 273(1585), 503–511 (2006)
20. Newman, M.E., Strogatz, S.H., Watts, D.J.: Random graphs with arbitrary degree distributions and their applications. Physical Review E 64(2), 026118 (2001)
21. Newman, M.E.: Assortative mixing in networks. Physical Review Letters 89(20), 208701 (2002)
22. Jespersen, S., Sokolov, I.M., Blumen, A.: Small-world Rouse networks as models of cross-linked polymers. The Journal of Chemical Physics 113(17), 7652–7655 (2000)
23. Gerdes, S., Scholle, M.D., Campbell, J.W., Balazsi, G., Ravasz, E., Daugherty, M.D., Osterman, A.L.: Experimental determination and system level analysis of Essential genes in Escherichia coli MG1655. Journal of Bacteriology 185(19), 5673–5684 (2003)
24. ADHD-200 global competition (2011),
   http://fcon1000.projects.nitrc.org/indi/adhd200

Motor Imagery EEG Signals Analysis Based on Bayesian Network with Gaussian Distribution

Liang-hua He[*] and Bin Liu

Department of Computer Science and Technology, Tongji University, Shanghai, 201804
helianghua@tongji.edu.cn

Abstract. A novel communication channel from brain to machine, the research of Brain-computer interfacing is attracted more and more attention recently. In this paper, a novel method based on Bayesian Network is proposed to analyze multi motor imagery task. On the one hand, the channel physical position and mean motor imagery class information are adopted as constrains in BN structure construction. On the other hand, continuous Gaussian distribution model is used to model the bayesian network nodes other than discretizing variable in traditional methods, which would reflect the real character of EEG signals. Finally, the network structure and edge inference score are used to construct SVM classifier. Experimental results on the BCI competition data and lab collected data show that the average accuracy of the two experiments are 93% and 88%, which are better comparing to current methods.

Keywords: EEG, Motor Imager, Bayesian Network, Gaussian Distribution.

1   Introduction

Brain-computer interfacing (BCI) is a new method with providing a novel communication channel from men to machines and is used to date primarily for intentional control. It has received increasing attention in recent years and more and more alternative applications of BCI technology are being explored [1]. Basically, BCIs require the users to follow a specific computer-generated cue before performing a specific mental control task. In order to analysis EEG signal, especially motor imagery(MI) EEG signal, Numerous analysis methods have been proposed for classification of two or multiple MI classes (e.g., imaginary movements of left hand, right hand, tongue, or foot). The most famous is the common spatial pattern method (CSP) [2] and its various extensions [3,4] are widely used for extracting discriminative spatial (or joint spatio-spectral) patterns that contrast the power features of spatial patterns in different MI classes. For tackling multi-class problems, an information theoretic feature extraction method [5] and other extensions of CSP [6,7] have been proposed.

There are still many useful discriminant methods have been proposed, including analysis based on self-regression model[8], algorithm based on wavelet transform[9], neural networks[10], etc.

---

[*] Corresponding author.

D.-S. Huang et al. (Eds.): ICIC 2014, LNBI 8590, pp. 241–247, 2014.

Among these methods, although the CSP is a popular method in BCI applications, it is very sensitive to noise, and often over-fits with small training sets. The weakness of SVM method is that the optimal parameters are manually selected which has much restriction during the parameters searching.

What's the most important is that all these methods have one thing in common, that is, they regard the problem of motor imagery EEG analysis as pattern classification and extract features of different imagery pattern, such as frequency, regression coefficients, and then build a discriminant analysis model. Under certain conditions these methods achieved good results. However, on the one hand, there are too much noise in EEG signals which affect the classification results. On the other hand, most methods do not use the channel space position and high time resolution.

Because of the powerful combination of prior knowledge and data distribution, as a kind of graphical model, bayesian network (BN)can accurately describe the causal relationship between variables [11]. At present, the applications of BN in EEG are mainly focus on analysis and discrimination. Guosheng Yang et al. [12] studied Bayesian network for emotion recognition by analyzing the EEG data under different emotion. Kwang-EunKO et al. [13] and X Li et al. [14] applied BN to identify the fatigue status of the vehicle driver.

In this paper, considering the space position of each EEG channels and low Signal to Noise Ratio of EEG signal, BN is modified to be suitable for multiclass motor imagery BCI analysis with event-related processing of accumulating. There are three major steps of this paper: constrains calculation of every node's parent and son set, optimal BN structure searching, SVM discrimination based on edge difference and score distribution. All three steps are finished automatically.

The paper is organized as follows: Section 2 introduces the methodology of the proposed method; Section 3 introduces the experiment and results; Section 4 is the discussion and conclusion.

2   Methodology

2.1   Modeling EEG Data with Bayesian Networks

A Bayesian network is a graphical model for probabilistic relationships among a set of variables. The learning task in Bayesian networks can be separated into two subtasks: structure learning and parameter estimation. The Bayesian network structure aims to identify the best topology and implies a set of conditional independence relations among the variable involved as long as these variable are valid. Besides independencies, the graph structure of a BN can also be used in certain domains to represent cause effect relationships through the edges and their directions. In these case, the parent of a node are taken to be the "direct causes" of the quantity represented by that node. The parameters define the conditional probability distributions for a given network topology.

In this paper, in order to make analysis logic as simple as possible, one node in the network is one EEG channel. Therefore, edges among the nodes in BN indicate the relationship among the corresponding channels.

Bayesian network structure learning proposed in this paper can be divided into the following three steps:

1. The mean signal for every class BCI is calculated, based on which the set of father and son of BN is studied.
2. The fisher criterion is used to determine whether any two nodes are independent or conditional independent, and then the parents-children node sets PC_1 of every node can be obtained.
3. Calculate the distribution of each node with Gaussian distribution, then search the optimal BN structure based on the BIC score with greedy method.

2.2   Scoring Based on Gaussian Distribution

In this paper, the Gaussian distribution is applied to simulate the probability density function of the continuous EEG signals. Given a channel x_i and its continuous parent Y, the conditional probability density function can be expressed as:

$$f(y|x) = \frac{1}{(2\pi)^{n/2}|\Sigma_i|^{1/2}} \exp\{-\frac{1}{2}(y - W_i x - \mu_i)^T \Sigma_i^{-1} (y - W_i x - \mu_i)\} \tag{1}$$

Where W_i is the weight matrix, μ_i is the mean value, and Σ_i is the covariance matrix.

Suppose that there exists m independently, identically distributed training cases D, so the log-likelihood is

$$L = \log \prod_{i=1}^{m} f(y_i|x_i, D) \tag{2}$$

Combining Eqs.(1) and(2), then we get the complete data log likelihood as follows:

$$L = -\frac{N}{2}\log|\Sigma_i| - \frac{1}{2}\sum_{i=1}^{N}(y_i - W_i x_i - \mu_i)^T \Sigma_i^{-1}(y_i - W_i x_i - \mu_i) \tag{3}$$

Then we can estimate the parameters of the Gaussian distribution via Eq.(3), and obtain the result

$$W_i = \frac{(N*E_i|YX\;'|) - \mu_i(N*E_i|X\;'|)}{N*E_i|XX\;'|}$$

$$\mu_i = \frac{(N*E_i|Y|) - W_i(N*E_i|X|)}{N} \tag{4}$$

$$\Sigma_i = \frac{N*E_i(YY' - Y\begin{bmatrix}X\\1\end{bmatrix}'[W_i \quad \mu_i]' - [W_i \quad \mu_i]\begin{bmatrix}X\\1\end{bmatrix}Y' + [W_i \quad \mu_i]\begin{bmatrix}X\\1\end{bmatrix}\begin{bmatrix}X\\1\end{bmatrix}'[W_i \quad \mu_i]')}{N}$$

Where $E[YX\;']$ is a conditional second moment; the other can be rewrite similarly. So given a training data set, the mean value, the weight matrix and the covariance matrix can be obtained by Eq.(4), and thus the probability density or the conditional probability density can be got by Eq.(1), with above conditions, the entire score of a network can be obtained.

2.3   Edge Difference

Definitely, there is a BN $G(i,j)$ for every try i MI BCI class j . Theoretically, different activation areas have different BN structure, i.e. G . After the simplest summation of G along all tries for given MI BCI class j , the statistics of every edge is acquired and the total edge matrix E_j are got. The value of E_j indicates the number tries that have edge $e(m,n)_j$ from node m to node n . The larger the $e(m,n)_j$ is, the more common it shows. If the value of $e(l,p)$ is much larger in MI class i than that in MI class j , it means that it has much discriminate ability between MI class i and j . Therefore, those edges with the largest difference between different MI classes are used to make classification.

3   Experiment and Results

3.1   Data Source

In order to test the proposed method performance, three experiments are made on three different datasets: Our own data set, Graz BCI competition III (dataset IIIa).

3.2   Data Preprocessing

The number of EEG channel in three datasets are different with 64, 11 respectively, which is shown in figure 2. Theoretically, more channels means more edges to be chosen. However, the complexity will also increase nonlinearly. According to the research results of neuroscience, the MI tasks are major correlated to Brodmann area 4 and 6, which are positioned at the channels of   FC3, FC4, C5, C3, C1, CZ, C2, C4, C6, CP3 and CP4 with symmetrically distributed around brain as shown in figure 2(b). Thus, these channels are adopted in this paper, which is shown as figure 2(b).

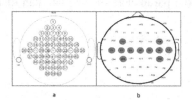

Fig. 1. Electrode montage of three datasets. a: IIIa dataset of Graz BCI competition III, b: our own.

The main work of preprocessing is to remove the Electro-Oculogram(EOG) and filtering .The EOG is removed by the Neuroscan software. And for the filtering work, this paper analyzes the frequency band of 8-30Hz, which is just the band of α wave and β wave. So an elliptic filter was designed, with band-pass from 8 to 30Hz.

3.3   BCI IIIa Experimental Results

As we all know, one trial indicates one imagery pattern in motor imagery task. Therefore, during analyzing the motor imagery EEG data, BN was constructed for each try.

The 20 tries statistical results of edges in BN for all the left and right imagery pattern are shown in figure 2 (for convenience, here only takes k3b as an example).The horizontal axis stands for edges made up by different channels, and the vertical axis represents the total number of occurrences of an edge in the 20 trials.

For all the subjects, the calculation results show that there exist significant different edges between the left and right motor imagery pattern, although the edge with significant difference is varying across subjects. Taking k3b as an example, the significant different edge is channel (1,4).

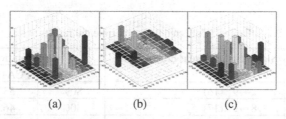

(a)   (b)   (c)

Fig. 2. Statistical results of BN edges of one subject (a) BN edges statistic on 20 left motor imagery trials (b)BN edges statistic on 20 right motor imagery trials (c) BN edges statistic difference on 20 left and right motor imagery trials

Table 1. BCI III Experimental Results

	Significant different Edges	Recognition rate	
		BN	PCA+Fisherscore
k3b	FC3→C3	85%	43.33%
k6b	C5→CP3	94%	53.33%
l1b	C4→C6	100%	40%
average		93%	45.55%

Table 2. BCI competition results for BCI III data IIIa

	k3b	k6b	l1b
1	0.8222	0.7556	0.8000
2	0.6872	0.4333	0.7111
3	0.9482	0.4111	0.5222
BN	0.7853	0.6931	0.8154

The experimental results of recognition rate for the proposed method are shown in table 1. Both the significant different edges and the corresponding recognition rate are provided. In order to evaluate the performance of BN, PCA+FisherScore[15] method is applied to make a comparing on the two data sets. The results are shown in table 1.

On the other hand, the results of *kappa coefficient* is listed on table 2 together with the top three results[16] of BCI competition for motor imagery data IIIa.

It can be seen from table 1 and table 2 that the average recognition rate of proposed method is 76.67%, which is much higher than PCA+Fisher Score method, whose performance is only 45.55%. As for the Comparing with the top three best winner, BN shows better performance on more than half sub-datasets.

3.4   The Experimental Results of Collected Data

For the collected experiment data of the five subjects, carrying out the same processing in accordance with the BCI IIIa data, and the experimental results are shown in Table 3.

Table 3. Collected data experimental results

	Significant different Edges	Recognition rate	
		BN	PCA+Fisherscore
Subject1	2→9 (16)	80%	53.33%
Subject2	8→9 (17)	80%	46.67%
Subject3	1→4 (13)	85%	40%
Subject4	4→10 (-20)	95%	53.3%
Subject5	8→9 (20) 8→11 (20)	100%	60%
average		88%	50.67%

It can be seen from table 3 that the proposed BN method overwhelm the PCA+Fisher Score method with 88% recognition rate, comparing with only 50.57% recognition rate of   PCA+Fisher Score method.

4   Discussion and Conclusion

In this paper, a method based on BN for the discriminate analysis of motor imagery EEG is introduced. And in order to prove the effect of the proposed method, PCA+Fisher Score is adopted to contrast. The experimental results indicate that the proposed improvements are very effective to improve the discriminant analysis results.

References

1. Blankertz, B., Tangermann, M., Vidau-rre, C., Fazli, S., Sannelli, C., Haufe, S., Maeder, C., Ramsey, L.E., Sturm, I., Curio, G., Müller, K.-R.: The Berlin brain-computer-interface: non-medical uses of BCI technology. Front. Neurosci. 4(198), 10–13 (2010)
2. Pfurtscheller, G., Neuper, C., Flotzinger, D., Pregenzer, M.: EEG based discrimination between imagination of right and left hand movement. Clin. Neurophysiol. 103, 42–651 (1997)

3. Lemm, S., Blankertz, B., Curio, G., Müller, K.-R.: Spatio-spectral filters for robust classification of single trial EEG. IEEE Trans. Biomed. Eng. 52, 1541–1548 (2005)
4. Blankertz, B., Losch, F., Krauledat, M., Dornhege, G., Curio, G., Müller, K.-R.: The Berlin brain-computer interface: accurate performance from first-session in BCI-naïve subjects. IEEE Trans. Biomed. Eng. 55, 2452–2462 (2008a)
5. Grosse-Wentrup, M., Buss, M.: Multiclass common spatial patterns and information theoretic feature extraction. IEEE Trans. Biomed. Eng. 55, 1991–2000 (2008)
6. Dornhege, G., Blankertz, B., Curio, G., Müller, K.-R.: Increase information transfer rates in BCI by csp extension to multi-class. Adv. Neural Inf. Process. Syst. 16 (2003)
7. Dornhege, G., Blankertz, B., Curio, G., Müller, K.-R.: Boosting bit rates in noninvasive EEG single-trial classifications by feature combination and multiclass paradigms. IEEE Trans. Biomed. Eng. 51, 993–1002 (2004)
8. Krusienski, D.J., McFarland, D.J., Wolpaw, J.R.: An evaluation of autoregressive spectral estimation model order for brain-computer interface applications. In: IEEE EMBS Ann. Int. Conf., vol. 1, pp. 1323–1326 (2006)
9. Hinterberger, T., Kubler, A., Kaiser, J.: A brain-computer interface (BCI) for the locked-in: comparison of different EEG classifications for the thought translation device. Clin. Neurophys. 114(3), 416–425 (2003)
10. Pfurtscheller, G., Kalcher, J., Neuper, C., On-line, E.E.G.: classification during externally-paced hand movements using a neural network-based classifier. Electroenceph. Clin. Neurophys. 99(5), 416–425 (1996)
11. Geiger, H.: Learning Bayesian Networks: The Combination of Knowledge and Statistical Data. Machine Learning 20(3), 197–243 (1995)
12. Guosheng, Y., Yingzi, L., Prabir, B.: A driver fatigue recognition model based on information fusion and dynamic Bayesian network. Information Sciences 180(10), 1942–1954 (2010)
13. Kwang-Eun, K., Hyun-Chang, Y., Kwee-Bo, S.: Emotion Recognition using EEG Signals with Relative Power Values and Bayesian Network. International Journal of Control, Automation and Systems 7(5), 865–870 (2009)
14. Xiangyang, L., Qiang, J.: Active Affective State Detection and User Assistance With Dynamic Bayesian Networks. IEEE Transactions on Systems, Man and Cybernetics 35(1), 93–105 (2005)
15. Cao, L., Li, J., Sun, Y., Zhu, H., Yan, C.: EEG-based vigilance analysis by using fisher score and PCA algorithm. In: IEEE Progress in Informatics and Computing (PIC), pp. 175–179 (2005)
16. Blankertz, B.: BCI Competition III Final Results (2006),
http://www.bbci.de/competition/iii/results/#winner

Prediction of Molecular Substructure Using Mass Spectral Data Based on Metric Learning

Zhi-Shui Zhang, Li-Li Cao, and Jun Zhang[*]

School of Electronic Engineering & Automation, Anhui University,
Hefei, Anhui 230601, China

Abstract. In this paper, some metric learning algorithms are used to predict the molecular substructure from mass spectral features. Among them are Discriminative Component Analysis (DCA), Large Margin NN Classifier (LMNN), Information-Theoretic Metric Learning (ITML), Principal Component Analysis (PCA), Multidimensional Scaling (MDS) and Isometric Mapping (ISOMAP). The experimental results show metric learning algorithms achieved better prediction performance than the algorithms based on Elucidation distance. Contrasting to other metric learning algorithms, LMNN is the best one in eleven substructure prediction.

Keywords: Data mining, molecular structure, metric learning.

1   Introduction

Gas chromatography coupled with mass spectrometry (GC-MS) is a key analytical technology for high-throughout analysis of small molecules [1]. A lot of mass spectral libraries have been created [2-5] and various mass spectral similarity measures [6-10] have been developed for the spectrum matching. When the spectrum of an unknown compound does not exist in the reference library, mass spectral classification is an important and complementary method to aid and benefit the mass spectral library searching.

So many classification methods based on mass spectral data have been developed. Varmuza first transform EI spectra into spectral features and then use a set of mass spectral classifiers to predict presence or absence of 70 substructure[11]. However, the chemical structure information contained in mass spectra is difficult to extract because of the relationship between MS data and chemical structures are too complicated. To improve the prediction performance, some feature selection methods were used: Genetic algorithm (GA) [12].As for the development of classifiers, from simple Artificial neural network (ANN)[13] , linear discriminant analysis (LDA) and partial least squares discriminant PLS (DPLS) to complex decision tree and Adaboost have all been used for prediction [14, 15]. Metric learning is a potentially effective method for the prediction of molecular sub-structure. In fact, the performance of many classification algorithms depends on the metric over the input space. Several existing methods were developed to explore distance information and showed excellent performance in standard data sets

---

[*] Corresponding author.

D.-S. Huang et al. (Eds.): ICIC 2014, LNBI 8590, pp. 248–254, 2014.

[16-18]. In this paper, total four metric learning algorithms are used to compare the prediction performance, among them are Information-Theoretic Metric Learning (ITML) [18, 19], Large Margin Nearest Neighbor (LMNN) [17, 20], Discriminative Component Analysis (DCA) [21, 22] and Isometric Mapping [23-25] algorithm.

2 Materials and Methods

2.1 Mass Spectra and Substructures Dataset

To evaluate the performance of different algorithms, a mass spectral features dataset with corresponding molecular substructure information have been taken from NIST mass spectral library. First, we randomly select 5172 molecules from NIST MS library. Software MassFeatGen was employed to transform the original mass peak data into an 862 mass features. The corresponding 11 molecular substructure are extracted from PubChem molecular fingerprint. The details of the molecular substructure are listed in table 1.

Table 1. Substructures used for the construction of datasets

Structure NO.	Chemical structure	Molecular equation	Number of objects
1		4-methylbenzenethiol	529
2		3-methylbenzenethiol	451
3		o-cresol	589
4		1-chloro-2-methylbenzene	527
5		4-methylcyclohexanol	670
6		4-methylcyclohexanethiol	691
7		3-methylcyclohexanol	819

Table 1. (*Continued.*)

8		3-methylcyclohexanethiol	620
9		2-methylcyclohexanol	927
10		2-methylcyclohexanethiol	535
11		1-chloro-2-methylcyclohexane	591

2.2   Algorithm

Information-Theoretic Metric Learning

Given a set of n points $\{x_1, x_2, ..., x_n\}$ in R^n, we seek a matrix A which parameterizes the Mahalanobis distance,

$$d_A(x_i, x_j) = (x_i - x_j)^T A(x_i - x_j) \tag{1}$$

Samples are similar: $d_A(x_i, x_j) \leq u$ for a relatively small value of u, samples are dissimilar: $d_A(x_i, x_j) \geq l$ for sufficiently large l, our problem is to learn a matrix A that parameterizes the corresponding Mahalanobis distance.

Given similar samples S and dissimilar samples D, the distance metric learning problem is

$$\min_A KL(p(x; A) \parallel p(x; A)) \tag{2}$$

Subject to
$$d_A(x_i, x_j) \leq u \qquad (i, j) \in S$$
$$d_A(x_i, x_j) \geq l \qquad (i, j) \in D$$

S represents the similar samples and D represents dissimilar samples, enlightened by low-rank kernel learning problem, it can be seen below:

$$KL(p(x; A) \parallel p(x; A)) = \frac{1}{2} D_{ld}(A_0^{-1}, A^{-1}) = \frac{1}{2} D_{ld}(A, A_0) \tag{3}$$

$$D_{ld}(A, A_0) = tr(AA_0^{-1}) - \log \det(AA_0^{-1}) - n \tag{4}$$

The step of this algorithm can be seen below:

Algorithm   Information-theoretic metric learning

Input: X: input d × n matrix;   S: set of similar pairs   D: set of dissimilar pairs;

u, l: distance thresholds; A_0: input Mahalanobis matrix; γ: slack parameter

c: constraint index function

Output: A: output Mahalanobis matrix

1. $A \leftarrow A_0, \lambda_{ij} \leftarrow 0 \forall i, j$

2. $\xi_{c(i,j)} \leftarrow u$ for $(i, j) \in S$; otherwise $\xi_{c(i,j)} \leftarrow l$

3. **repeat**

　3.1. Pick a constraint $(i, j) \in S$ or $(i, j) \in D$

　3.2. $p \leftarrow (x_i - x_j)^T A(x_i - x_j)$

　3.3. $\delta \leftarrow 1$ if $(i, j) \in S$, -1 otherwise

　3.4. $\alpha \leftarrow \min (\lambda_{ij}, \frac{\delta}{2}(\frac{1}{p} - \frac{\gamma}{\xi_{c(i,j)}}))$

　3.5. $\beta \leftarrow \dfrac{\delta \alpha}{1 - \delta \alpha p}$

　3.6. $\xi_{c(i,j)} \leftarrow \gamma \xi_{c(i,j)}/(\gamma + \delta \alpha \xi_{c(i,j)})$

　3.7. $\lambda_{ij} \leftarrow \lambda_{ij} - \alpha$

　3.8. $A \leftarrow A + \beta A(x_i - x_j)(x_i - x_j)^T A$

4. **until** convergence

return A

The parameter γ controls the tradeoff between satisfying the constraints and minimizing $D_{ld}(A, A_0)$.

Large Margin Nearest Neighbor (LMNN)
LMNN learn the matrix A with the help of semidefinite programming for every sample x_i, the similar samples should be close and the dissimilar samples should be far away, it can be represented as following:

$$\min_A \sum_{i, j \in N_i} d(x_i, x_j) \tag{5}$$

then constraining dissimilar sample x_l to be one point further away than similar sample x_j. The resulting can be stated as:

$$\forall_{i, j \in N_i, l, y_l \neq y_i} d(x_i, x_j) + 1 \leq d(x_i, x_j) \tag{6}$$

The final optimization problem becomes:

$$\min_A \sum_{i, j \in N} d(x_i, x_j) + \sum_{i, j, l} \xi_{ijl} \tag{7}$$

$$\forall_{i,j\in N_i,l,y_l\neq y_i} d(x_i,x_j)+1\leq d(x_i,x_j)+\xi_{ijl}, \xi_{ijl}\geq 0, A\succ=0 \qquad (8)$$

Here the variables ξ_{ijl} represent the amount of violations of the dissimilar samples. The sum is minimized.

3   Experiments and Discussions

We evaluated LMNN,DCA,ISOMAP and adaboost algorithm based on our data set, experimental results were obtained by averaging over multiple runs. and the weighting parameter was set to 0.5, maximum number of iterations was set to 1000,

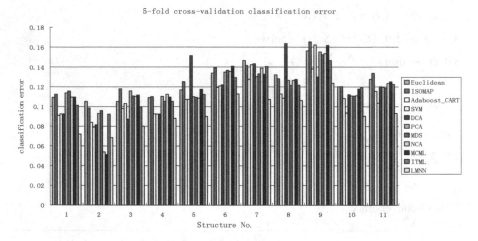

Fig. 1. The error of the algorithms for the classification of the substructure of molecules

Table 2. The classification error of the algorithms

5-fold cross-validation classification error								
No.	Euclidean	ISOMAP	Adboost	SVM	DCA	PCA	MDS	ITML	LMNN
1	0.1093	0.1123	0.0908	0.0925	0.0925	0.1138	0.1157	0.1012	0.072
2	0.1052	0.0985	0.084	0.079	0.0814	0.0929	0.0959	0.0923	0.0685
3	0.1051	0.118	0.098	0.103	0.0873	0.1159	0.1107	0.0995	0.0801
4	0.1091	0.11	0.0926	0.0924	0.0925	0.1104	0.1053	0.1054	0.088
5	0.1168	0.1251	0.1073	0.1073	0.1514	0.11	0.1094	0.1123	0.0901
6	0.134	0.1398	0.1194	0.1209	0.122	0.1349	0.1367	0.1294	0.1128
7	0.1466	0.1415	0.1278	0.1423	0.1434	0.1303	0.1331	0.1406	0.1073
8	0.1321	0.1283	0.1127	0.1086	0.1637	0.1266	0.1216	0.1217	0.1063
9	0.1563	0.1655	0.1382	0.1624	0.1301	0.1552	0.1525	0.1466	0.1237
10	0.1201	0.1203	0.1082	0.0937	0.1121	0.1109	0.1107	0.1191	0.0904
11	0.1277	0.1338	0.1154	0.1036	0.1201	0.1194	0.1188	0.1226	0.0932

validation step was set to 35 and suppress output was set to 1. As DCA algorithm, the percentage of positive constraints to be produced was set to 0.2. For all the algorithms, the output dimensions were set as 18. K value of KNN was set as 3. The main results on the data sets are shown in Fig. 1 and Table 2.

From the Fig.1 and Table 2, we can see that ITML, DCA, LMNN algorithms improves classification ability. We use the squared Euclidean distance as a baseline method. The results show that LMNN is the most effective algorithm to improve the KNN classification accuracy.

4   Conclusion

In this paper, we show the problem of metric learning with multiple features and compare several Metric Learning algorithms for the classification of the substructure of molecules. Our experimental results show that metric learning algorithms achieved better prediction performance than the algorithms based on Elucidation distance. The LMNN is the best one among these algorithms.

Acknowledgments. This work was supported by National Natural Science Foundation of China under grant nos. 61271098 and 61032007, and Provincial Natural Science Research Program of Higher Education Institutions of Anhui Province under grant no. KJ2012A005.

References

1. Denkert, C., Budczies, J., et al.: Mass Spectrometry-Based Metabolic Profiling Reveals Different Metabolite Patterns in Invasive Ovarian Carcinomas and Ovarian Borderline Tumors. Cancer Research 66(22), 10795–10804 (2006)
2. Horai, H., Arita, M., et al.: Massbank: A Public Repository for Sharing Mass Spectral Data for Life Sciences. Journal of Mass Spectrometry 45(7), 703–714 (2010)
3. Schauer, N., Steinhauser, D., et al.: GC-MS Libraries for The Rapid Identification of Metabolites in Complex Biological Samples. Febs Letters 579(6), 1332–1337 (2005)
4. NIST Mass Spectral Search for the NIST/EPA/NIH mass spectral library version 2.0. office of the Standard Reference Data Base, National Institute of Standards and Technology, Gaithersburg, Maryland (2005)
5. Stein, S.: Mass Spectral Reference Libraries: An Ever-Expanding Resource for Chemical Identification. Analytical Chemistry 84(17), 7274–7282 (2012)
6. Stein, S.E., Scott, D.R.: Optimization and Testing of Mass Spectral Library Search Algorithms for Compound Identification. Journal of the American Society for Mass Spectrometry 5(9), 859–866 (1994)
7. McLafferty, F.W., Zhang, M.Y., Stauffer, D.B., Loh, S.Y.: Comparison of Algorithms and Databases for Matching Unknown Mass Spectra. J. Am. Soc. Mass Spectrom. 9(1), 92–95 (1998)
8. Hertz, H.S., Hites, R.A., Biemann, K.: Identification of Mass Spectra by Computer-Searching a File of Known Spectra. Analytical Chemistry 43(6), 681 (1971)
9. Koo, I., Zhang, X., Kim, S.: Wavelet- and Fourier-Transform-Based Spectrum Similarity Approaches to Compound Identification in Gas Chromatography/Mass Spectrometry. Anal Chem. 83(14), 5631–5638 (2011)

10. Kim, S., Koo, I., Wei, X.L., Zhang, X.: A Method of Finding Optimal Weight Factors for Compound Identification in Gas Chromatography-Mass Spectrometry. Bioinformatics 28(8), 1158–1163 (2012)
11. Varmuza, K., Werther, W.: Mass Spectral Classifiers for Supporting Systematic Structure Elucidation. Journal of Chemical Information and Computer Sciences 36(2), 323–333 (1996)
12. Yoshida, H., Leardi, R., Funatsu, K., Varmuza, K.: Feature Selection by Genetic Algorithms for Mass Spectral Classifiers. Analytica Chimica Acta 446(1-2), 485–494 (2001)
13. Eghbaldar, A., Forrest, T.P., Cabrol-Bass, D.: Development of Neural Networks for Identification of Structural Features From Mass Spectral Data. Analytica Chimica Acta 359(3), 283–301 (1998)
14. Xiong, Q., Zhang, Y.X., Li, M.L.: Computer-Assisted Prediction of Pesticide Substructure Using Mass Spectra. Analytica Chimica Acta 593(2), 199–206 (2007)
15. He, P., Xu, C.J., Liang, Y.Z., Fang, K.T.: Improving The Classification Accuracy in Chemistry Via Boosting Technique. Chemometrics and Intelligent Laboratory Systems 70(1), 39–46 (2004)
16. Xing, E.P., Jordan, M.I., Russell, S., Ng, A.: Distance Metric Learning with Application To Clustering with Side-Information. Advances in Neural Information Processing Systems (2002)
17. Blitzer, J., Weinberger, K.Q., Saul, L.K.: Distance Metric Learning for Large Margin Nearest Neighbor Classification. Advances in Neural Information Processing Systems (2005)
18. Davis, J.V., Kulis, B., Jain, P., Sra, S., Dhillon, I.S.: Information-Theoretic Metric Learning. In: Proceedings of The 24th International Conference on Machine Learning. ACM (2007)
19. Bar-Hillel, A., Hertz, T., Shental, N., Weinshall, D.: Learning Distance Functions Using Equivalence Relations. In: ICML (2003)
20. Domeniconi, C., Gunopulos, D., Peng, J.: Large Margin Nearest Neighbor Classifiers. IEEE Transactions on Neural Networks 16(4), 899–909 (2005)
21. Schölkopf, B., Smola, A., Müller, K.-R.: Nonlinear Component Analysis As A Kernel Eigenvalue Problem. Neural Computation 10(5), 1299–1319 (1998)
22. Duchene, J., Leclercq, S.: An Optimal Transformation for Discriminant and Principal Component Analysis. IEEE Transactions on Pattern Analysis and Machine Intelligence 10(6), 978–983 (1988)
23. MacEachren, A.M., Davidson, J.V.: Sampling and Isometric Mapping of Continuous Geographic Surfaces. The American Cartographer 14(4), 299–320 (1987)
24. Ding, G.: The Isometric Extension Problem in The Unit Spheres of Lp (Γ)(P> 1) Type Spaces. Science in China Series A: Mathematics 46(3), 333–338 (2003)
25. Clements, J.C., Leon, L.: A Fast, Accurate Algorithm for The Isometric Mapping of A Developable Surface. SIAM Journal on Mathematical Analysis 18(4), 966–971 (1987)

Combine Multiple Mass Spectral Similarity
Measures for Compound Identification in GC-MS

Li-Huan Liao, Yi-Fei Zhu, Li-Li Cao, and Jun Zhang[*]

School of Electronic Engineering & Automation, Anhui University,
Hefei, Anhui 230601, China

Abstract. In this study, total seven similarity measures were combined to improve the identification performance. To test the developed system, 28,234 mass spectra from the NIST replicate library were randomly split into the training set and test set. PSO algorithm was used to find the optimized weights of seven similarity measures based on the training set, and then the optimized weights were applied into the test set. Simulation study indicates that the combination of multiple similarity measures achieves a better performance than single best measure, with the identification accuracy improved by 2.2 % and 1.7% for training and test set respectively.

Keywords: mass spectra, compound identification, similarity measures.

1 Introduction

Gas chromatography mass spectrometry (GC-MS) is one of the most widely used analytical tools for the analysis of chemical or biological samples in many fields [1]. One of the most important procedures for the analyses of GC-MS data is compound identification. Many commercial and academic mass spectral libraries have been created [2-5], and various mass spectral similarity measures have been developed for compound identification, including dot product, composite similarity[6], probability-based matching system [7], Hertz similarity index[8], normalized Euclidean distance and absolute value distance (ABS_VD) [9].

Stein and Scott compared five of the most popular spectral similarity metrics and concluded that the best performance was achieved by the proposed composite similarity[6]. Koo et al. [10] introduced a composite similarity measure that integrates wavelet and Fourier transform factors and showed that their similarity measures perform better than the dot product with its composite version. Kim et al. [11] developed a statistical approach to find the optimal weight factors through a reference library for compound identification. Kim et al. [12] also proposed a composite similarity measure based on partial and semi-partial correlations. Most recently, Koo et al. [13] compared the performance of several spectral similarity measures and found that the composite semi-partial correlation measure provides the best identification accuracy.

---

[*] Corresponding author.

D.-S. Huang et al. (Eds.): ICIC 2014, LNBI 8590, pp. 255–261, 2014.
© Springer International Publishing Switzerland 2014

In order to further improve the compound identification, we developed a method that combines the results of multiple mass spectral similarity measures. A filter method is used to define a subset of the reference spectral library [14, 15]. Particle swarm optimization (PSO) [16] algorithm is used to optimize the weight of each similarity measure. By using the combination of multiple similarity measures with the optimized weights, the final compound identification is implemented.

2   Materials and Methods

2.1   NIST EI Mass Spectral Library

The NIST/EPA/NIH Mass Spectral Library contains two EI mass spectral libraries, the main and the replicate EI MS library. In this study, the replicate EI mass spectra are used as a query library. A total of 28,234 mass spectra were extracted from the replicate library, of which 5844 mass spectra were randomly selected as training dataset while the remaining 23,290 mass spectra were used as test dataset. The main EI MS library of NIST/EPA/NIH Mass Spectral Library 2005 (NIST05) containing 163,195 mass spectra was used as reference library.

2.2   Similarity Measures

Let $X=(x_1,x_2,...,x_n)$ and $Y=(y_1,y_2,...,y_n)$ be the query and reference mass spectra, respectively. The weighted spectra are as follows [6]:

$$X^w = (x_1^w,......,x_n^w) \tag{1}$$

$$Y^w = (y_1^w,......,y_n^w) \tag{2}$$

where $x_i^w = x_i^a \bullet m_i^b$ and $y_i^w = y_i^a \bullet m_i^b$, $i=1,...,n$, m_i, is m/z value of the ith fragmention, n is the number of mass-to-charge ratios considered for computation, a and b are the weight factors for peak intensity and m/z value, respectively. Throughout this work, with $(a,b) = (0.5, 3)$.

Absolute Value Difference (ABS_VD)

$$S_{ABS\_VD}(X^w,Y^w) = \frac{1}{n}\sum_{i=1}^{n}\left|x_i^w - y_i^w\right| \tag{3}$$

The sum of the difference between the corresponding weighted intensity values of the query and reference mass spectra.

Euclidean Distance

$$S_{Euc}(X^w,Y^w) = \frac{1}{n}\sum_{i=1}^{n}\left(x_i^w - y_i^w\right)^2 \tag{4}$$

Cosine Correlation

$$S_c(X^w, Y^w) = \frac{\sum\limits_{i=1}^{n} x_i^w y_i^w}{(\sum\limits_{i=1}^{n} (x_i^w)^2)^{\frac{1}{2}} (\sum\limits_{i=1}^{n} (y_i^w)^2)^{\frac{1}{2}}} \tag{5}$$

Correlation

$$S_{Cor}(X^w, Y^w) = \frac{\sum\limits_{i=1}^{n} (x_i^w - \bar{x}^w)(y_i^w - \bar{y}^w)}{\sqrt{\sum\limits_{i=1}^{n} (x_i^w - \bar{x}^w)^2} \sqrt{\sum\limits_{i=1}^{n} (y_i^w - \bar{y}^w)^2}} \tag{6}$$

where $\bar{x}^w = \sum\limits_{i=1}^{s} x_i^w$ and $\bar{y}^w = \sum\limits_{i=1}^{n} y_i^w$ respectively.

Stein and Scott's Composite Similarity Measure

The similarity measure is derived from a weighted average of two items. First item is defined in equation (5). The second item is defined a ratio of peak pairs as follows:

$$S_R(X, Y) = \frac{1}{N_c} \sum\limits_{i=2}^{N_c} (\frac{y_i}{y_{i-1}} \bullet \frac{x_{i-1}}{x_i})^n \tag{7}$$

where n=1 if the first intensity ratio is less than the second, otherwise n=-1. x_i, y_i are non-zero intensities having common m/z value and N_c is the number of non-zero peaks in both the reference and the query spectra. The composite similarity is:

$$S_{ss}(X^w, Y^w) = \frac{N_x \bullet S_c(X^w, Y^w) + N_c \bullet S_R(X, Y)}{N_x + N_c} \tag{8}$$

where N_x is the number of non-zero peak intensities in the query spectrum.

Discrete Fourier and Wavelet Transform Composite Similarity Measure

The original spectral signal $X = (x_1, x_2, ..., x_n)$ is converted by Discrete Fourier transform (DFT) into a new signal $X_f = (x_1^f, x_2^f, ..., x_n^f)$ as follows:

$$x_k^f = \sum\limits_{d=1}^{n} x_d \cos(-\frac{2\pi i}{n} kd) + i \sum\limits_{d=1}^{n} x_d \sin(-\frac{2\pi i}{n} kd), \qquad k = 1, ..., n \tag{9}$$

The converted signal consists of real and imaginary part. We only use the real part of a signal is $X^{FR} = (x_1^{FR}, x_2^{FR}, ..., x_n^{FR})$.

The discrete wavelet transform (DWT) convert a discrete time domain signal into a time-frequency domain signal. A signal pass through a low-pass filter and a high-pass filter, two subsets of signals are formed: approximations and details:

$$\text{Approximation DWT:} \quad x_k^A = \sum_{d=1}^{n} x_d \, g\,[2k - d - 1] \qquad k = 1, \ldots, n \tag{10}$$

$$\text{detail DWT:} \quad x_k^D = \sum_{d=1}^{n} x_d \, h[2k - d - 1] \qquad k = 1, \ldots, n \tag{11}$$

where g and h are low-pass and the high-pass filter respectively. In literature [10] only use real part in DFT and detail part in DWT.

$$S_{DFT}(X^w, Y^w) = \frac{N_x \bullet S_c(X^w, Y^w) + N_c \bullet S_R(X^{FR}, Y^{FR})}{N_x + N_c} \tag{12}$$

$$S_{DWT}(X^w, Y^w) = \frac{N_x \bullet S_c(X^w, Y^w) + N_c \bullet S_R(X^D, Y^D)}{N_x + N_c} \tag{13}$$

2.3   Performance Measurement

The accuracy is the proportion of the spectra identified correctly in query spectra. Therefore, the accuracy of identification can be calculated by:

$$accuracy = \frac{number \quad of \quad spectra \quad matched \quad correctly}{number \quad of \quad spectra \quad queried} \tag{14}$$

3   Results and Discussion

3.1   Constructing the Sub-reference Library

In order to construct the sub-reference library, a similarity measure is selected from seven similarity measures based on its computation time. We randomly selected one hundred mass spectra as query data and change the size of reference library. As the size of reference library increase, the computation time is increased as shown in Fig.3. Since SS measure needs much more computation time than others, it will make the other measures cannot be clearly observed, we removed it from Fig.1.

Fig. 2. depicts the relationship between identification accuracy and the number of top ranked compounds. With the increase of the number of the top ranked compounds, the accuracy of compound identification is increased. The DFTR and DWTD both outperform the other five measures in every rank. Overall, except DFTR and DWTD, the rest similarity measures have similar identification performance.

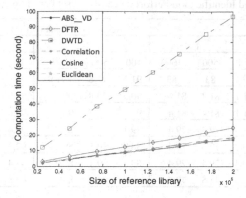

Fig. 1. Computational time of seven similarity measures

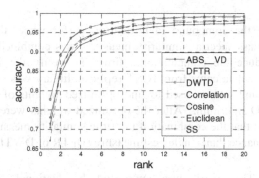

Fig. 2. Identification accuracy and corresponding rank number plot for seven similarity measures

3.2   Combine Multiple Similarity Measures (MUL_SM) for Compound Identification

Based on ABS_VD measure, the mass spectra of the top 100 ranked compounds identified by ABS_VD measure for each query spectrum were selected from the reference library NIST05 to construct the sub-reference library. PSO algorithm was used to find the optimized weights of multiple measures for training mass spectra. The optimized weights were then applied to the test dataset to find whether the identification performance of using multiple similarity measures (MUL_SM) is improved. From the training dataset the identification accuracy of MUL_SM exceeds the DFTR and DWTD about 2.2% and reaches to 80.0%.

Table 1 lists the identification results of the MUL_SM and each of the six similarity measures, respectively. The results show that the identification performance of MUL_SM outperforms any single spectral similarity measure. To study the influence of the size of filter subset on identification, the size of sub-reference library was set as 100, 500 and 1000, respectively. With the increase of the size of the sub-reference library from 100 to 1000, the identification performance of each similarity measure has a very smaller increment.

Table 1. Compound Identification Performance of test set based on ABS_VD filter

Size of filter Similarity subset Measures	Accuracy at Rank (%)								
	1			1-2			1-3		
	100	500	1000	100	500	1000	100	500	1000
MUL_SM	82.7	83	83	91.5	91.8	91.9	94.5	94.8	94.9
DFTR	81.1	81.3	81.4	90.5	90.8	90.9	93.9	94.2	94.4
DWTD	81.1	81.4	81.4	90.5	90.7	90.8	93.6	93.9	94
Correlation	79.3	79.3	79.4	89.1	89.1	89.2	92.4	92.5	92.6
Cosine	79.2	79.3	79.4	88.9	89.1	89.2	92.3	92.5	92.5
Euclidean	79.3	79.4	79.4	89	89.1	89.2	92.4	92.5	92.5
SS	78.3	78.5	78.5	88.7	89	89	92.5	92.8	92.9

4   Conclusion

In order to improve the compound identification performance, the identification difference of seven mass spectral similarity measures was combined. ABS_VD was used as filter to reduce the computational time. To verify the identification of combination, the query data came from NIST replicate library was split into training set and test set. Training set was used to find optimized weights of seven similarity measures through PSO algorithm.   After the optimized weights were applied into the test set, we concluded that the combination multiple similarity measures (MUL_SM) achieve better performance than single best measure (DFTR or DWTD).

Acknowledgments. This work was supported by National Natural Science Foundation of China under grant nos. 61271098 and 61032007, and Provincial Natural Science Research Program of Higher Education Institutions of Anhui Province under grant no. KJ2012A005.

References

1. Denkert, C., Budczies, J., et al.: Mass Spectrometry-Based Metabolic Profiling Reveals Different Metabolite Patterns in Invasive Ovarian Carcinomas and Ovarian Borderline Tumors. Cancer Research 66(22), 10795–10804 (2006)
2. Horai, H., Arita, M., et al.: Massbank: A Public Repository for Sharing Mass Spectral Data for Life Sciences. Journal of Mass Spectrometry 45(7), 703–714 (2010)
3. Schauer, N., Steinhauser, D., et al.: Gc-Ms Libraries for the Rapid Identification of Metabolites in Complex Biological Samples. Febs Letters 579(6), 1332–1337 (2005)
4. Ist, N.: Nist Mass Spectral Search for The Nist/Epa/Nih Mass Spectral Library Version 2.0. Office of the Standard Reference Data Base, National Institute of Standards and Technology, Gaithersburg, Maryland (2005)
5. Stein, S.: Mass Spectral Reference Libraries: An Ever-Expanding Resource for Chemical Identification. Analytical Chemistry 84(17), 7274–7282 (2012)

6. Stein, S.E., Scott, D.R.: Optimization and Testing of Mass Spectral Library Search Algorithms for Compound Identification. Journal of The American Society for Mass Spectrometry 5(9), 859–866 (1994)
7. Mclafferty, F.W., Zhang, M.Y., Stauffer, D.B., Loh, S.Y.: Comparison of Algorithms and Databases for Matching Unknown Mass Spectra. J. Am. Soc. Mass Spectrom. 9(1), 92–95 (1998)
8. Hertz, H.S., Hites, R.A., Biemann, K.: Identification of Mass Spectra by Computer-Searching a File of Known Spectra. Analytical Chemistry 43(6), 681 (1971)
9. Visvanathan, A.: Information-Theoretic Mass Spectral Library Search for Comprehensive Two-Dimensional Gas Chromatography with Mass Spectrometry (2008), Proquest
10. Koo, I., Zhang, X., Kim, S.: Wavelet- and Fourier-Transform-Based Spectrum Similarity Approaches to Compound Identification in Gas Chromatography/Mass Spectrometry. Anal Chem. 83(14), 5631–5638 (2011)
11. Kim, S., Koo, I., Wei, X.L., Zhang, X.: A Method of Finding Optimal Weight Factors for Compound Identification in Gas Chromatography-Mass Spectrometry. Bioinformatics 8(8), 1158–1163 (2012)
12. Kim, S., Koo, I., et al.: Compound Identification Using Partial and Semipartial Correlations for Gas Chromatography-Mass Spectrometry Data. Analytical Chemistry 84(15), 6477–6487 (2012)
13. Koo, I., Kim, S., Zhang, X.: Comparative Analysis of Mass Spectral Matching-Based Compound Identification in Gas Chromatography-Mass Spectrometry. J Chromatogr A 1298, 132–138 (2013)
14. Bjerga, J.M., Small, G.W.: Automated Selection of Library Subsets for Infrared Spectral Searching. Analytical Chemistry 62(3), 226–233 (1990)
15. Wang, C.P., Isenhour, T.L.: Infrared Library Search on Principal-Component-Analyzed Fourier-Transformed Absorption Spectra. Applied Spectroscopy 41(2), 185–195 (1987)
16. Kennedy, J., Eberhart, R.: Particle Swarm Optimization. In: Proceedings of the IEEE International Conference on Neural Networks (1995)

Metagenomic Phylogenetic Classification
Using Improved Naïve Bayes

Yuki Komatsu[1], Takashi Ishida[1], and Yutaka Akiyama[1,2]

[1] Graduate School of Information Science and Engineering,
Tokyo Institute of Technology, Japan
[2] Education Academy of Computational Life Sciences,
Tokyo Institute of Technology, Japan
{komatsu,t.ishida}@bi.cs.titech.ac.jp, akiyama@cs.titech.ac.jp

Abstract. The phylogenetic classification of DNA fragments from a variety of microorganisms is often performed in metagenomic analysis to understand the taxonomic composition of microbial communities. A faster method for taxonomic classification based on metagenomic reads is required with the improvement of DNA sequencer's throughput in recent years. In this research we focus on naïve Bayes, which can quickly classify organisms with sufficient accuracy, and we have developed an acceptably fast, yet more accurate classification method using improved naïve Bayes, Weightily Averaged One-Dependence Estimators (WAODE). Additionally, we accelerated WAODE classification by introducing a cutoff for the mutual information content, and achieved a 20 times faster classification speed while keeping comparable prediction accuracy.

Keywords: Metagenomic analysis, phylogenetic classification, naïve Bayes.

1 Introduction

Metagenomics is the relatively new study of analyzing the genomic information of microorganisms obtained directly from environmental samples, such as soils or human bodies, without the need for cell culture [1, 2, 3]. A major task of the analysis is elucidating the taxonomic composition of the sampled microbial communities. To understand this composition, the phylogenetic classification of raw sequence reads into groups representing the same or similar taxa needs to be performed. A biological classification defines the rank, such as phylum, class, order, family, genus, and often species; phylogenetic classification is performed at each taxonomic level [4, 5, 6, 7].

Metagenomic phylogenetic classification methods can be divided into two predominant approaches: homology-based versus composition-based.

The homology-based approach is accomplished by comparing metagenomic fragments against a reference database using a sequence homology search tool, such as BLAST [8, 9, 10, 11]. Basically, this approach finds similarities between sequences through a heuristic sequence alignment process. The approach generally has high accuracy, but requires excessive computation time, linearly proportional to the

D.-S. Huang et al. (Eds.): ICIC 2014, LNBI 8590, pp. 262–270, 2014.

amount of query data analyzed. The latest DNA sequencing technology, such as Illumina's HiSeq2500, can generate approximately 6 billion DNA fragments per run. The amount of metagenomic data generated, and requiring analysis, will become ever larger in the near future. Thus, reducing computational time for metagenomic phylogenetic classification is of upmost importance.

Composition-based approaches bypass the sequence alignment process to find similarities between a fragment and known sequences by extracting compositional features from DNA fragments. These features are generally used as inputs for supervised learning methods. The accuracy of composition-based approach is lower than that of homology-based approaches. However, once this approach constructs a model, the amount of calculation required for classification is much smaller than that for homology-based approaches. Therefore, this approach can classify reads more quickly than homology-based approaches. Currently, numerous composition-based metagenomic phylogenetic classification methods have been proposed based on various supervised machine learning methods, such as the support vector machine (SVM) [4] and naïve Bayes (NB) [5].

The SVM is a binary classification algorithm and generally has high accuracy. Even in the metagenomic phylogenetic classification problem, the SVM-based method, PhyloPythia [4], shows better performance than the other classification algorithms. However, SVM predictions are not as fast for complex classification problems, because it needs to use a non-linear kernel. It is also slow for problems with many classes, because it is a binary classifier and performs multiple predictions for such problems. Conversely, the classification accuracy of NB is relatively low, but its classification speed is much faster than the SVM.

We focus on the naïve Bayes method in this research. Naïve Bayes methods can perform taxonomic classification in a short time. Our aim is to develop a method faster than SVM-based methods, but more accurate than standard NB-based methods. To tackle these competing demands, we apply an extended NB algorithm to the problem. We use Weightily Averaged One-Dependence Estimators (WAODE) [12] for the metagenomic phylogenetic classification, because previous studies in other research fields have shown it to perform well in various extended NB applications [12, 13]. Unfortunately, the classification speed of our WAODE-based method is slower than that of standard NB-based methods. A major task in machine learning studies is reducing the learning time required for constructing the model. In contrast, only a small effort has been spent on improving machine learning classification times. Therefore, we attempt to improve classification speed in our WAODE algorithm implementation.

2   Methods

We applied WAODE to metagenomic phylogenetic classification, because previous studies have shown WAODE's performance to excel in extended naïve Bayes applications [12, 13].

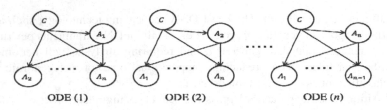

ODE (1)   ODE (2)   ODE (n)

Fig. 1. Structure of WAODE

2.1   Weightily Averaged One-Dependence Estimators (WAODE)

WAODE is an extended naïve Bayes classifier that relaxes the conditional independence assumption of NB, and consists of multiple one-dependence estimators [12].
One-dependence estimator (ODE) is a classifier with a single attribute that is the parent of all other attributes. In WAODE, ODEs are constructed for each attribute, and a
different weight is assigned for each ODE. WAODE averages the aggregate of the
weighted ODEs. Figure 1 shows the structure of WAODE.

Assume that an example E is represented by $E = (a_1, ..., a_n)$, where a_i is the value
of attribute A_i. The WAODE classifier for an example E is then defined as

$$c(E) = \operatorname*{argmax}_{c \in C} \left(\frac{\sum_{i=1}^{n} W_i P(a_i, c) \prod_{j=1, j \neq i}^{n} P(a_j | a_i, c)}{\sum_{i=1}^{n} W_i} \right), \tag{1}$$

where C is class variable, c is the value of class variable C, a_i is the value of attribute
A_i, and W_i is the weight of the ODE in which attribute A_i is the parent of all other
attributes.

In WAODE, the approach for determining the weight W_i uses the mutual information between attribute A_i and class variable C, as shown in Eq. (2).

$$W_i = I_P(A_i; C)$$
$$= \sum_{a_i, c} P(a_i, c) \log \frac{P(a_i, c)}{P(a_i)P(c)} \tag{2}$$

WAODE estimates the base probabilities $P(a_i, c)$ and $P(a_j | a_i, c)$ as follows:

$$P(a_i, c) = \frac{F(a_i, c) + 1.0/(n_i \cdot k)}{N + 1.0}, \tag{3}$$

$$P(a_j | a_i, c) = \frac{F(a_j, a_i, c) + 1.0/n_j}{F(a_i, c) + 1.0}, \tag{4}$$

where $F(\cdot)$ is the frequency with which a combination of terms appears in the training
data, N is the number of training examples, n_i is the number of values of attribute A_i,
and k is the number of classes.

2.2   Simplification of Weightily Averaged One-Dependence Estimators

In WAODE, ODEs are built for all attributes $A_1, ..., A_n$, and the aggregate of the
weighted ODEs are averaged. When the number of attributes in a dataset is large, the

number of ODEs comprising the WAODE, and the amount of calculation required by Eq. (2) both increase. Thus, we aimed to reduce classification time by decreasing the number of ODEs comprising the WAODE.

WAODE uses the mutual information between attribute A_i and class variable C as a measure of the importance of attribute A_i. In this study, we introduced the cutoff value of mutual information t_{WAODE} to WAODE. Our new algorithm uses nothing but those ODEs corresponding to the attributes which obtain mutual information higher than the cutoff value t_{WAODE}. We named the algorithm t-WAODE. For an example E the t-WAODE classifier is defined as:

$$c(E) = \underset{c \in C}{\text{argmax}} \left(\frac{\sum_{i:1 \leq i \leq n \wedge W_i > t_{WAODE}} W_i P(a_i, c) \prod_{j=1, j \neq i}^{n} P(a_j | a_i, c)}{\sum_{i:1 \leq i \leq n \wedge W_i > t_{WAODE}} W_i} \right). \tag{5}$$

2.3   Characterization Vectors

Many methods for metagenomic fragment classification use k-mer frequency as an input vector for supervised learning [4, 5]. We also used k-mer frequency as the input vector for our classifier. A popular method for computing k-mer frequency extracts k-mers while sequentially displacing the input DNA sequence one by one from the top, counting each k-mer as it proceeds (Fig. 2).

PhyloPythia uses 5-mer frequencies as an input vector at the rank of genus for optimum results [4]. Thus, we also employed 5-mer frequencies as our input vector.

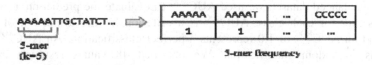

Fig. 2. Computing k-mer frequency

3   Results and Discussion

We compared WAODE and t-WAODE against the SVM and standard NB existing phylogenetic classification methods. We applied 10-fold cross-validation to evaluate the performance of the classifiers. All experiments were performed on a 2.93 GHz Intel Xeon X5670 CPU supplied with 54 GB of RAM.

As with PhyloPythia, we used the LIBSVM [14] package version 3.17 as a library for SVM, and employed a radial basis function (RBF), defined as $e^{-\gamma \|x_i - x_j\|^2}$. We wrote the code for the NB-based predictor and the WAODE-based predictors using the C programming language.

3.1   Dataset and Parameter Settings

We used simulated metagenomic samples drawn from existing sequences. We built a core library of Bacterial and Archaeal genomes derived from the NCBI reference sequence database (RefSeq) comprised 380 distinct organisms, containing 531 chromosomes and plasmids, belonging to 48 different genera, as our main data source. We used MetaSim software [15], which simulates metagenomic fragments from given genome sequences, with empirical error option to generate metagenomic reads with lengths of 100 bp. The total number of fragments was 319,972, and the dataset had 48 classes and 1,024 attributes.

The performance of the SVM with a Gaussian kernel depends on the regularization parameter C and the kernel width γ. Our t-WAODE algorithm depends on a cutoff value of mutual information, t_{WAODE}. To determine optimal values for C, γ and t_{WAODE}, we generated 16,000 fragments and applied 10-fold cross-validation. We determined the cutoff value of t-WAODE enabling the fastest prediction when accuracy is permitted to decrease 0.1 %.

3.2   Evaluation Method

We used prediction accuracy and classification time as our performance measurement. However, the deviation between the number of fragments in each class is quite large in the metagenomic dataset we used. For example, the maximum number of fragments belonging to a class is approximately 35 times as large as the minimum. Prediction accuracy, which is the ratio of correctly predicted cases to all cases, is inappropriate for the evaluation of such an unbalanced dataset. Because the area under the receiver operating characteristic (ROC) curve [16], AUC^{ROC}, is effective against such an unbalanced dataset, we used AUC^{ROC} to evaluate the prediction accuracy of each classifier for each class. AUC^{ROC} is a criterion for the evaluation of a ROC curve, and an AUC^{ROC} of 1.0 represents a perfect classification. An AUC^{ROC} of 0.5 represents a random classification. We obtained 48 values resulting from the AUC^{ROC} evaluation. Therefore, in this study we plotted the characteristic of each prediction method, based on these AUC^{ROC} values, and we used the area under the curve (AUC) of the plot obtained through the following steps to comprehensively evaluate a prediction accuracy of the classifiers:

1. A target class is defined as positive examples, and other classes are defined as negative examples. We calculate AUC^{ROC} for each class, and obtain values of AUC^{ROC} for each class $x_1, x_2, ..., x_n$, where n is the number of classes.
2. We sort $x_1, x_2, ..., x_n$ in ascending order.
3. For sorted values $x'_1, x'_2, ..., x'_n$ of AUC^{ROC}, we calculate the ratio of each classes whose AUC^{ROC} are more than x'_1. This ratio is plotted on a graph having the cutoff value of AUC^{ROC} as the abscissa and the rate of class whose AUC^{ROC} is more than cutoff value as the vertical axis.
4. The same operation as in step 3 is performed for the other sorted values $x'_2, ..., x'_n$.
5. We calculate the area under the curve obtained from the above steps.

To compute the classification times, we used the gettimeofday() function. For evaluating the classification time of each classifier, we performed the same calculation three times, and used their median value.

3.3   Results of Evaluation Tests

Our experiment compared WAODE and t-WAODE against NB and the SVM. Figure 3 shows the prediction accuracy characteristic curve for each prediction method. Table 1 summarizes AUC and classification times of the SVM, NB, WAODE and t-WAODE methods. The prediction accuracy of WAODE was lower than that of SVM but it much better than NB and the improvement was 0.02. Also, the prediction accuracy of t-WAODE slightly decreased compared with WAODE (the difference is 0.004) but it was still much better than NB (the improvement was 0.016).

We also checked statistical significance using a Wilcoxon signed rank test to evaluate the significance of the difference between the prediction accuracy of each method. We performed a Wilcoxon signed rank for the AUC^{ROC} values of the 48 classes. We used wilcox.test() function of R (version 3.0.1) for calculating the Wilcoxon signed rank test p-value. Table 2 shows the p-value for prediction accuracies. As shown in Table 2, WAODE and t-WAODE outperformed NB, in terms of prediction accuracy, and the differences are statistically significant because the p-values of the Wilcoxon signed rank test are smaller than 0.05 (7.11×10^{-14} and 1.42×10^{-14}, respectively). Although the SVM shows better prediction accuracy than WAODE and t-WAODE, the classification time of WAODE and t-WAODE was much shorter than that of SVM. Especially, the prediction of t-WAODE became approximately 20 times faster than that of WAODE. We expected that t-WAODE method keeps prediction accuracy compared with WAODE. However, the difference of the prediction accuracy of t-WAODE and that of WAODE was unfortunately significant (the p-value $1.68 \times 10^{-3} < 0.05$) even though the difference was small.

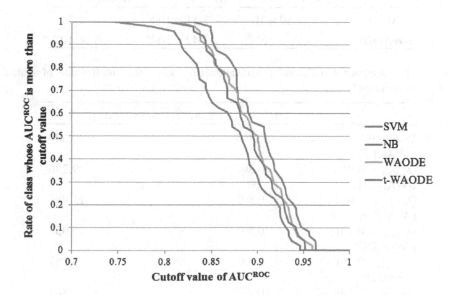

Fig. 3. The characteristic curve of prediction accuracy

3.4   Discussion

We propose t-WAODE as a simplification of WAODE to accelerate classification time by introducing a cutoff value for mutual information. We have determined the optimal cutoff value by applying a 10-fold cross-validation test to subset of our dataset. As described above, we determined the cutoff value of t-WAODE enabling the fastest prediction when accuracy is permitted to decrease 0.1 %. In our study t-WAODE's prediction accuracy was slightly lower than that of WAODE. However, as shown in Table 3, the optimum cutoff value enables a faster prediction without a decrease in prediction accuracy ($t_{WAODE} = 0.10$). Thus, methods for determining appropriate cutoff values that can speedup prediction while keeping acceptable prediction accuracies are important for future study.

Table 1. The accuracy (AUC) and classification time of each method

	Accuracy (AUC)	Classification time (sec.)
SVM	0.904	207,569
NB	0.875	125
WAODE	0.895	120,000
t-WAODE	0.891	6,053

Table 2. The p-value of the Wilcoxon signed rank test for prediction accuracy

	SVM	NB	WAODE
WAODE	2.19×10^{-5}	7.11×10^{-14}	
t-WAODE	3.63×10^{-10}	1.42×10^{-14}	1.68×10^{-3}

Table 3. The accuracy (AUC) and classification time when the cutoff value of mutual information is changed

	AUC	Classification time (sec.)
WAODE	0.895	120,000
t-WAODE ($t_{WAODE} = 0.01$)	0.894	79,296
t-WAODE ($t_{WAODE} = 0.05$)	0.892	15,986
t-WAODE ($t_{WAODE} = 0.10$)	0.891	6,053
t-WAODE ($t_{WAODE} = 0.15$)	0.885	1,287
t-WAODE ($t_{WAODE} = 0.18$)	0.879	387

The t-WAODE algorithm can be applied to other classification problems, although we have proposed t-WAODE only for the metagenomic phylogenetic classification problem. We expect that t-WAODE's prediction speed is also faster than that of WAODE and yet will maintain sufficient prediction accuracy for other classification problems as well.

4   Conclusions

In this study we applied WAODE to metagenomic phylogenetic classification, and compared it with a SVM-based predictor and a NB-based predictor. Our WAODE-based predictor achieved better prediction accuracy than the NB-based predictor and was a faster classifier than the SVM-based predictor.

Furthermore, we proposed t-WAODE for an even faster classification speed. The t-WAODE algorithm simplifies WAODE by introducing a cutoff value for mutual information content. As a result, t-WAODE's prediction speed is approximately 20 times faster than that of WAODE, yet it maintains comparative prediction accuracy as WAODE.

References

1. Daniel, R.: The Soil Metagenome – A Rich Resource for The Discovery of Novel Natural Products. Current Opinion in Biotechnology 15, 199–204 (2004)
2. Tyson, G.W., Chapman, J., Hugenholtz, P., Allen, E.E., Raml, R.J., et al.: Community Structure and Metabolism Through Reconstruction of Microbial Genomes From the Environment. Nature 428, 37–43 (2004)
3. Qin, J., Li, R., Raes, J., Arumugam, M., Burgdorf, K.S., et al.: A Human Gut Microbial Gene Catalogue Established by Metagenomic Sequencing. Nature 464, 59–65 (2010)
4. Mchardy, A.C., Martin, H.G., et al.: Accurate Phylogenetic Classification of Variable-Length DNA Fragments. Nature Methods 4(1), 63–72 (2007)
5. Rosen, G., Garbarine, E., Caseiro, D., Polikar, R., Sokhansanj, B.: Metagenome Fragment Classification Using N-Mer Frequency Profiles. Advances in Bioinformatics 2008(20), 59–69 (2008)
6. Brady, A., Salzberg, S.L., et al.: Metagenomic Phylogenetic Classification with Interpolated Markov Models. Nature Methods 6(9), 673–676 (2009)
7. Diaz, N.N., Krause, L., Goesmann, A., Niehaus, K., Nattkemper, T.W.: TACOA – Taxonomic Classification of Environmental Genomic Fragments Using a Kernelized Nearest Neighbor Approach. BMC Bioinformatics 10, 56 (2009)
8. Altschul, S.F., Gish, W., Miller, W., Myers, E.W., Lipman, D.J.: Basic Local Alignment Search Tool. Journal of Molecular Biology 215(3), 403–410 (1990)
9. Huson, D.H., Auch, A.F., Qi, J., Schuster, S.C.: MEGAN Analysis of Metagenomic Data. Genome Research 17(3), 377–386 (2007)
10. Suzuki, S., Ishida, T., Kurokawa, K., Akiyama, Y.: GHOSTM: A GPU-Accelerated Homology Search Tool for Metagenomics. Plos One 7(5), E36060 (2012)

11. Zhao, Y., Tang, H., Ye, Y.: Rapsearch2: A Fast And Memory-Efficient Protein Similarity Search Tool for Next-Generation Sequencing Data. Bioinformatics 23(1), 125–126 (2012)
12. Jiang, L., Zhang, H.: Weightily Averaged One-Dependence Estimators. In: Yang, Q., Webb, G. (eds.) PRICAI 2006. LNCS (LNAI), vol. 4099, pp. 970–974. Springer, Heidelberg (2006)
13. Koc, L., Mazzuchi, T.A., Sarkani, S.: A Network Intrusion Detection System Based on a Hidden Naive Bayes Multiclass Classifier. Expert Systems with Applications 39(18), 13492–13500 (2012)
14. Chang, C.-C., Lin, C.-J.: LIBSVM: A Library for Support Vector Machines. ACM Transactions on Intelligent Systems and Technology 2(27), 1–27 (2011)
15. Richter, D.C., Ott, F., Auch, A.F., Schmid, R., Huson, D.H.: Metasim - A Sequence Simulator for Genomics and Metagenomics. Plos One 3(10), P.E3373 (2008)
16. Zweig, M.H., Campbell, G.: Receiver-Operating Characteristic (ROC) Plots: a Fundamental Evaluation Tool in Clinical Medicine. Clinical Chemistry 39, 561–577 (1993)

Predicting Protein-Protein Interaction Sites by Rotation Forests with Evolutionary Information

Xinying Hu[2], Anqi Jing[2], and Xiuquan Du[1,2,*]

[1] Key Laboratory of Intelligent Computing & Signal Processing, Ministry of Education,
Anhui University, Anhui, China
dxqllp@163.com
[2] The School of Computer Science and Technology, Anhui University, Anhui, China
lehehehu@163.com, aqjing0224@gmail.com

Abstract. In this paper, according to evolutionary information and physicochemical properties, we selected eight features, combined with Rotation Forest (RotF) to predict interaction sites. We built two models on both balanced datasets and imbalanced datasets, named balanced-RotF and unbalanced-RotF, respectively. The values of accuracy, F-Measure, precision, recall and CC of balanced-RotF were 0.8133, 0.8064, 0.8375, 0.7775 and 0.6283 respectively. The values of accuracy, precision and CC of unbalanced-RotF increased by 0.0679, 0.0122 and 0.0361 over balanced-RotF. Precision values of unbalanced-RotF on our four selected testing sets were 0.907, 0.875, 0.878 and, 0.889, respectively. Moreover, experiment only using two physicochemical features showed evolutionary information has effective effects for classification.

Keywords: protein-protein interaction sites, Rotation Forests, evolutionary information, machine learning.

1 Introduction

On the basis of the sequence and structural information of protein, some methods have been proposed [1-6]. Kini and Evans [1] proposed a unique predictive method that detecting the presences of the "proline" because they observed that proline is the most common residue found in the flanking segments of interface residues. Zhu-Hong You.et al[6] have proposed a novel method only using the information of protein sequences, which used the PCA-EELM model to predict protein-protein interactions. Many methods to predict the protein-protein interacting sites are motivated by the different machine learning methods with characteristics of proteins [5-17]. Minhas F.U. et al. [10] presented a novel method called PAIRpred. They selected structure and sequence information of residue pairs, combined Support Vector Machine method, which achieved good and detailed result. Peng Chen and Jinyan Li [11] trained a SVM using an integrative profile by combining the hydrophobic and evolutionary information, where they used a self-organizing map (SOM) technique as input vectors. Based on the Random Forest method, B.L.et al. [12] presented a new method with the

---

* Corresponding author.

D.-S. Huang et al. (Eds.): ICIC 2014, LNBI 8590, pp. 271–279, 2014.

Minimum Redundancy Maximal Relevance method followed by incremental feature selection. What they took into consideration included the five 3D secondary structures.

2   Methods

2.1   Defining the Protein Interaction Sites

In our article, we adopted the Fariselli's [7] method to define the definition of surface residues and interface residues. If a residue's RASA is at least 16% of its MASA, it is defined to be a surface residue, or it is defined to be a non-surface residue. If a surface residue's difference between ASA and CASA is greater than 1 $\AA^2$, than it is defined to be an interface residue, otherwise it is defined to be a non-interface residue.

2.2   Features

In this paper, we adopt eight features to express interaction sites. These features as follows: sequence profiles, entropy, relative Entropy, conservation Weight, accessible surface areas, sequence variability, hydrophobicity [18] and polarity. The first six values of features could be obtained in HSSP database [19].

2.3   Creating Sample Sets

From what we have mentioned above, we use these features to describe a residue. Each residue is made up by 27 values (Sequence profile is 20 values, and the other features is one value.). We used sliding window of size 5. Therefore, there are 27*5 values in each residue's sample. If a residue doesn't have enough neighbors, we substitute the zero for its value.

2.4   Rotation Forests

In our paper, we constructed classifiers using Rotation Forests [20]. Rotation Forests, including many decision trees, is an ensemble learning method for classification. Its output decided by the mode of outputs of decision trees. In our experiment, we used Rotation Forest algorithm in Waikato Environment for Knowledge Analysis (WEKA) [21] to construct classifiers.

2.5   Datasets

In our experiment, we chose the proteins in bos Taurus organism as our training and testing datasets. We downloaded proteins of whose resolution is less than $3.5\AA^2$ in bos Taurus organism from the Protein Data Bank (PDB). Then we gave up those proteins whose length is less than 40 residues and sequence similarity is greater than 30%. Finally, we obtained 292 chains, 65185 residues. According to the definition of surface residues, there were 9291 interface residues and 30899 non-interface residues. Finally, we chose them as our datasets, named Bos. Then interface residues were labeled as "+1", and non-interface residues were labeled as "-1". We have created two training and testing datasets. One is unbalanced named unbalanced-Bos, containing all surface sites in Bos. The other one is balanced named balanced-Bos.

2.6   Measuring Method

Accuracy, F-Measure, Recall, Precision, Correlation Coefficient (CC) were calculated to evaluate the performance of our predictors. ROC Area and ROC curve were also used in our article.

$$Accuracy = (TP + TN)/(TP + TN + FP + FN) \quad Recall = TN/(TN + FP) \quad Pr\,ecision = TP/TP + FP$$

$$F - Measure = (2 * recall * precision)/(recall + precision)$$

$$CC = (TP*TN - FP*FN)\Big/\sqrt{(TP + FN)(TP + FP)(TN + FP)(TN + FN)}$$

3   Experimental Procedure and Results

3.1   Experiments on Different Machine Learning Methods

Experimental Procedure: We make experiments on both balanced Bos and unbalanced-Bos using Rotation Forests. We carried out experiments for 10 times and we created 10 models for balanced-Bos. We named the experiment balanced-RotF. For unbalanced-Bos, we carried out experiment for only once with10-cross validation and we named it unbalanced-RotF. Meanwhile we constructed other classifiers by some other machine learning methods in WEKA and LIBSVM [22] software. By comparing those results on different classifiers, we can make an observation which classifier that our sample sets perform on is better. From Figure 1 and Figure 2, we can see the value of accuracy, F-Measure and CC of Rotation Forests are higher than that of other machine learning methods. The values of accuracy, F-Measure, Precision, Recall and CC are 0.8133, 0.8064, 0.8375, 0.7775 and 0.6283，respectively.

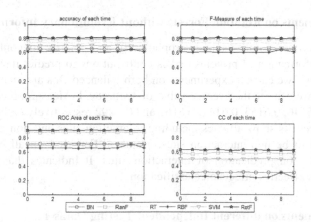

Fig. 1. The accuracy, F-Measure, and CC of different machine learning methods on the balanced-Bos. Figures on the top left corner, the top right corner, the bottom corner, show the accuracy values, F-Measure and CC of ten times of six machine learning methods on the balanced-Bos, respectively.

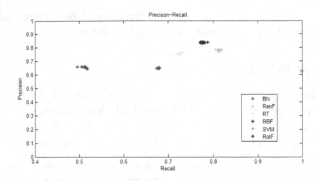

Fig. 2. The performances of Precision and Recall on the balanced-Bos. Ten black points show performances of ten balanced-RotF experiments we carried out. The vertical axis values show the value of recall and the abscissa axis values show the value of precision.

What we expected was it can achieve high accuracy and also get the high recall and precision. Figure 2 shows the values of precision and recall. Obviously, the closer that points can approach to the right top corner, the better performances they have. Black points in Figure 2, standing for Rotation Forest algorithm, we can observe that black points have highest precision. Figure 3 shows performances of different methods on unbalanced-Bos. It is obvious that unbalanced-RotF have better performances than other methods. The values of accuracy, F-Measure, precision, recall and CC were 0.8812, 0.7271, 0.8497, 0.6354 and 0.6644, respectively; expect precision of SVM was higher. From the three figures, we can make a conclusion that Rotation Forests are more suitable for our extracted features. From Table 1, what else we can observe was that the some indicator values on unbalanced-Bos were better than balanced Bos. It shows information that negative samples contained make irreplaceable contributions to the prediction of interaction sites and it should not be abandoned.

3.2   Experiments on Rotation Forests without Evolutionary Information

We make experiments only using hydrophobicity and polarity to confirm whether evolutionary information of proteins makes contributions to predict interaction sites. As the same way, we carried experiments on both balanced-Bos and unbalanced-Bos. From Table 2, we can see the average value of accuracy, F-Measure, precision, recall and CC was 0.6146, 0.6153, 0.6141, 0.6167 and 0.2292 respectively on balanced-Bos. However, the results show all sites including interaction sites and non-interface sites were predicted to be non-interaction sites. Rotation Forests with all eight features performed better on predication of interaction sites. It indicates that evolutionary information has effective effects on classification.

3.3   Experiments on different Independent Testing Datasets

In order to measure performances of RotF-classifiers we created in experiments on different machine learning methods, we built several independent testing sets, which came from escherichia coli (E.coli), bacillus subtilis (B.subtilis), rattus norvegicus

(R.norvegicus) and Yeast bacillus (Y.bacillus). We adopted the models which were produced by RotF-classifiers, including balanced-RotF and unbalanced-RotF. The following Table 3 and Table 4 present the performances of RotF-classifiers on independent testing sets, respectively.

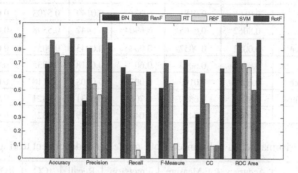

Fig. 3. Performances of unbalanced-Bos using different machine learning methods. It shows accuracy, F-Measure, Precision, Recall, CC and ROC Area using different machine learning methods on the unbalanced-Bos.

Table 1. Performances of Rotation Forests on balanced-Bos and unbalanced-Bos

	Accuracy	F-Measure	Precision	Recall	CC	ROC Area
balanced-Bos	0.8133	0.8064	0.8375	0.7775	0.6283	0.9077
unbalanced-Bos	0.8812	0.7271	0.8497	0.6354	0.6644	0.8790

Table 2. Performances of Rotation Forests only using hydrophobicity and polarity

	Accuracy	F-Measure	Precision	Recall	CC	ROC Area
balanced-Bos	0.6146±0.0030	0.6153±0.0061	0.6141±0.0026	0.6167±0.0123	0.2292±0.0059	0.6576
unbalanced-Bos	0.7509	—¹	—	0	—	0.5950

¹: "—" means all residues were predicted to be non-interface sites.

From the Table 3, we can observe that performances on imbalanced samples were good. Values of accuracy of balanced-RotF for these four organisms were 0.8198, 0.8062, 0.8093 and 0.8044, respectively. Values of ROC Area were 0.8441, 0.8278, 0.8030 and 0.8350, respectively. Table 4 shows the performances of unbalanced-RotF models. Values of precision of unbalanced-RotF models for four testing sets were 0.907, 0.875, 0.878 and 0.889, respectively. High precision means more positive samples were predicted correctly. Figure 4 shows the balanced-RotF models of ROC curves on four testing sets and Figure 5 shows the unbalanced-RotF model of ROC curves on four testing sets. We can make a conclusion that our classifiers performed well on independent testing sets, which confirms that our classifiers are suitable for not only the bos Taurus organism, but also for some other organisms. The results confirmed that our Rot-classifiers have extensive adaptation.

Table 3. Performances of Rotation Forests of balanced RotF models on independent testing datasets

	Accuracy	F-Measure	Precision	Recall	CC	ROC Area
E.coli	0.8198	0.7022	0.6976	0.7069	-0.1173	0.8441
variance	0.0101	0.0181	0.0219	0.0149	0.5703	0.0019
B.subtilis	0.8062	0.6665	0.6904	0.6442	0.5308	0.8278
variance	0.0022	0.0037	0.0045	0.0043	0.0052	0.0026
R.norvegicus	0.8093	0.6094	0.6074	0.6118	0.4835	0.8030
variance	0.0036	0.0100	0.0074	0.0208	0.0118	0.0025
Y.bacillus	0.8044	0.6850	0.7089	0.6631	0.5421	0.8350
variance	0.0088	0.0431	0.0435	0.0459	0.0326	0.0024

Table 4. Performances of unbalanced RotF model on independent testing datasets

	Accuracy	F-Measure	Precision	Recall	CC	ROC Area
E.coli	0.849	0.692	0.907	0.560	0.630	0.854
B.subtilis	0.831	0.645	0.875	0.511	0.578	0.839
R.norvegicus	0.856	0.615	0.878	0.473	0.574	0.814
Y.bacillus	0.830	0.674	0.889	0.543	0.598	0.847

According to results, we can also observe that values of accuracy, precision, CC and ROC Area of unbalanced-RotF models were better than balanced samples. The performances of Rot-classifiers in experiments on different machine learning methods also proved it, which means imbalanced samples contained the information of all sites in proteins, including interface sites and non-interface sites. We took the fully use of samples and achieved better results. It meant in our experiment information of non-interface sites should not be abandoned.

3.4   Compared to Other Methods

For comparison purpose, we make experiments with our sample sets using other methods. We make experiments on following websites: SPIDDER [23] (http://sppider.cchmc.org/): It uses solvent accessibility, based on artificial neural network method. InterProSurf [24] (http://curie.utmb.edu/usercomplex.html): It was based on solvent accessible surface area, a propensity scale for interface residues and a clustering algorithm to classify interaction sites.

In order to make a convenient comparison to the method of SPIDDER, we redefined interface residues according to the definition of SPIDDER and InterProSurf to calculate accuracy, F-Measure, precision, recall and CC. Table 5 shows performances on the two methods. The results of SPIDDER achieved high accuracy: 0.723, but the values of precision and recall are low. The results of InterProSurf were similar to the SPIDDER. Its precision was higher than SPIDDER, but similarity, the value of recall was unsatisfactory, only 0.4894. (There were some problems with our experiments on InterProSurf. There were 85 chains didn't obtain predicted results, so the results were obtained after deleting these 85 chains).

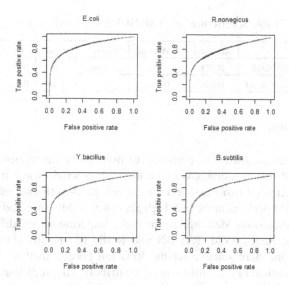

Fig. 4. Balanced ROC curves of four testing sets. It shows ROC curves of four testing sets, which produced by balanced-RotF classifiers from the experiment on Rotation Forests. E.coli stands for the Escherichia coli, which consists of ten curves, where each curve stands for the experimental result of each model from experiment on Rotation Forests. The same as E.coli, B.subtilis, R.norvegicus and Y.bacillus stand for the bacillus subtilis, rattus norvegicus and yeast bacillus, respectively.

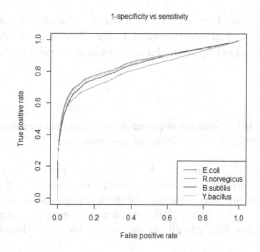

Fig. 5. Unbalanced ROC curves of four testing sets. It shows the ROC curves from four testing sets, which produced by unbalanced-RotF classifier from the experiment on Rotation Forests. There are four curves in the figure, where different color curves stand for different sample sets.

Table 5. Performances of SPIDDER and InterProSurf

	Accuracy	F-Measure	Precision	Recall	CC
SPIDDER	0.723	0.450	0.510	0.402	0.272
InterProSurf	0.851	0.608	0.802	0.489	0.226

4   Conclusion

In our paper, a new method was proposed to predict the interaction sites. At first, we extracted eight features, combined with the sliding window and it contained five amino acids. We created two classifiers named balanced-RotF and unbalanced-RotF, which showed good performances with high accuracy, F-Measure and CC, especially the Recall and Precision. Meanwhile, we make experiments on different machine learning methods: RanF, SVM, RT, BN and RBF. The results show that features that we selected are more suitable for the Rotation Forests method. What is more, we confirmed evolutionary information make contribution to prediction. Moreover, our models were tested on independent datasets, which achieved good results, as well, which proved that our models have extensive adaptation. For comparison, we made our datasets test on other methods. Performances show our results were better than theirs.

5   Funding

This project was supported by the National Natural Science Foundation of China (Grant No.61203290), Startup Foundation for Doctors of Anhui University (No.33190078) and outstanding young backbone teachers training (No.02303301).

References

1. Kini, R.M., Evans, H.J.: Prediction of potential protein-protein interaction sites from amino acid sequence identification of a fibrin polymerization site. FEBS Lett. 385(1-2), 81–86 (1996)
2. Tuncbag, N., Keskin, O., Nussinov, R., Gursoy, A.: Fast and accurate modeling of protein–protein interactions by combining template-interface-based docking with flexible refinement. Proteins: Structure, Function, and Bioinformatics 80(4), 1239–1249 (2012)
3. Zhang, S.W., Hao, L.Y., Zhang, T.H.: Prediction of protein–protein interaction with pairwise kernel Support Vector Machine. International Journal of Molecular Sciences 15(2), 3220–3233 (2014)
4. Konc, J., Janezic, D.: Protein-protein binding-sites prediction by protein surface structure conservation. J. Chem. Inf. Model. 47(3), 940–944 (2007)
5. Yuehui, C., Jingru, X., Bin, Y., Yaou, Z., Wenxing, H.: A novel method for prediction for protein interaction sites based on integrated RBF neural networks. Computers in Biology and Medicine 42(4), 402–407 (2012)
6. You, Z.H., Lei, Y.K., Zhu, L., Xia, J., Wang, B.: Prediction of protein-protein interactions from amino acid sequences with ensemble extreme learning machines and principal component analysis. BMC Bioinformatics 14(suppl. 8), S10 (2013)

7. Fariselli, P., Pazos, F., Valencia, A., Casadia, R.: Prediction of protein-protein interaction sites in heterocomplexes with neural networks. Eur. J. Biochem. 269, 1356–1361 (2002)

8. Sriwastava, B.K., Basu, S., Maulik, U., Plewczynski, D.: PPIcons: Identification of protein-protein interaction sites in selected organisms. J. Mol. Model. 19(9), 4059–4070 (2013)

9. Chen, C.T., Peng, H.P., Jian, J.W.: Protein-protein interaction site predictions with three-dimensional probability distributions of interacting atoms on protein surfaces. PLOS One 7(6), e37706 (2012)

10. Minhas, F.U., Geiss, B.J., Ben-hur, A.: PAIRpred: Partner-specific prediction of interacting residues from sequence and structure. Proteins: Structure, Function, and Bioinformatics (2013)

11. Chen, P., Li, J.: Sequence-based identification of interface residues by an integrative profile combining hydrophobic and evolutionary information. BMC Bioinformatics 11, 402–416 (2010)

12. Li, B.Q., Feng, K.Y., Chen, L., Huang, T., Cai, Y.D.: Prediction of Protein-Protein Interaction Sites by Random Forest Algorithm with mRMR and IFS. PLOS One 7(8), e43927 (2012)

13. Li, C.X., Drena, D., Vasant, H.: HomPPI: a class of sequence homology based protein-protein interface prediction methods. BMC Bioinformatics 12, 244–267 (2011)

14. Jordan, R.A., EI-Manzalawy, Y., Dobbs, D., Honavar, V.: Predicting protein-protein interface residues using local surface structural similarity. BMC Bioinformatics 13, 41–44 (2012)

15. Xu, B., Wei, X., Deng, L., Guan, J., Zhou, S.: A semi-supervised boosting SVM for predicting hot spots at protein-protein interfaces. BMC Syst. Biol. 6(suppl. 2) (2012)

16. Sriwastava, B.K., Basu, S., Maulik, U., Plewczynski, D.: PPIcons: identification of protein-protein interaction sites in selected organisms. J. Mol. Model. 19(9), 4059–4070 (2013)

17. Hwang, H., Vreven, T., Weng, Z.: Binding interface prediction by combining protein-protein docking results. Proteins 10, 1002 (2013)

18. Gallet, X., Charloteaux, B., Thomas, A., Brasseur, R.: A fast method to predict protein interaction sites from sequences. J. Mol. Biol. 302(4), 917–926 (2000)

19. Chris, S., Reinhard, S.: Database of homology-derived protein structures and the structural meaning of sequence alignment. Proteins Struct. Funct. Bioinforma. 9(1), 56–68 (1991)

20. Breiman, L.: Random forests. Machine Learning 45(1), 5–32 (2001)

21. Hall, M., Frank, E., Holmes, G., Pfahringer, B., Reutemann, P., Witten, I.H.: The WEKA Data Mining Software: An Update. SIGKDD Explorations 11(1) (2009)

22. Chang, C.C., Lin, C.J.: LIBSVM: a library for support vector machines. ACM Transactions on Intelligent Systems and Technology 2(27), 1–27 (2011)

23. Porollo, A., Meller, J.: Prediction-based fingerprints of protein-protein interactions. Proteins Struct. Funct. Bioinforma 66(3), 630–645 (2007)

24. Neqi, S.S., Schein, C.H., Oezquen, N., Power, T.D., Braun, W.: InterProSurf: a web server for predicting interacting sites on protein surfaces. Bioinformatics 23(24), 3397–3399 (2007)

Predicting Potential Ligands for Orphan GPCRs Based on the Improved Laplacian Regularized Least Squares Method

Yan Yan[1], Xinwei Shao[2], and Zhenran Jiang[1,*]

[1] Department of Computer Science & Technology,
East China Normal University, Shanghai 200241, China
[2] Department of Mathematics, East China Normal University, Shanghai 200241, China
zrjiang@cs.ecnu.edu.cn

Abstract. Predicting potential interactions between receptors and ligands can provide important clues to the discovery of ligands for orphan GPCRs (oGPCRs). In this paper, we develop an improved Laplacian Regularized Least Squares method (EstLapRLS) to predict potential receptor-ligand associations. The originality lies in the fact that we can utilize more valuable information for ligand-receptor interaction prediction based on two estimated matrices. Experimental results show that the proposed method can obtain a high specificity and sensitivity on cross-validation tests.

Keywords: G-protein coupling receptor, Ligand prediction, EstLapRLS method.

1   Introduction

GPCRs have been proved to be important targets for pharmaceutical treatment. Using computational methods to identify natural ligands associated with GPCRs can gain insights into the discovery of new targets. Many different methods have been proposed to predict the association between receptors and ligands during the past years. The traditional methods include text mining method [1] and molecular docking [2]. Text mining has high requirements on the organizational structure of data source. Furthermore, the redundant information existing in the literatures also have a significant impact on the accuracy of the prediction. Molecular docking method solely based on the crystal structure of the target binding site, but it is often difficult to obtain the 3-dimensional (3D) structure of GPCR by current experimental methods [3]. Therefore, it is hard to use it widely because the number of known crystal structures of receptors is limited [4-7].

In order to tackle the problem, a number of new methods including chemogenomics [8-9], kernel-learning method [10-15], and network-based diffusion methods [16-17] have been developed for receptor-ligand prediction recently. The motivation of most of these methods is to integrate more feature information from the receptors

---

* Corresponding author.

D.-S. Huang et al. (Eds.): ICIC 2014, LNBI 8590, pp. 280–287, 2014.
© Springer International Publishing Switzerland 2014

and ligands [18-19]. For instance, chemical genomics aims to seek all of the possible receptor-ligand pairs, which involves not only the feature information of receptors but also the information of ligands [20]. The bipartite model methods [16] integrated the chemical spaces and genomic spaces as well as the drug-protein interaction network into a pharmacological space [21]. As the methods mentioned above did not utilize a wealth of unlabeled information to assist prediction, the semi-supervised learning method was used to integrate known drug-protein interaction network information as well as chemical structure and genomic sequence data [14]. More recently, some methods analyzing the relationships between receptors and ligands based on network topological features emerged. Van Laarhoven [15] proposed a method calculating Gaussian interaction profile based on known receptor-ligand associations, which achieved a high accuracy by using RLS classifier. However, most available methods analyzed the features of receptors and ligands, separately [21]. For instance, they often neglected the feature relevance information between receptors and ligands, which may lead to a high false positive rate. Further, if the known receptor-ligand associations in dataset are not very adequate, using only the limited receptor-ligand associations or the chemical and genomic spaces information is not efficient. Therefore, most of the methods mentioned above can not be used to efficiently predict ligands for oGPCRs (GPCRs that have no ligands associated with yet).

In this paper, an improved Laplacian Regularized Least Squares method (EstLapRLS) is developed to utilize both the similarity information and known receptor-ligand associations to predict possible ligands of GPCRs (including oGPCRs). According to the method, we first construct two estimated value matrices, converting them into two weight matrices including inferred information. Then we apply the EstLapRLS method based on the semi-supervised learning framework to discovery potential associations from all of the receptor-ligand pairs. The results showed that the proposed method can obtain a high specificity and sensitivity on cross-validation tests.

2 Materials and Methods

2.1 Datasets

All of the receptors (80) and ligands (2,446) in this study were retrieved from the GLIDA database [22]. The corresponding number of the known interactions between receptor and ligand is 4,050. More information about the dataset can refer to previous reference [23]. Further, 71 orphan receptors are obtained from the same database above in order to embed oGPCRs into the new network. We constructed a receptor-ligand association matrix denoted $(A)_{n_r \times n_l}$ to demonstrate the relationship between each receptor and ligand. If the i_{th} receptor binds the j_{th} ligand, $(A)_{ij}$ will be set 1, otherwise 0.

A normalized Smith-Waterman score [24] was calculated to indicate the similarity between two amino acid sequences of GPCRs. A similarity matrix denoted $(S_r)_{n_r \times n_r}$ was constructed to measure the receptor-receptor similarity, where n_r represents the number of receptors.

The chemical structure similarity between compounds are calculated by SIMCOMP [25] using chemical structures fetched from KEGG LIGAND database [28]. A similarity matrix denoted $(S_l)_{n_l \times n_l}$ was constructed to measure the ligand-ligand similarity, where n_l represents the number of ligands.

2.2   Estimated Value Matrix

We constructed the estimated value matrices based on a basic premise: if a receptor binds a ligand, the receptors similar with the receptor have great possibility that they can bind with the ligand also. Similarly, if a receptor binds a ligand, ligands similar with the ligand have great possibility that they can be bind with by this receptor [26]. We define an estimated value matrix $(V_r)_{n_r \times n_l}$ as follows:

$$(V_r)_{ij} = \frac{\sum_{k=1}^{n_l}(S_l)_{ik} A_{kj}}{\sum_{k=1}^{n_l}(S_l)_{ik}} \tag{1}$$

$(V_r)_{n_r \times n_l}$ is the estimated value between the i_{th} receptor and the j_{th} ligand, which represent the possibility whether the i_{th} receptor binds the j_{th} ligand. Similarity, we define an estimated value matrix $(V_l)_{n_l \times n_r}$:

$$(V_l)_{ij} = \frac{\sum_{k=1}^{n_r}(S_r)_{ik} A_{ik}}{\sum_{k=1}^{n_r}(S_r)_{jk}} \tag{2}$$

This can be interpreted as: the ith receptor is more similar with receptors that bind the jth ligand, the estimated value between the ith receptor and the jth ligand is higher.

2.3   Constructing Weight Matrix

We constructed the weight matrix $(W_r)_{n_r \times n_l}$ based on the estimated value matrix $(V_r)_{n_r \times n_l}$:

$$(W_r)_{ij} = \exp\left(-p_r * \left\| (V_r)_i - (V_r)_j \right\|^2\right) \tag{3}$$

where $(V_r)_i$ is the i_{th} transversal vector of $(V_r)_{n_r \times n_l}$, $(V_r)_j$ is the j_{th} transversal vector of $(V_r)_{n_r \times n_l}$, p_r is the control parameter:

$$p_r = 1 \Big/ \left(\frac{1}{n_r} \sum_{i=1}^{n_r} \left\| (V_r)_i \right\|^2 \right) \tag{4}$$

Similarly, we constructed the weight matrix $(W_l)_{n_l \times n_r}$ based on the estimated value matrix $(V_l)_{n_l \times n_r}$:

$$(W_l)_{ij} = \exp\left(-p_l * \|(V_l)_i - (V_l)_j\|^2\right) \qquad (5)$$

where $(V_l)_i$ is the i_{th} transversal vector of $(V_l)_{n_l \times n_r}$, $(V_l)_j$ is the j_{th} transversal vector of $(V_l)_{n_l \times n_r}$, p_l is the control parameter :

$$p_l = 1 \Big/ \left(\frac{1}{n_l} \sum_{i=1}^{n_l} \|(V_l)_i\|^2\right) \qquad (6)$$

2.4   Algorithm Analysis

Given the weight matrices of receptors and ligands, the normalized graph Laplacian will be defined as follows:

$$L_r = D_r^{-1/2}(D_r - W_r)D_r^{-1/2} \qquad (7)$$

$$L_l = D_l^{-1/2}(D_l - W_l)D_l^{-1/2} \qquad (8)$$

where D_r and D_l are two diagonal matrices, and the element $(D_r)_{ii}$ or $(D_l)_{ii}$ is the sum of the i_{th} row of W_r or W_l.

We define a continuous classification function F that is estimated on the graph to minimize a cost function, the cost function is defined and derived as follows:

$$f^* = \arg\min \frac{1}{l} \sum_{i=1}^{l} (y_i - f(x_i))^2 + \gamma_A \|f\|_K^2 + \gamma_I \|f\|_I^2$$
$$= \arg\min \frac{1}{l} \sum_{i=1}^{l} (y_i - f(x_i))^2 + \gamma_A \|f\|_K^2 + \frac{\gamma_I}{(l+u)^2} f^T \qquad (9)$$

In our model, we have two regular terms $\gamma_A \|f\|_K^2$ and $\gamma_I \|f\|_I^2$, aiming at adding a low complexity correction to the original minimizing empirical error function model that is $\sum_{i=1}^{l} (y_i - f(x_i))^2$ in order to meet the complexity that it should possess, at the same time to keep the calculation simple.

We add the estimated value of each receptor-ligand pair v_i (which is in $\left(V_r\right)_{n_r \times n_l}$ or $\left(V_l\right)_{n_l \times n_r}$) to the model, which means $y_i = s_i, u = 0$. Therefore, we can get a new cost function:

$$f^* = \arg\min \frac{1}{n}\sum_{i=1}^{n}\left(y_i - f(x_i)\right)^2 + \gamma_A \|f\|_K^2 + \frac{\gamma_I}{n^2} f^T Lf \tag{10}$$

where n is the number of all the receptor-ligand pairs. According to Belkin 2006 [27], we can get:

$$F^* = W\left(W + \gamma_A lI + \frac{\gamma_I}{n^2}LW\right)^{-1} Y \tag{11}$$

2.5   Generate the Prediction Results

We calculated two different cost function matrices F_l and F_r by using the process described above based on $\left(V_r\right)_{n_r \times n_l}$ and $\left(V_l\right)_{n_l \times n_r}$. We carried out the bivariate correlation test by using SPSS, finding that the correlation coefficient between F_l and F_r was small, which means that the two different cost function value matrices could independently reflect the prediction results. In order to assess the comprehensive performance of two cost function, we define a linear combination model for the two cost function matrices:

$$F = \mu F_l + v F_r + \theta \tag{12}$$

where μ, v represent the degree of contribution of the two cost functions, θ is the small revision of the overall prediction. Furthermore, $\mu + v = 1, \theta \to 0$.

We found that there was an obvious difference between the distribution areas of two cost functions.

Table 1. Descriptive statistics of the two cost matrices

	Range	Minimum	Maximum	Mean	Std.Deviation	Variance
F_l	.25960	.0001189	.2597282	.031046781	.0415899143	.002
F_r	.7298054	.0009623	.7307677	.031933098	.0505467581	.003

As we can see from Table 1, the standard deviation of F_l is 0.0415899143 while the standard deviation of F_r is 0.0505467581. In order to combine the two cost functions more proportionate, we can select the parameters according to the ratio between the two standard deviations. Since $\mu{:}v$ =0.0505467581:0.0415899143 and $\mu + v = 1$, we chose $\mu = 0.5486$ and $v = 0.4514$. Finally, in order to make the minimum of F 0, we chose $\theta = -9.8037e-004$. Therefore, we confirmed the parameters of F:

$$F = 0.5486 \times F_l + 0.4514 \times F_r - 9.8037e-004 \qquad (13)$$

3   Results and Discussion

Fig.1 shows the ROC curves and Precision-Recall curves of the three different methods. Using the proposed method, we have predicted some receptor-ligand pairs such as P28222 (5-hydroxytryptamine receptor 1B) and L000736 (Mianserin), P18825 (Alpha-2C adrenergic receptor) and L000520 (ropinirole), which can be verified in KEGG [28] and DrugBank [29]. This approved the reliability of our prediction. Furthermore, as demonstrated in Table 2, the EstLapRLS method can achieve a better precision than two classical methods BLM and NetLapRLS. The proposed method increased by 2% and 4% on the AUC scores, and improved by 11% and 8% on the AUPR scores comparing with BLM and NetlapRLS methods. We can obtain the best results: AUC score of 96.15% and AUPR score of 75.17% with the EstLapRLS method.

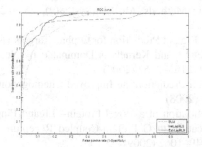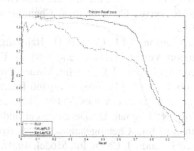

Fig. 1. Performance comparison between three methods

Table 2. Performance comparison of three methods

Method	AUC	AUPR	Sensitivity	Specificity	PPV
EstLapRLS	96.15	75.17	48.98	99.87	87.7
BLM	94.34	64.84	28.82	99.81	83.9
NetlapRLS	92.45	67.25	29.31	99.83	87.5

Acknowledgements. This work was supported by National Basic Research Program of China (Grants No. 2012CB910400) and the Fundamental Research Funds for the Central Universities (Grants No. 78260026).

References

1. Altman, R.B., Bergman, C.M., Blake, J., et al.: Text Mining for Biology-The Way Forward: Opinions From Leading Scientists. Genome Biol. 9(suppl. 2), S7 (2008)
2. Cheng, A.C., Coleman, R.G., Smyth, K.T., et al.: Structure-Based Maximal Affinity Model Predicts Small-Molecule Druggability. Nat. Biotechnol. 25(1), 71–75 (2007)
3. Lundstrom, K.: Structural Genomics of Gpcrs. Trends Biotechnol. 23(2), 103–108 (2005)
4. Jaakola, V.P., Griffith, M.T., Hanson, M.A., et al.: The 2.6 Angstrom Crystal Structure of a Human A2A Adenosine Receptor Bound to an Antagonist. Science 322(5905), 1211–1217 (2008)
5. Ballesteros, J., Palczewski, K.: G Protein-Coupled Receptor Drug Discovery: Implications From The Crystal Structure of Rhodopsin. Curr. Opin. Drug. Discov. Devel. 4(5), 561 (2001)
6. Cherezov, V., Rosenbaum, D.M., Hanson, M.A., et al.: High-Resolution Crystal Structure of an Engineered Human B2-Adrenergic G Protein-Coupled Receptor. Science 318(5854), 1258–1265 (2007)
7. Warne, T., Serrano-Vega, M.J., Baker, J.G., et al.: Structure of A &Bgr; 1-Adrenergic G-Protein-Coupled Receptor. Nature 454(7203), 486–491 (2008)
8. Van Der Horst, E., Peironcely, J.E., Ijzerman, A.P., Beukers, M.W., et al.: A Novel Chemogenomics Analysis of G Protein-Coupled Receptors (Gpcrs) and Their Ligands: A Potential Strategy for Receptor De-Orphanization. BMC Bioinformatics 11(1), 316 (2010)
9. Cheng, F., Zhou, Y., Li, J., et al.: Prediction of Chemical–Protein Interactions: Multitarget-QSAR Versus Computational Chemogenomic Methods. Mol. Biosyst. 8(9), 2373–2384 (2012)
10. Wassermann, A.M., Geppert, H., Bajorath, J.: Ligand Prediction for Orphan Targets Using Support Vector Machines and Various Target-Ligand Kernels is Dominated by Nearest Neighbor Effects. J. Chem. Inf. Model. 49(10), 2155–2167 (2009)
11. Jacob, L., Vert, J.P.: Protein-Ligand Interaction Prediction: an Improved Chemogenomics Approach. Bioinformatics 24(19), 2149–2156 (2008)
12. Weill, N., Rognan, D.: Development and Validation of a Novel Protein– Ligand Finger-print to Mine Chemogenomic Space: Application to G Protein-Coupled Receptors and Their Ligands. J. Chem. Inf. Model. 49(4), 1049–1062 (2009)
13. Iacucci, E., Ojeda, F., De Moor, B., Moreau, Y.: Predicting Receptor-Ligand Pairs Through Kernel Learning. BMC Bioinformatics 12(1), 336 (2011)
14. Xia, Z., Wu, L.Y., Zhou, X., Wong, S.T.: Semi-Supervised Drug-Protein Interaction Prediction From Heterogeneous Biological Spaces. BMC Syst. Biol. 4(suppl. 2), S6 (2010)
15. Van Laarhoven, T., Nabuurs, S.B., Marchiori, E.: Gaussian Interaction Profile Kernels for Predicting Drug–Target Interaction. Bioinformatics 27(21), 3036–3043 (2011)
16. Yamanishi, Y., Araki, M., Gutteridge, A., Honda, W., Kanehisa, M.: Prediction of Drug–Target Interaction Networks From The Integration of Chemical and Genomic Spaces. Bioinformatics 24(13), I232–I240 (2008)
17. Alaimo, S., Pulvirenti, A., Giugno, R., Ferro, A.: Drug–Target Interaction Prediction Through Domain-Tuned Network-Based Inference. Bioinformatics 29(16), 2004–2008 (2013)
18. Bock, J.R., Gough, D.A.: Virtual Screen for Ligands of Orphan G Protein-Coupled Receptors. J. Chem. Inf. Model. 45(5), 1402–1414 (2005)
19. Erhan, D., L'Heureux, P.J., Yue, S.Y., Bengio, Y.: Collaborative Filtering on A Family of Biological Targets. J. Chem. Inf. Model. 46(2), 626–635 (2006)

20. Doddareddy, M.R., Van Westen, G.J., Van Der Horst, E., et al.: Chemogenomics: Looking at Biology Through the Lens of Chemistry. Statistical Analysis and Data Mining 2(3), 149–160 (2009)
21. Bleakley, K., Yamanishi, Y.: Supervised Prediction of Drug–Target Interactions Using Bipartite Local Models. Bioinformatics 25(18), 2397–2403 (2009)
22. Okuno, Y., Yang, J., Taneishi, K., Yabuuchi, H., Tsujimoto, G.: GLIDA: GPCR-Ligand Database for Chemical Genomic Drug Discovery. Nucleic Acids Res. 34(suppl. 1), D673–D677 (2006)
23. Jacob, L., Hoffmann, B., Stoven, V., Vert, J.P.: Virtual Screening of Gpcrs: an in Silico Chemogenomics Approach. BMC Bioinformatics 9(1), 363 (2008)
24. Smith, T.F., Waterman, M.S.: Identification of Common Molecular Subsequences. J. Mol. Biol. 147, 195–197 (1981)
25. Hattori, M., Okuno, Y., Goto, S., Kanehisa, M.: Development of a Chemical Structure Comparison Method for Integrated Analysis of Chemical and Genomic Information in the Metabolic Pathways. J. Am. Chem. Soc. 125(39), 11853–11865 (2003)
26. Klabunde, T.: Chemogenomic Approaches to Drug Discovery: Similar Receptors Bind Similar Ligands. Br. J. Pharmacol. 152(1), 5–7 (2007)
27. Belkin, M., Niyogi, P., Sindhwani, V.: Manifold Regularization: A Geometric Framework for Learning From Labeled and Unlabeled Examples. Journal of Machine Learning Research 7, 2399–2434 (2006)
28. Kanehisa, M., Goto, S., Sato, Y., Furumichi, M., Tanabe, M.: KEGG for Integration and Interpretation of Large-Scale Molecular Data Sets. Nucleic Acids Res. 40(D1), D109–D114 (2012)
29. Knox, C., Law, V., Jewison, T., et al.: Drugbank 3.0: A Comprehensive Resource for 'Omics' Research on Drugs. Nucleic Acids Res. 39(suppl. 1), D1035–D1041 (2011)

Computational Evaluation of Protein Energy Functions

Nashat Mansour and Hussein Mohsen

Department of Computer Science and Mathematics Lebanese American University, Lebanon
{nmansour,hussein.mohsen}@lau.edu.lb

Abstract. Proteins are organic compounds made up of chains of amino acids that fold into complex 3-dimensional structures based on their chemical and physical properties. A protein is characterized by its 3D structure, which defines its biological function. Proteins fold into 3D structures in a way that leads to low-energy state. Predicting these structures is guided by the requirement of minimizing the energy value associated with the protein structure. However, the energy functions proposed so far by biophysicists and biochemists are still in the exploration phase and their usefulness has been demonstrated only individually. Also, assigning equal weights to different terms in energy has not been well-supported. In this project, we carry out a computational evaluation of putative protein energy functions. Our findings show that the CHARMM energy model tends to be more appropriate for *ab initio* computational techniques that predict protein structures. Also, we propose an approach based on a simulated annealing algorithm to find a better combination of energy terms, by assigning different weights to the terms, for the purpose of improving the capability of the computational prediction methods.

Keywords: CHARMM, force field, protein structure prediction, simulated annealing.

1 Introduction

Proteins are organic compounds that are made up of combinations of amino acids and are of different types and roles in living organisms. Initially a protein is a linear chain of amino acids, ranging from a few tens up to thousands of amino acids. Proteins fold, under the influence of several chemical and physical factors, into their 3-dimensional structures which determine their biological functions and properties. Misfolding occurs when the protein folds into a 3D structure that does not represent its correct native structure, which can lead to many diseases such as Alzheimer, several types of cancer, etc... [1]. Using computational methods for predicting the native structure of a protein from its primary sequence is an important and challenging task especially that this protein structure prediction (PSP) problem is computationally intractable. The protein's sequence of amino acids defines a unique native fold which normally corresponds to a minimum energy value [2]. In theory, this free energy minimum can be computed from quantum mechanics and, thus, should help in predicting the structure from the sequence. In practice, the theoretical foundation of such functions has not been fully established and several energy functions have been proposed.

D.-S. Huang et al. (Eds.): ICIC 2014, LNBI 8590, pp. 288–299, 2014.

The energy function models proposed so far depend on a number of biophysical factors. Their usefulness has been relatively demonstrated by different researchers. But, previous work has also shown that the precision of these energy models is not well-established [3]. Also, no serious comparative evaluation of these energy functions has been reported. Furthermore, limited work has been reported on the relative importance of the terms of the energy function; many decoys per protein, for a number of proteins, were generated from molecular dynamics trajectories and conformational search using the A-TASSER program minimizing the AMBER potential [4], [5].

In this work, we carry out a computational comparison of important energy functions that have appeared in the protein structure prediction literature in association with *ab initio* algorithms. We also design a simulated annealing algorithm for deriving values that should be used as weights for the energy terms based on the native structure knowledge on existing golden proteins in the 'protein data bank'. The ultimate goal is to yield better prediction of the tertiary structure of proteins.

This paper is organized as follows. Section 2 presents our methodology. Section 3 describes the energy models used for the comparative work. Section 4 explains the algorithm used for optimizing the weights of the energy terms. Section 5 presents the experimental results. Section 6 concludes the paper.

2   Methodology

The primary structure of a protein is a linear sequence of amino acids connected together via peptide bonds. Proteins fold due to hydrophobic effect, Vander Waals interactions, electrostatic forces, Hydrogen bonding, etc.... The protein structure prediction (PSP) problem is intractable [6]. Hence, the main computational approaches are heuristics for finding good suboptimal solutions and can be classified as: Homology modeling, threading, and ab initio methods [7]. For the latter methods, the only required input is the amino acid sequence whereas for the first two methods, data of previously predicted protein structures are used.

Ab initio methods predict the 3D structure of proteins given their primary sequences without relying on protein databases. The underlying strategy is find the best possible structure based on a chosen energy function. Based on the laws of physics, the most stable structure is the one with the lowest possible energy. We have identified three energy models/force fields as the most recognized models for pure ab initio PSP methods: the CHARMM model [8], the LINUS energy function [9], and AMBER [10]. The different energy functions include different terms and make a variety of assumptions. But, the relative merits of these functions in guiding computational protein structure prediction methods have not been well-studied. In particular, a computational investigation of their applicability has not been carried out. We believe that conducting such an investigation will serve the PSP research community by providing guidelines regarding the applicability of the recognized force fields.

Our methodology is based on the following steps and activities. We employ our recently developed computational method for PSP, namely the adapted scatter search metaheuristic [3], [11], as the basic platform for analyzing the behavior of the different energy functions. The selected energy functions are simulated and incorporated into the scatter search algorithm to create different versions of the scatter search based program. Then, real-world proteins are selected from a protein databank. The impact of the energy functions will be evaluated by computing the widely used root mean square deviation (RMSD) of the target structure with respect to the reference/golden protein structure. Then, we computationally derive sub-optimal weights for the energy terms in order to further improve the prediction. Then, for the 'winner' energy function, we find alternative weights for its terms to replace the commonly-used equal weights. This is done by adapting a simulated annealing algorithm that aims to simultaneously minimize the energy values of several (golden) proteins whose structure is already known.

3   Energy Functions/Models

The stability of the three-dimensional structure for protein is determined by the intra-molecular interactions and interactions with the external environment. The search for stable conformations of proteins is based on the minimum total energy of interaction. The three recognized energy models, which are selected for our experimental study, are described in the following subsections.

3.1   CHARMM Energy Model

The Chemistry at HARvard Molecular Mechanics (CHARMM) function [12] is based on the dihedral planes representation of proteins that can be defined by the degrees of freedom given by the torsion angles. There are four torsion angles present in each amino acid in a protein: phi φ, psi ψ, omega ω, and chi χ. Phi is the angle between the planes C-N-Cα and N-Cα-C, where N-Cα is the axis of rotation. This angle decides the distance of C-C of two amino acids. The chi angle is between the planes formed by the atoms of the side chains, and side chains can have as many as five chi angles. Fig. 1 shows a segment of a protein backbone.

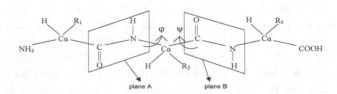

Fig. 1. Segment of a protein backbone with planes of bonds N-Cα and Cα-C, plane A and plane B, respectively

The CHARMM energy function is given by

$$E(\bar{c}) = \sum_{bonds} K_b (b - b_o)^2 + \sum_{angles} K_\theta (\theta - \theta_o)^2 +$$

$$\sum_{\substack{improper\\dihedrals}} K_{imp} (\varphi - \varphi_o)^2 + \sum_{dihedrals} K_\chi (1 + \cos(n\chi - \delta))$$

$$+ \sum_{hydrogen} \left(\frac{A_{ij}}{r_{ij}^{10}} - \frac{B_{ij}}{r_{ij}^{12}} \right) + \sum_{electrosta\ tic} \frac{q_i q_j}{4\pi\varepsilon_o \varepsilon_r r_{ij}}$$

$$+ \sum_{van\ der\ waals} 4\varepsilon_{ij} \left(\frac{\sigma_{ij}^{12}}{r_{ij}^{12}} - \frac{\sigma_{ij}^{6}}{r_{ij}^{6}} \right)$$

3.2 AMBER Energy Model

The AMBER99 model is composed of several all-atom force fields. These fields include parameters for bonded potential energy terms (stretching, bending, and torsion) and nonbonded terms (charge and van der Waals). The original version was AMBER94, which was developed to improve on peptide backbone torsion parameters; Kollman and co-workers used RESP charges derived from high-level ab initio calculations to parameterize energies [13]. The subsequent force field, denoted as AMBER99, is intended for use both with and without polarization effects [14]. AMBER99 includes the following terms:

$$V_{bounded} = \sum_{bonds} K_r (r - r_{eq})^2 + \sum_{angles} K_\theta (\theta - \theta_{eq})^2 + \sum_{dihedrals} \frac{Vn}{2} [1 + \cos(n\varphi - \gamma)]$$

$$V_{nonbounded} = \sum_{i<j} \left\{ \left[\frac{A_{ij}}{R_{ij}^{12}} - \frac{B_{ij}}{R_{ij}^{6}} \right] + \frac{q_i q_j}{4\pi\varepsilon R_{ij}} \right\}$$

$$V_{pol} = -\frac{1}{2} \sum_i \mu_i E_i^o$$

The total energy includes the sum of all the potential fields and the polarization potential energy added in AMBER99. In the first equation, three terms represent contribution to the total energy from "bond stretching, bond angle bending, and torsion angle", in the second one $V_{nonbonded}$ is the sum of non-bonded energy as "van der Waals and electrostatic energies". In the third equation, V_{pol} the polarization value is calculated for each pair of point charge and induced point dipole moment as μ_i and E_i is the electrostatic field at the ith atom generated by all other point charges q_j.

3.3   LINUS Energy Model

LINUS (Local Independently Nucleated Units of Structure) is an ab initio method for simulating the folding of a protein on the basis of simple physical principles. LINUS involves a Metropolis Monte Carlo procedure, represents a protein by including all its heavy atoms (i.e., non-hydrogen atoms). LINUS developed by Srinivasan and Rose in 1995 is based on simple scoring function includes three components: hydrogen bonding, scaled contacts, and backbone torsion. The hydrogen bonding and the hydrophobic contact scores are calculated between pairs of atoms from residues. The contact energy is given by

$$\text{Contact energy} = \text{maximum value} \times \left[1.0 - \frac{d_{ij}^2 - \sigma^2}{(\sigma + 1.4)^2 - \sigma^2} \right]$$

The scaled contact has both "Repulsive and attractive" terms. The repulsive term is implemented by rejecting conformations when the interatomic distance between any two atoms is less than the sum of their van der Waals radii. All pairwise interactions are evaluated except those involving carbonyl carbons and the attractive term is applied between the side chain pseudo-atoms. The total energy of the LINUS function scoring is given by the negative sum of the three preceding terms: hydrogen bonding, scaled contact, and backbone torsion [9].

4   Simulated Annealing Algorithm for Energy Terms' Weights

Simulated Annealing (SA) is a metaheuristic that deals with optimization problems with large search space to find near-optimal solutions. In this paper, simulated annealing is employed to assign appropriate weights to different energy terms. SA aims to yield a good solution with a minimized objective function value.

4.1   Algorithm Steps

The outline of the SA algorithm is shown in Fig. 2

```
Initialize Solution X and initial Temperature T
while (T > Steady State Temperature
            and iteration < MAX_ITERATIONs)
       for (NUMBER_OF_PERTURBATIONS)
       Y = Perturb(X)
       if (F(Y) < F(X) or e (-delta E/T) > random (0,1))
              X = Y
       // end if
       // end for
       Update (T)
// end while
```

Fig. 2. Outline of the SA algorithm

4.2   Solution Representation

Each energy term is given a random weight between 0 and 1, where the sum of weights must be 1 in any solution. The weight given to ES is called α, that to VW is called β, and to Torsion energy is δ. Thus, the obtained total energy for all solution is calculated according to the following formula:

$$E_{protein} = \alpha.Golden\text{-}ES_{protein} + \beta.Golden\text{-}VW_{protein} + \delta.Golden\text{-}Torsion_{protein}$$

4.3   Initial Solution

The initial solution is randomly generated. α, β, and δ are randomly generated with values between 0 and 1, such that $\alpha + \beta + \delta = 1$ and no single value falls below 1.

4.4   Initial Temperature, Maximum Iterations, and Number of Perturbation

Initial temperature is chosen as 400,000 and that of steady state is 15. The maximum number of iterations is chosen to be 200 with 3 perturbations in the 'for' loop of each iteration.

4.5   Perturbation Method

The implemented perturbation method alters the weights distribution among the energy terms. It either takes a certain percentage (0.1) from a target weight factor and distributes it to the other 2 weight factors or takes this percentage from two factors and adds it to the target third one.

The method has 3 decisions to take randomly. The first one is which of the weight factors (α, β, and δ) to target (whether to take from or add to). The second decision is whether to take from the chosen factor or give it more energy. The third decision is how to distribute the amount of energy taken/given.

For example, the algorithm may randomly first choose α as the target, then randomly choose to take from it 0.1 of its value, and then randomly chooses to give 0.3 of the amount to be taken from α to β and 0.7 to δ.

4.6   Objective Function

The objective function to be minimized is the following:

$$\sum (E_i - Avg_{Ei})^2, \qquad for\ i=1\ to\ n$$

where n is the number of the selected proteins, E_i (defined in subsection 4.2) is the total energy obtained according to the weights distribution by α, β, and δ, and Avg_{Ei} is the average of the calculated energies, E_i for i=1..n, in the set of proteins according to weight distributions. Effectively, we are minimizing the mean square deviation in the values of E_i over the n proteins as the values of the weights vary.

The SA metaheuristic algorithm enforces a lower bound of 0.1 for each of α, β, and δ in order not to prevent making any of the energy terms negligible. Thus, in any perturbed combination of values, the SA algorithm rejects any perturbation that yields weight values below 0.1.

5   Experimental Results

In this section, we demonstrate the performance of our proposed methods using the 3 different energy models for generating native-like structures for the backbones of the three target proteins.

5.1   Experimental Procedure for Energy Functions

In our experiments, we use three subject proteins with known structures in PDB. Our reference PDB is the Brookhaven database [15]. The 3 proteins are: 1CRN (CRAMBIN) is Plant seed protein (46 AAs); 1ROP (ROP Protein) is Transcription Regulation (56 AAs); 1UTG (UTEROGLOBIN) is Steroid Binding (70 AAs).

We run the scatter search program for predicting protein structures based on each of the three energy models. The results are evaluated by computing the target protein's structural difference from the reference/golden protein. This is accomplished by calculating the root mean square deviation (RMSD), in Angstrom, of the Cα atoms of the two proteins [16].

5.2   Experimental Results for Energy Functions

Table 1 gives the RMSD values by Scatter Search using the 3 types of potential energy function. These results show that CHARMM generates the lowest RMSD values for the 3 proteins. Also, the limited experiments reveal that the polarization term added in AMBER99 may not cause an improvement in the predicted protein structure. CHARMM also runs faster than AMBER and has comparable execution time to LINUS.

Although the results in Table 1 demonstrate a rather clear tendency in favor of CHARMM, this does not yield a final conclusion since the number of proteins that are used in the experiment is small. Future work should employ many proteins with various sizes and functions in order to establish whether our result may vary with protein size and type.

5.3   Experimental Procedure for Energy Weights

In order to experiment with weights for energy terms, the real energy values have to be obtained. These are the golden energy values obtained from the data retrieved from the Protein Data Bank (PDB) file of each protein. The data are the 3D coordinates of atoms, torsion angles and amino acids. The total energy value of a protein is the sum of the terms of the CHARMM energy function.

Two sets of non-homologous proteins have been chosen, where each is made up of 5 different proteins. The first set contains proteins each with less than 100 amino acids (AAs), whereas the second contains proteins with more than 100 AAs in each. We run the SA algorithm on the data obtained from each set of proteins to generate values for the weights of the energy terms. The variation in the weights is also plotted over the SA iterations until convergence. Finally, to give an indication of the validity of the weight results, we rerun the scatter search program of Mansour et al. [11] to predict the structure of a protein, by using the new weights, and compare the resulting RMSD with that of the structure produced by using equal weights for the energy terms.

Table 1. Experimental results for SS on 3 energy functions

Energy function	1CRN (46 AAs, 326 atoms)		1ROP(56 AAs, 420 atoms)		1UTG(70 AAs, 547 atoms)	
	Time (min)	RMSD	Time (min)	RMSD	Time (min)	RMSD
CHARMM	964	9.39	1059	11.52	1182	13.56
AMBER96	1140	11.80	1320	15.84	1800	16.21
AMBER99 with Polarization	3600	14.39	4200	16.04	5005	18.07
LINUS	960	13.05	1005	15.22	1200	18.36

5.4   Results for Energy Weights

Results of SA for Proteins of Less than 100 Amino Acids. For proteins with less than 100 amino acids (1RPO, 1UBQ, 1CRN, 1ROP, and 1UTG), SA converged after 20 iterations to the objective function value of 5.159×10^{15}. The initial randomly generated solution was of objective function value of 2.178×10^{17}. Fig. 3 shows the variations of α, β, and δ as a function of iterations of the SA. The values of the three weights at convergence are: $\alpha = 0.352$; $\beta = 0.105$; $\delta = 0.543$.

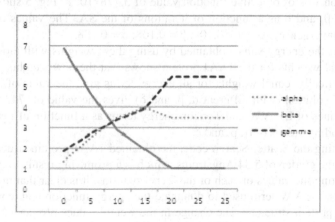

Fig. 3. Variations of α, β, and δ ($\times 10^{-1}$) as a function of iterations

Comparing the energy values obtained by using these weights with those obtained from the equal weights for the 1ROP protein show that the former ones (using the new weights) are lower. Equal weights (0.333) give the energy value of 1.125×10^6, whereas the obtained solution (with α, β, and δ values) gives the value of 426,072. Fig. 4 shows the values of ES, VW and Torsion energy terms as a function of iterations and the corresponding values of α, β, and δ.

After running the scatter search code, the obtained 1ROP protein structure has an RMSD with respect to the golden protein of 7 Angstrom in comparison with about 12 Angstrom, obtained with equal weights [11].

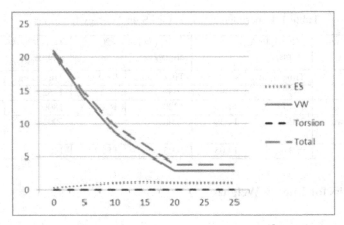

Fig. 4. Variations of ES, VW and Torsion Energies for 1ROP (in 10^5 charge units) as a function of iterations

Results of SA for Proteins of More Than 100 Amino Acids. For proteins with more than 100 amino acids (1AAJ, 1BP2, 1RPG, 1RRO, and 1YCC), SA converged after 43 iterations to the objective function value of 1.457×10^{12}. The initial randomly generated solution was of objective function value of 3.278×10^{13}. Fig. 5 shows the variations of α, β, and δ as a function of iterations of the SA. The values of the three weights at convergence are: $\alpha = 0.104$; $\beta = 0.108$; $\delta = 0.788$.

Comparing the energy values obtained by using these weights with those obtained from the equal weights for the 1AAJ protein shows that the new weights yield lower values. Specifically, equal weights for all energy terms give the value of: 2.305×10^6. The obtained solution (with different α, β, and δ) gives the value of: 742,844. Fig. 6 shows the values of ES, VW and Torsion energy terms as a function of iterations and the corresponding values of α, β, and δ.

After running the Scatter Search code, the obtained 1AAJ protein structure has an RMSD with the golden of 5.84 Angstroms, which is a promising result.

By inspecting the values of each of the 3 energy terms, it is clear that in the case of equal weights, the VW term used to dominate the energy function and, consequently, the resulting protein structure. The change in the weight values provides fairer shares to the other two terms and, thus, allows them to influence the evolution of the predicted structure. We also note that the relative weights are different for different protein sizes.

These results show that assigning equal weights to the energy terms does not yield the best possible protein structure prediction. But, more experiments are required to establish what weights should be assigned for what size-category of proteins. Also, it will be useful to apply our approach to other recognized energy functions.

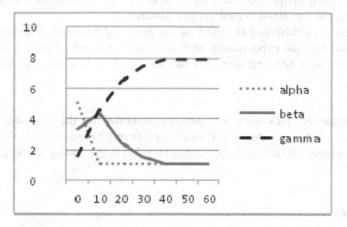

Fig. 5. Variations of α, β, and δ (x10⁻¹) as function of iterations

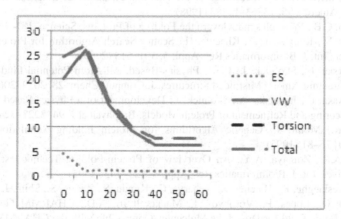

Fig. 6. Variations of ES, VW and Torsion Energies in 1AAJ (in 10^5 charge units) as a function of iterations

6   Conclusions

We have carried out a computational assessment of the ability of three recognized energy models for predicting the tertiary structure of proteins using a pure ab initio algorithm. We have also investigated the merit of assigning unequal weights to the terms included in energy functions employed for ab initio protein structure prediction.

Our experimental results show that the CHARMM energy model tends to yield better protein structures than the other two energy functions, next is AMBER without polarization, followed by LINUS and the polarization version of AMBER. We have also found that it is more favorable for computational protein prediction methods to assign unequal weights to the terms in the energy function. As a result, we recommend the following weight values for the CHARMM energy function: 0.1-0.3 for the electrostatic term, 0.1-0.2 for the Vander Waals term, and 0.6-0.8 for the Torsion term, when applied to small to medium size proteins.

This work has established the merit of the proposed approach. Further work can focus on extending the experimental work to a larger number of protein sets that include proteins with different sizes and functions and on extending to other energy models.

Acknowledgments. This work was partially supported by the Lebanese American University and Lebanon's National Council for Scientific Research. We thank Mirvat Sibai for guidance on biology issues and acknowledge the coding support of Rachid Sayed.

References

1. Prusiner, S.B.: Prions. Proceedings of the National Academy of Sciences of the United States of America 95, 13363–13383 (1998)
2. Anfinsen, C.B.: Principles that Govern the Folding of Proteins. Science, 181–187 (1973)
3. Mansour, N., Kehyayan, C., Khachfe, H.: Scatter Search Algorithm for Protein Structure Prediction. Int. J. Bioinformatics Res. Appl. 5, 501–515 (2009)
4. Wroblewska, L., Skolnick, J.: Can a Physics-Based, All-Atom Potential Find a Protein's Native Structure Among Misfolded Structures. J. Comput. Chem. 28, 2059–2066 (2007)
5. Wroblewska, L., Jagielska, A., Skolnick, J.: Development of a Physics-Based Force Field for the Scoring and Refinement of Protein Models. Biophysical J. 94, 3227–3240 (2008)
6. Unger, R., Moult, J.: Genetic Algorithms for Protein Folding Simulations. J. Mol. Biol. 231, 75–81 (1993)
7. Sikder, A.R., Zomaya, A.Y.: An Overview of Protein-Folding Techniques: Issues and Perspectives. Int. J. Bioinformatics Res. Appl. 1, 121–143 (2005)
8. Vanommeslaeghe, K., Hatcher, E., Acharya, C., Kundu, S., Zhong, S., Shim, J., Darian, E., Guvench, O., Lopes, P., Vorobyov, I., Mackerell Jr., A.D.: CHARMM General Force Field: A Force Field for Drug-Like Molecules Compatible with the CHARMM All-Atom Additive Biological Force Fields. J. Comput. Chem. 31, 671–690 (2009)
9. Srinivasan, R., Fleming, P.J., Rose, G.D.: Ab Initio Protein Folding Using LINUS. Methods in Enzymology 383, 48–66 (2004)
10. Cornell, W.D., Cieplak, P., Bayly, C.I., Gould, I.R., Merz, K.M., Ferguson, D.M., Spellmeyer, D.C., Fox, T., Caldwell, J.W., Kollman, P.A.: A Second Generation Force Field for the Simulation of Proteins, Nucleic Acids, and Organic Molecules. J. Am. Chem. Soc. 117, 5179–5197 (1995)
11. Mansour, N., Ghalayini, I., Rizk, S., El Sibai, M.: Evolutionary Algorithm for Predicting All-Atom Protein Structure. In: Int. Conf. on Bioinformatics and Computational Biology, New Orleans (2011)

12. Brooks, B.R., Bruccoleri, R.E., Olafson, B.D., States, D.J., Swaminathan, S., Karplus, M.: CHARMM: a Program for Macromolecular Energy, Minimization, and Dynamics Calculations. Journal of Computational Chemistry 4, 187–217 (1983)
13. Kollman, P.A.: Advances and Continuing Challenges in Achieving Realistic and Predictive Simulations of the Properties of Organic and Biological Molecules. American Chemical Society (1996)
14. Wang, J., Cieplak, P., Kollman, P.A.: How Well Does a Restrained Electrostatic Potential (RESP) Model Perform in Calculating Conformational Energies of Organic and Biological Molecules? J. Comp. Chem. 21, 1049–1074 (2000)
15. Bernstein, F.C., Koetzle, T.F., Williams, G.J., Meyer Jr., E.F., Brice, M.D., Rodgers, J.R., Kennard, O., Shimanouchi, T., Tasumi, M.: The Protein Data Bank: a computer-based archival file for macromolecular structures. J. Mol. Biol. 112, 535–542 (1977)
16. Carugo, O., Pongor, S.: A Normalized Root-Mean-Square Distance for Comparing Protein Three-Dimensional Structures. Protein Sci. 10, 1470–1473 (2001)

Selection and Classification of Gene Expression Data Using a MF-GA-TS-SVM Approach

Hernández-Montiel Alberto Luis[1], Bonilla-Huerta Edmundo[1],
Morales-Caporal Roberto and Guevara-García Antonio José[2].

[1] LITI, Instituto Tecnológico de Apizaco,
Av. Instituto Tecnológico s/n. C.P. 90300. Apizaco, Tlaxcala, México
edbonn@hotmail.fr
[2] Universidad Autónoma de Tlaxcala
Calzada Apizaquito S/N,Apizaco, Tlax C.P 90300, Apizaco, Tlaxcala, México

Abstract. This article proposes a Multiple-Filter (MF) using a genetic algorithm (GA) and Tabu Search (TS) combined with a Support Vector Machine (SVM) for gene selection and classification of DNA microarray data. The proposed method is designed to select a subset of relevant genes that classify the DNA-microarray data more accurately. First, five traditional statistical methods are used for preliminary gene selection (Multiple Filter). Then different relevant gene subsets are selected by using a Wrapper (GA/TS/SVM). A gene subset, consisting of relevant genes, is obtained from each statistical method, by analyzing the frequency of each gene in the different gene subsets. Finally, the most frequent genes are evaluated by the Multiple Wrapper approach to obtain a final relevant gene subset. The proposed method is tested in four DNA-microarray datasets. In the experimental results it is observed that our model work very well than other methods reported in the literature.

1   Introduction

In last years many researchers have been devoted to tackle the gene selection and classification of microarray gene expression data by proposing a lot of promising methods [1,2,3,4,5]. However, the experiment results are still not satisfying to solve very high dimensional gene expression data. One of the main reasons is that a DNA-microarray dataset contains ten thousands of genes and a very small number of experimental samples or observations about a cancer. This means that thousands of genes are irrelevant or noisy or redundant for typical gene selection and classification algorithms. To extract a subset of relevant genes from microarray data is necessary to reduce dimensionality and to explore this new reduce space to find a small gene subset with the higher classification accuracy. In order to overcome this obstacle, we propose a Multiple Filter a Genetic Algorithm combined with Tabu Search and Support Vector Machine (MF-GA-TS-SVM) approach that consists of 2 basic steps: in the first step, a preprocessing data is performed using 5 statistical filters to make an initial selection from biomedical databases. In the second step, the selection and classification of subsets features is performed, the selection is effected by a genetic

D.-S. Huang et al. (Eds.): ICIC 2014, LNBI 8590, pp. 300–308, 2014.

algorithm that combined with a tabu search as a local search method, and the classification of the subsets feature is made with a support vector machine and is validated using cross-Validation method. With this hybrid method, the most relevant genes are researched from 5 public databases obtained from DNA-microarray technology. This model performs a gene selection procedure to find subset of genes with higher classification accuracy in four microarray datasets. This paper is organized as follows. Methodology of our model is shown in section 2. Section 3 provides an analysis of the experimental results and finally conclusions are drawn in section 4.

2   Methodology

The problem of the feature selection can be defined, as the task of selecting a subset feature that maximizes the classifier capacity. In this paper, this problem is solved with a MRMR approach. Fig. 1 shows the general process of selection and classification of the genes, applying to the following DNA-microarray databases: leukemia, colon cancer, diffuse large B-cell lymphoma (DLBCL), Central Nervous System (CNS) and lung cancer.

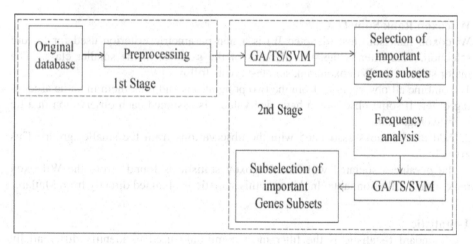

Fig. 1. Two main stages for gene selection and classification

2.1   Multiple-Filter

The pre-processing procedure is a very important task in gene selection and classification. In this process the noisy, irrelevant and inconsistent data have been eliminated. First, we normalize the gene expression levels of each dataset into interval [0,1] using the minimum and maximum expression values of each gene. Second, five methods of data filtering are used to gene selection: between sum square and within sum square (BSS/WSS), mutual information (MI), signal to noise ratio (SNR), Wilcoxon test (WT) y T-statistic (TS). The main idea is to select a subset of genes obtained by each method; each method of filtering uses a relevance value (Ranking) that is assigned to each gene. These five filters are used for their statistical capacity, since a filter prioritizes a gene and the other filter prioritizes the other genes (a description of each filter is given below).

BSS/WSS
We use the gene selection filter proposed by Dudoit [19], namely the ratio of the sums of squares between groups (Between Sum Square - BSS) and within groups (Within Sum Square – WSS). This ratio compares the distance of the center of each class to the over-all center to the distance of each gene to its class. The equation for a given gene j has the form:

$$\frac{BSS(j)}{WSS(j)} = \frac{\sum_i \sum_k I(y_i = k)(\bar{x}_{kj} - \bar{x}_{.j})^2}{\sum_i \sum_k I(y_i = k)(\bar{x}_{ij} - \bar{x}_{kj})^2} \tag{1}$$

Where $\bar{x}_{.j}$ denotes the average expression level of the gene j through all samples and $\bar{x}_{kj}$ denotes the average expression level of the gene j on all samples for the relevance of class k. In this work the top-p genes ranked by BSS/WSS are selected.

Wilcoxon Rank Sum Test
Wilcoxon rank sum test (denoted W) is a non-parametric criterion used for feature selection. This filter is the sum of ranks of the samples in the smaller class. The major steps of the Wilcoxon rank sum test are as follows [9]:
1. Combine all observations from the two populations and rank them in value ascending order. If some observation have tied values, is assigned each observation in a tie their average rank.
2. Add all the ranks associated with the observations from the smaller group. This gives W.
3. the p-value associated with the Wilcoxon statistic is found from the Wilcoxon rank sum distribution table. In this case this statistic is obtained directly from Matlab.

T-Statistic
The standard t-statistic is the filter most commonly used to identify differentially expressed genes. Each sample is labeled into interval {1, -1}. For each gene g_j, the mean is μ_j^1 and μ_j^{-1}, standard deviation δ_j^1 and δ_j^{-1} are calculated using only the samples labeled 1 and -1 respectively. Then a score $T(g_j)$ can be obtained by [20]:

$$t(g_j) = |\mu_j^1 - \mu_j^{-1}| / \sqrt{(\delta_j^1)^2 / n_1 + (\delta_j^{-1})^2 / n_{-1}} \tag{2}$$

Where n_1 and n_{-1} are the number of samples labeled as 1 and -1 respectively. Large absolute t-statistic indicates the most discriminatory genes.

Mutual Information

A and B are two random variables with a different probability distribution and a joint probability distribution. The mutual information between the two variables I (A; B) is defined as the relative entropy between the joint probability and the product of the probabilities [9].

$$I(A;B) = \sum_{a_i} \sum_{b_j} P(a_i, b_j) \log \frac{P(a_i, b_j)}{P(a_i)P(b_j)} \tag{3}$$

Where $P(a_i, b_j)$, are the joint probabilities of the variables, $P(a_i)$ are the probabilities of the variable A and $P(b_j)$ is the probability of the variable B.

Signal to Noise Ratio (SNR)

SNR Identifies the expression patterns with a maximum difference in the mean expression between two groups and the minimum variation of expression within each group. In this method, the genes are first ranked according to their expression levels [10].

$$SNR = |(\mu_1 - \mu_2)/(\sigma_1 + \sigma_2)| \tag{4}$$

Where μ_1 and μ_2 denotes the average values of expression of class 1 and class 2, respectively, σ_1 and σ_2 are the standard deviation of the samples in each class respectively.

2.2   GA/TS/SVM Wrapper

In first stage, $p=50$ genes with the highest top ranking score are selected from the multiple filters. In this second stage, a genes subset selection is performed using the wrapper method GA/TS/SVM.

2.3   Genetic Algorithm (GA)

The technique of Genetic Algorithms (GA's) was described by John Holland [14]. This technique is based on the selection mechanisms used by nature, according to the fittest individuals of a population are those that survive and can adapt more easily to the changes that are produced in their environment. The GAs used a population of chromosomes, where each chromosome is a solution to the problem of optimizing [10]. The step of the chromosomes to the next generation, is determined by its fitness. There are five principal components of a GA: the population, the fitness function, the selection operator, the crossover operator and the mutation operator.

A. Initial Population

The initial population of the GA, this constituted by a chromosome set orbit string, which are randomly generated to have a uniform distribution of the chromosomes, these chromosomes string represent the possible solutions of the problem.

B. Fitness Function and Support Vector Machine

The Support Vector Machine (SVM), are classifiers that discriminate linearly separable data classes through an optimum hyper plane, so that the separation margin between the positive and negative samples are maximized [13]. The fitness of the chromosome is used to select gene subsets with a high classification ratio. In the wrapper GA/TS/SVM, SVM is used as a classifier to evaluate the fitness of a each candidate gene subset.

C. Selection, Crossover,Tabu Search and Replacement

Tabu search (TS), was introduced by Fred Glover [17]. As a technique that implements a memory through simple structure with the objective guiding a local search procedure to solve problems of combinatorial optimization with a high degree of difficulty, exploring the solution space beyond the local optima [18]. It can get a basic TS algorithm through the use of a tabu list. At each iteration, the current solutions are replaced by the best found solution s' in their neighbourhood $N(s)$. $s' \in N(s)$ such a way $\forall s'' \in N(s), f(S'') \le f(s')$ and $s' \in \hat{S}$ where $\hat{S}$ is the solution set currently prohibited by the tabu list. Note that selected neighbor s' can or cannot be better than S. The TS algorithms stopped when a fixed maximum number of iterations are reached or when all movements have been converted in tabu. The main role of the tabu list is to prevent the search from cycling. In our case, the tabu list is implemented in the following way. Each time a movement (i,j) is carried out. The gene g_i is dropped and the gene g_j is selected, then g_i is saved in the tabu list for the next k iterations. Consequently, g_j cannot be reselected during the process. The k value is the residence time that the gene g_j will be within the tabu list and varies from k_{min} to k_{max}. The tabu list forbids a new gene selected, this gene can be removed from the tabu list in the next iteration if the classification coefficient of the new gene selected is very low. The GA/TS/SVM algorithm is described as follows.

Step 1: The GA starts with a population that is generated randomly following a uniform distribution and the length of the chromosome is equal to the number of genes selected by filter method, which is calculated by the fitness $(f(x))$ of each chromosome using a support vector machine and after is validated by the K fold cross validation method.

Step 2: Two genetic operators are applied, the selection operator and the crossover operator, the selection operator is based on the roulette wheel and the crossover operator is multi-uniform.

Step 3: The tabu search begins, the initial solution S is the solution obtained by the crossover operator.

Step 5: The neighborhood is generated from the initial solution S, Which is evaluated with the support vector machine.

Step 6: The best solution S' is searched in the neighborhood and is checked if it is restricted by the tabu list, if S' is tabu, the second best solution of the neighborhood is taken, if S' in not tabu, S' is taken as the best solution.

Step 7: It is verified that the solution S' is greater than or equal to the threshold (S' $>\alpha$), if it is greater, the solution S' is returned to the genetic algorithm to be applied as the replacement operator, if S' is not greater than the threshold (S' $<\alpha$), S' it becomes the initial solution (S=S') and is generated as a new neighborhood to form the solution S, this is repeated n times until S' is greater than the threshold.

Step 8: The worst chromosome is replaced from the population with the solution S', which been obtained with the tabu search, the new population goes to the next generation, the algorithm repeated these steps n times until the number of generations established is fulfilled. Fig. 2 shown the iteration process of GA/TS/SVM approach.

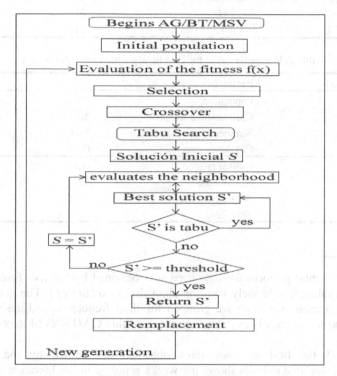

Fig. 2. GA/TS/SVM Wrapper

The combination of a tabu search and genetic algorithm is performed to obtain a good gene subset.

3   Experiments and Results

3.1   Experimental Protocol and Datasets

In order to perform the experimentations, 5 databases of public domain were used, the biomedical database of leukemia, colon cancer, lung cancer, CNS and DLBCL. Which are described in table 1, the parameters by the GA and the tabu search are shown in table 2.

Table 1. Description of Biomedical Datasets

Dataset	Genes/Samples	Reference
Leukemia	7128/72	[1]
Colon	2000/62	[2]
Lung	12533/181	[3]
CNS	7129/60	[4]
DLBCL	4026/47	[5]

Table 2. Parameters used for genetic algorithm and tabu search

Method	Parameters	
GA	Population	50
	Chromosome length	50
	Number of generations	100
	Crossover rate	0.85
	Elitism rate	0.5
TS	Size of tabu list	5
	Aspiration criteria	Yes
	Threshold	0.98

3.2   Results

In our experimental protocol the data used was obtained by the five filter methods, this data is evaluated separately with the algorithm GA/TS/SVM. The genes subsets resulting from each evaluation are grouped for their frequency, and the genes with greater frequency, are newly evaluated by the algorithm GA/TS/SVM to obtain a final gene subset.

In table 3 the best accuracy rates obtained are shown by the algorithm GA/TS/SVM, the first column shows the works reported in the literature with which the results obtained were compared   to the proposed method, the second, third, fourth fifth and   sixth columns, show the accuracy rates (%) and the number of genes (Ng) obtained for each biomedical database. To obtain a better classification rate, the algorithm GA/TS/SVM is run 10 times, which gives us different performances for each gene expression dataset.

Table 3. Comparison with different methods reported in literature

Authors	Leukemia	Colon % (Ng)	Lung % (Ng)	CNS % (Ng)	DLBCL % (Ng)
Hernández et al [6]	92.5 (6)	87.0 (8)	- - - -	- - - -	95.44 (12)
Luo et al [13]	71.3 (5)	80.0 (7)	- - - -	- - - -	82.13 (7)
Yu [14]	96.8 (10)	88.6 (10)	94.7 (10)	- - - -	- - - -
Yu et al [15]	- - - -	- - - -	- - - -	92.86 (71)	- - - -
Leung and Hung [16]	**100** (4)	**96.7**(6)	95.0 (**9**)	- - - -	- - - -
Our model	98.6 (8)	**96.7**(12)	**97.8** (10)	**93.92 (10)**	**97.61**(12)

As shown in Table 4, our model is very competitive on 4 from 5 biomedical databases, yielding small subsets of genes with high classification accuracy. Only the work of Leung and Hung [16] provides a classification rate of 100 for leukemia. For Colon tumor dataset our models have the same classification rate 96.7, they have a gene subset of 6 genes and we have a gene subset of 12 genes. With lung cancer, they have a small gene subset of 9 genes with a classification accuracy of 95%, but our model provides a higher rate of classification (97.8) with 10 genes. For CNS and DLBCL datasets and our model provides high classification rates with few genes.

4   Conclusions

In this article, we introduced a new method to select genes from the DNA-microarray technology. Five filter methods (Multiple-Filter) were used to make a first selection of the databases to have many relevant genes. In the Hybrid Wrapper a Genetic Algorithm was combined with a Tabu Search and a SVM classifier (AG/BT/SVM) to find a small gene subset. The proposed method is innovative, since it determines a small genes subset with high classification accuracy to the five microarray databases, which were compared with subsets found in different literatures shown in table 3. In future research the combination of other techniques of feature selection will be used, as other local search methods or other techniques of mining data, the goal is to maximize the classification accuracy and minimize the number of genes.

References

1. Golub, T., Slonim, D., Tamayo, P., et al.: Molecular Classification of Cancer: Class Discovery and Class Prediction by Gene Expression Monitoring. Science, 531–537 (1999)
2. Alon, U., Barkai, N., Notterman, D., et al.: Broad patterns of gene expression revealed by clustering analysis of tumor and normal colon tissues probed by oligonucleotide arrays. Proc. Nat. Acad. Sci. USA, 6745–6750 (1999)
3. Gordon, G.J., et al.: Translation of Microarray Data into Clinically Relevant Cancer Diagnostic Tests Using gene expression ratios in lung cancer and mesothelioma. Cancer Res. (2002)
4. Pomeroy, S.L., Tamayo, P., Gaasenbeek, M., Sturla, L.M., Golub, T.R.: Prediction of Central Nervous System Embryonaltumour Outcome Based on Gene Expression. Nature, 436–442 (2002)
5. Alizadeh, A.A., Eisen, B.M., Davis, R.E., et al.: Distinct Types of Diffuse Large (b)–Cell Lymphoma Identified by Gene Expression Profiling. Nature, 503–511 (2000)
6. Hernandez, J.C., Duval, B., Hao, J.K.: SVM-based Local Search For Gene Selection and Classification of Microarray Data. Communications in Computer and Information Science 13, 499–508 (2008)
7. Mohamad, M.S., et al.: A Hybrid of Genetic Algorithm and Support Vector Machine for Features Selection and Classification of Gene Expression Microarray. International Journal of Computational Intelligence and Applications, 91–107 (2005)

8. Dudoit, S., Fridlyand, J., Speed, T.P.: Comparison of Discrimination Methods for The Classification of Tmors Using Gene Expression Data. Journal of the American Statistical Association, 77–87 (2002)

9. Deng, L., Pei, J., Ma, J., Lee, D.L.: A Rank Sum Test Method for Informative Gene Discovery. In: Proceedings of the 10th ACM SIGKDD International Conference on Knowledge Discovery and Data Mining (KDD 2004), pp. 410–419. ACM Press, Seattle (2004)

10. Mishra, D., Sahu, B.: Feature Selection for Cancer Classification: A Signal-to-noise Ratio Approach. International Journal of Scientific & Engineering Research 2 (2011)

11. Hernández Montiel, L.A., Bonilla Huerta, E., Morales Caporal, R.: A multiple-filter-GA-SVM Method for Dimension Reduction and Classification of DNA-microarray data. Revista Mexicana de Ingenieria Biomedical XXXII, 32–39 (2011)

12. Li, L., Darden, T.A., Weinberg, C.R., Levine, A.J., Pedersen, L.G.: Gene Assessment and Sample Classification for Gene Expression Data Using a Genetic Algorithm/K-Nearest Neighbor Method. Combinatorial Chemistry & High Throughput Screening, 727–739 (2001)

13. Luo, L.K., Huang, D.F., Ye, L.J., Zhou, Q.F., Shao, G.F., Peng, H.: Improving the Computational Efficiency of Recursive Cluster Elimination for Gene Selection. IEEE/ACM Transactions on Computational Biology and Bioinformatics, 122–129 (2011)

14. Yu, L., Han, Y., Berens, M.E.: Stable Gene Selection from Microarray Data via Sample Weighting. IEEE/ACM Transactions on Computational Biology and Bioinformatics, 262–272 (2012)

15. Yu, G., Feng, Y., Miller, D.J., Xuan, J., Hoffman, E.P., Clarke, R., Davidson, B., Shih, I.M., Wang, Y.: Matched Gene Selection and Committee Classifier for Molecular Classification of Heterogeneous Diseases. Journal of Machine Learning Research, 2141–2167 (2010)

16. Leung, Y., Hung, Y.: A Multiple-filter-multiple-wrapper Approach to Gene Selection and Microarray Data Classification. IEEE/ACM Trans. Comput. Biol. Bioinformatics 7(1), 108–117 (2010), doi:10.1109/TCBB.2008.46

17. Glover, F., Melián, B.: Tabu Search. Revista Iberoamericana de Inteligencia Artificial (2003)

18. Vélez, M.C., Motoya, J.A.: Metaheurísticos: Una alternativa para la solución de problemas combinatorios en Administración de Operaciones. EIA 8, 99–115 (2007)

19. Dudoit, S., Fridlyand, J., Speed, T.: Comparison of Discrimination Methods for The Classification of Tumors Using Gene Expression Data. Journal of the American Statistical Association, 77–87 (2002)

20. Fu, X., Tan, F., Wang, H., Zhang, Y.Q., Harrison, R.: Feature Similarity Based Redundancy Reduction for Gene Selection. In: Proceedings of 2006 International Conference on Data Mining (DMIN 2006), Las Vegas, June 26-29 (2006)

Evaluation of Advanced Artificial Neural Network Classification and Feature Extraction Techniques for Detecting Preterm Births Using EHG Records

Paul Fergus, Ibrahim Olatunji Idowu, Abir Jaffar Hussain,
Chelsea Dobbins, and Haya Al-Askar

Liverpool John Moores University, Byrom Street, Liverpool, L3 3AF, UK
I.O.Idowu@2009.ljmu.ac.uk, H.Alaskar@2011.ljmu.ac.uk,
{P.Fergus,A.Hussain,C.M.Dobbins}@ljmu.ac.uk

Abstract. Globally, the rate of preterm births is increasing and this is resulting in significant health, development and economic problems. Current methods for the early detection of such births are inadequate. However, there has been some evidence to suggest that the analysis of uterine electrical signals, collected from the abdominal surface, could provide an independent and easier way to diagnose true labour and detect when preterm delivery is about to occur. Using advanced machine learning algorithms, in conjunction with electrohysterography signal processing, numerous studies have focused on detecting true labour several days prior to the event. In this paper however, the electrohysterography signals have been used to detect preterm births. This has been achieved using an open dataset that contains 262 records for women who delivered at term and 38 who delivered prematurely. Several new features from Electromyography studies have been utilized, as well as feature-ranking techniques to determine their discriminative capabilities in detecting *term* and *preterm* records. Seven artificial neural network algorithms are considered with the results showing that the *Radial Basis Function Neural Network* classifier performs the best, with 85% *sensitivity*, 80% *specificity*, 90% area under the curve and a 17% mean error rate.

Keywords: Electrohysterography (EHG), Preterm Delivery, Term Delivery, Artificial Neural Networks.

1 Introduction

The World Health Organisation (WHO) defines preterm birth as the delivery of any baby born alive before 37 weeks of gestation. In other words, births that occur before 259 days of pregnancy are defined as *preterm* and births that occur between 259 and 294 days, as *term*. Preterm births have a significant adverse impact on the newborn, including an increased risk of death and other health related defects. In 2009, preterm births accounted for approximately 7% of live births, in England and Wales [3].

During pregnancy, the monitoring of uterine contractions is vital in order to differentiate between those that are normal and those that may lead to premature birth. The early onset of such contractions can be caused by a number of conditions, including

D.-S. Huang et al. (Eds.): ICIC 2014, LNBI 8590, pp. 309–314, 2014.

abnormalities in the cervix and uterus, recurrent antepartum hemorrhage and infection [8]. In the USA, the cost of treatment is reportedly $25.6 billion, whilst in England and Wales, it is estimated to be £2.95 billion, annually [3]. Consequently, in the last twenty years, a great deal of research has been undertaken to detect and prevent the threat of preterm birth.

One promising technique, which has gained recognition in monitoring uterine activity, is the use of advanced machine learning algorithms and Electrohysterography (*EHG*). This method records signals from the abdominal surface of pregnant women. These readings are then used to study the electrical activity produced by the uterus. The results are convincing and suggest that it is an interesting line of enquiry to pursue.

In conjunction with *EHG* signal processing, the research carried out by Lucovnik *et al.* [8] and Hassan *et al.* [5] illustrates that extracting features from *EHG* signals is key to finding particular spectral information specific to *term* and *preterm* deliveries. The aim of this paper is to evaluate features and their use with several advanced artificial neural network classification algorithms and their ability to distinguish between *term* and *preterm* births. An open dataset has been used, which contains 300 records of pregnant subjects (262 *term* and 38 *preterm*). The results indicate that the selected classifiers, in conjunction with selected features, outperform a number of previous approaches.

The remainder of the paper is structured as follows. Section 2 discusses related studies. Section 3 describes the experimental methodology and the selected extracted feature sets, including the design of the experiment. The results are presented in section 4 before the paper is concluded in Section 5.

2   Related Studies

Over the past 20 years, research has focused on the use of pattern recognition techniques to extract features from *EHG* signals. These include *linear* and *nonlinear* methods, in both the *time* and *frequency* domains, to improve the results obtained from classification algorithms. The extraction of features often forms part of the data preprocessing stage. In our previous work [4], features such as *peak frequency, median frequency, root mean square* and *sample entropy*, performed particularly well when discriminating between *term* and *preterm* records.

However, it is in the Electromyography (*EMG*) field that we find some new and interesting works. In one study, Lucovnik *et al.* [8] investigated whether uterine *EMG* could be used to evaluate propagation velocity (*PV*). In this study, the electrical signals of the uterus were measured both in labour and non-labour patients who delivered at *term* and *prematurely*. The results indicate that, the combination of power spectrum (*PS*) and *PV* peak frequency parameters yielded the best predictive results in identifying true *preterm* labour. However, only one dimension of propagation is considered at a time, which is based on the estimation of time delays between spikes. In comparison, Lange *et al.* [6] estimate the *PV* of the entire *EHG* bursts that occur during a contraction by calculating the bursts corresponding to a full contraction event. The results illustrate that the estimated average propagation velocity is 2.18 (60.68) cm/s. No single preferred direction of propagation was found.

Meanwhile, Alamedine *et al.* [2] presented three techniques to identify the most useful features relevant for contraction classification. These included *linear* features, such as *peak frequency, mean frequency* and *root mean square*, and *nonlinear* features, such as the *Lyapunov exponent* and *sample entropy*. In order to choose the most suitable features that represent contractions, feature selection algorithms have been used. This process involved using a binary particle swarm-optimization (*BPSO*) algorithm and calculating the Jeffrey Divergence (*JD*) distance. This is a sequential forward selection (*SFS*) algorithm. The results show that the *BPSO* and *SFS* algorithms could select features with the greatest discriminant capabilities. In this case, out of the six features considered, *sample entropy* produced the best results.

Vasak *et al.* [12] studied whether uterine *EMG* can identify inefficient contractions. This can lead to first-stage labour and caesarean delivery in *term* nulliparous women, with the unplanned onset of labour. In this study, *EMG* was recorded during spontaneous labour in 119 such cases, with singleton *term* pregnancies in the cephalic position. Electrical activity of the myometrium, during contractions, is characterized by its power density spectrum (*PDS*). The diagnosis of labour was made if the patient was in active labour, with no increase in dilation, for at least two hours. The data was analysed to calculate the Intra-class correlation coefficients. This was achieved by comparing the variance of contraction characteristics, within subjects, to the variance between subjects.

3   Methodology

The TPEHG dataset contains the raw *EHG* signals that have been used in our study [10]. This data has been pre-processed using data segmentation, feature extraction and classification. The study in [7] illustrates how *EHG* signals can be pre-processed using various frequency related parameters. The study uses several *linear* and *non-linear* signal pre-processing techniques, via three different channels, to discern *term* and *preterm* deliveries. The pre-processing technique used in [7] passed the *EHG* signal through a Butterworth filter configured to filter 0.8-4 Hz, 0.3-4 Hz, and 0.3-3Hz frequencies. However, [9] found that uterine electrical activity occurred within 1Hz and that the maternal heart-rate was always higher than 1Hz. Furthermore, 95% of the patients measured had respiration rates of 0.33 Hz or less. Based on these findings, in this paper, the raw *TPEHG* signals have been passed through the same Butterworth filter to focus on data between 0.34 and 1Hz.

3.1   Raw Data Collection

The raw *EHG* signals, obtained from the Physionet database [10], have been recorded using four bipolar electrodes. These have been adhered to the abdominal surface and spaced at a horizontal and vertical distance between 2.5 and 7cm apart. The total number of records in the EHG dataset is 300 (38 *preterm* records and 262 *term* records). Each of the signals were either recorded early, <26 weeks (at around 23 weeks of gestation) or later, =>26 weeks (at around 31 weeks). Within the dataset, three signals have been obtained simultaneously, 'per record'. This has been achieved by recording through three different channels.

3.2   Feature Selection

The literature reports that *peak frequency*, *median frequency*, *sample entropy* and *root mean squares* have the most potential to discriminate between *term* and *preterm* records. Furthermore, the literature also reports that in *EMG* studies, features such as *waveform length*, *log detector* and *variance* are equally as good at discriminating between different muscle activities. To validate these findings, the above mentioned features have been ranked using *statistical significance*, *linear discriminant analysis using independent search (LDAi)*, *linear discriminant analysis using forward search (LDAf)*, *linear discriminant analysis using backward search (LDAb)* and *gram-schmidt (GS)* analysis.

The *Radial Basis Function Neural Network (RBNC)*, using the *Linear Discriminant Analysis Forward Search* feature ranking technique showed that, *sample entropy*, *waveform length*, *log detector*, and *variance* provide the best discriminant capabilities and are therefore used to evaluate the classifiers used in this paper.

3.3   Classifiers

This study evaluates the use of seven advanced artificial neural network classifiers. These are the Back-Propagation Trained Feed-Forward Neural Network Classifier (*BPXNC*), Levenberg-Marquardt Trained Feed-Forward Neural Network Classifier (*LMNC*), Perceptron Linear Classifier (*PERLC*), Radial Basis Function Neural Network Classifier (*RBNC*), Random Neural Network Classifier (*RNNC*), Voted Perceptron Classifier (*VPC*) and the Discriminative Restricted Boltzmann Classifier (*DRBMC*) (37steps, 2013).

4   Results

This section presents the classification results for *term* and *preterm* delivery records. This has been achieved using the extracted feature set from the 0.34-1 Hz filter on Channel 3. Using the 80% holdout technique, the initial validation results have been presented. This provides a baseline for comparison against all subsequent evaluations that have been performed, using the oversampled dataset.

4.1   Original Results for 0.34-1 Hz Filter on Channel 3

The performance of each classifier has been evaluated using the *sensitivity*, *specificity*, *errors*, and *AUC* values. In this trial, the experiments have been repeated 30 times. Randomly selected training and test sets have been used in each iteration.

Classifier Performance

The first evaluation uses the original *TPEHG* dataset, which contains 38 *preterm* and 262 *term* records. Table 1, below, illustrates the mean averages obtained over 30 simulations for the *sensitivity*, *specificity*, and *AUC* values. As it can be seen, the *sensitivities* (i.e. the ability to classify a *preterm* record), in this initial test, are low for all classifiers. This is expected because there are a limited number of *preterm* records from which the classifiers can learn. Consequently, *specificities* are higher than *sensitivities*.

Table 1. Original TPEHG Signal (262 *Term* And 38 *Preterm*)

Classifiers	Sensitivity	Specificity	AUC
BPXNC	0	0.9987	54%
LMNC	0.0667	0.9519	58%
PERLC	0.1619	0.8647	57%
RBNC	0.1286	0.9622	56%
RNNC	0.0667	0.9474	56%
VPC	0	1.0000	50%
DRBMC	0	0.9981	58%

4.2   Results for 0.34-1 Hz TPEHG Filter on Channel 3 – Oversampled Using SMOTE

In order to solve the class skew problem, the *preterm* records have been oversampled using the Synthetic Minority Oversampling Technique (*SMOTE*) [11]. This algorithm oversamples the minority class (38 *preterm* records) to 262, which equals the 262 *term* samples already provided by the *TPEHG* database. A new dataset now contains an even split between *term* and *preterm* records. Using this dataset, the experiment has been repeated a further 30 times.

Classifier Performance
Table 2, illustrates the mean averages obtained over 30 simulations for the *sensitivity*, *specificity*, and *AUC* values. As it can be seen, the *sensitivities*, for all of the algorithms, have significantly improved, while *specificities* have decreased. In addition, the *AUC* results also show a significant improvement in accuracy for all of the classifiers. In particular, the *RBNC* has dramatically improved with an accuracy of 90%.

Table 2. SMOTE TPEHG signal (262 *Term* and 262 *Preterm*)

Classifiers	Sensitivity	Specificity	AUC
BPXNC	79%	58%	72%
LMNC	82%	69%	82%
PERLC	46%	67%	63%
RBNC	85%	80%	90%
RNNC	86%	72%	83%
VPC	98%	2%	50%
DRBMC	59%	55%	56%

5   Conclusion

The development of medical information systems has played an important role in the biomedical domain. This has led to the extensive use of Artificial Intelligence (AI) techniques for extracting biological patterns in data. Furthermore, data pre-processing and validation techniques have also been used extensively to analyze such datasets for classification problems. In this paper, seven classifiers have been used to classify *term* and *preterm* records from the *TPEHG* dataset, filtered between 0.34 and 1 Hz. The results demonstrate that the best performing classifier was the *RBNC* with 85% *sensitivity*, 80% *specificity*, 90% *AUC* and a 17% mean error rate. These results are encouraging and suggest that the approach posited in this paper is a line of enquiry worth pursuing.

Perhaps one negative aspect of the work is the need to utilize oversampling to increase the number of *preterm* samples. A better way would have been to balance the dataset using actual recordings obtained from pregnant women who delivered prematurely. This will be the focus of future research, alongside a more extensive investigation into different machine learning algorithms and techniques.

References

1. 37steps, Pattern Recognition Tools. Version 5 (2013)
2. Alamedine, D., Khalil, M.: Marque.: Comparison of different EHG feature selection methods for the detection of preterm labor. Computational and Mathematical Methods in Medicine 10(6), 24–26 (2013)
3. Bulletin, S.: Statistical Bulletin Gestation-specific Infant Mortality inEngland and Wales. National Office for Statistics (2011)
4. Fergus, P., Cheung, P., Hussain, A., Al-Jumeily, D., Dobbins, C., Iram, S.: Prediction of Preterm Deliveries from EHG Signals Using Machine Learning. PloS One 8(10), 130–135 (2011)
5. Hassan, M., Muszynski, C., Alexandersson, A., Marque, C.: Nonlinear Correlation Analysis of External Uterine Electromyography. IEEE Transactions on BioMedical Engineering 60(4), 1160–1166 (2013)
6. Lange, L., Vaeggemose, A., Kidmose, P., Mikkelsen, E., Uldbjerg, N., Johansen, P.: Velocity and directionality of the electrohysterographic signal propagation. PloS One 9(1), 199–205 (2014)
7. Leman, H., Marque, C., Gondry, J.: Use of the electrohyster- ogram signal for characterization of contractions during pregnancy. IEEE Trans. Biomed. Eng. 46(10), 1222–1229 (1999)
8. Lucovnik, M., Maner, W.L., Chambliss, L.R., Blumrick, R., Balducci, J., Novak-Antolic, Z., Garfield, R.E.: Noninvasive uterine electromyography for prediction of preterm delivery. American Journal of Obstetrics and Gynecology 204(3), 156–162 (2011)
9. Maner, W.: Predicting term and preterm delivery with transabdominal uterine electromyography. Obstetrics & Gynecology 101(6), 1254–1260 (2003)
10. PhysioNet. The Term -Preterm EHG Database (TPEHG- DB). physionet.org (2012)
11. Richman, J., Moorman, J.: Physiological time-series analysis using approximate entropy and sample entropy. American Journal of Physiology 49, H2039–H2049 (2000)
12. Vasak, B., Graatsma, E.M., Hekman-Drost, E., Eijkemans, M.J., van Leeuwen, J.H.S., Visser, G.H., Jacod, B.C.: Uterine electromyography for identification of first-stage labor arrest in term nulliparous women with spontaneous onset of labor. American Journal of Obstetrics and Gynecology 209(3), 232.e1–232.e8 (2013)

Potential Driver Genes Regulated by OncomiRNA Are Associated with Druggability in Pan-Negative Melanoma

Di Zhang[1,2] and Junfeng Xia[1]

[1] Institute of Health Sciences, Anhui University, Hefei, Anhui 230601, China
[2] School of Life Sciences, Anhui University, Hefei, Anhui 230601, China
jfxia@ahu.edu.cn

Abstract. OncomiRNAs (oncomiRs) are small regulatory microRNAs (miRNAs) that play an important role in tumor formation and progression. These oncomiRs are found to regulate different types of tumor by targeting a large set of cancer driver genes (including oncogenes and tumor suppressor genes). In the present work, we have developed a pipeline for the identification of frequently occurring and clinically relevant driver genes in pan-negative melanoma (absence of mutations in BRAF (affecting V600), NRAS (G12, G13, and Q61), KIT (W557, V559, L576, K642, D816), GNAQ (Q209), and GNA11 (Q209) by integrating oncomiRs regulated genes and frequently mutated genes in melanoma pan-negative samples. The preliminary experience has identified 28 potential driver genes that are regulated by oncomiRs, of which 25 genes are associated with drugs, 3 differentially expressed genes are associated with metastasis. This analysis provides a method to mine clinically relevant driver genes in pan-negative melanomas.

Keywords: MicroRNA, OncomiRNA, Melanoma, Driver gene.

1 Introduction

MicroRNAs (miRNAs) are small noncoding RNAs that negatively regulate gene expression. Disregulation of miRNAs can contribute to cancer initiation, progression and metastasis. For example, miRNAs are found to regulate different hallmarks of cancer by targeting a large set of cancer related genes (including oncogenes and tumor suppressor genes). These miRNAs are usually termed oncomiRNAs (oncomiRs). In recent years, many databases aiming at annotating the cancer-related miRNAs have been developed [including miRCancer [1], PhenomiR [2], somamiR [3], and OncomiRD [4], providing information about miRNAs and their target genes in cancer.

Melanoma is a highly aggressive cancer of melanocytes and accounts for 80% of deaths from skin cancer [5], with an estimated 76,100 new patients and 9,710 deaths expected in the United States in 2014 [5]. The high mortality rate of advanced stage metastatic melanoma is largely due to its aggressive behavior and limited treatment options. Recently, novel effective molecular-based targeted therapies for the treatment of patients whose metastatic melanomas harbor specific driver mutations in *BRAF*,

D.-S. Huang et al. (Eds.): ICIC 2014, LNBI 8590, pp. 315–321, 2014.
© Springer International Publishing Switzerland 2014

NRAS, KIT, GNAQ, and *GNA11* have emerged. However, more than 30% of tumors lack any of these mutations and are called "pan-negative". Continued investigation for novel driver genes in these cases is critical to improve therapeutic outcomes for melanoma patients. For example, we recently identified 12 significantly mutated genes in "pan-negative" samples (*ALK, STK31, DGKI, RAC1, EPHA4, ADAMTS18, EPHA7, ERBB4, TAF1L, NF1, SYK,* and *KDR*).

To uncover other potentially targetable mutations, we analyzed frequently mutated genes in melanoma pan-negative samples to identify mutated genes associated with oncomiRs. Among the 28 potential driver genes that are regulated by oncomiRs, of which 25 genes are associated with drugs. Our findings provide important therapeutic implications for "pan-negative" melanomas patients.

2   Materials and Methods

2.1   Mutation Data in Pan-Negative Melanomas

The frequent mutated gene data set were obtained from our previous study [6]. We defined a highly mutated gene set in pan-negative melanoma samples. This set was defined by mutated gene occurred in at least 10% of pan-negative melanomas. This threshold led to selection of 681 highly frequently mutated genes.

2.2   OncomiRs and Their Target Genes

We obtained the experimentally verified oncomiRs data from the oncomiRDB database [4]. After filtering the duplicate data, 46 melanoma related oncomiRs were included in our study. A total of 739 target genes of these oncomiRs were obtained from the miRTarBase database [7], which provides the experimentally validated miRNA-target interactions.

2.3   Druggable Human Genes

The druggable genes are genes or gene products that are known or predicted to response to drug. We used the druggable gene set in MelanomaDB database [8], which includes the genes associated with drugs from 10 different sources.

2.4   Analysis of Differential Overlapping Genes

We obtained 28 over-lapping genes (Table 1) between the sets of highly mutated genes (mutation frequency ≥ 10%) and 739 miRNAs target genes. The functional annotation analysis of these 28 genes was executed using the DAVID tool [9].

Finally, to infer potential therapeutic targets for the treatment of malignant melanoma, the expression profiles of genes in melanoma cells were gathered from the collected gene expression data (GSE8401, including 31 primary melanomas and 52 melanoma metastases). We defined upregulation as a fold change of >2, and downregulation as a fold change of <-2.

3   Results and Discussions

3.1   Inferring Potential Therapeutic Targets Using Melanomadb

To infer potential therapeutic targets, we first filtered 739 miRNA targeted genes, and obtained 28 overlapped genes with a mutation frequency above 10%. In previous investigations on the druggability of highly recurrent mutated genes in breast cancer, the authors found that these possible driver genes are poorly targeted by known drugs.Of these 28 overlapped genes, 89.3% (25 of 28) are approved to be associated with drugs. Driver gene has been applied to clinic, such as RG7204 [10] is an effective agent in melanoma patients who harbor *BRAF* mutation. These overlapping genes have a great potential to be a new biomarker.

Table 1. Overlapping between genes in pan-negative and miRNA targets gene

Mutation frequency	miRNA targets gene
>0.1	ARID2 COL5A3 COL7A1 COL3A1 DMD ELAVL4 GRIN2A PTPRO SELE TCF4 TP53 TSHZ3 ZEB1 ZFPM2 ZNF804A CARD11 GRM7 CASR APC ACVR1C COL1A2 COL4A1 FLT1 NTRK3 PTPRD TP63 FBN1 SMARCA4

Table 2. The enriched GO terms in 28 overlapping genes

GO-ID	Description	Count	P value
43588	skin development	5	1.71E-04
8544	epidermis development	7	3.40E-04
7398	ectoderm development	7	3.59E-04
122	negative regulation of transcription from RNA polymerase II promoter	6	0.017645
10604	positive regulation of macromolecule metabolic process	9	0.020833
51172	negative regulation of nitrogen compound metabolic process	7	0.029598
45934	negative regulation of nucleobase, nucleoside, nucleotide and nucleic acid metabolic process	7	0.031407
51253	negative regulation of RNA metabolic process	6	0.033302
9890	negative regulation of biosynthetic process	7	0.033468
1501	skeletal system development	6	0.034081
31327	negative regulation of cellular biosynthetic process	7	0.035833
45892	negative regulation of transcription, DNA-dependent	6	0.037618
9891	positive regulation of biosynthetic process	7	0.049835
10557	positive regulation of macromolecule biosynthetic process	7	0.049967

Note: Count represents the number of genes in each GO category; *P* value was adjusted by using the Benjamini method.

We analyzed genes found to be highly mutated in a cohort of 69 "pan-negative" melanoma genomes. These targets genes are enriched in epidermis development, epidermis development, ectoderm development, regulation of transcription and so on(Table 2). These genes have been proved to play a crucial role in biological function. Such as ACVR1C involved in multiple signaling pathway, including MAPK and TGF-beta signaling pathway [11]. *CARD11* is a member of cascade recruitment domain family, which take part in T cell and B cell receptor signaling pathway [12]. The *CARD11* mutation is a common phenomenon in the pathogenesis of Primary CNS lymphoma (PCNSL). *COL5A3*, *COL3A1*, *COL1A2* and *COL4A1* are modulated by miR-29c in many cancers [13]. All missense mutations in *TP53* predicted to have an average effect on the protein function in melanoma [6].

3.2   Inferring Potential Therapeutic Targets Associated with Melanoma Metastasis

Different kinds of disease usually present vary features, such as gene methylation or expression profiles. Therefore, the inferred 28 potential target genes ought to be further filtered for a given progressing period. We utilized gene expression data from melanoma clinical samples, which includes 31 primary melanomas and 52 melanoma metastases, and obtained three target genes overexpressed in melanoma metastasis. Among them, *SELE* and *TP63* were the two most important genes studied by many researchers. All genes found differentially expressed in our results accord with report in breast cancer [14-16].

The *TP63* gene is a homologue of *TP53* family, which plays a role in tumor progression by dysregulating proliferation and differentiation. Overexpression of the *TP63* gene is strongly associated with the diagnosis of lung cancer and cervical cancer [17, 18], suggesting this marker can apply in assessing cancer risk. Moreover, the previous studies reveled that p63 was reckoned with a marker of epithelial derivation, as it was overexpressed in cutaneous tumors [19]. More importantly, in squamous carcinoma of the lung, patients with the amplification and overexpression of *TP63* have prolonged survival [13]. *TP63* contains one tumor suppressors isoform (*TATP63*) and two oncogenes isoforms (*ΔTP63*; *dNTP63*) [20]. The oncogenic activity of the *TP63* isoform may explain why we see its overexpression in melanoma.

E-selectin (*SELE*) is a soluble adhesion molecule and has low expression in normal endothelial cells [21, 22]. But the *SELE* expression is induced rapidly when it binds transcription factors such as NF-κB and AP-1. Increased expression of *SELE* has been widely reported on endothelial cells when a cancer occurred, such as colorectal cancer and lung cancer [23, 24]. *SELE* acts as a mediator of the adhesion cascade and improve the metastatic potential. In clinic, *SELE* expression was decreased by using Cimetidine and it improve therapeutic effects in colorectal metastasis cancer patients [25]. While many studies show that *SELE* participates in metastasis, the mechanism of its regulation is not fully understood. A study showed that the increased level of *SELE* in metastatic melanoma cells was two folds higher than the concentration found in primary melanoma cells[26]. The increased level of *SELE* in melanoma patients was a poor prognosis. Since *SELE* plays a vital role in metastasis, its levels can be a useful marker for the recurrence in melanoma. Hence, the detection of *SELE* may be a quick and auxiliary method to evaluate the metastatic potential of melanoma.

The third differential mutated gene was *COL7A1*, which encodes a component of type VII collagen. The study of Teresa Odorisio et al. [27] showed that the amount of type VII collagen indicate an involvement of TGF-β pathways in modulating disease variability. The research of *COL7A1* mainly aims at dystrophic epidermolysis bullosa, where *COL7A1* mutation predisposing to cutaneous squamous-cell carcinoma [28]. Though there is no evidence suggesting that it is associated with melanoma progression and metastasis, it has been found to be key determinant of lung metastasis in osteosarcoma and its encoding protein is a breast cancer bone metastasis-associated peptidase regulators [29]. Besides, recent study [30] suggested that VII collagen overexpressed in dystrophic epidermolysis bullosa patient group with a higher inherent risk of developing skin cancer. *COL7A1* plays a vital role in disease development. Whether it plays the same role in melanoma progression needs to be further verified.

In all, these three genes execute quite important biological functions. The aberrant mutations cause the dysregulation of normal cell and may cause cancer. Numerous studies have indicated that these three mutation genes are associated with risk of several cancers, including lung cancer, colorectal cancer [30-32]. Among these genes, only *COL7A1* was less reported in cancers. In our study, it has a potential to be targeted in melanoma.

4   Conclusion

With increasing knowledge of gene mutation profiles, we can use it to identify cancer driver genes. In this study, we systematically integrated different sources of data in melanoma "pan-negative" samples. Combining mRNA targets gene with highly mutated genes, we identified 28 potential drug target genes by overlapping these data sets.

These 28 identified genes may act as potential targets for therapeutic agents in melanoma patients without harboring *BRAF*, *NRAS*, *KIT*, *GNAQ*, and *GNA11* driver mutations. Though this method seems feasible, it inevitably missed other potential target genes in melanoma. Our study provides a new perspective of potential druggable mutation genes and 3 differentially expressed genes related to melanoma metastasis, especially in pan-negative melanoma samples.

In summary, we integrated oncomiRs regulated genes and frequently mutated genes in melanoma pan-negative samples. We identified 28 potential driver genes associated withmelanoma. Future biological experiments will be applied to determine whether these mutations are driver or passenger in melanoma. The strategies adopted in this study may also uncover targets that can be translated into clinical therapeutic for other cancers.

Acknowledgments. This work is supported by the grants from the National Science Foundation of China (31301101 and 61272339), the Anhui Provincial Natural Science Foundation (1408085QF106), and the Specialized Research Fund for the Doctoral Program of Higher Education (20133401120011). The authors appreciate the constructive criticism and valuables suggestions from the anonymous reviewers.

References

1. Xie, B., et al.: Mircancer: A Microrna–Cancer Association Database Constructed by Text Mining on Literature. Bioinformatics 29(5), 638–644 (2013)
2. Ruepp, A., Kowarsch, Theis, F.: Phenomir: Micrornas in Human Diseases and Biological Processes. In: Next-Generation Microrna Expression Profiling Technology, pp. 249–260. Springer (2012)
3. Bhattacharya, A., Ziebarth, J.D., Cui, Y.: Somamir: A Database for Somatic Mutations Impacting Microrna Function in Cancer. Nucleic Acids Research 41(D1), D977–D982 (2013)
4. Wang, D., et al.: Oncomirdb: A Database for The Experimentally Verified Oncogenic and Tumor-Suppressive Micrornas. Bioinformatics, Btu155 (2014), doi:10.1093/Bioinformatics/Btu155
5. Siegel, R., et al.: Cancer Statistics. CA: A Cancer Journal for Clinicians 64(1), 9–29 (2014)
6. Xia, J., et al.: A Meta-Analysis of Somatic Mutations From Next Generation Sequencing of 241 Melanomas: A Road Map for The Study of Genes With Potential Clinical Relevance. Molecular Cancer Therapeutics, Molcanther. 0804.2013 (2014), doi:10.1158/1535-7163.MCT-13-0804
7. Hsu, S.-D., et al.: Mirtarbase Update 2014: An Information Resource for Experimentally Validated Mirna-Target Interactions. Nucleic Acids Research 42(D1), D78–D85 (2014)
8. Trevarton, A.J., et al.: Melanomadb: A Web Tool for Integrative Analysis of Melanoma Genomic Information to Identify Disease-Associated Molecular Pathways. Frontiers in Oncology 3 (2013), doi:10.3389/Fonc.2013.00184
9. Dennis Jr., G., et al.: DAVID: Database for Annotation, Visualization, and Integrated Discovery. Genome. Biol. 4(5), P3 (2003)
10. Yang, H., et al.: RG7204 (PLX4032), A Selective BRAFV600E Inhibitor, Displays Potent Antitumor Activity in Preclinical Melanoma Models. Cancer Research 70(13), 5518–5527 (2010)
11. Weiss, A., Attisano, L.: The Tgfbeta Superfamily Signaling Pathway. Wiley Interdisciplinary Reviews: Developmental Biology 2(1), 47–63 (2013)
12. Egawa, T., et al.: Requirement for CARMA1 in Antigen Receptor-Induced NF-KB Activation and Lymphocyte Proliferation. Current Biology 13(14), 1252–1258 (2003)
13. Ueda, T., et al.: Relation between Microrna Expression and Progression and Prognosis of Gastric Cancer: A Microrna Expression Analysis. The Lancet Oncology 11(2), 136–146 (2010)
14. Smirnov, D.A., et al.: Global Gene Expression Profiling of Circulating Endothelial Cells in Patients With Metastatic Carcinomas. Cancer Research 66(6), 2918–2922 (2006)
15. Lerebours, F., et al.: NF-Kappa B Genes Have A Major Role in Inflammatory Breast Cancer. BMC Cancer 8(1), 41 (2008)
16. Ma, X.-J., et al.: Gene Expression Profiling of The Tumor Microenvironment During Breast Cancer Progression. Breast Cancer Res. 11(1), R7 (2009)
17. Massion, P., et al.: Recurrent Genomic Gains in Preinvasive Lesions As A Biomarker of Risk for Lung Cancer. Plos One 4(6), E5611 (2009)
18. Zhu, D., et al.: Amplification and Overexpression of TP63 and MYC As Biomarkers for Transition of Cervical Intraepithelial Neoplasia to Cervical Cancer. International Journal of Gynecological Cancer 24(4), 643–648 (2014)
19. Fox, M.D., et al.: Cutaneous Meningioma: A Potential Diagnostic Pitfall in P63 Positive Cutaneous Neoplasms. Journal of Cutaneous Pathology 40(10), 891–895 (2013)

20. Hibi, K., et al.: AIS Is An Oncogene Amplified in Squamous Cell Carcinoma. Proceedings of the National Academy of Sciences 97(10), 5462–5467 (2000)
21. Zetter, B.: Adhesion Molecules in Tumor Metastasis. Seminars in Cancer Biology 4(4), 219–229 (1993)
22. Meyer, T., Hart, I.: Mechanisms of Tumour Metastasis. European Journal of Cancer 34(2), 214–221 (1998)
23. O'hanlon, D., et al.: Soluble Adhesion Molecules (E-Selectin, ICAM-1 and VCAM-1) in Breast Carcinoma. European Journal of Cancer 38(17), 2252–2257 (2002)
24. Gogali, A., et al.: Soluble Adhesion Molecules E-Cadherin, Intercellular Adhesion Molecule-1, and E-Selectin As Lung Cancer Biomarkers. CHEST Journal 138(5), 1173–1179 (2010)
25. Kobayashi, K.-I., et al.: Cimetidine Inhibits Cancer Cell Adhesion to Endothelial Cells and Prevents Metastasis by Blocking E-Selectin Expression. Cancer Research 60(14), 3978–3984 (2000)
26. Xu, L., et al.: Gene Expression Changes in An Animal Melanoma Model Correlate With Aggressiveness of Human Melanoma Metastases. Molecular Cancer Research 6(5), 760–769 (2008)
27. Odorisio, T., et al.: Monozygotic Twins Discordant for Recessive Dystrophic Epidermolysis Bullosa Phenotype Highlight The Role of TGF-B Signalling in Modifying Disease Severity. Human Molecular Genetics, Ddu102 (2014), doi:10.1093/Hmg/Ddu102
28. Madan, V., Lear, J.T., Szeimies, R.-M.: Non-Melanoma Skin Cancer. The Lancet 375(9715), 673–685 (2010)
29. Jin, L., et al.: Differential Secretome Analysis Reveals CST6 As A Suppressor of Breast Cancer Bone Metastasis. Cell Research 22(9), 1356–1373 (2012)
30. Pourreyron, C., et al.: High Levels of Type VII Collagen Expression in RDEB Cscc Keratinocytes Increases PI3K and MAPK Signalling, Cell Migration and Invasion. British Journal of Dermatology (2013), doi:10.1111/Bjd.12715
31. Hosgood III, H.D., et al.: Genetic Variant in TP63 on Locus 3q28 Is Associated With Risk of Lung Adenocarcinoma Among Never-Smoking Females in Asia. Human Genetics 131(7), 1197–1203 (2012)
32. Alexiou, D., et al.: Serum Levels of E-Selectin, ICAM-1 and VCAM-1 in Colorectal Cancer Patients: Correlations With Clinicopathological Features, Patient Survival and Tumour Surgery. European Journal of Cancer 37(18), 2392–2397 (2001)

Classification of Ventricular Tachycardia and Fibrillation Based on the Lempel–Ziv Complexity and EMD

Deling Xia[1,2], Qingfang Meng[1,2,*], Yuehui Chen[1,2], and Zaiguo Zhang[3]

[1] The School of Information Science and Engineering,
University of Jinan, Jinan 250022, China
[2] Shandong Provincial Key Laboratory of Network Based Intelligent Computing,
Jinan 250022, China
[3] CET Shandong Electronics Co., Ltd., Jinan 250101, China
ise_mengqf@ujn.edu.cn

Abstract. Detection of ventricular tachycardia (VT) and ventricular fibrillation (VF) in electrocardiography (ECG) has clinical research significance. The complexity of the heart signals has changed significantly, when the heart state switches from normal sinus rhythm to VT or VF. With the consideration of the non-stationary of VT and VF, we proposed a novel method for classification of VF and VT in this paper, based on the Lempel–Ziv (LZ) complexity and empirical mode decomposition (EMD). The EMD first decomposed ECG signals into a set of intrinsic mode functions (IMFs). Then the complexity of each IMF was used as a feature in order to discriminate between VF and VT. A public dataset was utilized for evaluating the proposed method. Experimental results showed that the proposed method could successfully distinguish VF from VT with the highest accuracy up to 97.08%.

Keywords: ventricular fibrillation, ventricular tachycardia, the Lempel–Ziv complexity, empirical mode decomposition (EMD).

1   Introduction

Ventricular fibrillation (VF) and ventricular tachycardia (VT) are both life-threatening arrhythmia. Once a patient was regarded as VF, high-energy defibrillation is required [1]. Nevertheless, a patient with VT demands the low-energy cardio-version instead. However, if a normal sinus rhythm or VT is misinterpreted as VF, the patient will suffer an unnecessary shock that may damage the heart. Conversely, if VF is incorrectly interpreted as VT, the result is also life-threatening. Therefore, an effective detection method to distinguish VF from VT has clinical research significance [2].

Many VF detection methods have been proposed for ECG arrhythmia recognition in the literature, such as a sequential hypothesis testing algorithm [13], total least square-based prony modeling algorithm [16], correlation dimension method [6], Lyapunov exponent method [5], an approximate entropy and its improved

---

* Corresponding author.

D.-S. Huang et al. (Eds.): ICIC 2014, LNBI 8590, pp. 322–329, 2014.

approximate entropy method for automatic diagnosis of VF and VT [7,8], a modified sample entropy that measures the time series complexity [19], qualitative chaos analysis based on symbolic complexity [17,18], the method based on Lempel-Ziv (L-Z) computation complexity measure [9].

Zhang et al. [9] proposed a complexity-based method for VF and VT detection. However, this method appeared to some limitations [13]. It could achieve a satisfactory result only when the sample length was not very short. With the decreasing of the sample length, it was very hard to distinguish VT from VF.

Empirical mode decomposition (EMD) was first proposed in 1998. With well defined instantaneous frequency, a finite set of band-limited signals that is termed intrinsic mode functions (IMFs) are decomposed from original signal. It's a new technique to analysis nonlinear and non-stationary signals.

In this paper, we presented a novel method for detection and recognition of ECG using the LZ complexity and EMD. The method demonstrated a high accuracy rate in the classification of VF and VT. Furthermore, the proposed method suited short data length and noisy recording in physiological signals.

2   Detection of VF and VT Using the LZ Complexity and IMFs

2.1   Data Selection

We selected ECG signal files from MIT-BIH Malignant Ventricular Ectopy Database (MIT-BIH Database) and Creighton University Ventricular Tachyarrhythmia Database (CU Database). In CU Database, it contains a total of 35 single-channel records; we selected 100 episodes of VF from it. Similarly, 100 episodes of VT were taken from MIT-BIH Database. The four-second times of the data is selected. The frequency of all these signals is 250 Hz, resolution of 12 bit. We gave it a normalized before used these samples.

2.2   LZ Complexity

The LZ complexity algorithm was first proposed by Lempel and Ziv [3]. It has been widely applied in the biomedical signals including detects VF and VT, study the brain function and brain information transmission [4].

The detailed algorithm for the signal X (t) can be summarized as follows: [11]

(1) Given a discrete-time signal X of N samples ($X = x_1, x_2 \ldots x_N$), converted the original x_m ($m=1\sim N$) into a sequence of symbols $P = u(1), u(2), \ldots, u(n)$, in which each $u(i)$ is a character of a finite alphabet $a=0,1$. (n represents the length of the sample).

(2) Let S and Q denote two subsequences of the sequence P and SQ be the concatenation of S and Q, while sequence $SQ\pi$ is derived from SQ after its last character is deleted (π respects the operation to delete the last character in the sequence).

(3) W ($SQ\pi$) as the vocabulary of the sequence $SQ\pi$ that is formed by all its substrings.

(4) At the beginning, $c(n)$(the complexity counter)=1, $S = u(1), Q = u(2)$, $SQ = u(1)$, $u(2)$, and then $SQ\pi = u(1)$.

(5) In general, suppose that $S = u$ (1), u (2) . . ., u(r), $Q= u(r+1)$ and therefore, $SQ\pi$ = $u(1)$, $u(2)$, . . ., $u(r)$. If $Q \in w$ $(SQ\pi)$, then Q is a subsequence of $SQ\pi$, not a new sequence.

(6) The value of S is fixed and renew Q to be $u(r+1)$, $u(r+2)$, then judge if Q belongs to w $(SQ\pi)$ or not.

(7) Repeat the previous steps until Q does not belong to w $(SQ\pi)$. Now $Q= u(r+1)$, $u(r+2)$...., $u(r + i)$ is not a subsequence of $SQ\pi = u$ (1), u (2) . . ., $u(r + i-1)$, the counter c (n) is increased by one.

(8) Thereafter, S and Q are combined and renewed to be u (1), u (2) . . ., $u(r + i)$, and $u(r+i+1)$, respectively.

(9) Repeat the previous steps until Q is the last character. At this time, the number of different substrings is defined as c (n), c (n) is usually between zero and one [15].

2.3   Empirical Mode Decomposition (EMD)

The EMD [5, 12] can separate a segment of ECG signal x (t) into n IMFs: $E1$ (t), $E2$ (t)..., En (t) and a residue signal r. Only when each IMF satisfies two basic conditions, the signal x (t) can be reconstructed as a linear combination:

$$x(t) = \sum_{j=1}^{N} En(t) + r \tag{1}$$

Given an input signal x (t), r (t) $=x$ (t), $j=0$.

(1) Set g $(t) = x$ (t).

(2) Get the maxima and minima of the g (t).

(3) Generate the upper and lower envelopes $e_u(t)$ and $e_l(t)$, respectively by connecting the maxima and minima separately with cubic spline interpolation.

(4) The local mean m (t) is defined:

$$m(t) = (e_u(t) + e_l(t))/2 \tag{2}$$

(5) The m (t) value is subtracted from the original signal g (t), i.e., redefine g (t) as:

$$g(t) = g(t) - m(t) \tag{3}$$

(6) Decide whether g (t) is an IMF or not according to the two basic conditions as described in the above.

(7) Repeat steps (2)–(6).   When an IMF g (t) is obtained, jump to the next step.

(8) Define $E1$ $(t) = g$ (t) when the first IMF is got. $E1$ (t) is the smallest temporal scale in x (t). To find the rest of the IMF components, define the residue signal $r1$ (t) as: $r1$ $(t) = x$ (t) $-E1$ (t).

(9) Set g (t) $=r1$ (t). Repeat the previous steps and can get $E2$ (t), $E3$ (t)....En (t).

2.4   The Algorithm Based on LZ Complexity and EMD

EMD is a nonlinear and non-stationary signal processing technique. It can represent any temporal signal into a finite set of amplitude and frequency modulated (AM-FM) oscillating components [14].

Our proposed algorithm is defined as follows:

(1) Given a discrete-time signal X, $X = (X_1, X_2, \ldots\ldots, X_N)$, where N represents the samples of X. Define $X_M = \{ x_{(N-1)*m+1}, \ x_{(N-1)*m+2} \cdots\cdots x_{(N-1)*m+m} \}$ ($M=1\sim N$), where m represents the length of each sample.

(2) According to the following formula, make these samples be normalized.

$$X'_M = (X_M - \bar{x})/\sigma, \tag{4}$$

Where $\bar{x}$ and σ represent the mean and the standard deviation of the sample X_M.

(3) Repeat steps (2) until all samples are normalized. Calculate the complexity of VT and VF using those samples first, and then get the accuracy for detection of VT and VF according to the assessment formula of the algorithm performance.

(4) Get IMFs of ECG signals. EMD technique is applied to decompose ECG signals into five IMFs.

(5) For the first IMF of VT and VF, calculate the complexity of them and get the accuracy for detection. Repeat this step until the other IMFs are calculated.

3   Classification Performance on VF and VT

A sample of ECG epochs from MIT-BIH Database and CU Database are plotted in Fig.1. And the first IMF1–IMF5 of it showed in Fig.3. It's found the waveform of the first IMF of VT and VF is not uniform. This is exactly consistent with the theoretical.

When the LZ complexity analysis was performed, calculate the values of each episode with the method described previously. The results calculated from an episode of VF and an episode of VT is presented in Fig.2. Based on the assessment formula, we can draw that the classification results for 63.10% of accuracy from Fig.2. As we know, the clinical signals are very complex, so the results are not good.

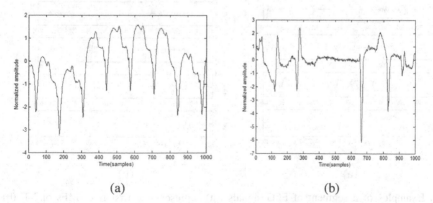

(a)   (b)

Fig. 1. Examples of ECG signal epochs: (a) VF time domain signal and (b) VT time domain signal

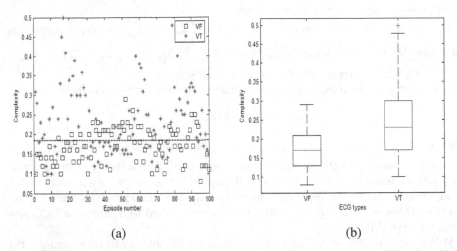

(a)   (b)

Fig. 2. (a)The complexity was calculated for different VT and VF episodes. The dotted horizontal line is the threshold. (b) The box-plot of the complexity of VT and VF from ECG data.

After EMD, the complexity of each IMF is computed. From the result, the first IMF1 accuracy for detection of VT and VF can reach 93.56%. The effect of the first IMF5 detection is shown in Fig.4. For the IMF1–IMF5, the performances on classification of VF and VT patterns are shown in Tables 1. The classification results using the LZ complexity-EMD algorithm methods can reach an accuracy of 97.08%, respectively.

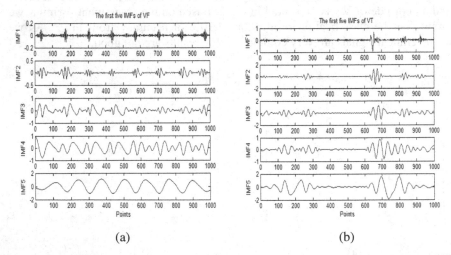

(a)   (b)

Fig. 3. Examples of a segment of ECG signals: (a) represent the first five IMFs of VF (b) represent the first five IMFs of VT

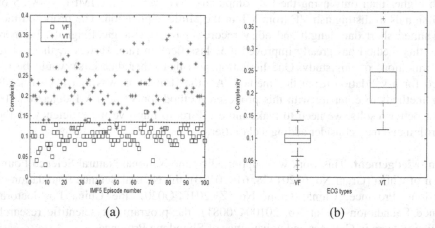

(a)   (b)

Fig. 4. (a) The complexity was calculated after EMD for different VT and VF episodes. The dotted horizontal line is the threshold (b) the box-plot of the complexity of VT and VF after EMD.

From Tables 1, it can be found the accuracy of each IMF for distinguish of VT from VF is higher than only using the LZ complexity. According to the relevant literature, the frequency of VF and VT is not the same. After EMD, ECG signal is decomposed into different frequency IMF. The same IMF of VT and VF are used as a feature in order to discriminate between VF and VT. So the results are good than only using the LZ complexity. The proposed method has greatly improved the effect of the classification. In the clinic application, we can use the IMF1 and IMF5 to distinguish VF from VT.

Table 1. The classification of VF and VT using EMD and complexity analysis

Method	Component	VF		VT		Accuracy (%)
		Sensitivity (%)	Specificity (%)	Sensitivity (%)	Specificity (%)	
Complexity		64.11	62.09	62.09	64.11	63.10
Complexity and EMD	IMF1	87.12	100.00	100.00	87.12	93.56
	IMF2	82.04	68.16	68.16	82.04	75.10
	IMF3	77.21	73.18	73.18	77.21	75.20
	IMF4	88.13	90.28	90.28	88.13	89.21
	IMF5	98.15	96.01	96.01	98.15	97.08

4   Discussion and Conclusions

In this paper, a method of VF and VT detection based on the LZ complexity and EMD was proposed. We used the complexity of each IMF as a feature to discriminate between VF and VT. The accuracy of each IMF in distinguishing of VT from VF is much higher than only using the LZ complexity. We can use the IMF1 or IMF5 of ECG signals to distinguish VF from VT in the clinic application. The proposed method suited short data length and noisy recording in physiological signals. Furthermore, this method has greatly improved the classification rate. However, there were two limitations of this study. One limitation was that other dataset(s) would be required for a validation using this method. Another limitation was that it also needs other methods to compare with this proposed method for VF and VT detection. To obtain better results, we need to make more efforts to improve the efficiency of the algorithm and may consider adding a classifier.

Acknowledgement. This work was supported by the National Natural Science Foundation of China (Grant No. 61201428, 61070130), the Natural Science Foundation of Shandong Province, China (Grant No. ZR2010FQ020), the China Postdoctoral Science Foundation (Grant No. 20100470081), the program for scientific research innovation team in Colleges and universities of Shandong Province.

References

1. Othman, M.A., Safri, N.M., Ghani, I.A., et al.: A New Semantic Mining Approach for Detecting Ventricular Tachycardia and Ventricular Fibrillation. Biomedical Signal Processing and Control 8, 222–227 (2013)
2. Kong, D.-R., Xie, H.-B.: Use of Modified Sample Entropy Measurement to Classify Ventricular Tachycardia and Fibrillation. Measurement 44, 653–662 (2011)
3. Lempel, A., Ziv, J.: On The Complexity of Finite Sequences. IEEE Trans. Inform. Theory 22, 75–81 (1976)
4. Kolmogorov, A.N.: Three Approaches to The Quantitative Definition of Information. Inform. Trans. 1, 3–11 (1965)
5. Owis, M.I., Abou-Zied, A.H., Youssef, A.B.M., Kadah, Y.M.: Study of Features Based on Nonlinear Dynamical Modeling In ECG Arrhythmia Detection and Classification. IEEE Trans. Biomed. Eng. 49, 733–736 (2002)
6. Small, M., Yu, D., Simonotto, J., Harrison, R.G., Grubb, N., Fox, K.A.A.: Uncovering Non-Linear Structure in Human ECG Recordings. Chaos Solitons Fract. 13, 1755–1762 (2002)
7. Pincus, S.M.: Approximate Entropy As A Measure of System Complexity. Proc. Natl. Acad. Sci. USA 88, 2297–2301 (1991)
8. Xie, H.B., Gao, Z.M., Liu, H.: Classification of Ventricular Tachycardia and Fibrillation Using Fuzzy Similarity-Based Approximate Entropy. Expert Systems with Applications 38, 3973–3981 (2011)
9. Zhang, X.S., Zhu, Y.S., Thakor, N.V., Wang, Z.Z.: Detecting Ventricular Tachycardia and Fibrillation by Complexity Measure. IEEE Trans. Biomed. Eng. 46(5), 548–555 (1999)
10. Leonardo, S., Abel, T., JosÉ, A.F., Josep, M., Raimon, J.: Index for Estimation of Muscle Force From Mechanomyography Based on the Lempel-Ziv Algorithm. Journal of Electromyography and Kinesiology 23, 548–557 (2013)
11. G´Omeza, C., Hornero, R., Ab´Asolo, D., Fern´Andez, A., L´Opez, M.: Complexity Analysis of the Magnetoencephalogram Background Activity in Alzheimer's Disease Patients. Medical Engineering & Physics 28, 851–859 (2006)

12. Pachori, R.B., et al.: Analysis of Normal and Epileptic Seizure EEG Signals Using Empirical Mode Decomposition. Computer Methods and Programs in Biomedicine 104, 373–381 (2011)
13. Thakor, N.V., Zhu, Y.S., Pan, K.Y.: Ventricular Tachycardia and Fibrillation Detection by A Sequential Hypothesis Testing Algorithm. IEEE Trans. Biomed. Eng. 37, 837–843 (1990)
14. Li, S.F., Zhou, W.D., Yuan, Q., Geng, S.J., Cai, D.M.: Feature Extraction and Recognition of Ictal EEG Using EMD and SVM. Computers in Biology and Medicine 43, 807–816 (2013)
15. Zhang, H.X., Zhu, Y.S., Wang, Z.M.: Complexity Measure and Complexity Rate Information Based Detection of Ventricular Tachycardia and Fibrillation. Medical & Biological Engineering &Computing 38, 553–557 (2000)
16. Chen, S.W.: A Two-Stage Discrimination of Cardiac Arrhythmias Using a Total Least Squares-Based Prony Modeling Algorithm. IEEE Trans. Biomed. Eng. 47, 1317–1327 (2000)
17. Zhang, H.X., Zhu, Y.S.: Qualitative Chaos Analysis for Ventricular Tachycardia and Fibrillation Based on Symbolic Complexity. Med. Eng. Phys. 23, 523–528 (2001)
18. Zhang, H.X., Zhu, Y.S., Xu, Y.H.: Complexity Information Based Analysis of Pathological ECG Rhythm for Ventricular Tachycardia and Ventricular Fibrillation. Int. J. Bifurcat. Chaos 12(10), 2293–2303 (2002)
19. Kong, D.R., Xie, H.B.: Use of Modified Sample Entropy Measurement to Classify Ventricular Tachycardia and Fibrillation. Measurement 44, 653–662 (2011)

Prediction of Protein Structure Classes with Ensemble Classifiers

Wenzheng Bao, Yuehui Chen[*], Dong Wang, Fanliang kong, and Gaoqiang Yu

School of Information Science and Engineering,
University of Jinan, Jinan, P.R. China
yhchen@ujn.edu.cn, baowz55555@126.com

Abstract. Protein structure prediction is an important area of research in bioinformatics. In this research, a novel method to predict the structure of the protein is introduced. The amino acid frequencies, generalization dipeptide composition and typical hydrophobic composition of protein structure are treated as candidate feature. Flexible neural tree and neural network are employed as classification model. To evaluate the efficiency of the proposed method, a classical protein sequence dataset (1189) is selected as the test dataset. The results show that the method is efficient for protein structure prediction.

Keywords: protein structure prediction, flexible neural tree, neural network.

1   Introduction

The structural classes are one of most important attributes of protein, which plays a significant role in both experimental and theoretical researches in Proteomics. On one hand, the data of protein sequence database has been growing so fast that corresponding research hardly catch up with the pace of it. On the other hand, the traditional methods can't meet the needs of users[1].

The concept of protein structural classes has been proposed by Levitt and Chothia ,which are divided proteins into four structural classes: *all-α*, *all-β*, *α+β* and *α/β* in 1976[2]. The definition by *K C Chou* is showed in Table 1.

Table 1. The definition of 4 categories of protein structural

	helical structure	folding structure	anti-parallel folding structure	parallel folding structure
all-α	≥40%	≤5%		
all-β	≤5%	≥40%		
α+β	≥15%	≥15%	≥60%	≤15%
α/β	≥15%	≥15%	≤15%	≥60%

---

[*] Corresponding author.

D.-S. Huang et al. (Eds.): ICIC 2014, LNBI 8590, pp. 330–338, 2014.

There are a variety of methods to prediction the structure of protein. These methods are put into 3 categories: classic prediction methods, experimental methods and machine learning methods. The classical prediction methods mainly include homology modeling[4], fold recognition[5-7] and *ab initio* prediction[8]. The experimental methods gradually became popular, since 1960. There are two kinds of experimental methods: the NMR and X-ray crystallography[9]. Nowadays, with the development of machine learning, the machine learning methods play an important role in protein structure prediction. A variety of machine learning algorithms, such as Support Vector Machine(*SVM*)[10], Hidden Markov Model(*HMM*)[11], Neural Network(*NN*)[12-13] and Naive Bayesian classification[14] are widely used in protein structure prediction.

2   Dataset

To validate our proposed classify mode, a classical datasets: 1189 dataset is selected[15]. 1189 dataset contains 1092 protein domains, including 223 *all-α* class, 294 *all-β* class, 241 *α+β* class and 334 *α/β* class. The sequence homology of this dataset is below 40%. It was found through long-term that the performance of classification is strongly affected by sequence homology of dataset. In this method, the results of classification will be more objective to value the validity of proposed result. The Fig.1 shows the four structural classes in the SCOP.

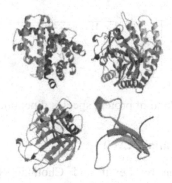

Fig. 1. Four kinds of protein structure in SCOP

3   Feature Selection

3.1   Amino Acid Frequency

Amino Acid Frequency (*AAF*) is based on statistical property to analysis of protein tertiary structure[16]. The feature include a protein as 20 elements of the vector, in which each element represents the corresponding frequency of amino acids. The feature vector of protein P can be represented by Eq.1.

$$P = [f_1, f_2, \cdots, f_{20}] \tag{1}$$

The N is the length of a protein .The f_i is the corresponding amino acid residues. Eq.2 stands for AAF a protein.

$$f_u = \frac{\sum_{i=1}^{N} p_i}{N} \qquad p_i = \begin{cases} 1, if & p_i = A(u) \\ 0, if & p_i \neq A(u) \end{cases} \tag{2}$$

For one thing, the feature of *AAF* has the ability to represent the amino acid type influence on protein structure. For another thing, *AAF* has a large number of information about protein structure.

3.2   Generalized Dipeptide Composition(GDC)

Amino acid composition information reflects the frequency of the amino acids in proteins, without considering the amino acid sequence information. *Idicula Thomas* and *Chou*[18] pointed out amino acids and amino acid sequence information is one of most important in large number of protein features. A protein sequence can be expressed as a 400-dimensional vector. Eq.4 show the amino acid composition.

$$X_k^\xi = \begin{bmatrix} x_k^1 \\ x_k^2 \\ \vdots \\ x_k^{400} \end{bmatrix} \quad \begin{array}{l} \xi = 1, 2, \cdots, 400 \\ k = 1, 2, \cdots, m \\ \sum_{\xi=1}^{400} x_k^\xi = 1 \end{array} \tag{3}$$

X_k^ξ is the frequency of the ξ kind of protein species dipeptide in the k protein.

3.3   Amino Acid Composition(AAC)

According to the definition by Levitt and Chothia[19], there are some major differences between the structure of helix and folding, which is amino acid molecules arrangement, in different structures of the protein sequence.

In this research, the amino acid side chains and water lead to the special composition of a protein sequences. According to *Lim's* research, 6 kinds of hydrophobic compositions(including (*i, i+2*), (*i, i+3*), (*i, i+2, i+4*), (*i, i+5*), (*i, i+3, i+4*), (*i, i+1, i+4*)) frequently exist in the protein. Based on the theory of *Rose's*[19], there are 7 categories of hydrophobic amino acid composition meet the requirements. The 7 categories of hydrophobic patterns show in Table 2.

Table 2. 7 categories of hydrophobic amino acid patterns

No.	Motifs	Occurrence in β	Occurrence in α
1	hhpphh	under represented and not frequent	over represented and frequent
2	pphhpp	under represented and not frequent	over represented and frequent
3	hhpp	under represented and not frequent	over represented and very frequent
4	pphh	under represented and not frequent	over represented and very frequent
5	hphp	over represented and frequent	under represented and not frequent
6	phph	over represented and frequent	under represented and not frequent
7	pphhh	over represented and very frequent	under represented and not frequent

4   Methods

4.1   Flexible Neural Tree

A function instruction set T and set F are used to generate a *FNT* model, which is described as $S = F \cup T = \{+_2, +_3, \cdots, +_N\} \cup \{x_1, \cdots, x_n\}$, where $+_i (i = 1, 2, \cdots, n)$ denote non-leaf nodes' instructions and taking i arguments, $x_1, x_2, \cdots, x_n$. The structure of a non-leaf node is showed as Fig. 2 and structure of a FNT is showed in Fig. 3.

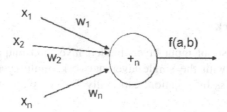

Fig. 2. Non-leaf node of flexible neural tree with a terminal instruction set $T = \{x_1, x_2, \ldots, x_n\}$

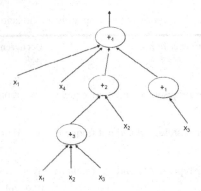

Fig. 3. Typical representation of FNT with function instruction set $\{+_1,+_2,+_3,+_4\}$ and terminal set $\{x_1,x_2,x_3,x_4\}$, which has four layers

Based on the defined function instruction set and terminal instruction set, the evolution process of *FNT* is recursively[21]. The general learning process of construct the *FNT* model can be described as follows:

STEP1 Randomly create an initial FNT population and its corresponding parameters.

STEP2 Find the proper tree structure with PI PE algorithm. In this step, considering the effect of parameters on the structure selection, before select the better structures of population we use PSO to simply optimize the parameters of every tree in population . This way, we can reduce the impaction of parameters on better structure select.

STEP3 If a proper structure is found, then go to STEP4, otherwise go to STEP2.

STEP4 Parameter optimization is achieved by the PSO. In this step architecture of FNT model is fixed.

STEP5 If no better parameter vector is found for a long time or the Specific maximum number of local search is reached, then go to STEP6, otherwise go to STEP4.

STEP6 If satisfactory solution is found, then the algorithm is stopped, otherwise go to STEP2.

4.2   Neural Network

Neural network consists of input layer, hidden layer and output layer. Experiments show that compared with the single-layer network, multilayer neural network has better ability to process information, especially for complex information processing ability.

The $\omega_{ih}^{(1)}$ is input layer of the *No.i* hidden layer neurons and the first h the weights of connections between neurons. The $\omega_{hj}^{(2)}$ is the first *h* hidden layer neurons connected to the output layer first *j* neuron weights. Eq.5 is the result of *No.h* neuron in the hidden layer.

$$M_h = f(\sum_{i=1}^{n} \omega_{ih}^{(1)} x_i - \theta_h^{(1)})$$

$$h = 1, 2, \cdots, k$$

(4)

Eq.6 is the result of No.*j* neuron in the output layer.

$$y_j = f(\sum_{h=1}^{k} \omega_{hj}^{(1)} M_h - \theta_j^{(1)})$$

$$j = 1, 2, \cdots, m$$

(5)

5   Classification Model

Based on four binary *NN* and *FNT* ensemble classification models are constructed a novel classification mode. So, *No.1* classification model ,the feature of the generalized dipeptide composition feature and *FNT* model are treated as classifier. *No.2* classification model, the feature of *AAF*, *AAC* and Hydrophobic Amino Acid Combination feature and *NN* model is employed. *No.3* classification model, the feature of generalized dipeptide composition feature and *NN* model are used. *No.4* classification ,the feature of *AAF*, *AAC*, Generalized Dipeptide Composition and Hydrophobic and *FNT* model are adopted.

The results of each classifier output using hamming distance. Calculating the minimum output to achieve the Hamming distances of the classification. Some cases have more than one category code equals the distance and the minimum distance, at this time will be different weighting the output of the classifier. Finally, the samples of unknown categories based on the specific situation for special treatment. The code of 4 classifiers show in Table 3.

Table 3. The coding of each classifiers

	No.1 classifier	No.2 classifier	No.3 classifier	No.4 classifier
all-α	*1*	*0*	*0*	*0*
all-β	*0*	*1*	*0*	*0*
α+β	*0*	*0*	*1*	*0*
α/β	*0*	*0*	*0*	*1*

6   Result and Analysis

In this research, we found that the parameter of each classifiers meet the requirement of Table 4 and Table 5, the accuracy of prediction of protein structure classes will reach the maximum. Curve according to the fitness of four classifiers is shown in Figure 4.

Table 4. The information of each classifiers

Classifier	Classification model	Feature	Input number	Training generation	Hidden layer notes of NN
No.1	NN	AAF+ GDC	420	1200	15
No.2	FNT	GDC	400	1000	NA
No.3	NN	GDC	400	1000	7
No.4	FNT	AAF+ AAC+ GDC	430	1400	NA

Table 5. The parameter of PSO algorithm

V_max	Position_max	Particles number	C1	C2
2	0.02	60	2	2

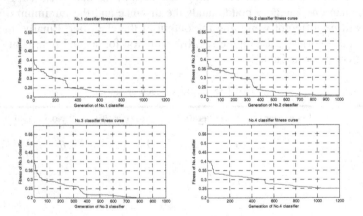

Fig. 4. The four categories of fitness function curve

Table 6. Comparison of accuracies between different methods(1189 dataset)

Algorithm	all-α(%)	all-β(%)	α+β(%)	α/β(%)	overall(%)
Logistic regression[19]	57.0	62.9	25.3	64.6	53.9
Stacking C ensemble[19]	NA	NA	NA	NA	58.9
PseAAC[20]	48.9	59.5	26.6	81.7	56.9
SVM+AA composition[21]	NA	NA	NA	NA	57.8
RQA & PCC[22]	63.0	77.5	24	88.5	63.6
This paper	65.32	80.23	45.2	86.12	65.2

7   Conclusion

In this paper, the hybrid feature extracted by *AAC*, *GDC*, *AA* Composition and Hydrophobic Amino Acid Combination were used to present a protein sequence. The 1189 databset protein sequences were used for conducting all the experiments. Compared with other traditional methods, the method will largely improve the classification accuracy. However, the model exists some drawbacks. Firstly, the number of feature is so large that waste a great many of storage space. Secondly, the NN model hardly explain the principle of biology. Thirdly, the feature is mostly based on the statistical feature. Since the experiment was not considered homologous extracted information, so that the information of dataset 1189 is enough. Therefore, in future work should focus on considering the information extracted protein homology.

Acknowledgments. This research was partially supported by the Natural Science Foundation of China (61070130) and National Natural Science Foundation Youth Project(61302128), the Key Project of Natural Science Foundation of Shandong Province (ZR2011FZ001), National Natural Science Foundation of China (61201428, 61070130) ,the Natural Science Foundation of Shandong Province (ZR2011FL022) and the Key Subject Research Foundation of Shandong Province and the Shandong Provincial Key Laboratory of Network Based Intelligent Computing.

References

1. Levitt, M., Chothia, C.: Structural patterns in globular proteins. Nature 261, 552–558 (1976)
2. Chou, K.C.: A novel approach to predicting protein structural classes in a (20-1)-D amino acid composition space. Proteins 21, 319–344 (1995)
3. Xu Y&Xu, D.: Protein threading using PROSPECT: Design and evaluation. Proteins: Structure, Function, and Genetics 40, 343–354 (2000)
4. Chothia, C., Lesk, A.M.: The relation between the divergence of sequence and structure in proteins. EMBO J. 5, 823–826 (1986)
5. Chothia, C., Lesk, A.M.: The relation between the divergence of sequence and structure in proteins. EMBO J. 5(4), 823–826 (1986)
6. Chung, S.Y., Subbiah, S.: A structural explanation for the twilight zone of protein sequence homology. Structure 4, 1123–1127 (1996)
7. Kaczanowski, S., Zielenkiewicz, P.: Why similar protein sequences encode similar three-dimensional structures. Theoretical Chemistry Accounts 125, 543–550 (2010)
8. Bairoch, A., Apweiler, R., Wu, C.H., et al.: The Universal Protein Resource (UniProt). Nucleic Acids Res. 33(Database Issue), D154–D159 (2005)
9. Helliwell, J.R.: Protein crystal perfection and its application. Acta Crystallographica D61(pt. 6): 793–798 (2005)
10. Nassif, H., Al-Ali, H., Khuri, S., Keirouz, W.: Prediction of protein-glucose binding sites using support vector machines. Proteins 77(1), 121–132 (2009)
11. Söding, J.: Protein homology detection by HMM-HMM comparison. Bioinformatics 21(7), 951–960 (2005)
12. Wang, Y., Wu, L.Y., Zhang, X.S., Chen, L.: Automatic classification of protein structures based on convex hull representation by integrated neural network. In: Cai, J.-Y., Cooper, S.B., Li, A. (eds.) TAMC 2006. LNCS, vol. 3959, pp. 505–514. Springer, Heidelberg (2006)
13. Zhang, X.S., Zhan, Z.W., Wang, Y., Wu, L.Y.: An Attempt to Explore the Similarity of Two Proteins by Their Surface Shapes. In: Operations Research and Its Applications. Lecture Notes in Operations Research, vol. 5, pp. 276–284. World Publishing Corporation, Beijing (2005)
14. Kohonen, J., Talikota, S., Corander, J., Auvinen, P., Arjas, E.: A Naive Bayes classifier for protein function prediction. Silico. Biol. 9(1-2), 23–34 (2009)
15. Wang, Z.-X., Yuan, Z.: How good is the prediction of protein structural class by the component-coupled method? Proteins 38, 165–175 (2000)
16. Zhang, C.T., Chou, K.C.: An optimization approach to predicting protein structural class from amino-acid composition. Protein Science 1, 401–408 (1992)
17. Zhang, C.T., Chou, K.C., Maggiora, G.M.: Predicting protein structural classes from amino acid composition: application of fuzzy clustering. Protein Engineering 8, 425–435 (1995)
18. Kedarisetti, K., Kurgan, L., Dick, S.: A comment on Prediction of protein structural classes by a new measure of information discrepancy (2006) (accepted)
19. Kedarisetti, K.D., Kurgan, L., Dick, S.: Classifier ensembles for protein structural class prediction with varying homology. Biochemical and Biophysical Research Communications 348, 981–988 (2006)
20. Liu, T., Jia, C.: A high-accuracy protein structural class prediction algorithm using predicted secondary structural information. J. Theor. Biol. 267, 272–275 (2010)
21. Shao, G., Chen, Y.: Predict the Tertiary Structure of Protein with Flexible Neural Tree. In: Huang, D.-S., Ma, J., Jo, K.-H., Gromiha, M.M. (eds.) ICIC 2012. LNCS, vol. 7390, pp. 324–331. Springer, Heidelberg (2012)

A Parameterized Algorithm for Predicting Transcription Factor Binding Sites

Yinglei Song[1], Changbao Wang[1], and Junfeng Qu[2]

[1] School of Computer Science and Engineering, Jiangsu University of Science and Technology,
Zhenjiang, Jiangsu 212003, China
syinglei2013@163.com, wangchangbao@126.com
[2] Department of Information Technology, Clayton State University, Morrow, GA 30260, USA
jqu@clayton.edu

Abstract. In this paper, we study the Transcription Factor Binding Sites (TFBS) prediction problem in bioinformatics. We develop a novel parameterized approach that can efficiently explore the space of all possible locations of TFBSs in a set of homologous sequences with high accuracy. The exploration is performed by an ensemble of a few Hidden Markov Models (HMM), where the size of the ensemble is the parameter of the algorithm. The ensemble is initially constructed through the local alignments between two sequences that have the lowest similarity value in the sequence set, the parameters of each HMM in the ensemble are revised when the remaining sequences in the set are scanned through by it one by one. A list of possible TFBSs are generated when all sequences in the set have been processed by the ensemble. Testing results showed that this approach can accurately handle the cases where a single sequence may contain multiple binding sites and thus has advantages over most of the existing approaches when a sequence may contain multiple binding sites.

Keywords: parameterized algorithm, Hidden Markov Model (HMM), Transcription factor binding site, dynamic programming.

1   Introduction

Transcription Factor Binding Sites (TFBS) are subsequences found in the upstream region of genes in DNA genomes. A transcription factor, which is a specialized protein molecule, may bind to the nucleotides in the subsequences and thus may affect some relevant biological processes. Research in molecular biology has revealed that transcription factor binding sites are important for many biological processes, including gene expression and regulation. An accurate identification of TFBSs is thus important for understanding the biological mechanism of gene expression and regulation. Classical experimental methods are time consuming and expensive [6,7]. Recently, a few new experimental methods such as ChIP-chip and ChIP-seq have been developed for TFBS identification [17]. Although the throughput of these methods is high, processing the large amount of complex data generated by

D.-S. Huang et al. (Eds.): ICIC 2014, LNBI 8590, pp. 339–350, 2014.
© Springer International Publishing Switzerland 2014

these methods remains a challenging task [17]. Computational methods that can accurately and efficiently identify TFBSs from homologous sequences are thus still convenient and important alternative approaches to rapid identification of TFBSs.

Since TFBSs for the same transcription factor have similar sequence content in homologous sequences, the most often used computational approaches make the prediction by analyzing a set of homologous sequences and identifying subsequences that are similar in content. The locations of a TFBS may vary in different homologous sequences. To determine the location of a TFBS in each sequence, we need to evaluate all possible starting locations among all sequences to find the optimal solution. The total number of combinations of subsequences that need to be examined is exponential and exhaustively enumerating all of them is obviously impractical when the number or the lengths of the sequences are large. To avoid exhaustive search, a large number of heuristics have been developed to reduce the size of the search space, such as Gibbs sampling based approaches AlignACE [19], BioProspector [16], Gibbs Motif sampler [15], expectation maximization based models [1, 2], greedy approaches such as Consensus [8], and genetic algorithm based approaches such as FMGA [14] and MDGA [4].

Of all these approaches and software tools, Gibbs Motif sampler is a tool based on a stochastic approach. It computes the binding site locations by Gibbs sampling [15, 16, 19]. Consensus uses a greedy algorithm to align functionally related sequences and applies the algorithm to identify the binding sites for the E. coli CRP protein [8]. MEME+ [2] uses Expectation Maximization technique to fit a two component mixture model and the model is then used to find TFBSs. MEME+ achieves higher accuracy than its earlier version MEME [1]. However, the prediction accuracy is still not satisfactory.

Genetic algorithm (GA) simulates the Darwin evolutionary process to find an approximate optimal solution for an optimization problem. GA based approaches have been successfully used to solve the TFBS predicting problem, such as FMGA [14] and MDGA [4]. FMGA was declared to have better performance than Gibbs Motif Sampler [15] in terms of both prediction accuracy and computation efficiency. MDGA [4] is another program that uses genetic algorithms to predict TFBSs in homologous sequences. During the evolutionary process, MDGA uses information content to evaluate each individual in the population. MDGA is able to achieve higher prediction accuracy than Gibbs sampling based approaches while using a less amount of computation time.

So far, most of the existing approaches use heuristics to reduce the size of the search space. However, heuristics employed by these approaches may also adversely affect the prediction accuracy. For example, GA based prediction tools cannot guarantee the prediction results are the same for different runs of the program. A well defined strategy that can be used to efficiently explore the search space and can generate deterministic and highly accurate prediction results is thus necessary to further improve the performance of prediction tools.

Recent work has shown that an ensemble of HMMs can be effectively used to improve the accuracy of protein sequence alignment [21]. In this paper, we develop a new parameterized algorithm that can predict the locations of TFBSs with an ensemble of Hidden Markov Models (HMMs), where the size of the ensemble is the parameter. The approach uses an ensemble of profile HMMs to generate a list of positions that are likely to be the starting positions of the TFBSs. As the first step, we construct the ensemble from the local alignment of two sequences. The ensemble consists of HMMs that represent the local alignments with the most significant alignment scores. We then align each profile HMM in the ensemble to each sequence in the data set, the parameters of the HMMs are also changed to incorporate the new information from the new sequence. This procedure is repeated until all sequences in the dataset have been processed. As a parameter, the number of HMMs in the ensemble can be adjusted based on the needs of users. We have implemented this approach into a software tool EHMM and our experimental results show that the prediction accuracy of EHMM is higher than or comparable with that of the existing tools. Our testing results suggest that EHMM has the potential to provide some assistance to the ENCODE Project.

2   Algorithms and Methods

The method selects the two sequences that have the lowest similarity to initialize the ensemble. The similarity between each pair of sequences in the set is computed by globally aligning the two sequences. A local alignment of the selected sequences is then computed. The alignment results are then used to construct an ensemble that consists of k HMMs, where k is a positive integer. The algorithm selects the local alignments with the k largest alignment scores and each of such local alignments can be used to construct an HMM. An ensemble of k HMMs can thus be constructed based on the local alignments with k most significant alignment scores.

We then progressively use the HMMs to scan through each remaining sequence in the set. Each sequence segment in a sequence is aligned to each HMM in the ensemble and the alignments with the k most significant scores are selected to update

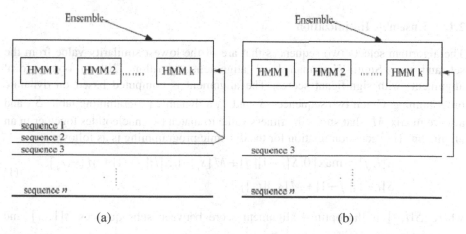

Fig. 1. (a) An ensemble is constructed from local alignments. (b) The ensemble is updated progressively.

the parameters of the HMM. This process will create up to k^2 HMMs, but only the alignments that have the k most significant alignment scores are selected to create a new ensemble of k HMMs. We repeat this procedure until all sequences in the set have been processed and the HMMs remained in the ensemble provide the candidate TFBS motifs. Figure 1 (a) shows the initialization of the ensemble and Figure 1 (b) illustrates how the ensemble is updated. Figure 2 shows the final stage of the approach, where the binding sites can be determined from the HMMs in the ensemble.

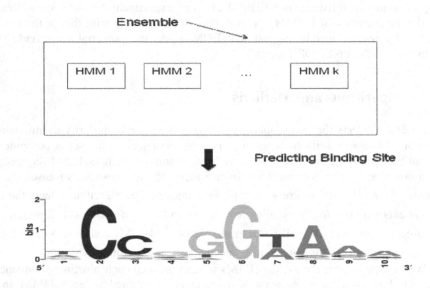

Fig. 2. Finally the binding sites can be inferred from the HMMs in the ensemble

2.1   Ensemble Initialization

The algorithm selects two sequences that are of the lowest similarity value from the set and uses Smith-Waterman local alignment algorithm [20] to obtain local alignments with significant scores. The alignment is computed based on dynamic programming. Given two sequences s and t, a dynamic programming table S, and a score matrix M that stores the fitness value to match two nucleotides together in an alignment. The recursion relation for the dynamic programming is as follows.

$$S[i, j] = \max\{0, S[i-1][j] + M[s_i, -], S[i][j-1] + M[-, t_j],$$
$$S[i-1][j-1] + M[s_i][t_j]\}$$
(1)

where $S[i, j]$ is the optimal alignment score between subsequences $s[1...i]$ and $t[1...j]$, s_i and t_j are the i th and j th nucleotides in s and t and '-' represents a possible gap that may appear in a local alignment.   After S is completely determined, the algorithm selects the alignments with the k largest alignment scores in S. An ensemble of k profile HMMs can then be constructed from these k alignments.

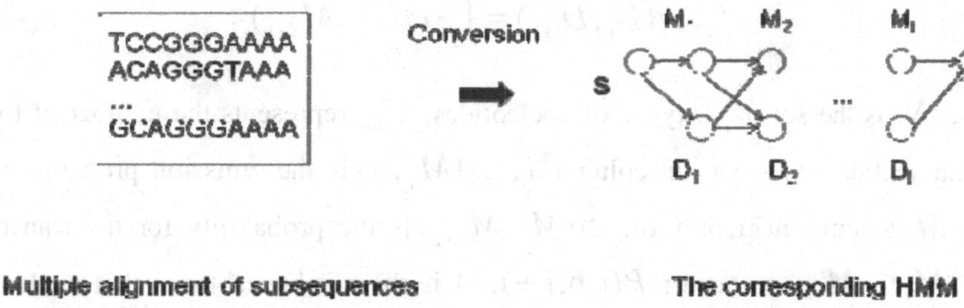

Fig. 3. A multiple alignment of subsequences can be converted into a profile HMM

Each column in an alignment contains a set of nucleotides and gaps that are aligned together. A profile HMM can be used to describe these columns. Specifically, a column i in the corresponding alignment can be modeled by two states, namely D_i and M_i, in a profile HMM. The deletion state D_i does not emit any nucleotide and is used to represent the gaps in column i; the matching state M_i emits a nucleotide and is used to describe the probabilities for each nucleotide to appear in column i. In addition, transitions in a profile HMM may occur only between states for columns consecutive in the corresponding alignment. The probabilities of emission and transition for each state can be computed from each alignment as well. Figure 3 shows that two sates can be created for each column in a multiple alignment of subsequences in the corresponding profile HMM and transitions may occur between the states for two consecutive columns. The parameters of a profile HMM can be computed as follows.

$$ep(M_i, a) = \frac{C_{ia}}{\sum_{b \in N} C_{ib}} \quad (2)$$

$$et(M_i, M_{i+1}) = \frac{\sum_{b \in N, c \in N} P(i,b,i+1,c)}{\sum_{b \in N, c \in N} P(i,b,i+1,c) + \sum_{b \in N} P(i,b,i+1,-)} \quad (3)$$

$$et(M_i, D_{i+1}) = 1 - et(M_i, M_{i+1}) \quad (4)$$

$$et(D_i, M_{i+1}) = \frac{\sum_{b \in N} P(i,-,i+1,b)}{\sum_{b \in N} P(i,-,i+1,b) + P(i,-,i+1,-)} \tag{5}$$

$$et(D_i, D_{i+1}) = 1 - et(D_i, M_{i+1}) \tag{6}$$

where N is the set of all types of nucleotides, C_{ia} represents the number of times that nucleotide a appears in column i, $et(M_i, a)$ is the emission probability for state M_i to emit nucleotide a. $et(M_i, M_{i+1})$ is the probability for the transition from M_i to M_{i+1} to occur; $P(i, b, i+1, c)$ is the number of times that nucleotide b appears in column i and nucleotide c appears in position $i+1$; $P(i, b, i+1, -)$ is the number of times that nucleotide b appears in column i and a gap appears in column $i+1$. $et(D_i, M_{i+1})$ is the probability for the transition from D_i to M_{i+1} to occur; $P(i, -, i+1, b)$ is the number of times that a gap appears in column i and nucleotide b appears in column $i+1$; $P(i, -, i+1, -)$ is the number of times that gaps appear in both columns i and $i+1$. More details of the algorithm can be found in [5].

2.2   Updating Ensemble

The remaining sequences in the set are processed based on the profile HMMs in the ensemble. For each of the remaining sequences, we evaluate the average similarity between it and the two sequences that have been selected to initialize the ensemble. The remaining sequences can thus be sorted based on an ascending order of this similarity value. This order is the execution order of the remaining sequences in the set.

Each of the remaining sequence is scanned through by each profile HMM in the execution order and subsequences that have the k most significant alignment scores are selected. The algorithm uses a window of certain size to slide through the sequence. The size of the window is set to be 1.5 times of the average lengths of all subsequences in the alignments used to construct the ensemble. The window moves by 1bp each time and each subsequence in the window is aligned to each HMM in the ensemble. The alignment can be computed with a dynamic programming algorithm. The recursion relation for the dynamic programming is as follows.

$$S[D_s, i, j] = \max\{et(D_s, D_{s+1})S[D_{s+1}, i, j], et(D_s, M_{s+1})S[M_{s+1}, i, j]\} \tag{7}$$

$$S[M_s, i, j] = \max\{et(M_s, D_s)ep(M_s, t_i)S[D_s, i+1, j],$$
$$et(M_s, M_{s+1})S[M_{s+1}, i+1, j]\} \tag{8}$$

where $0 \leq i \leq j \leq W$ are integers that indicate the location of subsequence t included in the window; $S[D_s, i, j]$ and $S[M_s, i, j]$ are the dynamic programming table cells that store the maximum probability for states D_i and M_i to generate the subsequence $t[i...j]$; t_i is the nucleotide at position i in t. More details of the algorithm can be found in [5].

The algorithm then selects k subsequences with the largest alignment scores. We thus obtain in total k^2 candidates for updating the HMMs in the ensemble. We pick k subsequences that correspond to the largest k alignment scores from the k^2 candidates. The parameters of each profile HMM are then updated based on these additional k subsequences. Specifically, the additional subsequence changes the counts that appear in (2), (3), (4), (5), and (6). The process is applied progressively to other remaining sequences in the set until each sequence in the set has been processed. The locations of the sequence segments used to construct each HMM in the ensemble are then output as the possible binding sites.

2.3   Computation Time

We assume the set contains m sequences, each sequence contains n nucleotides, and the binding site contains l nucleotides. The construction of the initial ensemble needs $O(m^2 n^2 + kn^2)$ time. The computation time needed to scan through a sequence with a single HMM is $O(l^2 n)$. The total amount of computation needed by the approach is thus $O(kml^2 n^2 + m^2 n^2 + kn^2)$.

3   Experimental Results

We have implemented this approach and integrated it into a software tool EHMM. We tested its accuracy on a biological dataset cyclic-AMP receptor protein (CRP). This dataset consists of 18 sequences, each of which consists of 105 bps [17]. Twenty three binding sites have been determined by using the DNA footprinting method, with a motif width of 22 [16].

Figure 4 compares the prediction accuracy of EHMM with three other computational methods: Gibbs Sampler [8], BioProspector [9], and MDGA [3]. The value of the parameter is set to be $k = 10$ in all the tests. It can be seen from the table that EHMM can achieve comparable accuracy with other tools in homologous sequences that contain a single binding site. However, sequences 1, 2, 6, 9, and 17 contain two TFBSs and all three other tools fail to recognize the second one. Table 1 shows the errors of the predicted locations of the second binding site in these sequences by EHMM. For most of them, EHMM can thus accurately identify the locations of both motifs. In particular, EHMM obtains excellent prediction results on sequence 17, where all three other methods fail to identify either of the two TFBSs. Our method is capable of identifying the locations of multiple binding sites since it uses an ensemble of HMMs to explore the alignment space of all subsequences, which significantly improves the sampling ability and the probability to accurately identify the locations of TFBSs.

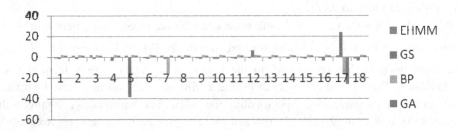

Fig. 4. The error of predicted locations of TFBSs by EHMM, GS(Gibbs Sampler), BP(BioProspector), GA(MDGA). The error is the deviation of the predicted starting positions from those obtained with fingerprint experiments.

In addition to the data set CRP, we also use EHMM ($k = 10$) and other tools to predict the binding sites for a few transcription factors including BATF [17], EGR1[9], FOXO1[3], and HSF1[18]. The prediction accuracy of a software tool is evaluated by computing its prediction accuracy on each single sequence in the set and taking the average of the prediction accuracy on all sequences in the set. The prediction accuracy on a single sequence is defined to be the percentage of correctly predicted part in the binding site. In other words, if we use B to denote the binding site and P to denote the predicted binding site, the accuracy of the prediction can be computed with

$$A = \frac{|P \cap B|}{|B|} \tag{9}$$

where $P \cap B$ denotes the intersection of P and B. For a set D of homologous sequences, the prediction accuracy of an approach on D is computed with

$$A_D = \frac{\sum_{s \in D} A_s}{|D|} \tag{10}$$

where s is a sequence in D and A_s is the prediction accuracy of the approach on s.

Figure 5 (a) shows and compares the prediction accuracy of EHMM, Gibbs Sampler, BioProspector, and MDGA on the four data sets. For each of the other three tools, we test its prediction accuracy for 100 times and use the average prediction accuracy for comparison. It is not difficult to see from the figure that EHMM achieves significantly higher prediction accuracy on data sets BATF, FOXO1, and HSF1 and achieves accuracy that is comparable with other tools on data set FOXO1.

Table 1. The errors of the locations of the second TFBS predicted by EHMM

Seq.#	1	2	6	9	17
Error	-1	-1	-1	1	-4

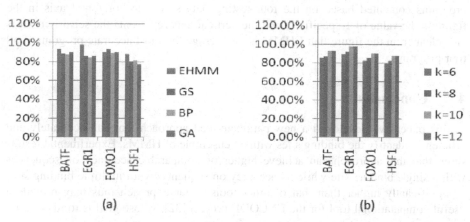

(a)   (b)

Fig. 5. (a) Prediction accuracy of the EHMM, GS, BP, GA on data sets BATF, EGR1, FOXO1, and HSF1. (b) Prediction accuracy of the EHMM when k is 6,8,10, and 12 respectively.

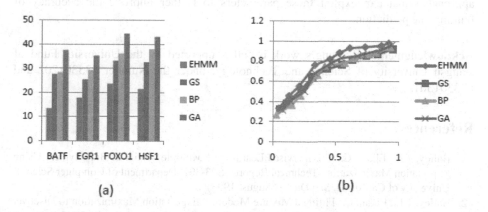

(a)   (b)

Fig. 6. (a) Computation time needed by the four programs on all data sets. (b) The ROC curve for the four programs.

The size of the ensemble can be changed by the user to balance the prediction accuracy and the computation time needed for prediction. Figure 5 (b) shows the prediction accuracy on data sets BATF, EGR1, FOXO1, and HSF1 when the value of the parameter k is 6,8,10, and 12. It can be seen from the figure that the prediction accuracy improves when the size of the ensemble increases and the prediction accuracy becomes steady when the value of the parameter is 10. The testing results also show that a parameter value of 10 is thus sufficient to achieve satisfactory prediction accuracy in practice.

Figure 6 (a) shows the computation time needed by the four programs on all data sets in seconds. It can be seen from the figure that EHMM is computationally more efficient than the other three programs. Figure 6 (b) shows the ROC curve of all four programs computed based on the four testing data sets. The horizontal axis in the figure is the value of 1-specificity and the vertical axis represents the sensitivity. It is also clear from the figure that EHMM is on average the most accurate program of all four programs.

4   Conclusions

In this paper, we developed a new parameterized approach that can accurately and efficiently identify the binding sites with an ensemble of HMMs. Experimental results show that this approach can achieve higher or comparable accuracy on sequences with a single binding site while its accuracy on sequences with multiple binding sites is significantly higher than that of other tools. Our approach thus may provide a useful computational tool for the ENCODE project [32], whose goal is to identify all functional elements in human genome sequences.

Our previous work has demonstrated that introducing additional parameters to the algorithms for some bioinformatics problems may significantly improve the accuracy of the results [10-13, 22-29]. Our future work will focus on the development of new approaches that can exploit these parameters to further improve the accuracy of binding site prediction.

Acknowledgments. Y. Song's work is fully supported by the University Fund of Jiangsu University of Science and Technology, under the Number 635301202 and 633301301.

References

1. Bailey, T.L., Elkan, C.: Unsupervised Learning of Multiple Motifs In Biopolymers Using Expectation Maximization. Technical Report CS93-302, Department of Computer Science, University of California, San Diego (August 1993)
2. Bailey, T.L., Elkan, C.: Fitting a Mixture Model by Expectation Maximization to Discover Motifs in Biopolymers. In: Proceedings of the Second International Conference on Intelligient Systems for Molecular Biology, pp. 28–36 (1994)
3. Brent, M.M., Anand, R., Marmorstein, R.: Structural Basis for DNA Recognition by Foxo1 and its Regulation by Posttranslational Modification. Structure 16, 1407–1416 (2008)
4. Che, D., Song, Y., Rasheed, K.: MDGA: Motif Discovery Using a Genetic Algorithm. In: Proceedings of the Genetic and Evolutionary Computation Conference, pp. 447–452 (2005)

5. Durbin, R., Eddy, S.R., Krogh, A., Mitchison, G.: Biological Sequence Analysis: Probabilistic Models of Proteins and Nucleic Acids. Cambridge University Press (1998)
6. Galas, D.J., Schmitz, A.: A DNA Footprinting: A Simple Method for the Detection of Protein-DNA Binding Specificity. Nucleic Acids Research 5(9), 3157–3170 (1978)
7. Garner, M.M., Revzin, A.: A Gel Electrophoresis Method for Quantifying He Binding of Proteins to Specific DNA Regions: Application to Components of the Escherichia Coli Lactose Operon Regulatory Systems. Nucleic Acids Research 9(13), 3047–3060 (1981)
8. Hertz, G.Z., Stormo, G.D.: Identifying DNA and Protein Patterns with Statistically Significant Alignments of Multiple Sequences. Bioinformatcs 15(7), 53–577 (1999)
9. Hu, T.C., et al.: Snail Associates with EGR-1 and SP-1 to Upregulate Transcriptional Activation of P15ink4b. The FEBS Journal 277, 1202–1218 (2010)
10. Liu, C., Song, Y., Shapiro, L.W.: RNA Folding Including Pseudoknots: A New Parameterized Algorithm and Improved Upper Bound. In: Proceedings of the 7th Workshop on Algorithms in Bioinformatics, pp. 310–322 (2007)
11. Liu, C., Song, Y., Burge III, L.L.: Parameterized Lower Bound and Inapproximability of Polylogarithmic String Barcoding. Journal of Combinatorial Optimization 16(1), 39–49 (2008)
12. Liu, C., Song, Y.: Parameterized Dominating Set Problem in Chordal Graphs: Complexity and Lower Bound. Journal of Combinatorial Optimization 18(1), 87–97 (2009)
13. Liu, C., Song, Y.: Parameterized Complexity and Inapproximability of Dominating Set Problem in Chordal and Near Chordal Graphs. Journal of Combinatorial Optimization 22(4), 684–698 (2011)
14. Liu, F.F.M., Tsai, J.J.P., Chen, R.M., Chen, S.N., Shih, S.H.: FMGA: Finding Motifs by Genetic Algorithm. In: IEEE Fourth Symposium on Bioinformatics And Bioengineering, pp. 459–466 (2004)
15. Liu, J.S., Neuwald, A.F., Lawrence, C.E.: Bayesian Models for Multiple Local Sequence Alignment and Gibbs Sampling Strategies. J. Am. Stat. Assoc. 90(432), 1156–1170 (1995)
16. Liu, X., Brutlag, D.L., Liu, J.S.: Bioprospector: Discovering Conserved DNA Motifs in Upstream Regulatory Regions of Co-Expressed Genes. In: Pacific Symposium of Biocomputing, vol. 6, pp. 127–1138 (2001)
17. Quigley, M., et al.: Transcriptional Analysis of HIV-Specific CD8+ T Cells Shows That PD-1 Inhibits T Cell Function by Upregulating BATF. Nature Medicine 16, 1147–1151 (2010)
18. Rigbolt, K.T., et al.: System-Wide Temporal Characterization of the Proteome and Phosphoproteome of Human Embryonic Stem Cell Differentiation. Science Signaling 4, RS3–RS3 (2011)
19. Roth, F.R., Hughes, J.D., Estep, P.E., Church, G.M.: Finding DNA Regulatory Motifs Within Unaligned Non-Coding Sequences Clustered by Whole-Genome Mrna Quantitation. Nature Biotechnology 16(10), 939–945 (1998)
20. Smith, T.F., Waterman, M.S.: Identification of Common Molecular Subsequences. Journal of Molecular Biology 147, 195–197 (1981)
21. Song, J., Liu, C., Song, Y., Qu, J., Hura, G.: Alignment of Multiple Proteins With an Ensemble of Hidden Markov Models. International Journal of Bioinformatics and Data Mining 4(1), 60–71 (2010)
22. Song, Y., Liu, C., Huang, X., Malmberg, R.L., Xu, Y., Cai, L.: Efficient Parameterized Algorithm for Biopolymer Structure-Sequence Alignment. In: Casadio, R., Myers, G. (eds.) WABI 2005. LNCS (LNBI), vol. 3692, pp. 376–388. Springer, Heidelberg (2005)

23. Song, Y., Liu, C., Malmberg, R.L., Pan, F., Cai, L.: Tree Decomposition Based Fast Search of RNA Structures Including Pseudoknots in Genomes. In: Proceedings of IEEE 2005 Computational Systems Bioinformatics Conference, pp. 223–234 (2005)
24. Song, Y., Zhao, J., Liu, C., Liu, K., Malmberg, R.L., Cai, L.: RNA Structural Homology Search with a Succinct Stochastic Grammar Model. Journal of Computer Science and Technology 20(4), 454–464 (2005)
25. Song, Y., Liu, C., Huang, X., Malmberg, R.L., Xu, Y., Cai, L.: Efficient Parameterized Algorithms for Biopolymer Structure-Sequence Alignment. IEEE/ACM Transactions on Computational Biology and Bioinformatics 3(4), 423–432 (2006)
26. Song, Y., Liu, C., Malmberg, R.L., He, C., Cai, L.: Memory Efficient Alignment Between RNA Sequences and Stochastic Grammar Models of Pseudoknots. International Journal on Bioinformatics Research and Applications 2(3), 289–304 (2006)
27. Song, Y.: A New Parameterized Algorithm for Rapid Peptide Sequencing. Plos ONE 9(2), E87476 (2014)
28. Song, Y., Chi, A.Y.: A New Approach for Parameter Estimation in the Sequence-Structure Alignment of Non-Coding Rnas. Journal of Information Science and Engineering (in press, 2014)
29. Song, Y.: An Improved Parameterized Algorithm for the Independent Feedback Vertex Set Problem. Theoretical Computer Science (2014), doi:10.1016/J.Tcs.2014.03.031
30. Stormo, G.D.: Computer Methods for Analyzing Sequence Recognition of Nucleic Acids. Annu. Rev. Biochem. 17, 241–263 (1988)
31. Stormo, G.D., Hartzell, G.W.: Identifying Protein-Binding Sites from Unaligned DNA Fragments. Proc. of Nat. Acad. Sci. 86(4), 1183–1187 (1989)
32. https://Www.Genome.Gov/Encode/

Road Network Construction and Hot Routes Inferring with Vehicular Trajectories

Junwei Wu[1,2], Yunlong Zhu[1], and Hanning Chen[1]

[1] Shenyang Institute of Automation, Chinese Academy of Sciences, Shenyang 110016, China
[2] University of Chinese Academy of Sciences, Beijing 100049, China
{wujunwei,ylzhu,chenhanning}@sia.cn

Abstract. This work proposes a novel hot routes inferring approach without the support of real road network. Discovery of hot routes is important to the applications that requiring classifies the traffic flow or profiles the dynamic of the city, such as targeted advertising, traffic management and control. The advances of location-acquisition technologies have led to a huge collection of objects' trajectories in the road network, which give us the chances to finding hot routes conveniently. However, it is difficult to effectively detect hot routes without the support of the available road map. To address this issue, we first develop a Road Network Constructing Algorithm (RNCA) that extract road network from vehicular trajectories using image processing methods, and then propose a Hot Route Inferring Algorithm (HRRA) based on the extracted road network. Meanwhile, a novel road matching operation is also developed to match trajectory points onto roads. We have conducted extensive experiments on real dataset of taxi trajectories. Simulation results show that the proposed RNCA and HRRA are both effective and efficient.

Keywords: Data mining, Image processing, Vehicular Trajectories, Hot routes, Road network.

1 Introduction

In recent years, as the mature of the positioning technology and the universal of the positioning device, a variety of mobile terminals in different application areas generate a large amount of trace data. These data is rich in knowledge that reflects people's movement regularity, the traffic conditions, and the structure of the road network. Today, the associated trajectory mining is getting hotter, one significant study of them is inferring hot route from vehicular trajectory. The hot route, which can be informally defined as the route that frequently followed by multiple objects during a certain time, reveals people's moving behavior patterns and attention/reliance to the geographical area.

Gaffney et al. [1] have proposed a hot route detection algorithm FlowScan, which is able to detect effectively the global hot route in the city, and correctly identify the splitting/joining, overlapping, and slack of the hot routes. However, this algorithm requires not only the support of a road network with good topology, but also the

D.-S. Huang et al. (Eds.): ICIC 2014, LNBI 8590, pp. 351–362, 2014.
© Springer International Publishing Switzerland 2014

accuracy of the road matching algorithm. That is, without the road network or the accurate road matching algorithm, this algorithm will be helpless.

How to address this problem? One naive solution is to divide the space into grid with small size, and map the GPS points into these grids. Then the hot route detection is converted to hot grid sequence detection. In this way, like the FlowScan, we can define the directly density-reachable grids according to the common trajectories between adjacent grids, and use the depth-first search or breadth-first search to detect hot routes. However, this approach has its defects. If the grid is large, one grid may cover more than one road, so that the final hot routes will be too large in width to express the finer actual path. If the grid is small, one grid may only cover a partial region of a road, so that the trajectory amount in one grid will be too few to mistakenly lose many hot routes.

In view of the above discussion, the key issue of the hot route detection is the support of the road network. If the road network can be constructed easily, the hot route detection will be no longer a problem. From this straightforward idea, this work develops a rapid road network constructing algorithm (RNCA), and then proposed an effective hot route inferring algorithm (HRRA) based on RNCA. The proposed hot routes detecting processes are roughly as follows: firstly, constructing the road network from vehicular trajectories using image processing methods; and then matching the trajectories to roads; finally detecting hot routes like the above naive solution.

2   Related Work

This section briefly introduces the previous works associated with the hot route detection, including the road network construction, route inferring, and trajectory pattern mining techniques.

2.1   Road Network Construction

There have been a few other existing algorithms for building maps with vehicular GPS trajectories such as image processing-based methods[2, 3], clustering-based methods [4-6], machine learning-based methods [7], and a few other methods [8-10]. However, these algorithms are either high time costly, or sensitive to the granularity and noise of the positioning points, or require an auxiliary reference map.

2.2   Route Inferring

Work [11] proposed a route inference method to identify the popular routes by the means of the routable graph, which is constructed on the basis of collective knowledge. Explicitly, given a location sequence, this algorithm find out the top-k routes, which sequentially passing these locations within the specified time span, from the routable graph. Work [12] also investigated the problem of popular route planning. This work designed a transfer network, and derived a reasonable transfer probability for each transfer node in the network. Then the most popular route between two given locations can be inferred by the transfer probability of each transfer node. However, the popular routes between given query locations only tell that these routes are popular among the optional paths between these locations, while may not most popular in the whole area.

3   Road Network Construction

3.1   Bitmap Construction

In order to extract road network with vehicular trajectories, we need to convert the geographical space including a tremendous amount of GPS points into a bitmap, i.e. discretize the geographical range into gridded space with cells of small size. In this way, each pixel in the bitmap corresponds to a grid cell, and the gray value of each pixel is equal to the number of points in the corresponding grid cell.

Definition 1: Trajectory Bitmap. Let S be a two-dimensional geographical space containing massive trajectories, the trajectory bitmap of S, denoted by G_{bit}, is defined as: $G_{bit}=\{\ g_1,g_2,...,g_{l \times c}\}$, $l>1$, $c>1$, $Gray(g_i) \geq 0$, $i>0$, where l is the number of grid lines in longitude direction, c is the number of grid columns in latitude direction, g_i is the ith pixel, and $Gray(g_i)$ denotes the gray value of pixel g_i. Here the pixels (or grid cells) are numbered line by line from the bottom of the bitmap.

For convenience, we consider the grid cell on the road as ROAD grid, and denote the grid cell not on the road as NON-ROAD grid. Then the corresponding pixels of them are represented as ROAD pixel and NON-ROAD pixel, respectively.

3.2   Binarization of Gray-Scale Image

The aim of image binarization is to converts a gray-level image to a black and white image with a suitable threshold. That is, this operation removes the grid cells not on the road and retains the cells on the road.

The key problem of the binarization is how to choose the threshold. Artificially choosing a fixed threshold is not appropriate, when the threshold is set too large, the ROAD grid with few points will be incorrectly removed; on the other hand, when threshold is set too small, many NON-ROAD grids with a lot of points may be retained improperly. To overcome this disadvantage, we use a hybrid thresholding method to take advantage of both global and local information. As the vehicle travelling along the road, the number of points in ROAD grid is commonly more than that in NON-ROAD grid, i.e. the gray scale of ROAD pixel is higher than that of the NON-ROAD pixel; consequently, when the $r \times r$ neighbors of a ROAD pixel include more than one NON-ROAD pixel, the gray scale of this ROAD pixel will be no less than the average gray scale of its $r \times r$ neighbors. In view of this analysis, we can easily differentiate the ROAD pixels from NON-ROAD pixels by the means of local average gray scale. Similarly, we can use the global average of all the nonzero pixels to filter out the dark pixels. After binarization, the final image will contain object pixels of 1s and background pixels of 0s.

Let Avg_{global} be the average value of all the non-zero pixels in the whole Gray-scale image, and $Avg_{r\times r}(g)$ be the average value of the $r\times r$ neighbors of pixel g, then the threshold of pixel g, denoted by $TH(g)$, is defined by:

$$TH(g)=t_1\times Avg_{global}+ t_2\times Avg_{r\times r}(g) \tag{1}$$

where $t_i\in[0, 1]$, $t_1+ t_2=1$, $r=2n+1$, $n\in N$. With the $TH(g)$ we can determine the binary value of pixel g, if $Gray(g)$ more than $TH(g)$, the value of pixel g is set to 1, otherwise set to 0. Note that, the weight t_1 should be less than t_2 in equation (1), because too large weight of the Avg_{global} will cause many grid cells on the light-traffic road to be incorrectly deleted.

3.3   Morphology

After the above binarization process, the resulting binary image will only contain the pixels on/near the roads, i.e. it shows a rough outline of the road network. However, the binarization process will inevitably lead to "lumps", "holes", "cracks" or "pits" in the binary image. The "lumps" may pull some disconnected roads too close, and the "cracks" or "holes" will cause the road disruption. To thin the bloated roads, we can use morphology erosion or thinning operation. In order to fill the road gaps and smooth the road borders, we use the morphology dilation or bridge operation. The detailed steps of morphology operation are as follows.

Thinning

Thinning is a morphological operation that is used to remove selected foreground pixels from binary image. The result of thinning operation is a single pixel thick, but topologically equivalent binary image. The thinning of a set X by structuring element B, denoted by $X\otimes B$, can be defined in terms of the hit-or-miss transform: $X\otimes B = X-(X \circledast B)$, where" $\circledast$ "denotes the hit-or-miss transform, $X\circledast B = (X\ominus E)\cap(X^c\ominus F)$, and $B=(E, F)$. The more usual process to thin X is using a sequence of structuring elements B^1, B^2, ..., B^n to generate output sequence $X^1 = X\otimes B^1, X^2 = X^1\otimes B^2,\cdots, X^n = X^{n-1}\otimes B^n$, where B^i is rotated version of B^{i-1}, $i=1, 2, ..., n$.

With the thinning process, we can greatly reduce the probability of connecting the disconnect roads in the dilation step, which is described in dilation process in next section.

Dilation

In this work we employ the dilation operation to fill gaps among ROAD pixels of each road. The dilation process is performed by laying the structuring element B on the image X and sliding it across the image in a manner similar to convolution. It also changes all pixels covered by the structuring element into object pixels whenever the origin of the structuring element coincides with an object pixel in the image. The dilation can be defined as: $X \oplus B = \{ p : B_p \cap X \neq \phi \}$, where B_p is the structuring element shifted with its reference point to pixel p in the image.

In most dilation algorithms, the typical structuring element is a symmetric 3×3 or 5×5 mask, and only one structuring element can be used throughout the dilation process. However, this methodology is not suitable for our situation of constructing road network. Because the road is a directional line and we can only dilate the ROAD pixels along the direction of the road, while the pixels in the roads in different directions will have different structuring element. For example, given a pixel p of an east-west road, then its structuring element should be "horizontal"; similarly, the structuring element of the south-north pixel should be "perpendicular". It is easy to get the direction of the road by checking the vehicular orientation in each ROAD grid.

Then we can calculate the structuring element of each pixel conveniently. Accordingly, every background (white) pixel that is touching an object (black) pixel in mask is changed into an object pixel.

Skeletonization

The skeleton of an object pattern is a line representation of the object, which can be interpreted as medial axis or symmetrical axis in mathematical morphology. It should preserve the topology of the object, be one-pixel thick.

Through above the thinning and dilation process, the binary image will become a shape-like skeleton, but dilation operation also brings some undesirable small "bumps". Therefore, we need to further skeletonize the binary image. Skeletonization is the skeleton extraction process by reducing foreground pixels in a binary image to a skeletal remnant. Let X denotes a binary image and let B be a structuring element. Then the skeletonization process of X can be defined as:

$$Skel(X) = \bigcup_{k=0}^{n} Skel_k(X)$$

(2)

where $Skel_k(X) = (X \ominus kB) - [(X \ominus kB) \circ B]$. Note that $X \ominus kB$ denotes k successive erosions of $X \ominus B$, and n is the final step before X is eroded to empty set.

Cleaning

This is the final step of binary image processing that cleaning up the noisy short segments, the lengths of which are less than 4 pixels. After this process, the image can be viewed as a map of the road network. The formal definition of the road network is detailed in the following.

Definition 2: Road Network. Given a trajectory bitmap G_{bit}, execute binarization and morphology operations to it, then the resultant bitmap will be a road network, which can be expressed as: $G_{road} = \{ g_1', g_2', ..., g_i', ... \}$, where $i \in (1, l \times c]$, $g_i' \neq g_j'$, $g_i' = g_k$, $i \neq j$, $k > 0$, $Gray(g_i') = 1$, $1 \leq |N(g_i')| \leq 4$, $G_{road} \subseteq G_{bit}$, and $N(g_i')$ denotes the directly adjacent grids of grid g_i' in G_{road}.

4   Road Matching

The purpose of road matching is to match the GPS points map onto the road that the vehicle traveling on. Many researchers have proposed a lot of effective, but high-complexity algorithms [13-17] to improve the matching accuracy. However, since our road network structure is simple, does not include the roundabout, flyovers, and other complex structures we do not need to use these complex algorithms.

In our situation, we can easily accomplish the road matching by just matching one point into the nearest grid within a specified r-neighborhood. For one GPS point p, if the grid g_i, where p is located in, is a constituent part of the road network, we match p into g_i directly; otherwise, if g_i is not a constituent part of the road network, we match p into the nearest grid g_j, within the $r \times r$ neighbors of grid g_i.

Definition 3: Road Matching. Given a GPS point p, a road network G_{road}, the matching of p, denoted by $Match_{road}(p)$, is defined by

$$Match_{road}(p) = \begin{cases} g_i, & g_i \in G_{road} \\ g_j, & g_i \notin G_{road}, g_j = \arg\min_{g \in N_r(g_i)} Dist(p, g) \end{cases} \tag{3}$$

where g_i is the grid the point p located in, $N_r(g_i)$ denotes the $r \times r$ neighbors of grid g_i in G_{bit}, $Dist(p, g_j)$ denotes the distance from point p to the center of grid g_j. Note that r should be adjusted according to the size of the grid cell. When the grid width is small, such as 30m, we may need to search the 5×5 neighbors; when the grid width is large, such as 50m, just searching 3×3 neighbors will be done, in the situation that the width of the urban roads are generally no more than 100m. After road matching process, any trajectory $T_i = \{p_1, p_2, ..., p_m\}$, $m > 1$, will be translated to $T_i = \{g_1^i, g_2^i, ..., g_n^i\}$, $g_j^i \in G_{road}$, $g_j^i \neq g_{j+1}^i$, $j \geq 1$, $n > 1$.

5   Hot Route Inferring

The hot route is a general path in the road network which contains heavy traffic. It represents a general flow of the moving objects in the network. If there is heavy traffic between two grid cells in the road network, then the two grids are very likely part of one hot route. Similarly, if a sequence of adjacent grids (i.e. a road segment) contains quite a number of common trajectories, we can consider this grid sequence to be a complete hot route. Based on this naive idea, we give several relative definitions and detailed algorithm of the hot route detection, which are introduced in the following.

5.1   Definitions

Definition 4: Hot route. Hot route can be expressed as a sequence of road segments which share a high amount of traffic in a period of time. Generally, it should have the following properties:

1. Direction: one hot route should have the start and end points.
2. Length: the geographic distance from the start to the end point. It should not be too short.
3. Weight: used to identify the popularity of one hot route.

Note that the hot route in this paper is no longer a sequence of road segments in the strict sense, but a sequence of grid cells due to the definition of road network G_{road}.

Definition 5: Traffic of gird. Let $Traf_{start}(g)$ denotes the set of trajectories started at grid g, $Traf_{finish}(g)$ denotes the set of trajectories ended in grid g, $Traf_{pass}(g)$ denotes the set of trajectories that passed through grid g, and $Traf(g)$ denotes the union of the three set, defined by $Traf(g) = Traf_{start}(g) + Traf_{finish}(g) + Traf_{pass}(g)$, then $|Traf(g)|$ denotes the traffic of gird g.

Definition 6: Directly traffic-reachable. Grid g_1 is directly traffic-reachable to an adjacent grid g_2, w.r.t. minimum traffic threshold λ, if all of the following hold true.

1. $|Traf(g_1) \cap Traf(g_2)| \geq \lambda$.
2. $\forall T \in \{Traf(g_1) \cap Traf(g_2)\}$, T must travel through g_1 and g_2 successively.

Definition 7: Route traffic-reachable. For a grid cell chain $L=(g_1, g_2, ..., g_n)$, grid g_1 is route traffic-reachable to an adjacent grid g_n w.r.t parameters λ and ε, if L satisfying the following conditions:

1. g_i is directly traffic-reachable to g_{i+1}.
2. For every sub-chain $L_i = (g_i, g_{i+1}, ..., g_{i+\varepsilon})$ of the chain L, $|Traf(g_i) \cap Traf(g_{i+1}) \cap ... \cap Traf(g_{i+\varepsilon})| \geq \lambda$, $1 \leq \varepsilon < n$, $i \geq 1$.
3. $\forall T \in \{Traf(g_i) \cap Traf(g_{i+1}) \cap ... \cap Traf(g_{i+\varepsilon})\}$, T must travel through $g_i, g_{i+1}, ..., g_{i+\varepsilon}$ successively.

Definition 8: Hot Route Start. A grid g is a hot route start w.r.t. λ, if any one of the following conditions is satisfied:

1. $\exists g' \in N(g)$, $|Traf_{start}(g) - Traf(g')| \geq \lambda$.
2. $\exists g' \in N(g)$, $|Traf_{pass}(g) - Traf(g')| \geq \lambda$, $\forall g'' \in N(g)$, g'' is not directly traffic-reachable to g.
3. $\exists g' \in N(g)$, $|Traf_{start}(g) + Traf_{pass}(g) - Traf(g')| \geq \lambda$, $|Traf_{start}(g) - Traf(g')| < \lambda$, $|Traf_{pass}(g) - Traf(g')| < \lambda$, and $\forall g'' \in N(g)$, g'' is not directly traffic-reachable to g.

5.2   Discovering Hot Routes

To find all the hot routes having complex behavior patterns, such as splitting, joining, and overlapping, requires only two steps: (1) finding out all the hot route starts based on Definition 8; (2) detecting hot routes from the hot route starts according to Definition 7.

The first step can be easily accomplished by simply traversing all grids of the road network, if one grid can meet one condition of Definition 8, this grid will be a hot route start, else just skip this grid and check the next grid. The second step is somewhat complicated. That is, it can be executed by initializing a hot route start to a hot route at first and then iteratively add all the route traffic-reachable grids to it. However, the key problem is how to effectively search the route traffic-reachable grids in the road network. Considering the directly traffic-reachability of ROAD grids, each grid has no more than four directly traffic-reachable grids, then we can construct a quad-tree for the searching space of each hot route start, in which the hot route start corresponding the root node and its directly traffic-reachable grids corresponding to the child nodes of the root node. Obviously, it's easy to find out all hot routes by traversing this tree using depth-first search or breadth-first search. During the searching, if the grids in the sliding window satisfy the conditions of Definition 7, add the end grid in the window to the hot route, and then slide the window forward one grid; otherwise, end the search in current branch (in this time one hot route is finished) and start the search in next branch. Repeat this process until all the branches are completed.

The complexity of the quad-tree construction is: *number of ROAD grids* × (*average traffic of ROAD grids*)^2, and the complexity of the depth-first search is: *number of hot route starts* × *average length of hot routes*.

6   Experiments

6.1   Dataset Description

In our experiments, we use a real trajectory dataset that generated by 13, 798 taxis traveling 3 hours in Shenzhen City. The dataset contains totally 2,448,245 GPS points, from which 94,824 trajectories are extracted.

6.2   Parameters Setting

There are two input parameters in the proposed RNCA: the lines l and the columns c of the grids, which control the size of the grid. They should be adjusted according to the size of the geographical space, as well as the width of the road. In this experiment, the length and width of the grid should be less than most of the width of the road, in order to ensure a grid can be included in one road. Hence, a non-strict range, namely 10m~50m, is usually reasonable.

There are two input parameters in the HRRA: the minimum traffic threshold λ, and the window width ε. The first parameter λ cannot be set a constant, because it is an application or traffic dependent threshold. Due to the lack of domain knowledge, we herein adopt an alternative approach that changing the first condition of Definition 6 to: $|Traf(g_1) \cap Traf(g_2)|/|Traf(g_1) \cup Traf(g_2)| \geq \lambda$, and $|Traf(g_1)| \geq | \cup \{Traf(g_i)\}|/n$, $n > 0$, where g_i is the ROAD grid, and n is the number of ROAD grids. In this way, λ will be a traffic-independent decimal in the range [0, 1], which can be determined based on the statistical data of the traffic.

The second parameter, ε controls how long the common objects must travel together to generate a hot route. It is closely related with the grid size. When the grid is small, such as the width of 20 meters, a value of 2 is too loose since it will lead to many overlong hot routes that too many roads contribute to one hot route; when the grid is large, such as the width of 100 meters, a value of 10 is too strict since it will cause too few hot routes. In common sense, the ε grids of 200~500 meters in a hot route is usually reasonable. That is, if the grid width is 50 meters, ε, should be in range of 4~10.

6.3   Effectiveness

In order to demonstrate the effectiveness of the proposed RNCA, we make two intuitive but empirical comparisons.

First of all, we compare the effects of different thresholding polices in bitmap binarization, as shown in Fig. 1. We can see that the identified roads amount increase dramatically with the decrease of the weight of global average, which explains the ineffectiveness of the binarization strategy with only global threshold, and the effectiveness of our composite thresholding scheme of global average and local average.

Secondly, the impacts of different structuring elements to dilation operation in morphology process are demonstrated in Fig. 2. It shows that the traditional 3×3 mask sticks many different road segments together too badly, and contrarily, our mask policy separate these segments from each other very well.

The final road network generated by RNCA is illustrated in Fig. 3, from which we can see most of the roads are identified except some backstreets or the railway due to too few or no trajectories in them.

Next, we analyze the effectiveness of the proposed HRRA. Fig. 5 shows the comparison of the hot route amounts with different parameter values. In Fig. 5(a), the numbers of the detected hot routes decrease with the increase of the window width, here $\lambda=0.10$, $\gamma=3$, and the grid width is about 50 meters. However, the "$\varepsilon=3$" generates too many short routes (length<5), the "$\varepsilon=5$" produces too few long routes (length≥5), and the "$\varepsilon=4$" detects most modest routes.

Fig. 5(b) illustrates the numbers of the detected hot routes with different directly traffic-reachable thresholds, here $\varepsilon=3$ and the other parameters are same to the above experiment. Through this comparison, we can carefully give a conclusion that $\lambda \leq 0.08$ will be a too loose condition, $\lambda \geq 0.12$ will be a too strict condition, and $0.08 < \lambda < 0.12$ could be a suitable range.

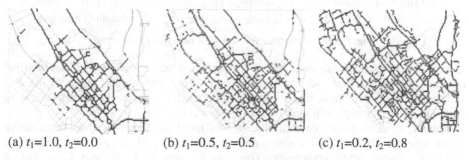

(a) $t_1=1.0$, $t_2=0.0$ (b) $t_1=0.5$, $t_2=0.5$ (c) $t_1=0.2$, $t_2=0.8$

Fig. 1. Road network comparison with different weight of equation (1)

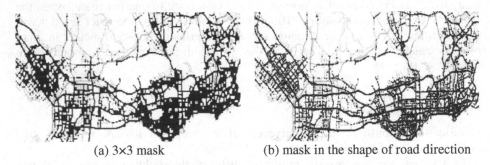

(a) 3×3 mask   (b) mask in the shape of road direction

Fig. 2. Comparison of different structuring elements in dilation operation

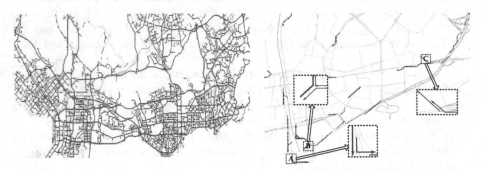

Fig. 3. Final road network   **Fig. 4.** Detected hot routes

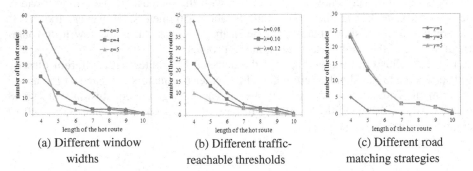

(a) Different window   (b) Different traffic-   (c) Different road
    widths   reachable thresholds   matching strategies

Fig. 5. Effectiveness evaluation with different parameters

Fig. 5(c) illustrates the numbers of the detected hot routes with different road matching strategies, here $\varepsilon=3$ and $\lambda=0.10$. In this Fig., we can see that both the 3×3 and the 5×5 neighbors matching strategies can effectively detect the hot routes, while the no neighbor strategy will miss most of the hot routes.

Finally, to demonstrate detection quality of the HRRA, we need to furthermore check whether HRRA can recognize complex behaviors of the hot routes such as: splitting, joining, and overlapping. The zoomed region A, B, and C in Fig. 4 respectively shows the three complex behaviors. From this Fig. we can see that the proposed HRRA can clearly identify these behaviors.

6.4   Efficiency

In this experiment, we also test the efficiency of RNCA and HRRA with respect to the number of GPS points. Fig. 6 shows the running time of them as the number of the points increases from 400,000 to 2,400,000. As the curve in Fig. 6(a) shows, the running time increases linearly with respect to the number of objects, and it is no more than 3 minutes when the data amount reaches 2.4 million. As the Fig. 6(b) shows, the running time, which is so small (only a few seconds) that even can be negligible, also increases linearly in a smoother manner with respect to the number of objects.

It should be noted that once the road network is completed, we can keep using it, without the need to execute the construction algorithm whenever detect hot routes, till the real road structure is changed. From this point, the time cost of RNCA could be neglected. Thus, the total process time of our solution is very small.

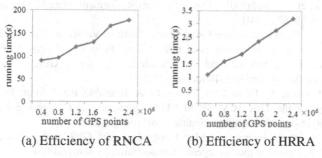

(a) Efficiency of RNCA   (b) Efficiency of HRRA

Fig. 6. Efficiencies of RNCA and HRRA

7   Conclusion

In this paper, we study the problem of hot route detection without available road network, by considering vehicular trajectories. We propose an effective road network construction algorithm based on the mathematical morphology, and present a suitable road matching method for the road network composed by grids. On the basis of these preprocessing, we propose a hot route detection algorithm, and give the normative definitions and the detailed description of which. To show the effectiveness of our solution, we perform comparable experiments using real data sets. The experimental results demonstrate that RNCA can extract most of the streets, and our HRRA can detect the hot routes effectively with a certain range of parameters. Furthermore, we study the efficiencies of RNCA and HRRA; the experimental results show that when the data amount reaches multimillion degree, the running times of them are only a few minutes or seconds.

Acknowledgment. This work was supported by NSFC (Grant No. 51205389, 61003208, 61174164, and 61105067), the S&T Program of Shenyang (Grant No. F11-264-1-08), and the National Key Technology R&D Program (Grant No. 2012BAF10B11 and 2012BAF10B06).

References

1. Li, X., Han, J., Lee, J.-G., Gonzalez, H.: Traffic Density-Based Discovery of Hot Routes In Road Networks. In: Papadias, D., Zhang, D., Kollios, G. (eds.) SSTD 2007. LNCS, vol. 4605, pp. 441–459. Springer, Heidelberg (2007)
2. Chen, C., Cheng, Y.: Roads Digital Map Generation with Multi-Track Gps Data. International Workshop on Presented at the Education Technology and Training 2008, and 2008 International Workshop on Geoscience and Remote Sensing, ETT and GRS 2008 (2008)
3. Shi, W., et al.: Automatic Generation of Road Network Map From Massive Gps Vehicle Trajectories. 12th International IEEE Conference on Presented at the Intelligent Transportation Systems, ITSC (2009)
4. Worrall, S., Nebot, E.: Automated Process for Generating Digitised Maps Through Gps Data Compression. Presented at the Australasian Conference on Robotics and Automation (2007)
5. Schroedl, S., et al.: Mining GPS Traces for Map Refinement. Data Mining and Knowledge Discovery 9, 59–87 (2004)
6. Liu, X., et al.: Road Recognition Using Coarse-Grained Vehicular Traces. HP Labs (2012)
7. Fathi, A., Krumm, J.: Detecting Road Intersections From Gps Traces. In: Fabrikant, S.I., Reichenbacher, T., van Kreveld, M., Schlieder, C. (eds.) GIScience 2010. LNCS, vol. 6292, pp. 56–69. Springer, Heidelberg (2010)
8. Cao, L., Krumm, J.: From GPS Traces to A Routable Road Map. Presented at the Proceedings of the 17th ACM SIGSPATIAL International Conference on Advances in Geographic Information Systems, Seattle, Washington (2009)
9. Bruntrup, R., et al.: Incremental Map Generation with GPS Traces. Proceedings of the 2005 IEEE Presented at the Intelligent Transportation Systems (2005)
10. Chen, Y., Krumm, J.: Probabilistic Modeling of Traffic Lanes From GPS Traces. Presented at the Proceedings of the 18th SIGSPATIAL International Conference on Advances in Geographic Information Systems, San Jose, California (2010)
11. Wei, L.-Y., et al.: Constructing Popular Routes From Uncertain Trajectories. In: Proceedings of the 18th ACM SIGKDD International Conference on Knowledge Discovery and Data Mining, pp. 195–203 (2012)
12. Chen, Z., et al.: Discovering Popular Routes From Trajectories. In: 2011 IEEE 27th International Conference on Data Engineering (ICDE), pp. 900–911 (2011)
13. Kim, S., Kim, J.-H.: Adaptive Fuzzy-Network-Based C-Measure Map-Matching Algorithm for Car Navigation System. IEEE Transactions on Industrial Electronics 48, 432–441 (2001)
14. Quddus, M.A.: High Integrity Map Matching Algorithms for Advanced Transport Telematics Applications, Imperial College London, United Kingdom (2006)
15. Yang, D., et al.: An Improved Map-Matching Algorithm Used in Vehicle Navigation System. In: Proceedings of the 2003 IEEE Intelligent Transportation Systems, pp. 1246–1250 (2003)
16. Brakatsoulas, S., et al.: On Map-Matching Vehicle Tracking Data. In: Proceedings of the 31st International Conference on Very Large Data Bases, pp. 853–864 (2005)
17. El Najjar, M.E., Bonnifait, P.: A Road-Matching Method for Precise Vehicle Localization Using Belief Theory and Kalman Filtering. Autonomous Robots 19, 173–191 (2005)

PSO Based on Cartesian Coordinate System

Yanmin Liu[1,2,*], Zhuanzhou Zhang[1], Yuanfeng Luo[1] and Xiangbiao Wu[1]

[1] School of Mathematics and Computer Science, Zunyi Normal College, Zunyi 563002
[2] School of Economics and Management, Tongji University, Shanghai, 200092, China
yanmin7813@gmail.com

Abstract. In order to deal with the problems of the slow convergence and easily converging to local optima, a classification learning PSO is proposed based on hyperspherical coordinates. The method of determination of poor performance particle is presented, and the swarm is divided into three parts where three learning strategies are introduced to improve the swarm to escape from local optima. Additionally, to decrease outside disturbance, the particle positions and velocities are updated in hyperspherical coordinate system, which improve the probability flying to the optimal solution. The simulation experiments of three typical functions are conducted, and the results show the effectiveness of the proposed algorithm. Consequently, CLPSO-HC can be used as an effective algorithm to solve complex multimodal problems.

Keywords: Particle swarm optimizer, Multimodal problem, Cartesian coordinate, Hyperspherical coordinates.

1 Introduction

Since Kennedy and Eberhart [1] proposed the particle swarm optimization (PSO), it has been widely used in science and engineering field, and achieved satisfactory effect [2]. Since PSO has simple concept and easily applied process, it received extensive attention in the academia. In [3] the author introduced a contraction factor, and then put forward a contraction factor PSO variant. In order to strengthen information exchange between particles, Mendes proposed the complete information PSO [4]. In [5] the author proposed an adaptive distance ratio with neighbor cooperative PSO (FDR-PSO). In [6] the author used one-dimensional (1-D) group to search each dimension variable, which will raise potential search space. In [7], the author presents a variant of particle swarm optimizer (PSO) based on the simulation of the human social communication behavior (HSCPSO). In HSCPSO, each particle initially joins a default number of social circles that consist of some particles, and its learning exemplars include three parts. In [8] the author gives a novel learning strategies, to enhance the capacity of exploration of particles.

Experience shows that PSO has good performance in solving most optimized problems, but for the complex multimodal optimization problems, PSO easily occurs

---

[*] Corresponding author.

D.-S. Huang et al. (Eds.): ICIC 2014, LNBI 8590, pp. 363–370, 2014.

"premature" phenomenon mainly due that the multi-peak problems contain more local optimal solution, and the probability of individuals get into a local optimal solution will increase. Additionally in order to solve the contradiction between population convergence rate and premature phenomenon, scholars generally use improved learning strategies [9], and mixed different algorithms [10], etc. At the existing various PSO, the updating strategy of the speed and position of particles is in the cartesian coordinate system. However, in the cartesian coordinate system, a small disturbances change of the particle in the process of flying will result in a great flight angle change of particle in D dimension space, which make particle be far away from the optimal orbit. Therefore, seeking a kind of particle velocity and position update coordinates which is less affected by the outside world, will improve the algorithm efficiency.

In conclusion, this paper proposes improved learning strategies, and it can guide the particles that fall into local optimal solution of the particles to seek a new learning sample and enhance population's ability to jump out of local optimal solution. In order to reduce the interference of external environment, the updating process of the particle's velocity and position proceed in spherical coordinates, which will improve the ability to escape from a local minimum.

2   Standard PSO

In the standard PSO, each particle represents a potential solution and each particle realize the best flight by its own 'cognitive' and 'communication' between groups. Assuming that population size N, at the iteration time t, each particle in D dimension can adjust its performance according to Eq.(1) and (2)

$$\overline{v_i}(t+1) = \overline{v_i}(t) + c_1 \cdot r_1(\overline{p_i}(t) - \overline{x_i}(t)) + c_2 \cdot r_2(\overline{p_g}(t) - \overline{x_i}(t))$$

$$\overline{x_i}(t+1) = \overline{x_i}(t) + \overline{v_i}(t+1)$$

(1)

$$\begin{cases} v_i^d = v_{max} \text{ , } if \text{ } v_i^d > v_{max} \\ v_i^d = -v_{max} \text{ , } if \text{ } v_i^d < -v_{max} \end{cases}$$

(2)

It can be seen that the particle's velocity consists of three parts: (I) $\overline{v_i}(t)$ is the particle velocity that has the ability of expanding the search space, which make the algorithm hold the global optimization ability; (II) $\overline{p_i}(t)$ is particle's history optimal position (*pbest*) called "self-knowledge" learning, which show particles thinking (their own learning ability); (III) $\overline{p_g}(t)$ is the best particle position in the swarm (*gbest*), called "social part" learning, which denotes the ability of learning particles to the entire population. Learning factor c_1 and c_2 represent the influence of *gbest* and *pbest*, which can adjust learning factor to change the convergent speed of particle swarm.

3   The Proposed Algorithm (CLPSO-HC)

3.1   The Identification and Classification of Poor Particles

PSO is a kind of swarm intelligence algorithm based on learning from each other between the swarms, and from basic evolution equation of PSO shown in Eq.(1) it means that once the learning samples of the particles in the population are in the state of local optimal solution, the entire population will easily to fall into local optimal solution. Based on this thought, finding and classifying the poor particle in the swarm and them, and taking the corresponding learning strategies according to the characteristics of each individual, will increase the ability of the particles jumping out of local optimal solution. Algorithm 1 gives the identification process of poor particle

---

Algorithm 1 identification of poor particles

// *WI*-the worst performance individual

// *MI*-the common performance individual

// *BI*-the best performance individual

Step 1 Initialize population size (*PS*)

Step 2 Determine the common performance
individual size (Num_wor)

Step 3 Individual ranking based on fitness value

Step 4 Determine *WP*

Step 5 Divide *WP* into 3 types: *WI, MI* 和 *BI*

Step 6 Replace *WI* with *gbest*

Step 7 Improve *MI* by *rand×gbest*

Step 9 Improve all *WP*, and then end program

After the identification of the poor populations (WP), according to their quality the swarm will be divided into three categories: (I) the worst performance individual WI; (II) the common performance individual MI; (III) the best performance individual BI.

3.2   Three Kinds of Learning Strategy

Based on observation of the social life, the members that affect the collective performance in a collective have the following classification according to work performance: (I) the most influence collective achievement individual; (II) the generally affected collective performance individual; (III) small affected collective achievement individual. Correspondingly the corresponding measures for these individuals commonly is that the worst capabilities in business should learn from the best employees in the collective, poor capabilities should be properly learn from the best employees in the collective and need affirm its own one; strongest capacity should continue to play its special features. Therefore, in CLPSO-HC, the poor individual performance is choose to update their learning exemplar. Figure 1 shows the particle update strategy.

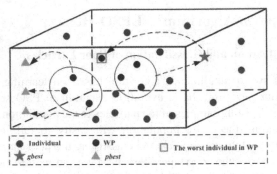

Fig. 1. Particles update strategy

3.3   Update of Particle Velocity and Position Based on the Spherical Coordinates

In basic PSO and various improved PSO versions, the particle's velocity and position update are proceed in cartesian coordinates, where its drawback is that the small coordinates changes will make individuals in the swarm deviate from the optimal solution orbit. So to reduce the external disturbance influence in flight process of the particles, the particle's velocity and position updating is proceed in spherical coordinates. Figure 2 shows in 2 dimension variable, the corresponding relation of cartesian coordinates and spherical coordinates for the individuals.

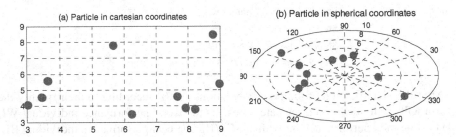

Fig. 2. Corresponding position particles in different coordinate system

---

Algorithm 2 coordinate transformation

// x-varialbe in cartesian coordinates

//(r, ø)-cartesian coordinates

// rand-[0 1]uniform random number

(1) Begin coordinate transformation

(2)   Compute $r \leftarrow \sqrt{\sum (x^2)}$

(3)   Compute $\phi \leftarrow (180/\pi) \times a\cos(x/r)$

(4)   Compute $\phi \leftarrow \phi + rand$

(5)   Compute $r \leftarrow rand \times r$

(6) End Begin

(7) Begin coordinate transformation

(8)   Compute $x \leftarrow r \times \cos((\phi \times \pi /180))$

(9) End Begin

The conversion process of D dimension variable x in cartesian coordinates and spherical coordinates $(r, \emptyset)$ is as follows:

$$x_1 = r\cos(\phi_1)$$

$$x_2 = r\sin(\phi_1)\cos(\phi_2)$$

$$x_3 = r\sin(\phi_1)\sin(\phi_2)\cos(\phi_3)$$

$$\vdots \qquad\qquad \vdots$$

$$x_{n-1} = r\sin(\phi_1)\sin(\phi_2)\cdots\sin(\phi_{n-2})\cos(\phi_{n-1})$$

$$x_n = r\sin(\phi_1)\sin(\phi_2)\cdots\sin(\phi_{n-2})\sin(\phi_{n-1})$$

Algorithm 2 shows the pseudo code in the transformation of cartesian coordinates and spherical coordinates

Based on the above strategies, the algorithm 3 shows the proposed CLPSO - HC pseudo code.

Algorithm 3 CLPSO-HC

    Initialize
(1) Initialize *Xmin, Xmax, PS, D, Num_wor, acceleration constant*
(2) Initialize all particle positions, velocity, *pbest, gbest, t=0, inertia weight*
(3) Compute the fitness function of the initialize particles
    Optimize
(4) **While** *t<maxT*
(5)   Record the the information about each particle position and velocity
(6)   **For each particle**
(7)   **For each dimension**
(8)   Updating velocity (1) according to algorithm 2
(9)   Updating position (2) according to algorithm 2
(10)   **End For**
(11)   **End For**
(12)   Evaluate fitness function for each particle
(13)   **If** fitness(x_i)<fitness(*pbest$_i$*)
(14)   *pbest$_i$= x_i*
(15)   *pbestval$_i$*=fitness(x_i)
(16)   **EndIf**
(17)   Find which particle is best according to fitness value (*Index*)
(18)   **If** fitness(*gbest*)>min(*pbestval$_i$*)
(19)   *gbestval= pbestval$_i$*
(20)   *gbest= x$_{index}$*
(21)   **End If**
(22)   Identify the worst particles (*WP*) according algorithm 1
(23)   Apply three strategies to improve *WP* taccording algorithm 1
(24)   **If** stop criteria not met
(25)   *t=t+1*
(26)   **EndIf**
(27) **End While**
(28) Report results
(29) Terminate

---

4   Simulation Experiments

In order to test the effectiveness of the proposed algorithm, we compared the proposed algorithm CLPSO-HC with the basic particle swarm optimization (BPSO) and CPSO algorithm [6]. Due to the space limitations in the article, we only give the convergence characteristics of the multimodal detection function (Rastrigin, Schwefel and Weierstrass function [3]). The experiment setting is: all algorithm iteration number is 200, the population size is 30, all testing function for 30 dimension, and other parameters setting is the same to initial one. The simulation platform is Pentium Core Duo, 1.8 GB of RAM CPU with 2 GB of RAM, and Matlab R2008B. Figure 3 shows the algorithm convergence characteristic curve, and in order to further test running effect of CLPSO-HC, the statistical analysis of computational results is carried out in independent running 30 times for each algorithm. Table 1 shows the statistical results of different algorithms in three test function, where B is the optimal value; W is the worst value, and B is average value.

Table 1. The results comparison for different algorithms

Algorithm	Weierstrass			Schwefel			Rastrigin		
	B	W	M	B	W	M	B	W	M
BPSO	5.2915	15	7.4	4.3e+003	9.2e+003	6.7e+003	111	134	126
CPSO	0.7500	4	2.6	2.1e+003	4.9e+003	3.6e+003	90	127	108
CLPSO-HC	1.9e-010	3.3e-004	1.6e-004	1.5e+003	2.1e+003	1.7e+003	54	60	58

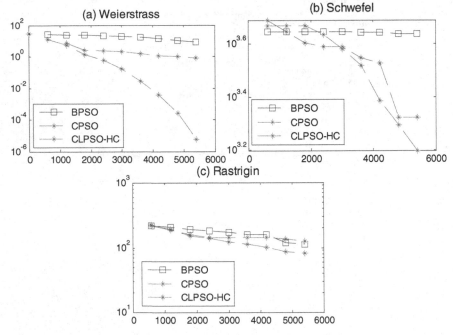

Fig. 3. Convergence characteristics

It can be seen from the convergence characteristic Figure 3 , CLPSO-HC has better convergence properties in complex multimodal problems, and Table 1 also show that the algorithm have better performance compared with the other two algorithms. Therefore, CLPSO - HC can be regarded as an effective method for solving complex multimodal problems.

5   Conclusions

In view of the defects of basic particle swarm optimization (PSO) in solving complex multimodal problems, we put forward a kind of classification learning strategy based on the spherical coordinates, and then propose a new particle swarm (CLPSO – HC for short). Each individual in the swarm choose different learning samples based on the particle operating characteristics, and the spherical coordinates is adopted to update position and speed of the particles instead of cartesian coordinates which reduce the outside disturbance to the flying trajectories of the particles. The simulation results of three multimodal problems show that the CLPSO-HC is an effective method for solving complex multimodal problems. In addition, hybrid approach with other new intelligent algorithm can effectively improve the performance, next, we will design CLPSO – HC hybrids with the one proposed by [11][12][13].

Acknowledgments. This work is supported by Guizhou province science and technology fund (Grant no. Qian Ke He J [2012] 2340, Qian Ke He J [2012] 2342, LKZS [2012]10, LKZS [2012]22, LKZS[2014]29, LKZS[2014]30); China Postdoctoral Science Foundation Funded Project (Grant no. 2012M520936, 2013T60466); Shanghai Postdoctoral Science Foundation Funded Project (Grant no. 12R21416000); Key project of teaching contents and curriculum system reform in Guizhou province education department (Grant no.[2013]446). Zunyi 15851 talents elite engineering in 2013 year.

References

1. Kennedy, J., Eberhart, R.C.: Particle swarm optimization. In: Proceedings of IEEE International Conference on Neural Networks, Piscataway, USA, pp. 1942–1948 (1995)
2. Ishaque, K., Salam, Z.: An improved Particle Swarm Optimization Based MPPT for PV with Reduced Steady-State Oscillation. IEEE Transactions on Power Electronics 27(8), 3627–3638 (2012)
3. Clerc, M., Kennnedy, J.: The particle swarm-explosion, stability, and convergence in a multidimensional complex space. IEEE Transactions on Evolutionary Computation 6(2), 58–73 (2002)
4. Mendes, R., Kennedy, J.: The fully informed particle swarm: Simpler, maybe better. IEEE Transactions on Evolutionary Computation 8(2), 204–210 (2004)
5. Peram, T., Veeramachanei, K.: Fitness-distance-ratio based particle swarm optimization. In: Proceedings of IEEE International Swarm Intelligence Symposium, Piscataway, NJ, pp. 174–181 (2003)

6. Van, D.B.F., Engelbecht, A.P.: A cooperative approach to particle swarm optimization. IEEE Transactions on Evolutionary Computation 8(3), 225–239 (2004)
7. Liu, Y.M., Niu, B.: A Novel PSO Model Based on Simulating Human Social Communication Behavior. Discrete Dynamics in Nature and Society, 1–22 (2013)
8. Liang, J.J., Qin, A.K., Sugaanthan, P.N.: Comprehensive learning particle swarm optimizer for global optimization of multimodal functions. IEEE Transactions on Evolutionary Computation 10(3), 281–295 (2006)
9. Li, C.H., Yang, S.X.: A Self-Learning Particle Swarm Optimizer for Global Optimization Problems. IEEE Transactions on Systems, Man, and Cybernetics 42(3), 627–646 (2012)
10. Jia, D.L., Zheng, G.X.: A hybrid particle swarm optimization algorithm for high-dimensional problems. Computers & Industrial Engineering 61(2), 1117–1122 (2011)
11. Niu, B., Wang, H., Chai, Y.J.: Bacterial Colony Optimization. Discrete Dynamics in Nature and Society 2012, Article ID 698057, 28 pages (2012)
12. Niu, B., Fan, Y., Xiao, H., Xue, B.: Bacterial Foraging-Based Approaches to Portfolio Optimization with Liquidity Risk. Neurocomputing 98(3), 90–100 (2012)
13. Niu, B., Wang, H., Wang, J.W., Tan, L.J.: Multi-objective Bacterial Foraging Optimization. Neurocomputing 116, 336–345 (2012)

An Improved PSO for Multimodal Complex Problem

Yanmin Liu[1,2,*], Zhuanzhou Zhang[1], Yuanfeng Luo[1], and Xiangbiao Wu[1]

[1] School of Mathematics and Computer Science, Zunyi Normal College, Zunyi 563002
[2] School of Economics and Management, Tongji University, Shanghai, 200092, China
yanmin7813@gmail.com

Abstract. As the multimodal complex problem has many local optima, basic PSO is difficult to effectively solve this kind of problem. To conquer this defect, firstly, we adopt Monte Carlo method to simulate the fly trajectory of particle, and conclude the reason for falling into local optima. Then, by defining distance, average distance and maximal distance between particles, an adaptive control factor (Adaptive rejection factor, ARF) for pp and pg was proposed to increase the ability for escaping from local optima. In order to test the proposed strategy, three test benchmarks were selected to conduct the analysis of convergence property and statistical property. The simulation results show that particle swarm optimizer based on adaptive rejection factor (ARFPSO) can effectively avoid premature phenomenon. Therefore, ARFPSO is available for complex multimodal problems.

Keywords: Particle swarm optimizer, Adaptive rejection factor, Monte Carlo simulation.

1 Introduction

Particle Swarm Optimization (PSO) [1] is a random search algorithm based on population which has been widely applied in the field of social science, natural science. Compared with other intelligence algorithm, PSO is easy to implement. But the basic PSO is easily fall into local optimal solution when in optimizing complex multimodal problems due to the loss of diversity of population, which affects the basic PSO apply in practical application. For better applying PSO to solve practical problems, many scholars proposed some improvement strategies in view of the basic PSO.

For example, Clerc [3] gives a shrinkage factor based on basic PSO, ant the author proposed PSO variants with contraction factor. Mendes [4] proposed a complete information PSO which fully use particle information in the each dimension of population to enhance the population of potential search space. Zhan [5] proposed a orthogonal learning PSO to improve the learning strategy. In [6], the author presents a variant of particle swarm optimizer (PSO) based on the simulation of the human social communication behavior (HSCPSO). In HSCPSO, each particle initially joins a default number of social circles that consist of some particles, and its learning exemplars include three parts. In [7], the author proposed an improved PSO based on dynamic

---

* Corresponding author.

D.-S. Huang et al. (Eds.): ICIC 2014, LNBI 8590, pp. 371–378, 2014.

neighborhood to improve the ability to escape from local optima. The above improved PSOs have achieved a satisfactory result, but at convergence velocity and precision.

Recently, Blackwell [8] put forward a kind of dynamic update rule to enhance the operation efficiency of PSO. Wan [9] proposed a hybrid algorithm to improve the performance of PSO. All in all, the existing improvement algorithm are derived from the population diversity and improved particle learning samples, the mixed algorithm which have obtained the certain effect, but there is still room for improvement on the precision.

Therefore, in order to effectively improve algorithm's ability to jump out of local optimal solution, and the precision of the algorithm, this paper proposes an adaptive rejection factor particle swarm (ARFPSO). Firstly, we used the Monte Carlo method to simulate the population flight path to conclude the reason why population is easily trapped in local optimal solution; secondly, by defining the distance, the average distance between and maximum distance between the particles, we put forward a kind of adaptive exclusive factor to control the distance between particle's history optimal position (p_p) and best particle position in the swarm (p_g) which can improve the population's ability to jump out of local optimal; Finally, the proposed algorithm is compared with several algorithms by the convergence of algorithms and statistical analysis.

2   Standard PSO

$$v_{id}(t) = w \cdot v_{id}(t-1) + c_1 r_1 (p_{p_{id}} - x_{id}(t-1))$$
$$+ c_2 r_2 (p_{gd} - x_{id}(t-1)) \tag{1}$$

$$x_{id}(t) = x_{id}(t-1) + v_{id}(t) \tag{2}$$

where $v_{id}(t)$ denotes the velocity d^{th} dimension of particles i^{th} at time t; $x_{id}(t)$ is the position d^{th} dimension of particles i^{th} at time t; r_1 and r_2 are evenly distributed random number between [0, 1]; w is inertia weight which decided the particle history velocity influence on the particle trajectories, and in this paper we selects a linear gradient method $w = 0.9 - t/(2 \times T)$ to determine its value which is a decreasing inertia from 0.9 to 0.4 to ensure convergence of the algorithm [4]. c_1 and c_2 are constant which determine p_{pid} (particle's history optimal position, p_p) and p_{gd} (best particle position in the swarm, p_g) learning ability, c1 = c2 = 2 here.

3   PSO Based on Adaptive Rejection Factor

3.1   Particle Velocity Factor Analysis Based on Monte Carlo Simulation

From population evolution equation shown in Eq (1), it can be seen that the particle's velocity will determine its flight path, which can decide whether the population can search to the global optimal solution. In addition, each dimension of a particle is independent, and the operation of each particle is independent for each other. Therefore, by studying motion trajectory of any dimension of any particle, and it is enough to explore the running rule of the whole population. In view of this, the evolution equation shown in Eq (1) and (2) can be equivalent to Eq (3) and (4) whose symbol significance is consistent with Eq (1) and (2).

$$v(t+1) = w \cdot v(t) + \phi_1(p_p - x(t)) + \phi_2(p_g - x(t)) \tag{3}$$

$$x(t) = x(t-1) + v(t) \tag{4}$$

After Eq (4) deformation, we can get Eq (5),

$$-x(t-1) = \frac{1}{\phi_3 + \phi_4}(v(t) - w \cdot v(t-1) - \phi_3 p_p - \phi_4 p_g) \tag{5}$$

Let Eq (4) and (5) be into Eq (3), we can obtain Eq (6),

$$v(t+1) = (w - k_1 + k_2) \cdot v(t) - wk_2 \cdot v(t-1) \\ - k_3(p_p - p_g) \tag{6}$$

$$\phi_i = c \cdot r_i, \ i = 1,2,3,4 \tag{7}$$

$$k_1 = \phi_1 + \phi_2 \tag{8}$$

$$k_2 = \frac{\phi_1 + \phi_2}{\phi_3 + \phi_4} \tag{9}$$

$$k_3 = \frac{\phi_1\phi_4 - \phi_3\phi_2}{\phi_3 + \phi_4} \tag{10}$$

It can be seen from the evolution equation (4), if the speed of individuals in the swarm is 0, which is individual to stop flying, the population will be lost their search ability. Therefore, to explore the influencing factors of population evolution, we should firstly understand the factors affecting population speed. Additionally, it can be seen from the evolution equation (6), the factors influencing particle velocity at time t contains two parts: (I) inertial part, namely the particle velocity $v(t)$ and $v(t-1)$ at last iteration; (II) learning part, at time t particle's history optimal position p_p, and best particle position in the swarm p_p.

There are four random variables in Eq(6), the population running track analysis in the existing literature [3-4] have almost omitted the evolution equation of random items, which lack the general. To overcome its shortcomings, we adopt the classical theory of random process-Monte Carlo simulation to determine the influence of inertia and learning part of algorithm and find the strategy jump out of local optimal solution.

Monte carlo simulation platform is: the Pentium Core Duo, 1.8 GB of RAM with 2 GB of RAM, CPU R2008B with Matlab. The simulation parameters setting is: maximum number iterations 5000; population size 200; random number generator for the machine running time, the rand (' state ', the sum (100 * clock)); inertia weight for a linear gradient; accelerated constant $c_1=c_2=2$ speed range between [-100 100]. Figure 1 shows the speed memory value simulation diagram in the hypothesis of $p_p= p_g$, and it can be seen that no matter how the initial speed after 2800 iterations, the speed of population individuals are 0 and the population stop evolution. Figure 2 shows the probability density distribution of k_3 of affecting learning ability factor in [-2 2].

In conclusion, when p_p is close to p_g (no matter how much the population the initial speed of the swarm), population will lose the ability to explore search space. Similarly, if the swarm did not converge to global optimal solution, the entire population will be trapped in local optimal solution.

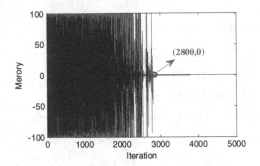

Fig. 1. Memory value changes Based on the monte carlo simulation

3.2   Adaptive Rejection Factor

On the above conclusions, this paper puts forward a kind of adaptive strategy to control the distance between p_p and p_g , which called adaptive rejection factor (Adaptive rejection factor, ARF), to improve the population's ability to jump out of local optimal. To better understand the strategy, three defined is introduced as follows:

Definition 1 (Distance between the particles):

$$D_{ij} = \sqrt{\sum_{k=1}^{d}(x_{ik} - x_{jk})} \quad \forall i, j \ i \neq j \tag{11}$$

Definition 2 (Maximum distance between the particles):

$$MAXD = \max(D_{ij}) \tag{12}$$

Definition 3 (Average distance between the particles):

$$AD = \sum_{i=1}^{PS}\sum_{j=1}^{PS}D_{ij}/N \tag{13}$$

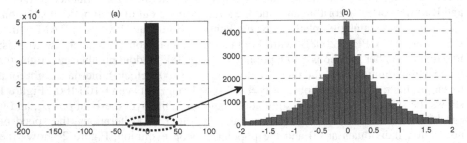

Fig. 2. Probability density distribution of learning factor

Table 1. Algorithm results comparison in 60 independent run

Algorithm	Rosenbrock			Ackley			Griewank		
	Best	Worst	Mean	Best	Worst	Mean	Best	Worst	Mean
ARFPSO	53.82	66.39	57.28	2.1203	3.0087	2.3487	5.32e-004	1.86e-003	1.2e-003
BPSO	265.37	297.27	281.84	8.0778	12.8761	11.7208	15.0541	17.2376	16.8635
FIPS	53.99	69.81	63.35	7.4823	11.2643	10.1862	0.1596	0.5071	0.3861

The proposed ideas are as follows: when the distance between the p_p and p_g is less than the average distance between particles in a population, it shows that they are relatively close to each other, but does not rule out an accident. Therefore, in order to prevent the population information loss caused by additional strategy, the distance between the p_p and p_g is lower than AD at N (1/10 of maximum number of iterations) consecutive generation, the exclusive factor is stimulated. Algorithm 1 gives exclusive factor pseudo code.

Algorithm 1. Pseudo-code of adaptive rejection factor

1: stay_num=0
2: **If** $D_{pg}<AD$
3:    stay_num= stay_num+1;
4:    **If** stay_num>N
5:      **For** each particle
6:         $p_p=p_p+rand()\times MAXD$;
7:      **End For**
8:    **End If**
9: **End If**

The proposed ARFPSO step is shown below :

【Step 1】 Initialization: population size(PS), w, position and velocity
【Step 2】 Initialization: particle's history optimal position(p_p), best particle position in the swarm(p_g)
【Step 3】 Initialization: *staynum*=0, Maximum iterations $MAXT$
【Step 4】 Computing: position and velocity for each particle
【Step 5】 Computing: fitness function value for each particle
【Step 6】 Computing and updating: each particle p_p and the swarm p_g
【Step 7】 Run algorithm 1
【Step 8】 If $MAXT$ is not, return step 4, else go to step 9
【Step 9】 Record result

4   The Simulation Experiment and Analysis

4.1   Design of Simulation Experiment

In order to test ARFPSO ability to jump out of local optimal solution, we adopted the combination of the qualitative and quantitative analysis for different test function, namely the convergence property and statistical analysis to test performance of the algorithm. ARFPSO is compared with PSO with inertia weight w (wBPSO) and complete information PSO (FIPS) [4]. Rosenbrock, Ackley and Griewank are selected to test the algorithm performance. Parameter settings of algorithm: maximum number of iterations of all algorithms (MAXT) is 1000; population size (PS) is 30; function dimension is 60; other parameters are the same to that proposed by author. Simulation platform is: Pentium Core Duo, 1.8 GB of RAM with 2 GB of RAM, CPU and Matlab R2008B. Figure 3 shows the algorithm convergence characteristics. Table 1 gives the optimal value, average value and the worst of each algorithm in 60 independent run from quantitative analysis. In order to further analyze ARFPSO performance statistically significant, we adopted the boxed statistic figure shown in figure 4.

4.2   Simulation Experiments for Convergence Characteristics

From the convergence characteristics (Figure 3), it can be seen that ARFPSO has obvious advantages compared with other algorithms in Ackley and Griewank function, and this conclusion is supported by the results shown in table 1. In Rosenbrock function, ARFPSO and FIPS had the similar performance, but the box statistical results shows that ARFPSO has the advantage compared with FIPS. In short, from the algorithm convergence characteristic and box statistical results (Figure 4), ARFPSO can effectively solve the multimodal problems.

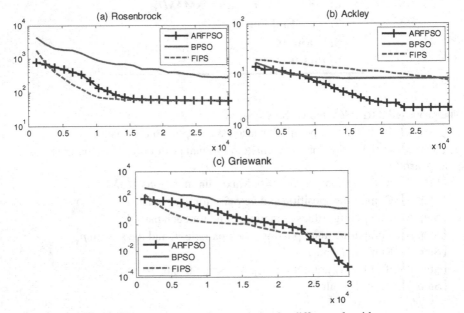

Fig. 3. The convergence characteristics for different algorithms

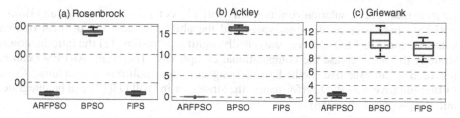

Fig. 4. Box statistical results in 60 independent run

4.3 Computational Complexity Analysis

As adaptive rejection factor of PSO (ARFPSO) stems from basic PSO and is introduced the corresponding strategy, we need analyze the computational complexity to explore whether the introduced strategies increase the computational complexity. With T denotes the maximum number of iterations; the total number of particles is N; D denotes dimensions of the decision variables. The computational complexity of the adaptive rejection factor is $T_1(N)=O(N\times T)$, the basic PSO computational complexity $T_2(N)=O(N\times D\times T)$, so ARFPSO computational complexity is $T(N)=O(N\times D\times T)+O(N\times T)\approx O(N\times D\times T)=T_2(N)$. Therefore, the complexity of ARFPSO and basic PSO are in the same order of magnitude, theoretically.

In order to further test algorithm computational complexity, three algorithms, Rosenbrock, Ackley and Griewank function are used to test averaged running time of each algorithm in 30 independent run based on simulation platform Pentium Core Duo, 1.8 GB of RAM CPU with 2 GB of RAM, Matlab R2008B, where each algorithm conducted at each iteration 3×10^4 function evaluation, Table 2 shows the independent running time of each algorithm, it can be seen that ARFPSO has the same order of magnitude as other algorithms at run time, which indicated the introduction of strategy did not increase the computational complexity.

Table 2. Algorithm running time (3×10^4FES) (Unit: seconds)

Algorithm	Rosenbrock	Ackley	Griewank
ARFPSO	58	69	74
BPSO	43	48	65
FIPS	62	72	79

5   Conclusions

In view of the defect of the basic PSO in solving complex multimodal problems, this paper proposes an adaptive rejection factor PSO. First of all, by Monte Carlo method to simulate the population trajectory, we can conclude that when the distance between particle's history optimal position (p_p) and best particle position in the swarm (p_g) is too close, the population flight velocity will be close to zero, which makes population lose the ability to explore further. On this conclusion, the paper puts forward a kind of exclusive factor to improve the population's ability to jump out of local optimum. Rosenbrock, Ackley and Griewank function are used to test the proposed algorithm performance, the simulation results show that: (1) compared with other algorithms, ARFPSO has faster convergence speed and the ability to jump out of local optimal solution, and ARFPSO achieves statistically significant results; (2) the introduction of strategy did not increase the computational complexity. Therefore, ARFPSO can be regarded as an effective method for solving complex multimodal problems; (3) to further improve ARFPSO performance, the strategies in [10][11][12] will be integrated into the proposed algorithm.

Acknowledgments. This work is supported by Guizhou province science and technology fund (Grant no. Qian Ke He J [2012] 2340, Qian Ke He J [2012] 2342, LKZS [2012]10, LKZS [2012]22, LKZS[2014]29, LKZS[2014]30); China Postdoctoral Science Foundation Funded Project (Grant no. 2012M520936, 2013T60466); Shanghai Postdoctoral Science Foundation Funded Project (Grant no. 12R21416000); Key project of teaching contents and curriculum system reform in Guizhou province education department (Grant no.[2013]446). Zunyi 15851 talents elite engineering in 2013 year.

References

1. Kennedy, J., Eberhart, C.: Particle swarm optimization. In: Proceedings of IEEE International Conference on Neural Networks, Washington, pp. 1942–1948 (1995)
2. Zhou, X.C., et al.: Remanufacturing closed-loop supply chain network design based on genetic particle swarm optimization algorithm. Journal of Central South University of Technology 19(2), 482–487 (2012)
3. Clerc, M., Kennedy, J.: The particle swarm-explosion, stability, and convergence in a multidimensional complex space. IEEE Transactions on Evolutionary Computation 6(2), 58–73 (2002)
4. Mendes, R., Kennedy, J., Neves, J.: The fully informed particle swarm: Simpler, maybe better. IEEE Transactions on Evolutionary Computation 8(3), 204–210 (2004)
5. Zhan, Z.H., et al.: Orthogonal Learning Particle Swarm Optimization. IEEE Transactions on Evolutionary Computation PP(99), 1 (2010)
6. Liu, Y.M., Niu, B.: A Novel PSO Model Based on Simulating Human Social Communication Behavior. Discrete Dynamics in Nature and Society, 1–22 (2013)
7. Liu, Y., Zhao, Q., Shao, Z., Shang, Z., Sui, C.: Particle swarm optimizer based on dynamic neighborhood topology. In: Huang, D.-S., Jo, K.-H., Lee, H.-H., Kang, H.-J., Bevilacqua, V. (eds.) ICIC 2009. LNCS, vol. 5755, pp. 794–803. Springer, Heidelberg (2009)
8. Blackwell, T.: A Study of Collapse in Bare Bones Particle Swarm Optimization. IEEE Transactions on Evolutionary Computation 16(3), 204–210 (2012)
9. Wan, Z.P., Wang, G.M.: A hybrid intelligent algorithm by combining particle swarm optimization with chaos searching technique for solving nonlinear bilevel programming problems. Swarm and Evolutionary Computation 8(1), 26–32 (2013)
10. Niu, B., Wang, H., Chai, Y.J.: Bacterial Colony Optimization. Discrete Dynamics in Nature and Society 2012, Article ID 698057, 28 pages (2012)
11. Niu, B., Fan, Y., Xiao, H., Xue, B.: Bacterial Foraging-Based Approaches to Portfolio Optimization with Liquidity Risk. Neurocomputing 98(3), 90–100 (2012)
12. Niu, B., Wang, H., Wang, J.W., Tan, L.J.: Multi-objective Bacterial Foraging Optimization. Neurocomputing 116, 336–345 (2012)

A Weighted Bacterial Colony Optimization
for Feature Selection

Hong Wang[1], Xingjing Jing[1], and Ben Niu[2]

[1] Department of Mechanical Engineering, The Hong Kong Polytechnic University, Hong Kong
xingjian.jing@{gmail.com, polyu.edu.hk}
[2] College of Management, Shenzhen University, Shenzhen 518060, China

Abstract. Feature selection is essentially important for high dimensional feature characterization problems. In this paper, we propose a weighted feature selection algorithm based on bacterial colony optimization (BCO) for dimensionality reduction. The weighted strategy is used for reducing the redundant features as well as increasing the classification performance, which considers the frequency of features being selected by bacterial colony optimization(BCO) as well as the repeated appearance in the same individual. The contributions of features in classification will be evaluated and kept in 'Achieve'. The learning mechanism used in BCO considers the randomness which avoids the ignorance of unseen features as well as disengages from the local optimal error. Benchmark datasets with varying dimensionality are selected to test the effectiveness of the proposed feature selection method. The significance of the proposed weight feature selection algorithm is verified by comparing with three recently proposed population based feature selection algorithms.

Keywords: Bacterial Colony Optimization, Feature Selection, Classification.

1 Introduction

Most problems in reality are described as high dimensional feature characterization, which is computationally expensive if it works directly with raw data in terms of computational cost, time consuming, storage cost as well as the performance influence.

Therefore, many techniques have been developed to address such issues. Among them, feature selection and feature extraction as the important preprocessing techniques are commonly used for dimensionality reduction. Feature selection is generally regarded as a special case of feature extraction, even though feature selection(FS) and feature extraction have something in common, and each of them has their unique set of methodologies. Feature extraction is to convert the existing high dimensionality features into lower space, and a new subset is created after the process of feature extraction. However, it is an irreversible process. While feature selection is to select a subset from the available features space and eliminate redundant features or features with little or no conducting information. Feature extraction methods like

D.-S. Huang et al. (Eds.): ICIC 2014, LNBI 8590, pp. 379–389, 2014.

Wavelets[1], PCA coefficients[2], etc, can be more accurate. In many practical cases, predefined features may be difficult to interpret, highly computational complexity, as well as could degrade the performance of algorithms or models[3]. Therefore, the need for Feature Selection(FS) approaches or Feature-based classifiers is imperative in such situations.

As there is no specific feature selection technique that can be applied for all types of issues, numerous feature selection methods are proposed by researchers for a variety of applications. In recent decades, biological intelligence approaches based on stimulating the intelligent behaviors of real organisms have been developed. More specifically, evolutionary computation based algorithms and swarm intelligence based algorithms have been implemented for feature selection, such as Genetic Algorithm(GA)[4], Differential Evolution(DE)[5], Particle Swarm Optimization(PSO) [6], Ant Colony Optimization(ACO)[7, 8] as well their combinations like the hybrid GA-ACO-PSO[9].

Even so, when confronting with high dimensional features, it also shows some difficulties to achieve higher performance and lower dimensional features simultaneously. To enhance the efficiency, the efforts have been made to seek the improvement. One of strategy is to embed the filters such as mutual information(MI) in biological intelligence learning methods[18, 19]. Admittedly, filters themselves are a group of feature selection algorithms[13,15,16]. The interest of filters is that they can provide the correlations between the features and the class labels, which guide the feature selection process. However, the shortcoming is that the computational demands are tough[17]. The combination of filters and biological intelligence learning methods(belonging to wrappers) surely can improve the classification performance, while the computational cost is largely increased at the same time. Actually, the computational cost is also an essential problem in high dimensional feature problems. Thus, minimization of both selected features and computational cost, maximization of classification performance needs to be considered simultaneously in further development of feature selection methods.

In this paper, a weighted bacterial colony optimization has been developed for feature selection in classification. Three objectives are considered in the process of feature selection. Classification performance is the most important objective to pursue. On the basis of considerable classification performance, the number of features will be reduced at large. Additionally, the computational cost is also considered in the proposed feature selection methods.

This paper is organized as follows. Section 2 gives a brief introduction of the original optimization--Bacterial Colony Optimization(BCO). Section 3 describes the main principle of the proposed BCO feature selection method. Experiments on benchmark datasets will be conducted in Section 4. Finally, the corresponding conclusion will be given in Section 5.

2   Bacterial Colony Optimization

Inspired by behaviors of E.coli bacteria, Bacterial Colony Optimization(BCO) is proposed by Niu[10], which absorbs the advantages of two well known bacterial based algorithms: Bacterial Foraging Optimization [11] and Bacterial Chemotaxis(BC) [12], imitates the foraging behavior of bacteria, and investigates the communication mechanism between artificial bacteria as well as the artificial bacterial colony. It is proved that the BCO is a superiority optimization algorithm in terms of the efficiency searching performance as well as computational cost. For that, it must be more interesting to apply it for feature selection in classification.

In BCO, the comprehensive lifecycle model of artificial bacteria consists of four sub-models, namely Chemotaxis & Communication model, Reproduction model, Elimination model, and Migration model. The main model is Chemotaxis & Communication which involves two unique behavior(tumbling and swimming) which lead to two different forms of position adjustment. Fig.1 shows the Chemotaxis & Communication behaviour of bacteria in BCO. At the very beginning, the bacterial colony is randomly distributed in the whole region. Except the globe best, there also exist many other local optimal positions which may create a barrier to search for the globe best. Thus, the communication strategy between the groups is added to reduce the computational cost as well as avoid the locally optimal solution.

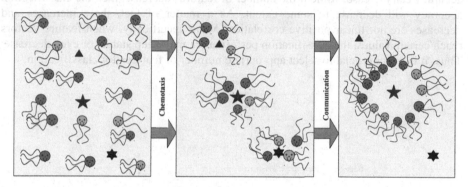

Fig. 1. The Chemotaxis & Communication mechanism in BCO[10]

As shown in Eq. 1 and Eq. 2, the difference is the the tumbling behavior by using $turbulent_i$. $turbulent_i$ is the turbulent direction variance of the ith bacterium. Actually, it represents the processing of tumbling that the bacterium changes the swimming direction randomly. $f_i \in [0,1]$, Eq.3 shows the changing of chemotaxis step size $C(i)$ with the iteration, and $iter_{max}$ is the maximal number of iterations, $iter_j$ is the current number of iterations.

$$Poistion_i(T) = Poistion_i(T-1) + C(i)*[f_i*(Gbest - Position_i(T-1)) + (1-f_i)*(Pbest_i - Position_i(T-1)) + turbulent_i] \tag{1}$$

$$Poistion_i(T) = Poistion_i(T-1) + C(i)*[f_i*(Gbest - Position_i(T-1)) + (1-f_i)*(Pbest_i - Position_i(T-1))] \tag{2}$$

$$C(i) = C_{min} + (\frac{iter_{max} - iter_j}{iter_{max}})^n (C_{max} - C_{min}) \tag{3}$$

While the remaining models: reproduction model, elimination model, and migration model are operated conditionally. More specifically, once the predefined rules are satisfied, then it can be realized. Since the conditional rules defined in proposed feature selection method are different, the descriptions are excluded in this section. More details can refer to [10].

3   Bacterial Colony Optimization Feature Selection

The purpose of the feature selection techniques in classification is to select a subset from the available features space by eliminating redundant features and maximizing the classification performance. Thus, two objects are normally considered, they are: minimization the number of features and maximization the classification performance. Fundamentally, as the number of features increase, the classification accuracy can increase, while if the number of features decrease, then the classification accuracy will decrease to some extent. As a matter of fact, these increases and decreases are not linear positive correlation. More specifically, when feature vectors reach certain values, the classification performance may keep stable, or even decrease. Thus, it is rather crucial to select appropriate number of features for classification.

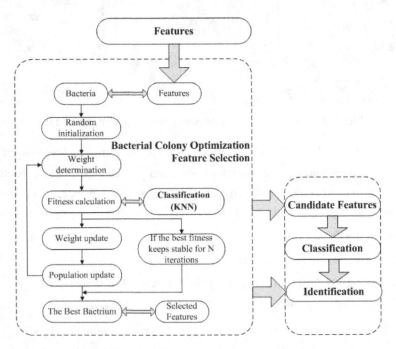

Fig. 2. The overall frame of the proposed methods

The proposed feature selection method in this paper adopts the weighted strategy to eliminate redundant features as well as improve the classification performance. The weights of each feature are changing with the selected frequency by BCO as well as mutual information between features and class label. Fig.2 also shows the overall frame of the proposed methods. In what follows, the mechanism of weighted BCO feature selection will be described in details.

3.1   Weight Determination

Weight of each feature in BCO feature selection method represents probability of being selected for replacing the repeated features. The larger weight means the higher probability being considered. In the process of optimization, the features selected by BCO may be repeated. To enhance the classification accuracy, the repeated ones will be deleted. However, the repeated features have shown their existence in population, so they will be assigned with lower weights to avoid the repeated appearance.

Assume that the weight of feature is: $W = [W_{f_1},...W_{f_H}]$, and H is the total number of features.. In the process of initialization, all the weight are equal to 1, namely $W_0 = [1,...1]$. After that, bacteria will select the better positions obey their rule to update the positions. Assume that f_i is a repeated feature in the process of optimization. For example, if the position of mth bacterium is $Pop_m = \{1,2,4,5,2,4\}$, then the 2 and 4 are repeated features. Thus, to obtain the unique features in population as well as enhance the optimization performance, the weight W_{f_i} will be updated correspondingly as follows:

$$W_{f_i} = W_{f_i} - \frac{\max_s(W_{f_s}) - \min_t(W_{f_t})}{H} \qquad (5)$$

By this way, the repeated features will keep lower values of weights, while features without being selected by population would have higher weights, which to some extent, efficiently enhances the feature distribution and effectively ensures more evaluated features in population. The weights of all features will be sorted in descending order, and save the resultant sequence of features $Sequence' = \{s_1',...,s_H'\}$ with the larger weights locate in the front and the smaller in the end, namely $W_{s_i} \geq W_{s_{i+1}}$ ($i = 1,...D-1$). Therefore, the new version of weight and the sequence are all updated again. By this way, the weight of each features $W = [W_{f_1},...W_{f_H}]$ will be updated consistently.

Since the features vectors in BCO represent the special positions that artificial bacteria find in the process of foraging, it is critical to ensure the unique of features in specific feature vector in order to effectively and efficiently enhance the classification performance. Suppose the position of mth bacterium is $Pop_m = \{f_1,...,f_D\}$, where D is the dimension of the position which equals to the expected number of features to be selected. Assume that the population of ith bacterium is $Pop_i = [f_1,...f_D]$, and there are n redundant features. So after deleting, it needs another different n features to feed the population. For that, those features will choose from sequence of weight.

After updating, the newly population is $Pop_i =[f_1,...f_{D-n}, f_{s_1},..., f_{s_n}]$. However, if the redundance still exists, the randomness of feature will be selected to realize the unique of the feature in population. Thus, in the third strategy, the features only with the frist n highest weights are provided for filling the gaps. To avoid the resultant feature vector still with certain features repeatedly, the randomness is added to update the population when the redundant feature occurs after the adding of n features with highest weights. Since the 'tumbling' behavior of bacteria has enhanced the occurrence of randomness, the probability of adding extra randomness, to some extent, is conditionally operated.

In this paper, both the weights and randomness are adopted in the process of feature selection. Even though the randomness in this updating process is conditionally operated, it also avoids the several repeated features distribution all the time. Besides, the BCO algorithm itself also considers the randomness to avoid local optimal.

3.2   Randomness Realization

As is illustrated previously, randomness is an critical strategy to realize the dynamic. In the proposed feature selection method, randomness has been realized in different ways. In the previous section, weighted determination adopts the conditional randomness to ensure that all the features are unique in each vector. The redundant features are replaced by features with higher weights. The detail realization has been illustrated in perviously section.

Besides, the tumbling behavior of bacteria employs the randomness direction selection to decide the new foraging orientation. The purpose of tumbling is to seek the better position, so not all features in a vector need to experience the tumbling process. A variable $Achieve$ is defined to mark the performance of features, that is to say, as long as the features occur in the population, it will be evaluated and the performance of it will be marked as well as kept in $Achieve$. The feature with higher value in $Achieve$ means the more critical it is than other features. Assume that the position of ith bacterium is $Pop_i =[f_1,...f_D]$, and the contribution of each feature in population is marked as $Achieve_i =[ac_1,...,ac_D]$. Firstly, sort the values $[ac_1,...,ac_D]$ with ascending order. Based on the ascending order, the features in datasets are optimized with varying dimensionality, e.g. the frist $round(3/D)$ features(with smaller values of 'Achieve') are updated.

The tumbling process in the proposed feature selection method is realized using the following equation:

$$Poistion_i^d(T) = Poistion_i^d(T-1)+turbulent_i \tag{6}$$

$$turbulent_i = C(i)\times \Delta(i) \Big/ \sqrt{\Delta^T(i)\Delta(i)} \tag{7}$$

$$C_k(i) = C_{min} + (\frac{iter_{max}-iter_j}{iter_{max}})^k (C_{max}-C_{min}) \tag{8}$$

The equation presents how the dth dimension of the position of ith bacterium is updated.Where $C(i)$ is the chemotaxis step, $C_k(i)$ is the chemotaxis step in the kth iteration. Here, a linear decreasing chemotaxis step is adopted. $\Delta(i)$ is a random direction angle of ith bacterium, which provides another randomness in the BCO feature selection method, $\Delta(i) \in [-1,1]$.

3.3   Fitness and Classifier

In BCO, population is initialized with random distribution of the features. For a given number of features, the objective for optimization is to maximize the classification performance or classification accuracy, which can be regarded as minimizing the classification error, it can represented as:

$$Minimize : Fitness = error\_rate \qquad (9)$$

In each datasets, the half of the samples are provided for training and the rest of them are for testing. With selected features chose by BCO, the classifier, i.e. k-Nearest Neighbor algorithm(KNN), offers the class categories for samples. Thus, the fitness is obtained by comparing the difference between the real class label and the class label obtained by classifier. The fitness is also considered as the error rate which can be used as the guidance for the optimization strategies for bacteria. Besides, the position of each bacterium is updated according to the principle of chemotaxis & communication and reproduction, while the rules of elimination and migration are not considered in this paper.

4   Experiment Results and Discussions

K-Nearest Neighbor algorithm(KNN) classifier(with $K = 4$) is used as the classifier to offer the class label in comparison with target class. Three population based feature selection methods: Ini_PSO[6], DEFS[5], and GA[14] are used to compare with the proposed feature selection method. The four benchmark datasets with different number of features and samples are introduced to test the effectiveness of the proposed feature selection algorithm, the detail information of the datasets has been shown in Table 1. The first three datasets are selected from the UCI machine learning repository(https://archive.ics.uci.edu/ml/datasets.html), the fouth dataset is available online from (http://cilab.ujn.edu.cn/datasets.html).

One deficiency in population based algorithm is the time consuming since the optimization performance largely depends on the randomness search process. So the total computational time need to be controlled to some extent. As is known to all, the larger population size it has, the better performance it may achieve, while the computational cost is also increasing at the same time. Thus, to solve the time consuming issue, the population of the algorithm needs to be controlled at certain level, e.g. no more than 100. Also, the number of iterations also impact the computational complex. So, the maximal number of iterations can not be too large. For that, the population size of all three compared feature selection methods are defined as $Pop = 50$, and the max_iterations is $iter = 50$. The minimization number of feature $min\_fea = 1$, and the maximization number is $max\_fea = 25$. The boundary chemotaxis step C_{min} and C_{max} in Equation 6 are set as 1 and 10 respectively.

As for PSO, parameters are set as: $w = 0.7298$, $c1 = c2 = 1.5$, $v_{max} = 6$. While for DEFS, and GA, crossover rate=0.8, mutation rate=0.001. For the proposed feature selection, the learning probability is equal to $f_i = rand(1)$, while the maximal and minimal chemotaxis step size are $C\,max = 10$, $C\,min = 1$ respectively. Fig.3 and Fig.4 show the average classification accuracy of eight benchmark datasets over the 10

Table 1. Description of Datasets

Dataset	Features	classes	instances
Wine	13	3	178
Lung	56	3	32
Madelon	500	2	1000(4400)
Colon	2000	2	62

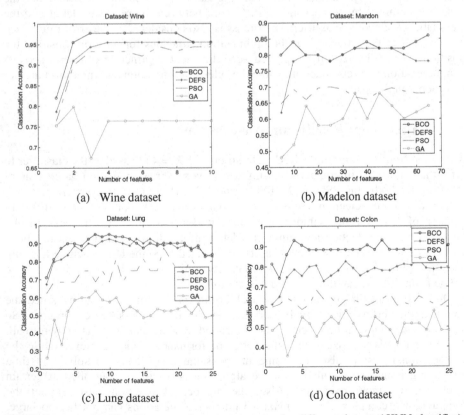

(a) Wine dataset

(b) Madelon dataset

(c) Lung dataset

(d) Colon dataset

Fig. 3. Average classification accuracies across ten runs for different datasets(KNN classifier)

repeated runs. Meanwhile, Table 2 also shows the average classification accuracy of the proposed feature selection with the given number of feature selection, while Tables 3 gives the corresponding computational time consuming to select the number of features in Tables 2.

The figures of all datasets show the effectiveness of the proposed weighted BCO feature selection algorithms since it can reach more classification accuracy in comparison with three other well known population based feature selection algorithms in most cases. Compared with the DEFS, the proposed feature selection algorithm BCO is not bad, instead, it can obtain the higher classification accuracy when the desired number of selected features are small. As is shown in Figs.3, when the number of features to be selected are small, BCO can get the highest classification accuracy. Besides, the first four datasets prove that the BCO can select the best features for classification in comparison to the compared three other population based algorithms. In contrast, the earlier proposed feature selection algorithm GA and PSO have poorer ability of feature selection, especially in high dimensional datasets. Among four feature selection algorithm, GA has the poorest feature reduction capacity, since it is the earliest contribution of feature selection, which ignores the difference of the feature dependence on the classification. Even though the PSO has better performance than GA, it also pays less attention to special features. In contrast, DEFS treats different features with different weights according to the results of fitness comparison. However, the weight determination of it is largely different from this paper. Overall, in terms of classification accuracy, the weighed BCO feature selection has shown the effectiveness for feature selection in classification.

Table 2. The average accuracy of classification achieved by BCO(KNN classifier)

datasets	Total features	Number of features						
		1	3	5	7	9	11	13
wine	13	0.8202	0.9551	0.9775	0.9775	0.9775	0.9775	0.9775
Lung	56	0.5075	0.9375	0.8750	0.9375	0.9375	0.9375	0.9375
Madelon	500	0.8000	0.8400	0.8000	0.8200	0.8400	0.8400	0.8600
Colon	2000	0.9535	0.9070	0.9767	0.9535	0.9302	0.9535	0.9535

It is difficult to select the fewer number of features with higher classification when the total number of features are very large, since the population size as well as the time of iterations in BCO is limited. Even so, with different number of total features, the computational complex is different. When handling the large available feature selection problems, the evaluation process will spend more time than smaller feature cases.

Table 3. The computational time (seconds) spend by BCO(KNN classifier)

datasets	Total features	Number of features						
		1	3	5	7	9	11	13
wine	13	2.1552	3.7801	2.4011	1.6119	1.6576	1.6930	1.0211
Lung	56	3.4345	2.8781	3.2143	2.0379	1.8814	1.6018	1.3815
Madelon	500	4.4089	3.5664	3.5883	5.8666	4.5184	3.7546	3.2486
Colon	2000	4.3592	4.4428	4.5511	3.7617	5.1396	4.0708	3.0188

The computational time of each dataset that BCO costs in each run are given in Tables 3. It is shown that the about 4 seconds that Colon dataset(with 2000 features) spends in each run. It is acceptable region of the time consuming. Admittedly, the PSO feature selection spends the smallest computational time, however, the classification performance of it is really unacceptable. Whatever, the performance of the classification is the more important than time consuming.

5   Conclusion and Future Work

A weighted feature selection using BCO has been proposed in this paper. The weight in the proposed feature selection methods is used to remove the repeated features in the same vector, as well as evaluate the contributions of the features in population which further determinate the probabilities of being selected to be updated by the randomness. A range of datasets have been introduced, and the proposed feature selection methods using BCO proves to be effective in selecting the small number of features. Compared to three other population based feature selection methods, the BCO feature selection method can achieve higher classification accuracy. Besides, the proposed method overcomes the biggest flaw that the common population-based swarm intelligence methods may involve. The highly computational costly is consistently reduced by avoiding the excessive iteration in the searching procedure.

Even though the proposed method can exceed the PSO and GA in feature selection, while in the datasets with large number of features(over ten thousand), BCO still need to spend more iterations to obtain the considerable classification accuracy. Thus, in our future study, under a prerequisite of keeping the classification performance, more efforts will focus on reducing the computational complex.

Acknowledgment. The authors would like to thank the handling editors and anonymous reviewers for your time and effort in reviewing this paper. The authors gratefully acknowledge the support from a CAST-funded project (H-ZG2D), a NSFC project (No 61374041) of China, Department General Research Funds and internal Competitive Research Grants of Hong Kong Polytechnic University.

References

1. Jin, X., Gupta, S., Mukherjee, K., Ray, A.: Wavelet-based feature extraction using probabilistic finite state automata for pattern classification. Pattern Recognition 44(7), 1343–1356 (2011)
2. Roislien, J., Brita, W.J.: Feature extraction across individual time series observations with spikes using wavelet principal component analysis. Statistics in Medicine 32(21), 3660–3669 (2013)
3. Deng, H., Runger, G., Tuv, E., Vladimir, M.: A time series forest for classification and feature extraction. Information Sciences 239, 142–153 (2013)
4. Zhou, L., Lai, K.K., Yen, J.: Bankruptcy prediction using SVM models with a new approach to combine features selection and parameter optimisation. Source of the Document International Journal of Systems Science 45(3), 241–253 (2014)

5. Khushaba, R.N., Al-Ani, A., Al-Jumaily, A.: Feature subset selection using differential evolution and a statistical repair mechanism. Expert Systems with Applications 38(9), 11515–11526 (2011)
6. Xue, B., Zhang, M., Browne, W.N.: Particle swarm optimisation for feature selection in classification: Novel initialisation and updating mechanisms. Applied Soft Computing (2013) (article in press)
7. Hu, Y., Ding, L., Xie, D., Wang, S.: The setting of parameters in an improved ant colony optimization algorithm for feature selection. Journal of Computational Information Systems 8(19), 8231–8238 (2012)
8. Sivagaminathan, R.K., Ramakrishnan, S.: A hybrid approach for feature subset selection using neural networks and ant colony optimization. Expert Systems with Applications 33(1), 49–60 (2007)
9. Sheikhan, M., Mohammadi, N.: Time series prediction using PSO-optimized neural network and hybrid feature selection algorithm for IEEE load data. Neural Computing and Applications 23(3-4), 1185–1194 (2013)
10. Niu, B., Wang, H.: Bacterial Colony Optimization. Discrete Dynamics in Nature and Society 2012(2012), 1–28 (2013)
11. Passino, K.M.: Biomimicry of bacterial foraging for distributed optimization and control. IEEE Control Systems Magazine 22(3), 52–67 (2002)
12. Müller, S.D., Marchetto, J., Airaghi, S., Koumoutsakos, P.: Optimization based on bacterial chemotaxis. IEEE Transactions on Evolutionary Computation 6(1), 16–30 (2002)
13. Peng, H., Long, F., Ding, C.: Feature Selection Based on Mutual Information: Criteria of Max-Dependency, Max-Relevance, and Min-Redundancy. IEEE Transactions on Pattern Analysis and Machine Intelligence 27(8), 1226–1238 (2005)
14. Raymer, M.L., Punch, W.F., Goodman, E.D., Kuhn, L.A., Jain, A.K.: Dimensionality reduction using genetic algorithm. IEEE Transaction on Evolutionary Computation 4, 164–171 (2000)
15. Battiti, R.: Using mutual information for selecting features in supervised neural net learning. IEEE Transactions on Neural Networks 5(4), 537–550 (1994)
16. Zhang, Y., Zhang, Z.: Feature subset selection with cumulate conditional mutual information minimization. Expert Systems with Applications 39(5), 6078–6088 (2012)
17. Schaffernicht, E., Gross, H.M.: Weighted mutual information for feature selection. In: Proceedings of Artificial Neural Networks and Machine Learning, pp. 181–188 (2011)
18. Dong, G., Guo, W.W., Tickle, K.: Solving the traveling salesman problem using cooperative genetic ant systems. Expert Systems with Applications 39(5), 5006–5011
19. Zhang, C., Hu, H.: Ant colony optimization combining with mutual information for feature selection in support vector machines. In: Zhang, S., Jarvis, R.A. (eds.) AI 2005. LNCS (LNAI), vol. 3809, pp. 918–921. Springer, Heidelberg (2005)

A Novel Method for Image Segmentation Based on Nature Inspired Algorithm

Yang Liu[1,2,3,*], Kunyuan Hu[1], Yunlong Zhu[1], and Hanning Chen[1]

[1] Shenyang Institute of Automation Chinese Academy of Sciences, 110016, Shenyang, China
[2] Shenyang University, 110044, Shenyang, China
[3] University of Chinese Academy of Sciences, 100049, Beijing, China
liuyang4@sia.cn

Abstract. Image segmentation is of great importance in the fields of computer vision, face recognition, medical imaging, digital libraries, and video retrieval. This paper presents a novel method for image segmentation based on a Hybrid particle swarm algorithm, which combines the advantages of swarm intelligence and the natural selection mechanism of artificial bee colony algorithm. Experimental results show that the proposed method can reach a higher quality adequate segmentation, reduce the CPU processing time and eliminate the particles falling into local minima.

Keywords: Image segmentation, Particle Swarm Optimization (PSO), Hybrid Particle Swarm Optimization (HPSO).

1 Introduction

There is a great source of inspiration for creating metaheuristic algorithms in nature and individuals interact constantly within a species or a population, which can obtain useful information to improve their adaptation by interacting with each other in the same species or population, such intraspecific interaction (heterogeneous coevolution) and interspecific interaction (homogeneous coevolution) in an ongoing cycle of adaptation, which are called symbiotic coevolution in biology[1].With the development and use of concepts, there are many algorithms have been used to solve difficult optimization problems, such as Genetic Algorithm (GA) ,Differential Evolution (DE), Particle Swarm Optimization (PSO) and so on.

Image segmentation is considered as an important basic operation for meaningful analysis and interpretation of images acquired, which is the first step for image understanding, feature extraction and recognition. There are four different types for image segmentation commonly, including texture analysis based methods, histogram thresholding based methods, clustering based methods and region based split and merging methods. In all of them, the thresholding method is a simple but effective method for the segmentation of images, which can divide an image into related sections

---

* Corresponding author.

D.-S. Huang et al. (Eds.): ICIC 2014, LNBI 8590, pp. 390–402, 2014.

or regions, consisting of image pixels having related data feature values. According to the selected threshold, each pixel belongs to a determined class is labeled, which is giving as a result pixel groups sharing visual characteristics in the image. The key of image segmentation is how to efficiently select the optimal thresholding. Many methods for segmentation have been proposed in these years[2].Particle swarm optimization is a kind of swarm intelligence algorithm proposed by Kennedy and Eberhart in 1995, which basically consists of a number of particles that collectively move in the search space in search of the global optimum. However, a general problem with the PSO algorithms is that of becoming trapped in a local optimum. In order to overcome this problem, we introduce a new bio-inspired image segmentation algorithm based on Hybrid Particle Swarm Optimization (HPSO) to compute threshold selection for image segmentation. In this approach, the segmentation process is considered as an optimization problem, we use domain search strategies to improve the traditional PSO algorithm. Results showed that the Hybrid Particle Swarm Optimization (HPSO) based image segmentation executed faster, eliminate the particles falling into local minima and were more stable than the traditional PSO algorithm.

2   Image Thresholding

There are two categories of thresholding techniques including bi-level and multi-level. One limit value is chosen to segment an image into the object and the background in bi-level thresholding techniques. The optimal multilevel thresholding problem can be configured as multi-level optimization problem. When an image is composed of several distinct objects, multiple threshold values have to be selected for proper segmentation [3][4].

Let there be L intensity levels [0, 1. . . L-1] of a given image .Then one can define:

$$p_i = \frac{h_i}{N}; \quad \sum_{i=1}^{N} p_i = 1 \tag{1}$$

Where I represents a specific intensity level, N represents the total number of pixels contained in the image. h_i represents the number of pixels for the corresponding intensity level I. The total mean μ_T can be calculated as:

$$\mu_T = \sum_{i=1}^{L} i p_i \tag{2}$$

The bi-level thresholding can be extended to generic n-level thresholding and assume t_j to generic n-level thresholding (j=1...n-1). The pixels of a given image will be divided into n classes $D_1...D_n$, which represent multiple objects or even specific features on such objects. The optimal threshold is the one that maximizes the between-class variance which is generally defined by:

$$\sigma_B^2 = \sum_{j=1}^{n} w_j (\mu_j - \mu_T)^2 \tag{3}$$

Where j represents a specific class in such a way that W_j and μ_j are the probability of occurrence and mean of class j, which can be defined by:

$$\begin{cases} W_j = \sum_{i=1}^{t_j} p_i, & j = 1 \\ W_j = \sum_{i=t_{j-1}+1}^{t_j} p_i, & 1 < j < n \\ W_j = \sum_{i=t_{j-1}+1}^{L} p_i, & j = n \end{cases} \tag{4}$$

$$\begin{cases} \mu_j = \sum_{i=1}^{t_j} \frac{ip_i}{w_j}, & j = 1 \\ \mu_j = \sum_{i=t_{j-1}+1}^{t_j} \frac{ip_i}{w_j}, & 1 < j < n \\ \mu_j = \sum_{i=t_{j-1}+1}^{L} \frac{ip_i}{w_j}, & j = n \end{cases} \tag{5}$$

The segmentation process is considered as an optimization problem, and the problem of n-level thresholding is reduced to an optimization problem to search for the thresholds t_j that maximizes the objective functions, generally defined as:

$$\emptyset = \max \sigma_B^2(t_j) \tag{6}$$

The standard deviation can evaluate the stability of the algorithm, the following index is used:

$$STD = \sqrt{\sum_{i=1}^{n} \frac{(\sigma_i - \mu)^2}{N}} \tag{7}$$

Where N is the repeated times of each algorithm, σ_i is the best fitness value of the ith run of the algorithm, μ is the average value of σ_i [5][11].

3   Image Segmentation Algorithm Based on Hybrid Particle Swarm Optimization (HPSO)

3.1   Traditional Particle Swarm Optimization (PSO)

In PSO model, the potential solutions of each optimization problem can be seen as a bird in the search space, which is called particle. Each particle has a velocity and searches the solution space iteratively which determines the direction and rate of particles fling and a position vector which determines the current position of the particle.

All particles have a fitness value determined by the function and need to be optimized. The particle swarm algorithm is initialized to be a group of random particles, and then we can search for the optimal solution through an iterative method. After several iterations, we can obtain the optimal solution of the optimization problem.

We focused on real-coded particle position. Each individual position of the initial population is randomly generated, which matches the corresponding fitness values of different sizes [4].

The PSO is a population-based technique, similar in some aspects to evolutionary algorithms [8], except that potential solutions (particles) move, rather than evolve, through the search space. The rules of particle dynamics that govern this movement are inspired by models of swarming and flocking. In PSO population, each particle has a position and a velocity, and experiences linear spring-like attractions towards two attractors: One is its previous best position, the other is best position of its neighbors.

In mathematical terms, each individual's direction of movement is manipulated according to the following equations:

$$v_i^{t+1} = \chi(v_i^t + c_1 r_1 (pbest_i - x_i^t) + c_2 r_2 (gbest_i - x_i^t)) \tag{8}$$

$$x_i^{t+1} = x_i^t + v_i^{t+1} \tag{9}$$

Where the ith particle is represented as $X_i = (x_{i1}, x_{i2}, \cdots x_{iD})$ in the D-dimensional space, the rate of velocity for particle i is represented as $v_i = (v_{i1}, v_{i2}, \cdots v_{iD})$, pbest is the best position found so far of the ith particle, gbest is the best position of any particles in its neighborhood, χ is known as constriction coefficient, c_1 and c_2 are learning rates, r_1 and r_2 are two random vectors uniformly distributed in [0, 1], and t is the time step[5][6].The PSO algorithm can be summarized in the table 1.

Table 1. The PSO algorithm

1. Initialize the population.
2. Calculate the fitness values of the particles
3. Update the best experience of each particle
4. Choose the best particle
5. Calculate the velocities of the particles.
6. Update the positions of the particles.
7.Until requirements are met
8.If the requirements are not met go back to step

3.2 Hybrid Particle Swarm Optimization (HPSO)

In this paper, a hybrid particle swarm optimization (HPSO) has been proposed, which combines the advantages of swarm intelligence and the natural selection mechanism of artificial bee colony algorithm, using the domain search strategies to the particle's best position to eliminate the particles falling into local minima [7].

For each particle, we should search population particle according to the formula (9), then the search in result as the domain particles. Search the entire field, if individual best of the domain particle is better than the historical individual best position; let the domain best as the local best of the particle.

$$new_{x_{ij}} = x_{ij} + r(x_{ij} - x_{kj})$$ (10)

Where $k \in (1, 2,..., size)$ and $j \in (1, 2,..., D)$ are randomly chosen indexes, and k has to be different from i, r is a random number between[-1,1].

With the increase of the number of iterations, the value of $(x_{ij} - x_{kj})$ will gradually decrease, In other words, the searching space of the particle will gradually shrink, which will also help improve the accuracy of the algorithm. To model the swarm, each particle moves in a multidimensional space according to position and velocity values which are highly dependent on information of the local best, the domain best and the global best[9].

3.3   Image Segmentation Algorithm Based on HPSO

The particles in the Hybrid Particle Swarm Optimization (HPSO) are evaluated for the fitness function, which is defined as the between-class variance σ_B^2 of the image intensity distributions previously represented in (6). The segmentation procedure can be summarized by the following steps:

(1)Initialize swarm: Initialize the particles' positions and velocities. In the beginning, the particles' velocities are set to zero and their position is randomly set within the boundaries of the search space. The search space will depend on the number of intensity levels L, i.e., if the frames are 8-bit images then the particles will be deployed between 0 and 255.

(2)For each particle in the swarm, update Particles' fitness according to the formula (4).

(3) Using formula (10), the fitness function is used to evaluate the domain best, if personality best of the domain particle is better than the historical best of the particle, let the domain best as the local best of the particle.

(4) Update Particles' velocity and position vectors according to the formula (8) and (9)

(5) Stopping criteria can be a predefined number of iterations without getting better results or other criteria, depending on the problem, then the global best is the Optimal threshold, else go to step (2);

(6)The Optimal threshold is used for image segmentation.

The flowchart of the Hybrid Particle Swarm Optimization (HPSO) process is given in Fig.1.

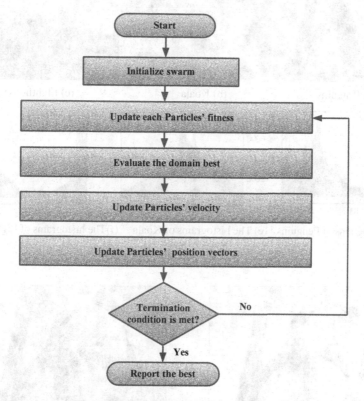

Fig. 1. The Flowchart of the proposed Algorithm

4   Experiment Result

In this section, the traditional Particle Swarm Optimization (PSO) and the Hybrid Particle Swarm Optimization (HPSO) based image segmentation which proposed in this paper was programmed in MATLAB [10]. The proposed methods are tested on a few common images including Penguins, Koala and Lighthouse. Fig. 2 illustrates different test cases along with the histograms of the images.

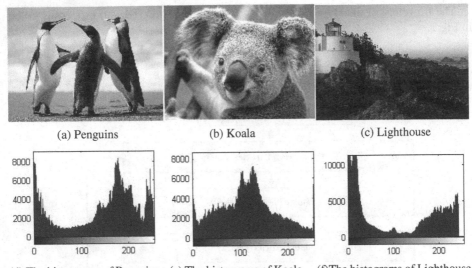

(a) Penguins   (b) Koala   (c) Lighthouse

(d) The histograms of Penguins (e) The histograms of Koala (f)The histograms of Lighthouse

Fig. 2. The images and the histogram

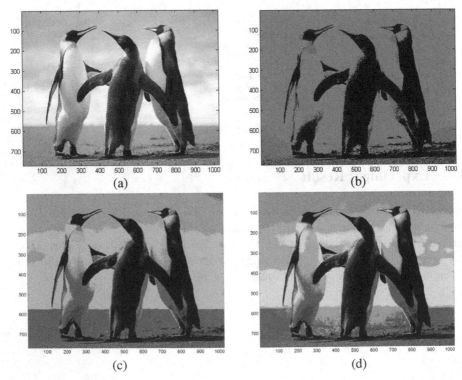

(a)   (b)

(c)   (d)

Fig. 3. The result of segmentation with 2, 3, 4 thresholds with PSO of 'Penguins' (a) Original
(b)(c)(d) The result of segmentation with 2, 3, 4 thresholds

The images are tested to evaluate the performance of the proposed algorithm. The Population size for the two methods are set to 30, the max iterations of the two methods are set to be 100, the learning rates are $c_1 = c_2 = 2.0$, a total of 20 runs are performed[8].

The first one is tested on the followed image of 'Penguins', the goal is to segment the image for 2, 3, 4 thresholds with the traditional Particle Swarm Optimization (PSO) and the Hybrid Particle Swarm Optimization (HPSO), the results are shown in Fig 3 and Fig 4 .The other one are tested on the image of 'Koala ' with the same method, the results are shown in Fig 5 and Fig 6. The last one are tested on the image of 'Lighthouse', the results are shown in Fig 7 and Fig 8.The conducted experiments show that the proposed method yields adequate segmentations.

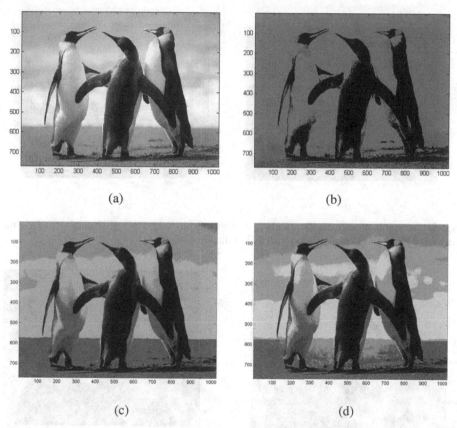

Fig. 4. The result of segmentation with 2, 3, 4 thresholds with HPSO of 'Penguins' (a) Original (b)(c)(d) The result of segmentation with 2, 3, 4 thresholds

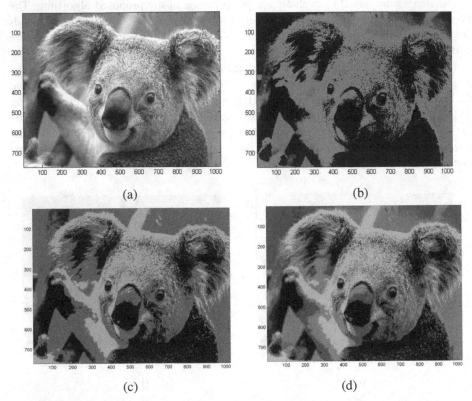

Fig. 5. The result of segmentation with 2, 3, 4 thresholds with PSO of 'Koala'   (a) Original (b)(c)(d) The result of segmentation with 2, 3, 4 thresholds

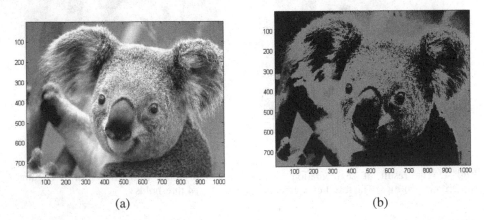

Fig. 6. The result of segmentation with 2, 3, 4 thresholds with HPSO of 'Koala' (a) Original (b)(c)(d) The result of segmentation with 2, 3, 4 thresholds

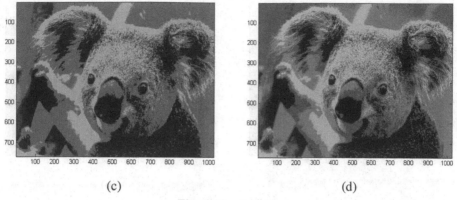

(c)   (d)

Fig. 6. (*Continued.*)

(a)   (b)

(c)   (d)

Fig. 7. The result of segmentation with 2, 3, 4 thresholds with HPSO of 'Lighthouse' (a) Original (b)(c)(d) The result of segmentation with 2, 3, 4 thresholds

Fig. 8. The result of segmentation with 2, 3, 4 thresholds with HPSO of 'Lighthouse' (a) Original (b)(c)(d) The result of segmentation with 2, 3, 4 thresholds

The standard deviation and CPU process time were selected as the measures for comparing the output of different methods. As we can see from the standard deviation and CPU processing times are brought in Table 1, the Hybrid Particle Swarm Optimization (HPSO) has the least the standard deviation values in comparison with the traditional Particle Swarm Optimization (PSO), which is the more stable. The Hybrid Particle Swarm Optimization (HPSO) has been proven in the literature to require less CPU processing time for finding thresholds in comparison to the traditional Particle Swarm Optimization (PSO), especially for higher threshold numbers. The results illustrate that the Hybrid Particle Swarm Optimization (HPSO) is more efficient than the traditional Particle Swarm Optimization (PSO), in particular, when the level of segmentation increases, thus being able to find the better thresholds with more stability in less CPU processing time.

Table 2. STD and CPU process time of different methods

Test image	Thresholds	PSO		HPSO	
		STD	Computational time	STD	Computational time
Penguins	2	0.0953	0.3912	0.0089	0.3635
	3	1.0951	0.4887	0.1039	0.4575
	4	2.8349	0.5965	0.2614	0.5067
Koala	2	0.0776	0.4134	0.0467	0.4352
	3	1.2658	0.4998	0.1953	0.4846
	4	2.6067	0.6047	0.6386	0.5575
Lighthouse	2	0.2586	0.3934	0.0278	0.3846
	3	1.5413	0.4967	0.1225	0.4569
	4	3.2364	0.5956	0.3576	0.5483

5   Conclusion

In this paper, it proposed a novel method for image segmentation based on a Hybrid particle swarm algorithm (HPSO) for solving the problem for delineating multilevel threshold values and to overcome the disadvantages of traditional Particle Swarm Optimization (PSO) in terms of trapping in local optimum. Results have been evaluated in terms of quality of the output images and computational time to obtain them, which indicate that the Hybrid Particle Swarm Optimization (HPSO) is more efficient than the traditional Particle Swarm Optimization (PSO), specifically when the level of segmentation increases, the novel method for image segmentation based on a Hybrid particle swarm algorithm (HPSO) can find the better thresholds with more stability in less CPU processing time.

Acknowledgment. This work was supported in part by the National Natural Science Foundation of China under Grant 61105067 and 61174164,the General Project of Education Department of Liaoning Province under Grant L2013446 and the Engineering research center of the IOT Information technology integration of Liaoning Province open-funded projects.

References

1. Frank, A.: Models of symbiosis. American Naturalist 150, 80–99 (1997)
2. Couceiro, M.S., Ferreira, N.M.F., Machado, J.A.T.: Application of fractional algorithms in the control of a robotic bird. Journal of Communications in Nonlinear Science and Numerical Simulation-Special Issue 15(4), 895–910 (2010)
3. Sezgin, M., Sankur, B.: Survey over image thresholding techniques and quantitative performance evaluation. Journal of Electronic Imaging 13(1), 146–168 (2004)

4. Das, S., Abraham, A., Konar, A.: Automatic clustering using an improved differential evolution algorithm. IEEE Transactions on Systems, Man, and Cybernetics-Part A: Systems and Human 38, 218–237 (2008)
5. Ghamisi, P., Couceiro, M.S., Benediktsson, J.A., Ferreira, N.M.F.: An efficient method for segmentation of images based on fractional calculus and natural selection. Expert Systems with Applications 39, 12407–12417 (2010)
6. Baßstürk, A., Günay, E.: Efficient edge detection in digital images using a cellular neural network optimized by differential evolution algorithm. Expert System with Applications 36(8), 2645–2650 (2009)
7. Chen, S., Wang, M.: Seeking multi-thresholds directly from support vectors for image segmentation. Neurocomputing 67(4), 335–344 (2005)
8. Guo, R., Pandit, S.M.: Automatic threshold selection based on histogram modes and discriminant criterion. Machine Vision and Applications 10, 331–338 (1998)
9. Sathya, P.D., Kayalvizhi, R.: Modified bacterial foraging algorithm based multilevel thresholding for image segmentation. Journal Engineering Applications of Artificial Intelligence 24(4) (2011)
10. Saha, P.K., Udupa, J.K.: Optimum image thresholding via class uncertainty and region homogeneity. IEEE Transactions on Pattern Analysis and Machine Intelligence 23, 689–706 (2001)
11. Zhang, Y., Li, S., Dong, X.: Multiple Neural Network Model Based on Data Partition Using Feature Clustering. Information and Control 42(6), 693–699 (2013)

Neural Network Based on Self-adaptive Differential Evolution for Ultra-Short-Term Power Load Forecasting

Wei Liu[1], Hui Song[2], Jane Jing Liang[2,*], Boyang Qu[2,3], and Alex Kai Qin[4]

[1] State Grid Henan Economic Research Institute, Zhengzhou, China
liuwei830610@163.com
[2] School of Electrical Engineering, Zhengzhou Univerisity, Zhengzhou, China
[3] School of Electric and Information Engineering, Zhongyuan University of Technology, Zhengzhou, China
hsong320@163.com, liangjing@zzu.edu.cn, qby1984@hotmail.com
[4] School of Computer Science and Information TechnologyRMIT University, Melbourne 3001, Victoria, Australia
kai.qin@rmit.edu.au

Abstract. Ultra-short-term power load forecasting, which is a complex and nonlinear optimization problem, is an important problem in power system. Self-adaptive Differential Evolution (SaDE), whose control parameter (mutation factor F, crossover factor CR) and mutation strategy are changed gradually and adaptively according to the previous search performance, has been a widely used optimization algorithm among so many improved Differential Evolutions for its strong ability of global numerical optimization and good convergence characteristic. SaDE is employed to optimize a two-layer Neural Network (NN) for the problem of Ultra-short-term power load forecasting. The result shows that SaDE has higher accuracy comparing with Back Propagation (BP) when it is applied in Ultra-short-term power load forecasting.

Keywords: Ultra-short-term power load forecasting, Self-adaptive Differential Evolution, Neural Network, Back Propagation.

1 Introduction

Power load forecasting plays a very important role in managing and researching power system, and it also makes the most use of electricity and eases the conflict between supply and demand for the analysis of the existing electric energy [1]. According to the time length of the prediction, the power load forecasting can be classified to ultra-short-term power load forecasting, short-term power load forecasting, medium long-term power load forecasting and long-term power load forecasting [2]. In terms of power system dispatching and management, ultra-short-term power load forecasting which varies from an hour to a week is the most important.

---

* Corresponding author.

D.-S. Huang et al. (Eds.): ICIC 2014, LNBI 8590, pp. 403–412, 2014.
© Springer International Publishing Switzerland 2014

Intelligent prediction methods do not need prior knowledge about parameters, the structure of process model, a complex system to establish a mathematical model, thus these methods are efficient for time-varying, nonlinear, multi-variables and uncertainty ultra-short-term power load forecasting [3]. Intelligent forecasting methods include Expert System (ES) [5], Support Vector Machine (SVM) [4][6][7], Back Propagation Neural Network(BPNN) [8][9] and so on. The main drawback of the ES is that it learns nothing from the environment and has ambiguous relationship between rules, low efficiency and adaptability. The main disadvantage of SVM is that it is difficult to handle large-scale training samples and solve multi-classification problems. BPNN is widely to calculate large-scale complex training samples as well as to slow the speed of convergence during training process used for power load forecasting in recent years.

The shortcomings exist both in classical and intelligent power load forecasting models, so more attentions are focused on various methods which combine optimization algorithms and predictive models. Many researchers have done a series of researches and many applications, and then make a conclusion that using optimization algorithms to optimize predicted models has a stronger ability to adapt the changes of the environment [1].

Recently, many heuristic algorithms have been proposed to be combined with neural networks to solve Ultra-short-term power load forecasting problem, such as Genetic Algorithm (GA), Particle Swarm Optimization (PSO), Tabu Search (TS)[1]. Evolutionary Algorithm (EA) which imitates the evolutionary process of individuals to find the optimal solution is based on the evolution theory of nature. Differential evolution (DE), which is a branch of EA, is one of the best heuristic algorithms proposed so far. It can find the global optimal solution effectively by mutation, crossover and selection operation with floating-point coded individuals. DE can be used to solve a variety of optimization problems in power system for its good robustness.

The success of Traditional DE in solving a specific problem crucially depends on appropriately choosing trial vector generation strategies and their associated control parameter values. What's more, its associated parameter settings require high computational costs and different strategies coupled with different parameter settings may be required in order to achieve the best performance at different stages of evolution [3]. So a Self-adaptive Differential Evolution (SaDE) [10], in which both trial vector generation strategies and their associated control parameter values are gradually self-adapted by learning from their previous experiences in generating promising solutions, is employed to optimize the weights in the neural network for solving ultra-short-term power load forecasting problem. The result shows that compared with BPNN, it is easier to find global optimum and has a higher accuracy with SaDE-NN in Ultra-short-term power load forecasting.

The rest of this paper is organized as follows. Section 2 gives a brief introduction about Back Propagation Neural Network. The main idea of Self-adaptive Differential Evolution and Neural Network Based on Self-adaptive Differential Evolution model employed in this work are described in detail in Section 3. Section 4 introduces the experimental setup and presents the results. Conclusions and future work are given in Section 5.

2   Back Propagation Neural Network

Back Propagation Neural Network was proposed by Dr. Werbos in 1974[11], which is the most widely used Feedforward Neural Network. BP Neural Network can approximate a highly nonlinear function in arbitrary precision, in which error back propagation algorithm is adopted to adjust the network parameters.

The basic idea of the algorithm is as follows: The learning process of BPNN includes signal transmission and error back propagation. During the signal transmission, the sample transmits from the input layer to output layer after calculating each hidden layer's neurons. If the actual output is different from desired output, then error back propagation process will work. Error passes through the hidden layer to output layer step by step in some units and is assigned to all unites of each layer to acquire the error of each layer. The error signal is regarded as the basic information for correcting weights of each unit. Signal transmission and error back propagation is repeated again and again. Adjusting weights is the learning process of neural network, which is conducted until the output error reaches to the target range or a predetermined number of iterations. Fig.1 is a typical three layer BPNN structure.

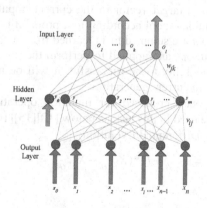

Fig. 1. Structure of BPNN

where, $x_0, x_1, ..., x_j ..., x_n$ is the input value of BPNN, $o_1, o_2, ..., o_k ..., o_l$ is predictive value, v_{ij} and w_{jk} $(i = 1, 2, ..., n, j = 1, 2, ..., m, k = 1, 2, ..., l)$ are the input and output weights of BPNN respectively. If the input node is n and the output node is l, BPNN expresses the mapping relationship from n independent input variables to l independent output variables. BPNN acquires associative memory and ability to predict through training the network.

3   Neural Network Based on Self-adaptive Differential Evolution

3.1   Self-adaptive Differential Evolution

Differential evolution (DE) was originally presented by R. Storn and K. V. Price in 1995 [12]. It has been proven to be one of the most competitive EAs [13][14]. The key control parameters are kept the same and are given in advance according to experience in traditional DE. So it is very difficult to determine the parameters in practice. F determines the rate of convergence. CR is sensitive to the complexity of the problem and has much to do with the characteristic of the optimization problem. In order to find the real global optimal solution, parameters should be changed for many runs. Generally speaking, it will spend a lot of time to find proper parameters. However, in the evolutionary process of SaDE, mutation strategy and control parameters can be gradually self-adapted according to their previous experiences of generating promising solutions.

The core of the SaDE is as follows:

　　a.   Trial Vector Generation Strategy Adaptation

A candidate pool with several different strategies is used. In the process of evolution, with respect to each target vector in the current population, one strategy will be chosen from the candidate pool according to a probability(all probabilities of strategies in the candidate pool are summed to 1) learned from its previous experience of generating promising solutions and applied to perform the mutation operation [9]. If one strategy has more possibility to be successful, it will be more possible to be selected to generate solution in current generation.

Various strategies have been proposed for mutation operation, and five most frequently used strategies are used in this task as below [10][15][16]:

Mode 1: DE/rand/1(Basic Differential Evolution)

$$V_{i,G} = X_{r_1^i,G} + F*(X_{r_2^i,G} - X_{r_3^i,G}) \tag{1}$$

Mode 2: DE/best/1

$$V_{i,G} = X_{best,G} + F*(X_{r_1^i,G} - X_{r_2^i,G}) \tag{2}$$

Mode 3: DE/rand_to_best/1

$$V_{i,G} = X_{i,G} + F*(X_{best,G} - X_{i,G}) + F*(X_{r_1^i,G} - X_{r_2^i,G}) \tag{3}$$

Mode 4: DE/ best/2

$$V_{i,G} = X_{best,G} + F*(X_{r_1^i,G} + X_{r_2^i,G}) + F*(X_{r_3^i,G} - X_{r_4^i,G}) \tag{4}$$

Mode 5: DE/ rand/2

$$V_{i,G} = X_{r_1^i,G} + F*(X_{r_2^i,G} + X_{r_3^i,G}) + F*(X_{r_4^i,G} - X_{r_5^i,G}) \tag{5}$$

where, $X_{best,G}$ is best individual achieved so far in the population at generation G. F is a control mutation factor while $r_1^i, r_2^i, r_3^i, r_4^i, r_5^i$ are mutually integers randomly generated within the range $[1, NP]$, which are different from the individual i. $V_{i,G}$ is the new position after mutation.

b.   Parameter Adaptation

F, CR, NP are very difficult to determine in traditional DE, so the parameter F which is described in detail how it changes in [9]is approximated by a normal distribution with mean value 0.5 and standard deviation 0.3, denoted by $N(0.5,0.3)$ in SaDE. CR, which generally falls into a small range for a given problem, but this algorithm can perform consistently well, is also a normal distribution with mean value CRm (which is initialized to 0.5 and then adjusted gradually according to the possibility of entering the next generation within the previous LP generations for every strategy).Standard deviation Std=0.1, denoted by $N(CRm, Std)$.

Using this method to determine the F and CR, a SaDE algorithm is developed and both trial vector generation strategies and their associated parameter values are gradually self-adapted by learning their previous experiences of generating promising solutions.

3.2 The Process of Neural Network Based on Self-adaptive Differential Evolution

Self-adaptive Differential Evolution which is applied to train the weights of NN includes the following steps:

a.   According to the input and output (x, o) determine the number of input layer nodes n, hidden layer nodes m and output layer nodes l. Randomly generate the initial population $P_G = \{X_{1,G}, \ldots X_{NP,G}\}$, NP is the population size, and $X_{i,G} = \{x_{i,G}^1, \ldots, x_{i,G}^D\}$, $i = 1, \ldots, NP$ uniformly comes from the range $[X_{min}, X_{max}]$, where $X_{min} = \{x_{min}^1, \ldots, x_{min}^D\}$ and $X_{max} = \{x_{max}^1, \ldots, x_{max}^D\}$, $D = n*m+m+m*l+l$ is the individual length. Set the initial median of $CR(CRm_k)$,generation counter $G = 0$, strategy probability $(p_{k,G}, k = 1, \ldots, K$, K indicates the number of available strategies), learning period(LP)

b.   Calculate the fitness values of the population individuals. $f(x) = \dfrac{1}{1+e^{-x}}$ is the excitation function. Normalize the original data input and output samples:

$$x_k^{new} = \frac{0.1+0.8\times(x_k^{old} - \min x_k^{old})}{\max x_k^{old} - \min x_k^{old}}$$

$$o_k^{new} = \frac{0.1+0.8\times(o_k^{old} - \min o_k^{old})}{\max o_k^{old} - \min o_k^{old}}$$

(6)

c. $K=1, 2,\ldots m$ is the number of samples. x_k^{old} and y_k^{old}, x_k^{new} and y_k^{new} represent the input and output of the network which are unprocessed and processed respectively. Firstly, calculate the output of hidden layer H according to the input data x, weights v_{ij} between input and hidden layer and threshold a.

$$H_j = f(\sum_{i=1}^{n} v_{ij} x_i - a_j) \quad j = 1, 2, ..., m \tag{7}$$

m is the nodes of hidden layer and f is the excitation function of hidden layer. Secondly, according to the output of hidden layer H, weights w_{jk} between hidden layer and output layer, threshold b calculate o which is the predicted output of BPNN.

$$o_k = \sum_{j=1}^{m} H_j w_{jk} - a_k \quad k = 1, 2, ..., l \tag{8}$$

Then, according to predicted output o and expected output p calculate predicted error e of neural network.

$$e_t^k = P_t^k - o_t^k \quad k = 1, 2, ..., l \ t = 1, 2, ...NP \tag{9}$$

The fitness function is set as:

$$fit(t) = \sum_{k=1}^{l} abs(e_t^k) \tag{10}$$

Calculate every particle's fitness value by (10), search for each particle's best position achieved so far.

d.   WHILE stopping criterion is not satisfied , DO

(i)   If $G > LP$, for each strategy, calculate strategy possibility $p_{k,G}$ ($k = 1, ... K$) by equation $P_{k,G} = \dfrac{S_{k,G}}{\sum_{k=1}^{K} S_{k,G}}$,

$$S_{k,G} = \dfrac{\sum_{g=G-LP}^{G-1} ns_{k,g}}{\sum_{g=G-LP}^{G-1} ns_{k,g} + \sum_{g=G-LP}^{G-1} nf_{k,g}} + 0.01$$ and update the *Success* and *Failure*

$(k = 1, 2, ..., K; G > LP)$

Memory by removing $ns_{k,G-LP}$ and $nf_{k,G-LP}$ from them, respectively.

(ii)   For each target vector $X_{i,G}$, select one strategy k using stochastic universal sampling, and assign a control parameter F_i by randomly sampling from a normal distribution $N(0.5, 0.3)$. Set the other control parameter CR according to the principles: if $G >= LP$, update the median of CR using $CRm_k = median(CRMemory_k)$ first; after that, with regard to each strategy k, for each individual X_i , assign a $CR_{k,i}$ value by sampling from a normal distribution $N(CRm_k, 0.1)$, and if $CR_{k,i} < 0$ or $CR_{k,i} > 1$, sample a new one.

(iii)   Produce a new population, and generate each trial vector $U_{i,G}^k$ using the associated trial vector generation strategy k and control parameters F_i, $CR_{k,i}$ set in (ii)

(iv)   For each $U_{i,G}^k$, if there is any variable outside its boundaries, randomly reinitialize this vector.

(v)   For each $U_{i,G}^k$, use (10) to evaluate it first, and go on selection afterwards. If $f(U_{i,G}^k) \leq f(X_{i,G})$, then $X_{i,G+1} = U_{i,G}^k$, $f(X_{i,G+1}) = f(U_{i,G}^k)$, $ns_{k,G} = ns_{k,G} + 1$, store $CR_{k,i}$ into $CRMemory_k$, and at the same time, if $f(U_{i,G}^k) \leq f(X_{best,G})$, then $X_{best,G} = U_{i,G}^k$, $f(X_{best,G}) \leq f(U_{i,G}^k)$; Otherwise, if $f(U_{i,G}^k) > f(X_{i,G})$, then $ns_{k,G} = ns_{k,G} + 1$.   After completing aforementioned operation, store $ns_{k,G}$ and $nf_{k,G}$ ($k = 1,\dots,K$) into the *Success* and *Failure Memory*, respectively.

(vi)   Update the generation count $G = G + 1$.

e.   END WHILE

4   Experimental Results

This experiment is carried out based on the electricity industry, whose data is obtained through the system of monitoring and analyzing key power industry. There are 96 sampling points for everyday. Two models which are BPNN and SaDE-NN are used to predict the power load of one day. According to the recorded load data of October, November, December, precious 29 days in December, related days (related days of everyday are 20 days) and related sampling points(related points for every sampling point are 34 points) of these 29 days are regarded as train data to predict the load of 30th, December. The related days are the same days in the previous two months, the same days in previous weeks, and the previous days except for the first two cases in these 20 days about the current day. The related sampling points are 9 points about yesterday, 9 points before and after the same sampling point(the sampling point is included) about the day before yesterday, 8 points about yesterday in last week, 9 points before and after the same sampling point(the sampling point is excluded) about the day before yesterday in last week. So the number of data used as training input is 54.What's more, the prediction of each algorithm concludes the whole day's prediction and every point's prediction during one day. They are defined as follows:

BPNN1: The data of the whole day is regarded as a whole prediction output (the dimension of the output is 96) and the predicted mode is BPNN.

SaDE-NN1: The data of the whole day is regarded as a whole prediction output and the predicted mode is SaDE-NN.

BPNN2: Every point in one day is regarded as the output (the dimension of the output is 1) and the predicted mode is BPNN. Each time only one point is predicted.

SaDE-NN2: Every point in one day is regarded as a whole prediction output and the predicted mode is SaDE-NN.

The parameters used in this task are set as follows:
The structure of NN1: 54 input nodes, 20 hidden nodes, 96 output nodes
The structure of NN2: 54 input nodes, 20 hidden nodes, 1output node
Dimension: 1121
Population size: 150
MaxFES (Maximum Fitness Evaluation): 40000

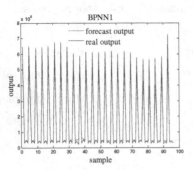
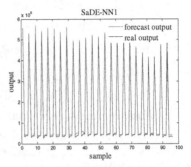

Fig. 2. The whole day as a sample to be optimized

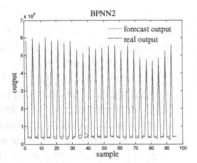
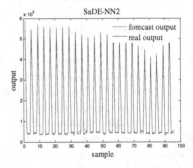

Fig. 3. Every point in one day as a sample to be optimized

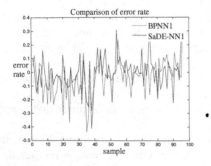
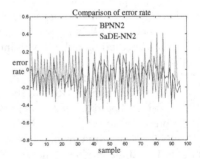

Fig. 4. Comparison of error rate under different conditions

Table 1. The error rate which is below 3%

	BPNN1	SaDE-NN1	BPNN2	SaDE-NN2
Error rate<3%	0.6146	0.6458	0.6874	0.8125

Some conclusions could be made from the result as follows:
- SaDE-NN performs better than BPNN which shows that Self-adaptive has improve the diversity of the solutions;
- To predict every point has a better result than regard the whole day as a sample;
- The accuracy of SaDE-NN is higher than BPNN obviously.

From these three points, we could know that SaDE has a better global search ability which helps it avoid being trapped into local optimum, and avoids finding suitable parameters which is very difficult. After applying SaDE to optimize the weights of the neural network, the prediction is much more better which shows that the accuracy of SaDE-NN is higher than BPNN obviously for Ultra-Short-Term Power load forecasting.

5   Conclusions

In this paper, an improved DE(SaDE) is applied to optimize the weights of the neural network. What's more, two experiments are used to test the property of SaDE-NN. The result shows that SaDE-NN has better global search ability to find optimal solution when it is used in ultra-short-term power load forecasting problems. The result of error rate also makes us know that when every point is regared as training sample, the result is much more better. Another phonomenan could be see is that the prediction arccuracy is a little worse which shows that the collected data is not good enough, so a better predited system to obtain data will be applied in ultra-short-serm power load forecasting, what's more, more algorithms will be used to predict power load and more better and fast algorithms will be used for online forcast.

Acknowledgment. This research is partially supported by The Second Batch Project of Science and Technology of Henan Electric Power Company in 2013 (5217L0135029)and National Natural Science Foundation of China (61305080) and Postdoctoral Science Foundation of China (20100480859) and Specialized Research Fund for the Doctoral Program of Higher Education (20114101110005).

References

1. Gross, G., Galiana, F.D.: Short-term power load forecasting [J]. Proceedings of the IEEE, Vol. 75(12), pp. 1558 – 1573(1987)
2. Hamadi, H. M. Al.: Long-Term Electric Power Load Forecasting Using Fuzzy Linear Regression Technique. In Power Engineering and Automation Conference (PEAM), 2011 IEEE, pp. 96-99(2011)

3. Zhao, S.B., Zhang, F.S., Zhong, J.Y., Tian, H.: An Adaptive Differential Evolution Algorithm and Its Application in Reactive Power Optimization of Power System, Power System Technology, Vol. 34(6), pp. 169-174(2010)
4. Zhang, Q.: Research on Mid-long Load Forecasting Based on SVM and Wavelet Neural Network. International Conference on Machine Vision and Human-Machine Interface (MVHI), pp. 283-287(2010)
5. Hsu, Y.Y.: Fuzzy expert systems: an application to short-term power load forecasting [J]. IEE Proceedings C: Generation Transmission and Distribution, 139(6). 471-477 (1992)
6. Francis, E., Tay, H.: Application of support vector machines in financial time series forecasting [J]. Omega, Vol. 29(4). pp. 309-317(2001)
7. Rüping, S.: Incremental learning with support vector machines. Proceedings-IEEE International Conference on Data Mining, ICDM. pp. 641-642(2001)
8. Luo, X., Zhou, Y.H., Zhou, H.: Forecasting the daily load based on ANN. In: Control theory and application. pp. 1–4(2007)
9. Kim, C.I., Yu, I. K.: Kohonen neural network and transform based approach to short-term power load forecasting. Elect Elecr Power Syst Res 63(3). pp. 169–1765 (2002)
10. Qin, A.K., Huang, V.L., Suganthan, P.N.: Differential Evolution Algorithm With Strategy Adaptation for Global Numerical Optimization, IEEE Transactions on Evolutionary Computation, VOL. 13(2),pp. 398-417(2009)
11. Werbos, P.J.: Beyond regression : New tools for predictions and analysis in the behavioral science, Ph D Thesis, Harvard University(1974)
12. Storn, R., Price, K.V.: Differential evolution: A simple and efficient adaptive scheme for global optimization over continuous spaces, ICSI, Tech. Rep. TR-95-012(1995)
13. Price, K.V.: Differential evolution vs. the functions of the 2nd ICEO, in Proc. IEEE Int. Conf. Evol. Comput., pp. 153–157(1997)
14. Price, K.V., Storn, R.: Differential evolution: A simple evolution strategy for fast optimization, Dr. Dobb's J., vol. 22, no. 4, pp. 18–24(1997)
15. Price, K.V., Storn, R., Lampinen, J.A.: Differential Evolution : A Practical Approach to Global Optimization, in Natural Computing Series Berlin: Springer(2005)
16. Price, K.V.: Differential evolution vs. the functions of the 2nd ICEO, in Proc. IEEE Int. Conf. Evol. Comput., pp. 153–157(1997)

Bacterial Foraging Optimization with Neighborhood Learning for Dynamic Portfolio Selection

Lijing Tan[1], Ben Niu[2,3,*], Hong Wang[3], Huali Huang[2], and Qiqi Duan[2]

[1] Management School, Jinan University, Guangzhou 510632, China
[2] College of Management, Shenzhen University, Shenzhen 518060, China
[3] Department of Industrial and System Engineering,
The Hong Kong Polytechnic University, Hong Kong
ben.niu@polyu.edu.hk

Abstract. This paper proposes a new variant of bacterial foraging optimization, called Bacterial Foraging Optimization with Neighborhood Learning (BFONL). In the proposed BFO-NL, information sharing among each individual can be realized by using a von Neumann-style neighborhood topology. To demonstrate the efficiency of BFO-NL in dealing with real world problem, this paper improves the original mean-variance portfolio model into Two-Period dynamic PO model considering risky assets for trading, then uses BFO-NL to automatically find the optimal portfolios in the advanced model. With a five stock portfolio example, BFO-NL is proved to outperform original BFO in selecting optimal portfolios.

Keywords: Neighborhood learning, bacterial foraging optimization (BFO), von Neumann-style, portfolio optimization.

1 Introduction

Bacterial foraging optimization (BFO) was firstly proposed by Passino in 2002 [1]. It inspired by the foraging behavior of E.coli bacteria. BFO has attracted increasing attention as its strong optimization capabilities in solving optimization problems. The analysis and improvement of this algorithm are mainly from two aspects. Some researchers redesigned mechanism of the algorithm to improve the efficiency, such as the behavioral model of bacteria(BCO) proposed by Niu [2] which contains Chemotaxis, Communication, Elimination, Reproduction and Migration, Tang [3] constructed a novel biologically methodology for complex system. On the other hand, researchers proposed hybrid algorithm by integrating other algorithms into BFO, such as a hybrid approach involving genetic algorithms (GA) and bacterial foraging (BF) algorithms presented by Kim [4], Bacterial Swarm Optimization(BSO) which combined Bacterial Foraging Optimization (BFO) algorithm with Particle Swarm Optimization (APSO) algorithm to balance between exploration and exploitation [5], Bacterial Foraging-Tabu Search Metaheuristics(BTS) incorporated Tabu Search into BFO [6] and so on.

---

* Corresponding author.

D.-S. Huang et al. (Eds.): ICIC 2014, LNBI 8590, pp. 413–423, 2014.

Untill date, BFO has been successfully applied to a number of engineering problems, such as economic load dispatch [7], optimal control [8], PID controller design [9] , machine learning [10] and some multi-objective optimization problems [11] etc. However, there are very few studies on BFO to deals with portfolio selection problem in the literature. The first mathematical formalization for portfolio selection problem is Mean-Variance model, which was proposed by Markowitz in 1952 [12]. The standard Markowitz portfolio framework explains the trade-off between returns and risk. As the high computational complexity and the far too many input parameters, this model is less used in practice. A large numbers of researchers dedicateed in the evolution of Markowitz model, such as Konno and Yamazaki introduced a Mean Absolute deviation (MAD) model [13], Speranza [14] introduced a more general model with a weighted based on MDA, Speranza [15] presented a general mixed integer model including real world constraints. However, the investors usually invest continuously rather than at intervals or only once in the real world. So this paper extend the original single-period mean-variance portfolio model into Two-Period dynamic PO model firstly, which consider a financial market with risky assets for trading

From the descriptions of BFO above, it can be seen that few literatures are considering the information communication to improve the performance of the algorithm. Based on our previous works [16], this paper proposes a novel communicational bacterial foraging optimization here called Bacterial Foraging Optimization with Neighborhood Learning (BFO-NL). With the neighborhood learning mechanism, the diversity of the swarm is increased and the search efficient is improved. Then, to verify the performance of the proposed BFO-NL, it is used to solve to solve the improved dynamic Markowitz model. The results were compared to those obtained from heuristic methods based on the original BFO.

2   An Overview of Bacterial Foraging Optimization

Bacterial foraging optimization (BFO) is a stochastic optimization technique that imitates the social foraging behavior of swarms of bacteria [1, 17]. Since its introduction in 2002, it has drawn increasing attention from researchers in different scientific and industrial fields. One of the attractive characteristics of BFO lies in the fact that it simulates the bacterial foraging behavior driven by an underlying control system at a micro level. The control system consists of chemotaxis, reproduction, and elimination-dispersal events. Its concrete biological context can be found in [1]. For saving space, here we omit it and mainly focus on the improvements and applications of BFO. The pseudo code of BFO is briefly presented as following. Note that the swarming mechanism in BFO is neglected here due to its expensive computation cost and low improvement in the solution quality [18].

Like other stochastic optimization algorithms, BFO does also suffer from the common problems of premature convergence and oscillation and so on [19]. In order to alleviate these issues, diverse BFO variants have been proposed which were mentioned in the introduction. This paper we attempt to hybridize the concept of 'neighbor topology' and the idea of 'neighbor learning' in the context of PSO to improve the performance of BFO, as presented below.

3   Bacterial Foraging Optimization with Neighborhood Learning

For most of swarm intelligence algorithms, learning from neighbor information is one of critical features and important driving forces for the efficient search. To achieve fast convergence and excellent exploitation, it is valuable, even for evolutionary algorithms, to obtain the direction information of neighborhood to guide the search [20]. In the context of PSO [21] and DE [20], it has been proved that neighbor learning could improve the performance on some problem instances (especially for multimodal functions), in terms of convergence rate and solution quality. Further, a neighborhood topology termed as von Neumann is more efficient over a variety of problems instances than other static topologies (e.g., ring, star and pyramid) in terms of solution quality [22]. Therefore, in this paper only the von Neumann-style neighborhood topology is explored in the context of BFO.

In this section, we investigate how to integrate the neighbor topology (i.e., von Neumann [22]) and the neighborhoods' position information into the search behavior of bacteria, and propose a bacterial forging optimization algorithm with neighbor leaning, which is named as BFO-NL. Inspired on the position update formula of PSO, we propose a novel bacterial position update equation as presented in the following:

$$P(i, j+1, k, ell) = P(i, j, k, ell) + W * C(i, k) * (NP(l, j, k, ell) - P(i, j, k, ell)) \quad (1)$$

where W is a system parameter that controls the tradeoff between exploration and exploitation, k-th reproduction, and ell-th elimination events, and $NP(i, j+1, k, ell)$ is the position information of the best-performing neighbor learned by bacterium i.

Note that the neighborhood topology is static for easy to program, which means that each bacterium cannot change its neighborhood indices during the entire course of optimization. The dynamic population topology is beyond the scope of this paper. Further, at the initialization stage of optimization, each bacterium's neighborhoods are decided based on the indices of population rather than the geographical locations of population for avoiding excessive distance calculations. Through the detailed description above, the pseudo-code of BFO-NL is given as Table 1.

Table 1. Pseudo code of the BFO-NL algorithm

```
Algorithm BFO-NL
Begin
```
Step 1. **Initialization.** The population P is randomly distributed in the search space with dimension D. The costs of all bacteria J are evaluated according to the cost function $f(P)$.

Step 2. **Elimination loop:** $ell = 1$ to N_{ed} (N_{ed} is the number of elimination-dispersal events)

Step 3. **Reproduction loop:** $k = 1$ to N_{re} (N_{re} is the number of reproduction operations)

Step 4. **Chemotaxis loop:** $j = 1$ to N_c (N_c is the number of chemotaxis operations)

  [a].For $i = 1$ to S (i and S are the index and total number of bacteria, respectively)

  [b].Cost calculation: $J(i,j,k,ell) = f(P(i,j,k,ell))$, and Let $J_t = J(i,j,k,ell)$,

  [c].Position update: according to equation (1) (where $C(i,k)$ is the step size for bacterium in the k-th reproduction loop, and is a D-dimensional vector randomly distributed in [-1,1]),

  [d].Cost calculation: $J(i,j+1,k,ell) = f(P(i,j+1,k,ell))$,

  [e].Swimming Operations: set $m = 0$ (where m is a counter for swimming),

    [1].While $m < N_s$ (where N_s is a maximum number of swimming)

    [2].Let $m = m + 1$,

    [3].If $J(i,j+1,k,ell) < J_t$ // if the bacterium finds a better position with lower cost

    [4].Let $J_t = J(i,j+1,k,ell)$,

    [5].Position re-update: according to equation (1),

    [6].Cost re-calculation: $J(i,j+1,k,ell) = f(P(i,j+1,k,ell))$,

    [7].Else set $m = 0$,

    [8].End While.

  [f]. End For i .

Step 5. **Reproduction:** calculate the bacterial health index $J_h = \sum_{j=1}^{N_c} J(i,j,k,ell)$, sort all bacteria in the increasing order, and then substitute the first half of bacteria for the remaining bacteria in one-to-one fashion.

Step 6. **Elimination-dispersal Events:** each bacterium is re-initialized within the whole problem space with probability P_{ed} .

```
End
```

4   BFO-NL for Dynamic Portfolio Model

4.1   Dynamic Portfolio Model

In this section, a multi-period and dynamic portfolio model based on the previous work [23] will be formulated. We consider a financial market including risky assets for trading. An investor intends to invest his wealth among the assets at the beginning of period 1 for a continuous T-period investment. And he can reallocate his wealth in every beginning of each of the following periods.

Suppose that the initial capital is M which remains constant in the later periods and the transaction costs of assets of all the transaction costs for buying or selling keep unchanged for all kinds of assets in each period. All the investment for each period is a consecutive time periods. Then the wealth is increased from the preceding period to the next period, and the investor expects that the cumulative fortune at the end of T period is great. Some notations are introduced as follows:

$x^t = (x_1^t, x_2^t, \ldots, x_n^t)$ is the proportion of money allocated in each asset at the t th period, and $\sum_{i=1}^{n} x_i^t = 1$.

$x_i^t \geq 0$ means there is no short sales.

$\xi^t = (\xi_1^t, \xi_2^t, \cdots, \xi_n^t)$ indicates the amount of each asset at the t th period the investor has invested.

p_i^t is the price of the i asset at the t th period.

R_i^t represents the expected rate of revenue of the i asset at the t th peirod, and $R_i^t = E(r_i^t), i = 1, 2, \cdots, n$.

r_i^t means the yield of the i asset at the t th period, and $r_i^t = \dfrac{p_i^t - p_i^{t-1}}{p_i^{t-1}}$.

$\sigma_{ij}^t = \mathrm{cov}(i^t, j^t)$ is the covariance of r_i and r_j.

k_i^b and k_i^s are the transaction fee for buying and selling the i asset respectively.

M^t is the total amount of the t th period.

Based on these assumptions, the total amount M^t and the investment proportion x_i^t at the t th period can be expressed as follows:

$$M^t = \sum_{i=1}^{n} p_i^t \xi_i^t$$

$$x_i^t = \frac{p_i^t \xi_i^t}{M^t}$$

Set I_t is the yield at the t th period. So the relationship of the revenue between the t th period and the $t-1$ th period can be formulated:

$$f^t(x) = (1 + I_t) f^{t-1}(x) \tag{2}$$

So at the end of the Tth period, the total revenue can be expressed by $f^T(x)$ as follow:

$$f^T(x) = M * \prod_{t=1}^{T} \{1 + (\sum_{i=1}^{n} R_i^t x_i^t - \sum_{i=1}^{n} [\mu_t k_i^b (x_i^t - x_i^{t-1}) + (1 - \mu_t) * k_i^s * (x_i^{t-1} - x_i^t)])\} \tag{3}$$

where $\mu_t = \begin{cases} 0, & x_i^t \leq x_i^{t-1} \\ 1, & x_i^t \geq x_i^{t-1} \end{cases}$

Based on these defined variables, the function $f^T(x)$ and $g^T(x)$ denote the revenue and risk of the dynamic T-period portfolio optimization problem can be obtained as below.

$$\max f^T(x) = M * \prod_{t=1}^{T} \{1 + (\sum_{i=1}^{n} R_i^t x_i^t - \sum_{i=1}^{n} [\mu_t k_i^b (x_i^t - x_i^{t-1}) + (1-\mu_t) * k_i^s * (x_i^{t-1} - x_i^t)])\} \quad (4)$$

$$\min g^T(x) = \sum_{i=1}^{n} \sum_{j=1}^{n} \sigma_{ij}^T x_i^T x_j^T \quad (5)$$

Then our dynamic portfolio optimization model can be formulated by introducing a preference coefficient:

$$\max F(x) = \max\{(1-\lambda) * f^T(x) - \lambda * g^T(x)\} \quad (6)$$

where λ is a preference coefficient, which distributes in [0,1]. Different λ represent different preference to estimate the terminal fortune.

4.2   Numerical Experiments

In this section, a two-period numerical example is given to verify the effectiveness of the proposed algorithm. Besides, we also compare the proposed model with four types of investors to identify the influence of different preferences.

We assume that an investor chooses five stocks from Shanghai Stock Exchange for his investment and intends to make two periods of investment with initial wealth 10, 000 yuan. The wealth can be adjusted at the beginning of each period. The historical data about the assets from Jan. to Jun. in 2011 are collected and set every three months as a period [24-25]. The relation number is as follows:

$$R_1 = [0.5750, 0.4650, 0.0775, 0.1450, 0.1125]$$
$$R_2 = [0.01675, 0.00859, 0.05146, 0.04227, 0.09462]$$
$$\sigma_1 = [0.5435, -0.0964, -0.0040, 0.0878, 0.0488;$$
$$-0.0964, 0.0492, 0.0084, -0.0185, -0.0090;$$
$$-0.0040, 0.0084, 0.0031, -0.0011, -0.0015;$$
$$0.0878, -0.0185, -0.0011, 0.0145, 0.0077;$$
$$0.0488, -0.0090, -0.0015, 0.0077, 0.0053;]$$
$$\sigma_2 = [0.01002, 0.00319, 0.01093, 0.00025, 0.01786;$$
$$0.00319, 0.00934, -0.00057, -0.01612, -0.01779;$$
$$0.01093, -0.00057, 0.02392, 0.01793, 0.04677;$$
$$0.00025, -0.01612, 0.01793, 0.05139, 0.07250;$$
$$0.01786, -0.01779, 0.04677, 0.07250, 0.15965;]$$

Table 2. Numerical results with different λ

| Algorithm | $\lambda = 0.15$ | | | | $\lambda = 0.3$ | | | |
| | BFO | | BFO-NL | | BFO | | BFO-NL | |
	t=1	t=2	t=1	t=2	t=1	t=2	t=1	t=2
x_1	0.5324	0.0068	0.4953	0.0022	0.4697	0.0009	0.3485	0.0644
x_2	0.3958	0.0249	0.4552	0.0000	0.4644	0.0803	0.5967	0.0112
x_3	0.0033	0.0164	0.0460	0.0293	0.0050	0.2576	0.0004	0.0535
x_4	0.0599	0.2224	0.0003	0.1240	0.0293	0.0376	0.0506	0.0063
x_5	0.0086	0.7296	0.0031	0.8444	0.0316	0.6236	0.0037	0.8646
Income percent	0.4994	0.0789	0.4997	0.0860	0.4935	0.0739	0.4849	0.0854
Risk percent	0.1263	0.1116	0.1003	0.1323	0.0916	0.0807	0.0455	0.1263
Terminal-max	2.064e+000		2.080e+000		1.501e+000		1.513e+000	
Terminal-min	1.979e+000		2.009e+000		1.451e+000		1.466e+000	
Terminal-mean	2.018e+000		2.055e+000		1.470e+000		1.494e+000	
Terminal-std	2.637e-002		6.488e-004		1.414e-002		1.422e-002	

Suppose that the investor has the same original proportion in every asset, i.e. $x_i^0 = 0$. And the transaction cost of each asset at each period maintain unchanged, i.e., $k_i^b = 0.00065$, $k_i^s = 0.00075$ in this two-period experiment. The parameters in these two algorithms are set below: the data of bacteria in the population is 50, and chemotactic steps are 100, the number of elimination-dispersal events is 2, the number of reproduction steps is 5. The value of λ is set as 0.15, 0.3, 0.5, 0.65 to represent different investors based on various preference to estimate the terminal fortune, respectively. After conducting a total of 20 runs for each experimental setting, the corresponding optimal investment strategies obtained are shown in Table 2~3.

4.3   Experimental Results

Tables 2~3 display the numerical results with four different λ which are obtained by the BFO and BFO-NL. The corresponding computational results including the optimal investment strategy, income percent and risk percent for each period, and the max value, the min value, the mean value and the standard deviation of the terminal wealth on this two-period portfolio selection are also listed as follows. And the mean relative performance by these two methods is shown in Figs 1~4. Note that all the results should be multiplied by the value of initial amount10,000.

In Tables 2~3, x_i repents the amount of i th (i =1,2,…,5) asset on the t th (t =1,2) investment periods. It can be seen that for almost of all the different risk preferences, BFO-NL can get the better mean value of the terminal wealth and the smaller standard deviation. And the Figures 1~4 also demonstrate the same results. According to these tables and figures, we can conclude that:

Table 3. Numerical results with different λ

Algorithm	$\lambda = 0.5$				$\lambda = 0.65$			
	BFO		BFO-NL		BFO		BFO-NL	
	t=1	t=2	t=1	t=2	t=1	t=2	t=1	t=2
x_1	0.3923	0.0323	0.2639	0.0214	0.3922	0.0155	0.2169	0.0304
x_2	0.5668	0.0144	0.6702	0.3257	0.5578	0.3642	0.6919	0.3851
x_3	0.0066	0.7257	0.0001	0.3257	0.0136	0.4083	0.0030	0.3851
x_4	0.0059	0.0439	0.0566	0.0016	0.0031	0.0987	0.0215	0.1178
x_5	0.0284	0.1837	0.0093	0.3257	0.0333	0.1134	0.0667	0.0815
Income percent	0.4930	0.0566	0.4719	0.0502	0.4894	0.0387	0.4566	0.0357
Risk percent	0.0577	0.0335	0.0273	0.0270	0.0579	0.0126	0.0211	0.0103
Terminal-max	8.936e-001		8.968e-001		5.333e-001		5.391e-001	
Terminal-min	8.600c-001		8.861e-001		5.190e-001		5.357e-001	
Terminal-mean	8.747e-001		8.908e-001		5.251e-001		5.370e-001	
Terminal-std	7.852e-003		1.975e-003		3.542e-003		1.126e-006	

i) Comparing the experimental results presented in Tables 2~3, it verifies that the modified algorithm outperforms BFO in terms of result qualify and result robustness, which illustrates the effectiveness of the proposed algorithm repeatedly. And the Figures 1~4 also testify this results.

ii) Based on the data of the related terminal value listed in Tables, we can find that the optimal investment profit depend on the value of λ. The fitness value decreases along with the increase of the preference coefficient λ and this trend consists with the structure of the fitness function. Moreover, all the income percent and risk percent reduce with the rise of λ.

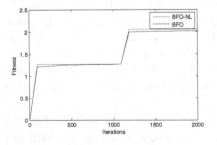

Fig. 1. $\lambda = 0.15$

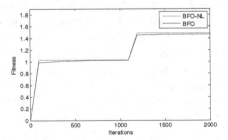

Fig. 2. $\lambda = 0.3$

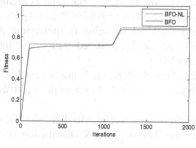

Fig. 3. $\lambda = 0.5$

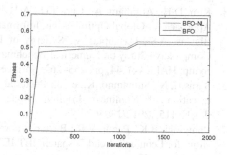

Fig. 4. $\lambda = 0.65$

5   Conclusions and Future work

This paper presents a new variant of original BFO algorithm that incorporates the information interaction based on a neighbor learning strategy. By introducing this mechanism, the search information can be made full use by bacteria and help to avoid trapping into local minima. The comparative experiment of the proposed algorithm (BFO-NL) is evaluated by testing on eight benchmark functions. Related results indicate that it can provide better quality solutions. In order to demonstrate the performance of BFO-NL, we apply it to a dynamic portfolio optimization model and compare the results with the original BFO. For the two-period portfolio model, numerical results show that BFO-NL is feasible and effective.

However, further work may focus on optimizing the performance of this proposed algorithm and extensive study of application in more complex problems to evaluate the performance of BFO-NL.

Acknowledgements. This work is partially supported by The National Natural Science Foundation of China (Grants nos. 71001072, 71271140), The Hong Kong Scholars Program 2012 (Grant no. G-YZ24), China Postdoctoral Science Foundation (Grant nos. 20100480705), Special Financial Grant from the China Postdoctoral Science Foundation (Grant nos. 2012T50584, 2012T50639) and the Natural Science Foundation of Guangdong Province (Grant nos. S2012010008668, S2012040007098, 9451806001002294).

References

1. Passino, K.M.: Biomimicry of Bacterial Foraging for Distributed Optimization and Control. IEEE Control Systems Magazine, 52–67 (2002)
2. Niu, B., Wang, H., Chai, Y.J.: Bacterial Colony Optimization. Discrete Dynamics in Nature and Society, 1–28 (2012)
3. Tang, W.J., Wu, Q.H., Saunders, J.R.: A Novel Model for Bacteria Foraging in Varying Environments. In: Gavrilova, M.L., Gervasi, O., Kumar, V., Tan, C.J.K., Taniar, D., Laganá, A., Mun, Y., Choo, H. (eds.) ICCSA 2006. LNCS, vol. 3980, pp. 556–565. Springer, Heidelberg (2006)

4. Kim, D.H., Abraham, A., Cho, J.H.: A Hybrid Genetic Algorithm and Bacterial Foraging Approach for Global Optimization. Information Sciences 177(18), 3918–3937 (2007)
5. Biswas, A.S., Dasgupta, A.: Synergy of PSO and Bacterial Foraging Optimization: A Comparative Study on Numerical Benchmarks. In: Corchado, E., et al. (eds.) Proc. 2nd Int. Symp. HAIS, vol. 44, pp. 255–263. Springer, Berlin (2007)
6. Sarasiri, N., Suthamno, K., et al.: Bacterial Foraging-Tabu Search Metaheuristics for Identification of Nonlinear Friction Model. Journal of Applied Mathematics (2012), doi:10.1155/2012/238563
7. Panigrahi, B.K., Pandi, V.R.: Bacterial Foraging Optimization: Nelder-Mead Hybrid Algorithm for Economic Load Dispatch. IET IET Generation Transmission & Distribution 2(4), 556–565 (2008)
8. Kim, D.H., Cho, J.H.: Adaptive Tuning of PID Controller for Multivariable System Using Bacterial Foraging Based Optimization. In: Szczepaniak, P.S., Kacprzyk, J., Niewiadomski, A. (eds.) AWIC 2005. LNCS (LNAI), vol. 3528, pp. 231–235. Springer, Heidelberg (2005)
9. Kou, P.G., Zhou, J.Z., He, Y.Y., Xiang, X.Q., Li, C.S.: Optimal PID Governor Tuning of Hydraulic Turbine Generators With Bacterial Foraging Particle Swarm Optimization Algorithm. In: Proceedings of the Chinese Society of Electrical Engineering, vol. 29(26), pp. 101–106 (2009)
10. Kim, D.H., Cho, C.H.: Bacterial Foraging Based Neural Network Fuzzy Learning. In: Proceedings of the Indian International Conference on Artificial Intelligence, pp. 2030–2036 (2005)
11. Niu, B., Wang, H., Tan, L.J., Xu, J.: Multi-Objective Optimization Using BFO Algorithm. In: Huang, D.-S., Gan, Y., Premaratne, P., Han, K. (eds.) ICIC 2011. LNCS, vol. 6840, pp. 582–587. Springer, Heidelberg (2012)
12. Markowitz, H.: Portfolio Selection. Journal of Finance 37, 77–91 (1952)
13. Konno, H., Yamazaki, H.: Mean-Absolute Deviation Portfolio in Optimization Model and its Application to Tokyo Stock Market. Management Science 37, 519–531 (1991)
14. Speranza, M.G.: Linear Programming Models for Portfolio Optimization. Finance 14, 107–123 (1993)
15. Speranza, M.G.: A Heuristic Algorithm for a Portfolio Optimization Model Applied to the Milan Stock Market. Computers and Operations Research 23, 433–441 (1996)
16. Gu, Q., Yin, K., Niu, B., Xing, K., Tan, L., Li, L.: BFO With Information Communicational System Based on Different Topologies Structure. In: Huang, D.-S., Jo, K.-H., Zhou, Y.-Q., Han, K. (eds.) ICIC 2013. LNCS, vol. 7996, pp. 633–640. Springer, Heidelberg (2013)
17. Liu, Y., Passino, K.M.: Biomimicry of Social Foraging Bacteria for Distributed Optimization: Models, Principles, and Emergent Behaviors. Journal Optimization Theory Application 115(3), 603–628 (2002)
18. Eberhart, R., Kennedy, J.: Performance assessment of foraging algorithms vs. evolutionary algorithms. Information Sciences 1(182), 243–264 (2012)
19. Dasgupta, S., Das, S., Abraham, A., et al.: Adaptive computational chemotaxis in bacterial foraging optimization: an analysis. IEEE Transactions on Evolutionary Computation 4(13), 919–941 (2009)
20. Kennedy, J., Mendes, R.: Differential evolution with neighborhood and direction information for numerical optimization. IEEE Transactions on Cybernetics 6(43), 2202–2215 (2013)

21. Liang, J.J., Qin, A.K., Suganthan, P.N., et al.: Comprehensive learning particle swarm optimizer for global optimization of multimodal functions. IEEE Transactions on Evolutionary Computation 3(10), 281–295 (2006)
22. Kennedy, J., Mendes, R.: Population structure and particle swarm performance. In: Proceedings of the Congress on Evolutionary Computation, pp. 1671–1676 (2002)
23. Wu, Y.: Modified Markowitz portfolio model and bacterial foraging algorithm solving research (Master Thesis) Shenzhen University (2011)
24. Niu, B., Tan, L., Xue, B., Li, L., Chai, Y.: Constrained portfolio selection using multiple swarms. In: IEEE Congress on Evolutionary Computation, pp. 1–7. IEEE Press, New York (2010)
25. Xue, B.: Research on portfolio selection model and particle swarm optimization (Master Thesis) Shenzhen University (2010)

Structure-Redesign-Based Bacterial Foraging Optimization for Portfolio Selection

Ben Niu[1,2,3,*], Ying Bi[1], and Ting Xie[1]

[1] College of Management, Shenzhen University, Shenzhen, China
[2] Hefei Institute of Intelligent Machine, Chinese Academy of Science, Hefei, China
[3] Department of Industrial and System Engineering,
Hong Kong Polytechnic University, Hong Kong
Drniuben@gmail.com

Abstract. In this paper structure-redesign-based Bacterial Foraging Optimization (SRBFO) is proposed to solve portfolio selection problem. Taking advantage of single-loop structure, a new execution structure is developed in SRBFO to improve the convergence rate as well as lower computational complexity. In addition, the operations of reproduction and elimination-dispersal are redesigned to further simplify the original BFO algorithm structure. The proposed SRBFO is applied to solve portfolio selection problems with transaction fee and no short sales. Four cases with different risk aversion factors are considered in the experimental study. The optimal portfolio selection obtained by SRBFO is compared with PSOs, which demonstrated that the validity and efficiency of our proposed SRBFO in selecting optimal portfolios.

Keywords: Bacterial foraging, portfolio selection, execution structure.

1 Introduction

Swarm intelligence is becoming important area of hi-tech research and its associated technology developing rapidly. Bacterial Foraging Optimization (BFO) as a new comer of swarm intelligence has obtained much attention from various areas, and widely applied to electrical engineering and control [1], artificial neural networking training [2] and image segmentation [3] and so on. Although BFO has succeeded in solving many real-world practical problems, it still has disadvantages of its slowly convergence rate and computational complexity. To improve the performance of BFO, many BFO's variants are developed, including parameters modification [4] and hybrid algorithms [5] etc.

This paper redesigned the structure of BFO, which provided a new idea to further improve the convergence performance of BFO. To demonstrate the effectiveness of SRBFO we proposed, experiments on portfolio selection problems with transaction costs and no short sales were conducted. Results obtained by SRBFO compared with PSOs are presented and testified the efficiency of SRBFO.

---

* Corresponding author.

D.-S. Huang et al. (Eds.): ICIC 2014, LNBI 8590, pp. 424–430, 2014.
© Springer International Publishing Switzerland 2014

2   Structure-Redesign-Based Bacterial Foraging Optimization

BFO is a population-based random search algorithm proposed by K. M. Passino [12] in 2002 according to the competition and collaboration mechanisms in the process of searching for food in the human intestinal of Escherichia coli groups. Main four bacterial-specific activities, chemotaxis, swarming, reproduction, elimination and dispersal are imitated to update position for bacteria to search for optimal solutions in BFO [6,7].

Although the BFO has been succeeded in solving many optimization problems, it still poses the slow convergence rate because of its nested implementation structure. To obtain fast convergence speed and low time consumption, SRBFO is proposed by redesigning the original BFO implementation structure.

The main idea of the structure in SRBFO is inspired from the structure executed in GA, PSO and some other intelligent algorithms. Taking advantage of single-loop execution structure, SRBFO uses single-loop structure to replace the original triple nested structure used in BFO.   The Pseudo-code of SRBFO is presented in Table 1.

The reproduction operation and elimination-dispersal operation are nested within chemotactic operation, which determined by the reproduction frequency (Fre), elimination-dispersal frequency (Fed) and the current number of chemotaxis. In addition, a cumulative value of fitness function is used in BFO to assess the health status of bacteria. However, this accumulated mechanism may eliminate the most current healthy bacterium, and thus affect the convergence rate. In SRBFO, the current value of fitness function replaced by the original cumulative value is employed to simplify the complexity of computation in the process of reproduction.

Table 1. Pseudo-code of SRBFO

SRBFO
Begin
For (Each run)
Calculate the fitness function J, and set $J = J_{last.}$;
For (Each chemotaxis)
Update the position of bacteria by tumbling (Chemotaxis);
Calculate fitness function J;
If ($J < J_{last;}$ and the maximum swimming steps are not met)
Swimming (Chemotaxis);
End If
If mod(the current number of chemotaxis, reproduction frequency Fre)==0
Reproduction operation;
End If
If mod(the current number of chemotaxis, disperse frequency Fed)==0
Dispersal operation;
End If
End For
End For
End

3   SRBFO for Portfolio Selection Problems

3.1   Portfolio Selection Model

Markowitz's 'Mean-Variance' model established the basic and complete analytical framework of portfolio, while it has many strict assumptions, including the effectiveness of markets, ignoring transaction costs and invertors risk aversion and so on. These limitations restrict it to be further widely applied into many realistic portfolio optimization problems. To address these problems, an improved model is proposed in [8]. In the model, the transaction fee of selling and buying assets and no short sales are considered, investors' return and risks can be expressed as:

$$Return \ f(x) = \sum_{i=1}^{n} r_i x_i - \sum_{i=1}^{n} \left[\mu * k_i^b * (x_i - x_i^0) + (1 - \mu) * k_i^s * (x_i^0 - x_i) \right] \tag{1}$$

$$and \quad \mu = \begin{cases} 1, \dots x_i \geq x_i^0 \\ 0, \dots x_i \leq x_i^0 \end{cases}$$

$$Risk \quad g(x) = \sum_{i=1}^{n} \sum_{j=1}^{n} \sigma_{ij} x_i x_j \tag{2}$$

Pursuing of maximizing benefit and minimizing risks are two tradeoff objectives in portfolio selection problems. A risk aversion factor λ was introduced to balance the two tradeoff objectives. The multi-objective problem is also transferred into single objective problem by using risk aversion factor. The mathematical model can be described as follow:

$$min \ F(x) = min(\lambda g(x) - (1 - \lambda)g(x))$$

$$s.t \begin{cases} \sum_{i=1}^{n} x_i = 1 \\ x_i > 0 \end{cases} \tag{3}$$

In this model, there are n assets can be selected to invest, r_i indicates the expected return vector, x_i is the investor's investment ratio in each asset, $x_i^0 > 0$ indicates the original investment ratio in asset. $x_i > 0$ represents there is no short sales. σ_{ij} represents the return covariance between asset i and asset j. k_i^b is the transaction expense ratio of buying asset , and k_i^s is the transaction expense ratio of selling asset . In general, the fee of selling assets in the financial market is greater than buying. $\lambda \in [0 \ 1]$ is risk aversion factor determined by investors, the smaller the value of λ is, the larger risk the investor can bear.

3.2   Encoding

Each bacterium represents a potential solution in solving the portfolio selection problem. The fitness function calculated according to Eq. (3). The encoding of a bacterium is given in Eq. (4) and the constraints dealing with Eq. (5).

$$\theta = \left[x_1, x_2, x_3, \cdots, x_n, fit(x) \right] \tag{4}$$

$$s = \sum_{i=1}^{n} x_i$$

$$\theta' = \left[\frac{1}{s}(x_1, x_2, x_3, \cdots, x_n), fit(x)' \right] \tag{5}$$

4   Experiment Result and Discussion

In the portfolio selection problems, we supposed there are eight assets can be chosen to invest. Parameters including the covariance of assets and the expected return of assets are simulated according to actual condition and our experiences. Four different risk aversion factors are considered in the portfolio selection problems. The parameters are shown as follow.

σ_{ij} = (0.0034, 0.0063, 0.0025, 0.0002, 0.0024, 0.0025, 0.0007, 0.0013;
    0.0063, 0.0027, 0.0059, 0.0029, 0.0069, 0.0039, 0.0062, 0.0044;
    0.0025, 0.0059, 0.0001, 0.0011, 0.0028, 0.0033, 0.0037, 0.0017;
    0.0002, 0.0029, 0.0011, 0.0061, 0.0019, 0.0004, 0.0029, 0.0003;
    0.0024, 0.0069, 0.0028, 0.0019, 0.0003, 0.0020, 0.0015, 0.0005;
    0.0025, 0.0039, 0.0033, 0.0004, 0.0020, 0.0024, 0.0013, 0.0005;
    0.0007, 0.0062, 0.0037, 0.0029, 0.0015, 0.0013, 0.0005, 0.0008;
    0.0013, 0.0044, 0.0017, 0.0003, 0.0005, 0.0005, 0.0008, 0.0017)
R = (0.0013, 0.0036, 0.0002, 0.0022, 0.0016, 0.0013, 0.0017, 0.0009)
λ = (0.15, 0.4, 0.65, 0.9)

The transaction expense ratio of buying asset is set as 0.00065, and selling asset is fixed at 0.00075 according to the paper [8].

In order to verify the performance of SRBFO, SPSO and PSO are selected for comparison. We set $c_1 = c_2 = 2$, and inertia weight $w = 1$ for PSO, $w_{start} = 0.9$ and $w_{end} = 0.4$ are used in PSO. In SRBFO, the length of chemotaxic step Csz=0.2, the swimming length is set to 2. The probability of elimination/dispersal is set to 0.3. The new parameters of reproduction frequency and elimination-dispersal frequency are set as: Fre=24, Fed=48. All the experiment runs 50 times, the iterations is 300, the size of population p=50. The initialized ratio of each asset is 0.125 to make the sum of all assets ratio equal to 1.

The experimental results of the best ratio invested in asset (the value of x), return, risk, maximum, minimum, mean, standard deviation obtained by three algorithms of $\lambda = 0.65$ and $\lambda = 0.9$ of 50 runs are given in Table 2. The convergence curves of BFO and PSOs of four different risk aversion factors are shown in Fig. 1 and Fig. 2.

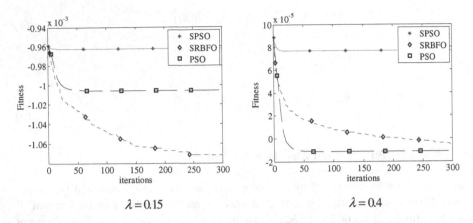

Fig. 1. Convergence curve of SRBFO and PSOs

Table 2. Experimental results of $\lambda = 0.65$ and $\lambda = 0.9$

	$\lambda = 0.65$			$\lambda = 0.9$		
	PSO	SPSO	SRBFO	PSO	SPSO	SRBFO
x_1	9.0247e-002	1.3272e-001	2.2527e-003	1.8845e-002	1.0237e-001	1.7415e-002
x_2	3.0378e-007	1.0102e-001	4.8515e-003	3.4078e-012	9.5280e-002	1.4952e-003
x_3	5.4316e-019	1.0683e-001	2.4028e-002	7.5124e-019	1.0912e-001	1.3949e-002
x_4	1.3466e-001	1.3664e-001	1.1544e-001	2.6916e-001	1.4036e-001	5.6223e-002
x_5	2.2599e-001	1.3709e-001	3.1322e-001	1.3989e-001	1.4178e-001	1.0352e-001
x_6	1.7900e-001	1.3364e-001	1.1544e-001	1.9494e-001	1.4889e-001	3.4477e-001
x_7	1.1017e-001	1.0407e-001	1.1544e-001	2.1799e-002	1.1328e-001	5.5388e-002
x_8	2.5994e-001	1.4799e-001	3.0932e-001	3.5537e-001	1.4892e-001	4.0724e-001
Return	1.0027e-003	1.4605e-003	8.7423e-004	8.0246e-004	1.4308e-003	5.3681e-004
Risk	1.3824e-003	2.3787e-003	1.3066e-003	1.3401e-003	2.3447e-003	1.2461e-003
Max	7.8282e-004	1.0870e-003	**7.0806e-004**	1.5692e-003	2.0762e-003	**1.3616e-003**
Min	5.4765e-004	1.0350e-003	**5.4331e-004**	1.1258e-003	1.9671e-003	**1.0678e-003**
Mean	6.5486e-004	1.0611e-003	**6.4973e-004**	1.3210e-003	2.0238e-003	**1.2573e-003**
Std	5.3968e-005	**1.2725e-005**	3.6809e-005	1.0488e-004	2.6525e-005	**6.6794e-005**

Analyzing the results, the performance of SRBFO is obviously better than that PSOs. SRBFO maintains good global search capability as well as convergence speed and may be more suitable for solving these difficult portfolio selection problems.

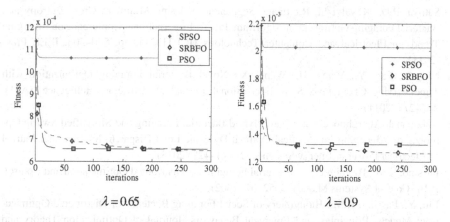

$\lambda = 0.65$ $\lambda = 0.9$

Fig. 2. Convergence curve of SRBFO and PSOs

5   Conclusion

In this paper, we developed SRBFO by redesigning the executive structure of original BFO to reduce its computational complexity and make it convergence to global optimum faster. SRBFO and other two PSOs were used to solve the complex portfolio selection problems with different risk aversion factors. Experimental results obtained verified the performance of the proposed SRBFO and indicated that SRBFO is more suitable for solving these difficult portfolio selection problems than SPSO and PSO.

Future work will continue pay attention to optimize the efficiency of SRBFO. In addition, more intelligence algorithms will be used to solve more difficult portfolio selection problems [9], such as Bacterial Colony Optimization [10], and Multi-objective Bacterial Foraging Optimization [11], etc.

Acknowledgements. This work is partially supported by The National Natural Science Foundation of China (Grants nos. 71001072, 71271140), The Hong Kong Scholars Program 2012 (Grant no. G-YZ24), China Postdoctoral Science Foundation (Grant nos. 20100480705), Special Financial Grant from the China Postdoctoral Science Foundation (Grant nos. 2012T50584) and the Natural Science Foundation of Guangdong Province (Grant nos. S2012010008668, S2012040007098, 9451806001002294).

References

1. Tang, W.J., Li, M.S., Wu, Q.H., Saunders, J.R.: Bacterial Foraging Algorithm for Optimal Power Flow in Dynamic Environments. IEEE Transactions on Circuits and Systems I: Regular Papers 55(8), 2433–2442 (2008)
2. Ulagammai, M., Venkatesh, P., Kannan, P.S., Prasad Padhy, N.: Application of Bacterial Foraging Technique Trained Artificial and Wavelet Neural Networks in Load Forecasting. Neurocomputing 70(16), 2659–2667 (2007)

3. Sathya, P.D., Kayalvizhi, R.: Image Segmentation Using Minimum Cross Entropy and Bacterial Foraging Optimization Algorithm. In: 2011 International Conference on Emerging Trends in Electrical and Computer Technology (ICETECT), pp. 500–506. IEEE Press (2011)
4. Niu, B., Fan, Y., Wang, H., Wang, X.: Novel Bacterial Foraging Optimization with Time-Varying Chemotaxis Step. International Journal of Artificial Intelligence 7(A11), 257–273 (2011)
5. Azizipanah-Abarghooee, R.: A New Hybrid Bacterial Foraging and Simplified Swarm Optimization Algorithm for Practical Optimal Dynamic Load Dispatch. International Journal of Electrical Power & Energy Systems 49, 414–429 (2013)
6. Passino, K.M.: Biomimicry of Bacterial Foraging for Distributed Optimization and Control. IEEE Control Systems Magazine, 52–67 (2002)
7. Liu, Y., Passino, K.M.: Biomimicry of Social Foraging Bacteria for Distributed Optimization: Models, Principles, and Emergent Behaviors. Journal of Optimization Theory and Applications 115(3), 603–628 (2002)
8. Li, L., Xue, B., Tan, L., Niu, B.: Improved Particle Swarm Optimizers with Application on Constrained Portfolio Selection. In: Huang, D.-S., Zhao, Z., Bevilacqua, V., Figueroa, J.C. (eds.) ICIC 2010. LNCS, vol. 6215, pp. 579–586. Springer, Heidelberg (2010)
9. Niu, B., Fan, Y., Xiao, H., Xue, B.: Bacterial Foraging-Based Approaches to Portfolio Optimization with Liquidity Risk. Neurocomputing 98(3), 90–100 (2012)
10. Niu, B., Wang, H., Chai, Y.J.: Bacterial Colony Optimization. Discrete Dynamics in Nature and Society 2012, 28 (2012)
11. Niu, B., Wang, H., Wang, J.W., Tan, L.J.: Multi-objective Bacterial Foraging Optimization. Neurocomputing 116, 336–345 (2012)

Bacterial Colony Optimization for Integrated Yard Truck Scheduling and Storage Allocation Problem

Ben Niu[1,2,3,*], Ting Xie[1], Ying Bi[1], and Jing Liu[1]

[1] College of Management, Shenzhen University,
Shenzhen 518060, China
[2] Department of Industrial and System Engineering,
The Hong Kong Polytechnic University, Hong Kong, China
[3] Hefei Institute of Intelligent Machines, Chinese Academy of Sciences,
Hefei 230031, China
drniuben@gmail.com

Abstract. This research is motivated by both the indispensable need for optimization in container terminals and the recent advances in swarm intelligence. In this paper, we try to address the Integrated Yard Truck Scheduling and Storage Allocation Problem (YTS-SAP), one of the major optimization problems in container port, which aims at minimizing the total delay for all containers. Bacterial colony optimization (BCO), a recently developed optimization algorithm that simulates some typical behaviors of E. coli bacteria, is introduced to address this NP-hard problem. In addition, we designed a mapping schema by which the particle position vector can be transferred to the scheduling solution. The performance of the BCO is investigated by an experiment conducted on different scale instances compared with PSO and GA. The results demonstrate the competitiveness of the proposed approach especially for large scale and complex problems.

Keywords: Yard truck scheduling, Storage allocation, Container terminal, Bacterial Colony Optimization (BCO).

1 Introduction

As an intermodal interfaces between sea and land in the global transportation network, container terminals are forced to study the optimal logistics management in marine transportation faced with competitive environment. The comprehensive review on operations research at container terminals can be found in [1]. Yard cranes (YCs), quay cranes (QCs), and yard trucks (YT) are three fundamental equipments in typical container terminals. Two important decisions related to the logistics cost and operational efficiency of container terminals are developing strategies for scheduling yard truck and allocating storage space to discharging containers. Therefore, the variant that will be discussed here is the Integrated Yard Truck Scheduling and Storage

---

* Corresponding author.

D.-S. Huang et al. (Eds.): ICIC 2014, LNBI 8590, pp. 431–437, 2014.

Allocation Problem (YTS-SAP). The YTS-SAP problem is a very prominent field of research, and various researchers have employed different approaches. e.g., the exact solution algorithms (linear programming et al.) and heuristic algorithms (genetic algorithm et al) [2,3,4,5].

The YTS-SAP has been proved to be a NP-hard problem. Regarding such NP-hard problem, exact solution methods are only suitable for small sized problems. To deal with large scale problems, recent research has focused on developing efficient heuristics, in which swarm intelligence is one of the promising one. Bacterial Colony Optimization (BCO) is a relatively new swarm intelligence algorithm, which simulates some typical behaviors of E. coli bacteria. To the best of our knowledge, BCO-based approach for YTS-SAP hasn't been presented in the literature so far. Therefore, a BCO-based approach is proposed for this task by comparing the performance with GA and PSO.

2   Problem Description

The YTS-SAP model used in this paper is the same as that used in literature [4] and the notations and mathematical model are given as follows.

J^+: the set of loading jobs with the cardinality of n^+. J^- : the set of discharging jobs with the cardinality of n^-. J : the set of all jobs $(J^+ \cup J^-)$ with $|J| = n$.

$[a_i, b_i)$: a soft time window for container i based on the crane schedules. a_i is the starting time of job i, that is, job i should be processed at or after a_i . The due time of job i, b_i can be violated with a penalty. d_i : delay of job i. w_i : start time of service at job i. R : the set of all routes indexed by r, where $|R| = m$. ι_r, κ_r : two dummy jobs to denote the initial and final location of each YT. o_i, d_i : denote the origin and destination of job i, respectively. $J' = J \cup \{\iota_r\}_{r \in R}$. J'' $= J \cup \{\kappa_r\}_{r \in R}$

L : the set of all yard locations for all loading and discharging jobs with indices p and q. τ_{pq} : the travel time of YT along the shortest route between yard location p and q. ζ_k: where $k \in K$, the index for the storage location (SL) k, where K is the set of all SLs.

t_i the processing time of job i

$$t_i = \begin{cases} \tau_{o_i, d_i} & \text{if Request } i \text{ is a loading request} \\ \\ \tau_{o_i, \zeta_k} & \text{if Request } i \text{ is a discharging request and allocated to SL} k \end{cases}$$

S_{ij} the setup time from the drop-off location of job i to the pick-up location of job j

$$S_{ij} = \begin{cases} \tau_{d_i, o_j} & \text{if Request } i \text{ is a loading request} \\ \\ \tau_{\xi_k, o_j} & \text{if Request } i \text{ is a discharging request and allocated to SL} k \end{cases}$$

x_{ik} $= 1$, if job i is allocated to SL k

        $= 0$, otherwise

y_{ij} $= 1$, if job i is connected to job j in the same route

        $= 0$, otherwise

Mathematical model:

Minimize $\sum_{i \in J} d_i$

Subject to

$$\sum_{i \in J^-} x_{ik} = 1, \quad \forall k \in K \qquad (1) \qquad \sum_{k \in K} x_{ik} = 1, \quad \forall i \in J^- \qquad (2)$$

$$\sum_{j \in J''} y_{ij} = 1, \quad \forall i \in J' \qquad (3) \qquad \sum_{i \in J'} y_{ij} = 1, \quad \forall j \in J'' \qquad (4)$$

$$w_i \geq a_i, \quad \forall i \in J' \cup J'' \qquad (5) \qquad d_i \geq w_i + t_i - b_i, \quad \forall i \in J' \cup J'' \qquad (6)$$

$$w_j + M(1 - y_{ij}) \geq w_i + t_i + s_{ij}, \quad \forall i \in J' \text{ and } J \in J'' \qquad (7)$$

$$t_i = \tau_{o_i, d_i}, \quad \forall i \in J^+ \qquad (8) \qquad t_i = \sum_{k \in K} \tau_{o_i, \xi_k} x_{ik}, \quad \forall i \in J^- \qquad (9)$$

$$s_{ij} = \tau_{d_i, o_i}, \quad \forall i \in J^+ \text{ and } j \in J \qquad (10)$$

$$s_{ij} = \sum_{k \in K} \tau_{\xi_k, o_j} x_{ik}, \quad \forall i \in J^- \text{ and } j \in J \qquad (11)$$

$$x_{ik}, y_{ij} \in \{0, 1\}, \quad \forall i \in J', j \in J'' \text{ and } k \in K \qquad (12)$$

$$w_i \in \Re, \quad \forall i \in J' \cup J'' \qquad (13) \qquad t_i \in \Re, \quad \forall i \in J^- \qquad (14)$$

$$s_{ij} \in \Re, \quad \forall i \in J^- \text{ and } j \in J \qquad (15)$$

3   Methodology

3.1   The Background of Bacterial Colony Optimization

Bacterial colony optimization (BCO) is a recently developed optimization algorithm which is inspired by a lifecycle model of Escherichia coli bacteria[6,7]. The lifecycle model of E.coli bacteria contains four key stages: chemotaxis and communication, elimination, reproduction, and migration. In chemotaxis and communication stage, bacteria tumble toward optimum directed by two kinds of information: personal previous information, group information, and a random direction. Tumbling and swimming are two activities of bacteria chemotaxis. Optimal searching director and turbulent director altogether decide the searching director while bacteria tumbling, the position is updated using (16). In the process of swimming, turbulent director does not participate in it as shown in (17).

$$Position_i(T) = Positin_i(T-1) + C(i)$$
$$* [f_i * (G_{best} - Positin_i(T-1)) + (1-f_i) \qquad (16)$$
$$* (P_{best_i} - Positin_i(T-1)) + turbulent_i]$$

$$Position_i(T) = Positin_i(T-1) + C(i)$$
$$* [f_i * (G_{best} - Positin_i(T-1)) + (1-f_i) \qquad (17)$$
$$* (P_{best_i} - Positin_i(T-1))]$$

where i represent the ith bacterium. P_{best} and G_{best} denote the best previous position of the ith bacterium and the historically best position of the entire swarm. $f_i \in \{0,1\}$ and $turbulent_i$ is the stochastic direction employed in the ith bacterium. $C(i)$ represents the chemotaxis step size. The detail introduction and the whole computational procedure can be referred to [6].

3.2   Total Solution Representation

Fig. 1 is an example to illustrate our mapping mechanism. In this example, we assign two trucks to handle three discharging jobs and three loading jobs, in the situation that three potential locations is available to the discharging jobs. In addition, we assume that the first three jobs are discharging jobs. According to the scheduling results, the first truck will handle jobs 4, 1, 6, sequentially, while the second truck is assigned to handle jobs 3, 2, and 5, sequentially. The location solution is that the first discharging job is located in ς_2, the second discharging job is located in ς_1, the last discharging job is located in ς_3, as shown in Fig. 2.

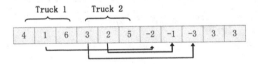

Fig. 1. An example for encoding scheme of YTS-SAP

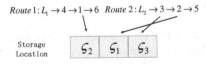

Fig. 2. Decoding of encoding scheme illustrated in Fig. 1

3.3 Job and Storage Allocation Solution Representation

In order to convert the position vector to a job permutation, Smallest Position Value (SPV) rule is introduced which is firstly proposed by Tasgetiren et al [8]. We sort the elements of position vector in ascending order so that the job permutation is constructed. For example if a particle with six dimensional vector is given as following: 9.0 -5.3 2.1 -0.2 7.8 5.2. After using SPV rule the particle becomes: 6 1 3 2 5 4. Similarly, SPV rule is applied to construct the permutation of storage locations.

3.4 Truck Solution Representation

The algorithm used for this mapping named Truck Assignment Algorithm is described in the following flow chart.

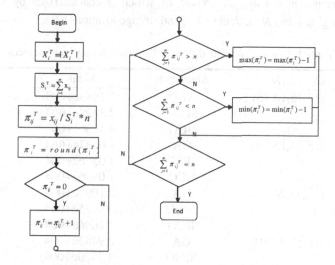

Fig. 3. Flowchart of the Truck Assignment Algorithm

3.5 Fitness Evaluation

In YTS-SAP, the delay of job k processed by truck m implied by particle i, $d_{im}(k)$ equal to $\max\{0, C_{im}(k) - b_{im}(k)\}$, where $C_{im}(k)$ is the completion time and $b_{im}(k)$ is the due time of job k. Let $o_m(i)$ be the summation of delay generated by jobs assigned to truck m $(m = 1, 2, \cdots, M)$ based on the schedule π_i implied by particle i, the objective of YTS-SAP is to minimize the total delay of jobs, i.e.

$$O(i) = \sum_{m=1}^{M} o_m(i) \quad m = (1, 2, \cdots, M).$$

4   Computational Experiments

The effectiveness of the BCO was evaluated compared with other well-known algorithms, namely GA and PSO. Based on the recommendation by Shi et al. [9], the parameters of SPSO with linear inertia weight is set as follows: $w_{start} = 0.9$, $w_{end} = 0.4$, $c_1 = c_2 = 2$. The parameters involved in GA were set to be the same as literature [10]. The parameters for BCO are recommended by Ref. [6]. Considering both the required computational time and the quality of the solution, we set the population size and the maximum number of iterations of three algorithms as 200 and 80, respectively. All algorithms were tested on a set of instances with their data generated from the same manner that literature [4] generates. All algorithms are run 10 times on six different size instances. The obtained means and variances by all algorithms are presented in Table 1. Each problem is denoted as (N^+, N^-, M, L) which is characterized by loading jobs (N^+), discharging jobs (N^-), trucks (M) and storage locations (L).

Table 1. Comparison with different algorithms for six test instances

No.	(N^+, N^-, M, L)	Algorithm	Mean	STD
1	(15,15,10,15)	GA	3.1983e+003	900
		SPSO	**2.3328e+003**	663
		BCO	4.1066e+003	1217
2	(25,25,15,25)	GA	**1.0437e+004**	2566
		SPSO	1.0596e+004	1793
		BCO	1.0806e+004	1873
3	(38,37,20,37)	GA	2.2093e+004	2340
		SPSO	2.4925e+004	2440
		BCO	**2.1606e+004**	1442
4	(50,50,30,50)	GA	2.9443e+004	3408
		SPSO	3.2520e+004	2199
		BCO	**2.6582e+004**	3495
5	(100,100,40,100)	GA	1.2872e+005	3912
		SPSO	1.3517e+005	5573
		BCO	**1.1973e+005**	7594
6	(150,150,50,150)	GA	2.5533e+005	7866
		SPSO	2.6523e+005	7856
		BCO	**2.4735e+005**	9664

According to Table 1, BCO surpasses all other algorithms on problem 3, 4, 5 and 6, while SPSO performs best only on problem 1 and GA dominates only on problem 2. Obviously, BCO performs better than PSO and GA. It may be attributed to the fact that with the help of communication and the ability of migration, BCO is able to keep the tradeoff between the local exploitation and the global exploration [6], while GA and PSO are easy to be trapped in local optima. Furthermore, we can observe that the larger and more complex the problem is, the better BCO will perform.

5   Conclusion and Future Work

This paper presents a BCO method for Integrated Yard Truck Scheduling and Storage Allocation Problem employing an effective problem mapping mechanism in which Smallest Position Value rule and a novel Truck Assignment Algorithm are used to transfer the particle position vector to the job scheduling solution. Based on the result of the three algorithms on the six chosen test instances, we can draw a conclusion that BCO algorithm can find the optimal area in the search space especially for large scale problems compared with GA and PSO. In our future study, this work would be extended to apply the Multi-objective Bacterial Foraging Optimization [11] to solve multi-objective scheduling problems in container terminal.

Acknowledgments. This work is partially supported by The National Natural Science Foundation of China (Grants nos. 71001072, 71271140), The Hong Kong Scholars Program 2012 (Grant no. G-YZ24), China Postdoctoral Science Foundation (Grant nos. 20100480705), Special Financial Grant from the China Postdoctoral Science Foundation (Grant nos. 2012T50584, 2012T50639) and the Natural Science Foundation of Guangdong Province (Grant nos. S2012010008668, 9451806001002294).

References

1. Stahlbock, R., Voß, S.: Operations research at container terminals: a literature update. Or Spectrum 30(1), 1–52 (2008)
2. Bish, E.K., Thin-Yin, L., Chung-Lun, L., Ng, J.W.C., Simchi-Levi, D.: Analysis of a new vehicle scheduling and location problem. Naval Research Logistics 48(5), 363–385 (2001)
3. Wu, Y., Luo, J., Zhang, D., Dong, M.: An integrated programming model for storage management and vehicle scheduling at container terminals. Research in Transportation Economics 42(1), 13–27 (2013)
4. Lee, D.-H., Cao, J.X., Shi, Q., Chen, J.H.: A heuristic algorithm for yard truck scheduling and storage allocation problems. Transportation Research Part E: Logistics and Transportation Review 45(5), 810–820 (2009)
5. Sharif, O., Huynh, N.: Storage space allocation at marine container terminals using ant-based control. Expert Systems with Applications 40(6), 2323–2330 (2013)
6. Niu, B., Wang, H.: Bacterial Colony Optimization. Discrete Dynamics in Nature & Society, 1–28 (2012)
7. Niu, B., Wang, H., Duan, Q.Q., Li, L.: Biomimicry of Quorum Sensing Using Bacterial Lifecycle Model. BMC Bioinformatics 14(8), 1–13 (2013)
8. Fatih Tasgetiren, M., Liang, Y.-C., Sevkli, M., Gencyilmaz, G.: Particle swarm optimization and differential evolution for the single machine total weighted tardiness problem. International Journal of Production Research 44(22), 4737–4754 (2006)
9. Shi, Y., Eberhart, R.: A Modified Particle Swarm Optimizer. In: Proceedings of 1998 IEEE International Conference on Evolutionary Computation Proceedings, pp. 69–73 (1998)
10. Sumathi, S., Hamsapriya, T., Surekha, P.: Evolutionary Intelligence: An Introduction to Theory and Applications with Matlab. Springer Publishing Company, Incorporated (2008)
11. Niu, B., Wang, H., Wang, J.W., Tan, L.J.: Multi-objective Bacterial Foraging Optimization. Neurocomputing 116, 336–345 (2012)

Improving Fusion with One-Class Classification and Boosting in Multimodal Biometric Authentication

Quang Duc Tran and Panos Liatsis

Information Engineering and Medical Imaging Group, Department of Electrical and Electronic Engineering, City University London, London, UK
{quang.tran.1,p.liatsis}@city.ac.uk

Abstract. Class imbalance poses serious difficulties to most standard two-class classifiers, when applied in performing classification in the context of multimodal biometric authentication. In this paper, we propose a system, which exploits the natural capabilities of one-class classifiers in conjunction with the so-called Real AdaBoost to handle the class imbalance problem in biometric systems. Particularly, we propose a decision rule for the fusion of one-class classifiers to effectively use the training data from both classes. By treating this decision rule as the base classifier, the Real AdaBoost is then employed to further improve its performance. An important feature of the proposed system is that it trains the base classifiers with different parameter settings. Hence, it is able to reduce the number of parameters, which are normally set by the user. An empirical evaluation, carried out on the BioSecure DS2 database, demonstrates that the proposed system can achieve a relative performance improvement of 5%, 13%, and 14% as compared to other state-of-the-art techniques, namely the sum of scores, likelihood ratio based score fusion, and support vector machines.

Keywords: Class imbalance, one-class classification, boosting, Real AdaBoost.

1   Introduction

Biometric authentication is the process of verifying a human identity using his/her behavioural and physiological characteristics. It is well-known that multimodal biometric systems can further improve the authentication accuracy by combining information from multiple biometric traits at various levels, namely, sensor, feature, matching score, and decision levels. Fusion at matching score level is generally preferred due to the trade-off between information availability and fusion complexity [1].

A common practice in many reported works on multimodal biometrics is to view fusion at matching score level as a two-class classification problem, where the vector of matching scores is treated as a feature vector, and can be classified into one of two classes: genuine user/impostor [1]. However, recent studies have indicated that most standard two-class classifiers are inadequate, when applied to problems, characterized by class imbalance [2]. Class imbalance is a common problem in multimodal biometric authentication, where the samples of the impostor class greatly outnumber the samples of the genuine user class. It is not uncommon for class imbalances to be in

D.-S. Huang et al. (Eds.): ICIC 2014, LNBI 8590, pp. 438–444, 2014.

the order of 500:1. The skew data distribution makes standard two-class classifiers less effective, particularly when predicting genuine user class samples. Under-sampling has been widely used to counteract the class imbalance problem in the bio-metric literature [1]. An obvious shortcoming of under-sampling is that it may cause the classifiers to miss important aspects in the data, pertaining to the impostor class, since the optimal class distribution is usually unknown.

Over the years, the machine learning community has addressed the issue of class imbalance in many different ways. Among others, the two most popular techniques are one-class classification and boosting. One-class classification is naturally quite robust to the class imbalance problem by defining the decision boundary using single class samples rather than distinguishing between samples of the two classes [3]. In [4], [5], the authors suggested that one-class classifiers are particularly useful in han-dling extremely imbalanced data sets in feature spaces of high dimensionality, while two-class classifiers are suitable for data sets with relatively moderate degrees of imbalance. On the other hand, boosting is the technique, which can be used to im-prove the classification performance of the classifier regardless of whether the data is imbalanced [6], [7]. The aim of boosting is to combine multiple (base) classifiers in order to develop a highly accurate classifier system. It is known to reduce bias and variance errors as it focuses on the samples, which are harder to classify [6]. Particu-larly, boosting weighs each sample to reflect its importance, and places the most weights on those samples, which are most often misclassified by the preceding clas-sifiers [6], [7]. Boosting is very effective at handling the class imbalance problem because the small class samples are most likely to be misclassified. The Real Ada-Boost [8] seems to be the most representative boosting algorithm. It is also resistant to classification noise, which appears very naturally in biometric applications.

In this paper, we propose a system, which inherits both virtues of one-class classifica-tion and the Real AdaBoost in order to advance the classification performance of imba-lanced biometric data sets. The system works by firstly developing a decision rule, based on Bayesian decision theory as applied to the fusion of one-class classifiers to efficiently and effectively use the training data from both the genuine user and impostor classes. Next, the Real AdaBoost is employed, which treats the above decision rule as the base classifier to further improve its performance. The conventional Real AdaBoost trains the base classifiers on a variety of data sets, constructed from the original training data. In our technique, a new training procedure is introduced to train these classifiers on the same data set, but with different parameter settings. The target is to reduce the number of free parameters, which have to be specified by the user. An empirical evaluation is car-ried out using the BioSecure DS2 [9], which demonstrates that the proposed system achieves significantly improved results in terms of Half Total Error Rate (HTER) as compared to state-of-the-art techniques, including the sum of scores [1], likelihood ratio based score fusion [10], and support vector machines (SVM).

The remainder of the paper is organized as follows: Section 2 discusses in detail the proposed system. Section 3 presents extensive experiments using data from the BioSecure DS2, and discusses the results. Section 4 is dedicated to conclusions and further work.

2   The Proposed System

This section will begin by introducing the decision rule, used for the fusion of one-class classifiers. Next, the Modified Real AdaBoost will be presented to enhance the verification accuracy and reduce the number of free parameters.

2.1   The Decision Rule

A large number of one-class classifiers have been proposed in the literature. Among others, the initial one-class classifier that was selected is Gaussian Mixture Models (GMM), which has been demonstrated to successfully estimate the biometric matching score distributions and converge indeed to the true density with a sufficient number of training samples [3], [10], [11]. Let us assume that $p(\mathbf{x} \mid w_G) (p(\mathbf{x} \mid w_I))$ is the density estimates of the genuine (impostor) matching scores, where $\mathbf{x}$ is a test matching score vector, and w_G (w_I) is the genuine (impostor) target class. Generally, $p(\mathbf{x} \mid w_G)$ and $p(\mathbf{x} \mid w_I)$ can be directly utilized to render a biometric decision as in [3]. In this work, we are interested in combining these probability estimates to effectively exploit both genuine user and impostor class samples. Based on Bayesian decision theory [12], the combination can be given as:

$$\text{Assign } \mathbf{x} \rightarrow w_G \text{ if } p(\mathbf{x} \mid w_G) - p(\mathbf{x} \mid w_I) \geq \tau \tag{1}$$

where τ is the decision threshold. Equation (1) holds by assuming that the prior probabilities are equal (i.e., $p(w_G) = p(w_I)$), and different costs are assigned to the False Rejection Rate (FRR) and False Acceptance Rate (FAR) [1]. In practice, it is possible to combine the one-class classifiers using the log-likelihood ratio test [10] as:

$$\text{Assign } \mathbf{x} \rightarrow w_G \text{ if } \log\left(p(\mathbf{x} \mid w_G) / p(\mathbf{x} \mid w_I)\right) \geq \tau \tag{2}$$

Although the log-likelihood ratio test is the optimal test for deciding that test sample $\mathbf{x}$ corresponds to a genuine user or an impostor, it is a bad idea to employ it as the base classifier in the Real AdaBoost as rescaling it may have a detrimental effect on the overall generalization error [8]. The decision rule in (1) has a distinct advantage since its outputs lie in the range $[-1,+1]$. In general, such decision rule has three parameters to be set by the user, namely: the numbers of mixture components, i.e., N_G and N_I, used to model the densities of genuine and impostor matching scores, and the fraction rejection f_T. By definition, f_T controls the percentage of target samples, rejected by the classifier during training. While the number of mixture components can be found using the GMM fitting algorithm in [13], there is no effective means for the optimal selection of f_T. In [3], the value of f_T was optimized on the training set. However, the fraction rejection value obtained through the optimization process does not necessarily provide the optimal performance on the test set. One straightforward reason for this is that biometric data suffers from various forms of degradation, caused by the manner a user interacts with a biometric device, and changes in the acquisition environment [14]. In what follows, we present the idea of exploiting the Real AdaBoost to reduce the computational effort used to estimate such parameters.

2.2   Modified Real AdaBoost

Real AdaBoost [8] is the generalization of Discrete AdaBoost [15], where each of the base classifiers generates not only hard class labels, but also real valued "confidence-rated" predictions. It is observed to be tolerant with regards to classification noise, and is capable of providing better performance, as compared to the Discrete Ada-Boost.

Given $X = \{(\mathbf{x}_1, y_1), (\mathbf{x}_2, y_2), ..., (\mathbf{x}_m, y_m)\}; y_i \in \{-1, +1\}$

1. Initialize $D_1(i) = 1/m$

2. For $t = 1, ..., T$

   (a) Train the base classifier $g_t(\mathbf{x}) = p(\mathbf{x} \mid w_G) - p(\mathbf{x} \mid w_I)$ using $f_T = 0.01t$.

   (b) Determine the weight updating parameter α_t

$$\alpha_t = \frac{1}{2} \log \frac{\sum_{i=1}^{m} D_t(i)(1 + y_i g_t(\mathbf{x}_i))}{\sum_{i=1}^{m} D_t(i)(1 - y_i g_t(\mathbf{x}_i))}$$

   (c) Update and normalize $D_{t+1}(i)$ such that

$$D_{t+1}(i) = \frac{D_t(i) \exp(-\alpha_t y_i g_t(\mathbf{x}_i))}{\sum_{i=1}^{m} D_t(i) \exp(-\alpha_t y_i g_t(\mathbf{x}_i))}$$

3. Output the final hypothesis

$$G(\mathbf{x}) = sign\left(\sum_{t=1}^{T} \alpha_t g_t(\mathbf{x})\right)$$

Fig. 1. The Real AdaBoost algorithm

Let $X = \{(\mathbf{x}_1, y_1), (\mathbf{x}_2, y_2), ..., (\mathbf{x}_m, y_m)\}$ be a sequence of m training samples, where $\mathbf{x}_i$ is a vector of matching scores, and y_i is its associated class label, i.e., $y_i \in \{-1, +1\}$, where -1 denotes an impostor, and +1 denotes a genuine user. Fig. 1 shows the Real Adaboost algorithm. In step (1), the weights of each sample are selected to be uniformly distributed for the entire training data set, i.e., $D_1(i) = 1/m$. In step (2), T base classifiers are trained, as shown in steps (2a)-(2c). In step (2a), the base classifier $g_t(\mathbf{x}) = p(\mathbf{x} \mid w_G) - p(\mathbf{x} \mid w_I)$ is trained using the entire training data set and a different $f_T = 0.01t$. This is the key difference from the conventional Real AdaBoost, which trains the base classifiers using a variety of data sets or feature sets. In step (2b), the weight updating parameter α_t is determined such that the bound on the generalized training error is minimized as in [8], [15]. Next, the weight distributions of the genuine user and impostor classes for the next iteration (i.e.,

$D_t(i)$) are updated and normalized (steps (2c)). After T iterations of step (2), the final hypothesis $G(\mathbf{x})$ is obtained as a linear combination of the T weak hypotheses (step (3)). As can be seen, the base classifiers are generated using various values of f_T. Hence, no training is required to find its optimal value. In general, each base classifier is known to make errors, however the patterns, which are misclassified by the different classifiers are not necessarily the same.

3   Experiments

Experiments were carried out on the BioSecure DS2 [9], which is the desktop scenario subset of the BioSecure database. The database contains still face, 6 fingerprint (i.e., thumb, middle, and index fingers of both hands) and iris matchers from 333 persons. A detailed description of the BioSecure DS2 database can be found in [9]. It should be noted that the BioSecure DS2 database has a class imbalance in the order of 524:1. By exhaustively pairing the available face, fingerprint, and iris matchers with respect to multimodal fusion (using different biometric traits), we obtain 13 possible combinations. Experiments were conducted using the functions provided by the Data Description Toolbox 1.9.1 [16]. The performance in terms of the a priori Half Total Error Rate (HTER) was evaluated using the tools, proposed in [17].

We first evaluate the influence of the number of rounds of boosting T on the proposed system. It should be noted that when T is increased, the range of the fraction rejection f_T, used by the base classifier, is increased accordingly. For example, if $T = 10$, then the range of f_T should be from 0.01 to 0.1 (i.e., 0.01×10). Fig. 2 depicts the matching performance of the proposed system as a function of T. It can be empirically observed that the proposed system does not overfit, even when $T = 50$. This clearly contradicts the spirit of the bound on the generalized error, which suggests that boosting will overfit if it runs for too many rounds [8], [15]. In fact, the HTER across the 13 possible combinations do not change for $T = [10,...,50]$.

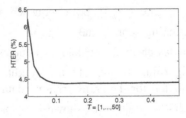

Fig. 2. The HTER (%) of the proposed system as a function of $T = [1,...,50]$

Table 1 shows the detailed results of the proposed system across 13 fusion possibilities, which are then compared with other state-of-the-art techniques, including the sum of scores (abbreviated as SUM) [1], likelihood ratio based score fusion (abbreviated as LR) [10], and SVM. In Table 1, Dr-Tr and Dr-Te denote the decision rule, described in Section 2.1, when f_T is optimized on the training set and when

f_T is directly optimized on the testing set, respectively. The following observations can be made:

- When appropriate f_T is selected, the Dr-Te offers a significant advantage as it outperforms other state-of-the-art techniques. In practice, it is not easy to estimate the appropriate value of f_T even when it is optimized because biometric training data is usually different from testing data. The results of the Dr-Tr further confirm this observation. Nevertheless, it is important to note that the Dr-Tr achieves significant lower error rates, with respect to the SUM and SVM.
- The proposed system performs best as it provides a performance improvement in terms of average HTER of 5%, 13% and 14% as compared to the LR, SVM, and SUM. Indeed, it is shown to achieve higher verification accuracy, relative to the Dr-Te, which optimizes f_T directly on the testing set.

Table 1. The HTER (%) of different techniques accross 13 possible combinations of the BioSecure DS2 datababase. Note that * indicates the lowest HTER.

	SUM	LR	SVM	Dr-Tr	Dr-Te	Proposed System
Face + Right thumb finger	5.34	4.46	5.16	4.81	4.36*	4.54
Face + Right index finger	3.49	3.44	3.12	3.59	2.92*	2.92*
Face + Right middle finger	5.42	4.94	6.10	5.56	5.15	3.79*
Face + Left thumb finger	4.27	3.74	3.74	4.36	3.84	3.64*
Face + Left index finger	3.18	3.75	3.17*	3.71	3.47	3.44
Face + Left middle finger	3.95	3.42*	4.37	4.00	3.44	3.88
Face + Iris	5.67	4.80	4.70	4.63	4.63	4.46*
Iris + Right thumb finger	6.85	6.39	6.58	6.65	6.14*	6.21
Iris + Right index finger	4.15	3.42	3.76	3.26	3.26	3.25*
Iris + Right middle finger	6.53	5.38	6.81	5.76	5.35*	5.58
Iris + Left thumb finger	6.55	6.16	6.19	6.06	6.06	5.57*
Iris + Left index finger	4.98	4.75	5.19	4.74	4.61	4.49*
Iris + Left middle finger	5.72	5.14	6.34	5.57	5.44	5.04*
Mean	**5.08**	**4.60**	**5.01**	**4.82**	**4.51**	**4.37**

4   Conclusions

In this paper, a new system has been proposed by first developing a decision rule for the fusion of one-class classifiers. Next, the Real AdaBoost is employed, where this decision rule is treated as the base classifier and is trained using the entire training data, but with different parameter settings (i.e., fraction rejection). In general, this system offers many distinct advantages. It is shown that it can effectively exploit the entire set of the training data, and efficiently handle the class imbalance problem, while reducing the computational effort for estimating the optimal value fraction rejection, which is difficult to achieve in practice. Experiments carried out on the

BioSecure DS2 database, demonstrate that the proposed system can provide significantly better performance as compared to other state-of-the-art techniques, including the sum of scores, likelihood ratio based score fusion, and support vector machines.

References

1. Ross, A., Nandakumar, K., Anil, K., Jain, A.K.: Handbook of multibiometrics, vol. 6. Springer (2006)
2. He, H., Garcia, E.A.: Learning from imbalanced data. IEEE Transaction on Knowledge and Data Engineering 21(9), 1263–1284 (2009)
3. Tax, D.M.J.: One-class Classification: Concept-learning in the absence of counter-examples. Ph.D. dissertation, Dept. Intelligent Systems, Univ. TU Delft (2001)
4. Raskutti, B., Adam, K.: Extreme re-balancing for SVMs: a case study. ACM Sigkdd Explorations Newsletter 6(1), 60–69 (2004)
5. Japkowicz, N.: Supervised versus unsupervised binary-learning by feed forward neural networks. Machine Learning 42(1-2), 97–122 (2001)
6. Galar, M., Fernandez, A., Barrenechea, E., Bustince, H., Herrera, F.: A review on ensembles for the class imbalance problem: bagging-, boosting-, and hybrid-based approaches. IEEE Transaction on Systems, Man, and Cybernetics, Part C: Applications and Reviews 42(4), 463–484 (2012)
7. Seiffert, C., Khoshgoftaar, T.M., Van Hulse, J., Napolitano, A.: RUSBoost: A hybrid approach to alleviating class imbalance. IEEE Transaction on Systems, Man and Cybernetics, Part A: Systems and Humans 40(1), 185–197 (2010)
8. Schapire, R.E., Singer, Y.: Improved boosting algorithms using confidence-rated predictions. Machine Learning 37(3), 297–336 (1999)
9. Poh, N., Bourlai, T., Kittler, J.: A Multimodal Biometric Test Bed for Quality-dependent, Cost-sensitive and Client-specific Score-level Fusion Algorithms. Pattern Recognition 43(3), 1094–1105 (2010)
10. Nandakumar, K., Chen, Y., Dass, S.C., Jain, A.K.: Likelihood ratio-based biometric score fusion. IEEE Transaction on Pattern Analysis and Machine Intelligence 30(2), 342–347 (2008)
11. Silverman, B.W.: Density Estimation for Statistical and Data Analysis. Chapman and Hall (1986)
12. Duda, R.O., Hart, P.E., Stork, D.G.: Pattern classification. John Wiley & Sons (2012)
13. Figueiredo, M.A., Jain, A.K.: Unsupervised learning of finite mixture models. IEEE Transaction on Pattern Analysis and Machine Intelligence 24(3), 381–396 (2002)
14. Poh, N., Merati, A., Kittler, J.: Adaptive client-impostor centric score normalization: A case study in fingerprint verification. In: IEEE 3rd International Conference on Biometrics: Theory Applications, and Systems, pp. 1–7 (2009)
15. Freund, Y., Schapire, R., Abe, N.: A short introduction to boosting. Journal of Japanese Society For Artificial Intelligence 14(5), 771–780 (1999)
16. Tax, D.M.J.: DDtools, the Data Description Toolbox for Matlab (2012)
17. Poh, N., Bengio, S.: Database, protocols and tools for evaluating score-level fusion algorithms in biometric authentication. Pattern Recognition 39(2), 223–233 (2006)

Integrative Analysis of Gene Expression and Promoter Methylation during Reprogramming of a Non-Small-Cell Lung Cancer Cell Line Using Principal Component Analysis-Based Unsupervised Feature Extraction

Y.-h. Taguchi

Department of Physics, Chuo University, 1-13-27 Kasuga, Bunkyo-ku, Tokyo 112-8551, Japan
tag@granular.com

Abstract. Cancer cells are to some extent regarded as similar to undifferentiated cells, such as embryonic stem cells and induced pluripotent cells. However, cancer cells can be reprogrammed using standard reprogramming procedures. Thus, it would be interesting to observe the result of cancer cell reprogramming. In this paper, we reanalyzed publically available mRNA expression and promoter methylation profiles during reprogramming of non-small-cell lung cancer cell lines, using the recently proposed principal component analysis-based unsupervised feature extraction. Six genes, *TGFBI, S100A6, CSRP1, CLDN11, PRKCDBP*, and *CRIP1*, were commonly found (P = 0.003) in the 100 top-ranked genes with aberrant expression or aberrant promoter methylation. Because all six genes were related to cancer in the literature, they might be new therapeutic targets for treatment of non-small-cell lung cancer.

Keywords: principal component analysis, feature extraction, non-small-cell lung cancer, aberrant promoter methylation, reprogramming.

1 Introduction

Because cancers are regarded to be similar to undifferentiated cells to some extent [1], it would be interesting to observe the outcome of cancer cells that are further reprogrammed. Mahalingam et al. [2] recently measured gene expression and promoter methylation profiles during non-small-cell lung cancer (NSCLC) cell line reprogramming. They observed that reprogramming drastically changed both gene expression and promoter methylation profiles and concluded that reprogramming could reverse aberrant gene expression and promoter methylation profiles that might cause cancer progression. However, the integration of gene expression analysis and promoter methylation profiles for multiple sample classes has remained partial. In this paper, we applied recently proposed principal component analysis (PCA)-based unsupervised feature extraction (FE) [3,4,5,6,7] to gene expression and promoter methylation profiles. This allowed us to integrate gene expression and promoter methylation analysis over multiple sample classes. We identified six genes with aberrant gene expression and promoter methylation that were negatively correlated with each other.

D.-S. Huang et al. (Eds.): ICIC 2014, LNBI 8590, pp. 445–455, 2014.

These genes were extensively reported to be related to cancers. This suggests the usefulness of PCA-based unsupervised FE for the multiclass problem.

2   Approaches

Gene expression and promoter methylation profiles were downloaded from Gene Expression Omnibus (GEO) using GEO ID: GSE35913. The file including gene expression, GSE35911_SampleProbeProfile.txt.gz, was provided as a supplementary file in the subseries GEO ID: GSE35911. Columns annotated as "AVG_Signal" were used. Promoter methylation profiles were obtained from "Series Matrix File(s)" in the subseries GEO ID: GSE35912. They consisted of eight cell lines, H1 (ES cell), H358 and H460 (NSCLC), IMR90 (Human Caucasian fetal lung fibroblast), iPCH358, iPCH460, iPSIMR90 (reprogrammed cell lines), and piPCH358 (re-differentiated iPCH358) with three biological replicates. In total, there were 3 replicates × 8 cell lines × 2 properties (gene expression and promoter methylation) = 48 samples.

Probes were embedded into a two-dimensional space by applying PCA to either gene expression or promoter methylation. Based on biological considerations, PC2s were employed for FE. The top 100 outliers were selected for gene expression and promoter methylation profiles.

Disease associations with genes were investigated by Gendoo [8], a literature-based disease-gene association database.

For gene expression, probe annotations were based on the "Accession" column (for RefSeq gene ID) or "Symbol" column (for gene symbol) in the GSE35911_SampleProbeProfile.txt.gz file. For promoter methylation, GPL8490-65.txt available from the GEO ID: GSE35912 file was used and the "Accession" column was used to assign a Refseq gene ID to each probe.

To confirm a negative correlation between promoter methylation and gene expression based on PCA, a two-step analysis is required as follows:

1. Compute correlation coefficients of selected principal components (PCs) between gene expression and promoter methylation.
2. If the correlation coefficients are negative (positive), probes corresponding to the same gene should have equally (oppositely) signed PC scores between gene expression and promoter methylation.

To confirm this point, the first 100 top-ranked probes having positively (negatively) larger PC scores were extracted for PC1 (PC2) of gene expression. Then, PC1 (PC2) scores for promoter methylation of probes corresponding to genes attributed to the selected probes by gene expression were extracted. If PC scores selected for promoter methylation were significantly negative (positive) and if correlation coefficients of PC1 (PC2) between promoter methylation and gene expression were positive (negative), or if PC scores selected by promoter methylation were significantly positive (negative) and if correlation coefficients of PC1 (PC2) between promoter methylation and gene expression were negative (positive), PC1 (PC2) represented a negative correlation between gene expression and promoter methylation. Significance was tested using one sample t-test of PC scores in promoter methylation of the selected probes.

3   Results

Figure 1 shows the two-dimensional embedding of probes when applying PCA to either gene expression or promoter methylation. Contributions of PC1 and PC2 to overall gene expression (promoter methylation profile) were 91 (84)% and 3 (6)%, respectively. Figure 2 shows the contribution from each sample to PC1 and PC2 for gene expression and promoter methylation. To apply PCA-based unsupervised FE to gene expression/promoter methylation, it is important to determine which PC is biologically meaningful. First, because promoter methylation is thought to suppress gene expression, selected PCs for gene expression and promoter methylation should be negatively correlated.

Table 1 shows the correlation coefficients of PC1 and PC2 between promoter methylation and gene expression. Because PC1s are positively correlated, probes corresponding to the same gene should have oppositely signed PC scores for gene expression and promoter methylation (see Approaches). To determine this, we selected the 100 top-ranked probes with high PC1 scores for gene expression, and tested whether PC1 scores for promoter methylation in 100 probes that shared genes with the selected 100 probes for gene expression were negative. PC1 scores for promoter methylation were significantly positive ($P = 2.2 \times 10^{-8}$). PC1s therefore do not represent a negative correlation between gene expression and methylation, and were thus   excluded as PCs for FE. Because PC2s were negatively correlated, probes corresponding to the same gene should have equally signed PC scores for gene expression and promoter methylation. To determine this, we selected the 100 top-ranked probes with low PC2 scores for gene expression and tested whether PC2 scores for promoter methylation of the 100 probes that share genes with the selected 100 probes for gene expression were negative. PC2 scores for promoter methylation were significantly negative ($P = 0.0001$). PC2s therefore represent a negative correlation between gene expression and methylation, and thus were used as PCs used for FE.

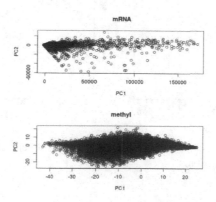

Fig. 1. Two-dimensional embedding of probes when applying PCA to gene expression (top) or promoter methylation (bottom). Horizontal (vertical) axis: PC1 (PC2).

Although PC2s represented a global negative correlation between gene expression and promoter methylation, the contribution of PC2s was as low as a few percent, thus, it was not clear whether each gene reflected a negative correlation. To confirm this, we selected 100 top-ranked probes with high PC2 scores for gene expression and promoter methylation and identified six probes sharing the same genes for gene expression and promoter methylation. The probability that six probes were accidentally included in both sets was 0.003. Thus, the two sets of 100 probes had significant overlap. Figure 3 shows the sample contributions to PC2 for gene expression and promoter methylation of individual genes. Generally, individual gene base correlations between gene expression and promoter methylation were more significant than that between PC2s (−0.62, Table 1). Thus, our PCA-based unsupervised FE system successfully selected genes with a negative correlation between gene expression and promoter methylation.

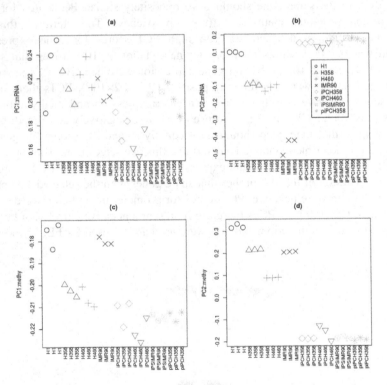

Fig. 2. Contributions from samples to PCs. (a) PC1, (b) PC2 for gene expression, (c) PC1, and (d) PC2 for promoter methylation.

Table 1. Pearson correlation coefficients (P-values) of PCs between gene expression and promoter methylation profiles

		Promoter methylation profile	
		PC1	PC2
Gene expression	PC1	0.58 (0.003)	0.59 (0.002)
	PC2	−0.59 (0.002)	−0.62 (0.001)

4   Discussion

4.1   Biological Significance

Although our PCA-based unsupervised FE system successfully selected six genes with a negative correlation between gene expression and promoter methylation, the biological significance was not clear. Table 2 shows disease association with the six genes reported by Gendoo [8].

Table 2. Disease association with the six selected genes related to cancer/tumors only reported by the Gendoo server

Gene Symbol	Disease Associations (P-values)
TGFBI	Neoplasms, Radiation-Induced (3×10^{-5}); Neoplasm Invasiveness (2×10^{-4}); Cell Transformation, Neoplastic (6.7×10^{-3}); Bronchial Neoplasms (0.02); Cocarcinogenesis (0.03)
S100A6	Skin Neoplasms (1.1×10^{-11}); Pancreatic Neoplasms (1.8×10^{-11}); Adenocarcinoma (3.6×10^{-8}); Melanoma (6.4×10^{-8}); Precancerous Conditions (9.1×10^{-8});
CSRP1	Carcinoma, Hepatocellular (1.3×10^{-2}); Liver Neoplasms (0.014); Prostatic Neoplasms (0.017)
CLDN11	No associations
PRKCDBP	Lung Neoplasms (4.9×10^{-4}); Hamartoma (5.0×10^{-4}); Glioblastoma (7.9×10^{-3}); Adenoma (0.012); Carcinoma, Non-Small-Cell Lung (0.013)
CRIP1	Carcinoma, Hepatocellular (0.025), Liver Neoplasms (0.028), Prostatic Neoplasms (0.033)

Table 2 shows that many disease associations have been reported for *TGFBI*, *S100A6, CSRP1, PRKCDBP*, and *CRIP1* genes. Among the six selected genes, only *CLDN11* was not related to cancer disease. Thus, the PCA-based unsupervised FE system successfully selected genes that appear to be important during reprogramming of NSCLC.

4.2   Gene Expression/Promoter Methylation Profile of Individual Genes

Generally, induced pluripotent stem cell (iPC/iPS/piPC) lines exhibited similar gene expression and promoter methylation profiles, with suppressed gene expression and hypermethylated promoters (Fig. 3). This observation is coincident with the idea that promoter methylation suppresses gene expression and the conclusion by Mahalingam et al. that reversal of gene expression during reprogramming is mediated by hypermethylation. However, the behavior of other cell lines, H1, H358, H460, and IMR90, were not straightforward. For example, *TGFBI* had the highest upregulation in the IMR90 cell line while *S100A6* was most upregulated in the H358 cell line. This divergence is often observed in genes/cell lines for both gene expression and promoter methylation. This suggests that cancer cell lines could be successfully reprogrammed into specific cell types, possibly pluripotent cells.

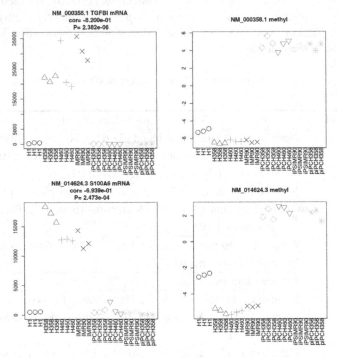

Fig. 3. Gene expression (first and third columns)/promoter methylation profile (second and fourth columns) of individual genes. "cor" represents Spearman correlation coefficients between gene expression and promoter methylation. "P" represents associated P-values.

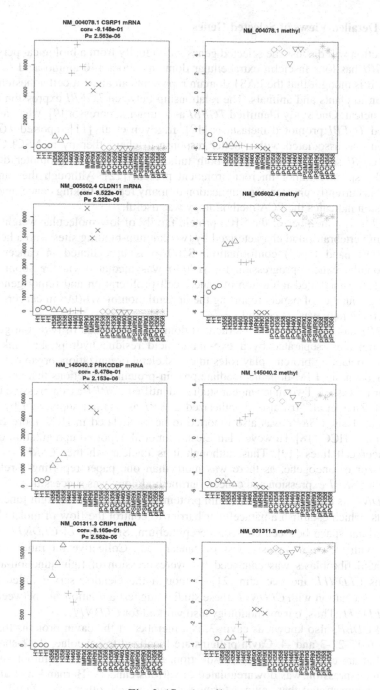

Fig. 3. (*Continued.*)

4.3   Detailed Views of Selected Genes

This section will discuss the selected genes individually from a biological perspective.

TFGBI has four fasciclin extracellular domains about 140 amino acid residues in length. It is thought that the FAS1 domain represents an ancient cell adhesion domain common to plants and animals. The relationship between *TGFBI* expression and cancer is unclear. One study identified *TGFBI* as a tumor suppressor [9], whereas another reported *TGFBI* promoted metastasis [10]. Irigoyen et al. [11] reported *TGFBI* expression was associated with a better response to chemotherapy in NSCLC. Therefore, *TGFBI* seems to function as both tumor suppressor and promoter depending upon the specific tumor microenvironment present [12]. Although the function of *TGFBI* is currently unclear, the publication of many reports linking cancer and *TGFBI* expression indicates the PCA methodology was useful.

S100A6 is a member of the S100 protein family of low-molecular-weight proteins found in vertebrates and characterized by two calcium-binding sites with a helix-loop-helix ("EF-hand type") conformation. S100A6 is upregulated in cancer [13,14]. Functionally, cancer progression by *S100A6* was mediated via the suppression of CacyBP/SIP-mediated inhibition of cancer cell proliferation and tumorigenesis [15]. The large number of papers reporting the upregulation of *S100A6* in cancers suggests our methodology was successful.

CSRP1 has two LIM protein structural domains, composed of two contiguous zinc finger domains, separated by a two-amino acid residue hydrophobic linker. LIM-domain containing proteins play roles in cytoskeletal organization, organ development and oncogenesis. LIM-domains mediate protein-protein interactions that are critical to cellular processes. Two independent studies identified *CSRP1* as suppressive in tumors [16,17]. Zhou et al. [16] also hypothesized *CSRP1* as a tumor suppressor by literature search analysis. *CSRP1* was also reported to be methylated in HCC more frequently than in non-HCC [18]. However, Hu-Lieskovan et al. reported upregulation of *CSRP1* in cancer cell lines [19]. Thus, although it is unclear whether *CSRP1* is a tumor suppressor or oncogene, as there was more than one paper reporting a relationship between *CSRP1* expression and cancer, our methodology was successful.

CLDN11 is a member of the claudin proteins that are important tight junction components, which establish a paracellular barrier to control the flow of molecules in the intercellular space between cells in the epithelium. Silencing of *CLDN11* was associated with increased invasiveness of cancer [20]. Collective migration of cancer-associated fibroblasts was enhanced by overexpression of tight junction-associated proteins *CLDN11* and occludin [21]. Although the Gendoo server failed to report cancer association with *CLDN11*, these studies suggest a relationship between cancers and *CLDN11*. Thus, our methodology also worked for *CLDN11*.

PRKCDBP, also known as cavin-3, is a member of the cavin proteins that consist of cavin-1, -2, -3 and -4. Cavin proteins are localized to caveolae, flask-shaped lipid rafts that are critical for signal transduction. *PRKCDBP* is also a tumor suppressor, since its expression was downregulated in various cancers. Hernandez et al. [22] recently demonstrated that cavin-3 forms a complex with other cavin family proteins. They also showed that the cavin-3 lacking NSCLC cell line H1299 exhibited a 7.6-fold increase in surface caveolae by restoration of cavin-3. In their hypothesis, cavin-3 mediated signal transduction of the ERK/Akt signaling pathway, which is critical for oncogenesis. As seen in Fig.3, the expression of *PRKCDBP* in cancer cell lines was less than that of IMR90, a fully differentiated cell line, which is coincident with the hypothesis that *PRKCDBP* is a tumor suppressor. However, *PRKCDBP* expression is reduced in ES/iPS cell lines. Thus, currently it is not clear whether a reduction of *PRKCDBP* expression always mediates cancer progression. A more detailed investigation is required. All of these studies suggest *PRKCDBP* has a potentially critical role in NSCLC, supporting the correctness and/or usefulness of our methodology.

CRIP1 contains a LIM domain, as does *CSRP1*. Similar to *CSRP1*, the relationship between *CRIP1* expression and cancer is unclear. Although *CRIP1* is expressed in various tumors, suggesting it is oncogenic, a lack of *CRIP1* expression is also correlated with a worse prognosis of patients, indicating *CRIP1* is a tumor suppressor [23]. However, hypomethylation of *CRIP1* in cancer was also observed, suggesting *CRIP1* is oncogenic [24]. In addition, its cellular role is still unclear. Since many articles reported a relationship between aberrant *CRIP1* expression and cancer, our methodology to detect NSCLC-related genes was successful.

5 Conclusion

In this study, we applied recently proposed PCA-based unsupervised FE to publically available gene expression/promoter methylation samples during reprogramming of NSCLC cell lines. Our unsupervised method identified a number of cancer-related genes. This demonstrates the superiority of PCA-based unsupervised FE, because the results were more robust compared with previous studies as there was reduced arbitrariness. For PCA-based unsupervised FE, only PCs that need to be considered for further analyses should be specified, e.g., FE. We identified six genes with a negative correlation between gene expression and promoter methylation. All six genes were related to cancer disease. Because these genes were not previously reported as related to NSCLC, they might be new drug targets for the treatment of NSCLC.

Acknowledgments. This work was supported by the Japan Society for the Promotion of Science KAKENHI (grant number 23300357, 26120528), and a Chuo University Joint Research Grant.

References

1. Kim, J., Orkin, S.H.: Embryonic Stem Cell-Specific Signatures in Cancer: Insights Into Genomic Regulatory Networks and Implications for Medicine. Genome. Med. 3, 75 (2011)
2. Mahalingam, D., Kong, C.M., Lai, J., Tay, L.L., Yang, H., Wang, X.: Reversal of Aberrant Cancer Methylome and Transcriptome Upon Direct Reprogramming of Lung Cancer Cells. Sci. Rep. 2, 592 (2012)
3. Ishida, S., Umeyama, H., Iwadate, M., Taguchi, Y.-H.: Bioinformatic Screening of Autoimmune Disease Genes and Protein Structure Prediction with FAMS for Drug Discovery. Protein Pept. Lett. (in press, 2014)
4. Kinoshita, R., Iwadate, M., Umeyama, H., Taguchi, Y.-H.: Genes Associated with Genotype-Specific DNA Methylation in Squamous Cell Carcinoma as Candidate Drug Targets. BMC. Syst. Biol. 8(suppl. 1), S4 (2014)

5. Murakami, Y., Toyoda, H., Tanahashi, T., Tanaka, J., Kumada, T., Yoshioka, Y., Kosaka, N., Ochiya, T., Taguchi, Y.-H.: Comprehensive Mirna Expression Analysis in Peripheral Blood Can Diagnose Liver Disease. PLOS One 7, E48366 (2012)
6. Taguchi, Y.-H., Murakami, Y.: Principal Component Analysis Based Feature Extraction Approach to Identify Circulating Microrna Biomarkers. PLOS One 8, E66714 (2013)
7. Taguchi, Y.-H., Okamoto, A.: Principal Component Analysis for Bacterial Proteomic Analysis. In: Shibuya, T., Kashima, H., Sese, J., Ahmad, S. (eds.) PRIB 2012. LNCS, vol. 7632, pp. 141–152. Springer, Heidelberg (2012)
8. Nakazato, T., Bono, H., Matsuda, H., And Takagi, T.: Gendoo: Functional Profiling of Gene and Disease Features Using Mesh Vocabulary. Nuc. Acid. Res. 37, S2, W166–W169 (2009)
9. Li, B., Wen, G., Zhao, Y., Tong, J., Hei, T.K.: The Role of TGFBI in Mesothelioma and Breast Cancer: Association with Tumor Suppression. BMC Cancer 12, 239 (2012)
10. Ma, C., Rong, Y., Radiloff, D.R., Datto, M.B., Centeno, B., Bao, S., Cheng, A.W.M., Lin, F., Jiang, S., Yeatman, T.J., Wang, X.-F.: Extracellular Matrix Protein BIg-H3/TGFBI Promotes Metastasis of Colon Cancer by Enhancing Cell Extravasation. Genes. Dev. 22, 308–321 (2008)
11. Irigoyen, M., Pajares, M.J., Agorreta, J., Ponz-SarvisÉ, M., Salvo, E., Lozano, M.D., Pío, R., Gil-Bazo, I., Rouzaut, A.: TGFBI Expression is Associated with a Better Response to Chemotherapy in NSCLC. Mol. Cancer 9, 130 (2010)
12. Ween, M.P., Oehler, M.K., Ricciardelli, C.: Transforming Growth Factor-Beta-Induced Protein (TGFBI)/(BIg-H3): A Matrix Protein with Dual Functions in Ovarian Cancer. Int. J. Mol. Sci. 13, 10461–10477 (2012)
13. Yang, Y.Q., Zhang, L.J., Dong, H., Jiang, C.L., Zhu, Z.G., Wu, J.X., Wu, Y.L., Han, J.S., Xiao, H.S., Gao, H.J., Zhang, Q.H.: Upregulated Expression of S100A6 in Human Gastric Cancer. J. Dig. Dis. 8, 186–193 (2007)
14. Ohuchida, K., Mizumoto, K., Ishikawa, N., Fujii, K., Konomi, H., Nagai, E., Yamaguchi, K., Tsuneyoshi, M., Tanaka, M.: The Role of S100A6 in Pancreatic Cancer Development and its Clinical Implication as a Diagnostic Marker and Therapeutic Target. Clin. Cancer. Res. 11, 7785–7793 (2005)
15. Ning, X., Sun, S., Zhang, K., Liang, J., Chuai, Y., Li, Y., Wang, X.: S100A6 Protein Negatively Regulates Cacybp/SIP-Mediated Inhibition of Gastric Cancer Cell Proliferation and Tumorigenesis. PLOS One 7, E30185 (2012)
16. Zhou, C.Z., Qiu, G.Q., Wang, X.L., Fan, J.W., Tang, H.M., Sun, Y.H., Wang, Q., Huang, F., Yan, D.W., Li, D.W., Peng, Z.H.: Screening of Tumor Suppressor Genes on 1q31.1-32.1 in Chinese Patients with Sporadic Colorectal Cancer. Chin. Med. J. 121, 2479–2486 (2008)
17. Mandal, S., Curtis, L., Pind, M., Murphy, L.C., Watson, P.H.: S100A7 (Psoriasin) Influences Immune Response Genes in Human Breast Cancer. Exp. Cell. Res. 313, 3016–3025 (2007)
18. Hirasawa, Y., Arai, M., Imazeki, F., Tada, M., Mikata, R., Fukai, K., Miyazaki, M., Ochiai, T., Saisho, H., Yokosuka, O.: Methylation Status of Genes Upregulated by Demethylating Agent 5-Aza-2'-Deoxycytidine in Hepatocellular Carcinoma. Oncology 71, 77–85 (2006)
19. Hu-Lieskovan, S., Zhang, J., Wu, L., Shimada, H., Schofield, D.E., Triche, T.J.: EWS-FLI1 Fusion Protein Up-Regulates Critical Genes in Neural Crest Development and is Responsible for the Observed Phenotype of Ewing's Family of Tumors. Cancer Res. 65, 4633–4644 (2005)

20. Agarwal, R., Mori, Y., Cheng, Y., Jin, Z., Olaru, A.V., Hamilton, J.P., David, S., Selaru, F.M., Yang, J., Abraham, J.M., Montgomery, E., Morin, P.J., Meltzer, S.J.: Silencing of Claudin-11 Is Associated with Increased Invasiveness of Gastric Cancer Cells. PLOS One 4, E8002 (2009)

21. Karagiannis, G.S., Schaeffer, D.F., Cho, C.K., Musrap, N., Saraon, P., Batruch, I., Grin, A., Mitrovic, B., Kirsch, R., Riddell, R.H., Diamandis, E.P.: Collective Migration of Cancer-Associated Fibroblasts is Enhanced by Overexpression of Tight Junction-Associated Proteins Claudin-11 And Occludin. Mol. Oncol. 8, 178–195 (2014)

22. Hernandez, V.J., Weng, J., Ly, P., Pompey, S., Dong, H., Mishra, L., Schwarz, M., Anderson, R.G.W., Michaely, P.: Cavin-3 Dictates The Balance Between ERK and Akt Signaling. Elife 2, E00905 (2013)

23. Ludyga, N., Englert, S., Pflieger, K., Rauser, S., Braselmann, H., Walch, A., Auer, G., Höfler, H., Aubele, M.: The Impact of Cysteine-Rich Intestinal Protein 1 in Human Breast Cancer. Mol. Cancer. 12, 28 (2013)

24. Wang, Q., Williamson, M., Bott, S., Brookman-Amissah, N., Freeman, A., Nariculam, J., Hubank, M.J.F., Ahmed, A., Masters, J.R.: Hypomethylation of WNT5A, CRIP1 and S100P in Prostate Cancer. Oncogene 26, 6560–6565 (2007)

Predicting the Subcellular Localization of Proteins with Multiple Sites Based on Multiple Features Fusion

Xumi Qu[1,2], Yuehui Chen[1,2,*], Shanping Qiao[1,2], Dong Wang[1,2], and Qing Zhao[1,2]

[1] The School of Information Science and Engineering, University of Jinan, Jinan 250022, China
[2] Shandong Provincial Key laboratory of Network Based Intelligent Computing,
Jinan 250022, China
952173250@qq.com

Abstract. Protein sub-cellular localization prediction is an important and meaningful task in bioinformatics. It can provide important clues for us to study the functions of proteins and targeted drug discovery. Traditional experiment techniques which can determine the protein sub-cellular locations are almost costly and time consuming. In the last two decades, a great many machine learning algorithms and protein sub-cellular location predictors have been developed to deal with this kind of problems. However, most of the algorithms can only solve the single-location proteins. With the progress of techniques, more and more proteins which have two or even more sub-cellular locations are found, it is much more significant to study this kind of proteins for they have extremely useful implication in both basic biological research and drug discovery. If we want to improve the accuracy of prediction, we have to extract much more feature information. In this paper, we use fusion feature extraction methods to extract the feature information simultaneously, and the multi-label k nearest neighbors (ML-KNN) algorithm to predict protein sub-cellular locations, the best overall accuracy rate we got in dataset s1 in constructing Gpos-mploc is 66.1568% and 59.9206% in dataset s2 in constructing Virus-mPLoc.

Keywords: N-terminal signals, pseudo amino acid composition, Physicochemical properties, Amino acid index distribution, multi-label k nearest neighbor.

1   Introduction

Protein is the bearer of life activities, it takes responsibility for the whole life process. But it can only work normally when they are in special and correct localizations. Since the post-genomic age, large number of protein sequences were generated, relying on biochemical experiment to determine the subcellular locations of proteins is unpractical. A lot of classifiers and predictors which can only deal with single-location proteins have been developed, but some proteins may belong to two or even more subcellular locations, according to the report of DBMloc, more than 30% of proteins have more than one subcellular locations [1], so it is a common phenomenon for proteins to have multiple sub-cellular locations [2], however, there are only a handful of predictors can deal with this kind of proteins.

---

* Corresponding author.

D.-S. Huang et al. (Eds.): ICIC 2014, LNBI 8590, pp. 456–465, 2014.
© Springer International Publishing Switzerland 2014

In this paper, we use four feature extraction methods simultaneously, they are N-terminal signal [3], pseudo amino acid composition, physical and chemical properties and amino acid index distribution. Then use multi-label k nearest neighbor algorithm to predict the subcellular locations and got satisfied results by Jack Knife test.

2   Dataset

In this paper, we choose to use two datasets. One is dataset s1 in constructing Gpos-mploc [4], it was established specialized for Gram-positive bacteria proteins and includes both singleplex and multiplex sub-cellular location proteins. This benchmark dataset includes 523 gram-positive bacteria protein sequences (519different proteins), classified into 4 sub-cellular locations. Among the 519 different proteins, 515 belong to one location and 4 to two locations. None of the proteins has ≥25% sequence identify to any other in the same subset. The four subcellualr locations are shown in Fig.1.

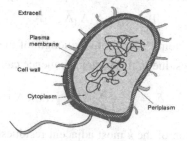

Fig. 1. Four subcellular locations of Gram-positive bacteria proteins

The other dataset is s2 in constructing Virus-mPLoc [5]. It includes both singleplex and multiplex subcellular location proteins and was established specialized for viral proteins. This benchmark dataset includes 252 locative protein sequences (207 different proteins), classified into 6 subcellular locations. Among the 207 different proteins, 165 belong to one subcellular location, 39 to two locations, 3 to three locations, and none to four or more locations and none of the proteins has ≥25% sequence identity to any other in the same subset (subcellular location). The six subcellular locations are shown in Fig.2.

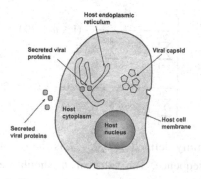

Fig. 2. Six subcellular locations of virus proteins

3   Feature Extraction Mehtods

3.1   Pseudo Amino Acid Composition

Most of the feature extraction methods are based on the frequency of single or several residues in a protein sequence, but ignored the position information between residues. To avoid losing the protein sequence order information, Chou proposed a kind of protein descriptor, it is pseudo amino acid composition [6]. In this kind of feature extraction model, the feature vector is expressed by the following equation:

$$F = [v_1, v_2, \cdots v_{19}, v_{20}, v_{20+1}, \cdots v_{20+\eta}](\eta < N) \tag{1}$$

The first twenty components is the same as amino acid composition method, reflect the information of protein composition. The following η sections reflect the protein position information which can incarnate its unique advantage.

Use A to represent amino acid residue, then the protein sequence can be expressed as:

$$P = A_1 A_2 A_3 A_4 A_5 \cdots A_N \tag{2}$$

A_1 is the first residue of protein P, N denote the length of the protein sequence. The k correlation factor of each residue in this protein sequence can be represented as:

$$\delta_k = \frac{1}{N-k} \sum_{i=1}^{N-k} \Omega_{i,i+k}, (k < N) \tag{3}$$

The sequence information of the k most adjacent residues are contained in the k th correlation factor, $\Omega_{i,i+k}$ is coupling factor,

$$\Omega_{i,i+k} = \frac{1}{3} \left\{ [S_1(A_{i+k}) - S_1(A_i)]^2 + [S_2(A_{i+k}) - S_2(A_i)]^2 + [T(A_{i+k}) - T(A_i)]^2 \right\} \tag{4}$$

Here $S_1(A_i)$, $S_2(A_i)$ and $T(A_i)$ is the value of normalized hydrophobicity, hydrophilicity and the side chain mass for amino acid residue A_i respectively. While $S_1(A_{i+k})$, $S_2(A_{i+k})$ and $T(A_{i+k})$ are those values for amino acid residue A_{i+k}.

If the k correlation factor is calculated, each dimension of the protein feature vector can be represented as:

$$p_u = \begin{cases} \dfrac{f_u}{\sum\limits_{i=1}^{20} f_i + \omega \sum\limits_{k=1}^{\eta} \delta_k} & (1 \le u \le 20) \\[3ex] \dfrac{\omega \delta_{u-20}}{\sum\limits_{i=1}^{20} f_i + \omega \sum\limits_{k=1}^{\eta} \delta_k} & (20+1 \le u \le 20+\eta) \end{cases} \tag{5}$$

ω is weight factor, generally defined as 0.05, f_i is the occurrence frequency of the residues in this protein sequence. The value of η should neither too small nor too big. In this paper, we set it to be 20.

3.2   Physicochemical Properties Model

In this model, all the protein amino acid residues are divided into three groups including neutral, hydrophobic and polar according to their seven physicochemical properties. The seven physicochemical properties are hydrophobicity, normalized vander Waals volume, polarity, polarizibility, charge, secondary structures and solvent accessibility.

According to the seven properties of amino acids residues, compute occurrence frequency of the residues manifested as polar, neutral and hydrophobic in a protein sequence. The calculation formula is:

$$f_{i,polar} = \frac{n_{polar}}{N} \tag{6}$$

$$f_{i,neutral} = \frac{n_{neutral}}{N} \tag{7}$$

$$f_{i,hydrophobic} = \frac{n_{hydrophobic}}{N} \tag{8}$$

$i = 1,2 \cdots 7$. $f_{i,polar}$ represents the frequency of amino acid which are characterized by polar, the other two represents the frequency of neutral and hydrophobic amino acid, N is the length of the protein sequence. So in this feature extraction model, we get a 21 dimension feature vector. Each protein sequence will be represented by a 21 dimension feature vector. The distribution situation of amino acids properties are showed in table 1.

Table 1. The distribution situation of amino acids properties

Property	polar	neutral	hydrophobic
hydrophobicity	RKEDQN	GASTPHY	CLVIMFW
normalized vander Waals	GASCTPD	NVEQIL	MHKFRYW
polarity	LIFWCMVY	PATGS	HQRKNED
polarizibility	GASDT	CPNVEQIL	KMHFRYW
charge	KR	ANCQGHILMF PSTWYN	DE
secondary structures	EALMQKRH	VIYCWFT	GNPSD
solvent accessibility	ALFCGINW	RKQEND	MPSTHY

The 20 capitals denote the 20 amino acids respectively, the left column shows the seven properties of the amino acids, and the line represents the distribution situation of the 20 amino acids under a property.

3.3   Amino Acid Index Distribution

In this kind of model, the feature vector of the protein sequence can be represented by the following formula:

$$F_{AAID} = [x_1, x_2, \cdots x_{20}; y_1, y_2, \cdots y_{20}; z_1, z_2, \cdots z_{20}] \tag{9}$$

Firstly, we introduce the first 20 dimension vectors. It is the combination of statistical information and physicochemical values which can be represented by the following formula:

$$x_i = J_i f_i \quad i = 1, 2, \cdots 20 \tag{10}$$

J_i is the physicochemical values of the 20 amino acids, the physicochemical values of the 20 amino acids are as follows: JA=0.486, JC=0.2, JD=0.288, JE=0.538, JF=0.318, JG=0.12, JH=0.4, JI=0.37, JK=0.402, JL=0.42, JM=0.417, JN=0.193, JP=0.208, JQ=0.418, JK=0.262, JS=0.2, JT=0.272, JV=0.379, JW=0.462, JY=0.161, f_i is the frequency of the 20 amino acids in the corresponding protein sequence. J_i and f_i are independent to each other.

Secondly, the following 20 dimension feature vectors is 2-order center distance information, it does not only includes the statistical information and physicochemical values, but also contains position information. The formula is as follows:

$$y_i = \sum_{j=1}^{N_{n_i}} \left(\frac{p_{i,j} - \bar{p}_i}{T} J_i \right)^2 \quad i = 1, 2, \cdots 20 \tag{11}$$

Where $p_{i,j}$ is the position number of i th amino acid. $\bar{p}_i$ is the mean position number of i th amino acid. T is the total number of protein sequence.

Last, if the 2-order center distance information cannot cover sufficient location information, we can extract 3-order center distance information. The formula is as follows:

$$z_i = \sum_{j=1}^{N_{n_i}} \left(\frac{p_{i,j} - \bar{p}_i}{T} J_i \right)^3 \quad i = 1, 2, \cdots 20 \tag{12}$$

The 3-order center distance information is almost the same as 2-order center distance excetp the order number, we can get much more and different protein information through change the order number. We may get unsatisfied results with the increasing order for it may contain much redundant information. In this paper, we used the first 40 dimension vectors.

4   Multi-label k Nearest Neighbor

Design an effective algorithm is an important step in the process of protein subcellular localization. Most algorithms existed can only deal with proteins with one subcellular location, such as nearest neighbor, neural network and so on. Seldom algorithms can be used to handle protein multi-site localization problem. Zhou and Zhang developed the multi-label k nearest neighbor [7-8] on the basis of traditional k nearest neighbor algorithm, which can deal with multi-label learning [9] problems.

There are also some other multi-label algorithms, such as OVR-kNN and BP-MLL [10]. The OVR-k NN algorithm is also transformed from the traditional k nearest neighbor algorithm, it needs to statistic the proportion of all the labels after the k nearest neighbor are determined, then the labels whose proportion is bigger than half the threshold will be the label of the test sample. It is derived from the popular back-propagation algorithm and it introduced a novel error function to capture the characteristics of multi-label learning. But using this method exist the long prediction time problem.

For a test sample, we can find out the k nearest neighbor easily, then according to the statistical information of the train sample labels, conditional probability and Bias decision theory to predict the labels of the test sample. For detail, firstly, compute the prior probability of all the labels no matter it is train or test sample,

$$G(L_1^l) = \frac{(s + \sum_{j=1}^{n} \delta_{X_j}(l))}{s \times 2 + n} \tag{13}$$

$$G(L_0^l) = 1 - G(L_1^l) \tag{14}$$

L_1^l represents that the sample have label l , correspondingly, L_0^l represents that the sample do not have label l, $\delta_{X_j}(l)$ is the membership of label l, s is smoothing exponential.

Secondly, compute the posterior probability.

$$G(E_j^l \mid L_1^l) = \frac{s + e[j]}{s \times (k+1) + \sum_{i=0}^{k} e[i]} \tag{15}$$

$$G(E_j^l \mid L_0^l) = \frac{s + e'[j]}{s \times (k+1) + \sum_{i=0}^{k} e'[i]} \tag{16}$$

E_j^l represents that there are exactly j samples have label l among the k nearest neighbor, $e[j]$ counts the number of those there are exactly j samples have label l among the k nearest neighbor in all training sets. $e'[j]$ counts the number of those there are exactly j samples without label l among the k nearest neighbor in all training sets.

Last, compute the label vector and label membership vector of the test sample.

$$v(l) = \arg \max_{c \in \{0,1\}} G(L_c^l)G(E_{C_T(l)}^l \mid L_c^l) \tag{17}$$

$$\lambda(l) = \frac{G(L_1^l)G(E_{C_T(l)}^l \mid L_1^l)}{\sum_{c \in \{0,1\}} G(L_c^l)G(E_{C_T(l)}^l \mid L_c^l)} \tag{18}$$

$C_T(l)$ is the number of samples which have label l among the k nearest neighbor.

5   Results and Conclusions

In multi-label learning system, the popular evaluation metrics used in single–label system are unsuitable, it is much more complicated. Evaluation metrics for multi-label learning include the following five items.

Hamming Loss:

$$HLoss(h) = \frac{1}{n_t} \sum_{i=1}^{n_t} \frac{1}{m} \mid h(x_i)\Delta L_i \mid \tag{19}$$

Where n_t is the number of test sample, $h(x_i)$ and L_i represent predicted label and actual label, respectively, Δ is symmetric difference between two sets. It is used to evaluate the degree of inconsistency between the predicted label and actual label.

One-error:

$$One - Error(f) = \frac{1}{n_t} \sum_{i=1}^{n_t} E(x_i) \tag{20}$$

The value of $E(x_i)$ is 1 if the top-ranked label is in the set of proper labels, otherwise it is 0. It is used to evaluate the probability of top-ranked label of sample is not in the proper label set.

Coverage:

$$Coverage(f) = \frac{1}{n_t} \sum_{i=1}^{n_t} \max_{l \in L_i} rankf(x_i, l) - 1 \tag{21}$$

It is used to evaluate how many labels we need, on the average, to go down the list of labels in order to cover all the proper labels of the test sample.

Ranking Loss:

$$RLoss(f) = \frac{1}{n_t} \sum_{i=1}^{n_t} \frac{1}{\mid L_i \parallel \bar{L}_i \mid} \left\{ (l_1, l_2) \mid f(x_i, l_1) \leq f(x_i, l_2), (l_1, l_2 \in L_i \times \bar{L}_i) \right\} \tag{22}$$

$\bar{L_i}$ is the complementary set of L_i. It is used to evaluate average fraction of label pair that are reversely ordered for the samples.

Average Precision:

$$APre(f) = \frac{1}{n_t} \sum_{i=1}^{n_t} \frac{1}{|L_i|} \sum_{l \in L_i} \frac{|l'| rankf(x_i,l') \le rankf(x_i,l), l' \in L_i|}{rankf(x_i,l)} \quad (23)$$

It is used to evaluate the average prediction accuracy of sample label.

For the first four evaluates metrics, smaller value indicates better performance, for the last one, on the contrary, bigger value indicates better performance.

In multi-label learning statistical prediction, there are three cross-validation methods which are often used to evaluate the performance and effectiveness of the classifiers, they are independent dataset test, sub-sampling test and jackknife test. Jackknife test is considered to be the most objective and rigorous test method, so in this paper, we used the Jack knife test method which can reflect higher efficiency of the predict algorithm,

Protein precursors include special sorting signals [11] which is called N-terminal signal and can instruct the protein enter into special subcellular locations, so it contains large amount of protein information, but it is not very closely linked to the rest amino acids, so we divide the protein sequence into two parts (the N-terminal signal and the rest amino acid sequence) to extract much more protein information. In this paper, we use the following four feature extraction models to extract the protein features simultaneously: N-terminal signals, PseAAC [12], physicochemical property and amino acid index distribution, then use the multi-label k nearest neighbor algorithm to predict the subcellular locations of virus and Gram-positive bacteria proteins. For we have extracted relative enough feature information, so we got satisfied results by Jack knife test. We can get a label set from the test process each time, if the predicted label set is the same as the original label set totally, it is regarded as correct, or it is not correct even if there is only one label is wrong. The experimental results on the two datasets are showed in the following two tables, k varies from one to five. The best results on each metrics are shown in bold face.

Table 2. Comparision results of ML-KNN with different number of nearest neighbors considered for s1 dataset

k	\multicolumn{5}{c}{Evaluation criterion}
	Hamming Loss	One-error	Coverage	Ranking Loss	Average Precision
1	0.164	0.329	0.518	0.169	0.809
2	0.173	0.275	*0.398*	*0.129*	*0.845*
3	*0.144*	0.285	0.415	0.135	0.839
4	0.152	*0.273*	0.413	0.134	0.844
5	0.152	0.287	0.422	0.137	0.838

Table 3. Comparision results of ML-KNN with different number of nearest neighbors considered for s2 dataset

k	Evaluation criterion				
	Hamming Loss	One-error	Coverage	Ranking Loss	Average Precision
1	*0.123*	*0.377*	*1.048*	*0.133*	*0.775*
2	0.167	0.409	1.143	0.152	0.756
3	0.179	0.413	1.167	0.153	0.748
4	0.179	0.401	1.218	0.165	0.748
5	0.179	*0.377*	1.214	0.159	0.753

It can be seen from the table 2 that the best performance is when the number of nearest neighbor is 2 for s1 dataset, the best overall accuracy rate we have achieved is 66.1568%. It combined the following three feature extraction models: N-terminal signals, PseAAC, physicochemical property, if the four models are used to extract features simultaneously, the overall accuracy rate is only 63.2887%, From table 3 we can see that we can get the best results when the number of nearest neighbor is 1 for s2 dataset, the four models are combined simultaneously and the best overall accuracy rate 59.9206%. For dataset s1, the 4 protein sequences which have 2 subcellular locations are predicted accurately, 338 protein sequences of the 515 protein sequences which localized to only one subcellular location are predicted accurately. For the dataset s2, all the protein sequences which have two or more subcellular locations(the 39 protein sequences localized to two subcellular locations and the 3 protein sequences localized to 3 subcellular locations), we have predicted all their subcellular locations accurately, for the 165 proteins which have only one subcellular location, 65 of them are predicted accurately.

Table 4. Comparision results of different feature extraction method

dataset	Feature extraction method		
	N+PseAAC	N+PseAAC+PC	N+PseAAC+PC+AAID
S1	55.0669%	*66.1568%*	63.2887%
S2	55.9524%	58.7302%	*59.9206%*

As we can see from the table 4, only rely on single feature extraction model to extract features is far from enough, remarkable performance may be achieved if several models are combined, but if inappropriate model is included in, the result may be opposite for large amount of redundant information have affected and disturbed the computation to some extent. So it is important to choose the appropriate feature extract methods for different datasets.

Although the feature extraction methods and algorithm used in this paper have got satisfied performance, seeking much more efficient and accurate methods are still a difficult and meaningful task which need much more efforts.

Acknowledgment. This research was partially supported by the Natural Science Foundation of China (61070130), the Key Project of Natural Science Foundation of Shandong Province (ZR2011FZ001), the Key Subject Research Foundation of Shandong Province and the Shandong Provincial Key Laboratory of Network Based Intelligent Computing, the Youth Project of National Natural Science Fund (61302128). The Natural Science Foundation of Shandong Province (ZR2011FL022) and was also supported by the National Natural Science Foundation of China (Grant No. 61201428).

References

1. Du, P.F., Xu, C.: Predicting Multisite Protein Subcellualr Locations: Progress and Challenges. Expert Rev. Proteomics 10(3), 227–237 (2013)
2. Shen, H.B., Chou, K.C.: Virus-Mploc: A Fusion Classifier for Viral Protein Subcellular Location Prediction by Incorporating Multiple Sites. J. Biomol. Struct. Dyn. 28, 175–186 (2010)
3. Emanuelsson, O., Nielsen, H., Brunak, S.: Predicting Subcellular Localization of Proteins Based on Their N-Terminal Amino Acid Sequence. Mol. Biol. 300, 1005–1016 (2000)
4. http://Www.Csbio.Sjtu.Edu.Cn/Bioinf/Gpos-Multi/Data.Htm
5. http://Www.Csbio.Sjtu.Edu.Cn/Bioinf/Virus-Multi/Data.Htm
6. Chou, K.C., Shen, H.B.: A New Method for Predicting the Subcellular Localization of Eukaryotic Proteins with Both Single and Multiple Sites: Euk-Mploc 2.0. Plos ONE 5, E9931 (2010)
7. Zhang, M.L., Zhou, Z.H.: ML_KNN: A Lazy Learning Approach to Multi-Label Learning. Pattern Recognition 40(7), 2038–2048 (2007)
8. Zhang, S., Zhang, H.X.: Modified KNN Algorithm for Multi-Label Learning. Application Research of Computers 28(12), 4445–4446 (2011)
9. Duan, Z., Cheng, J.X., Zhang, L.: Research on Multi-Label Learning Method Based on Covering. Computer Engineering and Applications 46(14), 20–23 (2010)
10. Zhang, M.L.: Multilabel Neural Networks with Applications to Functional Genomics and Text Categorization. IEEE Trans. Knowl. Data Eng. 18, 1338–1351 (2006)
11. Nakai, K.: Protein Sorting Signals and Prediction of Subcellular Localization. Adv. Protein Chem. 54, 277–344 (2000)
12. Gao, Q.B., Jin, Z.C., Ye, X.F., Wu, C., He, J.: Prediction of Nuclear Receptors with Optimal Pseudo Amino Acid Composition. Anal. Biochem. 387, 54–59 (2009)

Global Voting Model for Protein Function Prediction from Protein-Protein Interaction Networks

Yi Fang[1], Mengtian Sun[2], Guoxian Dai[1], and Karthik Ramani[2]

[1] Electrical Engineering, New York University Abu Dhabi, UAE
{yfang,guoxian.dai}@nyu.edu
[2] Mechanical Engineering, Purdue University, USA
{sun84,ramani}@purdue.edu

Abstract. It is known that the observed PPI network is incomplete with low coverage and high rate of false positives and false negatives. Computational approach is likely to be overwhelmed by the high level of noises and incompleteness if relying on local topological information. We propose a global voting (GV) model to predict protein function by exploiting the entire topology of the network. GV consistently assigns function to unannotated proteins through a global voting procedure in which all of the annotated proteins participate. It assigns a list of function candidates to a target protein with each attached a probability score. The probability indicates the confidence level of the potential function assignment. We apply GV model to a yeast PPI network and test the robustness of the model against noise by random insertion and deletion of true PPIs. The results demonstrate that GV model can robustly infer the function of the proteins.

Keywords: Diffusion Geometry, PPI Network, protein function prediction.

1 Introduction

The advancement in high-throughput technologies has resulted in a rapidly growing amount of data in many genome research fields [16], [21], [12], [30], [9], [29], [15]. Then, inference of protein functions is one of the most important aims in modern biology [26]. However, in spite of the advancement in protein function characterizing techniques, even for the most-studied model species, such as yeast, there is a proportion of about 10% to 75% uncharacterized proteins [26], [27]. We are therefore facing an increasing demand of approaches for functional annotation for ever-growing amount of proteins. The vivo methods are usually labor-intensive and associated with high rate of false measurement of protein functions [2], [11]. In addition, it is somehow impractical to experimentally identify the functions for all individual proteins within one cell [2]. Therefore, the development of more sophisticated silico models assisting the interpretation of the wealth of observed data has been receiving more and more attention to meet this demanding challenge in recent years [2], [27], [28].

The traditional approaches in computational functional annotation first characterize each protein by a set of features, for example, the sequence and structure, and use machine learning algorithms to predict annotation based on those features [1], [23]. Recent developments in large-scale experiments have led to the new representation for protein

D.-S. Huang et al. (Eds.): ICIC 2014, LNBI 8590, pp. 466–477, 2014.
© Springer International Publishing Switzerland 2014

relationship, protein-protein interaction (PPI) network, with nodes representing proteins and edges representing the identified interactions [16], [21], [12], [30], [9], [29], [15], [27]. Many approaches have been proposed to computationally predict the protein functions based on the PPI network [26], [25], [16], [28]. Those approaches basically aim at predicting the function of unannotated proteins from functional annotated ones in the network by which the connections among all proteins are described. We can break the approaches into two broad categories: direct methods and module-assisted methods as reviewed in [26]. For the direct methods, the basic assumption behind is that the closer the two proteins in the network the more likely they have similar function. The majority rule (MR) algorithm proposed in [25], also known as neighborhood counting, predicts the function of a protein from the known functions of its neighbors in the network. MR assigns a protein the function which is most common to its neighbors. There are variants of MR algorithm proposed in [3], [10]. Apparently the simplicity and effectiveness give MR a distinct advantage over other approaches. However, its performance can be easily affected by the false measurement in the network due to its dependency on local neighborhood [26]. In [20], [13], [31]; the cut-based and flow-based algorithms exploit the entire topology of the network and provide a more robust strategy to predict protein function. Vazquez [31] predicts the function of a protein by maximizing the number of edges that link proteins assigned with the same function. This type of methods can predict the function of protein with a relatively higher precision but normally have computational difficulty for solving the optimization problem. The probabilistic approaches based on Markov random field (MRF) are other kind of methods for protein annotation [14], [5], [6]. The pioneering MRF based method and its variants have shown good performance in the prediction of protein function in the network. For the module-assisted methods, also known as indirect method, the basic assumption is that the coherent subset of proteins in the network is a functional module in which unannotated components can be characterized by functional known ones. As our approach is not in this category, we refer interested readers to [26] for a review of the module-assisted methods.

Here, we develop a global voting model for the protein function prediction solely based on the topology of PPI network. Along with the development of GV model, we introduce six new concepts for protein: protein function vector, protein function matrix, protein voting vector, protein voting matrix, predicted function vector and predicted function matrix. The GV model elegantly finishes the procedure of the function prediction for all unannotated proteins by a simple matrix product of protein function matrix and protein voting matrix. The predicted function vector assigns each unannotated protein a list of potential functions with each attached a probability score. To exploit the entire topology of the network, we integrate the heat diffusion weighting scheme into global voting model to enhance its understanding of the PPI network. Fig. 1 illustrates the basic idea of proposed global voting model for the application of protein function prediction. Fig. 1(A) demonstrates a toy PPI network consisting of 7 proteins and 9 PPI in the network. The line between two proteins indicates there is a PPI between them. Fig. 1(B) demonstrates the mechanism of the function prediction by global voting model. To predict the function for protein Pi, all of annotated proteins in the network vote based their weight with Pi, for example, Wij denotes the weight between protein Pi and Pj. Global voting model would basically assign the function to unannotated protein based on weighting the functions of all annotated proteins in the network. This voting strategy is efficient since it predicts function for all unannotated proteins at once.

2   Methods

2.1   Global Voting Model

To present global voting model for the prediction of the proteins in the network, we introduce a set of the new definitions to understand the voting process. We define three vectors, namely protein function vector, protein voting vector and predicted function vector, and three matrices, namely protein function matrix, protein voting matrix and predicted function matrix. In Fig. 2, we can see the three matrices with columns in each matrix representing the corresponding vectors.

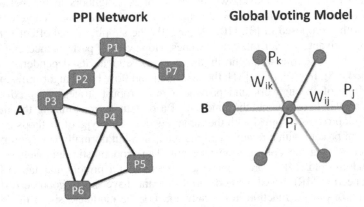

Fig. 1. Global voting model for function prediction of PPI network

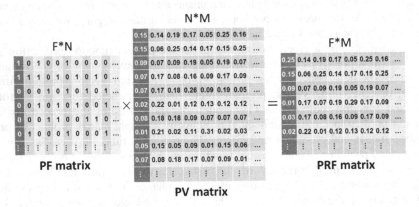

Fig. 2. Global voting procedure

Protein Function Vector and Matrix. We define protein function (PF) vector for representing the function of a protein. The PF vector for a protein is defined as a high-dimensional vector with the dimensionality equal to the total number of the functional categories. For example, 424 functional categories, determined by the finest grain classification scheme in MIPS, will give a 424 dimensional PF vector for each protein in the network. The component of a PF vector is either '1' or '0'. The '1' denotes that the protein has the corresponding function and '0' denotes the protein does not have the corresponding function. The PF vector is a compact form in representing all possible functions for one protein. We define the protein function (PF) matrix for representing the function of all annotated proteins. The PF matrix is formed by placing the PF vector of each annotated protein at the column of the matrix. Therefore, the PF matrix is a F by N matrix, where F denotes the dimensionality of the PF vector and N denotes the number of the annotated proteins in the network. The left matrix in Fig. 2 illustrates the PF vector and PF matrix, and how they are related to each other. In addition, as the PF vector and PF matrix are normally sparse with few ones and lots of zeros, they can be easily stored as a sparse vector / matrix for computational efficiency.

Protein Voting Vector and Matrix. We define protein voting (PV) vector for representing the similarities between one specific unannotated protein and all annotated ones in the network. The PV vector for a protein is defined as a high-dimensional vector with the dimensionality equal to total number of the annotated proteins in the network. The component of a PV vector is a floating value measuring the similarity between the unannotated protein and one annotated protein in the network. We define the protein voting (PV) matrix for representing the similarities between all unannotated proteins and all annotated ones in the network. The PV matrix is formed by placing the PV vector of each unannotated protein at the column of the matrix. Therefore, the PV matrix is a N by M matrix, where N denotes the number of the annotated proteins and M denotes the number of unannotated proteins in the network. The middle matrix in Fig. 2 illustrates the PV vector and PV matrix, and how they are related to each other.

Predicted Function Vector and Matrix. We define predicted function (PRF) vector for representing the probability of the potential function assignments to an unannotated protein. The PRF vector for a protein is defined as a high-dimensional vector with the dimensionality equal to the total number of functional categories. The PRF vector is normalized to have a length of one. The component of a PRF vector is a floating value measuring the probability to assign a specific function to the unannotated protein. The higher the value is, the more likely the protein has the corresponding function. For example, if the second component in PRF vector has the largest value among all components, the function defined by the second functional category is of the highest probability to be assigned to the protein. We define the predicted function (PRF) matrix for the probabilities of the potential function assignments to all unannotated proteins in the network. The PRF matrix is formed by placing the PRF vector of each unannotated protein at the corresponding column of the matrix. Therefore, the PRF matrix is a F by M matrix, where F denotes the number of the dimensionality of the PF vector and M denotes the number of unannotated proteins in the network. The right matrix in Fig. 2 illustrates the PF vector and PF matrix, and how they are related to each other.

Based on the definition of the vectors and matrices above, the global voting model elegantly predicts all unannotated proteins at once in the network by matrix product, the product of PF matrix and PV matrix. The produced PRF vector in PRF matrix records the probabilities of all potential functions for each unannotated protein. The PV matrix is critical for the prediction of functions of unannotated proteins in network as it basically transfers the similarity among proteins in the network to functional similarity among proteins. A good PV matrix should reflect the intrinsic similarity among proteins insensitive to false positive and false negative PPIs in the network. The use of diffusion based concepts demonstrates good performance in bioinformatics applications [17], [18]. We therefore use the heat diffusion based weighting strategy to form the PV matrix. We present the details of how heat diffusion based PV matrix can be formed below.

2.2   Diffusion Based PV Vector and Matrix

Heat kernel measures the amount of the heat that passes from node i to any other node j within a certain period of time. The amount of heat transferred between a pair of nodes can thus be used to represent the affinity of two nodes and thus serve as the corresponding entry in PV matrix.

Heat Kernel. The *PPI* network is denoted as a graph $G=(V, E)$, where V is the set of notes, E is a set of edges. We define the adjacency matrix A below.

$$A(i, j) = \begin{cases} 1 & if \ i \neq j \\ 0 & if \ i = j \end{cases} \tag{1}$$

Where $A_{i,j}$ represents the connectivity between node i and node j and 1 indicates an interaction exists between a pair of nodes. The heat kernel can be expressed as the eigenfunction expansion by graph Laplacian described below.

$$H_t = \exp(-t\hat{L}) \tag{2}$$

Where H_t is the heat kernel and $\hat{L}$ is the normalized graph Laplacian. By Spectral Theorem, the heat kernel can be further expressed as follows:

$$H_t(i, j) = \sum_{k=1}^{|V|} e^{-\lambda_k t} \phi_k(i) \phi_k(j) \tag{3}$$

where λ_k is the k_{th} eigenvalue of the Laplacian and ϕ_k is the k_{th} normalized eigenfunction, $H_t(i, j)$ is defined as heat affinity between node i and j in this paper.

PV Vector and Matrix. Heat kernel qualitatively measures the intrinsic relationship between all pairs of nodes in the network since it exploits the topology of the entire network. Our PV vector and matrix, defined based the heat diffusion similarity, reflects the hidden relationships among the nodes in the nodes. Suppose we have a set of proteins with N annotated ones and M unannotated ones. We have a N *M PV matrix while each column of the matrix is a PV vector. The entry (i,j) in PV matrix is given by the heat affinity between ith annotated protein and jth unannotated protein. The higher the value is, the stronger the pair of proteins is connected to each other, the more likely they have similar function. The description of global voting algorithm is explained in Algorithm 1.

Algorithm 1. Global voting for protein function prediction

- Given PPI network with N annotated proteins and M unannotated proteins. The level of functional categories is F
- Define the graph representation G for PPI network
- Compute the graph Laplacian $\hat{L}$ for the PPI network
- Compute the heat kernel H by exponentiating the graph Laplacian and produce the heat affinity matrix
- Define a $F*N$ PF matrix and a $N*M$ PV matrix for the global voting model according to the description in this section.
- Compute the $F*M$ PRF matrix for the protein function prediction for each unannotated protein.
- The PRF vector is normalized to length '1' and each of its components represents the probability of a specific functional assignment to an unannotated protein.
- The predicted functions of an unannotated protein can be assigned according to the descending order of probability in a PRF vector.
- Return the predicted functions

---

3   Results

We evaluate the predictive performance using the area under ROC curve (AUC) [24], [22]. Second, we evaluate the success rates (percentage of predictions that are correct) [31], [20] in the original network for the different fractions of unannotated proteins. Third, we evaluate the success rates in the noisy network at different rates of false positive and false negative PPIs in network. We verify our approach on two PPI networks: DIP-Core (S. cerevisiae) [4] and Yeast network [31]. We call DIP and VAZ, respectively. The functional classification is adopted from the MIPS classification scheme [19] and consists of 17 high level functional categories. The functional classification is obtained from the finest MIPS classification scheme [19] and comprises 424 functional categories.

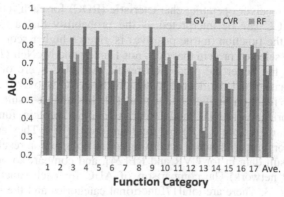

Fig. 3. Prediction performance evaluated by AUC

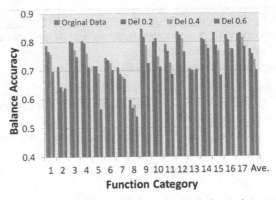

Fig. 4. Prediction performance evaluated by Balance Accuracy

3.1   Cross-Validation and Prediction Performance

We performed cross-validation test on the DIP network to examine the accuracy of our prediction of the protein function. A C-folds cross-validation function-prediction approach randomly divides all annotated proteins with C folds with equal number of members. The validation test starts with assuming that a given subset of annotated proteins is classified as unannotated ones, and then predicts them by remaining annotated proteins. The prediction performance is evaluated by comparison between the original annotations and predicted annotations. The above procedure is performed on every set of proteins and thus is able to evaluate generalized performance of the prediction method. We follow the experimental details of cross-validation in [8] to design our validation. The 10-fold (C=10) cross-validation is used to evaluate and compare our method to existing methods in this test. Two tests are carried out to assess the function prediction result for each functional category: assessment by area under ROC and assessment by balance accuracy. Both assessments are based on the four performance indexes [8], whose definitions are as follows: True Positive (TP), True Negative (TN), False Positive (FP), False Negative (FN).

Assessment by area under ROC. We first assess the performance by the area under curve (AUC) of receiver operating characteristic (ROC) for each functional category. The value of AUC can be interpreted as the probability that a randomly selected protein that has the function (a true positive) is given a higher score by the predictor than a randomly selected protein that does not Hanley and McNeil (1982). The higher the AUC value, the better the prediction result. An AUC score of 0.50 indicates a prediction by chance and the degree to which the AUC is over 0.50 indicates how much better our function prediction are than [3]. In our test result, we compare the prediction performance of GV model with two other protein function predictors: classification via regression (CVR) and random forests (RF). They are reported as the best two predictors in performance according to the comparison result in [24]. We use experimental result data in for CVR and RF[24], and compare to our method on the same data (DIP network).The comparison of AUC for each functional category is shown in the Fig. 3. There are total17functional categories and the last three bars are the average AUC for all functional categories of each method used in comparison. As we can see from the Fig. 3, the AUC scores for our method are consistently higher than the other two methods (CVR and RF) in all functional categories, with most of scores over 0.80. It indicates that GV is a better predictor for protein function prediction in all possible functional categories.

Assessment by Area under ROC. We then assess the performance by balance accuracy (BA) for each functional category, which is defined as the square root of the product of sensitivity, (TP/(TP+FN)) and specificity, TN/(TN+FP). As in the case of real protein data, links (true positive PPIs) are often missing due to various reasons, it is a desirable quality for the predictors to be robust against incompleteness. In order to demonstrate this robustness of GV method, we test GV method on the DIP network at four different levels of the removal of true PPIs original network. The assessment results are shown in Fig. 4. 'Del' denotes the ratio of the number of the removed PPIs to the number of the total PPIs in original network, which are 0.2, 0.4, 0.6, 0.8, respectively. In the Fig. 4, BA values are displayed for all 17 functional categories with bars. The last three column bars indicate the average value of BA for all functional categories under certain level of deletions of PPI. As we can see from the Fig. 4, for each individual functional category, most BA scores are above 0.70. As for the average value, average BA is 0.77 for the original data, and is 0.69 even for the data with 60% removal ratio. The test result indicates that GV is a good predictor for each possible individual functional category. In addition, it is encouraging that the BA remains to be a good predictor as the removal ratio increases. It indicates that GV model is able to address the problem of incompleteness of PPI network.

Table 1. Success rates in DIP network test

	GV			MR		
K\FOU	0.2	0.4	0.6	0.2	0.4	0.6
2	0.8718	0.8239	0.7692	0.7059	0.7273	0.5812
3	0.9167	0.8611	0.8699	0.7955	0.7870	0.7671
4	0.8974	0.9091	0.8829	0.8125	0.7424	0.7477
5	0.9091	0.9524	0.9242	0.8571	0.8810	0.8333
6	0.9565	0.9412	0.8889	0.9000	0.9412	0.7460
≥7	0.9180	0.9214	0.9345	0.9146	0.9214	0.8996
SR	0.9046	0.8816	0.8670	0.8233	0.8127	0.7527

Table 2. Success rates in VAZ network test

	GV			MR			GO
K\FOU	0.2	0.4	0.6	0.2	0.4	0.6	0.4
2	0.5745	0.5979	0.5455	0.4286	0.3918	0.3542	0.4600
3	0.6061	0.6984	0.6500	0.5313	0.5873	0.4343	0.6500
4	0.7059	0.6111	0.6441	0.6818	0.6111	0.5789	0.6200
5	0.7273	0.7333	0.7045	0.7222	0.5667	0.6667	0.6600
6	0.8000	0.7692	0.7333	0.6667	0.6154	0.6154	0.7400
≥7	1.0000	0.8537	0.8833	0.7826	0.7317	0.6812	0.7227
SR	0.6929	0.6821	0.6556	0.5929	0.5429	0.4941	0.5887

3.2   Function Prediction in Clean PPI Network

In this experiment, success rates test is carried out on DIP and VAZ data for our method and other methods (MR mainly) in comparison. Success rates are defined as percentage of predictions that are correct [31], [20]. We first randomly choose a percentage of annotated proteins and classify them as unannotated ones. The remaining annotated proteins are used to predict the function for them. There are several criteria to judge whether a protein is correctly assigned function [8]. In this work, the function protein is correctly predicted if more than half of the functions are correctly predicted.

We first test GV method on DIP network and compare to MR. The comparison result is shown in Table 1. In the table, 'FOU' denotes the ratio of unannotated protein number to total original protein number while K represents the group of protein with K degree of connectivity in the PPI network. We test two methods at three different 'FOU' levels (0.20, 0.40, 0.60). In addition, we show success rate (SR) for the proteins at different levels of degree (the number of direct interacted proteins, denoted as K). The case $K=1$ is not considered because the MR method finds only a trivial implementation in this case. It is clearly to find out the GV method outperforms the MR method with a higher success rates at different test conditions. For detailed comparison, the experimental result is analyzed in the following two perspectives: 1) the success rates at different K, 2) the success rates at different level of 'FOU'. We are interested in the prediction performance at different degree of K, particularly smaller K. Based on the result on the table, the performance of GV and MR is comparable at a higher level K, for example, larger than6. It is reasonable because the directly linked neighbors are able to provide enough information for function prediction when the degree K for an unannotated protein is large enough. However, the success rates for MR drops quickly when K goes down to a lower level, for example, less than 3. The success rates for GV remains reasonably stable when the degree K for an unannotated protein goes down to a lower level (even 2). The performance comparison of two methods at lower K is obvious and can be explained as follows. Because the MR is heavily dependent on the local topological connection and blind to the global view of the structure of network, therefore, when K is at a small scale, MR loses the basis of prediction. However, GV predicts the protein function in a globally consistent manner, therefore is less affected by the degree of a protein. The comparison result highlights the global property of our GV methods. We are also interested in the prediction performance at different levels of 'FOU'. We can see from the table, the GV method consistently performs better than MR method at all levels of the 'FOU'. We are particularly interested in the predictive performance at a higher level of 'FOU'. Our GV method is able to correctly predict about 87%functions even when 'FOU' is at 0.60, while MR gives about 75% success rates. This advantage of GV model is contributed by the global voting based on considering all of possible annotated proteins in the network.

We then test GV method on a more challenging network (VAZ) and compare to method of MR and GO. The comparison result is shown in table 2. The 'FOU' and Kin the table have the same notation as the table 1. We test two methods at three different 'FOU' levels (0.20, 0.40, 0.60). In addition, we show success rate (SR) for the proteins at different levels of degree (the number of direct interacted proteins, denoted as K). We are expecting the success rates are worse than that of DIP network, because the functional categories used in this test are the finest one (424). Other than the experimental setting used in the Table 1, we compare GV method to GO (global optimization) method [31] at 'FOU' of 0.40. For GO method, we used the success rates reported in [31] at 'FOU' of 0.40. Although the success rates for all of three methods are relatively lower, GV method is still consistently higher than other two methods.

4   Discussion and Conclusion

The advancement in high-throughput technologies for identification of PPIs has prompted the need for the computational annotation of protein functions in various organisms to reduce the costly and labor-intensive web-lab experiments. It is a challenging problem of computational prediction as the experimental data are inherently associated with high rates of false positive and false negative and somewhat incomplete observation for the entire PPI network. Those properties of PPI network data stirs up many concerns incomprehensive analysis in understanding the PPI network [7], [32]. We propose global voting model for systematic functional annotation using PPI network.

References

1. Altschul, S.F., Madden, T.L., Schaffer, A.A., Zhang, J., Zhang, Z., Miller, W., Lipman, D.J.: Gapped blast and psi-blast: a new generation of protein data base search programs. Nucl. Acids Res. 25, 3389–3402 (1997)
2. Chen, X., Liu, M.: Prediction of protein-protein interactions using random decision forest framework. Bioinformatics 21, 4394–4400 (2005)
3. Chua, H.N., Sung, W.K., Wong, L.: Exploiting indirect neighbors and topological weight to predict protein function from protein-protein interactions. Bioinformatics 22, 1623–1630 (2006)
4. Deane, C.M., Salwinski, L., Xenarios, O., Eisenberg, D.: Protein interactions: two methods for assessment of the reliability of high through put observations. Molecular & Cellular Proteomics: MCP 1, 349–356 (2002)
5. Deng, M., Zhang, K., Mehta, S., Chen, T., Sun, F.: Prediction of protein function using protein-protein interaction data. Journal of Computational Biology 10, 947–960 (2003)
6. Deng, M., Tu, Z., Sun, F., Chen, T.: Mapping gene ontology to proteins based on protein C protein interaction data. Bioinformatics 20(6), 895–902 (2004)
7. Edwards, A., Kus, B., Jansen, R., Greenbaum, D., Greenblatt, J., et al.: Bridging structural biology and genomics: assessing protein interaction data with known complexes. Trends in Genetics 18, 529–536 (2002)
8. Freschi, V.: Protein function prediction from interaction networks using a random walk ranking algorithm. In: Proceedings of the 7th IEEE International Conference on Bioinformatics and Bioengineering, BIBE 2007, pp. 42–48 (2007)
9. Giot, L., Bader, J., Brouwer, C., Chaudhuri, A., Kuang, B., et al.: A protein interaction map of drosophila melanogaster. Science 302, 1727–1736 (2003)

10. Hishigaki, H., Nakai, K., Ono, T., Tanigami, A., Takagi, T.: Assessment of prediction accuracy of protein function from protein-protein interaction data. Yeast 18, 523–531 (2001)

11. Hu, P., Bader, G., Wigle, D.A., Emili, A.: Computational prediction of cancer-gene function. Nature Reviews Cancer 7, 23–34 (2007)

12. Ito, T., Tashiro, K., Muta, S., Ozawa, R., Chiba, T., et al.: Toward a protein-protein interaction map of the budding yeast: A comprehensive system to examine two-hybrid interactions in all possible combinations between the yeast proteins. Proceedings of the National Academy of Sciences of the United States of America 97, 1143–1147 (2000)

13. Karaoz, U., Murali, T., Letovsky, S., Zheng, Y., Ding, C.: Whole-genome annotation by using evidence integration in functional-linkage networks. Proceedings of the National Academy of Sciences of the United States of America 101, 2888–2893 (2004)

14. Kourmpetis, Y.A.I., van Dijk, A.D.J., Bink, M.C.A.M., van Ham, R.C.H.J., ter Braak, C.J.F.: Bayesian markov random field analysis for protein function prediction based on network data. PLoS One 5 (2010)

15. Krogan, N., Cagney, G., Yu, H., Zhong, G., Guo, X., et al.: Global landscape of protein complexes in the yeast saccharomyces cerevisiae. Nature 440, 637–643 (2006)

16. Kuchaiev, O., Rasajski, M., Higham, D., Przulj, N.: Geometric de-noising of protein-protein interaction networks. Plos Computational Biology 5 (2009)

17. Lafon, S., Keller, Y., Coifman, R.: Data fusion and multi cue data matching by diffusion maps. IEEE Transactions on Pattern Analysis and Machine Intelligence 28, 1784–1797 (2006)

18. Lerman, G., Shakhnovich, B.: Defining functional distance using manifold embeddings of gene ontology annotations. Proceedings of the National Academy of Sciences of the United States of America 104, 11334–11339 (2007)

19. Mewes, H.W., Frishman, D., Guldener, U., Mannhaupt, G., Mayer, K., Mokrejs, M., Morgenstern, B., Munsterkotter, M., Rudd, S., Weil, B.: Mips: a database for genomes and protein sequences. Nucleic Acid Research 30, 31–34 (2002)

20. Nabieva, E., Jim, K., Agarwal, A., Chazelle, B., Singh, M.: Whole proteome prediction of protein function via graph-theoretic analysis of interaction maps. Bioinformatics 21, i302–i310 (2005)

21. Pawson, T., Gish, G., Nash, P.: Sh2 domains, interaction modules and cellular wiring. Trends in Cell Biology 11, 504–511 (2001)

22. Provost, F.J., Fawcett, T.: Analysis and visualization of classier performance: Comparison under imprecise class and cost distributions. In: KDD, pp. 43–48 (1997)

23. Punta, M., Ofran, Y.: The rough guide to insilico function prediction, orhow to use sequence and structure information to predict protein function. PLoS Computational Biology 4 (2008)

24. Rahmani, H., Blockeel, H., Bender, A.: Predicting the functions of proteins in ppi networks from global information. JMLR: Workshop and Conference. In: Proceedings, International Workshop on Machine Learning in Systems Biology, Ljubljana, Slovenia, vol. 8, pp. 82–97 (2010)

25. Schwikowski, B., Uetz, P., Field, S.: A network of protein-protein interactions in yeast. Nature Biotechnology 18, 1257–1261 (2000)

26. Sharan, R., Ulitsky, I., Shamir, R.: Network-based prediction of protein function. Molecular Systems Biology 3, 1–13 (2007)

27. Shoemaker, B.A., Panchenko, A.R.: Deciphering protein c protein interactions. part i. experimental techniques and databases. PLoS Comput. Biol. 3 (2007a)

28. Shoemaker, B.A., Panchenko, A.R.: Deciphering protein c protein interactions. part ii. computational methods to predict protein and domain interaction partners. PLoS Comput. Biol. 3 (2007b)
29. Stelzl, U., Worm, U., Lalowski, M., Haenig, C., Brembeck, F., et al.: A human protein-protein interaction network: A resource for annotating the proteome. Cell 122, 957–968 (2005)
30. Uetz, P., Giot, L., Cagney, G., Mansfield, T., Judson, R., et al.: A comprehensive analysis of protein-protein interactions in saccharomyces cerevisiae. Nature 403, 623–627 (2000)
31. Vazquez, A., Flammini, A., Maritan, A., Vespignani, A.: Global protein function prediction from protein-protein interaction networks. Nature Biotechnology 21, 697–700 (2003)
32. Von Mering, C., Krause, R., Snel, B., Cornell, M., Oliver, S., et al.: Comparative assessment of large-scale data sets of protein-protein interactions. Nature 417, 399–403 (2002)

Comparative Assessment of Data Sets
of Protein Interaction Hot Spots
Used in the Computational Method

Yunqiang Di[1,2], Changchang Wang[1,3], Huan Wu[1,2], Xinxin Yu[1,4], and Junfeng Xia[1]

[1] Institute of Health Sciences, Anhui University, Hefei, Anhui 230601, China
[2] College of Electrical Engineering and Automation, Anhui University,
Hefei, Anhui 230601, China
[3] School of Computer Science and Technology, Anhui University, Hefei, Anhui 230601, China
[4] School of Life Sciences, Anhui University, Hefei, Anhui 230601, China
jfxia@ahu.edu.cn

Abstract. It seems that every biological process involves multiple protein-protein interactions. Small subsets of residues, which are called "hot spots", contribute to most of the protein-protein binding free energy. Considering its important role in the modulation of protein-protein complexes, a large number of computational methods have been proposed in the prediction of hot spots. In this work, we first collect lots of articles from 2007 to 2014 and select nine typical data sets. Then we compare the nine data sets in different aspects. We find that the maximum number of interface residues used in the previous work is 318, which can be selected as the fittest training data set used in predicting hot spots. At last, we compare and assess the features used in different works. Our result suggests that accessibility and residue conservation are critical in predicting hot spots.

Keywords: proteins-protein interaction, hot spots, computational method, training data.

1   Introduction

Protein-protein interactions play an important role in almost all biological processes such as signal transduction, transport, cellular motion, and regulatory mechanisms. Researches of residues at protein-protein interfaces has shown that only a small portion of all interface residues is actually essential for binding [1]. These residues are termed as hot spots which contribute a large fraction of the binding free energy and are crucial for preserving protein functions and maintaining the stability of protein interactions. Recent years, several studies discovered that small molecules which bound to hot spots in protein interfaces can disrupt protein-protein interactions [2]. So, identifying hot spots and revealing their mechanisms can provide promising prospect for medicinal chemistry and drug design [3-4].

Experimental methods have been used to identify hot spot residues at protein-protein interfaces. For example, alanine scanning mutagenesis has been used to

D.-S. Huang et al. (Eds.): ICIC 2014, LNBI 8590, pp. 478–486, 2014.

identify protein-protein interface hot spots [5]. Because of the high cost and low efficiency of experimental method, public databases of experimental results such as the Alanine Scanning Energetic Database (ASEdb) [6] and the Binding Interface Database (BID) [7] contain only a limited number of complexes.

Besides the experimental methods, a large number of computational methods have been proposed in the prediction of hot spots. Tuncbag *et al.* [8] constructed a web server Hotpoint to predict hot spots effectively. Darnell *et al.* [9] also provided a web server KFC to predict hot spots by using decision trees. Cho *et al.* [10] developed two feature-based predictive support vector machine (SVM) models for predicting interaction hot spots with features including weighted atom packing density, relative accessible surface area, weighted hydrophobicity and molecular interaction types. Xia *et al.* [11] introduced both a SVM model and an ensemble classifier to boost hot spots prediction accuracy. Recently, Ye *et al.* [12] used network features and microenvironment features to predict hot spots.

Although these approached have obtained good performance, there are still some problems remaining in this field. Though many features have been used in the previous studies, effective feature subsets have not been found yet. Moreover, most existing approaches use very limited data from experiment-derived databases, therefore the training data is insufficient, which may lead to pool prediction performance. Cheng *et al.* [13] also found that a rational selection of training sets had a better performance than random selection.

To assess their data sets, we compare the methods with each other and with a overlapping set of hot spots.In this paper, we collect 9 data sets about hot spots from 2007 to 2014. Firstly, we compare their training sets and analysis the same subsets they used. Then, we list the features they used and give a heuristic conclusion.

2   Datasets and Methods

(a)   Datasets

We collect 2600 articles with a simple query of protein-protein interactions, hot spots prediction and computational methods on PubMed. Then we obtain 30 articles by cutting off the remaining ones whose topics are not concerning about hot spots. Finally, we select nine typical articles which are used the computational methods to predict hot spots, including APIS [11], KFC2 [14], RF [15], NFMF [12], ELM [16], KFC1 [17], MINERVA [10], DSP [18], and βACVASA [19].

Then we get data sets from the nine articles from the tables in the main text or from their supplements. The training data sets in these studies were all extracted from ASEdb [6] and the published data by Kortemme and Baker [1]. Then filtering methods were used to eliminate data redundancy by querying sequence identity. As a result, only a subset of the interface residues was chosen, and the interface residues with binding free energy ($\Delta\Delta G$) ≥ 2.0 kcal/mol are defined as hot spots [15, 17, 21]. The dataset from BID was used as test sets. BID categorizes the effect of mutations as strong, intermediate, weak or insignificant. The residues having strong interaction strengths are considered as hot spots in this study. Details of the data sets are listed in supplement Table S1-S9.

(b)   Framework

As described in Fig.1. We first collect data from literature which is explained in section 2.1. Then we compare their data in different aspects such as their scale and features. We use Venn Diagrams [22] to analysis these complexes. At last we obtain the overlapping data in the nine works.

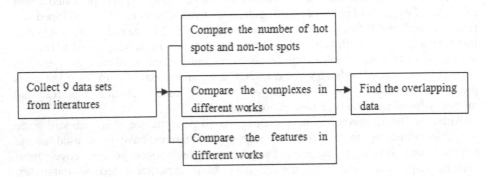

Fig. 1. The framework of our method. Firstly, we collect 9 data sets from literatures. Then we compare the number of hot spots and non-hot spots, the complexes and features respectively. Finally, we obtain the overlapping data.

3   Results and Discussions

(a)   Comparison of the Number of Training and Test Data Sets

Table 1 and 2 shows the number of training and test data sets in different works. From Table 1, we find that the number of training data sets really make a big difference. The KFC2 method has only 132 interface residues while RF, NFMF and ELM have the largest number (318) of interface residues. Then we also find that the number of hot spots and the number of non-hot spots are different in different works except NFMF, RF and ELM (the training data set of them are the same) However, the training data sets used in creating machine learning methods, such as APIS, RF, KFC1, MINERVA, DSP, and βACVASA, contain more non-hot spot residues than hot spot residues. To avoid biased predictions, the training data set of interface residues in KFC2 contains 65 hot spot residues and 67 non-hot spot residues.

From Table 2, we can see that almost all the number of test data sets is the same. Test data sets do not exist in DSP and βACVASA. The number of test data set in RF is the same as that in ELM, which is original from MINERVA. Two residues which are not in protein interfaces have been removed, so there are 125 residues in RF, not the number 127. Xia *et al.* [11] used exactly the same dataset as the one used in Cho *et al.* [10] for the purpose of comparing APIS and MINEVAR. So the number of their test data sets is also 127.

Table 1. The number of training data sets in different works

Dataset	Number of hot spots	Number of non-hot spots	Total number
APIS	62	92	154
KFC2	65	67	132
RF	77	241	318
NFMF	77	241	318
ELM	77	241	318
KFC1	60	189	249
MINERVA	119	146	265
DSP	76	145	221
βACVASA	86	148	234

Table 2. The number of test data sets in different works

Dataset	Number of hot spots	Number of non-hot spots	Total number
APIS	39	88	127
KFC2	39	87	126
RF	38	87	125
NFMF	38	86	124
ELM	38	87	125
KFC1	50	62	112
MINERVA	39	88	127
DSP	NA	NA	NA
βACVASA	NA	NA	NA

NA: Not Available

(b)   Comparison of the Protein Complexes Used in the Previous Works

We list the complexes in each work. Considering the training data sets of NFMF, RF and ELM are same, so we just list the other 7 data sets in Table 3. The overlapping complexes are underlined. Then we use Venn Diagrams [22] to distinguish each other. Because the works in DSP and βACVASA do not contain test data sets, we don't use these data sets. We first divide the rest 5 data sets into 2 groups. The one group is combining the data from APIS, KFC2 and ELM, the other is combining those from the remaining two methods KFC1 and MINERVA. From Fig.2, we can see that the dataset in ELM has the widest range of complexes among the three works (APS, KFC2, and ELM). So we choose the dataset from ELM as an additional set to join into the other group and use Venn Digrams to obtain the overlapping data. Apparently, from Fig.3, we also find that the complexes used in ELM contain the widest range of the whole. To further study, we list all the training data in supplement Table S 1-7 and the same data in supplement Table S8. We find that the data set of ELM contains the maximum amount of complexes and almost cover every data set of the rest.

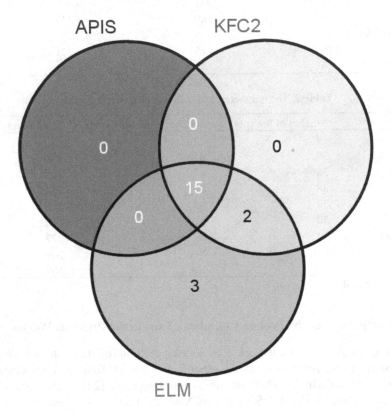

Fig. 2. The number of complexes in APIS, ELM and KFC2.The 3 complexes only exist in ELM are 1dn2, 1jck and 1jtg. 1f47 and 1nmb only exist in ELM and KFC2. The 15 complexes which all works contain are 1a22, 1a4y, 1ahw, 1brs, 1bxi, 1cbw, 1dan, 1dvf, 1fc2, 1fcc, 1gc1, 1jrh, 1vfb, 2ptc, and 3hfm.

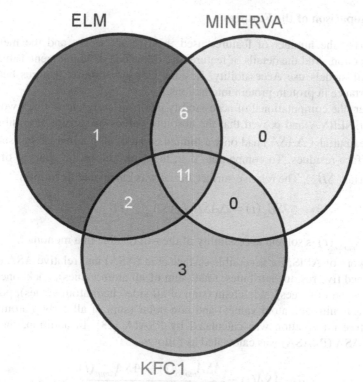

Fig. 3. The number of complexes in KFC1, ELM and MINERVA. The complex only exists in ELM is 1jck and those only in KFC1 are 1bsr, 1dx5 and 3hhr. The 2 complexes only exist both in ELM and KFC1 are 1dn2 and 1jtg and those only exist in ELM and MINERVA are 1a22, 1f47, 1fc2, 1fcc, 1jrh and 2ptc. All works contain 1a4y, 1ahw, 1brs, 1bxi, 1cbw, 1dan, 1dvf, 1gc1, 1nmb, 1vfb, and 3hfm.

Table 3. The complexes used in the previous works

Method	Complexes
APIS	1a22, <u>1a4y</u>, <u>1ahw</u>, <u>1brs</u>, <u>1bxi</u>, 1cbw, <u>1dan</u>, <u>1dvf</u>, 1fc2, 1fcc, <u>1gc1</u>, 1jrh, <u>1vfb</u>, 2ptc, <u>3hfm</u>
KFC2	1a22, <u>1a4y</u>, <u>1ahw</u>, <u>1brs</u>, <u>1bxi</u>, 1cbw, <u>1dan</u>, <u>1dvf</u>, 1f47, 1fc2, 1fcc, <u>1gc1</u>, 1jrh, 1nmb, <u>1vfb</u>, 2ptc, <u>3hfm</u>
ELM	1a22, <u>1a4y</u>, <u>1ahw</u>, <u>1brs</u>, <u>1bxi</u>, 1cbw, <u>1dan</u>, 1dn2, <u>1dvf</u>, 1f47, 1fc2, 1fcc, <u>1gc1</u>, 1jck, 1jrh, 1jtg, 1nmb, <u>1vfb</u>, 2ptc, <u>3hfm</u>
KFC1	<u>1a4y</u>, <u>1ahw</u>, <u>1brs</u>, 1bsr, <u>1bxi</u>, 1cbw, <u>1dan</u>, 1dn2, <u>1dvf</u>, 1dx5, <u>1gc1</u>, 1jtg, 1nmb, <u>1vfb</u>, <u>3hfm</u>, 3hhr
MINERVA	1a22, <u>1a4y</u>, <u>1ahw</u>, <u>1brs</u>, <u>1bxi</u>, 1cbw, <u>1dan</u>, <u>1dvf</u>, 1f47, 1fc2, 1fcc, 1jrh, 1nmb, <u>1gc1</u>, <u>1vfb</u>, 2ptc, <u>3hfm</u>
DSP	1a22, <u>1a4y</u>, <u>1ahw</u>, <u>1brs</u>, <u>1bxi</u>, 1cbw, <u>1dan</u>, <u>1dvf</u>, 1f47, 1fc2, 1fcc, <u>1gc1</u>, 1jrh, 1jtg, 1nmb, <u>1vfb</u>, 2ptc, <u>3hfm</u>, 3hhr
βACVASA	1a22, <u>1a4y</u>, <u>1ahw</u>, <u>1brs</u>, <u>1bxi</u>, 1cbw, <u>1dan</u>, 1dfj, <u>1dvf</u>, 1dx5, 1f47, 1fc2, 1fcc, <u>1gc1</u>, 1jck, 1jrh, 1jtg, 1nmb, <u>1vfb</u>, 2ptc, <u>3hfm</u>, 3hhr

The same complexes in all works are underlined.

3.1   Comparison of the Features

Table 4 gives the number of features used in different works and the methods of feature selection. And the details of features are described in supplement Table S9.We find that all models use Accessibility, Residue Conservation as features because of their importance in protein-protein interactions.

However, the computational of accessibility is a little different in the 5 works. The work in MINERVA had proved that the absolute values of solvent accessibility and surface area burial (ΔASA) had only a limited capacity to distinguish hot spots from other interface residues. To compensate that, they introduced the concept of relative surface burial (SB_r). The relative surface burial was calculated as follows:

$$SB_r(i) = \Delta ASA_i / ASA_{mono}(i) \tag{1}$$

Here $ASA_{mono}(i)$ is solvent accessibility of the i-th residue in a monomer.

In the work of APIS, for accessible surface area (ASA) and relative ASA (RASA), they obtained five residue attributes: total (sum of all atom values), backbone (sum of all backbone atom values), side-chain (sum of all side-chain atom values), polar (sum of all oxygen, nitrogen atom values) and non-polar (sum of all carbon atom values). The structure information was calculated by PSAIA [23]. In addition, the relative change in ASA (RcASA) was calculated as follows:

$$rel\_ASA(i) = \frac{ASA_{mono}(i) - ASA_{comp}(i)}{ASA_{mono}(i)} \tag{2}$$

Here $ASA_{comp}(i)$ is solvent accessibility of the i-th residue in a complex.

In the work of KFC2 and NFMF, they calculated the solvent accessible surface area using the program NACCESS [24]. In RF, they computed the relative accessible surface area (rel_ASA) of the ith residue is described in formula (2).

Table 4. The number of features used in different works

Methods	Initial number	Final number	Feature selection
MINERVA	54	12	Tree-decision
APIS	62	9	F-score
KFC2	47	14	SVM
RF	57	19	RF
NFMF	75	10	RF

4   Conclusions

In our work, we compared nine data sets from previous work. And we discuss the same training data set they all used. We think that the training data set of ELM may be the most suitable subsets to predict hot spots. In the end, we compare the features and find two features used in all works are important for protein-protein interactions. We hope that this paper can give a possible way to select training data sets and features for researchers in this field. In our future work, we will build a database that contains data both from the experimentally detected hot spots and computationally predicted hot spots.

Acknowledgments. This work is supported by the grants from the National Science Foundation of China (31301101 and 61272339), the Anhui Provincial Natural Science Foundation (1408085QF106), and the Specialized Research Fund for the Doctoral Program of Higher Education (20133401120011). The authors appreciate the constructive criticism and valuables suggestions from the anonymous reviewers.

References

1. Kortemme, T., Baker, D.: A Simple Physical Model for Binding Energy Hot Spots In Protein–Protein Complexes. Proceedings of the National Academy of Sciences 99(22), 14116–14121 (2002)
2. Walter, P., et al.: Predicting Where Small Molecules Bind at Protein-Protein Interfaces. Plos One 8(3), E58583 (2013)
3. Liu, Q., et al.: Structural Analysis of the Hot Spots in the Binding Between H1N1 HA and The 2D1 Antibody: Do Mutations of H1N1 From 1918 to 2009 Affect Much on This Binding? Bioinformatics 27(18), 2529–2536 (2011)
4. Liu, Z.-P., et al.: Bridging Protein Local Structures and Protein Functions. Amino Acids 35(3), 627–650 (2008)
5. Cunningham, B.C., Wells, J.A.: High-Resolution Epitope Mapping of Hgh-Receptor Interactions by Alanine-Scanning Mutagenesis. Science 244(4908), 1081–1085 (1989)
6. Thorn, K.S., Bogan, A.A.: Asedb: a Database of Alanine Mutations and their Effects on the Free Energy of Binding in Protein Interactions. Bioinformatics 17(3), 284–285 (2001)
7. Fischer, T., et al.: The Binding Interface Database (BID): a Compilation of Amino Acid Hot Spots in Protein Interfaces. Bioinformatics 19(11), 1453–1454 (2003)
8. Tuncbag, N., Keskin, O., Gursoy, A.: Hotpoint: Hot Spot Prediction Server for Protein Interfaces. Nucleic Acids Research 38(suppl. 2), W402–W406 (2010)
9. Darnell, S.J., Legault, L., Mitchell, J.C.: KFC Server: Interactive Forecasting of Protein Interaction Hot Spots. Nucleic Acids Research 36(suppl. 2), W265–W269 (2008)
10. Cho, K.-I., Kim, D., Lee, D.: A Feature-Based Approach to Modeling Protein–Protein Interaction Hot Spots. Nucleic Acids Research 37(8), 2672–2687 (2009)
11. Xia, J.-F., et al.: APIS: Accurate Prediction of Hot Spots in Protein Interfaces by Combining Protrusion Index with Solvent Accessibility. BMC Bioinformatics 11(1), 174 (2010)
12. Ye, L., et al.: Prediction of Hot Spots Residues in Protein–Protein Interface Using Network Feature and Microenvironment Feature. Chemometrics and Intelligent Laboratory Systems 131, 16–21 (2014)
13. Cheng, J., et al.: Training Set Selection for The Prediction of Essential Genes. Plos One 9(1), E86805 (2014)
14. Zhu, X., Mitchell, J.C.: KFC2: A Knowledge-Based Hot Spot Prediction Method Based on Interface Solvation, Atomic Density, and Plasticity Features. Proteins: Structure, Function, and Bioinformatics 79(9), 2671–2683 (2011)

15. Wang, L., et al.: Prediction of Hot Spots in Protein Interfaces Using a Random Forest Model With Hybrid Features. Protein Engineering Design and Selection 25(3), 119–126 (2012)
16. Wang, L., et al.: Prediction of Hot Spots in Protein Interfaces Using Extreme Learning Machines with the Information of Spatial Neighbour Residues (2014)
17. Darnell, S.J., Page, D., Mitchell, J.C.: An Automated Decision-Tree Approach to Predicting Protein Interaction Hot Spots. Proteins: Structure, Function, and Bioinformatics 68(4), 813–823 (2007)
18. Nguyen, Q., Fablet, R., Pastor, D.: Protein Interaction Hotspot Identification Using Sequence-Based Frequency-Derived Features. IEEE Transactions on Biomedical Engineering 60(11), 2993–3002 (2013)
19. Liu, Q., et al.: Integrating Water Exclusion Theory Into ß Contacts to Predict Binding Free Energy Changes and Binding Hot Spots. BMC Bioinformatics 15(1), 57 (2014)
20. Xu, B., et al.: A Semi-Supervised Boosting SVM for Predicting Hot Spots at Protein-Protein Interfaces. BMC Systems Biology 6(suppl. 2), S6 (2012)
21. Tuncbag, N., Gursoy, A., Keskin, O.: Identification of Computational Hot Spots in Protein Interfaces: Combining Solvent Accessibility and Inter-Residue Potentials Improves the Accuracy. Bioinformatics 25(12), 1513–1520 (2009)
22. Oliveros, J.C.: VENNY. An Interactive Tool for Comparing Lists with Venn Diagrams (2007)
23. Mihel, J., et al.: PSAIA–Protein Structure and Interaction Analyzer. BMC Structural Biology 8(1), 21 (2008)
24. Hubbard, S., Thornton, J.: Department of Biochemistry and Molecular Biology, University College London (1993)

The Intrinsic Geometric Structure of Protein-Protein Interaction Networks for Protein Interaction Prediction

Yi Fang[1], Mengtian Sun[2], Guoxian Dai[1], and Karthik Ramani[2]

[1] Electrical Engineering, New York University Abu Dhabi, UAE
{yfang,guoxian.dai}@nyu.edu
[2] Mechanical Engineering, Purdue University, USA
{sun84,ramani}@purdue.edu

Abstract. Recent developments in the high-throughput technologies for measuring protein-protein interaction (PPI) have profoundly advanced our ability to systematically infer protein function and regulation. To predict PPI in a net-work, we develop an intrinsic geometry structure (IGS) for the network, which exploits the intrinsic and hidden relationship among proteins in the net-work through a heat diffusion process. We apply our approach to publicly available PPI network data for the evaluation of the performance of PPI prediction. Experimental results indicate that, under different levels of the missing and spurious PPIs, IGS is able to robustly exploit the intrinsic and hidden relationship for PPI prediction with a higher sensitivity and specificity compared to that of recently proposed methods.

Keywords: Diffusion Geometry, PPI Network, protein function prediction.

1 Introduction

Protein-protein interactions play important roles in assembling molecular machines through mediating many essential cellular activities [12], [14], [8], [18], [6], [17], [11]. It is of important biological interest to analyze protein-protein interaction (PPI) network for deep understanding protein functions in cellular processes and biochemical events. The recent advancement in high-throughput technologies such as two-hybrid assays, tandem affinity purification, and mass spectrometry have provided tremendous amounts of PPIs in biological networks [15], [16]. The wealth of experimentally identified PPIs provides more opportunities in the exploration of protein functions and regulation in various organisms. However, the labor-intensive experimental data are inherently associated with high false positives and false negatives which stir up many concerns in comprehensive analysis in understanding the PPI network [5], [20]. In addition, the identified PPI networks are somewhat incomplete as it is impractical to experimentally verify all individual PPIs within one cell [1]. These limitations can be complemented by the computational models for predicting PPIs from noisy experimental observations [16]. The complementary in silico approaches have been receiving more and more attentions in the assistance of PPI network analysis [1], [16], [12], [9], [21], [7], [10].

The computational approaches for the prediction of PPIs have been developed over the years [16]. One of well-established propagation method, the shortest path

D.-S. Huang et al. (Eds.): ICIC 2014, LNBI 8590, pp. 487–493, 2014.
© Springer International Publishing Switzerland 2014

propagation, has been recently introduced for the prediction of the PPI in networks [12]. Their approach achieves a good performance in PPI prediction with specificity of 85% and sensitivity of 90%. However, although it is able to capture the global structure of the network, it should be noticed that the shortest path propagation is known to be sensitive to the short-circuit topological noise. The addition of spurious PPI would significantly affect the shortest path propagation. The random walk based diffusion propagation gains its advantage by progressively exploiting all possible linkages among proteins in the network [13], [22]. It is therefore robust to the local noisy interactions. Authors in [22] introduce this propagation strategy to PPI prediction in the network and demonstrate good performance in their experiments. However, it is an open research for choosing an appropriate parameter of steps for the propagation process. This parameter determines the degree to which the global structure of a network is exploited. A higher step of the propagation allows exploiting more global structure however reduces the resolution to differentiate proteins. A smaller step of the propagation allows preserve a relatively higher resolution but the revealed structure is more sensitive to noise [19]. Contrast to random walk based diffusion propagation, the heat diffusion, governed by the eigenfunctions of the Laplacian operator on network, can take account all of the local information at once to produce a consistent global solution.

In this paper, the heat diffusion is used to define the intrinsic geometric structure (IGS) of PPI network. Because the heat diffusion across the network aggregates structural information about all the possible paths connecting two nodes in network, it captures the intrinsic relationship among nodes. Similar to random walk based diffusion propagation, the extent to which heat diffuses across the network is scaled by the parameter of the dissipation time, which controls how globally the network structure is exploited. We propose a maximum likelihood based algorithm to determine the optimal dissipation time to balance the exploitation of the local and global structure of the entire PPI network. And the intrinsic geometric structure (IGS) of PPI is defined as the revealed structure in the heat diffusion process by the optimal dissipation time. Basically, the IGS organizes the proteins in the heat featured space according to their interactions in the network and has the following three desirable properties: 1) it organizes information about the intrinsic geometry of a PPI network in an efficient way; 2) it is stable under a certain number of missing and spurious interactions. 3) it faithfully interprets the implicit relationship with physics meaning supported.

2   Methods

2.1   Heat Kernel on Network

Heat transfer is a flow process of thermal energy from one region of matter or a physical system to another, which is mathematically governed by the heat equation. Heat Kernel provides a fundamental solution to heat equation in the mathematical study of heat conduction and diffusion. The heat kernel records the evolution of temperature in a region whose boundary is held fixed at a particular temperature (typically zero), such that an initial unit of heat energy is placed at a point at some time. Intuitively, we could imagine that applying a unit amount of heat at one node i and allow the heat flow on the network across all of the edges, heat kernel measures the amount of the heat that passes from the node i to any other node j within a certain unit of time.

Given a graph constructed by connecting pairs of data points with weighted edges, the heat kernel quantitatively codes the heat flow across a graph and is uniquely defined for any pair of data points on the graph. Suppose there is an initial heat distribution on network at time 0. The heat flow across the network is governed by the heat equation u(x, t), where x denotes one node in the network and t denotes the time after the application of unit heat. The heat kernel provides the fundamental solution of the heat equation [2]. The heat kernel is closely associated with graph Laplacian by:

$$\frac{\partial H_t}{\partial t} = LH_t \tag{1}$$

Where H_t denotes the heat kernel, L denotes the graph Laplacian and t denotes time.

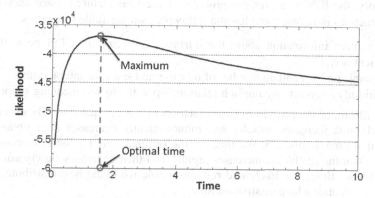

Fig. 1. Determination of optimal heat dissipation time

2.2   Intrinsic Geometric Structure

Heat kernel provides a transform by which the relationship among the data points is redefined according to the re-organization of all of the data simultaneously. The transform thus define a new relationship among proteins according to their topological connections. However, the heat kernel dynamically characterizes the proteins in the network from a local to global structure in the original network because it encapsulates the information about the heat flow over the time. The heat flow gradually aggregates information from local to global regions. At short time, heat kernel captures the local connectivity or topology of the network, while for long times the solution gauges the global geometry of the manifold on which the graph resides. However, there is one question remaining to answer: how to determine an appropriate time to balance how globally the structure of the entire network is exploited. The statistical interpretation of $H_t(i, j)$ arises from an exploration process: starting at node i, and exploring the entire network in all possible connections, the probability that j has been reached at the time t is $H_t(i, j)$ [19]. Based on the statistical interpretation, we proposed an approach to determining the time at which the likelihood for all of the observed PPIs is maximized. We formulate the optimization problem as follows. The likelihood function for the

$$L(t \mid PPI_1, PPI_2, \ldots, PPI_n) = \prod_{k=1}^{n} P(PPI_k \mid t) \tag{2}$$

Where PPI_k denote the k_{th} pair of the protein-protein interaction, n is the number of the total observed PPI in the network, t denotes the heat dissipation time and $P(PPI_k | t)$ denotes the probability that, starting from one node in k_{th} pair of PPI, another node is reached by the time t, and equals to the value provided by heat kernel $H_t(PPI_k)$. In practice, it is convenient to convert to logarithm of likelihood function, defined as:

$$\ln L(t | PPI_1, PPI_2, ..., PPI_n) = \sum_{k=1}^{n} \ln P(PPI_k | t) \qquad (3)$$

We are about to solve the following optimization problem to find the optimal time.

$$t = arg\ max \ln L(t | PPI_1, PPI_2, ..., PPI_n) \qquad (4)$$

Basically, the IGS organizes the proteins in the heat featured space according to their interactions in network and has the following two desirable properties:

1. It organizes information about the intrinsic geometry of a PPI network in an efficient way,
2. It is stable under a certain number of missing and spurious interactions,
3. It faithfully interprets the implicit relationship with physics meaning supported.

Fig. 1 illustrates the process of determination of the optimal time. By observation, likelihood value increases initially and monotonically decreases after obtaining its maximum at time around 1.5. We then set the optimal time for the PPI network 1.5. We notice that the likelihood increases rapidly and then decreases slowly after crossing the optimal time. The likelihood remains stable while the heat distributes evenly on the network after a long dissipation time.

3   Results

To test the performance of IGS in PPI prediction in network, we carry out two experiments based on the experimental setting in [3], [12] and our new design of experiments against false positive and false negative PPIs in network. First, Two-class classifier test to differentiate the protein-protein interaction (PPI) and protein-protein non-interaction (NPPI) at different noise levels. For the evaluation of the performance, we use the ROC (receiver operating characteristic curve, a graphical plot of the sensitivity versus (1-specificity)) curve and precision-recall curve. We verify our approach on a publicly available and a high confidence S. cerevisiae network [4]. It consists of 9,074 interactions amongst 1,622 proteins (we denoted it as CS2007 hereafter).

3.1   Two-Class Classifier Test

To validate the performance of IGS for differentiating the PPI and NPPI, we use the receiver operating characteristic (ROC) curve and precision recall (PR) curve as the criteria. Both curves reflect how well IGS can robustly differentiate the PPI from the NPPIs based on the revealed and intrinsic relationship among proteins. To plot the ROC curve and PR curve, we should first define true position (TP), false positive (FP), true negative (TN) and false negative (FN). The TP measures the intersection between the new assigned PPIs set and the ground truth PPIs set, FP denotes the assigned edges which are not in the set of ground truth PPIs set, TN denotes the intersection of new assigned NPPIs and ground truth of NPPIs, and FN denotes new assigned NPPIs which are not in the set of ground truth NPPIs. The ROC and PR curve are computed based on heat affinity given by IGS as follows.

1. We vary the threshold from minimum to maximum value in the heat affinity set among all pairs of proteins.
2. For a given threshold, we compute the true positive (TP) function, true negative (TN) function, false positive (FP) function and false negative (FN) function.
3. Based on the values obtained in the previous step, we compute the sensitivity rate (TP/(TP+FN)) and specificity rate (TN/(TN+FP)), precise (TP(TP+FP)) and recall (TP/(TP+FN)). To plot the ROC curve, the horizontal axis represents (1-specificity), and the vertical axis represents sensitivity. To plot the PR curve, the horizontal axis represents recall, and the vertical axis represents precision.

To demonstrate the robustness of IGS, we remove a fraction of true positive PPIs in the original network and plot the ROC curve at different levels of the removal of edges. The ROC curves are shown in the Fig. 2. The illustrated results are encouraging in terms of the prediction performance of PPI from the incomplete network. Without the removal of true PPI, the area under the ROC is nearly 1.00 and we can have specificity and sensitivity both over 0.95. The corresponding false positive rate (1-specificity) and false negative rate are all below 0.05. In addition, we find the IGS is very robust to the removal of the true PPIs in the network. As we can see from the Fig. 2, IGS performs pretty well even with 60% edges removed from the network. This result is appealing as most of the PPI network is incomplete with a large fraction of missing PPI in the observation in real scenario. Furthermore, IGS outperforms the MDS embedding method in this test [12]. They report a specificity 0.85 and sensitivity 0.90 in the experiment [12].

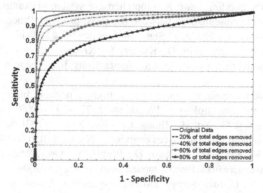

Fig. 2. Sensitivity-Specificity test of IGS method

4   Discussion and Conclusion

The silico approaches for prediction of PPI in network have been receiving more and more attentions, however, are facing challenging because of the inherently spurious and missing PPIs presence in observed measurements. The geometric based approaches, which are only based on the topology of the PPI network, are very promising as those approaches are fully independent from other prior knowledge except for topology of the PPI network. We proposed a novel geometric description, intrinsic geometric structure for the protein-protein interaction network. IGS reflects the hidden and implicit relationship among proteins.

References

1. Chen, X., Liu, M.: Prediction of protein-protein interactions using random decision forest framework. Bioinformatics 21, 4394–4400 (2005)
2. Chung, F.: Spectral graph theory. American Mathematical Society (1997)
3. Clauset, A., Moore, C., Newman, M.E.J.: Hierarchical structure and the prediction of missing links in networks. Nature 453, 98–101 (2008)
4. Collins, S., Kemmeren, P., Zhao, X., Greenblatt, J., Spencer, F., et al.: Toward a comprehensive atlas of the physical interactome of saccharomyces cerevisiae. Mol. Cell. Proteomics 6, 439–450 (2007)
5. Edwards, A., Kus, B., Jansen, R., Greenbaum, D., Greenblatt, J., et al.: Bridging structural biology and genomics: assessing protein interaction data with known complexes. Trends in Genetics 18, 529–536 (2002)
6. Giot, L., Bader, J., Brouwer, C., Chaudhuri, A., Kuang, B., et al.: A protein interaction map of drosophila melanogaster. Science 302, 1727–1736 (2003)
7. Hwang, D., Rust, A., Ramsey, S., Smith, J., Leslie, D., et al.: A data integration methodology for systems biology. Proceedings of the National Academy of Sciences of the United States of America 102, 17296–17301 (2005)
8. Ito, T., Tashiro, K., Muta, S., Ozawa, R., Chiba, T., et al.: Toward a protein-protein interaction map of the budding yeast: A comprehensive system to examine two-hybrid interactions in all possible combinations between the yeast proteins. Proceedings of the National Academy of Sciences of the United States of America 97, 1143–1147 (2000)
9. Jansen, R., Yu, H., Greenbaum, D., Kluger, Y., Krogan, N., et al.: A bayesian networks approach for predicting protein-protein interactions from genomic data. Science 302, 449–453 (2003)
10. Koyutürk, M.: Algorithmic and analytical methods in network biology. Wiley Interdisciplinary Reviews: Systems Biology and Medicine 2, 277–292 (2009)
11. Krogan, N., Cagney, G., Yu, H., Zhong, G., Guo, X., et al.: Global landscape of protein complexes in the yeast saccharomyces cerevisiae. Nature 440, 637–643 (2006)
12. Kuchaiev, O., Rasajski, M., Higham, D., Przulj, N.: Geometric de-noising of protein-protein interaction networks. Plos Computational Biology 5 (2009)
13. Lafon, S., Lee, A.: Diffusion maps and coarse-graining: A unified framework for dimensionality reduction, graph partitioning, and data set parameterization. IEEE Transactions on Pattern Analysis and Machine Intelligence 28, 1393–1403 (2006)
14. Pawson, T., Gish, G., Nash, P.: Sh2 domains, interaction modules and cellular wiring. Trends in Cell Biology 11, 504–511 (2001)

15. Shoemaker, B.A., Panchenko, A.R.: Deciphering proteincprotein interactions. part i. experimental techniques and databases. PLoS Comput. Biol. 3 (2007a)
16. Shoemaker, B.A., Panchenko, A.R.: Deciphering proteincprotein interactions. part ii. computational methods to predict protein and domain interaction partners. PLoS Comput. Biol. 3 (2007b)
17. Stelzl, U., Worm, U., Lalowski, M., Haenig, C., Brembeck, F., et al.: A human protein-protein interaction network: A resource for annotating the proteome. Cell 122, 957–968 (2005)
18. Uetz, P., Giot, L., Cagney, G., Mansfield, T., Judson, R., et al.: A comprehensive analysis of protein-protein interactions in saccharomyces cerevisiae. Nature 403, 623–627 (2000)
19. Vaxman, A., Ben-Chen, M., Gotsman, C.: A multi-resolution approach to heat kernels on discrete surfaces. ACM Trans. Graph. 29, 121:1–121:10 (2010)
20. Von Mering, C., Krause, R., Snel, B., Cornell, M., Oliver, S., et al.: Comparative assessment of large-scale data sets of protein-protein interactions. Nature 417, 399–403 (2002)
21. Wang, J., Li, C., Wang, E., Wang, X.: Uncovering the rules for protein-protein interactions from yeast genomic data. Proceedings of the National Academy of Sciences of the United States of America 106, 3752–3757 (2009)
22. Yu, H., Paccanaro, A., Trifonov, V., Gerstein, M.: Predicting interactions in protein networks by completing defective cliques. Bioinformatics, 22(7), 823–829 (2006)

Identification of Novel c-Yes Kinase Inhibitors

C. Ramakrishnan[1], A.M. Thangakani[2], D. Velmurugan[2], and M. Michael Gromiha[1]

[1] Department of Biotechnology, Indian Institute of Technology Madras,
Chennai 600 036, Tamilnadu, India
gromiha@iitm.ac.in
[2] CAS in Crystallography and Biophysics,
University of Madras, Chennai 600025, Tamilnadu, India

Abstract. c-Yes is a member of Src tyrosine kinase family and it is over expressed in human colorectal cancer cells. c-Yes tyrosine kinase is an attractive target due to its inhibition controls colon tumorigenesis, metastasis and angiogenesis. High throughput virtual screening and docking methods were employed to identify novel inhibitors based on the three dimensional structure of c-Yes. Kinase domain of c-Yes is modelled with reference to the crystal structure available for Src kinase structure and simulated for 100 ns to obtain ensembles with distinct conformation of the active site. Seven ensembles obtained from molecular dynamics (MD) trajectory and one homology model were used to screen library of the 2 million Enamine HTS compounds. A library of 159 Src kinase inhibitors and 6319 associated decoys is used for validation. Based on the score values, 25 compounds were shortlisted and reported as novel inhibitors of c-Yes kinase for further development of potent drugs to treat colorectal cancer.

Keywords: c-Yes kinase inhibitors, Src family, high throughput virtual screening, molecular dynamics simulation.

1 Introduction

Many cell processes are controlled by the protein phosphorylation driven activation and inaction of tyrosine kinases. The cytoplasmic tyrosine kinase family includes c-Src, c-Yes, fyn, c-Fgr, lyn, lck, hck, blk, and yrk. Three of these (c-Src, c-Yes and Fyn) are widely expressed in human colorectal cancer cells (1, 2). Many studies confirm the role of c-Src kinase in cancer and chances exist for each member of this family to have a non-redundant role. Evidently, gene knock-down studies confirm that silencing of c-Yes reduces cancer cell migration while c-Yes oncogenic signaling is not shared with c-Src (3-5). In addition, the c-Yes is the cellular complement of the v-Yes protein expressed by Yamaguchi avian sarcoma virus and it is also found to be over-expressed in the WNV infected cells (6). These findings confirm the role of c-Yes in viral assembly and propagation, as well. c-Yes has high homology with the other Src family members. Structures of Src kinase family members invariantly contain SH2, SH3 and kinase domains. The crystal structure of c-Src kinase (PDB entry 2SRC) reveals the structural organization and active and inactive conformations

D.-S. Huang et al. (Eds.): ICIC 2014, LNBI 8590, pp. 494–500, 2014.

of the active site (7). The active site cleft has the Try416 which undergoes phosphorylation during activation of the kinase. This residue is located at the activation loop which adopts different conformations associated with the activated and deactivated states. This loop is made up of 404-432. A short helix formation in this loop buries Tyr416 and influences the inactive conformation of the active site (auto-inhibition). The crystal structure of c-Yes kinase is not reported yet. Hence, the homology modeling and MD simulation methods were employed to build the three dimensional structure and to generate the ensembles for identifying novel inhibitors specific to c-Yes kinase. Many potent inhibitors of Src kinase family are available in the literature (8-16) and they are more specific to c-Src kinase and only few show c-Yes kinase inhibition. In this study, the molecular modeling and simulation methods were employed to find novel inhibitors specific to c-Yes kinase.

2   Computational Methods

The protocol shown in figure 1 explains the method of identification of the potential inhibitors of c-Yes kinase. The workflow is discussed in detail in the following subsections.

2.1   Preparation of Compound Library

Enamine collection of 2.2 million compounds for advanced HTS was downloaded. The 2D to 3D conversion was performed using Ligprep program (17) to generate number of possible states (tautomers, stereoisomers), ionization at a selected pH range (7±2), and ring conformations (1 ring conformer). Energy minimization of the 3D conformers was performed with the OPLS_2005 force field (18). For each ligand molecule, 32 stereoisomers and tautomers were generated and the stereoisomers for specified chiralities was retained. Only one low energy ring conformation was generated. The data set of about 460 c-Yes kinase specific inhibitors (downloaded from Bindingdb database) was analyzed for the level of diversity using the Tanimoto principle. With the resultant diverse set of actives, the physico chemical properties were calculated using the Qikprop module (Table 1).

Table 1. Physico-chemical properties of known inhibitors of c-yes/src kinase inhibitors

Property	Molecular Weight	Polar surface area	Hydrogen bond donor	Hydrogen bond acceptor	Molar refractivity
Cut-off values	450 ±75	100 ±20	2 ±1	5 ±1	120 ±10

Based on these physico-chemical parameters the initial compound library was filtered and the subset was made with about 5283 compounds satisfying drug-like properties. The Ligfilter module was used for filtering based on the cut-off values given in the Table 1. Along with the resultant library of 5283 compounds, 159 Src kinase inhibitors (actives) and 6319 decoys (inactives) were included to validate the screening protocol as well as to identify the early matching of novel hits from the

Enamine compound library (subset). A total of 11761 compounds were subjected for High Throughput Virtual Screening (HTVS), Standard Precision (SP) and Extra Precision (XP) screening methods available with Glide module (19, 20) of Schrodinger Suite.

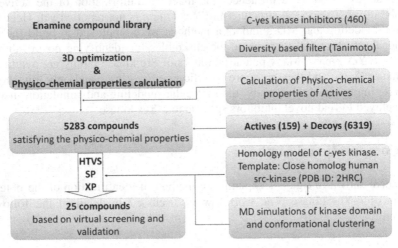

Fig. 1. Protocol used to screen the compound library and find the novel c-yes kinase inhibitors

2.2 Preparation of Target Protein (c-yes Kinase)

Since the crystal structure c-yes kinase is not yet reported, the three dimensional structure was built using homology modeling technique with reference to the close homolog human Src kinase. Many crystal structures of human c-Src kinase are available in protein databank. Particularly, the crystal structure (PDB ID: 2SRC) taken as template adopts more open conformation of the catalytic cleft compared to others. Sequence alignment for target (Uniprot id: P07947) and the template shows that 84% residues are identical and 92% are similar. The model was built using Modeller software package and the final model was chosen based on the DOPE score. The model was then subjected for "Protein preparation wizard" to assign proper bond order, charge, protonation state and for minimization prior to screening process. Optimization of the hydrogen bond network and His tautomers were performed and proper ionization states were predicted. 180° rotations of the terminal angle of Asn, Gln, and His residues were assigned, and hydroxyl and thiol hydrogen atoms were sampled as per the regular protocol. An all-atom constrained energy minimization was performed using the Impref module with RMSD cutoff of 0.30 Å. The grid was generated based on active site amino acids Val281, Lys295, Glu339, Met341, Asp386, Arg388, Asp404 and Tyr416. Same procedure was followed for preparing all eight structures.

2.3   MD Simulation and Virtual Screening

In addition to screening based on the homology model, there are seven ensembles with open conformation of active site of c-Yes kinase domain and these were selected using conformational clustering of the 100 ns MD simulation trajectory. The SH2 and SH3 domains were excluded from the calculations. MD Simulation was carried out using Gromacs simulation package (21) with OPLS force field. Minimization and equilibration were performed to attain the system free of steric clashes and to have constant temperature and pressure. Unrestrained production runs were carried out for 100 ns with 2fs time step and the coordinates were saved at 1 ps time interval. From the 100ns trajectory 10 ensembles were obtained using the conformational clustering. Out of these only 7 adopt open conformation (Figure 2) and the remaining 3 are with closed conformation. All the ensembles with open conformation were used to screen the 11761 compounds using screening methods discussed above.

3   Results and Discussion

Homology model of c-Yes kinase is validated by Ramachandran plot (22) and confirmed the accuracy of the model by 89.5%, 8.9% and 1.6% residues, which are in most favourable, additionally allowed and generously allowed regions, respectively. Important segments such as loop (339-345) at the hinge region which is known to interact with many Src kinase inhibitors, catalytic loop (381-388) and activation loop (404-432) together make the active site/ATP binding site of c-Yes and c-Src. Amino acids in these segments are more conserved and hence these segments are structurally conserved throughout the Src family. Particularly, Tyr416 exists in activation loop of both c-Yes and c-Src kinases and it is important for phosphorylation driven switching of kinase between active and inactive forms. From the 100 ns trajectory formed by simulation of c-Yes kinase in explicit solvent system, seven ensembles were selected were selected and identified by conformational clustering with 2.5Å rmsd cut-off value. Each ensemble has different active site conformation from others with respect to the orientation of the activation loop. Each of them subjected for screening a library of 11761 compounds includes subset of Enamine compound library, actives and decoys.

Each screening process produced respective hit list that includes actives, decoys and the new compounds from the library. The compounds with glide score lesser than -8.8 kcal/mol were selected as novel c-Yes kinase inhibitors. In addition, selection was made when their score supercedes that of the actives and when their score values are lesser than that of decoys. The resultant compounds were subjected for further screening using SP and XP docking methods to assess the mode of binding at the active site. Finally, 25 compounds satisfying above criteria were selected (Figure 3).

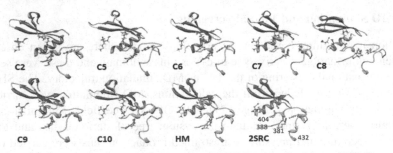

Fig. 2. Seven MD ensembles (C#), homology model (HM) and c-Src kinase (2SRC) are shown. The activation loop and catalytic loop are shown in cyan and green, respectively.

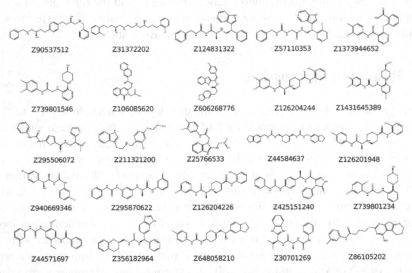

Fig. 3. List of compounds selected based on the score from high throughput virtual screening

4   Conclusion

In silico methods expedite the process of identification of novel inhibitors of target protein. Present study employed MD simulation and HTVS to identify inhibitors of c-Yes tyrosine kinase for which the X-ray crystal structure is not available. Simulation of modelled c-Yes kinase yielded 7 ensembles with distinct active site conformations and they were subjected for independent virtual screening of library of ~2 million compounds. Physicochemical parameters of known Src kinase inhibitors were used for initial filtering. The resultant compound library along with actives and decoys was subjected for HTVS, SP and XP methods, subsequently. As a result, 25 compounds were shortlisted based on scores and reported as a potent c-Yes kinase inhibitors. Present study helps further experimental studies for development of potent drugs based on the shortlisted compounds for treatment of human colorectal cancer.

Acknowledgments. This research was supported by Indian Institute of Technology Madras (BIO/10-11/540/NFSC/MICH) and, the Department of Biotechnology research grant (BT/PR7150/BID/7/424/2012) and Bioinformatics Infrastructure Facility, University of Madras.

References

1. Summy, J.M., Gallick, G.E.: Src family kinases in tumor progression and metastasis. Cancer Metastasis Reviews 22, 337–358 (2003)
2. Pena, S.V., Melhem, M.F., Meisler, A.I., Cartwright, C.A.: Elevated c-yes tyrosine kinase activity in premalignant lesions of the colon. Gastroenterology 108, 117–124 (1995)
3. Sancier, F., Dumont, A., Sirvent, A., Paquay de Plater, L., Edmonds, T., David, G., Jan, M., de Montrion, C., Coge, F., Leonce, S., Burbridge, M., Bruno, A., Boutin, J.A., Lockhart, B., Roche, S., Cruzalegui, F.: Specific oncogenic activity of the Src-family tyrosine kinase c-Yes in colon carcinoma cells. PloS One 6, e17237 (2011)
4. Stein, P.L., Vogel, H., Soriano, P.: Combined deficiencies of Src, Fyn, and Yes tyrosine kinases in mutant mice. Genes & Development 8, 1999–2007 (1994)
5. Roche, S., Fumagalli, S., Courtneidge, S.A.: Requirement for Src family protein tyrosine kinases in G2 for fibroblast cell division. Science 269, 1567–1569 (1995)
6. Hirsch, A.J., Medigeshi, G.R., Meyers, H.L., DeFilippis, V., Fruh, K., Briese, T., Lipkin, W.I., Nelson, J.A.: The Src family kinase c-Yes is required for maturation of West Nile virus particles. Journal of Virology 79, 11943–11951 (2005)
7. Xu, W., Doshi, A., Lei, M., Eck, M.J., Harrison, S.C.: Crystal structures of c-Src reveal features of its autoinhibitory mechanism. Molecular Cell 3, 629–638 (1999)
8. Lombardo, L.J., Lee, F.Y., Chen, P., Norris, D., Barrish, J.C., Behnia, K., Castaneda, S., Cornelius, L.A., Das, J., Doweyko, A.M., Fairchild, C., Hunt, J.T., Inigo, I., Johnston, K., Kamath, A., Kan, D., Klei, H., Marathe, P., Pang, S., Peterson, R., Pitt, S., Schieven, G.L., Schmidt, R.J., Tokarski, J., Wen, M.L., Wityak, J., Borzilleri, R.M.: Discovery of N-(2-chloro-6-methyl- phenyl)-2-(6-(4-(2-hydroxyethyl)- piperazin-1-yl)-2-methylpyrimidin-4-ylamino)thiazole-5-carboxamide (BMS-354825), a dual Src/Abl kinase inhibitor with potent antitumor activity in preclinical assays. Journal of Medicinal Chemistry 47, 6658–6661 (2004)
9. Chen, P., Doweyko, A.M., Norris, D., Gu, H.H., Spergel, S.H., Das, J., Moquin, R.V., Lin, J., Wityak, J., Iwanowicz, E.J., McIntyre, K.W., Shuster, D.J., Behnia, K., Chong, S., de Fex, H., Pang, S., Pitt, S., Shen, D.R., Thrall, S., Stanley, P., Kocy, O.R., Witmer, M.R., Kanner, S.B., Schieven, G.L., Barrish, J.C.: Imidazoquinoxaline Src-family kinase p56Lck inhibitors: SAR, QSAR, and the discovery of (S)-N-(2-chloro-6-methylphenyl)-2-(3-methyl-1-piperazinyl)imidazo- [1,5-a]pyrido[3,2-e]pyrazin-6-amine (BMS-279700) as a potent and orally active inhibitor with excellent in vivo antiinflammatory activity. Journal of Medicinal Chemistry 47, 4517–4529 (2004)
10. Guan, H., Laird, A.D., Blake, R.A., Tang, C., Liang, C.: Design and synthesis of aminopropyl tetrahydroindole-based indolin-2-ones as selective and potent inhibitors of Src and Yes tyrosine kinase. Bioorganic & Medicinal Chemistry Letters 14, 187–190 (2004)
11. Noronha, G., Barrett, K., Cao, J., Dneprovskaia, E., Fine, R., Gong, X., Gritzen, C., Hood, J., Kang, X., Klebansky, B., Li, G., Liao, W., Lohse, D., Mak, C.C., McPherson, A., Palanki, M.S., Pathak, V.P., Renick, J., Soll, R., Splittgerber, U., Wrasidlo, W., Zeng, B., Zhao, N., Zhou, Y.: Discovery and preliminary structure-activity relationship studies of novel benzotriazine based compounds as Src inhibitors. Bioorganic & Medicinal Chemistry Letters 16, 5546–5550 (2006)

12. Hu, S.X., Soll, R., Yee, S., Lohse, D.L., Kousba, A., Zeng, B., Yu, X., McPherson, A., Renick, J., Cao, J., Tabak, A., Hood, J., Doukas, J., Noronha, G., Martin, M.: Metabolism and pharmacokinetics of a novel Src kinase inhibitor TG100435 ([7-(2,6-dichloro-phenyl)-5-methyl-benzo[1,2,4]triazin-3-yl]-[4-(2-pyrrolidin-1-y l-ethoxy)-phenyl]-amine) and its active N-oxide metabolite TG100855 ([7-(2,6-dichloro-phenyl)-5-methylbenzo[1,2,4]triazin-3-yl]-{4-[2-(1-oxy-pyrrolid in-1-yl)-ethoxy]-phenyl}-amine). Drug Metabolism and Disposition: the Biological Fate of Chemicals 35, 929–936 (2007)
13. Palanki, M.S., Akiyama, H., Campochiaro, P., Cao, J., Chow, C.P., Dellamary, L., Doukas, J., Fine, R., Gritzen, C., Hood, J.D., Hu, S., Kachi, S., Kang, X., Klebansky, B., Kousba, A., Lohse, D., Mak, C.C., Martin, M., McPherson, A., Pathak, V.P., Renick, J., Soll, R., Umeda, N., Yee, S., Yokoi, K., Zeng, B., Zhu, H., Noronha, G.: Development of prodrug 4-chloro-3-(5-methyl-3-{[4-(2-pyrrolidin-1-ylethoxy)phenyl]amino}-1,2,4-benzotria zin-7-yl)phenyl benzoate (TG100801): a topically administered therapeutic candidate in clinical trials for the treatment of age-related macular degeneration. Journal of Medicinal Chemistry 51, 1546–1559 (2008)
14. Remsing Rix, L.L., Rix, U., Colinge, J., Hantschel, O., Bennett, K.L., Stranzl, T., Muller, A., Baumgartner, C., Valent, P., Augustin, M., Till, J.H., Superti-Furga, G.: Global target profile of the kinase inhibitor bosutinib in primary chronic myeloid leukemia cells. Leukemia 23, 477–485 (2009)
15. Huber, K., Brault, L., Fedorov, O., Gasser, C., Filippakopoulos, P., Bullock, A.N., Fabbro, D., Trappe, J., Schwaller, J., Knapp, S., Bracher, F.: 7,8-dichloro-1-oxo-beta-carbolines as a versatile scaffold for the development of potent and selective kinase inhibitors with unusual binding modes. Journal of Medicinal Chemistry 55, 403–413 (2012)
16. Urich, R., Wishart, G., Kiczun, M., Richters, A., Tidten-Luksch, N., Rauh, D., Sherborne, B., Wyatt, P.G., Brenk, R.: De novo design of protein kinase inhibitors by in silico identification of hinge region-binding fragments. ACS Chemical Biology 8, 1044–1052 (2013)
17. Chen, I.J., Foloppe, N.: Drug-like bioactive structures and conformational coverage with the LigPrep/ConfGen suite: comparison to programs MOE and catalyst. Journal of Chemical Information and Modeling 50, 822–839 (2010)
18. Peng, Y., Kaminski, G.A.: Accurate determination of pyridine-poly(amidoamine) dendrimer absolute binding constants with the OPLS-AA force field and direct integration of radial distribution functions. The Journal of Physical Chemistry B 109, 15145–15149 (2005)
19. Friesner, R.A., Banks, J.L., Murphy, R.B., Halgren, T.A., Klicic, J.J., Mainz, D.T., Repasky, M.P., Knoll, E.H., Shelley, M., Perry, J.K., Shaw, D.E., Francis, P., Shenkin, P.S.: A New Approach for Rapid, Accurate Docking and Scoring. 1. Method and Assessment of Docking Accuracy. Journal of Medicinal Chemistry 47, 1739–1749 (2004)
20. Halgren, T.A., Murphy, R.B., Friesner, R.A., Beard, H.S., Frye, L.L., Pollard, W.T., Banks, J.L.: Glide: a new approach for rapid, accurate docking and scoring. 2. Enrichment factors in database screening. Journal of Medicinal Chemistry 47, 1750–1759 (2004)
21. Pronk, S., Pall, S., Schulz, R., Larsson, P., Bjelkmar, P., Apostolov, R., Shirts, M.R., Smith, J.C., Kasson, P.M., van der Spoel, D., Hess, B., Lindahl, E.: GROMACS 4.5: a high-throughput and highly parallel open source molecular simulation toolkit. Bioinformatics 29, 845–854 (2013)
22. Ramachandran, G.N., Ramakrishnan, C., Sasisekharan, V.: Stereochemistry of polypeptide chain configurations. J. Mol. Biol. 7, 95–99 (1963)

A New Graph Theoretic Approach for Protein Threading

Yinglei Song[1] and Junfeng Qu[2]

[1] School of Computer Science and Engineering
Jiangsu University of Science and Technology
Zhenjiang, Jiangsu 212003, China
syinglei2013@163.com
[2] Department of Information Technology
Clayton State University
Morrow, GA 30260, USA
jqu@clayton.edu

Abstract. In this paper, we develop a novel graph theoretic approach for protein threading. In order to perform the protein sequence-structure alignment in threading both efficiently and accurately, we develop a graph model to describe the tertiary structure of a protein family and the alignment between a sequence and a family can be computed with a dynamic programming algorithm in linear time. Our experiments show that this new approach is significantly faster than existing tools for threading and can achieve comparable prediction accuracy.

Keywords: protein threading, graph theoretic approach, dynamic programming.

1 Introduction

Threading is one of the most important computational approaches to determining the tertiary structure of a newly sequenced protein molecule [3, 4, 6, 12]. Threading based methods align a sequence to each available tertiary structure template in a database and the template that is most compatible with the sequence is its predicted tertiary structure. The set of sequences that fold into the same tertiary structure is a *protein family*.

A threading based method often uses the statistical information from both the primary sequence content of the sequences in a protein family and their tertiary structures [3, 6]. Recent work [4, 12] has shown that the prediction accuracy can be significantly improved by including the two-body interactions between amino acids while aligning a sequence to a structure template.

Heuristics have been incorporated into the alignment process to reduce the computational cost [3]. On the other hand, threading algorithms based on optimal sequence-structure alignment have also been developed [4, 12]. However, these algorithms are not guaranteed to be computationally efficient in all cases. An accurate alignment algorithm that has low computational complexity is thus highly desirable for protein threading.

D.-S. Huang et al. (Eds.): ICIC 2014, LNBI 8590, pp. 501–507, 2014.

Our previous work has shown that efficient and accurate parameterized algorithms are available for some NP-hard problems in practice [7-10]. In this paper, we introduce a new approach for efficient sequence-structure alignment. We model a structure template with a conformational graph and preprocess a sequence to construct an image graph. Aligning a sequence to a structure template corresponds to finding the minimum valued subgraph isomorphism between the conformational graph and the image graph. We show that the sequence-structure alignment can be performed in linear time based on a tree decomposition of the conformational graph.

In order to test and evaluate the efficiency and accuracy of the algorithm, we implemented the algorithm into a program PROTTD and compared its performance with that of PROSPECT II [4] and RAPTOR [12]. Our experiments showed that, on average, PROTTD is about 50 times faster than PROSPECT II to obtain better or same alignment accuracy. In addition, we compared the accuracy of our approach with that of RAPTOR at all similarity levels. Our testing results showed that PROTTD achieved significantly improved fold recognition accuracy on both superfamily and fold levels.

2   Threading Models

(a)   Energy Function for Protein Threading

Alignments are scored with a given energy function and the goal of protein threading is to find the alignment with the minimum score. We used an energy function that is the weighted sum of mutation energy E_m, singleton energy E_s, pair-wise energy E_p, gap penalty E_g and an energy term E_{ss} that arises from the secondary structure matching respectively. The overall alignment score E_t can be computed as follows.

$$E_t = W_m E_m + W_s E_s + W_p E_p + W_q E_q + W_{ss} E_{ss} \tag{1}$$

where W_m, W_s, W_p, W_g and W_{ss} are relative weights for the corresponding energy terms.   A detailed description of these energy terms can be found in [12].

(b)   Problem Description

Structural units in a structure template include cores and loops. A core contains a row of residue locations where the tertiary structure is highly conserved during the evolution. In contrast, a loop consists of the residue locations in between two consecutive cores and its tertiary structure can be highly variable during the evolution. To reduce the computational difficulty for the sequence-structure alignment, gaps are not allowed to appear in core regions.

In our new threading algorithm, we define the possible residue locations that can be aligned to a given core to be its images. To determine the images for a given core, we use its profile specified in the structure template to scan its mapped region and select the residue locations with the k lowest alignment scores, where k is a small parameter that can be determined with a statistical cut-off.

Based on the structure units contained in a structure template, we model the two-body interactions among them with a conformational graph. In particular, we use vertices to represent cores in the structure template and cores next to each other in the backbone are joined with directed edges from left to right.

In contrast, undirected edges connect two vertices if there exists a two-body interaction with its interacting amino acids contained in the two corresponding cores. For a given sequence that needs to be aligned, the images of each core can be efficiently determined in linear time. Using vertices to represent images, two vertices are joined with an undirected (directed) edge if the vertices of their corresponding cores are joined with an undirected (directed) edge in the conformational graph. In addition, values are assigned to vertices and edges in an image graph, the value associated with a vertex is its alignment score on the corresponding core profile; the value of a directed edge is the score of aligning the sequence part between its two ends to the corresponding loop profile in the structure template; the value of an undirected edge is the sum of the energies of all two-body interactions with two ends from the two cores respectively.

An alignment thus corresponds to an embedding of the conformational graph into the image graph. The alignment score is the sum of the values of vertices and edges selected in the image graph to embed the conformational graph. The problem of optimally aligning a sequence to a structure profile thus can be formulated as a minimum valued subgraph isomorphism problem.

3   Threading Algorithms

(a)   Tree Decomposition and Tree Width

Definition 3.1. ([6]) *Let* $G = (V, E)$ *be a graph, where* V *is the set of vertices in* G, E *denotes the set of edges in* G. *Pair* (T, X) *is a tree decomposition of graph* G *if it satisfies the following conditions:*

1. $T = (I, F)$ *defines a tree, the sets of vertices and edges in* T *are* I *and* F *respectively,*

2. $X = \{X_i \mid i \in I, X_i \subseteq V\}$ *and* $\forall u \in V$, $\exists i \in I$ *such that* $u \in X_i$,

3. $\forall (u, v) \in E$, $\exists i \in I$ *such that* $u \in X_i$ *and* $v \in X_i$,

4. $\forall i, j, k \in I$, *if* k *is on the path that connects* i *and* j *in tree* T, *then* $X_i \cap X_j \subseteq X_k$.

The tree width of the tree decomposition (T, X) *is* $\max_{i \in I} |X_i| - 1$. *The tree width of* G *is the minimum tree width over all possible tree decompositions of* G.

(b)   Algorithm for Optimal Alignment

A dynamic programming table with up to k^t entries is maintained in each tree node in a tree decomposition of the conformational graph G. For a tree node that contains t vertices, each entry in the table stores the validity and the partial alignment score associated with a certain combination of the images of all t vertices. The table thus contains a column for each tree node to store its image in a certain combination and two auxiliary columns V and S to store the validity of the combination and its partial alignment score. Figure 1(a) shows the flowchart to fill all tables in a tree.

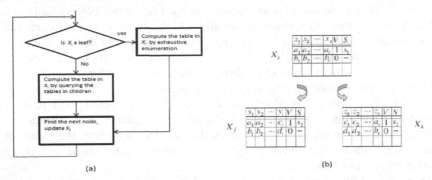

(a)   (b)

Fig. 1. (a) The flowchart of the approach. (b) For each entry in the table of X_i, the tables in its children X_j and X_k are queried tocompute its validity and partial alignment score.

Starting with the leaves of the tree, the algorithm follows a bottom-up fashion to compute the v and S for each entry in the table contained in all tree nodes. For a leaf X_l that contains t vertices $\{x_1, x_2, ..., x_t\}$, a combination of their images $\{i_1, i_2, ..., i_t\}$ is valid if they follow the same relative order as the t vertices the leaf contains, and its partial alignment score can be computed with

$$S(i_1, i_2, ..., i_t) = \sum_{m=1}^{g} w(s_m) \qquad (2)$$

where $s_1, s_2, ..., s_g$ are the corresponding structure units that are determined from the combination of images $i_1, i_2, ..., i_t$ and have X_l marked, $w(s_m)$ is the value associated with the structure unit s_m.

For an internal node X_i, without loss of generality, we assume that it has two children nodes X_j and X_k, and the vertices contained in X_i, X_j, and X_k are $\{x_1, x_2, ..., x_t\}$, $\{y_1, y_2, ..., y_t\}$ and $\{z_1, z_2, ..., z_t\}$ respectively. The sets $X_i \cap X_j$ and $X_i \cap X_k$ are often not empty and we assume them to be $\{u_1, u_2, ..., u_p\}$ and $\{v_1, v_2, ..., v_q\}$ respectively.

As can be seen from Figure 1 (b), to determine the validity of a combination of images $i_1, i_2, ..., i_t$ for vertices $x_1, x_2, ..., x_t$ in X_i, the algorithm first checks if it follows the same relative order as that of vertices in X_l. Secondly, the images for vertices in $X_i \cap X_j$ and $X_i \cap X_k$ are determined from the combination.

The algorithm then enumerates and queries the entries in the dynamic programming tables of X_j and X_k that contain the same image assignments for vertices in $X_i \cap X_j$ (for the table in X_j) and $X_i \cap X_k$ (for the table in X_k). The combination is set to be valid if at least one valid entry is found in each table during the query procedure. The partial alignment score for a valid combination can be computed with

$$S(i_1, i_2, ..., i_t) = MS(i_{u_1}, ..., i_{u_p}, X_j) + MS(i_{v_1}, ..., i_{v_q}, X_k) + \sum_{m=1}^{g} w(s_m) \qquad (3)$$

where $i_{u_1}, ..., i_{u_p}$ and $i_{v_1}, ..., i_{v_q}$ are the image assignments for vertices in $X_i \cap X_j$ and $X_i \cap X_k$ respectively. $MS(i_{u_1}, ..., i_{u_p}, X_j)$ and $MS(i_{v_1}, ..., i_{v_q}, X_k)$ are the minimum alignment scores over all the valid entries in the tables for X_j and X_k that assign $i_{u_1}, ..., i_{u_p}$ to vertices $u_1, ..., u_p$ and $i_{v_1}, ..., i_{v_q}$ to vertices $v_1, ..., v_q$ respectively. s_m's ($m = 1, 2, ..., g$) form the set of structure units with X_i marked and $w(s_m)$ is the value associated with s_m.

The optimal alignment can be obtained by searching the table in the root node for a valid entry with the minimum alignment score. The running time of the algorithm is $O(k'n)$, where n is the number of vertices in a conformational graph. The overall time complexity for the algorithm is thus $O(MN + k')$, where M and N are the sizes of the sequence and the structure template respectively.

4   Experiments and Results

We have implemented this algorithm into a program PROTTD. We constructed the conformational graph for each of the 3890 available structure templates compiled using PISCES [11]. Table 1 provides the statistics on the tree widths of all available 3890 structure templates obtained with PROTTD. Table 1 suggests that the tree decomposition based alignment can achieve a high computational efficiency.

We varied the value of the parameter k in PROTTD and performed sequence-structure alignment for protein pairs in the DALI test set [2]. The alignment accuracy is evaluated based on the structural alignments provided by FAST [14]. We obtain the alignment accuracy by computing the percentage of residues that are aligned with no error and those aligned with a shift of less than four amino acids. Table 2 shows the percentage of pairs where PROTTD outperforms PROSPECT II in alignment accuracy for different values of k. It can be clearly seen from the table that, compared with PROSPECT II, PROTTD can achieve satisfactory alignment accuracy when its parameter k is greater than 5.

Table 1. The distribution of tree widths for 3890 structure templates

Tree Width	0	1	2	3	4	5	6	>6
Percentage(%)	2.85	5.91	12.03	17.81	21.85	15.60	10.77	13.18

Table 2. The percentage of sequence-structure pairs in DALI test set where PROTTD outperforms PROSPECT II

Parameter	k=3	k=5	k=7	k=9
Percentage(%)	39.57	55.64	85.32	86.91

Table 3 shows the amount of relative speed up gained with PROTTD averaged on all pairs in the DALI data set. It can be seen from the table that PROTTD is significantly faster than PROSPECT II for sequence-structure alignment.

Table 3. The average amount of speed up PROTTD achieved on the DALI data set

Parameter	k=3	k=5	k=7	K=9
Average Speed-up	97.52×	57.83×	39.73×	23.61×

Table 4. The fold recognition performance for both PROTTD and RAPTOR. Top1 and Top5 are percentages of correctly identified protein pairs and those among the top 5 in the ranking of Z-scores.

PROTTD						RAPTOR					
Family		Superfamily		Fold		Family		Superfamily		Fold	
Top1	Top5	Top1	Top5	Top1	Top5	Top1	Top5	Top1	Top5	Top1	Top5
82.0	86.1	56.3	68.9	40.2	63.2	84.8	87.1	47.0	60.0	31.3	54.2

We evaluated the fold recognition performance of PROTTD using the lindahl dataset [6], which contains 941 structure templates and protein sequences. In the dataset, 555, 434, and 321 sequences have at least one matching structural homolog at the family, superfamily, and fold levels. Since Z-score provides a confident measure for an alignment score, we ranked all structure templates based on the Z-scores associated with each sequence-structure alignment. Table 4 compares the prediction accuracy of PROTTD with that of RAPTOR [12] in lindahl data set at family, superfamily and fold levels respectively. It is clear from the table that PROTTD has significantly improved recognition accuracy at both superfamily and fold levels.

5   Conclusions

In this paper, we introduce an efficient parameterized graph algorithm for protein threading. Based on this algorithm, we are able to efficiently align a sequence to a structure template with high accuracy. Since HP model [1] and protein structure alignment [13] have been extensively used for structure analysis. Exploring the potential of our approach to be applied to them would be the goal of our future work.

Acknowledgments. Y. Song's work is fully supported by the University Fund of Jiangsu University of Science and Technology under the number: 635301202 and 633301301.

References

1. Chen, L., Wu, L., Wang, Y., Zhang, S., Zhang, X.: Revealing Divergent Evolution, Identifying Circular Permutations and Detecting Active-sites by Protein Structure Comparison. BMC Structural Biology 6(1), 18 (2006)
2. Holm, L., Sander, C.: Decision Support System for Evolutionary Classification of Protein Structures. In: Proceedings of International Conference on Intelligent Systems for Molecular Biology, vol. 5, pp. 140–146 (1997)
3. Jones, D.T.: Protein Secondary Structure Prediction Based on Position-specific Scoring Matrices. Journal of Molecular Biology 292(2), 195–202 (1999)
4. Kim, D., Xu, D., Guo, J., Ellrott, K., Xu, Y.: Prospect II: Protein Structure Prediction Program for Genome-scale Applications. Protein Engineering 16(9), 641–650 (2003)
5. Robertson, N., Seymour, P.D.: Graph Minors II. Algorithmic Aspects of Tree-Width. Journal of Algorithms 7, 309–322 (1986)
6. Shi, J., Blundell, T.L., Mizuguchi, K.: FUGUE: Sequence-structure Homology Recognition Using Environment-specific Substitution Tables and Structure- dependent Gap Penalties. Journal of Molecular Biology 310(1), 243–257 (2001)
7. Song, Y.: A New Parameterized Algorithm for Rapid Peptide Sequencing. PLoS One 9(2), e87476 (2014)
8. Song, Y.: An Improved Parameterized Algorithm for the Independent Feedback Vertex Set Problem. Theoretical Computer Science (2014), doi:10.1016/j.tcs.2014.03.031
9. Song, Y., Liu, C., Huang, X., Malmberg, R.L., Xu, Y., Cai, L.: Efficient Parameterized Algorithms for Biopolymer Structure-Sequence Alignment. IEEE/ACM Transactions on Computational Biology and Bioinformatics 3(4), 423–432 (2006)
10. Song, Y., Chi, A.Y.: A New Approach for Parameter Estimation in the Sequence-structure Alignment of Non-coding RNAs. Journal of Information Science and Engineering (in press, 2014)
11. Wang, G., Dunbrack Jr., R.L.: PISCES: A Protein Sequence Culling Server. Bioinformatics 16, 257–268 (2000)
12. Xu, J., Li, M., Kim, D., Xu, Y.: RAPTOR: Optimal Protein Threading by Linear Programming. Journal of Bioinformatics and Computational Biology 1(1), 95–117 (2003)
13. Zhang, X., Wang, Y., Zhan, Z., Wu, L., Chen, L.: Exploring Protein's Optimal HP Configurations by Self-organizing Mapping. Journal of Bioinformatics and Computational Biology 3(2), 385–400 (2006)
14. Zhu, J., Weng, Z.: FAST: A Novel Protein Structure Alignment Algorithm. Proteins: Structure, Function and Bioinformatics 58(3), 618–627 (2005)

Author Index